VICTIMS

VICTIMS

The LDS Church and the Mark Hofmann Case

Richard E. Turley, Jr.

UNIVERSITY OF ILLINOIS PRESS
Urbana and Chicago

This book is printed on acid-free paper.

Quotations from the *Saints Herald* are used by permission of Herald Publishing House, Independence, Missouri.

Original sources from the collections of the Reorganized Church of Jesus Christ of Latter Day Saints are used by permission of RLDS Archives, Independence, Missouri.

Library of Congress Cataloging-in-Publication Data

Turley, Richard E. (Richard Eyring)
    Victims : the LDS Church and the Mark Hofmann case / Richard E. Turley, Jr.
        p.   cm.
    Includes bibliographical references (p.   ) and index.
    ISBN 0-252-01885-0
    1. Hofmann, Mark. 2. Criminals—Utah—Salt Lake City—Bibliography.
3. Murder—Utah—Salt Lake City—Case studies. 4. Forgery of manuscripts—Utah—Salt Lake City—Case studies. 5. Mormon Church—History. 6. Church of Jesus Christ of Latter-day Saints—History.
    I. Title.
    HV6248.H467T87   1992
    364.1′523′0979225—dc20   91-43248
                                                                        CIP

Contents

Preface

In October 1985, three bombs exploded in Utah's Salt Lake Valley, home to the headquarters of the Church of Jesus Christ of Latter-day Saints. The ensuing investigation unmasked a killer and a complex scheme of deception that would capture public attention like few other criminal cases in late twentieth-century America. The bizarre story spawned several books, hundreds of newspaper and magazine articles, and many hours of television and radio reports, interviews, and commentary. With all this attention, why one more book?

For two reasons.

First, no book has adequately approached the case from a victim's view. Besides the criminal, no one has been closer to the crimes than the victims. Tragically, two victims in this case did not survive to tell their stories. Their memory in part has been eclipsed by the media's focus on another victim: the Church of Jesus Christ of Latter-day Saints. Relying primarily on documentation created contemporaneously with the events in question and secondarily on recollections, this book helps fill a historical gap by relating the experiences and feelings of the church leaders and employees most involved in the case.

This volume has a second purpose. The pressures and competition of news reporting and law enforcement led to speculation about the case. Though later research has undermined much of the speculation, it remains a part of the media record, destined to last as long as paper, film, and tape survive. In the absence of accurate data, speculation uncritically hardens into "fact" to become the footnotes of tomorrow's histories. Relying on the best available historical evidence, this book corrects some misconceptions about the case. And unlike previous books, it provides readers with detailed source notes to help them understand and evaluate the evidence on which the narrative rests.

Although I serve as managing director of the Historical Department of the Church of Jesus Christ of Latter-day Saints, I am solely responsible for the content of this book. The church has a well-established process through which publications pass before acquiring the church's imprimatur, and in the earliest stages of my work, church officials agreed to cooperate fully with me without requiring that this volume pass through that process.

Committed to the idea that review by persons other than the author helps improve the accuracy and flow of historical writing, however, I submitted the manuscript of this book to a range of persons both inside and outside the church, including some involved in the case. This work benefited substantially from the comments of the reviewers, yet in no case did it lead to the omission of any material information about church officials' roles in the story. All of the church officials who read the manuscript honored my desire to retain editorial control over its contents.

Latter-day Saints have their own vocabulary and peculiar forms of address. I have tried to make this book comprehensible both to Latter-day Saints and to those outside the church. Active Latter-day Saints (of whom I am one) customarily refer to current church leaders by such titles as "President" or "Elder," followed by the leaders' last names. Church members sometimes refer to their early leaders by just first names. In this book, however, I have elected to follow scholarly custom and refer to all persons named in the story by their last names alone, except where titles or first names are necessary to introduce persons in the narrative, to avoid ambiguity (such as when characters share a surname), or to remind readers of individuals' identities.

I have also followed accepted scholarly practice in retaining the original spelling of the sources I quote. Exceptions for the sake of clarity (such as expanding initials to full names) are marked with square brackets.

Some readers of earlier works about this complex case have complained of becoming mired in a morass of names. To help readers keep the major characters in the story straight, I have relegated the names of many minor figures to the notes.

To understand this story fully, readers must have a basic grasp of the church's early history. The Introduction briefly recounts this history in terms that will already be familiar to Latter-day Saints. In recounting this history, I have relied largely on canonized sources because it is the tension between these sources and later documents that produces much of the drama in the case.

To make the narrative as realistic as possible, I have chosen to recount most events chronologically. Many questions that may naturally occur to readers of the first part of the book find their answers in the second part. Thus, the story unfolds much like a mystery novel with an important difference: The events recounted really happened.

Introduction

In 1980, the Church of Jesus Christ of Latter-day Saints commemorated its 150th anniversary. As jubilant members recalled key events from the church's history, a skillful forger had already begun a career of deception that would alter the way many viewed that history. The career would culminate in a series of grisly pipe bombings, followed by a criminal investigation and preliminary hearing unmatched in Utah history. To fully understand this bizarre criminal episode requires a leap backward in time to the days of Joseph Smith, Jr., founding prophet, seer, and revelator of the church.

In the late 1830s, Smith oversaw the beginnings of an official history, portions of which would become scripture for millions of future church members.[1] The history described Smith's quest for religious truth. As a teenager concerned with his spiritual standing and questioning which church to join, he was deeply moved by a New Testament passage. "If any of you lack wisdom," it read, "let him ask of God." Smith explained that he took the writer at his word and, walking into the woods near his home, knelt to pray.[2]

"I had scarcely done so," he recalled, "when immediately I was seized upon by some power which entirely overcame me, and had such an astonishing influence over me as to bind my tongue so that I could not speak. Thick darkness gathered around me, and it seemed to me for a time as if I were doomed to sudden destruction. But, exerting all my powers to call upon God to deliver me out of the power of this enemy which had seized upon me, and at the very moment when I was ready to sink into despair and abandon myself to destruction . . . , I saw a pillar of light exactly over my head, above the brightness of the sun, which descended gradually until it fell upon me.

"It no sooner appeared than I found myself delivered from the enemy which held me bound. When the light rested upon me I saw two Personages, whose brightness and glory defy all description, standing above me in the air. One of them spake unto me, calling me by name and said, pointing to the other—*This is My Beloved Son. Hear Him!*

"My object in going to inquire of the Lord was to know which of all the sects was right, that I might know which to join. No sooner, therefore, did I get possession of myself, so as to be able to speak, than I asked the

Joseph Smith's First Vision, depicted in stained glass. (Jed Clark/LDS Church)

Personages who stood above me in the light, which of all the sects was right . . . and which I should join. I was answered that I must join none of them, for they were all wrong."[3]

After recounting this First Vision (as it came to be called), Smith in his history described another heavenly visitation, this one occurring in September 1823 as he prayed to have his sins forgiven. "While I was thus in the act of calling upon God," he related, "I discovered a light appearing in my room, which continued to increase until the room was lighter than at noonday, when immediately a personage appeared at my bedside, standing in the air, for his feet did not touch the floor. . . .

"He called me by name, and said unto me that he was a messenger sent from the presence of God to me, and that his name was Moroni; that God had a work for me to do; and that my name should be had for good and evil among all nations, kindreds, and tongues, or that it should be both good and evil spoken of among all people.

"He said there was a book deposited, written upon gold plates, giving an account of the former inhabitants of this continent, and the source from whence they sprang. He also said that the fulness of the everlasting Gospel was contained in it, as delivered by the Savior to the ancient inhabitants; Also, that there were two stones in silver bows—and these stones, fastened to a breastplate, constituted what is called the Urim and Thummim—deposited with the plates; and the possession and use of these stones were what constituted 'seers' in ancient or former times; and that God had prepared them for the purpose of translating the book."[4]

The next day, Smith recounted, "I . . . went to the place where the messenger had told me the plates were deposited; and owing to the distinctness of the vision which I had had concerning it, I knew the place the instant that I arrived there." The site was on the tallest hill in the neighborhood. "On the west side of this hill, not far from the top," Smith said, "under a stone of considerable size, lay the plates, deposited in a stone box. This stone was thick and rounding in the middle on the upper side, and thinner towards the edges, so that the middle part of it was visible above the ground, but the edge all around was covered with earth."

He scraped the dirt from the edge of the stone and used a lever to lift it up. "I looked in," he explained, "and there indeed did I behold the plates, the Urim and Thummim, and the breastplate, as stated by the messenger. . . . I made an attempt to take them out, but was forbidden by the messenger, and was again informed that the time for bringing them forth had not yet arrived, neither would it, until four years from that time; but he told me that I should come to that place precisely in one year from that time, and that he would there meet with me, and that I should continue to do so until the time should come for obtaining the plates."[5]

In his history, Smith recorded that he finally received the ancient relics in September 1827. Then word leaked out that he had them. "The persecution became more bitter and severe than before," he recalled, "and multitudes were on the alert continually to get them from me if possible." Meanwhile, "rumor with her thousand tongues was all the time employed in circulating falsehoods about my father's family, and about myself. If I were to relate a thousandth part of them, it would fill up volumes."[6]

To escape the turmoil, Joseph Smith and his new bride, Emma, moved to Pennsylvania, aided financially by a well-to-do farmer named Martin Harris. In Pennsylvania, Smith recounted, he began to copy and translate characters from the gold plates. A few weeks later in February 1828, Harris visited the young couple, obtained a transcript of some of the characters, and traveled to New York City to show them to some of the most learned men of the day, including Charles Anthon of Columbia College, a scholar of whom Edgar Allan Poe would write, "If not absolutely the best, he is at least generally considered the best classicist in America." Harris and Anthon would disagree on what happened during their meeting, but Harris returned home more willing than ever to assist the young prophet. By mid-April 1828, he was acting as scribe to Smith in his translation of the gold plates.[7]

Harris's wife and other family members, however, remained skeptical and pressured him for evidence to justify his devotion to the project. Harris, in turn, pressed Smith for an opportunity to show family members the completed pages of the translation. Eventually, Smith relented, permitting him to take 116 manuscript pages, provided he show them to a few designated persons and no others. As Smith explained in his history, however, "he did show them to others, and by stratagem they got them away from him, and they never have been recovered."[8]

The loss of the 116 pages proved a temporary setback to the work in which Smith was engaged. It received fresh impetus, however, the following spring, when he found a new scribe to assist him. "On the 5th day of April, 1829," Smith recalled in his history, "Oliver Cowdery came to my house, until which time I had never seen him. He stated to me that having been teaching school in the neighborhood where my father resided, and my father being one of those who sent to the school, he went to board for a season at his house, and while there the family related to him the circumstance of my having received the plates, and accordingly he had come to make inquiries of me."[9]

Cowdery agreed to write for Smith as he dictated his translation of the plates, and over the next several weeks, the work proceeded rapidly. The major obstacle the two men faced was finding means to live while they worked. "Shortly after commencing to translate," Smith explained in his history, "I became acquainted with Mr. Peter Whitmer, of Fayette, Seneca county, New York, and also with some of his family. In the beginning of the month of June [1829], his son, David Whitmer, came to the place where we were residing, and brought with him a two-horse wagon, for the purpose of having us accompany him to his father's place, and there remain until we should finish the work."[10]

With the support of the Whitmers, the work rapidly moved to completion. "In the course of the work of translation," Smith recounted, "we ascertained that three special witnesses were to be provided by the Lord, to whom He would grant that they should see the plates from which this work (the Book of Mormon) should be translated; and that these witnesses should bear record of the same. . . . Almost immediately after we had made this discovery, it occurred to Oliver Cowdery, David Whitmer and the aforementioned Martin Harris (who had come to inquire after our progress in the work) that they would have me inquire of the Lord to know if they might not obtain of him the privilege to be these three special witnesses."[11]

Smith said he inquired and received an affirmative answer and that within a few days, he and his three associates experienced the promised manifestation. In a published statement, Oliver Cowdery, David Whitmer, and Martin Harris would subsequently testify that they had heard God's voice declaring that the plates had "been translated by the gift and power of God." "And we declare with words of soberness," they attested, "that an Angel of God came down from heaven, and he brought and laid before our eyes, that we beheld and saw the plates, and the engravings thereon; and we know that it is by the grace of God the Father, and our Lord Jesus Christ, that we beheld and bear record that these things are true." Because of this confirming testimony, Cowdery, Whitmer, and Harris became known to successive generations as the Three Witnesses of the Book of Mormon.[12]

When the translation of the plates was finally completed, Smith struggled to find a publisher for the volume. He applied to Palmyra, New York, publisher Egbert B. Grandin, who at first refused to print the book even though Harris (whom he knew to be a man of means) offered to guarantee his profit. A skeptical contemporary associated with Grandin later recalled that "Mr. Grandin at once expressed his disinclination to entertain the proposal to print at any price, believing the whole affair to be a wicked imposture and a scheme to defraud Mr. Harris, who was his friend, and whom he advised accordingly."

Harris assured Grandin he was not being deceived and that someone else would print the book if he did not. The skeptical contemporary observed that when a Rochester publisher offered to print the book, "Mr. Grandin, on taking the advice of several discreet, fair-minded neighbors, finally reconsidered his course of policy, and entered into contract for the printing and binding of five thousand copies of the Book of Mormon at the price of $3,000, taking Harris's bond and mortgage as offered in security for payment." On March 26, 1830, Grandin advertised the book as complete and available for sale.[13]

Shortly after the Book of Mormon was published, Smith organized a church founded on the belief that God continues to reveal his will to those on earth. In a later revelation, the fledgling church would be named the Church of Jesus Christ of Latter-day Saints, often abbreviated "LDS Church," or, colloquially among its members, simply "the church." Church members would become known as "Latter-day Saints," "saints," or, more popularly, "Mormons," reflecting their belief in the Book of Mormon.[14]

As the church grew, new revelations enhanced its organizational structure, until it eventually came to be headed by a First Presidency (made up of the President of the Church and two counselors, each bearing the title "President"), a Quorum of Twelve Apostles (officiating under the First Presidency's direction), and a First Quorum of Seventy (officiating under the direction of the First Presidency and Twelve Apostles). These church leaders, with a few others who were also authorized to preside in the church worldwide, became known as "general authorities" (often referred to by their surnames prefixed with the title "Elder").[15]

In his history, Joseph Smith explained that on the day the church was formally organized, he received a revelation commanding the church to keep a record. Thereafter, church officials began collecting historical information about the church and its members, a practice reinforced by later revelations. The acquisition of historical materials became for them a divinely mandated assignment. Over the next century and a half, however, forgeries would persistently hinder efforts to collect accurate information about the church's past.[16]

Part One

You cannot always tell the wicked from the righteous.
—Doctrine and Covenants 10:37

1

Alterations of the Past

"I would inform you," Joseph Smith wrote in his preface to the Book of Mormon, "that I translated, by the gift and power of God, and caused to be written, one hundred and sixteen pages, . . . which . . . some person or persons have stolen and kept from me, notwithstanding my utmost exertions to recover it again." Alluding to the thieves and the stolen pages, he explained he had been "commanded of the Lord . . . not [to] translate the same over again, for Satan had put it into their hearts to tempt the Lord their God, by altering the words, that they did read contrary from that which I translated and caused to be written."[1] By Smith's account, the first attempt to alter or forge Mormon documents actually preceded the formal organization of the church. For members of the church interested in its history, an ever-looming hindrance would be forgery, a term some would apply not just to bogus documents, but also to ideas that skewed the past. Over the next century and a half, both kinds of forgeries would plague the church.

In the fall of 1830, Mormon missionaries traveling through Ohio approached Sidney Rigdon, who had been a prominent Campbellite minister. One of the missionaries, who had been converted to Mormonism in New York, had once been a religious associate of Rigdon and had returned to tell him about the Book of Mormon and the new church. The missionary found that it was only "with much persuasion and argument" that he could get Rigdon to read the new book, and that even after that, Rigdon "had a great struggle of mind, before he fully believed and embraced it." Eventually, however, Rigdon joined the church, and soon many in the region followed his example.[2] Anti-Mormons in Ohio reacted to these conversions by underwriting a book titled *Mormonism Unvailed*, a volume intended to "prove the '*Book of Mormon*' to be a work of *fiction* and *imagination* . . . and completely divest Joseph Smith of all claims to the character of an honest man."[3]

To a large extent, *Mormonism Unvailed* reprinted, reiterated, and elaborated on arguments that had already been made against Joseph Smith and the Book of Mormon. Its most original claim, however, was the one for which it became most famous. The book theorized that one Solomon Spalding (sometimes spelled Spaulding), a former minister then deceased, had once written a historical romance, which he left with a Pittsburgh printer, who (after Spalding's death) conspired to publish it with Sidney Rigdon, who then embellished the manuscript and (after the printer's death) conspired to publish it with Joseph Smith, who faked his religious experiences and published the book under his own name as the Book of Mormon, with Rigdon later feigning his Ohio conversion.[4]

Mormons denounced the Spalding theory as "a base forgery" by those "who had long strove to account for the Book of Mormon, in some other way beside the truth." They pointed out that Joseph Smith and Sidney Rigdon had not met until after the Book of Mormon was printed and that other links in the Spalding manuscript's purported chain of possession were also flawed. In response, anti-Mormons collected affidavits and recollections to support the theory.[5]

In 1884, the Spalding manuscript was located, published, and found to be quite unlike the Book of Mormon. E. D. Howe, the nominal author of *Mormonism Unvailed,* had actually seen the Spalding manuscript before he published his book but had dismissed it by theorizing that it was merely an early draft of the version that became the Book of Mormon. Careful study of the rediscovered manuscript, however, would prove it was written late in Spalding's life. Eventually, a wide range of scholars, including some critical of Joseph Smith, concluded the theory was based on an untenable sequence of events and doubtful evidence, including affidavits shaped by those who gathered them.[6]

The Spalding theory, however, was not the only dubious effort to discredit Joseph Smith and the Book of Mormon. In 1843, a Mormon newspaper reported the discovery of six bell-shaped plates of brass near Kinderhook, Illinois. The Kinderhook plates garnered considerable attention among Latter-day Saints because they contained seemingly ancient inscriptions. At one point, they were shown to Joseph Smith to see if he could translate them. Years later, they were proved to be fake, however, and controversy swirled around whether the prophet ever purported to have translated them. Two Mormon contemporaries recorded that he had, but their statements disagreed, suggesting they were based on hearsay and not first-hand knowledge.

One of the perpetrators of the Kinderhook plate fraud later wrote that Joseph Smith "would not agree to translate them until they were sent to the Antiquarian society at Philadelphia, France, and England." Decades

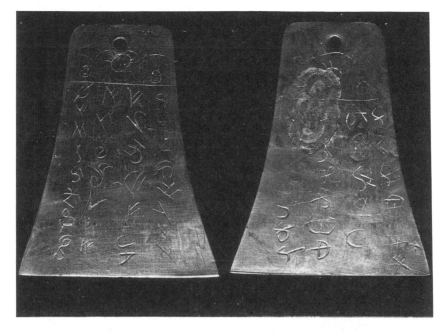

One of the Kinderhook plates (front and back). (Chicago Historical Society, Negative 1.1920.487)

later, an Illinois history professor researching the episode would write, "It has been suggested that the whole Kinderhook plate incident was . . . a heavy-handed frontier-style 'joke.' On the other hand, the conspirators' objective might have been more pointed—to produce a bogus set of plates and then reveal the hoax in a shower of ridicule *after* the Prophet made a purported 'translation.' In either case, they were frustrated in their scheme because no translation ever appeared."[7]

In 1844, Joseph Smith and his brother Hyrum were shot to death by anti-Mormons in Carthage, Illinois. Several suspects were tried for murder but acquitted, partly because defense lawyers were able to discredit the testimony of key prosecution witness William M. Daniels, whom they portrayed as an opportunist who joined the church after the Smiths' deaths in hopes of profiting from his testimony about the murders. Before Daniels testified at the trial, a pamphlet appeared under his name giving what was supposed to be his recollections of the murders. "The Daniels booklet," modern scholars would note, "gave the defense an unequaled opportunity for impeachment of this chief prosecution witness."[8]

Daniels's pamphlet, titled *A Correct Account of the Murder of Generals Joseph and Hyrum Smith,* asserted that after Joseph Smith died, a ruffian "gathered a bowie knife for the purpose of severing his [Joseph Smith's] head from his body. He raised the knife and was in the attitude of striking, when a light, so sudden and powerful, burst from the heavens upon the bloody scene, (passing its vivid chain between Joseph and his murderers,) that they were struck with terrified awe and filled with consternation. This light, in its appearance and potency, baffles all powers of description. The arm of the ruffian, that held the knife, fell powerless; the muskets of the four, who [had] fired [at Joseph Smith], fell to the ground, and they all stood like marble statues, not having the power to move a single limb of their bodies."[9]

At the murder trial, however, Daniels acknowledged the account contained fabrications, which he attributed to the typesetter who took down and published the story. When defense counsel questioned Daniels about the miraculous light the pamphlet described, Daniels maintained he had seen a light but conceded that it was "represented in the book rather different than what it was." Defense counsel also asked Daniels about the ruffian who supposedly tried to behead Joseph Smith. Asked if the man had a bowie knife in his hand, Daniels answered, "I did not see any." Counsel also asked if he saw the ruffian "stand like a marble statue." "No," Daniels conceded. When defense counsel then read the account from the pamphlet, Daniels insisted, "I did not write that, neither did I authorise it to be written."[10]

The Daniels pamphlet influenced the church historians who completed Joseph Smith's official history after his death and published it in serial form. When the history was republished in book form, however, most details from the Daniels story had been eliminated as unreliable by editor B. H. Roberts, a general authority and assistant historian of the church.[11] "The story of Daniels is incredible," Roberts wrote, "not because it involves incidents that would be set down as 'miraculous,' but because the story is all out of harmony with what in the nature of things would happen under the circumstances, and the incidents he details are too numerous, too complicated, too deliberate, and would have occupied too much time to be crowded into the space within which necessarily they must have happened, if they happened at all."[12]

"It was inevitable, perhaps," he remarked, "that something miraculous should be alleged as connected with the death of Joseph Smith; that both myth and legend, those parasites of truth, should attach themselves to the Prophet's career." But Roberts also lamented that "this whole fabric of myth and legend . . . has, unfortunately, found its way into some of our otherwise acceptable church works, and still more unfortunately has entered into the beliefs of many Latter-day Saints."[13]

Two general authorities of the church had been with Joseph and Hyrum Smith when they were killed, and within weeks, each had published an account of the murders, neither of which mentioned the sensational details described in the later Daniels pamphlet.[14] "Fortunately for the church," Roberts wrote, and "fortunately for the truth of history, the church placed on record at an early date, following the event, an official declaration of the accepted facts and incidents attending upon the martyrdom of her two chiefest men and prophets: and it is with deep satisfaction that one can note the absence of the myths and legends that ignorance and superstition would all too willingly attach to the tragedy of their martyrdom."[15]

Decades after the Daniels pamphlet was written, however, copies began to circulate of a letter supposedly written on October 14, 1844, by the ruffian described in the pamphlet. Though the letter did not mention the most sensational points of the Daniels account, it corroborated other details found in it and thus helped raise the pamphlet's overall credibility among church members.[16]

B. H. Roberts questioned the authenticity of the corroborating letter, which purportedly was written to a midwestern newspaper in an attempt to scuttle the congressional campaign of Thomas Sharp, a man credited with inciting the Smiths' murder. "It was not published by the unknown paper to which ostensibly it was sent," Roberts noted, "but it is alleged to have remained in the office of said paper until a change of owners was effected. The purchaser of the unknown paper, and himself unknown, found the letter among the rejected papers of his predecessor—handed it to a friend (name not given) with permission to keep it over night. The borrower happened to be friendly towards the 'Mormons' and allowed two visiting 'Mormon' elders . . . to copy it, and they certify on their copy that it is a true copy of the original. This copy comes to the hands of one . . . who furnishes [an LDS author] with a copy of it, and so it gets into our literature to appear and reappear *ad nauseam*."[17]

Decades later, another historian would write, "While the letter appears to be of nineteenth century vintage, internal inconsistencies raise a question of its authenticity. In the opening lines of his letter (dated October 14, 1844), for example, the author gives the impression he is writing to dissuade voters from supporting Thomas Sharp in a congressional election. But Sharp was not a candidate for congress until 1856."[18]

After Joseph Smith was killed in 1844, a large body of Latter-day Saints felt Brigham Young was the church's rightful leader and eventually followed him westward to what became Utah. Others challenged Young's leadership, and of those, none proved a greater threat than James J. Strang. Strang, a recent convert to Mormonism, claimed that Smith had sent a letter before his death appointing Strang as his successor. Young denounced the letter

as a "base and wicked forgery" and declared it "surprisingly strange that
Joseph Smith should appoint a man to succeed him . . . and yet not tell it
. . . to any of the authorities of the church." Still, Strang eventually succeeded in converting several church leaders and hundreds of others to follow
him.[19]

Some challenged Strang's appointment letter by claiming the postmark
on it was the wrong size and color and contained a dot that should not
have been there. When genuine postmarks were gathered for comparison,
however, not only did Strang's match in size and color, but even the stray
dot was present. "How could the forger know that on that particular day
. . . a little splinter would get into the mailing stamp, and mark every letter
with one dot which ought not to be there?" Strang exulted. "This dot, once
the sole ground of impeachment of this letter of appointment, has thus
established its genuineness."[20]

In course of time, Strang was killed, and his followers scattered. Eventually, the famed letter of appointment made its way to Yale University,
where modern scholars concluded that, despite Strang's claim, the letter
was not in Joseph Smith's hand. And what of the postmark? The letter was
written on two sheets, which under scrutiny, proved to be of different paper.
Some scholars theorized that Strang may have received a genuinely postmarked letter, retained the cover sheet (which bears the postmark but was
likely blank on one side), replaced the real inside sheet with one containing
the beginning of the forged message, and then finished the message on
the genuine sheet to persuade others that the sheets had come together.[21]

Careful study of Strang's life showed that he had perpetuated his fraud
by masking and controlling his true feelings. His sister would explain that
during his teens, he "seemed to lose his spirituality and become somewhat
skeptical." In a coded diary entry, Strang himself recorded that he would
pray and discuss religious subjects at church, but it had been "a long time
since I have really believed these dogmas." A biographer wrote that Strang
envied a debate colleague who "could appear sincere and reasonable in
uttering the greatest absurdities and was so skillful that he did not care
which side he took in a debate. Strang stored that trait for future reference.
Later in life, he would learn to use fabrication for a cause: his cause."[22]

In 1838, Book of Mormon scribe and witness Oliver Cowdery had been
excommunicated from the church.[23] In 1906, an anti-Mormon tract included
a "reprint" of a pamphlet purportedly published by Cowdery in 1839 under
the title *Defence in a Rehearsal of My Grounds for Separating Myself from
the Latter Day Saints*. In the pamphlet, Cowdery maintained that he was
sincere in his early religious professions but later wondered if Joseph Smith
had deceived him. He noted, for example, that his 1829 baptism at the
hands of Joseph Smith came "by the direction of the Angel of God whose

voice, as it has since struck me, did most mysteriously resemble the voice of Elder Sidney Rigdon."[24]

For years, many treated the pamphlet as genuine. Critics of Joseph Smith and the church reprinted its text repeatedly, and Latter-day Saints also cited it.[25] Over the next half century, however, serious questions about its authenticity gradually arose. No one, it seemed, could locate a copy of the pamphlet published before the 1906 "reprint," nor could anyone find the least reference to it before 1906, even though the early Mormon press would likely have refuted it, and anti-Mormons would hardly have let it go unnoticed. On the contrary, acquaintances of Cowdery left statements suggesting he did *not* publish any statements against the church following his excommunication.

Additional research failed to turn up any proof that the printing office ever existed from which the pamphlet was supposed to have issued. Furthermore, both Mormons and anti-Mormons began to point out aspects of the pamphlet's contents that seemed incongruous with Cowdery. Finally, the weight of evidence led both Mormon and anti-Mormon researchers to conclude that the pamphlet was the bogus production of an anti-Mormon sometime between 1887 and 1906.[26]

In October 1848, ten years after his excommunication, Oliver Cowdery returned to the church and petitioned for readmission. He spoke at a church conference in Iowa, where Reuben Miller was present and recorded that Cowdery said, "I wrote with my own pen the intire book of Mormon (save a few pages) as it fell from the Lips of the prophet. . . . That book is true. Sidney Rigdon did not write it. Mr Spaulding did not write it. I wrote it myself as it fell from the Lips of the prophet." Soon afterward, Cowdery was rebaptized and became a church member once again.[27]

Decades later, a typed statement began circulating that seemed to cast doubt on the historicity of Cowdery's return to the church. The purported author of the statement, Oliver Overstreet, maintained it was he, not Oliver Cowdery, who appeared at the Iowa conference, and that he impersonated Cowdery because Reuben Miller, representing Brigham Young, offered him five hundred dollars to do so. Overstreet said Miller told him "that I resemble Cowdery so much in form and features, notwithstanding our differences in tone of voice that I could easily personate him without danger of being caught and exposed," and that "to enable me to know what to say and do, Bro. Miller had me read some articles written by Cowdery and also gave me some voice drill, assuring me that he would make a *verbatim* record of my remarks . . . to be preserved for future use under Bro. Brigham Young's direction." Appended to Overstreet's statement was a typed "Certificate of Chirography" attesting that its three signers were familiar with Overstreet's handwriting and "that the above confession (shown to us by its recipient in strict confidence that we will not disclose his identity without first obtaining his permission) is in Mr. Overstreet's own handwriting." The certificate noted that Overstreet died "a few days after he penned the confession." Following this certificate appeared a statement of a probate judge asserting that the three signers had appeared before him on April 7, 1857, to acknowledge their signatures.[28]

In 1927, an anti-Mormon pamphlet cited the Overstreet confession and characterized it as "seemingly genuine."[29] Several aspects of the confession document, however, would raise suspicions of forgery. The confession did not begin to circulate until decades after it was supposedly recorded. Then only typescript copies appeared, and attempts to locate the original failed. The detailed records of the court in which the signers of the "Certificate of Chirography" supposedly had their signatures certified showed no evidence they had ever done so.

Most convincing of all, however, were the numerous and varied statements from the midnineteenth century that contradicted the Overstreet confession. Apparently, whoever forged the confession knew only of Reuben Miller's account of Oliver Cowdery's return and mistakenly assumed Cowdery's appearance was fleeting and thus could be easily faked. In reality, Cowdery spent weeks in the area mingling with Mormons, many of whom had known him personally before his excommunication and thus would not have been deceived by an impostor. Moreover, even persons who knew Cowdery but opposed Brigham Young left records corroborating Cowdery's return to the church. Ultimately, both Mormons and anti-Mormons would find the Overstreet confession to be a forgery.[30]

On June 15, 1878, assistant church historian Wilford Woodruff (who later became the church's fourth president) spent most of the day in the church Historian's Office. Later, he recorded in his journal that while he was in the office, he "had a vary strange vision Copied." In the same journal entry, Woodruff transcribed a copy of the peculiar vision. It described a desolating sickness afflicting communities from Salt Lake City to the eastern coast of North America and graphically detailed crimes, carnage, death, and destruction, together with the establishment of a temple in the New Jerusalem.[31] Because the copy Woodruff made in his journal was written in the first person, some later readers attributed the vision to Woodruff.[32]

Several factors, however, suggested Woodruff had not authored the vision but had simply made a copy of a curious but anonymous document that had been circulating. His journal entry introducing the vision explained that he had the vision *copied* but did not say he had experienced the vision himself. Although he made the journal copy in mid-1878, the vision itself was dated December 16, 1877, and nowhere in his journal for December 1877 did Woodruff, a meticulous journal keeper, record receiving such a vision. Moreover, even though Woodruff's journal copy of the vision began in the first person with the words "I went to bed at the usual hour," Woodruff left a large blank between the words "I" and "went," showing an intention to fill in the name of the vision's author when he learned it. Similarly, the church Historian's Office clerk whom Woodruff had copy the vision added a filing notation to the document that included a large blank after the words "Vision had by." Finally, the text of the purported vision claimed its recipient was "reading the Revelations in the French language" when the vision occurred, and Woodruff did not know French.[33]

Before long, other copies of the vision were circulating, attributed this time, however, to Joseph F. Smith, a nephew of Joseph Smith, Jr.[34] Joseph F. Smith would become the church's seventh president in 1901 and was second counselor in its First Presidency on November 17, 1880, when he publicly disclaimed the vision in an open letter published under the title "A Fraud" in the church-owned *Deseret Evening News.* "For some time," he wrote, "I have heard rumors of a document going the rounds . . . purporting to be a 'Vision by Joseph F. Smith.' A copy of this document was to-day handed to me by a friend. Having read it, I deem it my duty to announce through the News, that so far as this pretended vision has been connected with my name it is a fraud. I never had such a vision and am wholly ignorant of its author, and my name has been used in connection with it entirely without my knowledge." Smith's letter was reprinted by a church periodical in England whose editor, also a church general authority, felt it important to publicize "lest copies of the forgery therein mentioned, should have found their way this side the water."[35]

Meanwhile, another startling prophecy was attracting the attention of church members. In 1893, two Latter-day Saint periodicals ran articles by a member who quoted a remarkable statement purportedly published in 1739 in Basel, Switzerland. The statement mourned the loss of the "old true gospel and the powers thereof" and predicted that within a hundred years, God would speak again. "He will restore the old Church again. I see a little people led by a Prophet and faithful Elders," the statement had purportedly prophesied. "They are persecuted, burnt out and murdered; but in a *valley that lies towards a great lake* they will grow up, make a beautiful . . . land, have a temple of magnificent splendor, have all the old Priesthood, with Apostles, Prophets, Teachers and Deacons."[36]

Because the statement precisely reflected aspects of Mormon history, many saw it as a remarkable prophecy validating their belief in the church. In 1908, however, a general authority of the church published an article titled "A Fraudulent Prophecy Exposed" in which he expressed skepticism about the statement's authenticity. "For my part," he opined, "I am free to admit, that I regard it as a 'fake' and a fraud." He had been to Basel

and had found the book he felt was supposed to contain the statement. The
prophecy was not in it. He discouraged readers from using the statement,
adding that "there is enough of real prophecy without using any that is
bogus."[37]

A year and a half later, James E. Talmage, a Utah geologist and museum
director, saw an intriguing clay tablet in the museum of a midwestern
university. The tablet proved similar to several other objects unearthed
over the previous two decades in Michigan, and later that year, he traveled
to Michigan to meet the persons "who," he later wrote, "had made themselves prominent in the exploitation of these finds." Talmage, a Latter-day
Saint who would become one of the church's best-known general authorities, was fascinated by the "striking parallelism" between the depictions
on the Michigan artifacts and "the historical story embodied in the Book
of Mormon," which he felt would "be seen at once by anyone familiar with
the book named." He felt that "were the Michigan 'relics' what they purport
to be, they would furnish strong external evidence of the main facts set
forth in the Book of Mormon narrative." After carefully investigating the
new finds, however, Talmage concluded that "the Michigan 'relics' are
forgeries, and the seeming confirmation of the Book of Mormon story is
fictitious and false." In 1911, he published his findings under the title "The
'Michigan Relics': A Story of Forgery and Deception."[38]

Talmage learned that all of the remarkable discoveries could be traced
to one man and his associates. "Now," he reasoned, "were these 'relics'
actually of ancient burial, and were they as generally distributed as reports
of the discoveries would indicate, there would surely be some accidental
finds" by others. Yet none had ever been reported. Curiously, the first
relics unearthed by these men were made of unbaked clay. Then, Talmage
noted, early critics of the discoveries pointed out "that such tablets could
not have held together in moist earth for even a period of months, to say
nothing of years and centuries," whereupon "the discoverers ceased to
find objects of clay, and forthwith produced . . . artifacts of slate and copper"
with inscriptions "strikingly similar to the earlier and more perishable
sort."[39]

Applying his scientific skills, Talmage discovered other reasons for re-
jecting the slate and copper relics. He observed that lines on some of the
slate tablets, "when examined microscopically, show fresh fractures, practically indistinguishable from others made in the course of experiment at
the time of the examination." He found that the copper artifacts, "while
generally of an attractive greenness," had "evidently been corroded by
rapid chemical treatment and not by the slow processes of time." "As a
result of my investigation," he concluded, "I am thoroughly convinced that

the alleged 'relics' are forgeries and that they are made and buried to be dug up on demand."[40]

Meanwhile, the bogus vision document that Joseph F. Smith had hoped to unmask by his 1880 letter to the *Deseret Evening News* continued to mislead church members. Its circulation became so prominent as to merit inclusion in talks given at the church's October 1918 general conference by Joseph F. Smith himself (then church president) and his son Joseph Fielding Smith, Jr., a member of the Quorum of the Twelve who was then serving as an assistant church historian (and would someday become president also).

"In my travels in the stakes of Zion," related Joseph Fielding Smith, Jr., "my attention has been called, on a number of occasions, to a purported revelation or vision or manifestation, whatever it may be called, supposed to have been received by President Smith sometime in the distant past, in regard to events of great importance dealing with the nations of the earth and the Latter-day Saints. Many things in that purported vision, or revelation, are absurd. My attention has been called to this thing, and good brethren and good sisters have inquired of me to know whether or not there was any truth in that which had come to their attention. It is in printed form; and I have been under the necessity of telling them that there was no truth in it."[41]

The recipient of the spurious vision was supposed to have been reading in French at the time he received it. When President Joseph F. Smith arose to speak, he pointed out, "I never knew but two or three words in French in my life; consequently, I could not have been the originator of that revelation. I want you to understand that. I have denied it, I suppose, a hundred times, when I have been inquired of about it. It was gotten up by some mysterious person who undertook to create a sensation and lay the responsibility upon me."[42] After the conference, yet another copy of the document was sent to the church president's office to be added to those already in the church's collection.[43] On a copy received earlier that year, the president had written along the margins, "Not a word of truth in it. [Signed] Joseph F. Smith."[44]

In April 1931, more than a dozen years after his father's death, Joseph Fielding Smith, Jr., then church historian, once again felt compelled to discuss the letter in a general conference of the church. "Several times within the past three months," he said, broaching the subject, "I have been approached by individuals and have received communications through the mails, making inquiry concerning a certain purported revelation said to have been given many years ago to President Joseph F. Smith, in which he saw the destruction of many great cities and many countries of the world and other very unusual things." He then reviewed what he and his father had said in 1918 about the spuriousness of the vision and expressed his bewilderment that copies of the document continued to circulate.[45]

In 1945, copies of a typed story began circulating among Latter-day Saints about a "Great White Chief" whose people lived in a remote mountain region in southern Mexico and who were described in terms reminiscent of the Book of Mormon. The story asserted that the chief had become the leader "of all Indian tribes and nations of the western hemisphere" and was preparing them to build a great temple in the United States. The author of the story, a member of the church, attributed his information to a Navajo described as a tribal historian.[46]

The story was soon denounced by various church leaders. By 1953, however, copies of the story had continued to circulate so widely among church members that Spencer W. Kimball (a member of the Quorum of the Twelve who would become church president in 1973) found it necessary to publish an article about it. "In spite of the fact that the people have been repeatedly warned by letter, through their local Church authorities and from pulpit and press, there are still some who persist in spreading the fictional story of 'The Coming of the Great White Chief,' " he wrote. Although he attributed the story's prominence to "well-meaning people" who had "copied and distributed far and wide this fanciful story," he noted that the most evocative elements of the story had been "thoroughly investigated" and "found to be misleading, and most elements totally untrue." He concluded the article by expressing hope "that further duplication and circulation of this fictional story will cease."[47]

Yet the story continued to circulate, and in 1966, the church issued another statement, this time to local church leaders. "Although this story has been repudiated numerous times and found to be untrue in practically all of its major allegations," the statement explained, "uninformed persons continue to duplicate and distribute copies of this mythical composition. It is requested, therefore, that members be instructed to refrain from duplicating and distributing copies of this fictional story."[48]

In the early 1960s, a dozen tiny metal plates came to the attention of Mormon scholars. Supposedly discovered in a Mexican tomb between 1952 and 1956, the Padilla Gold Plates (as they were called, after one of the reported finders) engendered excitement among some who recognized that inscriptions on the plates paralleled the Book of Mormon characters Martin Harris showed to Charles Anthon in 1828.[49]

Scholars at church-owned Brigham Young University greeted news of the plates' discovery with skepticism. From their preliminary studies, the scholars tentatively concluded "that these gold plates from Mexico are forgeries, and that a serious fraud has been committed, since the plates are reported to have been sold for a large sum of money, on the testimony of the 'discoverer' that they are of ancient origin."[50]

More than a decade later, a professor of archaeology and anthropology at the university delivered a paper reporting a careful study of the plates. "If authentic," he posited, "these twelve postage stamp-size plates represent the most significant archaeological evidence of the Book of Mormon yet to appear. If not authentic, they are an embarrassing fraud." Reviewing the results of several scientific tests that revealed several "major technological anachronisms," the professor concluded "that the Padilla Plates are not authentic." He suggested that "given all of the factors considered, the case against the authenticity of the Padilla Plates should be closed once and for all."[51]

In 1977, the Spalding theory, condemned as a "base forgery" by early Mormons and rejected by a wide range of scholars, briefly captured headlines once again when three California researchers claimed to have evidence that Solomon Spalding wrote twelve pages of the original Book of Mormon manuscript. The researchers reported that they had provided enlarged reproductions of the disputed pages, along with sample handwriting from the Spalding manuscript rediscovered in 1884, to three handwriting analysts who, the *Los Angeles Times* reported, were "all well known in their field, worked independently and did not know of the Book of Mormon connection."[52]

The first analyst, who had "analyzed thousands of cases," reportedly told the *Times* that it was his "definite opinion that all of the questioned handwriting . . . [was] written by the same writer known as Solomon Spaulding." The second analyst, who "said he has been a questioned-documents examiner for the Milwaukee police department and the U.S. Treasury as well as serving as chairman of several national document and identification organizations," was said to have concluded, "This is one and the same writer," although he did condition his answer on whether the copies he had were good. The third analyst, who also was "frequently called to testify in court cases," offered his "considered opinion and conclusion that all of the writings were executed by Solomon Spaulding." While reporting these statements, however, the *Times* also raised questions about the supposed Spalding link and noted that "the research project is not altogether a disinterested study."[53] The most vocal of the three researchers, it turned out, was an ex-Mormon, and a prominent anti-Mormon had paid the fees for two of the three handwriting experts.[54]

Meanwhile, church historians in Salt Lake City adamantly denied that the disputed pages of the Book of Mormon were written by Spalding. "We have compared this writing in the Book of Mormon manuscript with the handwriting of Spaulding which was made more than 20 years earlier and there is absolutely no resemblance," responded Leonard J. Arrington of the church's Historical Department.[55] Arrington found the proposed theory "completely untenable." "It would require us to believe that Spaulding had written 12 pages in his copybook," Arrington continued, "that those 12 pages somehow drifted 14 years later into the hands of an unrelated young farm hand (Joseph Smith) a long distance away, that this young man while dictating the Book of Mormon inserted those 12 pages into his manuscript part of the way through his narrative and that those 12 pages matched exactly the size and texture of the paper which is just ahead of it and after it in the manuscript."[56] "We have unshakable confidence," Arrington said, "that the Book of Mormon was written by scribes in 1829 as it came from the lips of Joseph Smith."[57]

Before long, the hired handwriting experts began to appear less united in their views than the earliest reports had suggested. One soon withdrew from the project, maintaining that the press had misrepresented his opinion and that the anti-Mormon who helped finance the research "has a vendetta against the church."[58] The other two took positions opposite from each other.[59] "So," an Associated Press story quipped, "the score is one to one, with one abstaining."[60]

While these experts disagreed, Dean C. Jessee, a senior researcher for the church Historical Department, published a lengthy article that church officials felt conclusively proved their point. Jessee pointed out dissimilarities in the two sets of handwriting and raised other objections to the California researchers' theory. He observed, for example, that the person who wrote the disputed pages of the Book of Mormon also penned an 1831 document in church possession. The scribe could not have been Spalding because he died in 1816.[61] "To the lay eye," a *Los Angeles Times* writer acknowledged, "the examples selected by Jessee look quite similar. And both seem dissimilar to samples from a known Spaulding manuscript."[62]

To Book of Mormon skeptics, it may actually have been two of the church's severest critics whose statements persuaded them that church officials were right. Jerald Tanner and Sandra Tanner, described in *Christianity Today* as "ex-Mormons who now operate a Salt Lake City publishing firm that specializes in anti-Mormon research," had taken an interest in the California researchers' claims. Jerald had even accompanied one of the hired handwriting experts to the Historical Department to examine the pages in question. Though the expert he accompanied eventually remained the only one to support the California researchers, Jerald could not agree with his conclusions. The Tanners published a lengthy study of their own stating that though "nothing could have pleased us more than to have seen the conclusions of the California researchers verified," they had "grave doubts" about the researchers' claims and ultimately "were forced to the conclusion that the discovery would not stand up under rigorous examination."[63]

Despite encountering opposition in many forms, the Church of Jesus Christ of Latter-day Saints had grown from only six official members at the time of its formal organization in 1830 to more than four million by 1980.[64] That year in April, the month marking the 150th anniversary, a church magazine carried an essay by Gordon B. Hinckley of the Quorum of the Twelve Apostles, who was then serving as an adviser to the Historical Department. Entitled "150-Year Drama: A Personal View of Our History," the essay reviewed key events from the founding days of the church, including "the pressures of unrelenting persecution, the falsehood and vicious innuendo of public speakers and public press, the struggles against poverty and the harshness of nature" that contributed to "the great drama, with its own peculiar elements of tragedy and triumph, of a century and a half of The Church of Jesus Christ of Latter-day Saints." Hinckley also projected forward in time.

"Looking to the future," he declared, "the challenges we see facing the Church are immense." The church would continue to grow, he predicted, but not without opposition. "Let us hope and pray that the days of burnings, drivings, and murders are forever behind us. But there will likely continue to be criticism and attacks of many kinds on the Church and its people. It will be of a more sophisticated nature than it has been in the past; and in the future, as before, we may expect much of it to come from those within the ranks of the Church—members of record while apostate in spirit."[65]

His words would prove prophetic.

2

The Anthon Transcript

On Wednesday, April 16, 1980, Mark W. Hofmann sat in the front room of his Logan, Utah, apartment, leafing through the pages of a 1668 Bible he had bought. Where the Psalms ended and the Proverbs began, he found two pages that would not fully separate.

"These pages are stuck together," he remarked to his wife, Doralee, as he worked to pull them apart.

She studied the stubborn pages, then observed, "It looks like there's a piece of paper in there."

"Oh yes," he replied. "I think you're right."

The left page pulled away, revealing a single sheet of yellowed paper, repeatedly folded and sealed at one edge by a black adhesive that affixed it to the right page. The sheet tore as they worked to remove and open it. Not wanting to damage it more, the couple decided not to unfold it further without expert help. Still, they wondered together about its worth, for even with it partly folded, they could see it bore the signature "Joseph Smith Jr."[1]

The next day, Mark Hofmann took the manuscript to A. J. "Jeff" Simmonds, curator of special collections and archives at Utah State University, where Hofmann was a student. Simmonds was an Episcopalian who also served as historiographer and registrar for his diocese, but he had some LDS ancestors and administered a university collection that included many Mormon works. Hofmann, a member of the LDS Church, had spoken to Simmonds frequently about Mormonism. Hofmann showed Simmonds the document and asked if he thought the Joseph Smith signature was authentic.

"I'm not an expert on Joseph Smith's handwriting," Simmonds later recounted, "but it looked genuine to me." They compared the signature to another in the university's collections. "Similar, but not conclusive," Simmonds noted. "But it wasn't the signature that interested me," he added. "It was the markings on the other side of the paper. To anyone

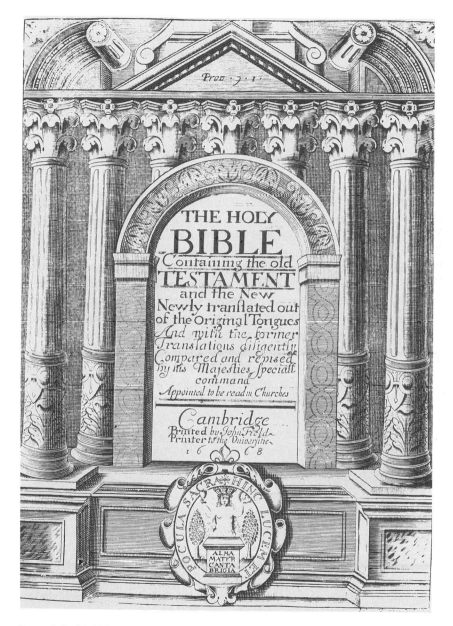

Samuel Smith Bible. (Paul L. Swensen)

who knows anything about Mormon history, they were clearly recognizable as the hieroglyphics Joseph Smith said he copied from the Golden Plates."[2] Simmonds was referring to the characters that Joseph Smith's scribe Martin Harris showed to Charles Anthon in New York. Both manuscript and printed copies of characters from the plates had survived into the twentieth century, but some scholars had puzzled over apparent discrepancies between the extant copies and Anthon's accounts of what he saw. The document Hofmann brought to Simmonds matched Anthon's description well and would soon be heralded as "the Anthon transcript."[3]

"Mark and I just sort of collapsed when it dawned on us that this, indeed, might have been the original paper which Martin Harris took to New York," Simmonds later reminisced. "I told Mark that he should take the paper to [the] LDS Church Archives for final verification. But Mark had already settled upon that course."[4]

Hofmann next took the document to Danel W. Bachman, an instructor at the LDS Institute of Religion near the Utah State University campus. Bachman had become acquainted with Hofmann a few weeks earlier when one of Hofmann's relatives, also on the institute faculty, had introduced Hofmann to him as a young collector of Mormon historical materials.[5] Hofmann had brought other finds to Bachman, but when he approached the religion instructor that day, Hofmann seemed especially elated. "You'd be interested in what I have," he said, reaching into a grey, legal-size document box and pulling out the Anthon transcript. Hofmann said he found the document in a Bible purchased from a Salt Lake City man who got it from a granddaughter of Joseph Smith's sister Katharine. (The Bible was also found to contain the signature of a Samuel Smith. Joseph Smith's great-grandfather, born 1714, and great-great-grandfather, born 1666, had both been named Samuel.)[6]

Bachman had spent much of his life studying Joseph Smith and immediately recognized the document's value. "Here's this kid running around campus with this grey folder in his hand," he later remembered thinking to himself, "and who knows what this thing is worth."

"Do you have any Joseph Smith signatures to verify this?" Hofmann asked, showing Bachman the signature on the back of the document.

"Well, I'm not a handwriting expert; so I couldn't do that," Bachman explained. "But I have some examples in my file." Bachman pulled out photocopies of documents from a later period in Joseph Smith's life. He had obtained them at the LDS Church Historical Department in Salt Lake City, eighty miles to the south. Bachman and Hofmann compared the file copies to Hofmann's discovery. "I was a little worried," Bachman later recalled, "because they didn't seem to look all that good."

The Anthon transcript. (Paul L. Swensen)

"What we really ought to do here, Mark," Bachman suggested, "is call Dean Jessee and have him look at it. He's the handwriting expert." Hofmann agreed.[7]

Among Mormon scholars, Dean Jessee of the Historical Department was recognized as the leading expert on Joseph Smith holographs, documents written in the church founder's own hand. Bachman reached Jessee by phone and made an appointment for Hofmann and him to show the document the following afternoon. "He seemed excited about it," Bachman wrote about Jessee in his journal. "My own view is that this must have been a copy made and kept in the Smith Family and handed down until the man in Salt Lake purchased it." Still, Bachman described the document with cautious optimism as "perhaps . . . one of the most important and significant documents of church history to be discovered in this century!"[8]

Bachman's optimism gradually grew the next day as he watched Jessee examine the document. "He is so calm and cool that he didn't react overtly at first," Bachman wrote in his journal, "but it wasn't long after he examined the note on the back of the characters that he felt pretty confident that it was Joseph Smith's handwriting. He said it was like looking a friend in the face."[9]

Jessee had spent years studying the handwriting of early church officials and recognized the general characteristics of Joseph Smith's handwriting on the document. "Just off the top of my head it looks like a Joseph Smith," he preliminarily concluded after seeing the document, but he wanted more time to be sure.[10]

"Well, Dean," Bachman began, voicing his reservations, "it doesn't look like the ones I've got."

"Joseph's signature changed over time," Jessee explained, "and this looks like an early one. I'd like to study it." He asked Hofmann and Bachman if he could make a copy of the document to study over the weekend.[11]

Describing the document in his journal, Jessee wrote, "The writing is characteristic of Joseph Smith's." Besides noting that the document fit Anthon's description better than another copy previously thought by some to be the original, Jessee also recorded the document's provenance, or genealogy, explaining that Hofmann said he found it in a "Bible obtained from someone who obtained it from a descendant of Katherine Smith."

"I asked him what he is going to do with it if it is genuine," Jessee also wrote. "He said he thought it ought to be in the archives of the Church. A marvelous find if authentic; it would be the oldest Joseph Smith holograph."[12]

While Hofmann and Bachman were in Salt Lake City seeing Jessee, Leonard Arrington, Jessee's supervisor, was up north at Utah State University giving a paper at a history symposium. Arrington, director of the History (i.e., history-writing) Division of the church's Historical Department, had been a professor at Utah State, and Jeff Simmonds had been one of his students. Simmonds also attended the symposium and recounted to Arrington how he had helped Hofmann open the document earlier that week. Later that day, Simmonds gave Arrington a photocopy of it.

"Received a call from Dan Bachman suggesting I not tell anyone about their discovery," Jessee wrote in his journal the next day, a Saturday. Bachman told Jessee he had spoken to Jan Shipps, the non-Mormon president of the independent Mormon History Association, about announcing the find at the association's upcoming meetings in New York. "Her reaction was one of caution," Jessee wrote, "urging that it be verified as authentic." Jessee told Bachman he ought to discuss the document with Arrington, who he assumed had not seen it. Jessee learned from Bachman that Simmonds and another man already knew about the document. "It appears to me the cat is already out of the bag," Jessee observed.[13]

First thing Monday morning when Arrington arrived at church headquarters, he took his photocopy of the document to Jessee. "I told him what I knew about it," Jessee recorded in his journal. "He agreed that if authentic it appears to be a very significant find."[14]

"What do you think?" Arrington later remembered asking Jessee. Jessee said it looked real, but he added that the ink and other properties of the document would have to be examined before reaching a firmer conclusion. "If the chances are it is real," Arrington replied, "we ought to call it to the attention of Elder Durham."[15] G. Homer Durham had been managing director of the LDS Church Historical Department since shortly after his call to the First Quorum of the Seventy in April 1977. Earlier, he had been a college professor, as well as vice-president of the University of Utah, president of Arizona State University, and Utah's first commissioner of higher education.[16]

Like other general authorities, Durham worked Tuesday through Friday in the office, then spent most weekends of the year traveling on assignment at church conferences. Monday was his only day off, and Arrington waited until Tuesday to describe the discovery to him. When Durham heard the news, he suggested telling the department's advisers of the discovery.[17] Gordon B. Hinckley and Boyd K. Packer of the Quorum of the Twelve had been appointed as advisers to the Historical Department in 1978. Besides having close ties in church administration, Hinckley and Durham had known each other since grade school and had remained close friends.[18]

At 10:30 A.M., Durham, Arrington, and Jessee of the Historical Department met with Hinckley in his office in the Church Administration Building, a five-story Greek revival structure situated just south of the twenty-eight-story Church Office Building in which the Historical Department was housed. Packer joined them a few minutes later. Though intrigued by the discovery, the advisers were also cautious. "Questions were asked about Hofmann, his feelings about the church, background, etc.," Jessee recorded. "Also, from whom he obtained the manuscript and its provenance back to Joseph Smith; and what disposition he would make of the document."

The questions caught the Historical Department personnel off guard. "We weren't able to answer these questions," Jessee wrote, "as none of us had spent that much time with Hofmann; he had expressed interest in the church getting the document, but the matter had not been dealt with in any detail." Hinckley and Packer agreed to meet Hofmann in the early afternoon.[19]

Bachman and Hofmann drove to church headquarters that morning with the document, arriving at Jessee's office about 11:30. Jessee took his visitors to meet with Arrington and then briefly with Durham.[20] Durham already had a tenuous connection with Hofmann. Durham's wife, mother-in-law, and daughter were all named Leah Eudora. The Durhams nicknamed their daughter Doralee. A young woman who once boarded with the Durhams later married and named her own daughter Doralee. That daughter married Mark Hofmann.[21]

After the brief meeting with Durham, Arrington and Jessee took the two visitors to lunch. "At lunch," Jessee wrote, "I asked Hofmann if the person he obtained the manuscript and bible from knew that the document was in it, and what his reaction would be when he found out. He stated that the fellow didn't know and he couldn't predict what his reaction would be." Jessee had hoped to get more information from Hofmann about the document's provenance, but he was disappointed. "Hofmann would not tell the name of the man he purchased the bible from," Jessee recorded, "which appeared a little strange to me, but evidently he has reasons." Without Hofmann's cooperation, Jessee would have to pursue the issue of provenance independently.

After lunch, Jessee began tracing descendants of Katharine Smith. As he noted later in his journal, the research revealed that Katharine Smith "had a granddaughter (Mary Hancock) who had resided many years in Carthage, Illinois and that she is the most likely candidate for the person who sold the bible to the unnamed Salt Laker who bought it from her in the 1950s."

At about 1:30 P.M., Durham, accompanied by Arrington and Jessee, took Hofmann and Bachman to meet Hinckley and Packer. "In conversation," Jessee wrote of the meeting, "details of Hofmann's background and obtaining of the bible were clarified. He is a collector of Mormon artifacts and documents—mainly coins. He bought the bible some time ago; but only discovered the document inserted in it last Thursday. He is a returned missionary from England; is now married, and pursuing a premed course at Utah State."

Hofmann agreed to lend the document and Bible to the church to have them preserved and authenticated. Though he remained tight-lipped about who sold him the Bible, what he did say tended to confirm what Jessee had discovered on his own. "The previous owner," Jessee wrote, "who he preferred not to name, had obtained it in the 1950s from a granddaughter of Katherine Smith in Carthage, Illinois."[22] Hinckley quizzed Hofmann about the discovery. "He encouraged Mark to do all he could to trace the history of the Bible because he felt that it was impo[r]tant to know as much as possible about its pedigree," Bachman recorded. "He secondly recommended that Mark obtain a notarized statement from Jeff Simmonds[,] the staff member of USU library who helped him unfasten the edges of the document so he could open it and read it. He stressed that this was 'very important, very important.[']"[23] Jessee also wrote in his journal that Hinckley was concerned about documenting the discovery. "He placed great emphasis upon the importance of keeping an accurate record of what has transpired," Jessee recorded. "He urged Hofmann or Bachman to get an affidavit from Jeff Simmonds at USU stating just how he removed the document from the bible, what he used to do it with, and all the pertinent facts."[24]

About forty-five minutes after the meeting began, the entire group left Hinckley's office and went to meet with the three members of the First Presidency, Spencer W. Kimball, N. Eldon Tanner, and Marion G. Romney. During the meeting, Romney asked, "Do you know where this Bible came

Examining the Anthon transcript, April 22, 1980. *From left to right:* Mark W. Hofmann, N. Eldon Tanner, Spencer W. Kimball, Marion G. Romney, Boyd K. Packer, Gordon B. Hinckley. (Jed Clark/LDS Church)

from?" A little later, Bachman noted, "Elder Packer ask[ed] if Mark would give the name of the man from whom he purchased the Bible but Mark said he would like to get his permission first." "At this point," Bachman added, "Dean Jessee testified that he believed the handwriting was that of Joseph Smiths. In his remarks he mentioned characteristic 'pen lifts' or places where a person lifts the pen in writing as he moves his hand across the page. He said that they had learned that Mary Hancock who lived in Carthage was a grand daughter of Catherine Smith and was a collector of antiques etc."[25]

Describing the meeting in his journal, Tanner explained that the transcript "to all present seemed to be very authentic and informative" and "appeared to be the original paper copied by Joseph Smith from the plates and given to Martin Harris to take to New York City for examination by Professor Anthon."[26]

After the meeting with the First Presidency, Hofmann signed an agreement lending the transcript to the Historical Department for two years to authenticate and conserve, and Jessee wrote out a statement expressing his belief that the document was a Joseph Smith holograph.[27]

The next day, Durham wrote Hofmann to confirm the loan of the document, expressing hope that it might someday become the permanent property of the church. Yet Durham remained cautious. "Bro. Durham pulled me aside," Jessee recorded of that day, "and asked what I see in the fact that Hofmann refuses to mention the name of the person he purchased the bible from. I don't know what to make of it; told him the provenance ought to be checked carefully." Jessee also suggested that the document be studied from both "the standpoint of the characters and physical properties."[28]

On Thursday, April 24, in a regular council meeting of the First Presidency and the Twelve, Hinckley reported on the document. The minutes of the council noted that the document "appears to have been written by the Prophet Joseph Smith" and bore characters "supposedly copied from the plates Joseph Smith had in translating the Book of Mormon." The church had received the document on loan for two years from Hofmann, "who found it in an old Bible he purchased that traces through the family of Samuel Smith." The minutes explained that Historical Department personnel, "who have special skill in identifying the handwriting of the Prophet Joseph Smith, have expressed the opinion that the document is authentic, and could be the document that Martin Harris delivered to Professor Charles Anthon."[29]

On April 28, the church issued a news release about the document under the heading "Newly Discovered Transcript May Be 1828 Example of Joseph Smith's Writing."[30] The day of the release, Durham received a letter from

Hofmann, who wrote that he had decided not to negotiate with the church for permanent acquisition of the transcript until it had been authenticated, deacidified, and "laminated." By laying down these conditions, he felt he would "provide motivation for the Church to take steps towards authentication and preservation as soon as possible since I am sure that you are anxious to permanently acquire this material."[31]

Durham referred Hofmann to Donald T. Schmidt, director of the Historical Department's Library-Archives Division, whose responsibilities included administering one of the largest private archival institutions in the United States.[32] Later, Durham sent Schmidt a memorandum explaining that a church member who had once worked as an FBI handwriting expert recommended that the church retain a certified handwriting expert to study the document. The man also recommended that the church obtain filtered photographs that would enhance the document's features and reduce the need for handling the fragile record. A few days earlier, Hofmann too had recommended photographing it.[33]

Durham invited Jessee into his office when the former FBI analyst was there. "I showed him Joseph Smith holographs," Jessee recorded in his journal. "He studied them a while and compared them with the transcript and felt the handwriting was the same."[34]

The same day, a church manuscript conservator reported he had spoken to a conservation scientist from the Mellon Institute of Carnegie-Mellon University in Pittsburgh who was also a member of the American Institute for Conservation. The Pittsburgh expert had said scientific tests would reveal only the general characteristics of the paper and ink, not the precise date on which the document was actually written, and would require destruction of a sizeable portion of the document. "If we want further information on ink dating," the church conservator reported, "he suggested we contact Walter McCrone whose commercial company has done legal work in dating of documents by ink."[35]

Schmidt later discussed the church conservator's report with Dean Jessee. Referring to the Pittsburgh expert, Jessee recorded in his journal, "He said he could make such a test but would need a piece of the original document to do it. But even after the test, all we would have is a rough estimate, probably within 25–30 years, for the age of the paper. The test is not foolproof. Same with the ink. Tests would not be conclusive evidence of authenticity. So as of now the inclination is to forego paper and ink tests and concentrate on comparative tests only. We don't feel it advisable to destroy segments of the original document for tests that are not conclusive anyway. A local person working at the Library of Congress has looked at the document and agrees that the best test at this time is handwriting comparison."[36]

On May 6, a professor at Brigham Young University proposed that the Anthon transcript be examined by a team of experts who could assess it from historical, physical, literary, and linguistic perspectives.[37] Durham responded that church officials wanted to be cautious about the transcript, avoiding interpretations and comments except for brief presentations in a church magazine. But he said he saw no reason why the document should not be studied or discussed by scholars who did not speak for the church.[38]

Over the next several months, the team of scholars assembled by the BYU professor evaluated and rejected proposed translations of the document, including one by a non-Mormon who was a Harvard professor emeritus of biology. The group reported their findings to Historical Department officials, who passed them on to Hinckley and Packer.[39]

As these scholars evaluated translations, Bachman, Jessee, and other historians compared the handwriting and content of the document against known data. During the summer, Bachman published his findings, declaring there were "compelling reasons for accepting it as genuine." Relying in part on Jessee's analysis, Bachman concluded that the spelling, word divisions, character formation, pen lifts, and even syntax were characteristic of Joseph Smith's writing. The document also fit Anthon's extant descriptions of the document and appeared, on close examination, to be the source from which later copies of the transcript had been prepared.[40]

Meanwhile, the physical aspects of the document were also being examined. On June 4, Schmidt took the transcript to the photography studios at Brigham Young University, where he obtained infrared and ultraviolet photographs of it.[41] A week later, Schmidt's supervisors, Homer Durham and Earl E. Olson (assistant managing director of the Historical Department), met with Gordon Hinckley and Boyd Packer in their regular monthly advisory meeting. The meeting minutes recorded that the photographs showed "no additional writing or changes on the document and this helps to verify its authenticity."[42]

Church officials also pressed Hofmann for further evidence of the document's provenance. In late May, Hofmann sent them an affidavit dated April 25, 1980, in which he recounted finding the document and described buying the Bible in which it was found from a Salt Lake man who said he had gotten it in Carthage, Illinois, in the 1950s from a granddaughter of Katharine Smith. Hofmann said the man could not remember the granddaughter's name but described her as "an elderly lady whose home was full of antiques."[43]

On May 23, church magazine editor Jay M. Todd telephoned Hofmann to get more information about the man who sold him the Bible. Hofmann refused to give the seller's name. "I do not believe that giving his name will in anyway authenticate the document," he wrote Todd four days later.

"I have carefully questioned this gentleman and he cannot tell you anything that I have not told you." Furthermore, the man did not want his identity known, an attitude Hofmann considered "more often the rule than the exception when dealing with collectibles, usually for security reasons, tax, etc." Hofmann said he felt obligated to respect the man's privacy. Besides, he reasoned, in his own experience with collectibles, he had rarely learned an item's pedigree. "If an item cannot stand on its own merits," he declared, "it is not worth owning."

To illustrate his point, Hofmann described two pieces of Mormon money he had recently bought. He thought the crudely printed notes would be "relatively easy to counterfeit except for the fact that they were hand-signed." Yet he willingly paid more than twenty-five hundred dollars for them with only limited information on their previous owners. "If a single signature can be authenticated with enough certainty as to command this kind of money on the open market, then the holographic manuscript in question can, of course, be authenticated," he wrote. "I have given the Church full rights to conduct, or have conducted, any such tests as they desire. I think that any expert will tell you that a manuscript such as this is self-proving."[44]

Confronted with Hofmann's secrecy, Todd called Dean Jessee to see what he knew about the document's provenance. Jessee told Todd that Joseph Smith's sister Katharine had a granddaughter named Mary Hancock who lived in Carthage, Illinois, where Joseph Smith had been killed. Jessee told Todd that Hancock was "the most likely source for verifying Hofmann's story." Todd asked Jessee if he knew a good genealogist who might be able to track down Hancock's descendants. Jessee recommended Noel R. Barton of the church's Genealogical Department, and Todd called him.[45]

On June 4, Barton phoned Carthage and spoke to Dorothy Dean, Mary Hancock's daughter. She had heard about Hofmann's discovery and had concluded that the granddaughter with the Bible must have been her mother. Dean had assumed that her great-grandmother Katharine Smith must have had a Bible, but she could not recall her mother having it and thought it would have passed to another relative. A few hours later, Barton spoke to one of Dean's relatives who said he remembered seeing and talking about an old Bible but could not remember much more about it.[46]

Church officials decided to pursue the Bible's provenance one step further. On June 19, Don Schmidt temporarily returned the Bible to Hofmann to help him gather more information about its pedigree.[47] Hofmann took it to Carthage, where he showed it to Smith family relatives. On June 27, he knocked on Dorothy Dean's back door. When Dean answered, Hofmann showed her the Bible. In an affidavit signed a few weeks later, Dean attested that Hofmann told her he had purchased the book from a man named White who claimed to have acquired it in the 1950s from a granddaughter of Katharine Smith who lived in Carthage and sold antiques. Dean said Hofmann asked her if she could locate any evidence of the sale.

Dean told Hofmann she would check her mother's sales records and let him know what she found. In the records, Dean discovered a 1954 entry documenting a six-dollar sale of an unspecified item on August 13 to a "Relative to Ansel White from California." She invited Hofmann back to her home the next day and showed him the entry. Though she felt her mother would not knowingly sell the family Bible, she knew her mother had many old books and supposed she might have sold it without realizing its significance.[48]

When Hofmann returned the Bible to the Historical Department after visiting Carthage, he discussed with Dean Jessee how he had located the information in the sales record kept by Dorothy Dean's mother. "He seemed gratified," Jessee recorded in his journal. "He has obviously been pushed hard to reveal the name of his source." A week later, Jessee asked Hofmann why he still would not reveal the exact name of his source. Jessee recorded that Hofmann "said the man has other materials in his home and to identify him would mark him for thieves."[49]

Meanwhile, Noel Barton had continued trying to trace the Bible's provenance. He telephoned Smith family relatives he thought might have useful information. He phoned Dorothy Dean again both before and after Hofmann visited her and thus knew about the Ansel White entry before Hofmann returned to the Historical Department with the Bible on July 2. Barton immediately set to work locating Ansel White.[50]

There was no one with that name in the Salt Lake City phone directory, but over the next few months, Barton learned that an Ansel White had indeed lived in California. He had died in 1952, two years before the entry Dorothy Dean had found; yet it was a relative of Ansel White, not White himself, who reportedly had bought the Bible. Barton was unsuccessful in locating White's relatives. "At the same time," Barton wrote to Todd, "I made contacts thru a friend of mine with all manner of collectors of Mormon memorabilia and he made enquiries concerning Ansel White & Hofmann, but no one ever heard of Ansel or any relatives. My friend even went to the extent of making friends with Hofmann, but he will not divulge anything."[51]

Still, the efforts to trace the Bible's provenance had yielded corroborating evidence. There really had been an Ansel White from California. And, as Dorothy Dean had affirmed again in a letter to Barton on July 25, Hofmann had given her the name *White* before she found the entry on Ansel White's relative. Dean explained in her letter that her mother had so many books that she may have sold the Bible without realizing how important it was. Dean noted that Katharine Smith's name was not in the

Bible and finding the Samuel Smith signature would have required carefully paging through the volume. Hofmann had told her that he had gone through the book repeatedly himself before he discovered the transcript. Referring to the information Barton collected, Dean Jessee later said church officials "found out enough to satisfy our minds" that the Anthon transcript indeed did come from Carthage, Illinois.[52]

By mid-August, Don Schmidt had affidavits from Hofmann, Jeff Simmonds, and Dorothy Dean attesting to what they knew of the Bible's provenance. Schmidt had also received another affidavit verifying Hofmann's account. It was signed by Jeffrey P. Salt, Hofmann's childhood friend and former roommate. Dated April 28, weeks before Hofmann's trip to Carthage, the affidavit attested that Hofmann had shown Salt the Bible a few weeks before and had told him a Mr. White bought it in the 1950s for $6 from a granddaughter of Joseph Smith's sister. At the time, the affidavit explained, Hofmann was trying to decide whether it was worth buying for $325. Later, Hofmann called to tell Salt he had bought the book and discovered the Anthon transcript in it.[53]

On August 13, 1980, Don Schmidt summarized in a memorandum some of the steps taken to authenticate the transcript. Infrared and ultraviolet photography "did not indicate any problems with the document." The infrared photographs showed "no indication that there was anything else on the paper at any time prior to the characters being written on it." Hofmann had visited Dorothy Dean and found the entry in her mother's account book. "The original statements by Mark Hofmann indicating how he obtained the Bible and its origin fits this latest documentation which he has obtained," Schmidt wrote. At the end of the report, Schmidt commented, "Although the research and documentation is moving along slowly, we feel that it is important that the research be done thoroughly and carefully without any hasty conclusions drawn from incomplete information." Schmidt's interim report was reviewed at the regular monthly meeting of Gordon Hinckley, Boyd Packer, Homer Durham, and Earl Olson held the same day.[54]

By the end of August 1980, the Historical Department had spent four months evaluating the document. Dean Jessee, the foremost expert on Joseph Smith's handwriting, had concluded the document was written in Smith's hand. Historical research studies showed the document fit what was known about Martin Harris's visit to Anthon. Textual studies suggested the recently discovered transcript was the source from which later copies were made. Infrared and ultraviolet photography revealed no evidence of forgery. The paper and ink of the transcript seemed consistent with those of other documents from the same time period, and further paper and ink analyses would not yield a precise date for the document's composition and would also require partial destruction of the document. Finally, affidavits from four witnesses, together with Noel Barton's research, tended to corroborate Hofmann's story of the document's provenance. On balance, the evidence weighed in favor of the document's authenticity.

On August 28, Hofmann wrote Schmidt to explain he had received offers for the document that he was "finding hard to turn down." Not wanting to deprive the church of "the opportunity to acquire this important manuscript," he proposed a "tax-free exchange." He would give the church the Anthon transcript, the Bible in which it was found, and supporting documentation. In return, he would receive "your duplicate set of six Mormon gold pieces hand-picked by myself." Hofmann said he felt that if Schmidt compared the significance of the document and the coins, he would agree the offer was fair.[55]

Schmidt did not agree. Complete sets of Mormon gold pieces, minted in the midnineteenth century, were extremely rare and had a market value far exceeding what Schmidt felt the Anthon transcript to be worth. On September 2, Schmidt replied, "I have just received your letter of 28 August 1980 in regards to the Anthon Transcript. In view of your proposal, I think that it is quite necessary for us to discuss this in person. There are several aspects of this proposal which need to be clarified before anything can be done." He asked Hofmann to contact him for an appointment at his earliest convenience.[56]

Three days later they met, but Hofmann apparently remained firm in his demand that Schmidt trade for a set of gold pieces. On September 19, still convinced that Hofmann was asking too much, Schmidt obtained two outside appraisals, which set the Anthon transcript's value at twenty-five thousand dollars. A week later, Hofmann wrote Schmidt, protesting that an independent appraisal would not affect his own estimation of the document's worth. "As you know," he wrote, "each manuscript must be judged by it's own merits in terms of how much someone wants it—and frankly, I will not sell it for less. If, however, you are not able to trade your duplicate gold set then the important thing is not so much that you have the original, but that the Church will still have access to photographs of the transcript for research and study." Hofmann said he would call again after the church's general conference in early October.[57]

When Hofmann visited him on October 9, however, Schmidt told Hofmann the church was "not in a position to dispose of" the gold pieces. "We discussed the situation for a few minutes," Schmidt wrote after the meeting, "and I asked him why he was expecting at least twice as much from the Church for the document as he could possibly get from anyone else. He did not have a real good answer to that question and at that point we started discussing other possibilities." At the end of the meeting,

Schmidt felt Hofmann would eventually consider accepting duplicate historic Mormon money of lesser value in trade. Schmidt told Hofmann he
would make a list of potential trade items, and the men agreed to meet
again the next week. "Our discussion was in a very cordial atmosphere,"
Schmidt recorded, "and I felt that he was in a mood to actually get down
to what he might be willing to accept for the document. He indicated that
his intention still is that the Church retain the document."[58]

Hofmann returned on October 13, and he and Schmidt reached an agreement. Hofmann agreed to give the church all rights to the document. In
turn, Schmidt agreed to give Hofmann one five-dollar Mormon gold coin,
several historic Mormon notes, and a first edition of the Book of Mormon
missing its title page. All were duplicates of items in the Historical Department's collection. Hofmann obtained fair value for his document, and
the church acquired what was felt to be not only the earliest Joseph Smith
holograph but also the earliest Latter-day Saint document in existence.[59]

But Hofmann was not done dealing with the church.

3

The Joseph Smith III Blessing

"I fully expected to relinquish ownership immediately," Mark Hofmann later said of the document he offered Don Schmidt in February 1981.[1] It purported to be a transcript of a blessing pronounced by church founder Joseph Smith, Jr., on his son Joseph Smith III in 1844. Its key passage read as follows:

> Blessed of the Lord is my son Joseph, who is called the third,—for the Lord knows the integrity of his heart, and loves him, because of his faith, and righteous desires. And, for this cause, has the Lord raised him up;—that the promises made to the fathers might be ful-filled, even that the anointing of the progenitor shall be upon the head of my son, and his seed after him, from generation to generation. For he shall be my successor to the Presidency of the High Priest-hood: a Seer, and a Revelator, and a Prophet, unto the Church; which appointment belongeth to him by blessing, and also by right.[2]

The document appeared to be primarily in the hand of early church clerk Thomas Bullock, with the notation "Joseph Smith 3 blessing" in Joseph Smith, Jr.'s, hand.[3]

Though a large body of Latter-day Saints followed Brigham Young westward after Joseph Smith, Jr., died, some who opposed Young began a movement in the early 1850s that became known as the Reorganized Church of Jesus Christ of Latter Day Saints (RLDS Church). In 1860, they appointed Joseph Smith III as their leader.[4] Some in this movement claimed Joseph III's right to lead them derived at least in part from one or more blessings he had received from his father, though opinions about the timing and nature of the blessings differed and no one had a contemporaneous transcription of any of them.[5]

Over the years, members of the LDS and RLDS churches occasionally debated the historicity of the blessings. Some RLDS members attributed

Joseph Smith III (1832–1914). (LDS Church)

great significance to them, viewing them as important to their claim of
authority. LDS members, on the other hand, felt that if blessings had
occurred at all (and many doubted they had), their terms were not nearly
so expansive as claimed and that, in any case, the blessings hinged on

A blessing, given to Joseph Smith, 3rd, by his father, Joseph Smith, Junr, on Jany 17 1844.

Blessed of the Lord is my son Joseph, who is called the third,— for the Lord knows the integrity of his heart, and loves him, because of his faith, and righteous desires. And, for this cause, has the Lord raised him up;— that the promises made to the fathers might be fulfilled, even that the anointing of the progenitor shall be upon the head of my son, and his seed after him, from generation to generation. For he shall be my successor to the Presidency of the High Priesthood: a Seer, and a Revelator, and a Prophet, unto the Church; which appointment belongeth to him by blessing, and also by right.

Verily, thus saith the Lord: if he abides in me, his days shall be lengthened upon the earth, but, if he abides not in me, I, the Lord, will receive him, in an instant, unto myself.

When he is grown, he shall be a strength to his brethren, and a comfort to his mother. Angels will minister unto him, and he will be. wafted as on eagle's wings, and be as wise as serpents, even a multiplicity of blessings shall be his. Amen.

The Joseph Smith III blessing. (LDS Church)

conditions never fulfilled by Joseph III.[6] Without transcripts of these blessings, acceptance or rejection of them became largely a matter of personal conviction, and by 1981, debate about them had waned as the two churches focused on mutual goodwill and cooperation.[7] Now, suddenly, Mark Hofmann claimed to have discovered the transcript of such a blessing, a document that threatened to rekindle past contention.

Though Hofmann expected Schmidt to snap up the blessing document, Schmidt was not easily impressed. All worthy members of the church were entitled to receive blessings from officials called patriarchs, as well as from their fathers. As director of the church's archives, Schmidt oversaw a huge collection of blessing transcripts gathered from around the world, a collection that already included blessings to Smith family members, though none like the one being offered. Besides, Hofmann showed him only a photocopy, not an original, and until Schmidt saw the original, he was not prepared to negotiate. In order to "boost Don's estimation" of the document, Hofmann later said, "I remarked that I thought the RLDS Church might possibly trade a *Book of Commandments* for it. After a short chuckle Don said, 'If you think you can get a *Book of Commandments* for it then you ought to try.' "[8]

When an agitated crowd of anti-Mormons destroyed the church's Missouri printing establishment in 1833, the printing of A Book of Commandments, a volume of scripture, was nearing completion. Risking personal injury, some Mormons gathered up a few sets of the unbound pages that had been tossed out in the fracas. The sheets were bound into books by those lucky enough to obtain a set and were cherished both because of their content and their rarity. By 1981, genuine copies of A Book of Commandments were coveted by collectors, commanding high prices whenever one of the few extant copies was offered for sale. To Schmidt, the document Hofmann offered him was not worth a copy of A Book of Commandments.[9]

By Friday, February 20, Hofmann had shown the blessing document to Dean Jessee. "Hofmann is apparently about to buy the document," Jessee wrote in his journal, "but wants to be sure it is authentic. Says he obtained it from Bullock family descendants in the Colesville area."[10] Coalville was a small Utah community northeast of Salt Lake City.

On Monday, Hofmann called Jessee to ask if the blessing might have been copied into the Book of the Law of the Lord, which Jessee later described in his *Personal Writings of Joseph Smith* as "a large leather-bound letterbook-diary-account book containing copies of letters, revelations, and other documents of historical importance intermixed with Joseph Smith's diary entries and a record of donations to the Church during the Prophet's [later] years." Recording his response to Hofmann, Jessee wrote in his journal, "I told him he would have to look at the book."[11]

Hofmann then went to visit Francis M. Gibbons, secretary to the First Presidency, and showed him the document. Gibbons went into the First Presidency's vault, a small but secure room in the Church Administration Building that housed records of the First Presidency, as well as a small collection of historical records and artifacts, most of which came into the First Presidency's possession when Joseph Fielding Smith, Jr., long-time church historian, became president in 1970. Gibbons looked at the Book of the Law of the Lord but found no mention of the blessing. He had no reason to doubt Hofmann, however, and assumed the blessing might well be authentic. Gibbons felt it had no theological significance for the church because Joseph Smith III had not fulfilled conditions described in the blessing and had not been sustained by a vote of the church's members as required by its scriptures.[12]

The next day, Hofmann called the RLDS Church History Commission in Independence, Missouri, and spoke with an archivist. Hofmann described the blessing to her and said Dean Jessee had already verified the Bullock handwriting and thought the inscription "Joseph Smith 3 blessing" might be in Joseph Smith, Jr.'s, hand. Hofmann offered to trade the document for a copy of A Book of Commandments.[13]

Shortly after Hofmann hung up, the assistant commissioner of history for the RLDS Church called him and had him read the blessing over the phone. Hofmann allowed him to tape-record the reading and told him he wanted a copy of A Book of Commandments for the document but would consider other offers. Hofmann said if the RLDS Church was seriously interested in acquiring the document, he would bring it to the church's headquarters in Independence. He also mentioned that at least one other party was interested in buying it.[14]

Richard P. Howard, RLDS historian, had been unavailable when Hofmann first called. He later listened to the recording of Hofmann reading the document and then phoned Hofmann, who asked, "Would you be willing to trade a Book of Commandments for the blessing?"

"If I could be sure of the blessing's authenticity," Howard responded, "I know something could be worked out, yes."[15] Eventually, Howard arranged to meet Hofmann at the LDS Church archives in Salt Lake City on Monday, March 2, 1981, at 9:00 A.M.[16]

"Received a telephone call from Richard Howard," Dean Jessee recorded in his journal on Thursday, February 26. "He is coming to Salt Lake City Monday to look at the Joseph Smith blessing. Said he is in the process of determining whether or not to buy it. He must present the matter to his First Presidency. He said the direction of the thinking among their hierarchy is away from the lineal descent idea. He asked if I would make a statement about the handwriting. He also suggested bringing in a disinterested handwriting authority. He asked about the Bullock writing and the paper, and the signature on the back. Was Bullock employed by Joseph Smith at the time? What did Bullock and Joseph say in their diaries on Jan. 17? I told him he would have to explore the details when he came. He wants to proceed cautiously with no advertising of his visit."[17]

The next day, Hofmann visited the Historical Department. Jessee asked him if he could see the original of the blessing. Around 3:00 P.M., Hofmann gave the document to Jessee and told him he would pick it up Monday. An hour later, Jessee went to see Earl Olson, assistant managing director of the Historical Department, about another matter. While in Olson's office, Jessee mentioned that Howard would be in town on Monday and wanted access to historical papers that would help him evaluate handwriting on the document. Olson said access would be no problem. Jessee told Olson he had the blessing document in his possession.

"When he found I had the original he asked to see it," Jessee recorded. "He was startled with the content and asked if I had showed it to Bro. Durham. I told him I had not but Don may have. Earl then showed the blessing to Bro. Durham who read it and was concerned. Said Bro. Hinkley should be notified, so called him."[18]

Hinckley was unavailable, so Durham left a message with Hinckley's secretary, describing the blessing, quoting excerpts from it, and requesting that information about it be kept confidential because Hofmann did not know Durham had seen it. The message also downplayed the blessing's uniqueness, explaining that Jessee had said a similar blessing was given to another of Joseph Smith's sons. The secretary who took down the message for Hinckley summarized Durham as saying that although the document had not yet been acquired by Historical Department personnel, "if it eventually gets into their hands, they will have to do extensive research on it." After giving her the message, Durham told the secretary that he and the other men would walk over to Hinckley's office in the hope he would be available when they arrived.[19]

Before going to Hinckley's office, however, Durham tried to find out more about the document. "He called Don Schmidt in," Jessee recorded, "and asked why he had not obtained it for the Church. Don said he thought the Book of Commandments was too high a price. Bro. Durham then raised the question of how to react to the issue if the RLDS make a big news announcement about the blessing. I pointed out that Joseph Smith's last charge to the Twelve took place in March 1844, and would supercede the blessing; also, the blessing, like all blessings, is contingent upon faithfulness." The LDS Church taught that Joseph Smith, Jr., bestowed authority on the Quorum of the Twelve that allowed the group to succeed him at his death. Brigham Young, President of the Twelve at Joseph's death, thus became the church's highest leader.[20]

After this discussion, Durham, Olson, Schmidt, and Jessee walked over to Hinckley's office and found him available. "Upon arriving there," Jessee recorded, "Bro. H[inckley] slowly read the document aloud and was fascinated." According to Durham's account, "Dean Jessee gave his opinion that it was in the handwriting of Thomas Bullock, and that the signature on the reverse side appeared to be that of the Prophet Joseph Smith."[21]

All the men present knew the RLDS Church was familiar with the blessing's contents, and therefore, according to Jessee's journal, Hinckley "wondered if we really needed the original." Durham, Jessee wrote, "responded that in reality the blessing does not constitute an ordination." Hinckley, apparently concerned about how the public would perceive the document, told Durham he didn't think his opinion would hold up. After some discussion of the document's monetary value, Hinckley called the Historical Department's other adviser, Boyd Packer, who was at home.[22]

Ultimately, Hinckley decided to confer with a member of the First Presidency on the matter. Spencer Kimball was out of town on church business, and Marion Romney was also unavailable, but Hinckley reached N. Eldon Tanner at home by phone. After listening to Hinckley's description of the document, Tanner responded, "We have to have it." Hinckley hung up the phone and said, "That settles it." Schmidt was then authorized and directed to acquire the document.[23]

Returning to the Historical Department at about 5:30 P.M., Durham and Schmidt began trying to locate Hofmann. Finding Hofmann's telephone number to be unlisted, they called Hofmann's local church leaders, one of whom learned through a neighbor that Mark's wife, Doralee, had had a baby and that Mark was at the hospital visiting her. Later that evening, Schmidt located Mark at the hospital, and they agreed to meet the next morning at Mark's house.[24]

They met as scheduled and Hofmann explained how he had offered the document to RLDS officials. "They had not fully accepted his offer," Schmidt wrote of the meeting, "but they offered to fly him to Independence, Missouri with the material to let them see it. Because his wife was expecting, he decided that he could not do that and so Richard Howard was coming out here and supposedly bringing a copy of the Book of Commandments. In view of the situation with the negotiations of the Reorganized Church, I did not make a counter offer at that time."[25]

Schmidt returned to his office and telephoned Durham to discuss the matter. Durham called Hinckley and then phoned Schmidt back, asking him to call Hofmann to discuss, in Schmidt's words, "whether or not we could, in fact, discuss a counter offer with him prior to his meeting with Richard Howard." Schmidt tried unsuccessfully to reach Hofmann and then returned home.[26]

On Sunday afternoon, March 1, Schmidt finally got through to Hofmann and arranged to meet with Durham and him in the Historical Department an hour before Hofmann's 9:00 A.M. meeting with Howard. "I learned," Schmidt wrote, "that he is probably having second thoughts about permitting the Reorganized Church to obtain the copy of the blessing. I hope that he will be agreeable to making some arrangements for the document."[27]

Monday morning, Hofmann picked up the document from Jessee and then met with Durham and Schmidt at 8:00 as scheduled in Durham's office. Durham later wrote, "I explained our desire to obtain the document for the Church; suggested to Brother Hoffman that he was a member, had served a mission, been to the temple, and undoubtedly would like to see it in our hands. He said he would. Further, that he would make it available to us."[28]

When Hofmann left the meeting, Durham called Jessee, who recorded that Durham had just met with Hofmann and that Hofmann had agreed to sell the manuscript to the church. Durham told Jessee that Hofmann and Howard would probably approach him anyway to identify the writing on the document. According to Jessee's journal, Durham pointed out that if he were to do so, they could anticipate the press would report "that a Mormon authority on handwriting had verified the authenticity of a document that disproves their Church." Durham urged Jessee not to sign any statements.

"I told him I had already told Howard that the document was written by Bullock," Jessee recorded, "and I didn't think my opinion would make that much difference, and besides Howard plans to have forensic people look at it anyway." Just as Jessee hung up the phone, Howard walked in. Jessee took him into the archives reading room so he could begin to look at materials he needed to see. Jessee also pointed out that Joseph Smith's diary did not mention the blessing and that, so far as he knew, Bullock did not keep a diary for that period.[29] After helping Howard get started on his research, Jessee dismissed himself from attending the meeting between Howard and Hofmann, saying, "I'm going to just stay in my office. I can't go."[30]

At 8:45 A.M., Durham reported the results of his meeting with Hofmann to Hinckley. Then Schmidt returned to his office, where at 9:00 A.M., as Hofmann went into his meeting with Howard and others, Schmidt recorded the events of the past hour: "Mark Hofmann met with Elder Durham and myself at eight o'clock and discussed the blessing which he had. After discussing the implications of the Reorganized Church obtaining this document, he agreed that he did not want it to go to them and that he would refuse their offer, and offer it to the Historical Department." Durham eventually returned home and left Schmidt to conclude the transaction later in the day.[31]

Despite what he told LDS officials, however, when Hofmann met with Howard, he did not withdraw his offer. Instead, he informed him, as Howard later explained, "that I was competing with the LDS Church for ownership of the document. I had earlier suspected this from an oblique comment by Hofmann over the phone on February 25, but came to know it for sure on March 2."[32]

During Hofmann's meeting with Howard, an LDS historian who was present pointed out that Thomas Bullock, the blessing's apparent scribe, had been dismissed from the Historian's Office in the 1860s after being suspected by Brigham Young of pilfering or destroying documents. He also guessed that the original blessing would have been in a different scribe's hand. These statements increased Howard's concern to verify the document fully.[33]

Later that morning, Hofmann and Howard approached Jessee as anticipated to discuss handwriting on the document. "I told Howard I thought it was Bullock's hand, and that the signature on the back could be Joseph Smith's," Jessee recorded, "but I would not like to make that definite as there are details that are not typical. I told Richard he ought to get a professional analysis of the paper, ink, and handwriting, and that I could write a statement but he still wouldn't have anything in the eyes of the people he has to convince. When Richard left, he was friendly, but I could sense he felt somewhat betrayed."[34]

With increased concerns about the document's authenticity and no handwriting expert to assist him, Howard told Hofmann he would return to Missouri and contact a handwriting expert in Kansas City. Hofmann agreed to visit Independence when the expert was available to examine the document.[35]

Sometime after his meeting with Hofmann, Howard ran into Earl Olson, who asked Howard how he felt about the document. Howard expressed concern about its price and authenticity, and Olson interpreted his response to mean the RLDS Church had lost interest in buying it. The Historical Department's office journal (which Olson oversaw) would record, "Mr. Howard had some reservations about the authenticity of the document and the amount Mark Hofmann was requesting for it, and so he returned to Independence."[36]

LDS Historical Department officials then assumed not only that Hofmann had withdrawn his offer to sell the document to the RLDS Church but also that Howard was no longer interested in purchasing it. These impressions were confirmed at 12:30 that afternoon when Hofmann met with Schmidt, declared he was ready to negotiate, and asked Schmidt what he had to offer. Schmidt offered him a first edition of the Book of Mormon and several pieces of historic Mormon money and other notes. Hofmann accepted, signed an acquisition form, and left. Schmidt then called Durham at home to report the transaction had been completed.[37]

On Tuesday, March 3, Durham was back in the office, and Schmidt met with him to detail Monday's transaction. After the meeting, Schmidt wrote, "I just concluded a discussion of yesterday's events with Elder Durham in his office. He appreciated the fact that we do have the document and had contacted Elder Hinckley who also was quite pleased that it had not gone to the RLDS Church."[38]

When Durham first informed Hinckley about the blessing, he had said that if the Historical Department acquired the document, it would have to conduct extensive research on it.[39] With the document in their possession, LDS officials began their research.

Meanwhile, on March 3, Howard, who had returned to Independence, telephoned Hofmann and the Kansas City handwriting expert to arrange a meeting between them. Hofmann agreed to meet on March 17 and promised to call Howard back to confirm the arrangements. Howard later met with the president of his church to discuss the document. They decided to trade Hofmann one of their three copies of A Book of Commandments when the blessing was authenticated. Hofmann did not call back, but Howard did not worry. "After all," he later said, "he was a new father, and I was sure he was up to his neck in the meaning of that event." On the afternoon of March 6, Howard decided to call Hofmann to tell him about a price quote from Walter C. McCrone Associates in Chicago for a scientific paper analysis of the document.[40]

As Howard reached for the phone, it rang. The caller introduced herself as a reporter and said, "We've heard that you have a copy of a blessing given by Joseph Smith, Jr., to his son, designating him as his successor to the presidency of the church. What can you tell me about this blessing?" Howard declined comment, suggesting the reporter speak to the document's owner. The reporter said she had heard that the LDS Church was acquiring the document, but that no one at the LDS Church archives would provide her any information. Howard simply replied, "Well, then, you need to get your information from the Mormon Church."

Proceeding with his plans, Howard called Hofmann to finalize arrangements for authenticating the document. As Howard began to speak, Hofmann interrupted, "Mr. Howard, I have some disappointing news for you. I presented the blessing to the Mormon Church this morning." Disturbed, Howard called Schmidt, whom he had known for a long time, and requested a certified copy of both sides of the document and permission to publish it. Schmidt asked him to put his request in writing and said he would forward the matter to his supervisors. Howard also canceled the appointment with the Kansas City document examiner.[41]

Howard slept little that night. The next day, he prepared a letter to Hofmann, chastising him for selling the blessing to the LDS Church while still negotiating with the RLDS Church. On Monday he mailed it to Hofmann and sent a copy to Schmidt.[42] With Schmidt's copy, Howard enclosed his formal written request for a copy of the blessing document and permission to publish it because of its "singular importance to the history of the RLDS Church from its inception to the present day."[43]

That same Monday, Leonard Arrington wrote Gordon Hinckley seeking access to material in the First Presidency's vault that might help him and his staff historians place the blessing in its proper context in "anticipation of the inevitability that the blessing pronounced by the Prophet Joseph Smith on his son Joseph III will become public knowledge."[44]

On Wednesday, Hinckley, Packer, Durham, and Olson met in their regular monthly meeting. Durham reported the details of the transaction with Hofmann, Howard's telephone request for a copy of the document, and Schmidt's instruction that Howard put his request in writing. Hinckley said that Howard's written request, when received, would be taken to the First Presidency for consideration. The minutes of the meeting also noted the research that had been going on since the document was acquired, as well as Arrington's request for access to material in the First Presidency's vault. The next day Hinckley wrote Arrington, agreeing to take up the matter of access with the First Presidency after Spencer Kimball's return the following week.[45]

It quickly became apparent, however, that news of the document would become public before the research was finished. That same morning, a long-time critic of the church telephoned Schmidt to say that someone in the Historical Department had told him about the document. Word was traveling fast.[46]

Meanwhile, Hofmann received Howard's letter of March 9, which quoted a February 24 letter from Hofmann in which he had offered the Joseph Smith III blessing to the RLDS Church, pledging, "You may consider the above trade offer binding on myself until 8 March 1981, at which time I will be free to sell it to the highest bidder." Howard wrote that he felt subsequent dealings had by implication extended the deadline to March 17, the date on which the Missouri handwriting specialist was to examine the document.[47]

Howard's letter also attacked Hofmann's ethics and expressed concern over what he assumed to be purposeful complicity on the part of LDS officials. "Perhaps then," he wrote, "you can appreciate my surprise and dismay at your demonstrated lack of ethical conduct in honoring agreements made. That the Mormon Church would involve itself in such a transaction . . . is an added insult and cause for sorrow . . . in view of the integrity and cordiality characterizing relationships between the respective historical agencies of the two churches during my tenure as Church Historian." Howard's letter would disturb LDS officials, who had been unaware that Hofmann had bound himself to hold open his offer to the RLDS Church. Howard's letter further informed Hofmann of the request made to Schmidt for copies of the document and permission to publish it. If the LDS Church did not grant his request, Howard explained, he would retain and use a photocopy Hofmann had already lent to him.[48]

Hofmann called Schmidt on March 12 after receiving the letter and asked to meet with Durham and him to discuss it.[49] When they met, Durham found Hofmann to be "somewhat agitated in his mind." Hofmann told LDS officials details they had not heard before. "All that we knew of February 27," Durham later explained in his journal, "was that [Richard Howard] had been approached, and that he was coming to Salt Lake City for a scheduled conference with Mark Hofmann. . . . Later events demonstrated that we did not have the full story of the involvement with our RLDS friends. For, they had a signed letter from Mark W. Hoffman stating that they could consider as a firm understanding, that he would exchange the document to them for a *Book of Commandments,* and that that firm offer stood until March 8, 1981."[50]

"Basically," Schmidt recorded, "Mark Hofmann broke an agreement with the Reorganized Church because he had made a written statement that they would have until March 8th to accept or reject his offer to exchange the document for the Book of Commandments." The manifestly penitent Hofmann proposed a solution. "Brother Hoffman was greatly disturbed by the letter," Durham wrote, "and proposed he receive back the document. In turn, he would return artifacts to us. Anxious to clear his name of unethical conduct." Hofmann would then trade the document to the RLDS Church for a copy of A Book of Commandments that he would give to the LDS Church.[51]

Durham felt the matter ought to be discussed with Gordon Hinckley, but he was out of town at the time, as was Boyd Packer, the other adviser to the Historical Department. Durham telephoned Hinckley's secretary and arranged a meeting with him the following Tuesday.[52]

Friday morning, March 13, Durham met with N. Eldon Tanner of the First Presidency to discuss the document. "To maintain good relations all around," Durham wrote, "I suggested to President Tanner we do return it and keep [a] photograph which will serve our purpose as well." With a photograph, research could still continue. Tanner counseled Durham to discuss the matter with Hinckley when he returned on Tuesday and to avoid making any hasty decisions over the weekend.[53] While waiting for Tuesday, Durham suggested that Earl Olson call Howard, a long-time friend, to explain that LDS officials did not understand all the details of Hofmann's negotiations with the RLDS Church. Olson called Howard and told him LDS officials wanted to acquire the document but were unaware of Hofmann's binding commitment to the RLDS Church. "When you and I talked on the street," Olson said, referring to their chance encounter on March 2, "I assumed from what you said that maybe you didn't want it because you were concerned with its authenticity."

Howard described the steps he had been planning to authenticate the document and his impressions that Hofmann had consented to carrying them out. "I can see from your letter here that you had gone to all those steps," Olson said. "We did not know any of that." He offered to take the matter up the line for further consideration. "If any kind of an agreement could be renegociated, will you still be willing to negotiate with Mark Hoffman on your original offer?"

"I think not," Howard responded. "Under the circumstances I would rather deal with you." Howard voiced continued interest in obtaining the document, or at least good photographs.

"I do not know whether we can do anything or not," Olson said. "Let's consider the door isn't closed quite yet." The matter would have to be discussed with others. "We will not be able to get any answer on any action until next week, probably the middle of the week," Olson explained, "at which time we will let you know if anything can be done."

Howard said he appreciated the goodwill that had characterized the two churches' relationship in the past and wanted to see those good relations continue.

"We want to keep it that way," Olson agreed. "Let's stand back and see if anything can be done next week, at which time I will let you know. We will do what we can."[54]

On Tuesday, March 17, at 7:30 A.M., the First Presidency met with Hinckley, Durham, Olson, and Schmidt, as well as Francis Gibbons, secretary to the First Presidency, and another secretary. Durham summarized how the church acquired the document. He said preliminary studies suggested the document was authentic, and he explained Howard's recent request for copies of it. Hinckley endorsed Durham's recommendation that the LDS Church give the document to the RLDS Church "in exchange for reimbursement for the amount which the Church paid to Mr. Hofmann."[55]

Discussion then turned to the blessing's significance. According to the minutes of the meeting, the discussion "brought out that even assuming the authenticity of this blessing, in order for the blessing to have been realized it would have been necessary for Joseph Smith, III, to have followed the procedure defined in the revelations for the call to priesthood service: namely, call, sustaining, and setting apart." No one saw any problem with the document except "with respect to the use that may be made of the document by the enemies of the Church," particularly Jerald Tanner and Sandra Tanner, who would probably "endeavor to make use of it to try to damage the Church."[56]

Ultimately, the First Presidency reached a decision about what to do with the document. They would offer it to the Reorganized Church for an amount equal to what Hofmann was paid, "with the understanding that the [LDS] Church will be permitted to retain a copy." They talked about what to include in a press release and concluded that, among other things, the release should "elaborate on the historical background of the document and upon the question of succession which the document raises." Finally, they decided to grant access to records in the First Presidency's vault that might aid in research on the document.

After Hinckley, Durham, Olson, and Schmidt had left the meeting, Gibbons told the First Presidency that Hofmann had contacted his office to see if the First Presidency's vault contained a record of the blessing. "There is no such record in the Office of the First Presidency," Gibbons reported.[57]

In his journal, N. Eldon Tanner of the First Presidency mentioned the meeting and recorded doubts he had about the document's authenticity. "This morning," he dictated to his secretary, "the First Presidency met with Gordon B. Hinckley at 7:30 to discuss a statement purported to be a blessing by Joseph Smith, Jr. on his son, Joseph Smith, III, naming him as his successor. It is supposed to have been given by Joseph Smith in 1844. It is hard to understand why it was not brought up at the time of the discussion on succession. It is in the handwriting of President Smith's secretary or clerk. We are trying to authenticate it or otherwise."[58]

On March 19 in Salt Lake City, representatives of the two churches signed an agreement in which the LDS Church transferred the Joseph Smith III blessing to the RLDS Church in exchange for a copy of A Book of Commandments. The agreement gave the RLDS Church ninety days in which it could "abrogate the agreement if, in its sole judgment, sufficient questions persist regarding the authenticity of the document."[59]

At a news conference held after the signing, Earl Olson and Richard Howard answered questions for their respective churches. A reporter asked if the document, assuming it proved to be authentic, would "foreshadow any change" in either church's leadership. "As far as we can determine," Olson answered for the LDS Church, "we would not foresee any change. We would still feel that the apostolic succession as we now have it would be continued to [be] carried out. This would not really hold any substantial meaning for any change in procedure, as far as we're concerned."

"I doubt that there would be any material change at all," Howard added, "so far as the RLDS Church goes. The RLDS Church, of course, has had a tradition of lineal descent in Presidency, but it has been very clear to the membership all the way through that that is not a mandatory principle. The prophets, presidents, of the RLDS Church who have occupied [the office] since 1860—each one of them has said in turn that qualification for the office is just as important [as], or perhaps more important than, some sort of birthright."[60]

Howard returned to Missouri that evening, and his assistant met him at the airport. Together, they returned to RLDS Church headquarters to deliver the document. Howard later reminisced that as they left the building that evening, "we both expressed hope that the same grace, fraternity, and good will that had characterized the dealings between Mormon officials and us in those past six days would also typify the manner in which our members everywhere would deal with the fact of this new acquisition. Now the task of authenticating it lay before us."[61]

Despite their own staff's preliminary conclusions that the document was authentic, some LDS general authorities remained skeptical of the blessing's authenticity. Bruce R. McConkie of the Quorum of the Twelve, con-

Joint LDS-RLDS news conference, March 19, 1981. *From left to right:* Donald T. Schmidt, Richard P. Howard (holding Joseph Smith III blessing), Earl E. Olson (holding copy of A Book of Commandments). (LDS Church)

sidered one of the church's foremost authorities on doctrine, expressed his concerns about the document in a memorandum to Gordon Hinckley. McConkie noted that the blessing document was "carefully and painstakingly written in longhand, and clearly could not have been recorded in its present form as the spoken words were being uttered."

He also had doubts about its provenance. "We have no knowledge of the source from which it was copied," he wrote, "whether it is an accurate transcription of an earlier record, or for that matter whether any prior record did or does exist, or even if any such blessing was ever given." He described the "purported blessing" as "an unsigned document of uncertain origin." "If it has any validity at all," he contended, "a thing that is by no means certain, it may well be a paraphrase, digest, condensation, or recollection of what was said. Essential and qualifying statements may well have been left out by design, inadvertence, faulty memory, or honest human error."

"Assuming, which is by no means clear, that it is an accurate account," he continued, "either in verbatim form or in substance and thought content, of a blessing actually given, certain explanations need to be made." He then listed ten reasons why the blessing ought not to be used to justify claims of succession through Joseph Smith III. The promises were conditional, he wrote, and he did not feel Joseph III met the conditions. He also viewed the document as doctrinally inconsistent. For example, a portion of it promised that if Joseph III "abides not in me, I, the Lord, will receive him, in an instant, unto myself." McConkie pointed out that the Lord receives only the obedient unto himself. The disobedient have "an entirely different destiny."[62]

On April 4, during the LDS Church's world general conference, Gordon Hinckley spoke about the blessing document, describing it briefly and explaining how it was obtained and traded. He reviewed the scriptural and historical sources justifying the church's position that God intended the Quorum of the Twelve and Brigham Young to succeed Joseph Smith, Jr., in leading the church. He described how Young had led the church to the valley of the Great Salt Lake under tremendous adversity. Among those who followed Young and the Twelve, he pointed out, was Thomas Bullock, in whose handwriting the blessing document was supposed to be written. Bullock later served a mission in England.

From these facts, Hinckley said, a "question naturally follows: Would he have been willing to pay so heavy a price for his membership in the Church and to have suffered so much to advance its cause as a missionary at the call of Brigham Young if he had any doubt that President Young was the proper leader of the Church and that this right belonged to another according to a blessing which he had in his possession and which he had written with his own pen?"[63]

Despite these doubts, LDS officials cooperated with the RLDS Church in its attempts to authenticate the document, furnishing an original document in the handwriting of Thomas Bullock and negatives of several signatures of Joseph Smith, Jr., that experts could use in making comparisons. "Without these samples," Howard later said, "the authentication process could not have been concluded."[64]

The RLDS Church submitted these exemplars and the blessing document to two document examiners, James R. Dibowski, retired chief of the Cincinnati Postal Crime Laboratory, and Albert W. Somerford, retired head of the Questioned Documents Laboratory of the Bureau of the Chief Postal Inspector, Washington, D.C. Dibowski had examined over a quarter million documents, testified in more than five hundred courts, and lectured and written extensively on questioned document examination. Somerford, an expert certified by the American Board of Forensic Document Examiners, had spent about forty years in the same profession.[65] After careful analysis, both experts concluded that the text of the blessing document was in the handwriting of Thomas Bullock, and that the notation "Joseph Smith 3 blessing" was written by Joseph Smith, Jr.[66]

Somerford microscopically examined the inks on the blessing and comparison documents and found them indistinguishable. All were iron gallotannic inks, which he noted had remained in common use into the midtwentieth century. The document had been folded, and Somerford observed that discoloration of the exposed surfaces of the document provided additional proof of its age, as did fractured paper fibers along its folds.[67]

The RLDS Church also furnished a one-inch-by-two-millimeter sample of paper from the document to Walter C. McCrone Associates for a scientific analysis. The analysis found the paper was made from cotton, hemp, and straw, suggesting it was produced between 1800 and 1890. The paper filler was mostly crushed mica, an additive that had come into use beginning about 1807. The sizing was starch, something used for that purpose for centuries. The report found nothing to suggest the paper was not made during the midnineteenth century.[68]

Howard reported these findings to LDS officials through Don Schmidt. Schmidt showed the reports to Durham, who forwarded copies of them to Hinckley and Packer. Schmidt also responded to a request from Howard for information about the document's provenance.[69]

On April 6, Hofmann had answered Howard's March 9 letter questioning his ethics. "If, rather than attacking my integrity," Hofmann had replied, "you would have thanked me for bringing this document to your attention, I would have been a great help in providing your Church with a pedigree back to Thomas Bullock," as well as "associate[d] material, some of which provides an important insight into the circumstances surrounding Thomas Bullock acquiring it." But no longer. "Many such details I now intend to keep to myself."[70]

Howard had responded, "Having read your letter of April 6 I find nothing of either importance or veracity in it sufficient to warrant specific response. Therefore I simply acknowledge the effort and imagination you expended in creating it."[71]

Having severed relations with Hofmann, Howard turned to the LDS Church for answers about the document's origin. Schmidt furnished Howard a copy of a notarized memorandum Hofmann had earlier given to LDS officials. In the affidavit, dated March 28, 1981, the signer, Alan Bullock, declared to whom it may concern: "Between Oct. 1980 and Feb. 1981 I sold several books and documents to Mark Hoffman. One of these was a blessing of Joseph Smith dated Jan. 17, 1844."[72]

In his April 6 letter to Howard, Hofmann mentioned giving the affidavit to LDS officials "on condition that they do not disclose the name of the individual who signed it." Having turned the blessing document over to the

RLDS Church, Schmidt felt obligated to furnish a copy of the affidavit to Howard, but because of the condition Hofmann imposed, Schmidt asked Howard to keep it confidential. "I will admit," Schmidt wrote to Howard, "that I do not know the man . . . who signed the document. We have not attempted to locate him but I understand he lives in the Salt Lake City area. We had an agreement with Mark Hofmann that we would not personally contact him concerning this document. I am sending you this copy with the understanding that it will not be released to the public at any time without prior permission of the Historical Department."[73]

In an August 1981 magazine article, Howard summarized all the tests that had been conducted on the blessing document. He acknowledged that "there remain some unresolved issues pertaining to its pedigree," but he concluded that the "Joseph Smith III blessing is authentic, beyond reasonable question."[74]

After the Anthon transcript had been authenticated in 1980, RLDS officials had removed from their museum a transcript of Book of Mormon characters that did not match Anthon's description but had been thought by many before Hofmann's discovery to be the original Anthon transcript. After authenticating the Joseph Smith III blessing, RLDS officials placed the blessing document on display in their newly remodeled museum. Twice in two years, Hofmann influenced the interpretation of history.[75]

The next year, the RLDS Church appended the Joseph Smith III blessing to a book of its scripture.[76]

4

On the Trail

"Mark is now on the trail of the 116 pages," wrote Kenneth W. Godfrey in his journal on April 13, 1981. Godfrey, an educational administrator for the church, had his office at the LDS Institute of Religion near Utah State University, where Hofmann had brought the Anthon transcript to show to Dan Bachman a year earlier. Since that time, Godfrey had spoken repeatedly to Hofmann, who had firmly established himself as the premier dealer in Mormon documents.[1] The Anthon transcript and Joseph Smith III blessing had been impressive finds, but they would hardly compare to the 116 lost and unpublished pages of the Book of Mormon manuscript—if they could be located. Over the years since the pages' disappearance, rumors of their existence repeatedly surfaced, but the pages eluded discovery.[2]

Even the manuscript of the published portion of the Book of Mormon was extremely valuable. On Friday, June 12, 1981, Gordon Hinckley, Boyd Packer, Homer Durham, and Earl Olson met in their regular monthly meeting. Durham reported that Hofmann was "on the trail of a one-half page of the original manuscript of the Book of Mormon which may be in the possession of the Summerhay' Family."[3]

In 1841, Joseph Smith had placed the original manuscript of the published Book of Mormon in the southeast corner of the Nauvoo House, a building then under construction in Nauvoo, Illinois. In 1882, the second husband of Joseph's widow, Emma, tore down a portion of the never-completed building and salvaged the contents of the cornerstone, including the Book of Mormon manuscript, which during four intervening decades had severely deteriorated. Emma and her husband gave away the surviving portions of the manuscript to interested visitors over the next few years.

One lucky recipient was Joseph W. Summerhays, a Utah businessman, who obtained a single leaf from the manuscript. In 1884, Summerhays gave half the sheet to a man whose papers were later donated to the University of Utah. Though most other surviving fragments from the Book of Mormon manuscript eventually made their way to the LDS Church Historical Department, no one seemed to know if the other half of Summerhays's sheet had done so. Now Hofmann claimed to know where it was.[4]

Though the Book of Mormon manuscript was esteemed among the most precious of church documents, those at the June 12 meeting decided not to buy the proffered fragment "if the price requested is for a high amount." Despite the manuscript's value to the church, its leaders were unwilling to pay an exorbitant price for any document.[5]

Yet for the most part, it was unnecessary to pay Hofmann money for documents. The Historical Department housed many thousands of books, pamphlets, manuscripts, and artifacts, some of which were duplicates. When dealing with the church, Hofmann generally was willing to accept duplicate material in trade. Church officials often preferred trading because it permitted them to upgrade their collections without spending money.[6]

As a rich repository of primary research materials, the Historical Department had numerous visitors each year. Most came for research, many to donate materials, a few to sell or trade. Hofmann's face became a familiar one around the department. On some days, he would do research or engage the department's employees in conversation. Other times, he came to deal.[7] On one such visit, Hofmann sold Schmidt four handwritten pieces of early Utah currency and related materials. *Handwritten* "valley notes" or "white notes" were known to have been issued in Utah in 1849, but Schmidt was unaware of any extant examples of them until Hofmann offered some to him. Like the Joseph Smith III blessing, the notes were in the hand of Thomas Bullock. They were also embossed with the seal of the Quorum of the Twelve Apostles, just as were the 1849 printed valley notes that had been in the church's collections for years.[8]

Hofmann did not take all his finds to the Historical Department. On September 4, 1981, he visited Gordon Hinckley, who had been called as a counselor to President Spencer W. Kimball on July 23. Hinckley greeted Hofmann and asked what he could do for him. Hofmann expressed concern and surprise about adverse public reaction to the Joseph Smith III blessing.[9]

In a memorandum to his file dictated later that day, Hinckley recounted the discussion that followed. "I responded," he said, "that I felt we might expect some such reactions because people were too prone to accept a document of this kind without considering the context of the circumstances under which the blessing was given."

Hofmann thanked Hinckley for his April conference address on the document and said he had referred several persons to it. He told Hinckley he had offered the document to the LDS Church two weeks before offering it to the RLDS Church. He also said he was disappointed word had gotten out about what he received in exchange for the document.

The Bullock-Young letter. (Paul L. Swensen)

"I asked how the word had gone out," Hinckley recorded.

Hofmann said a reporter had told him the information came from the spouse of a Historical Department employee.

"I simply responded," Hinckley noted, "by saying that I knew nothing about this."

Hofmann said he had gotten thirty-six other documents when he acquired the Joseph Smith III blessing, some of which the Historical Department had acquired.

"He then went on to say," Hinckley explained, "that one of the documents he acquired, which he still had, related directly to the blessing. He then handed me a typed transcript of a letter to President Brigham Young dated January 27, 1865. I read it with interest."[10]

The badly water-stained letter, marked "*Private*" and "*Not Sent*," read as follows:

> My Rhemnatism being very much improved to day, I sit down to write you a letter, hoping that we may be reconciled. I have attempted to speak with you privately, but on account that you are too busy to chat with me, since my dismissal from the Historian's Office, I resort to paper and ink.
>
> I have only the kindest regards for you, and for brother G. A. Smith [the church historian], altho' I must confess that I felt insulted at being turned out, without advance notice, nor warning; and this after nearly 17 years of faithful employment. I have never said that you are not the right man to head the Church, and if any man says otherwise, he is a *liar;* I believe that you have never pretended to anything that did not belong to you. Mr. Smith (Young Joseph) has forfeited any claim which he ever had to successorship, but *I do not believe* that this gives you licence to destroy every remnant of the blessing which he received from his Father, those promises *must* be fulfilled by some future generation.
>
> I will not, nay I can not, surrender that blessing, knowing what its certain fate will be if returned, even at the peril of my own livelihood and standing. I regret the necessity of disobeying your instructions, altho' I believe that you understand my feeling of loyalty towards brother Joseph, as well as towards yourself.
>
> You will please to excuse the warmth of my sentiment, my earnest desire is for the good of the Martyre, his heirs, the First Presidency, and all of the Saints of God. My conscience is "clear as Rocky Mountain water," I do not want a stink, and trust that you do not want one either.
>
> Dear Brother, when again we meet, may our hands strike in mutual respect and affection, our long friendship unchanged, is the prayer of
>
> Thomas Bullock
>
> P.S.
> I would to write more, but my hand smarts. Can we talk privately?[11]

After Hinckley read the document, Hofmann said he was a believing, active Latter-day Saint, that he wanted to give the original document to Hinckley, and that he did not want to blackmail the church. Trying to clarify what Hofmann meant, Hinckley asked, "Are you telling me that you wish to give this document to the Church without cost?"

Yes, Hofmann answered. He also told Hinckley he had not kept a copy of the document for himself.

"I thanked him," Hinckley recorded, "and told him that the First Presidency would be advised and also Elder Durham, Managing Director of the Historical Department. We shook hands when he left and I said, 'Thank you and the Lord bless you.' "[12]

Hinckley later showed the document to Durham and then gave it to Francis Gibbons, secretary to the First Presidency. The next Tuesday, Hinckley discussed the matter with his fellow counselors in the First Presidency, N. Eldon Tanner and Marion Romney. President Spencer Kimball had undergone surgery the previous Saturday and remained unconscious in a hospital room. The men decided to file the document in the First Presidency's vault.[13]

None of the First Presidency recorded reasons for the decision. Ordinarily, members of the First Presidency would routinely forward historical materials they acquired to the Historical Department. In this case, however, Hofmann had deliberately avoided working through the Historical Department and had lamented to Hinckley that the department had breached an earlier confidence. The concern he expressed over public reaction to the Joseph Smith III blessing implied he feared a similar reaction to the Bullock-Young letter.

The members of the First Presidency were undoubtedly not anxious themselves to revive the animosity expressed by church critics after the Joseph Smith III blessing became public. With Kimball hospitalized, Romney and Tanner struggling with the handicaps of old age, and Hinckley (the newest member of the presidency) shouldering the day-to-day responsibility for administering the church, the simplest resolution of the issue was to postpone making the document public.[14]

Hofmann's decision to bypass the Historical Department on the Bullock-Young letter did not keep him from dealing with the department on other items. A few months later, for example, Hofmann offered the church through Don Schmidt four denominations of scrip redeemable at the Spanish Fork Co-operative Institution, a merchandising cooperative established in Spanish Fork, Utah, in 1867. Schmidt had seen a Spanish Fork Co-op note before, but he had never seen any quite like the ones Hofmann offered to him.[15]

Hofmann was not the only collector to offer materials to the church. Among the other occasional visitors to Don Schmidt's office was Lyn Jacobs, a young collector who specialized in foreign-language editions of LDS books. Jacobs and Hofmann knew each other well. They had first met in a bookstore in 1979 and before long discovered they shared many of the same interests and points of view. Though they sometimes found themselves competing to acquire the same items, at other times they worked together.[16]

In 1982, Schmidt traded Jacobs an incomplete, duplicate copy of the church's first hymnal, which was compiled at least in part by Emma Smith and published in 1835. In return, the church received an 1852 French edition of the Book of Mormon unlike any it owned. Later, Hofmann told Jacobs he knew someone who would be willing to sell an original page from an Emma Smith hymnal. The page would complete the copy Jacobs got from Schmidt. Hofmann said he could then sell the completed copy to Brent F. Ashworth for around ten thousand dollars. Jacobs agreed to the deal on the condition that Hofmann explain to Ashworth that the page had been added.[17]

Ashworth was an LDS attorney and businessman whose pastime since 1961 had been collecting historical documents. By May 1981, Ashworth had heard so many stories about Hofmann's discoveries that he telephoned the document dealer to introduce himself. Before long, Ashworth became perhaps Hofmann's best customer.[18]

One day in late summer 1982, Hofmann asked Ashworth if he had any documents from criminals. Coincidentally, Ashworth had done his senior history paper in college on the St. Valentine's Day massacre. After he graduated, Ashworth thought it would be fun to have an Al Capone autograph. About the same time, Charles Hamilton, one of the best-known document dealers in the United States, happened to offer an autographed Al Capone photograph for sale at an auction, and Ashworth bought it.

When Hofmann expressed an interest, Ashworth dug the photograph out of a filing cabinet and showed it to him. Hofmann seemed fascinated by it and implored Ashworth to sell it to him. Ashworth agreed to part with it for about two thousand dollars, roughly twice what he paid for it originally. On the morning of August 13, 1982, just a short time after selling the photograph to Hofmann, Ashworth was surprised to hear Hofmann's name in a radio news story reporting that the photograph had been sold at a Hamilton auction the previous day. The autograph fetched $4,675, a world-record price for a signed photograph.[19]

The story also made the *Salt Lake Tribune* and national television news. Yet something about the news stories bothered Ashworth. The media reported that Hofmann had paid less than fifty dollars for the picture. The next time they met, Ashworth asked Hofmann why reports claimed he had paid so little when he had really paid two thousand dollars. Hofmann replied with a blank stare that implied he did not know what Ashworth was talking about.[20]

Two weeks before the Capone autograph sold at the Hamilton auction, Ashworth had acquired from Hofmann a letter that would interest church officials. In the late spring of 1982, Hofmann had told Ashworth about a letter he had seen while looking through a large collection of postmarks in an estate being liquidated in the eastern United States. Hofmann said the letter bore a postmark from Palmyra, New York, where Joseph Smith's family lived during many of the events leading to the establishment of the church. The letter was signed "Lucy Smith." Joseph Smith's mother and a sister were named Lucy, and Hofmann said he was uncertain which of the two had written the letter. (Later, the letter was attributed to Lucy Mack Smith, Joseph's mother.)

On July 29, Hofmann brought the letter to Ashworth's house in Provo, Utah, forty-five miles south of Salt Lake City. "As we sat that night in my living room," Ashworth recorded a few months later, "and I read it for the first time, I remember nearly falling out of the chair I was sitting in."[21]

"It is my pleasure to inform you," began the body of the letter, "of a great work which the Lord has wrought in our family, for he has made his paths known to Joseph in dreams and it pleased God to show him where he could dig to obtain an ancient record engraven upon plates made of pure gold and this he is able to translate." The letter also mentioned the loss of the 116 pages of the Book of Mormon. "Those favoured of God in all ages have had to suffer persecutions for his name's sake and so it is with us there being such a determined effort in this place to thwart the translation that Joseph was obliged to remove his wife to Pensylvania, nevertheless on account of negligence the translation of the first part of the record was carried off by some unknown person but God is faithfull and the work is now about to proceed."[22]

More important than mere mention of the lost pages, however, were two pieces of information that fit well into the Book of Mormon saga but were not part of the published record. One was that Lehi and Ishmael, two Book of Mormon patriarchs, were brothers-in-law. The other was that an evil secret society mentioned later in the book helped contribute to the fall of Jerusalem. It seemed obvious the information came from the 116 pages. "I knew there were things I was reading which were not in my copy of the Book of Mormon," Brent Ashworth wrote, "and I was greatly moved."[23]

Ashworth was determined not to let the new discovery leave his possession. He immediately began bargaining with Hofmann for it. When he finished, Ashworth had traded away several important items from his collection, including letters of Andrew Jackson and John Brown and a very valuable early copy of the Thirteenth Amendment signed by the members of Congress who voted for it.

Ashworth originally intended to keep the Lucy Mack Smith letter quiet so he could study it for a year or two and then, if it proved to be authentic, write an article on it. But word of the purchase began leaking out, and he decided to show it to others. On August 19, Ashworth had to travel to Salt Lake City for a deposition and decided to discuss the letter with Dean Jessee.[24]

Jessee had become aware of the letter before Ashworth arrived. Nearly four months earlier, Jessee had recorded that Noel Barton told him "that Mark Hofmann has obtained a Lucy Smith letter dated 1828 that contains material from the Book of Mormon manuscript prior to the loss of the 116 pages." Then, just eight days before Ashworth visited him, Jessee learned that Hofmann had sold the letter to Ashworth.[25]

Ashworth wrote that when Jessee saw the letter, he showed "great interest and excitement which seemed very unusual for Dean" and that Jessee told him that "after seeing that letter it would not surprise him some day if someone came into his office and laid the 116 pages themselves on his desk."[26]

"I asked about the letter's origin," Jessee wrote in his journal. "He said it had been part of a large estate containing some 4000 documents from the New England and New York area." That evening after Ashworth arrived home, Jessee called to discuss publication of the letter. Ashworth would record that during the conversation, Jessee "said he had done some checking and did believe this to be the earliest letter and earliest dated document (besides newspapers) dealing with the history of the Church." (The Anthon transcript did not count because, though older, it was not dated.)[27]

Jessee would later summarize reasons for accepting the letter as genuine. "Its authenticity," he wrote, "is supported by the handwriting and signature which match another letter Lucy wrote to her brother Solomon at Gilsum, New Hampshire, dated 6 January 1831. In addition, the black, double-line oval, handstamped postmark from Palmyra, New York, is the same as that used there between 1829 and 1834. Furthermore, the postage designation of 18¾ cents corresponds with the zone rate in effect then for distances from 150 to 400 miles."[28]

Saturday morning, August 21, 1982, Brent Ashworth was working in his yard when he got a call from Heber G. Wolsey, who headed the church's Public Communications Department. Wolsey chatted with Ashworth about having a news conference on Monday morning and about issuing a press release on the document at that time. "By the way," Wolsey said, "President Hinckley would like to meet you and see the letter." Wolsey wondered if Brent and his wife, Charlene, could come to Gordon Hinckley's office at 3:30 P.M. that very day. Brent said that they could, "and we were both excited as we headed up to Salt Lake that afternoon," he later wrote.[29]

Before Brent and Charlene Ashworth left Provo, Brent, the inveterate autograph collector, asked Charlene if he should take his copy of the Book of Mormon for Hinckley to sign. "Oh dear, come on," she answered, fearing her husband might embarrass them. Brent put the book in his briefcase anyway just in case the opportunity presented itself.[30]

When they arrived in Salt Lake City, the Ashworths drove to church headquarters and pulled into the underground parking area. For the Ashworths, as for most Latter-day Saints used to viewing church leaders largely from a distance, the opportunity to meet such officials personally was both exciting and imposing. Thus, they were surprised when Wolsey, for whom Saturday was normally a day off, showed up wearing a yellow golf shirt. Brent thought Wolsey's attire was "rather relaxed," given whom they were about to meet. To Charlene, Wolsey's casual dress was proof that "these people are human over here."

Wolsey led the Ashworths into the Church Administration Building, which was mostly dark because the offices were closed weekends. They reached Hinckley's office and knocked on the door. The Ashworths were a bit nervous when Hinckley answered, but he lightheartedly said to Wolsey, "Well, you look like you've been out working in the yard."

"It was a very down-to-earth comment," Brent later recalled. "It kind of set us all at ease."[31]

The group chatted together for an hour about the letter and early church history. After Hinckley had studied the letter briefly, Brent said, "Oh, by the way, President, would you mind signing my Book of Mormon?"[32]

"Not at all," Hinckley answered, pulling out a sheet of paper and drafting a message. "This is what I would like to write in your book. Is this all right?"

"That's great, President," Brent replied. Hinckley then inscribed the message and signed it.[33]

Charlene was embarrassed by her husband's request but later said she thought Hinckley was "very kind" in agreeing to sign the book. "And I know it thrilled Brent."[34]

"This is one of the great days and events of my life!" Brent wrote that day in his journal. A few months later, he described his and Charlene's experience as "one of the highlights of our married life."[35]

Hinckley had met with the Ashworths on Saturday because he was scheduled to spend the next week in the Philippines at a temple groundbreaking and knew he would not be present for the Monday news conference. On Monday as requested, the Ashworths arrived at church headquarters well before the press conference was to begin. They were then thrilled to learn that the other members of the First Presidency wished to meet with them. According to minutes of the meeting, someone asked Brent about the letter's provenance, and Brent "said that he purchased the letter from a man who had acquired it from a resident of Palmyra, New York."[36]

Brent wrote in his journal that the meeting with the First Presidency was "most sacred" to Charlene and him and that they "were both practically moved to tears." He would later call the experience "one of the greatest highs I've ever had in my life." Charlene would describe the meeting as "just beautiful." For both of the Ashworths, the news conference to which they went next was by comparison anticlimactic.[37]

The conference was held in the Historical Department conference room. Brent displayed and discussed the document but refused to answer specific questions about where he had obtained it or how much he had paid, other than to say it came "through another collector in the east . . . out of a very old collection of postmarks, rare, early postmarks." When a reporter asked about the document's authenticity, Ashworth relinquished the floor to Dean Jessee, who opined that the document was authentic and explained its significance to the church.[38]

"Would you consider this a priceless document?" a reporter asked Jessee, who was given to understatement.

"Oh . . . ," said Jessee, pausing briefly to clear his throat, ". . . no." The droll tone in his voice evoked laughter from the audience.

"You want to ask me that?" Ashworth chimed, spurring yet more laughter.

"I don't think too many things are priceless," Jessee continued. "It's a very valuable document no doubt. I don't know how you'd put a price on it. That's out of my bailiwick."

Jessee's reply prompted a reporter to comment, "If a private collector can discover and acquire a document of this significance, it makes me wonder why the church doesn't have a more aggressive acquisitions policy so that it can obtain these documents."

Jessee said he could not respond to the comment, but a later press question returned to the same theme: "Sir, do you attach any significance to the fact that three important documents have seemed to surface in about an eighteen-month period?"

"Well, yes," Jessee answered half humorously, "there's a lot of stuff laying around out there and we ought to get busy. Gosh, this is a marvelous time to live in. We ought to be home looking in our attics instead of sitting here in this room."

"Who authenticates something like this, and how do you do that?" a reporter asked a little later.

Jessee acknowledged it was possible to "pay a lot of money" to have someone "put a stamp on it." He added, however, that by spending a long time in archives, "you become associated with people's handwriting much like you do their faces. And that's been my experience here. So on the basis of that, I have grown to become acquainted with certain individuals by the way they write, as well as by their faces. As a matter of fact, some of these I could recognize better by their handwriting than I could if I saw them."

Later, a reporter asked, "Is Mark Hofmann involved in this in any way?"

Jessee deferred to Ashworth. "As I said earlier," Ashworth replied, "I just won't respond to that. There were two different collectors or groupings of material. I'd rather not go into that. I'm working on other things, too."

"Mr. Ashworth, is the reason that you don't want to go into the details of where you got it to protect your sources?"

"That's correct."[39]

An article about the document in the next morning's *Salt Lake Tribune* reported that Ashworth "refused to say how much he paid for it, but a

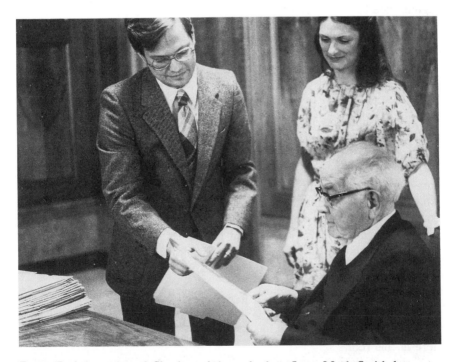

Brent F. Ashworth and Charlene Ashworth show Lucy Mack Smith letter to Spencer W. Kimball (seated), August 23, 1982. (Eldon Linschoten/LDS Church)

church source who wished to remain unidentified said Mr. Ashworth obtained it from a Salt Lake City collector, Mark William Hofmann, for about $30,000." Hofmann was believed to have obtained it from an eastern postmark collector.[40]

In an interview on September 17, Hofmann referred to the *Tribune* article when asked how he ascertained if an item is genuine. Explaining that forgeries plague the market for Abraham Lincoln letters, he said, "To date that hasn't been a real problem with Mormon documents. Now, however, with the publicity that's been given the tremendous amount of money to be realized (for example, the *Trib* mentioned a $30,000 figure for the Lucy Mack Smith letter), there may be some temptation to forge."[41]

In another interview published September 28, Hofmann said of his document hunting, "I am amazed that the Church doesn't have someone doing this, because the material is there to be found."[42]

And before long, yet another remarkable find came to church officials' attention. It surfaced after Boyd Packer delivered an address on Sunday, October 3, 1982, during a world general conference. In his talk, Packer

News conference of October 5, 1982, called to announce Harris-Conrad letter. *From left to right:* G. Homer Durham, Brent F. Ashworth, Jerry P. Cahill. (Eldon Linschoten/LDS Church)

described some of the history of the publication of the Book of Mormon and announced that church leaders had recently decided the book would bear the subtitle "Another Testament of Jesus Christ."[43]

Nine months earlier, Ashworth had acquired a document that purported to be a letter from Martin Harris to Walter Conrad, a son-in-law of Brigham Young, in which Harris solemnly affirmed his testimony of the truthfulness of the Book of Mormon. When Ashworth heard Packer's talk, he thought of the letter. "I felt that I did have a letter which substantiated that new subtitle," Ashworth later wrote, "a letter which would be of benefit to the mission of the Church at this particular time." He decided to bring the letter to church officials' attention.[44]

On Monday, October 4, Homer Durham arrived at his office in the morning and received an unexpected phone call from Ashworth, who described the letter to him. Durham invited Ashworth to his office and notified Gordon Hinckley. They decided a news conference should be held to announce the find. Ashworth met with Hinckley, Durham, Earl Olson, and Don Schmidt to show them the letter. Ashworth explained that the body of the letter appeared to be in the hand of Martin Harris's son. But the signature itself had been verified as Martin's own by comparing it to a signature found on a pension application in the National Archives.[45]

At the news conference held the next morning in the Historical Department, a press release was issued explaining why the letter was felt to be authentic and noting that Ashworth had spent months researching the letter. The release also said Ashworth had discovered that the letter had "passed through the hands of at least three prior owners," the first of whom had "kept the letter in a collection of postmarked covers from early Utah and apparently didn't realize its import." The release reiterated that Ashworth was also the owner of the Lucy Mack Smith letter. Referring to the two letters, the release added, "He declined to identify the collectors from whom he has obtained the documents."[46]

The first question posed by reporters at the press conference was "Mr. Ashworth, would you explain how you came by this letter, what the circumstances were?" Without naming his sources, Ashworth reiterated that the document had been owned by three previous collectors of which he was aware.

A little later in the news conference, a reporter directed a question to Homer Durham, the most senior church official at the conference. "I'm curious," the reporter commented. "Does the church have any plans to take an active role in trying to discover some of these documents themselves?"

Durham explained that one Historical Department staff member spent part of his time acquiring documents for the department, but that "being office confined, more or less, limits his activities."

Later questions sought more details from Ashworth on the prior owners of the document. When a reporter mentioned Mark Hofmann as a possible source, Ashworth refused to give further information. Analogizing to reporters' own tendency to keep some of their news sources confidential, Ashworth declined to name his sources, explaining that he was constantly trying to obtain additional material from them and did not want to jeopardize his opportunities.[47]

Though Ashworth remained publicly silent about the source of his discovery, he privately gave church officials more information. "The document was purchased by Brother Brent Ashworth from Mark Hofmann for $33,000," the Historical Department Office Journal recorded. In an October 5 meeting of the First Presidency, Hinckley reported his meeting of the previous day with Ashworth. He also described why the letter appeared to be authentic.[48]

The same day, Durham wrote Ashworth to thank him for making copies of the letter available to the church. On October 9, Ashworth responded to Durham's thank-you letter, expressing appreciation for the "historical professionalism and the apparent respect shown me by your staff in this instance to my professed desire to keep my source confidential."[49]

Two days later, Hofmann brought another letter to the church's attention through Don Schmidt. This letter, a companion to the one Ashworth had acquired, was written to Walter Conrad by David Whitmer, another of the Three Witnesses to the Book of Mormon. The letter was discussed at the regular monthly meeting of Hinckley, Packer, Durham, and Olson on October 13. The minutes recorded, "Elder Durham showed an original letter written in 1873 by David Whitmer testifying of the truthfulness of the Book of Mormon. This original letter is being offered for sale by Mark Hofmann and he is requesting $15,000 for it."[50]

At the October 5 news conference, a reporter had once again asked if the church had any plans to actively pursue the acquisition of documents.[51] During the October 13 meeting, the frequency and expense of Hofmann's discoveries engendered further reflection on how the church acquired documents. "The coming to light of this document and others in recent months," the minutes explained, "prompted a discussion as to how such documents might be best procured by the Church and whether the Church should have a field representative or an independent agent working for us who would search for and procure, when possible, important documents pertaining to the Church. Mark Hofmann has been in to see President Hinckley and expressed his opinion that there are many other items still in the field that might be procured."

This proposal would be discussed further at a later time. Meanwhile, the pressing issue was whether to accept Hofmann's sale offer. Hinckley

suggested that Hofmann be asked if he could wait a few days so the First
Presidency could consider his offer.[52]

On Friday, October 15, Hofmann wrote Hinckley, thanking him for taking
the time to speak with him that afternoon about the letter. Hinckley had
told Hofmann he would like to discuss the letter with Durham, and Hofmann
wrote to say that Durham would be absent for three weeks and he would
hold his offer open only until Friday, October 22. Hofmann also defined
the terms of the offer, explaining he would trade the letter either for two
blank pages from the original Book of Mormon manuscript or for a copy
of A Book of Commandments.[53]

The following Tuesday, Hinckley brought up the offer in a meeting of
the First Presidency. He reported that the letter being offered contained
David Whitmer's testimony of the Book of Mormon. He read Hofmann's
trade offer but said Hofmann would settle for fifteen thousand dollars cash
instead. The First Presidency authorized accepting the cash purchase
option.[54]

Hinckley called Earl Olson in the Historical Department, explained the
options in Hofmann's offer, and said the First Presidency wished to purchase the document for fifteen thousand dollars cash and did not want to
trade away the other items Hofmann sought. Olson explained the terms to
Schmidt, who tried unsuccessfully to reach Hofmann before noon. Just
before 1:00 P.M., Hofmann walked into Schmidt's office, and Schmidt relayed the decision.

"After some discussion," Schmidt wrote of Hofmann, "he made the
statement that he would not charge the Church $15,000 but rather
$10,000. Actually Mark Hofmann would prefer to have items for trade
[rather] than cash. I think that it has hurt his conscience to think that the
Church would give him money. He feels that the documents or other items
which he gets from the Church are really not costing us anything. He
mentioned such things as the Book of Mormon or again, the end sheets of
the Book of Mormon manuscript, or even a gold coin."

Schmidt told Hofmann to retrieve the document from his safe-deposit
box, saying they would reach a final decision on terms when he returned
with it. Hofmann returned about 3:00 P.M. Meanwhile, Schmidt had discussed the matter with Olson and decided to offer Hofmann ten thousand
dollars cash. Hofmann made out an invoice, he and Schmidt completed the
transaction, and they discussed another document Hofmann knew about
that might become available for purchase in the future.[55]

On Wednesday, November 24, Hinckley, Packer, Durham, and Olson
again met in their regular monthly meeting. In October, they had discussed
having a church field representative or other agent to procure materials
for the church. During the November meeting, discussion resumed on this

subject, and the participants reviewed the draft of an agreement that Hofmann wished the church to enter.[56] Under the terms of the proposal, Hofmann would promise "to actively (although not on a full time basis) search out Folded Letters and Covered Letters of historical interest on behalf of the Church." He would also agree to move himself and his family to New York by May 1, 1983, where he would live for at least a year while seeking this material. By a given date, the church would pay him thirty thousand dollars, half of which he would be obligated to repay. Hofmann would then price any discovered documents and offer them to the Historical Department on a thirty-day approval basis. If the Historical Department retained the material, it would deduct Hofmann's set price from his fifteen-thousand-dollar repayment obligation. If the Historical Department decided not to accept an item, Hofmann would pay the church 120 percent of his assigned price, and the payment would be deducted from his obligation.

Once the fifteen-thousand-dollar obligation was paid, a new "private auction" arrangement would go into effect, under which Hofmann and the church would bid against each other until one of them dropped out. The party submitting the highest bid would get the item and pay the other party in cash 50 percent of the bid amount. The agreement covered only items acquired after the signing of the agreement "which bear postal markings (either in manuscript or handstamped)," but it excluded "any other type of material which Hofmann may acquire, even if it is of historical interest to the Church."[57]

At the November 24 meeting, copies of the draft agreement were given to Hinckley and Packer for study. They were to evaluate the proposal and respond to Durham.[58] By December 8, Durham had not yet heard from them and sent a follow-up memorandum. He reported that Don Schmidt, "who maintains regular contact with Mark Hofmann," had told him that Hofmann was already in New York state and was planning to move his family there in the spring. Hofmann had told Schmidt that he would visit him by December 10 to find out what had happened to his proposal. "I have advised Brother Schmidt," Durham wrote, "that each of you have copies of same and have it under advisement. Further, that I will convey your feelings or the decision made when received."[59]

A final decision on the proposed agreement did not come until Wednesday, December 22, when Hinckley, Packer, Durham, and Olson met in their next monthly meeting. According to the minutes, "The proposal from Brother Hofmann that he be retained to search for Mormon materials was considered and it was decided that it was best for the Church not to get involved with his proposal." Still, the minutes continued, "It would be appropriate that we consider any individual items which he may find."[60]

Before long Hofmann brought in another item to be considered. It was
a letter purporting to reach back into the period before the church was
formally organized.

Joseph Smith hailed from a poor family, and he and his family members
had to work odd jobs to support themselves. In October 1825, Smith hired
himself out to work for a man named Josiah Stowell. Smith later described
his work for Stowell and the label it earned him. "He had heard something
of a silver mine having been opened by the Spaniards in Harmony, Sus-
quehanna county, state of Pennsylvania," Smith explained, "and had, previous to my hiring to him, been digging, in order, if possible, to discover
the mine. After I went to live with him, he took me, with the rest of his
hands, to dig for the silver mine, at which I continued to work for nearly
a month, without success in our undertaking, and finally I prevailed with
the old gentleman to cease digging after it. Hence arose the very prevalent
story of my having been a money digger."[61] Innocuous as Smith's money-
digging appears in this description, his detractors tried to associate it with
folk magic in hopes of undermining his prophetic claims.[62]

The item Hofmann offered the church was a letter addressed to Mr.
Josiah Stowell of Harmony, Pennsylvania. It read as follows:

Canandagua June 18th 1825

Dear Sir
My Father has Shown me your letter informing him and me of your
Success in locating the mine as you Suppose but we are of the oppinion
that Since you cannot asertain any particulars you Should not dig
more untill you first discover if any valluables remain you know the
treasure must be guarded by Some clever Spirit and if such is discovered So also is the treasure So do this take a hasel Stick one yard
long being new but and cleave it Just in the middle and lay it asunder
on the mine so that both inner parts of the stick may look one right
against the other one inch distant and if there is treasure after a
while you shall See them draw and Join together again of themselves
let me know how it is Since you were here I have almost deccided
to accept your offer and if you can make it convenient to come this
way I shall be ready to accompany you if nothing happens more than
I know of I am very respectfully

Joseph Smith Jr[63]

If authentic, the letter was potentially both a bane and a blessing to the
church.

Its description of divining treasure with a hazel stick reflected the superstition or pseudo-science of the period. Though faithful church members
might see Joseph Smith's involvement in such activity as no more harmful

than someone in the 1980s carrying a rabbit's foot, other persons would undoubtedly capitalize on the letter to revive and enhance the money-digging allegations Smith battled in his lifetime.[64] On the other hand, if authentic, the letter would be the oldest known document in Smith's hand, superseding Hofmann's earlier discovery, the Anthon transcript. As such, it would be an important document to add to the church's collection.

As he had sixteen months earlier with the Bullock-Young letter, Hofmann once again bypassed Don Schmidt and other regular Historical Department employees, taking the Stowell letter directly to a general authority of the church. This time it was Homer Durham, who in turn took Hofmann to meet with Gordon Hinckley. Hofmann later said he bypassed Schmidt on the document "because of its controversial nature."[65]

On Thursday, January 6, 1983, the First Presidency authorized the purchase of the letter. The transaction was not concluded immediately, however, because of concerns about the document's authenticity. To eliminate the concerns, Hofmann flew to New York and had the document authenticated by dealer Charles Hamilton. On Tuesday, January 11, Hofmann obtained a letter from Hamilton certifying that the Stowell letter was an authentic Joseph Smith holograph. Hamilton appraised the letter as worth fifteen thousand dollars. On Wednesday, Hofmann was back in Salt Lake City and visited briefly with Hinckley in his office. Hofmann presented him the certificate from Hamilton, and Hinckley then agreed that the church would buy the Stowell letter.[66]

Later that day, Francis Gibbons sent a memorandum to the managing director of the church's Finance and Records Department, describing the letter, explaining the First Presidency's January 6 decision to purchase it, and asking him to prepare a check to Hofmann for fifteen thousand dollars. On Thursday, a check in the requested amount was issued, drawn on a church bank account. On Friday, the transaction was completed. Hinckley gave the document to Gibbons, who, as he did with the Bullock-Young document, placed it in the First Presidency's vault for safekeeping.[67]

On Monday, February 28, 1983, Mark Hofmann brought Don Schmidt a document purporting to be the original agreement between Joseph Smith and Egbert B. Grandin for the publication of the Book of Mormon. Hofmann claimed to have bought the document for twenty thousand dollars from a Grandin family member. He offered to sell it to the church for that amount plus other items in trade worth approximately ten thousand dollars.

On Tuesday, March 1, Schmidt wrote a memorandum to Durham explaining the offer and noting that Hofmann needed an answer by Thursday. At noon, Durham discussed the offer with Hinckley. Durham worried that the price for the document would seriously deplete his department's budget,

Canandagua June 18th - 1825

Dear Sir

My Father has shown me your letter informing him and me of your success in locating
the mine as you suppose but we are of the
oppinion that since you cannot asertain any
particulars you should not dig more untill
you first discover if any valluables remain
you know the treasure must be guarded by
some clever spirit and if such is discovered
so also is the treasure so do this take a
hasel stick one yard long being new but
and cleave it just in the middle and lay it
asunder on the mine so that both inner parts
of the stick may look one right against the
other one inch distant and if there is treasure
after a while you shall see them draw and
join together again of themselves let me know
how it is since you were here I have almost
decided to accept your offer and if you can
make it convenient to come this way I shall
be ready to accompany you if nothing happens
more than I know of I am very respectfully

Joseph Smith Jr

The Josiah Stowell letter. (Paul L. Swensen)

This Agreement made this seventeenth day of August in the year of our Lord one thousand eight hundred and twenty-nine.— Between Joseph Smith, Jun. and Martin Harris both of Palmyra in the county of Wayne and State of New York of the one part—and Egbert Bratt Grandin of the same village, county and State of the other part— Whereas the said Joseph Smith, Jun. has secured right as author to a Book entitled "The Book of Mormon".— Now These Presents Witnesseth that the said Egbert Bratt Grandin for the consideration hereinafter contained, and at the request and on behalf of him the said Joseph Smith, Jun. agrees to execute five thousand copies of the said Book in the manner and form following—The volume to consist of six hundred octavo pages, (more or less,)—edited and closely printed on new type and fine paper—The full edition to be bound in calf, completed and delivered on or before the first day of July in the year of our Lord one thousand eight hundred and thirty— In Consideration whereof the said Joseph Smith, Jun. and the said Martin Harris do jointly and severally agree to pay the said Egbert Bratt Grandin the sum of three thousand dollars in the manner and form following—one equal undivided third part of the said money in hand paid at and before the signing and sealing of these presents the receipt whereof he does hereby acknowledge—one third part to be paid in the month of November next—and the remaining one third part when the aforesaid work is completed and delivered, with any money arising from the sale of the said Books before the said work is completed and delivered to be applied to the discharge of the sum of money so owing by the said Joseph Smith Jun. and the said Martin Harris—In Consideration whereof the said parties agree to faithfully execute, fulfill and perform the several articles herein contained binding themselves in the penal sum of one thousand dollars damages—In Witness whereof the said parties have hereunto set their hands and seals the day and year first herein before mentioned.

Signed and Sealed
in the presence of }

B. J. Reeves

Joseph Smith Jr.

Martin Harris

Egbert Bratt Grandin

The Grandin contract. (Paul L. Swensen)

and Hinckley agreed to see if additional funds could be authorized for the document's purchase.[68]

On Thursday, in a meeting of the First Presidency and the Twelve, Hinckley read a copy of the Grandin contract and explained that Hofmann, "a member of the Church who deals in old documents," had offered the original to the church. Hinckley said he thought the document could be obtained for twenty-five thousand dollars. The ensuing discussion justified purchasing the document because of its historical significance and because the document would likely increase in value over time. Those present approved paying twenty-five thousand dollars for it. Suggestions followed that the document be exhibited at the new Museum of Church History and Art, then under construction, and that a replica be displayed at the Grandin Building in Palmyra, New York, which had recently been purchased by the church and was being renovated. The Grandin Building was where the first edition of the Book of Mormon had been printed.[69]

The next day, the transaction was closed in Hinckley's office. Hofmann signed a receipt, the First Presidency issued the check, and the document itself, which had been temporarily housed in the Historical Department vault for safekeeping, was formally returned to the Historical Department for storage.[70]

In addition to the few major documents Hofmann brought to church leaders' attention, Hofmann brought many more minor documents to the Historical Department in 1983 as he had done over the previous three years.[71] As the year wound to a close, he was also discussing with Lyn Jacobs how to sell the church what would become perhaps the most famous document to be associated with the name *Mark Hofmann.*

5

The Salamander Letter

On Tuesday, January 3, 1984, the church offices in downtown Salt Lake City reopened after the New Year's vacation. That morning, Lyn Jacobs visited the Historical Department to talk to Don Schmidt. He showed Schmidt a letter he said he got from a stamp or postmark collector in the east whose name had been supplied by Mark Hofmann. The letter, dated October 23, 1830, was signed "Martin Harris" and addressed to W. W. Phelps of Canandaigua, New York, who joined the church in 1831 and became one of its prominent members.[1]

In the letter, Harris described how he first noticed Joseph Smith in 1824 when Smith's father agreed to build a fence for him. As the work progressed, Harris asked Smith "how it is in a half day you put up what requires your father & 2 brothers a full day working together." Smith replied that he had "not been with out assistance but can not say more only you better find out." Later, Smith's father told Harris that "Joseph can see any thing he wishes by looking at a stone" and that "Joseph often sees Spirits here with great kettles of coin money." The spirits "brought up rock because Joseph made no attempt on their money." Harris dreamed that he spoke "with spirits which let me count their money." He awoke to find a dollar coin in his hand, "which I take for a sign." Smith recounted Harris's dream to him "in every particular," adding "the spirits are grieved." Harris threw away the coin.

The letter then recounted the discovery of the Book of Mormon plates in terms, which like much of the letter, contrasted with official church histories:

> In the fall of the year 1827 I hear Joseph found a gold bible I take Joseph aside & he says it is true I found it 4 years ago with my stone but only just got it because of the enchantment the old spirit come to me 3 times in the same dream & says dig up the gold but when

> I take it up the next morning the spirit transfigured himself from a
> white salamander in the bottom of the hole & struck me three times
> & held the treasure & would not let me have it because I lay it down
> to cover over the hole when the spirit says do not lay it down

In a similar vernacular of folk magic, the letter described the eventual receipt
of the gold plates, the visit to Charles Anthon, the translation and publication
of the Book of Mormon, and the experience of the Three Witnesses. But
the most singular element of the letter remained its reference to a white
salamander. Over time, the document was dubbed "the salamander letter."[2]

Showing the letter to Don Schmidt, Lyn Jacobs suggested it might be
one the church would like to own. Jacobs said he wanted a ten-dollar Mormon gold piece for it. The most coveted item among collectors of Mormon
money, the rare coin was extremely valuable. Schmidt thought Jacobs had
an inflated idea of the letter's worth and told him he would never get what
he was asking. Jacobs also showed the letter to Homer Durham, who wrote
in his journal, "These collectors are charging very, very high prices for what
they find and when the Church buys such a document, it establishes a market
price which then skyrockets thereafter." Knowing that the price he was
asking exceeded what Schmidt and Durham were authorized to spend for
acquisitions, Jacobs had already made an appointment with Gordon Hinckley.
Soon he was on his way to the Church Administration Building.[3]

At 11:30 A.M., Jacobs and Hinckley met. Jacobs told Hinckley that he
owned the letter, that it had been located in New York, and that Mark
Hofmann had been involved in its discovery. Jacobs again offered to give
the letter to the church in exchange for a ten-dollar Mormon gold piece,
whose value Jacobs would later approximate at from sixty to over one
hundred thousand dollars. Like Schmidt and Durham, Hinckley said he felt
the asking price was too high. Jacobs then offered to trade the letter for
a copy of A Book of Commandments, valued by Jacobs at thirty to forty
thousand dollars. Hinckley considered the offer briefly, then said of the
letter, "I don't know if we really want it."[4]

Jacobs suggested, "Well, perhaps Brent Ashworth would be interested
since he has purchased some of these sorts of things in the last little while."
Jacobs said he thought Ashworth might be willing to donate it to the church.

"Well, that's a possibility," Hinckley replied. The meeting ended, and
Jacobs left, letter in hand.[5]

What neither Jacobs nor Hinckley knew, however, was that Hofmann
had already offered the letter to Ashworth, and Ashworth had turned it
down.[6]

"This letter is a fake, Mark," Ashworth had concluded after reading a
typescript of it weeks earlier. Ashworth had recently finished reading the

The salamander letter (front). (Paul L. Swensen)

early anti-Mormon book *Mormonism Unvailed*, one portion of which
claimed that when Joseph Smith opened the box in which the gold plates
had been deposited, "he saw in the box something like a toad, which soon
assumed the appearance of a man, and struck him on the side of his head."

The salamander letter (back). (Paul L. Swensen)

Ashworth thought the letter was probably an early forgery based on *Mormonism Unvailed*.[7]

"No, it's authentic," Hofmann maintained, defending the letter to Ashworth. "Dean Jessee is going to see it, and he's going to authenticate it. And then Ken Rendell is going to be offered it, and he'll authenticate it.

And what's more," Hofmann added, reaching a crescendo, "it's going to make *Time* magazine, Brent."[8] Kenneth W. Rendell, a document dealer from Massachusetts, was well known among collectors. Just a few months earlier, Rendell's reputation as a manuscript expert had received a boost when he had helped unmask the Hitler diaries as forgeries.[9]

After Jacobs failed to persuade Hinckley to buy the letter, he went back to see Schmidt. Schmidt tried to convince Jacobs that he was asking too much for the document, explaining that only if he dropped his price to a reasonable figure would the church consider buying it.

"What's that?" Schmidt recalled Jacobs saying when he mentioned a "reasonable figure."

"Well," Schmidt responded, "you get down there, and I'll tell you when it's reasonable."

"You have to have it," Jacobs insisted of the letter.

"No, I don't have to have it," Schmidt replied. "No such thing."[10]

Later, Hofmann tried his own hand at offering it to the Historical Department through Schmidt. Hofmann left the document with Schmidt, who took it in to his supervisor, Earl Olson. "He and I read it carefully," Olson recalled. "I remarked that it did not ring true, and that it bore too much resemblance to the story in Howe's 'Mormonism Unveiled.' We invited Elder Durham to sit down with us and read it, then brought out Howe's book and compared the stories. This was reported to Pres. Hinckley. It was decided that we should not purchase the letter, and Hofmann proceeded to sell it to Steve Christensen."[11]

Steven F. Christensen was a young LDS businessman with a deep interest in the church's history. Christensen served as the lay bishop of his church ward (local congregation). Hofmann sold the letter to Christensen on Friday, January 6, 1984, for forty thousand dollars, to be paid in installments.[12]

As they waited to sign the purchase contract, Christensen and Hofmann discussed how to handle the research and authentication of the letter. They thought it would be good to have Kenneth Rendell evaluate the physical aspects of the document. They also felt that both Dean Jessee and Ronald W. Walker should somehow participate in researching the historical issues it presented. Walker was a historian with degrees from Brigham Young University, Stanford, and the University of Utah. Both Walker and Jessee were senior research associates with the new Joseph Fielding Smith Institute for Church History at Brigham Young University. The Smith Institute had been created from the History Division, formerly a unit of the church Historical Department. Leonard Arrington, who had directed the History Division, became the institute's first director.[13]

On Monday, January 9, Christensen wrote Homer Durham, who had spoken to him by phone about the document. In his letter, Christensen explained what he planned to do with it. First, he wished to retain "one or two competent and faithful historians" to research the historical issues the document presented. Second, he desired to publish the document, complete with photographs and an "annotated commentary," when the research was completed. Finally, "At such point in time as the research and writing is completed," he wrote, "it is my intention and desire to donate the document to the Church of Jesus Christ of Latter Day Saints."[14]

On Friday, Durham replied in writing to Christensen's letter. "As stated in our telephone conversation," Durham wrote, "the Historical Department is available for any possible help as your plans progress." He expressed appreciation for Christensen's offer to donate the document to the church and concluded by thanking Christensen "for your letter, your service, and your willingness to make this future contribution to the Church."[15]

Christensen ultimately engaged three persons to study the historical aspects of the letter. One was Brent Metcalfe, who had helped Hofmann bring the document to Christensen's attention. Metcalfe was a former church Security Department employee who had left church employment and then gone to work for Christensen.[16] The other two researchers were Dean Jessee and Ron Walker.

Neither Jessee nor Walker was anxious to participate in the project. Metcalfe, representing Christensen, had contacted Jessee the day after Christensen had acquired the salamander letter and had solicited his help. Jessee had been devoting his time to the publication of Joseph Smith's writings and told Metcalfe to talk to his supervisor, Leonard Arrington. "Leonard asked what I thought," Jessee recorded in his journal for January 11. "My feeling is I have enough to do on the Joseph Smith writings without another project, but something is going to be done with the Harris letter whether or not we are involved in it. The issue from my standpoint is whether our involvement is necessary to assure a responsible statement."[17]

Six days later, Walker approached Jessee and mentioned that Leonard Arrington had asked to see him. Arrington had mentioned Jessee's name, and Walker asked Jessee if he knew what Arrington wanted. "Told him about the Martin Harris letter," Jessee recorded in his journal, "and Steve Christensen's desire for R[on] W[alker] to address the issue. Ron didn't seem too anxious. Its doubtful anything can be said that will soften the document's impact."[18]

The next morning, Walker went to see Arrington, who showed him a copy of the letter. "At face value," Walker recorded in his journal that night, "it is explosive. It is a letter from Martin Harris to W. W. Phelps [written in] 1830, describing the early origins of the Church in spiritualistic or cabalistic terms. It confirms several other documents that have been recently found, indicating the 'treasure-hunting' activity of Joseph Smith prior to the organization of the Church. These 'finds' will require a reexamination and rewriting of our origins."[19] Virtually all of the recent finds had resulted from the work of one man: Mark Hofmann.

The next day, Walker and Jessee both went to Arrington's house. "Ron Walker and I met at Leonard's," Jessee wrote in his journal. "Discussed the options regarding the Harris letter. It was Leonard's feeling that something should be written and we should do it, possibly an article as soon as possible, and then a longer study afterward. Felt its not plausible to think a monograph or book can be produced in less than a year. Rumors about the letter and its content demand more urgency than that."[20]

On Wednesday, January 25, 1984, during the monthly meeting of Gordon Hinckley, Boyd Packer, Homer Durham, and Earl Olson, "Elder Durham reported that Bishop Steven F. Christensen has purchased the 1830 Martin Harris letter from Lynn Jacobs." Those present at the meeting "hoped that Brother Christensen will eventually donate this letter to the Church." Hinckley mentioned that Peggy Fletcher, the publisher-editor of *Sunstone* magazine, wished to publicize the letter. *Sunstone* and *Sunstone Review* were independent publications that focused on the church from a variety of perspectives, including some quite critical. The group agreed that because Christensen owned the letter, he would have to decide on "any release for publicity."[21]

On Thursday, February 16, Hinckley mentioned the salamander letter in a council meeting of the First Presidency and Quorum of the Twelve. The minutes of the meeting noted that a church member had obtained the letter and offered it to the church "in exchange for a $10 gold piece minted by the Church (appraised at $80,000 or more) and a copy of the first edition of the Book of Commandments (appraised at $20,000 or more)." The minutes reported that Hinckley felt "the Church would not be justified in paying such an amount for this letter."

A discussion ensued in which someone pointed out that the letter was becoming rather widely known and that "a major magazine in the East" intended to publish an article about it. The council decided the letter could create misunderstandings without adequate historical context and agreed that research ought to be conducted in anticipation of the article's publication. Hinckley said he would speak to Homer Durham about the matter.[22]

The next day, Richard N. Ostling, religion editor of *Time* magazine, spoke to Christensen by phone and wrote him a letter. Christensen had told Ostling he felt obligated to coordinate the letter's public release with Peggy Fletcher of *Sunstone*. Ostling said he had talked to Fletcher and learned how soon she could run a story on the document in *Sunstone Review*.

Ostling proposed running a *Time* story shortly thereafter on March 12. He said he would try to prevent publicity before that date but would have to publish his story if someone broke the news before then. Ostling said Fletcher had told him that Jerald Tanner and Sandra Tanner knew about the letter but would not discuss it in their next newsletter. Ostling also said George Smith of Signature Books had called him to volunteer several details about the letter. Ostling said he called Smith back later and urged him to hold off talking to other journalists for a while. Smith agreed.[23]

George D. Smith (no relation to Joseph) was a Mormon skeptic who had recently written an article on Joseph Smith and the Book of Mormon for *Free Inquiry*, a journal published quarterly by the Council for Democratic and Secular Humanism. In his article, he had referred to the Book of Mormon account of Christ visiting the New World. "Many nineteenth-century theologians, of course, scoffed at the idea that Christ had visited the Americas," he had written, "but the more credulous welcomed the news. . . . The 'Reformed Egyptian' inscriptions upon the *Book of Mormon* plates were carefully concealed. Witnessed 'in a vision' and authenticated only by Joseph Smith's close associates, the gold plates were taken away 'by an angel' and were never available for scholarly examination. . . . In spite of all the evidence to the contrary, faithful Mormons still accept Joseph Smith's 'translations' from the Egyptian as literally 'true.' " The article expressed the view that Joseph Smith had engaged in "occult practices" and that there were "many cabalistic undertones in both the *Book of Mormon* and in Joseph Smith's 'revelations' to the church."[24]

Meanwhile, Mark Hofmann was cooperating in efforts to authenticate the salamander letter. On February 19, Dean Jessee recorded in his journal that Brent Metcalfe had telephoned him. "M. Hofmann had contacted him with the names of two forensics experts—James Di[b]owski and Albert S[o]merford," Jessee recorded. "Wondered what I knew of them. Said that Hofmann is willing to cover the costs incurred in authenticating the Harris letter by someone with the highest credentials."[25] Dibowski and Somerford were the experts who had evaluated the Joseph Smith III blessing.

On Friday, February 24, Christensen wrote to Gordon Hinckley about his purchase of the salamander letter and the problems it was causing him. "It is with some reluctance that I write to someone as busy as yourself," Christensen began. "However, I believe that under the circumstances you should be informed of events to which I am a party."

Christensen assumed Hinckley might not know who he was and so used part of the letter to introduce himself. "I am a thirty year old businessman who spends most of his time doing legal and security law work for investments," Christensen wrote. "Since the age of 16 I have been vigorously collecting books, pamphlets, journals, theses and dissertations, etc. which relate to religion and history, but Mormonism in particular." The extent of Christensen's interest became apparent when he described his collection as filling thirty-four eight-foot bookcases and forty-four filing cabinet drawers.

In his letter, Christensen also described buying the salamander letter from Hofmann, who had bought it from Jacobs. "I found out about the availability of the letter through an associate who works for me," Christensen explained, alluding to Brent Metcalfe. "The purchase contract and note were very specific on the issue of confidentiality," Christensen wrote. "Unfortunately in the weeks since that purchase a wide variety of individuals have become aware of the letter's existence." Christensen gave three reasons for the rapid spread of information about the document. First, several persons knew about the letter before he bought it. One in Idaho had even agreed to buy a typescript from an Indiana dealer. Second, Jacobs had told an unnamed "friend to anti-Mormons" about the letter in early January. Third, "Excited individuals both in and out of the Church have been busy in 'calling around' to see who knows what of the document."[26]

"My specific reason for writing this letter," Christensen explained, "is to inform you that the Religion Editor of *Time Magazine,* Richard Ostling, is very close to printing a story on the letter." Christensen said he had declined Ostling's request to cooperate on a story, saying he wanted to conduct further research before publication. "He is full aware that I am working independently of the Church and that the decision to not cooperate is strictly my own."

Christensen referred Hinckley to an enclosed copy of his January 9 letter to Homer Durham in which he had expressed his intention to research the document, publish it, and then donate it to the church. "My letter of January 9 still accurately reflects my intentions for the document," Christensen affirmed. However, he expected that "someone such as Jerald Tanner" might publish an article about the letter before he did. "I consider myself a faithful member of the Church," Christensen wrote, "and as such I have empathy for the Leaders of my Church whom certain members of the media would place in an embarassing position if possible." Accordingly, he was "willing to consider any suggestions which you (or your designees) may have as it relates to a public announcement of the existence of the letter."

"Unfortunately," Christensen also wrote, "collecting early Mormon documents appears to be a dangerous business."

"The bottom line," Christensen said, "is that I want to be helpful to the Church." He felt the salamander letter drew deeply from the early experiences of Joseph Smith, the Smith family, and the environment in which they and Martin Harris lived. "Unless it is dealt with appropriately," Christensen warned, "what may have seemed common to Martin Harris in his missionary work with William W. Phelps could be misunderstood by twentieth century readers."[27]

Hinckley received Christensen's letter of February 24 the day it was written and dictated a memorandum for his file: "I talked to Steven F. Christensen by telephone. He reiterated what he had set forth in his letter, that he is having it [the salamander letter] researched and that he is paying Ron Walker and Dean Jessee to do this. I told him that I wouldn't be rushed by pressure from Time or anybody else and that in response to their inquiries I would simply say that I am having it researched and when I get through with this I may be in a position to say something."[28] Meanwhile, *Time*'s interest in the story became manifest in other ways.

On March 1, Jerry P. Cahill, director of public affairs in the church's Public Communications Department, wrote a memorandum to his supervisor, Richard P. Lindsay, who was the department's managing director. By assignment, Cahill had called Ostling, as well as Christine Rigby Arrington (Leonard Arrington's daughter-in-law), a *Time* Los Angeles bureau reporter, to ask what information they wanted from the church on the letter. They were aware Hinckley had seen the letter and wanted some kind of church statement on it. "We need a determination if any statement will be made," Cahill wrote to Lindsay, "and in what form."[29]

On March 2, Lindsay sent Cahill's memorandum to Hinckley.[30] Later that day, Hinckley prepared a statement that read as follows:

> It is true that I saw the letter.
>
> I felt that no public comment was in order until the matter had been thoroughly researched in the context of the time and the environment in which it was written. I was pleased to learn that the owner has engaged professionals to do such research. Until such is completed it would be improper for me or anyone else to speculate on the contents or any interpretation of the meaning of various statements. I would think that no reputable individual or journal would issue a speculative story until such had been done.[31]

Hinckley read the statement to Boyd Packer, Homer Durham, and Richard Lindsay. He also read it over the phone to Steve Christensen, who said he felt good about having it issued. Hinckley then gave the statement to Jerry Cahill, who said he would give it to Chris Arrington.[32]

On Monday, March 5, Cahill wrote to Ostling and included Hinckley's statement, which he noted had already been given to Arrington. He also provided Ostling some pictures he had requested for his story. Cahill offered Ostling some dictionary definitions of *salamander* that showed the term could be taken to mean a person living in or capable of enduring fire. To these, he appended several scriptural references in which God and angels had been described as surrounded by fire. He tried to show Ostling that the term *salamander*, interpreted as a being surrounded by fire, was not necessarily inconsistent with the church's official account of how Joseph Smith found the gold plates.[33]

On the morning of Wednesday, March 7, a church representative in New York City delivered Cahill's March 5 response to Ostling. Reporting to Richard Lindsay about the delivery, Cahill wrote, "There will be a certain air of mystique about the authenticity of the letter. Ostling indicates that he is not sure of the authenticity of the letter, dated October 1830, and it is possible, he thinks, the letter could be either an 1983 forgery or an 1830's forgery." When Lindsay received Cahill's report, he forwarded it to Hinckley.[34]

Meanwhile, as anticipated, the March issue of the Tanners' newsletter beat *Time* to the punch. In an article titled "Moroni or Salamander? Reported Find of Letter by Book of Mormon Witness," the Tanners described the letter, said it was "apparently purchased by Mark Hofmann," and noted that Hofmann sold it to Christensen, who planned to publish it. Surprisingly, the article concluded, "While we would really like to believe that the letter attributed to Harris is authentic, we do not feel that we can endorse it until further evidence comes forth. If any of our readers have any information about the matter we would appreciate hearing about it. We understand that an article concerning the subject will be published in Time magazine."[35]

The Tanners' article prompted Steve Christensen to issue his own press release on March 7. "While it is hoped that the letter is authentic," Christensen wrote, "professional tests have not yet been performed on the document." He explained that he did not wish to release transcripts or photographs of the letter until he had completed further tests and research, and he was relying on skilled historians to assist him. "It is unfortunate," Christensen added, "that publicity of the document has preceded its historical authentication. This has lead to some cases of misstatement as well as numerous phrases being taken out of context." He concluded his release by saying he looked forward to being able to give more information to the media and the public in the future.[36]

On March 16, church-owned KSL Television broadcast a story about the letter. "Another significant Mormon history document has apparently surfaced," announced the news anchor as a lead-in to the story. "A Salt Lake City businessman says he has acquired the letter, said to be one of the earliest known handwritten accounts of events surrounding the coming forth of the Book of Mormon." Then followed a report by the station's religion specialist, who heavily quoted Christensen's press release. "Despite issuing a 'press statement,' " the reporter noted, "Christensen has declined to be interviewed and does not want the letter itself nor its contents made public at this time. He told Channel Five that he acquired the letter in January and is currently working with historians to authenticate the recently discovered document."

After briefly describing the document, the reporter added, "Speculation and rumors about the letter's contents are rampant in certain circles. Christensen said, 'This has led to some cases of misstatement as well as numerous phrases being taken out of context.' A source who has seen the document calls Christensen's acquisition extremely significant if the letter is determined to be authentic. Christensen said he will not release transcripts or photographs of the letter until his research and tests of authenticity have progressed further. He said that should occur in the next couple of months."[37]

Over the next several months, Christensen and his researchers studied the document. Meanwhile, Mark Hofmann offered the Historical Department some rare, typeset Deseret Currency Association notes, a kind of Mormon scrip that had been issued in various denominations in early Utah. Months before, Hofmann had told Lyn Jacobs he was researching a Deseret Currency Association account book for names of families whose ancestors had once held the association's notes. Eventually, Hofmann told Jacobs the research helped him locate a collector near New York City who had accumulated some of the currency, including higher-denomination notes. Jacobs later served as Hofmann's consignee in offering at least a one-hundred-dollar note to the church.

Though the church already had examples of typeset Deseret Currency Association notes, it had no examples of the higher denominations known to have been issued. The notes obtained from Hofmann included higher denominations and were quite valuable. Like the bulk of documents Hofmann provided to the church, the Deseret Currency Association notes were handled directly by the Historical Department without involving Gordon Hinckley.[38]

Ron Walker had been bishop of the church ward in which Hinckley resided and thus knew him as a neighbor and ward member. On Monday, August 6, 1984, Walker wrote Hinckley to update him on the progress he and Jessee were making in their study of the salamander letter. Their research had progressed well, and they hoped to be writing soon. Walker offered to sit down with the church leader to discuss his and Jessee's views. Walker also mentioned that some anti-Mormons had information on the Josiah Stowell letter and predicted that Jerald Tanner and Sandra Tanner would probably deal with it soon. Walker explained that he had received a copy of the letter's text several months earlier and that the persons who sent the copy to him might also have sent one to others. He noted that other documents were said to exist that would affect how the church's early history was interpreted.[39]

In mid-August 1984, the church's Public Communications Department contacted Historical Department officials about a call it had received from Chris Arrington of *Time*. Arrington had phoned to ask if the church owned a June 18, 1825, letter written from Canandaigua, New York, by Joseph Smith to Josiah Stowell. She said she had a typescript of the purported letter and described some of its contents. Historical Department officials said they had heard rumors about the document but had not seen it. Public Communications then relayed that message to Arrington.[40]

A few days later, Arrington again phoned Public Communications. She said informed sources had told her the church obtained the letter sometime during the last year, possibly in January 1984. She also said that Brigham Young University historians had been invited to study it. She asked, "Does the Church own the letter, when was it acquired, from whom and for how much?"

Richard Lindsay wrote to Gordon Hinckley, explaining Arrington's repeated inquiries and the responses that his department had gotten from Historical Department personnel. He asked Hinckley for direction on formulating a response to Arrington's questions.[41]

Later, when Lindsay saw Hinckley, he reiterated that Historical Department officials said they did not have the Stowell letter. Lindsay later recalled that Hinckley replied something like, "Yeah, that's right. They don't have it." Lindsay reported this response to Jerry Cahill, who had fielded Arrington's question. Meanwhile, Hinckley prepared to issue a news release on the Stowell letter.[42]

In a meeting of the First Presidency held Thursday, August 23, Hinckley observed that typescripts of the letter were reportedly circulating and that interested persons had asked the Historical and Public Communications departments about the document. He explained that few persons knew the church had bought the letter, which was being housed in the First Presidency's vault, and that this lack of knowledge accounted for why callers had been told that the Historical Department did not have it. Hinckley proposed that the church publish a statement explaining that the document had been "placed in the First Presidency's vault pending an examination and analysis of the letter to determine its authenticity."[43]

The same day, Hinckley prepared a statement, one portion of which read as follows:

> I am advised that questions are being raised concerning the location of a letter presumably written in 1825 by Joseph Smith to Josiah Stowell, typescripts of which I am told are now in circulation.

In response to queries, personnel of the Historical Department of the Church have indicated that they do not have the letter. This is true. I have it. I handled the purchase when it was brought to me by a dealer and put it in the vault adjacent to my office pending the time when we may have it studied to determine its authenticity. Meanwhile I would assume that no reputable scholar would draw conclusions concerning it and no journalist of integrity would wish to publish it.[44]

Hinckley sandwiched the writing of this statement between many other church administrative matters, but before he could finalize it and have it issued, the media went ahead with big stories about both the salamander and Stowell letters.

On Saturday, August 25, *Los Angeles Times* religion writer John Dart published a lengthy article in which he wrote that the salamander letter was "threatening to alter the idealized portrait of church founder Joseph Smith." He explained that although "Church leaders have declined to comment on the letter or its contents until its authenticity has been determined . . . some leading historians who study Mormon origins believe the letter would add to existing evidence that Smith was not only a dynamic religious leader, but also a treasure seeker who believed in magical spirits. And among conservative Protestant critics of the Mormon Church, the letter has been hailed as 'one of the greatest evidences against the divine origin of the Book of Mormon.' "

Despite his statement about the views of "conservative Protestant critics," Dart did not mention any avowed church critics by name except Jerald Tanner and Sandra Tanner, who he noted were treating the salamander letter with "unusual caution." Instead, he spent most of his article focusing on how the leading historians he mentioned were attempting to harmonize the newly discovered letters with evidence that antedated the discoveries. Dart quoted Richard L. Bushman, a widely published Latter-day Saint historian, who, Dart said, "urged Mormons to be tolerant 'about this culture of magic invading the life of the prophet.' "

He also quoted Jan Shipps, a Methodist who had been president of the Mormon History Association. Shipps, Dart said, "made what may have been the first public talk about the letter in Mormon circles . . . and simultaneously offered the church hierarchy a way to deal with the explosive issue. . . . Her studies led her to conclude that magic and religion are 'really two ends of the spectrum.' Further, she said, her reading 'makes it clear that Joseph Smith himself moved from hunting treasure to searching for a treasure of much higher magnitude and seems to me to provide a basis for a story of an honorable religious tradition.' "

Dart reported that Steve Christensen felt the document was authentic but would not release it until tests had been concluded. Dart also mentioned the Stowell letter, citing a reference to it Shipps had made and pointing out that typescripts of the letter had been circulating among historians and reporters. The letter itself, Dart said, "has not been confirmed publicly to exist."[45]

The comments by Bushman and Shipps that Dart quoted were made at a Sunstone theological symposium. Shipps would later recall, "While there were those in the audience who were excited by the Stowell and salamander letters because they thought they contained evidence that could be used to impugn the LDS foundation story, many responsible historians—Ron Walker, Dean Jessee, Marvin Hill, to name a few—were making a sincere effort to integrate this new evidence into the story without calling the integrity of the prophet into question. At the same time, of course, Brent Metcalfe's interpretation was moving in the other direction."

Metcalfe lacked the graduate training in history that the others Shipps mentioned had, and "without the apprenticeship that graduate training provides," she said, "his interpretations of the data in the historical record were generally very wide of the mark." Shipps recalled that at the symposium, "Brent was clearly intoxicated . . . with the idea that he possessed knowledge that would alter the world's understanding of the beginnings of Mormonism."

"An 'after hours' gathering for discussion was attended by lots of young Latter-day Saints (including Chris Arrington)," Shipps remembered. "But there was no discussion. Brent took the floor and dispensed his 'secret knowledge' with such an air of authority that the kind of general discussion that normally characterizes such gatherings was quite impossible. . . . John Dart was there for a while, but he apparently lost interest in Metcalfe's monologue and left. When it became clear that Brent was not willing to have his interpretation challenged in any way, I left as well."[46]

The *Salt Lake Tribune* picked up John Dart's article, as did other newspapers across the nation and the world. Thomas S. Monson of the Quorum of the Twelve was in Frankfurt, Germany, on church business and noted that the *International Herald Tribune* ran Dart's article under the title "The Mormons and the White Salamander: 1830 Letter, If Authenticated, Would Prove Founder's Interest in the Occult."[47]

On Sunday, September 2, the *Salt Lake Tribune* printed another article on the salamander letter. The article cited varied opinions on the letter's potential impact on the faith of church members. For example, the reporter asked Dean Jessee whether the document would shake his faith if it proved authentic. "Oh no," Jessee replied, "it wouldn't bother me at all." The article also quoted Wesley P. Walters, a Protestant minister and long-time critic of Joseph Smith, who reportedly "said that the letter would be significant because it is the first evidence from a 'friendly source' that connects Joseph Smith with money digging combined with magic."[48]

On September 5, Neal A. Maxwell of the Quorum of the Twelve wrote a letter to Quorum members addressed to its president, Ezra Taft Benson. Maxwell proposed initiating another study on historical aspects of the salamander letter, even though it might duplicate what Christensen's researchers were already doing. At the beginning of a working paper that he attached to the letter, Maxwell also pointed out, "We do not yet know *if* the publicized letter (October, 1830) from Martin Harris to W. W. Phelps is authentic."[49]

A month later, Maxwell addressed the inadequacies of history in a talk at the church's general conference. He quoted Winston Churchill's November 12, 1940, tribute to Neville Chamberlain: "History with its flickering lamp stumbles along the trail of the past, trying to reconstruct its scenes, to revive its echoes, and kindle with pale gleams the passion of former days." Members of the church, Maxwell explained, must patiently await the complete unfolding of the past to understand it fully. "Meanwhile," he continued, "unevenness in the spiritual development of people means untidiness in the history of people, and we should not make an individual 'an offender for a word' . . . as if a single communication could set aside all else an individual may have communicated or stood for!" "The finished mosaic of the history of the Restoration," he said, "will be larger and more varied as more pieces of tile emerge, adjusting a sequence here or enlarging there a sector of our understanding." Because "history deals with imperfect people in process of time, whose imperfections produce refractions as the pure light of the gospel plays upon them," some tiles may seemingly not fit the mosaic. Yet ultimately, "the fulness of the history of the dispensation of the fulness of times will be written," and when it is, the "final mosaic of the Restoration will be resplendent, reflecting divine design."[50]

During the conference, Gordon Hinckley gave a talk describing the church's "basic cornerstones." Elaborating on one of these cornerstones, Joseph Smith's vision of God the Father and his Son Jesus Christ, Hinckley said, "For more than a century and a half, enemies, critics, and some would-be scholars have worn out their lives trying to disprove the validity of that vision. Of course they cannot understand it. The things of God are understood by the Spirit of God."

Turning to another cornerstone, the Book of Mormon, he proclaimed, "The evidence for its truth, for its validity in a world that is prone to demand evidence, lies not in archaeology or anthropology, though these may be helpful to some. It lies not in word research or historical analysis, though these may be confirmatory. The evidence for its truth and validity lies within the covers of the book itself. The test of its truth lies in reading it. It is a book of God."[51]

That same day, Bruce McConkie spoke, observing that in Christ's day, some defamed Jesus' name and cursed him as a false prophet, thereby separating themselves from true Christians. "In our day," he continued, "the same approach is made by ill-disposed persons to the name of Joseph Smith. The way men feel about him and his prophetic successors divides true believers from those who serve another master." Later in his talk, he said, "No Latter-day Saint who is true and faithful in all things will ever pursue a course, or espouse a cause, or publish an article or book that weakens or destroys faith." Near the end of his discourse, he likened the church to a great caravan traveling to the celestial city of God. "What does it matter," he asked, "if a few barking dogs snap at the heels of the weary travelers? Or that predators claim those few who fall by the way? The caravan moves on."[52]

On Tuesday, October 16, Steve Christensen wrote Gordon Hinckley to update him on the salamander letter research and to ask his advice. Christensen began by reviewing how he had retained Jessee, Walker, and Metcalfe to study the letter. "My motive from the beginning," he wrote, "was to contribute the financial support necessary to purchase the Harris letter and see that the appropriate research was completed which would need to accompany a document of such varied contents." Tests on the letter, he said, had now been completed. "It is authentic by the way," he added in parentheses without further elaboration.

Initially, the three researchers intended to write a scholarly article, but "later it was felt that perhaps a book would be more suitable in light of the tremendous amount of material which had been discovered." While research and testing were going on, Christensen wrote, he had generally shunned the media because he "did not want to comment 'while the jury was still out.' "

All this information, he continued, was background to the events of the previous week. "Last Thursday," he revealed, "I had the unpleasant experience of terminating the working relationship with Brent Metcalfe." Christensen explained that he and his business associate, Gary Sheets, felt uncomfortable about Metcalfe's personal opinions on church history and doctrine and did not want to be in a position of underwriting a book on early Mormonism "if the work had the potential of doing more harm than good." Though they had terminated Metcalfe, they had also provided him a generous severance pay. Christensen said he had met his financial commitments to all the researchers and had encouraged each of them "to take their separate paths as it relates to finishing their work should they so choose."[53]

Christensen's next paragraph referred directly to Hinckley's conference address and also echoed the words of Bruce McConkie and Neal Maxwell:

> I was extremely impressed with your Conference talk, Sunday, October 7th. I am concerned that some of Brent Metcalfe's research, as interpreted by himself and perhaps others, would challenge some of the basic concepts to three out of four of the "foundations of the . . . Church" addressed in your talk. Most likely we will always be learning new things historically from our past; however, I believe that the Church has more pressing work to accomplish than to be consumed by questions and contradictions from the past. While it is better that we lead forth in historical inquiry rather than leaving the task to our enemies, those so engaged must have sufficient faith that the day will come when all is revealed and then the pieces will all fit together.

Watching Metcalfe's research erode his faith in the church disturbed Christensen, for whom study and faith were allies.

Christensen also sought advice on what to do with the salamander letter. He explained that his "current intention" was to release the document to the church-owned *Deseret News* when the researchers published their findings. Another option, he felt, would be to resell the document to Hofmann, who had offered him over fifty thousand dollars for it. "Mr. Hofmann has been approached by a representative of Yale University," Christensen explained, "who would like to seriously consider having the Yale Library purchase the document were it to become available." Christensen had not, however, forgotten his original intention to give the document to the church. "What I would appreciate knowing," he wrote, "is whether or not the Church feels strongly about owning the letter. If it would be more of a thorn than a rose I would gladly let Mr. Hofmann sell it to Yale or some other institution which would pay his 'highway robbery' prices. If the Church would like it, it is yours for the asking—just tell me when."[54]

The following day, Hinckley attended a luncheon to help church employees kick off their annual drive for contributions to the United Way. One of Christensen's friends happened to be vice-chairman of the employees' United Way committee that year. The committee customarily invited two or three local business leaders to contribute money for the kick-off luncheon, and Christensen's friend had invited him to donate for that purpose. Traditionally, the business leaders who donated were also invited to the luncheon and seated at the head table with a member of the First Presidency and other general authorities in attendance.[55]

"By chance," Christensen recorded after the luncheon, "I was placed at a table between Pres. Hinckley and Bishop Clark[e]," another general authority. Hinckley had spoken to Christensen by phone but had not met him in person and so did not recognize him until they were introduced. "Once he discovered who I was," Christensen wrote, "we talked of the Martin Harris letter and Brent Metcalfe. He also referred to my letter of 10/16/84 and indicated that he would like to see the letter come to the Church."[56]

Four months later on February 26, 1985, Christensen again wrote to Hinckley about the salamander letter. He explained that studies of eastern experts had authenticated it.[57] Christensen gave Hinckley no details about who the experts had been or how they had carried out their work. Among the experts, however, had been Albert H. Lyter III, a forensic chemist considered by many to be among the best ink analysts in the country. Lyter had looked for anachronistic coloring in the letter and had found none. He had identified the ink used in the letter as of the iron gallotannic type commonly used when the letter was said to have been written. The letter had compared well with other documents of the period, and Lyter had concluded, "There is no evidence to suggest that the examined document was prepared at other than during the stated time period."[58]

In his February 26 letter to Hinckley, Christensen said he had no plans for publicly releasing the letter but thought Walker and Jessee might deal with it at the May meetings of the Mormon History Association. "What may at one time have been a 'united research/writing effort' has now evolved to a point of each researcher pursuing his own course with regard to the letter," he wrote.[59]

Christensen's letter had another purpose. He explained he had received offers to buy the salamander letter. Earlier financial security had allowed him to disregard such offers, but recent reverses had made them tantalizing. He wrote that if the church still wanted the letter, he would honor his original commitment and donate, not sell, it to the church. He asked Hinckley to let him know what to do, adding, "I would be happy in either case."[60]

On March 1, Hinckley phoned Christensen. "I told him," Hinckley recorded in a memorandum, that "I was appreciative of the circumstances set forth in his letter, that I felt strongly that the Church should have the Martin Harris letter, and that I would like to see what we could do to work things out so that we could get it and he could take care of his problems."

But before Hinckley could discuss particulars of a sale, Christensen said he was now financially able to donate the letter. "With great appreciation to the Lord," Hinckley wrote, "he told me that since he had written his letter to me, in fact only yesterday, certain matters of his business had taken a turn which has taken care of his financial problem. Accordingly he wants the Church to have the Martin Harris letter. He is waiting for the letter from the group who have authenticated the document, and when that arrives he will bring both the original letter and the letter of authentication to my office. I thanked him for his great kindness and concern."[61]

Around March 1985, members of the Mormon History Association began receiving copies of the most recent issue of the *Journal of Mormon History*, published annually by the association.[62] The issue included a book review by Marvin S. Hill, professor of history at Brigham Young University, in which he referred both to the Stowell and salamander letters and the discussion they had evoked on money-digging. The salamander letter, Hill said, "makes it clear that even among the faithful a money digging interpretation of the coming forth of the Book of Mormon was in vogue" in the early days of the church. Hill also wrote that the Stowell letter proved Joseph Smith exhibited "no reluctance to search for gold with his magical powers."

Later in his review, Hill noted that Martin Harris was quoted in an 1829 newspaper report as saying that "Joseph Smith . . . had been visited by the spirit of the Almighty in a dream and informed that in a certain hill in that town was deposited a Golden Bible, containing an ancient record of divine origin." Hill puzzled, "Just why Martin Harris should tell the money diggers version of the story to W. W. Phelps is obscure. But it seems evident that Harris does not feel uncomfortable with the two versions and tells them interchangeably. My point is that it is very difficult indeed at this point to separate magic and religion in Joseph Smith and early Mormonism."[63]

On April 12, Steve Christensen visited Gordon Hinckley to make his promised donation of the salamander letter. The two men met in Hinckley's office at 2:00 P.M., along with two secretaries and a church photographer, who took pictures of Christensen giving the document to Hinckley.[64]

Christensen also gave Hinckley a letter written by Kenneth Rendell to Mark Hofmann. Rendell had examined the letter under ultraviolet light and had studied the paper, the ink, the seal, the folds, the postmark, and the handwriting. "It is my conclusion," Rendell wrote, "based upon all of this evidence, as well as the ink and paper tests undertaken independently of me, that there is no indication that this letter is a forgery."[65]

Christensen asked Hinckley how he should respond to questions that might come to him about the letter. The minutes of the meeting record, "President Hinckley indicated that he should respond that the letter has been given to the Church and has been placed in the archives of the Church. President Hinckley further expressed the feeling that one of the best responses to questions which might be raised about the letter and its contents is the history of Martin Harris and W. W. Phelps who, although they both became temporarily disaffected from the Church, returned to the Church and died in full fellowship, having rendered years of faithful, devoted service."

Steven F. Christensen (*right*) presents salamander letter to Gordon B. Hinckley, April 12, 1985. (Eldon Linschoten/LDS Church)

The meeting adjourned at 2:10 P.M., ten minutes after it began. It was the first and last time Christensen would visit Hinckley's office.[66] On April 18, the First Presidency sent Christensen a letter thanking him for donating the document and also for providing Rendell's report. The First Presidency noted that the report "gives the opinion of the examiner that the letter is authentic insofar as such authenticity can be proven, given the long passage of time, the intervening deaths of the parties involved, and certain nebulous features of its contents."[67]

Later that month, church officials published the complete text of the salamander letter in the weekly *Church News,* along with an article by a staff writer and a First Presidency statement. The article noted that "Dean Jessee, research historian and handwriting expert at the Joseph Fielding Smith Institute for Church History at BYU, and others have studied and tested the letter extensively for almost a year." Regarding the document's provenance, the article explained, "The letter was part of a stamp collection in New England until discovered by Lyn Jacobs, an LDS collector. The letter was purchased in late 1983 by Jacobs and Mark Hofmann, another LDS collector. They sold it to Steven F. Christensen on Jan. 6, 1984."

The article announced that Jessee's studies would be discussed in a paper he would give May 2 at the Mormon History Association's annual meeting.[68]

The First Presidency statement that accompanied the article described the salamander letter as "purportedly written by Martin Harris" and explained that the donated letter was accompanied by a report from an examiner concluding "that there is no indication that this letter is a forgery." The First Presidency statement further noted that typescripts of the letter had been widely circulated and discussed, that researchers would soon be making public statements about the letter, and that the original had been placed "in the archives of the First Presidency as another appreciated addition to documents and artifacts dating back to the early history of the Church."

The statement also quoted Gordon Hinckley. "No one, of course, can be certain that Martin Harris wrote the document," Hinckley said. "However, at this point we accept the judgment of the examiner that there is no indication that it is a forgery. This does not preclude the possibility that it may have been forged at a time when the Church had many enemies. It is, however, an interesting document of the times."

Hinckley offered the public the same perspective he had shared with Christensen. "Actually," he said, "the letter has nothing to do with the authenticity of the Church. The real test of the faith which both Martin Harris and W. W. Phelps had in Joseph Smith and his work is found in their lives, in the sacrifices they made for their membership in the Church, and in the testimonies they bore to the end of their lives."[69]

When the salamander letter was published, the *Salt Lake Tribune* carried the first of two articles on recently discovered Mormon documents. It described and commented on the salamander letter and explained some of the tests that had been conducted on the document: "Tests included where the paper had been milled. Ink, sealing wax and the stamp were also studied, along with seemingly insignificant determinations such as whether the letter had been folded after it had been written and pressure points in drawing individual letters." The article quoted Signature Books president George Smith as saying that the salamander letter connected Joseph Smith and the early church to folk magic. It also explained that several historians would discuss the letter at the May Mormon History Association meetings, which were "expected to attract national attention."[70]

On Monday, April 29, the two-part series concluded with an article on the Stowell letter. The article began, "A letter reportedly written by Mormon church founder Joseph Smith describing money-digging pursuits and treasure guarded by a clever spirit seems to have disappeared from view." Besides citing Marvin Hill's piece in *Journal of Mormon History*, the article quoted Hill as saying he thought the letter was authentic and had been "buried." It also quoted Brent Metcalfe as saying the church had the letter. Metcalfe said his information came from "very reliable, first-hand sources." According to the article, however, church spokesman Jerry Cahill denied church ownership. "The church doesn't have the letter," Cahill reportedly said. "It's not in the church archives or the First Presidency's vault."

The article said George Smith disagreed. "The church clearly has possession of the letter," Smith reportedly declared. "If the exact question isn't asked, someone can wink and say the church doesn't have it." Despite Smith's insistence, the article said Cahill still maintained the church did not have the letter.[71] Cahill was wrong, but unwittingly so. The responses to his earlier inquiries had led him to genuinely believe that the church did not have the letter.[72]

By Friday, May 3, Hinckley became aware of Cahill's public denials about the church owning the letter and invited Cahill to his office to discuss the matter. Hinckley informed Cahill that the church did in fact own the document. The two men decided to discuss the matter with Cahill's supervisor, Richard Lindsay, who was traveling in Europe. They reached Lindsay by phone, and after discussing the best way to set the record straight, they settled on having Cahill write a letter correcting his earlier statements.[73]

Cahill then drafted a letter to the editor of the *Salt Lake Tribune* explaining that the paper had quoted him correctly in denying church ownership of the Stowell letter. "My statement, however," he continued, "was in error, for which I apologize and for which I alone am responsible." In stating he was solely responsible, Cahill accepted more blame than he deserved. He had been a victim of circumstances and had not been personally negligent. In his letter, Cahill explained that Hinckley informed him of the error and affirmed that the church had acquired the document, which was being "stored in the First Presidency archives and perhaps some day may be the subject of the kind of critical study recently given to the purported letter of Martin Harris to W. W. Phelps."[74]

Monday morning, the *Salt Lake Tribune* incorporated Cahill's correction letter in an article titled "LDS Church Has Purported Smith Letter."[75] The *Tribune* also published a letter to the editor from George Smith that was obviously written before Smith became aware of Cahill's retraction. Smith wrote in part that he did not challenge Cahill's claim that the church did not own the Stowell letter. Smith said he had heard that Hinckley bought the document "in his own name" from Hofmann so that even though the letter had been seen at church headquarters, it "remained 'in private hands.' "[76] Smith's source of information, whoever it may have been, was in error. The letter had been purchased for the church with church funds using a church check. Smith's inaccurate depiction of the purchase, however, would soon take on a life of its own.[77]

Later that week, the church issued photographs and a transcript of the Stowell letter along with a news release bearing the cautious title "Church Releases Text of Presumed Letter of Joseph Smith to Josiah Stowell." The release, which tracked the one Hinckley had intended to issue months earlier, included a statement from the First Presidency describing the letter as "presumably written by Joseph Smith."[78]

On Saturday, May 11, John Dart of the *Los Angeles Times* published a lengthy article about the Stowell letter, characterizing it as "new evidence that the origins of Mormonism were interwoven with magical lore." Dart reported that Charles Hamilton, "a prominent New York City autograph collector," said Hofmann had shown him the letter two years earlier. Hamilton said, "I've seen hundreds of letters signed by 'Joseph Smith,' a very common name, but the second I saw this one I recognized it as the Mormon prophet's signature." Hamilton also said he told Hofmann the letter was worth around fifteen thousand dollars, but that Hofmann later told him he had sold it to the church for twenty-five thousand dollars.

Dart also quoted George Smith as saying that the Stowell letter added weight to the salamander letter. "Some church members," Dart wrote, "were starting to discount the Harris letter by speculating that Harris got the story wrong from young Smith, or had heard the salamander version from Smith's father instead." According to Dart, George Smith asked rhetorically, "If we say that the white salamander letter emerged from the occult culture of Joseph Smith's day, what about the origin of the church?"[79]

The article that Richard Ostling and Chris Arrington had been preparing finally ran in *Time* magazine. Entitled "Challenging Mormonism's Roots," the article began with comments from disenchanted church members and then described the salamander and Stowell letters. The article also said the Stowell letter "was released by Gordon Hinckley, acting president of the Latter-day Saints, who had previously denied church ownership of the document."[80]

Cahill wrote *Time* to correct its report that Hinckley had denied church ownership of the Stowell letter. "When your reporter Christine R. Arrington asked me about the letter in August, 1984, and again more recently," Cahill wrote, "I responded that the Church did not then possess the letter. My replies to her and others were in error, as I have since learned, because I misunderstood the response that came to me through channels from the First Presidency."[81]

Meanwhile, on Thursday, May 2, 1985, Dean Jessee and Ron Walker delivered their long-awaited papers on the salamander letter at the Mormon History Association's annual meeting. Though journalistic responses to the talks varied, an Associated Press article reported that Jessee and Walker felt the salamander letter, though apparently authentic, did not undermine Joseph Smith's image or the church's divine origin.[82]

At the Mormon History Association meetings, George Smith responded to Jessee's and Walker's talks. In his response, he said the salamander and Stowell letters offered early evidence from sympathetic persons that Joseph Smith was involved in folk magic and that this evidence suggested more consideration be given to less friendly accounts often disregarded by Mormon writers.[83]

The letters' publicity prompted responses from persons who still doubted the documents were authentic. Rhett S. James, an instructor at the LDS Institute of Religion at Utah State University, had been following the debate about the letters for months and offered his opinion that the salamander letter was a fraud and that the Stowell letter might be too. He based his conclusions on the language of the documents, which he felt differed from what either Martin Harris or Joseph Smith would have written. Siding with James were Jeff Simmonds of Utah State University, to whom Hofmann had first shown the Anthon transcript, and Ronald Vern Jackson, a genealogist.[84]

"Public objections to the Harris and Smith letters have clouded perceptions of the letters and include statements that are untrue and misleading," Dean Jessee would write in the published version of his Mormon History Association remarks. Jessee spent several pages evaluating the arguments of James and Jackson and presenting his views on why they were not persuasive. Jessee and his colleagues had weighed the evidence for and against the letters' authenticity and had concluded that the evidence tilted toward authenticity.[85]

Philatelic evidence favored the Stowell letter's authenticity. The letter contained "the circular, red, Canandaigua handstamp in use at the time, and the handwritten number 12½ is the designated amount for sending a single page letter between 80 and 150 miles in 1825, which would include the distance between Canandaigua, New York, and Harmony, Pennsylvania."

Jessee wrote that the Stowell letter exhibited "writing skill on a par with anything [Joseph Smith, Jr.] later wrote." Though the fluidity of the letter's wording raised questions about whether the less-educated Joseph, Jr., or his schoolteacher father had composed it, "a comparison of prose of the two men and a study of the autograph writings known to be the Prophet's suggest that the document could well have been produced by the younger Joseph. The personal pronouns used in the letter and the use of certain connectives—typical of Joseph's style—bear this out." Jessee also noted that though Emma Smith said late in life that Joseph "could neither write nor dictate a coherent and well-worded letter," her statement "was made in response to a question about the authorship of the Book of Mormon and in that context is more clearly a rhetorical defense of its divine origin than a precise statement of Joseph's writing ability." Jessee added his view that Joseph's "personal writings do not portray the illiterate frontiersman some have perceived." He also said the Stowell letter's "handwriting, spelling, grammar, and punctuation compare favorably with other Joseph Smith writings."[86]

Evidence for the authenticity of the salamander letter was even more compelling. Although the letter's content, attributed to Martin Harris, "seems to differ from what he said elsewhere, both before and after 1830," Jessee's evaluation of the letter's provenance, physical characteristics, and handwriting favored viewing the letter as genuine. Jessee felt he had traced the letter's genealogy from Lyn Jacobs to Elwyn Doubleday, a New Hampshire "dealer in rare postal memorabilia." Jessee wrote, "According to Doubleday, the Harris letter was very probably a part of a large collection of New York handstamped letters he obtained in 1982."[87]

Relying in part on the work of Albert Lyter and Kenneth Rendell, Jessee listed five observations suggesting the letter was authentic. First, tests on the paper found it consistent with genuine samples of the period. Rendell had even identified the New York paper mill in which the paper for the letter may have been manufactured. Second, ink samples were taken, and the ink proved "to be of the iron-gall type in wide use at the date appearing on the letter." Third, "The wax seal which produced the hole in the paper when the Harris letter was opened and the missing paper that had adhered to the wax match perfectly." Fourth, the postmark "matches in size, color, and wording the postmark on letters mailed at Palmyra, New York, between 1829 and 1834." Fifth, the postage charge written on the letter "agrees with the zone rate in effect in 1830 for sending a single sheet a distance of not more than thirty miles."

Finally, Jessee noted that although these characteristics "illustrate a number of technical requirements necessary if one were to try to duplicate a letter written in 1830, they do not prove Harris's authorship," which "ultimately rests upon an analysis of the handwriting." Jessee had gathered all the examples he could find of Martin Harris's rare handwriting and had studied them carefully. The salamander letter compared favorably with them.[88]

On Wednesday, May 22, Steve Christensen wrote to Gordon Hinckley. Christensen noted with interest the church's publication of the Stowell letter, adding, "Perhaps you are already aware of the existence of an 'Articles of Agreement', which evidently, was the legal document which followed the correspondence of Joseph Smith, Jr. to Stowel." Christensen had not seen the original of the document, dated November 1, 1825, but he enclosed a transcript of it that he had received from Mark Hofmann, who had certified it to be accurate.

The agreement was a contract signed by Joseph Smith, Jr., Joseph Smith, Sr. (the church founder's father), Josiah Stowell, and others regarding a proposed money-digging venture. Christensen wrote of the document:

> From my point of view, it shows that Joseph Smith, Jr. and Sr., looked upon the so called "money digging adventures" as a business. The legal document is very businesslike and it appears that they were fairly serious and precise in the manner inwhich they conducted their business affairs. I believe the articles of agreement are further strengthened by the fact that additional individuals were involved, both as participants, as well as witnesses. Those enemies of the Church who would do us harm by leaning upon the crutch of magic and occultism being involved in the early beginnings of the Church do not give due credit to the way inwhich this activity was perceived in Joseph Smith's day.

Christensen volunteered to assist "on this issue" should Hinckley want him to. He said he did not intend to publicize the document but that Walker, Jessee, and Metcalfe had all had access to the transcript over a year earlier when they began their research on the salamander letter.[89]

On Tuesday, May 28, Hinckley responded to Christensen's letter of May 22 containing the transcript of the 1825 Articles of Agreement. "This is an interesting document," he wrote. "I do not recall ever hearing of it before." Hinckley then expressed his long-range view of the recent publicity surrounding document discoveries: "The enemies of the Church seem to be having a great time. Their efforts will fade while the work moves forward."[90]

When Hinckley wrote his letter, the church's critics were ecstatic over word of yet another historical bombshell. When the church was organized in 1830, Oliver Cowdery became its first historian. John Whitmer, who succeeded Cowdery as historian, described his own record as a continuation of Cowdery's, which he said began "at the time of the finding of the plates" and continued "up to June 12, 1831." Whitmer's description led later historians to believe that Oliver Cowdery had written an early narrative history of the church.[91] In the latter part of the nineteenth century, church historians tried repeatedly to locate Cowdery's narrative history, but they were unable to find it. Though the church owned several other records written by Cowdery, the "Oliver Cowdery history," as the lost narrative became known, was never seen again.[92]

In the twentieth century, long-time church historian Joseph Fielding Smith, Jr., repeatedly referred to some Oliver Cowdery records that the church owned, leading some persons to believe the church had found the lost Cowdery history. In 1961, Jerald Tanner and Sandra Tanner began to claim the church owned the history and was hiding it. In the December 1982 issue of their newsletter, the Tanners asserted that the church owned the history, that it was housed in the First Presidency's vault, and that it contained references to magic. In 1983, they repeated their assertions, claiming the church had suppressed the history.[93]

When Steve Christensen introduced himself by letter to Gordon Hinckley in February 1984, he requested access to the Cowdery history so his researchers could use it in studying the salamander letter.[94] Months later, the subject apparently came up again, and Ron Walker offered the statement of Joseph Fielding Smith as proof that the history existed and was in church possession. Walker knew that Joseph Fielding Smith had later become president of the church and had kept with him a small group of historical materials that became the core of the collection housed in the First Presidency's vault.

On September 11, 1984, Francis Gibbons wrote a memorandum to Gordon Hinckley about the passage Walker cited and about the Cowdery history, concluding that it was not in the First Presidency's vault and that Earl Olson knew of no such history. "As you doubtless know," Gibbons wrote, "the safe that President Smith kept in his office when he was the Church Historian was transferred to the First Presidency's vault when he became the President of the Church, but that safe did not contain a history of Oliver Cowdery."[95]

It was significant that neither Gibbons, who had sole charge of the First Presidency's vault, nor Olson, who oversaw the Historical Department's collections, had ever seen the history. Yet it was not beyond possibility that the record might be lost somewhere among the church's extensive collections. Though Gibbons had charge of the First Presidency's vault, he had numerous other responsibilities as secretary to the First Presidency and had not yet been able to spend the time necessary to become fully acquainted with every item in it, even though the collection was comparatively small.

Earl Olson had spent five decades in the Historical Department and knew a great deal about its collections. Still, the collections were so vast that no human being could ever hope to read through them all in a lifetime. Furthermore, many of the collections were uncatalogued. Conceivably, a volume like the Oliver Cowdery history could be lost among all those items.

The next month, Homer Durham wrote a letter to Gordon Hinckley that followed up on an earlier memorandum. "On September 11, 1984," Durham began, "I wrote you, in response to an inquiry, that the Historical Department and archives contain no journals of Oliver Cowdery. This was written after a thorough search was made by myself and Donald T. Schmidt, both in our catalogs and in the vault." But since writing that memorandum, Durham explained, he and his staff had "re-discovered a journal of Oliver Cowdery for the period January 1, 1836 to March 27, 1836." During a period when paper was scarce in the church, the empty leaves of the journal had been used as a minute book, and the spine of the volume had been labeled with the name of the entity that kept the minutes rather than with Cowdery's name. Forwarding photocopies and a typescript of Cowdery's journal entries, Durham wrote, "I think you will find the reading of the journal a very interesting and uplifting experience."[96]

The rediscovered Oliver Cowdery sketchbook was a significant church history resource, but it was not the long-lost Cowdery history. Nor was it secret. In fact, the sketchbook, apparently forgotten in the interim, had been published in its entirety just a dozen years earlier.[97]

At church headquarters, the only evidence anyone could find that the church might own the narrative Cowdery history was the group of statements Joseph Fielding Smith had made about records kept by Oliver Cowdery. These statements, however, were ambiguous and could just as easily be interpreted as referring to other well-known records in church possession and not to a narrative history. Despite the Tanners' claims, no living person seemed to have ever seen the lost history, together with its purported references to magic.

No one, that is, until Brent Metcalfe's secret source came along. In early May 1985, Metcalfe spoke to Historical Department employee Ronald O. Barney about the alleged Cowdery history, using a description the source gave him. Metcalfe said the history was written on lined paper in a volume approximately 8¼ inches wide, 10 inches long, and ¾ inch thick. The volume was half bound in brown leather, had marbled boards, and was "written border to border." Metcalfe said his source had read the volume, that Gordon Hinckley would know where it was unless it had been moved in the last year and a half, and that information corroborating the salamander letter could be found about one-fourth of the way into it.[98]

On May 13, Brent Metcalfe and George Smith appeared together on a program broadcast by Salt Lake television station KUTV. Near the end of the program, Metcalfe said he had recently learned the contents of the long-lost Oliver Cowdery history. He said the history recounted the coming forth of the Book of Mormon "very much in the same terms as Martin Harris does" in the salamander letter. According to Metcalfe, the Cowdery history thrice referred to a salamander, which first appeared to Joseph Smith's brother Alvin, who, contrary to traditional church teachings, found the golden plates on which the Book of Mormon was engraved.[99]

"I had several calls from the Tribune about an announcement made on TV by Brent Metcalfe," wrote Glenn N. Rowe about his workday on May 14. Rowe had succeeded the retiring Don Schmidt as director of the Historical Department's Library-Archives Division. The next day, Rowe wrote, "I stayed home thinking I would get a jump on my cold, but I read the morning news on Brent Metcalfe's release and went in to work. The phone was busy all day."[100]

The article to which Rowe referred appeared in the *Salt Lake Tribune* that morning under the title "Researcher Says LDS History Disputes Golden Plates Story." The story repeated Metcalfe's assertions of May 13, as well as Metcalfe's claim that the church owned the history. The article noted the consistency between Metcalfe's story of the Cowdery history and the contents of the recently discovered salamander and Stowell letters. "Early Mormon letters recently released by LDS Church officials," it explained, "link Joseph Smith to folk magic and to an 'old spirit' that commanded Mr. Smith to return with his brother Alvin, who was dead at the time."[101]

The *Tribune*'s report once again prompted Gordon Hinckley to ask the Historical Department what it knew about the Oliver Cowdery history. Afflicted with heart problems, Homer Durham had passed away in January and had been replaced by Dean L. Larsen of the First Quorum of Seventy.[102] Larsen responded to Hinckley's request with a report citing a 1971 Dean Jessee article that concluded Cowdery's history had never been found. Larsen added, "We have never had this record in the Historical Department and no one has made a claim to having located it." He listed Cowdery's other papers in the department. "These," he reported, "have all been searched, and none of them contain any reference to Joseph or Alvin receiving the plates, nor of the visitation of the Angel Moroni, nor to any such things as spirits or salamanders." He also cited other records that supported the church's traditional account of its history and contradicted Metcalfe's claim. "As far as we can tell from current research," Larsen concluded, "the record referred to by Brother Metcalfe is not in the Church Archives."[103]

On May 15, Metcalfe told Ron Barney that his source (who he said was perhaps the best source he ever had) did not view the Cowdery history surreptitiously but apparently saw it about a year and a half earlier and was one of the few persons who could have seen it. The source had said Hinckley knew where the document was and had felt the First Presidency could figure out the source's identity if they knew when the volume had been seen. Metcalfe claimed to have corroborated his source's information through secondary means and also said his source was worried about having his name connected with the information.[104]

Public interest in both Metcalfe's announcements and the recent *Time* magazine article on Mormon documents was still high on Thursday, May 16. "We continued to receive many telephone calls concerning the items in the news," Glenn Rowe wrote of his day at work. "Most were not too bad. One woman however was so emotional that I really could not even discuss it with her."[105]

The same day, the Brigham Young University student newspaper published an article about the Oliver Cowdery history that provided additional clues about the source of Metcalfe's information. "While going through several private collections," a reporter wrote of Metcalfe, "he found a first-hand account of someone who had seen this early history written by Oliver Cowdery. A friend of Metcalfe, who had access to the church archives, wrote the account, Metcalfe said. He refused to release information about his friend or how the documents came into his friend's hands."[106]

Also on that day, Salt Lake radio station KUER broadcast an interview with Metcalfe and George Smith. Referring to the salamander and Stowell letters, one of two interviewers asked the pair, "Are both of you gentlemen convinced that these letters are authentic?" Both said they were.

Later in the interview, Smith commented on the letters' potential impact on the church. He felt they would not bother most good Latter-day Saints, but that "secular humanists, if there are such in the community of Mormons—I'm not sure—would obviously be quite put off." Smith also said that though the letters may not affect most current church members, they would present "a more difficult problem" to potential converts.

Toward the end of the interview, Metcalfe talked about the Oliver Cowdery history and its reportedly sensational contents. "Let's just take this one step at a time," one interviewer said, "because this is rather remarkable information. You have not seen this document?"

Metcalfe confirmed he had not but said he knew a source who had. The interviewers pressed him to name his source specifically or at least categorically. "All I can say," Metcalfe replied, "is it's an extremely reliable source, and I know—personally, I don't know other sources that are more reliable than this one."[107]

On May 24, the *Salt Lake Tribune* printed a letter signed by George Smith. Smith pointed out that the Cowdery history corroborated the salamander letter and illuminated the role that Joseph Smith's brother Alvin may have played in the discovery of the golden plates from which Joseph later translated the Book of Mormon. Citing the church's earlier release of the Stowell and salamander letter, he encouraged the church to make the Oliver Cowdery history available for study in order to contribute to the body of knowledge about the church's origin.[108]

The same day, Jerry Cahill wrote Richard Lindsay about a call he had received from John Dart, religion writer for the *Los Angeles Times*. Dart too was preparing a story on the Oliver Cowdery history and was basing it on an interview Metcalfe had arranged between Dart and Metcalfe's secret source. Dart told Cahill the interview had been granted on conditions of anonymity but that the source was trustworthy and reliable.

Dart said the source told him the Cowdery history included a taunting salamander that appeared once to Alvin and twice to Joseph, and that Alvin first located the golden plates with a seer stone. Alvin, the source said, had led a party to find the plates, and Joseph was among the group. The history reportedly contained no mention of a vision preceding the group's expedition. Dart said his source stepped forward because he felt the church was covering up a significant historical record.

Cahill challenged Dart on the adequacy of his information. "I questioned," Cahill wrote, "why he would go with a story based on an anonymous source who did not show him any copies or other documentation. He said in view of the other letters and interests, he felt he should write the story and bring it to his editors for decision on whether to proceed to publication."[109]

Four days later, Wesley Walters wrote a letter to Gordon Hinckley, explaining that he planned to visit Salt Lake City during the summer and seeking permission to study the Cowdery history, which he described as being in the First Presidency's vault.[110]

On Tuesday, June 4, Francis Gibbons responded to Walters's request for access to the Cowdery history. "Since the report of the existence of this history, purportedly written by Oliver Cowdery, surfaced," Gibbons wrote, "a thorough inspection has been made of both the archives in the Historical Department and of the First Presidency's vault. These searches have failed to reveal the existence of a record such as the one referred to [by Metcalfe]."[111]

On June 13, John Dart's anticipated article on the Cowdery history appeared in the *Los Angeles Times*, complete with detailed descriptions of the purported size and contents of the record. Dart wrote that a "highly reliable source told The Times in an interview . . . that he has viewed it in the church's headquarters" but "insisted on anonymity in order to preserve his standing in the church." The source said the Cowdery history helped to corroborate earlier discoveries, "which portray Joseph Smith's involvement in occult methods to find hidden treasures without any references to religious events so familiar to present-day Mormons."

The article quoted Jerry Cahill as saying he assumed the First Presidency had the history but did not intend to ask about it. After innocently but wrongly denying church ownership of the Stowell letter, Cahill had become cautious about denying church ownership of historical materials. His assumption that the church owned the item was based on the statements of Joseph Fielding Smith that reporters had read to him.

Dart's article, however, described Cahill as unwilling to accept claims about what the history might contain. "Church spokesman Cahill noted that the claim about the Cowdery history, made by a person unwilling to be identified publicly, is not supported by another witness or photographs of the pages in question. 'We can't ignore Joseph Smith's first-hand accounts,' he said." Dart then quoted George Smith as saying, "The church's silence damages its credibility."[112]

On Tuesday morning, June 25, at 10:30, Wesley Walters spoke to Francis Gibbons about the Cowdery history. Gibbons told him the First Presidency's vault contained nothing like the history described in Dart's *Los Angeles Times* article. Gibbons said the vault did contain a brief manuscript history of the church from 1829 to 1831 that was possibly in Cowdery's hand. But the history said nothing about salamanders. (The document, later published by Dean Jessee, turned out not to be in Cowdery's hand).[113]

On the matter of Metcalfe's secret source, Gibbons knew that no one, including Gordon Hinckley, could get access to the First Presidency's vault unless he, Gibbons, let the person in. And he knew that he had not shown anyone anything like what the media had described. While he had Gibbons's ear, Walters also inquired about another item that Gibbons assured him he had not seen. It was something called "the McLellin collection."[114]

6

The McLellin Collection

William E. McLellin met missionaries from the church in 1831, the year
after it was organized. Impressed by their teachings, he gave up his business
and was baptized and ordained to a church office. In time, he became
acquainted with Joseph Smith. During his years in the church, McLellin
wavered between devotion and dissidence. During periods of devotion, he
preached, suffered persecution, and even became a member of the Quorum
of the Twelve. But dissidence eventually overcame him, and he was first
disfellowshipped, then later excommunicated.[1]

Both before and after his excommunication, McLellin collected materials
about the church. At one time or another, he reportedly owned the original
record of the Quorum of the Twelve, two copies of A Book of Commandments, manuscript revelations, certificates from early church members,
and various books, pamphlets, and periodicals containing church information.[2] McLellin was also a writer. Late in his life he worked on a book about
Mormonism that he nearly finished but never published. He also wrote
essays on polygamy and faith.[3]

Some of McLellin's books and papers eventually fell into the hands of
a man named J. L. Traughber. In 1901, an anti-Mormon lawyer wrote
Traughber, who was then living in Texas, to obtain information about the
church. The men corresponded repeatedly that year, and gradually Traughber informed the lawyer of valuable records he had in his possession. In
one letter, he wrote that he owned one of McLellin's two copies of the
rare Book of Commandments.[4]

Later that year, Traughber explained he also had "some little manuscript
books written by Dr. W. E. McLellin," as well as McLellin's journals for
parts of 1831 through 1836, and some letters. Would he sell them? "Yes,"
he answered, "I could be induced to part with what I have on the subject
of Mormonism, provided I could get enough for it to do me some good."
But he would not sell the material piecemeal. "If I dispose of any of it,"

William E. McLellin (1806–83). (LDS Church)

he wrote, "I want to make a clean sweep and wipe my hands forever from all that pertains to the matter." Traughber encouraged the lawyer to make him an offer, provided he could offer "anything that amounts to anything" for the materials. "If I can't get enough out of my possessions on Mormonism to do me some good in a financial sense," he warned, "I don't care to part with any of it."[5]

Eventually, the lawyer died, and the New York Public Library acquired his papers. A few scholars read them and learned of Traughber's offer to sell McLellin's journals and other papers to him. Interesting as the late lawyer's papers were, they offered no proof he ever bought the proffered McLellin materials. One Mormon scholar attempted to contact Traughber's descendants about them but received no response.[6]

McLellin's books and papers remained elusive as ever to the few researchers who knew they had even existed. Despite McLellin's prominence in the early church, by the late twentieth century, he had largely been forgotten by most officials and members, who, if they remembered him at all, knew him as an obscure figure whose name (often written M'Lellin and mispronounced) occasionally appeared in church writings. The 1980s, however, would bring a series of events that would once again catapult McLellin's name into prominence.

In 1984 church officials heard a rumor about the discovery of a copy of an early revelation Joseph Smith had purportedly received. The revelation itself had been mentioned in historical sources for years, but no copies of it had been thought to survive. Two church historians who visited McLellin in 1878 had mentioned the revelation. One wrote that McLellin had "said Joseph had given a false revelation in 1829, ordering Oliver Cowdery to go to Canada and get the copyright of the Book of Mormon, and afterwards acknowledged it was false, now, therefore, he (McLellin) doubted all of Joseph's revelations subsequently given."[7]

Assistant church historian B. H. Roberts described the "Canadian copyright episode" in detail in his *Comprehensive History of the Church.* "May this . . . incident and the Prophet's explanation be accepted and faith still be maintained in him as an inspired man, a Prophet of God?" Roberts queried, replying, "I answer unhesitatingly in the affirmative."[8] Relying largely on Roberts, Francis Gibbons described the incident in his 1977 biography of Joseph Smith. "The Canadian incident merely demonstrated that Joseph was human and therefore subject to error," he wrote. Gibbons added, however, that this "isolated instance of error" should not lead "to the unwarranted conclusion that Joseph was not a prophet—or was a fallen prophet."[9]

On August 9, 1984, the president of Brigham Young University dictated a message for Gordon B. Hinckley. Among other things, he mentioned that

Jerald Tanner and Sandra Tanner might have the original copy of a revelation in which Joseph Smith asked Oliver Cowdery and others to try to sell the copyright of the Book of Mormon in Canada. "The effort was unsuccessful," he explained, "and was later described as a false revelation." From the message, it was not clear who the source of the document was or whether it was part of a larger collection of materials.[10]

A few months later in January of 1985, Brent Metcalfe passed on another rumor to Ron Barney of the church Historical Department. "Brent Metcalfe says the Church (probably the First Presidency) has been given some documents," Barney recorded in his notes, "one of which is Facsimile #2 of the Book of Abraham. Evidently these would have been given to the Church (or sold) in Nov/Dec 1984."[11]

In the 1830s, Joseph Smith began translating some papyrus records taken from mummies found in Egypt. Smith's published history explained that he "commenced the translation of some of the characters or hieroglyphics, and . . . found that one of the rolls contained the writings of Abraham," the Old Testament prophet. Joseph's translation was later published as the Book of Abraham and accepted as scripture by the church. The published Book of Abraham contained three facsimiles, or reproductions, that were made from the papyrus and printed along with the English text. After Joseph Smith's death, the mummies and papyrus were lost. In 1967, some of the papyrus was rediscovered at the Metropolitan Museum in New York City and presented to the church. The rediscovered pieces included Facsimile No. 1 from the published Book of Abraham but not Facsimiles No. 2 or No. 3.[12]

Now, according to Metcalfe, Facsimile No. 2 had also been discovered and was among a larger collection of documents rumored to have been purchased by the First Presidency. On Wednesday, January 23, 1985, Glenn Rowe was confronted with a rumor like the one Barney had heard from Metcalfe. Rowe wrote in his journal that he "had several questions about a purchase of facsimile #2 papyri."[13]

The questions Rowe fielded may have been prompted by the January 1985 issue of Jerald Tanner's and Sandra Tanner's newsletter, which passed on a rumor "that Mark Hofmann has obtained the original Egyptian Papyrus which Joseph Smith used as Fac. No. 2 in the Book of Abraham" and "that Hofmann plans to secretly sell the document to the Church so that it can remain hidden from the eyes of the public." The Tanners also reported that a "prominent Mormon scholar" (whom they did not name) told them "he had heard the Church was buying the document," but "he was not aware of any plans for a cover-up." Hofmann, the Tanners added, had confirmed that the facsimile was "in existence and that paste up work has been done on it." Another unnamed source confirmed Hofmann's statement.[14]

Meanwhile, another rumor was afloat. On May 3, 1985, church magazine editor Jay Todd telephoned Brent Ashworth, who later recalled that "Jay said that there were rumors floating around the Church Office Building . . . that the Tanners had just bought the 116 pages, or that they had acquired a copy of it." Ashworth recalled Todd saying that "several of us up here are concerned about it," though Todd did not name who the concerned persons were. Ashworth assumed the concerned persons were general authorities of the church. (Todd, however, would later say that although he could not remember the source of the information that prompted the call, he was certain no general authority had assigned him to make it.)[15]

Ashworth checked with Hofmann about the rumor. Hofmann said that a manuscript did exist in Bakersfield, California, but it was a fake. After Hofmann described the fake to him, Ashworth felt intrigued and thought to himself, "I would like to own that as a collectible."

"Mark," Ashworth later recalled asking Hofmann, "what do you think that thing could be had for?"

Eventually, Hofmann answered, "Oh, I think we'd have to have at least five thousand [for it] even as a forgery."

"Well, look," Ashworth said, "I'll pay you ten thousand if you can get it."

Later, Ashworth called Todd. "Mark told me that the Tanners do not have a copy of it," Ashworth said, explaining how he offered Hofmann ten thousand dollars for the fake. The offer dumbfounded Todd. Ashworth recalled that "there was kind of a sigh like, 'Well, . . . you don't expect us to pay that for it!' "

"Oh no. Heck no," Ashworth said. "I did that on my own." Despite Ashworth's repeated entreaties, however, Hofmann never delivered the document to him.[16]

Rumors about manuscript discoveries continued over the next six months. On Monday, June 3, Richard Lindsay of the church's Public Communications Department wrote a memorandum to his supervisors, who included Gordon B. Hinckley and Dallin H. Oaks. Oaks, fifty-two years old, had become the newest member of the Quorum of the Twelve just a year earlier. Before then, he had served as a United States Supreme Court clerk, University of Chicago law professor, American Bar Foundation executive director, Brigham Young University president, and Utah Supreme Court justice.[17]

In his memorandum, Lindsay mentioned telephone calls his department had received from a reporter who had called repeatedly to ask questions about a "McLellin Collection." "This collection," Lindsay summarized, "is supposed to include a number of historical documents including three diaries of William E. McLellin, an early member of the Quorum of the Twelve;

copies of some early revelations, a Book of Commandments, and artifacts including Facsimile #2 and four papyri fragments.''

The reporter had said the collection was reportedly sold in Texas and recently transported to Utah. She had asked if the church owned or possessed the collection, noting that an unidentified person, perhaps one of the church's general authorities, had reportedly paid $100,000 for it. Lindsay concluded, ''It is our understanding that the material is not in possession of the Historical Department. This is another 'Historical Item' I presume we will continue to hear about. We would appreciate direction on a suggested response.''[18]

In the late afternoon on Tuesday, June 11, a secretary in the Church Administration Building received a telephone call from Alvin E. Rust, a Salt Lake City coin dealer. She recorded that Rust seemed ''quite agitated and expressed the opinion that there was a 'collection' in Pres. Hinckley's hands given him by Mark Hoffman.'' Rust said little about the collection itself but asked to speak to someone who worked with Hinckley on confidential matters. The secretary transferred Rust to Francis Gibbons.

Before long, Rust called her back. He said he had spoken to Gibbons and that Gibbons told him he was not aware of the collection and felt the story about Hinckley's having it was not true. ''Brother Rust was again very agitated,'' the secretary wrote, ''and indicated that he had put up a 'lot of money,' that it would threaten his business if he did not get it back. He mentioned the name of Mark Hoffman but said he couldn't tell me more because he had promised total confidentiality. Brother Rust expressed concern that he was getting the 'run-around' from Mark Hoffman because a period of several weeks had passed and he did not feel he was getting 'straight' answers from Bro. Hoffman.'' Because Rust was a coin dealer, the secretary assumed he was talking about a coin collection.

Rust told her his son had traveled with Hofmann to pick up the collection and was to have brought it back to Rust's store for evaluation. The son had returned without Hofmann and without the collection. Rust said the financial crisis created by the situation was harming his health. He told the secretary he would be leaving town June 15 and wanted to clear up the matter before he left.

The secretary asked Rust to hold the line for a moment. She then called Gibbons to discuss the matter. Gibbons suggested she have Rust put his concerns in a letter. The secretary then talked to Rust and passed on the suggestion, assuring him that if he marked the envelope ''Confidential,'' she would give it directly to Hinckley without opening it. Rust said he would do so and would drop the letter off the next morning.[19]

Rust sat down that day and wrote a letter in which he explained that Hofmann had asked him to help finance the purchase of the McLellin collection. He had helped Hofmann with similar transactions in the past. Hofmann had agreed that Rust's son would go with him to buy the collection, that the most valuable items in the collection would be hand-carried by them to Rust's store, and that the rest of the items would be shipped back to the same location.

"Now the problem," Rust wrote. "Mark by-passed my son where he was not involved at all. The entire collection was sent back to Mark instead of to me." About a week later, Rust explained, Hofmann called him to say the church wanted to buy the whole collection but would need a few days to conclude the transaction. At first, Rust thought this arrangement satisfactory, but as time dragged on, he became less comfortable. "Now a month later," he wrote, "I still have no idea what is going on."

When Hofmann first approached Rust, he said nothing to him about keeping the transaction confidential. But when Hofmann called to say the church wanted to buy the collection, he told Rust it was imperative to keep the transaction quiet. Neither he nor his son had said a word about the deal, Rust wrote. He assured Hinckley he did not want to create a problem, but Hofmann was avoiding him, and he felt entitled to an explanation. "A phone call or something to ease my concern prior to our family leaving on vacation this Saturday would be appreciated," Rust concluded.[20]

The next day, June 12, Rust dropped his letter off at the Church Administration Building. From Rust's perspective, the request for an explanatory phone call seemed reasonable under the circumstances. But his letter baffled Hinckley. Hofmann had never talked to him about any McLellin collection.

At 4:30 P.M. that day, Hofmann visited Hinckley and asked if he had gotten a letter from Rust. Hinckley said he had and asked Hofmann about the letter and his dealings with Rust. Hofmann said that a couple of years earlier, he had spoken to Don Schmidt about McLellin's papers. Schmidt had told him he knew about the papers but would not pursue them if Hofmann was going after them. Hofmann told Hinckley he had learned the papers were available and that they had been put up as security for a loan. A bank had them in its possession, but they could be purchased for $185,000. Hofmann said Rust had put up $175,000. "Mark went East and got the papers," Hinckley wrote in a memo to his file that day, adding parenthetically, "I suppose it was East[;] he stated that he had flown in from New York today."

Hofmann told Hinckley that Rust had not kept the papers confidential, even though he had promised Hofmann he would. Hofmann implied Rust's breach of confidence had led to publicity aimed at getting the church to disclose if it had bought the collection. Hofmann said he intended to repay Rust by borrowing money from Chase Manhattan Bank against his inventory of historical materials. After repaying Rust, he intended to donate the McLellin collection to the church. He would then repay the Chase Manhattan loan using what Hinckley described as "a very substantial fee coming from the Library of Congress in connection with finding some materials for the library."[21]

Sifting through materials in a New York bookstore, Hofmann had purportedly found a copy of *The Oath of a Freeman*, the first English document known to have been printed in the Western Hemisphere. Working through New York dealers Justin G. Schiller and Raymond M. Wapner, he had offered it to the Library of Congress for $1.5 million, an amount that was more than enough to repay any debt incurred in buying the McLellin collection.[22]

Hinckley recorded that although they did not discuss the contents of the papers in detail, he learned that they contained Facsimile No. 2, as well as "journals and diaries, some affidavits, and quite a number of things." "We concluded our conversation," Hinckley wrote, "by again saying that when he was all in the clear with Rust, that he could then get in touch with me and we could talk about his making this contribution. I thanked him and told him to keep in touch with me."

"Earlier in our conversation," Hinckley also wrote, "I raised a question concerning the so-called Oliver Cowdery history of the Church which we are alleged to have and which we have been unable to find. He said that all he knew was that Brent Metcalfe had told him that an individual knew of this and had typescripts of two pages of this. He said he thought he could get a copy of the typescript."

"He said further," Hinckley wrote, "that Brent is employed by George D. Smith and that it was George D. Smith who talked with the Los Angeles Times about the matter."[23]

The next day, June 13, in the weekly meeting of the First Presidency and the Twelve, Hinckley announced he had been approached by a church member who said he had acquired important papers of William E. McLellin. "These papers," the minutes recorded, "are now the subject of a controversy between this man and another, which, it is expected, will be resolved soon. This member has indicated a desire and intention to give these documents to the Church when the controversy has been resolved, documents which he reportedly purchased for $185,000."

The minutes also recorded how the council felt the offer should be treated: "President Hinckley indicated that it is his disposition to accept this gift when it is tendered and, because there have been public announcements that the Church already has this collection, to make announcement of the receipt of the gift and merely to indicate that the documents will be retained by the Church pending the time when they can be analyzed and appraised. The Council approved this procedure."[24]

THE OATH OF A FREEMAN.

I ·AB· being (by Gods providence) an Inhabitant, and Freeman, within the iurifdictiō of this Common-wealth, doe freely acknowledge my felfe to bee fubject to the governement thereof; and therefore doe heere fweare, by the great & dreadfull name of the Everliving-God, that I will be true & faithfull to the fame, & will accordingly yield affiftance & fupport therunto, with my perfon & eftate, as in equity I am bound: and will alfo truely indeavour to maintaine and preferve all the libertyes & privilidges thereof; fubmitting my felfe to the wholefome lawes, & ordres made & ftablifhed by the fame; and further, that I will not plot, nor practice any evill againft it, nor confent to any that fhall foe do, butt will timely difcover, & reveall the fame to lawefull authoritee nowe here ftablifhed, for the fpeedie preventing thereof. Moreover, I doe folemnly binde my felfe, in the fight of God, that when I fhalbe called, to give my voyce touching any fuch matter of this ftate, (in which freemen are to deale) I will give my vote & fuffrage as I fhall judge in myne owne confcience may beft conduce & tend to the publick weale of the body, without refpect of perfonnes, or favour of any man. Soe help mee God in the Lord Iefus Chrift.

The Oath of a Freeman. (*Deseret News*)

Late in the afternoon on June 24, Brent Metcalfe once again visited Ron Barney in the Historical Department. He mentioned the Oliver Cowdery history and McLellin collection, and Barney pressed him for clues on the source of his information about the two items. Barney wrote that Metcalfe said his source "has not only seen the Oliver Cowdery history but has also seen the original documents of the McLellin papers in the First Presidency vault." Moreover, "Metcalfe also said that there are photographs available of the McLellin papers and also of a 'gag order' placed on the participants of the transaction of the McLellin papers going to the First Presidency."

Believing Metcalfe's source was telling the truth, Barney wrote, "If the church were to make a public statement now—which they were going to do—that we can't find the Oliver Cowdery history and that we do not have the McLellin material the availability of the above mentioned photographs would be very devastating as per our image of being honest." Concerned about Metcalfe's information, Barney met with F. Michael Watson, a secretary in the First Presidency's office. "I told him," Barney wrote, "that while laying in bed this morning and ruminating over these things everything fell into place, for me, that Mark Hofmann is the 'source'. Michael felt the same thing."[25]

On Thursday, June 27, Hofmann called Steve Christensen and told him he had a serious matter to discuss. Christensen agreed to meet with him the next morning. At 10:30 A.M. on June 28, the two met, and Hofmann unraveled a complicated tale about his attempts to acquire the McLellin collection. The collection, he said, was in Texas. The church had once tried to obtain it from the father of the current owner, but he would not sell. Hofmann said he agreed with Don Schmidt that if the church would back off the deal, Hofmann would offer the collection to the church first if he acquired it. Hofmann had finally acquired an option to purchase the collection but needed $195,000 to conclude the deal. He had already put up $10,000 earnest money and had thought the balance would be lent by a private party. Recently, however, the party withdrew his support, and the option would expire in two days. Hofmann asked Christensen if he could put up the money to close the transaction.[26]

Hofmann had approached Christensen because he seemed to be well-off. Just a year and a half earlier, Christensen had bought the salamander letter for forty thousand dollars and had then helped finance its authentication. Hofmann assumed the young businessman might once again be able to provide money for important historical material. Hofmann was wrong. Steve Christensen's financial success had been rapid but short-lived. Steve had been working at Mr. Mac's, a chain of clothing stores owned by his father, Mac Christensen, when he was hired away by Gary Sheets, a salesman who developed a burgeoning investment and financial planning business called CFS Financial Corp. Steve had worked his way up from being Sheets's administrative assistant to being his partner in J. Gary Sheets and Associates. On January 1, 1985, Christensen became senior executive vice-president of CFS. Confident of CFS's success, Christensen had invested his time and assets heavily in the business. CFS, however, went into a tailspin, and Christensen knew he was tied too closely to the business to escape crashing with it. Thus, when Hofmann called, the young businessman was not in a position to provide money. But he could at least point Hofmann toward someone who might help.

"After a thirty minute review of the facts and potential options," Christensen recorded in his journal, "I suggested to Mark that we contact Elder Hugh Pinnock, not necessarily because he was a General Authority, but more particularly because he was a man of financial expertise with a wide circle of friends & contacts."[27]

Hugh W. Pinnock, fifty-one years old, was a member of the First Quorum of the Seventy who had been a successful insurance executive before his call to full-time church service. Pinnock had known Christensen's business associate, Gary Sheets, since high school and had maintained a close relationship with him. Several years earlier, Sheets had been one of Pinnock's insurance agents before venturing out on his own. One day after Sheets established his own business, he told Pinnock he had hired the greatest man in the world to work for him. Sheets later introduced Steve Christensen to him as that man. After meeting Christensen, Pinnock also saw him in other settings. Pinnock had belonged to a religious study group for many years, and a member of the group had invited Christensen to speak to it about church history. Through this and similar experiences, the two men gradually became acquainted so that on June 28, 1985, Christensen felt he could call Pinnock to help out Mark Hofmann.[28]

"The purpose for going to Elder Pinnock," Christensen recorded of his June 28 meeting, "rather than someone like President Hinckley, was due to the fact that President Hinckley was dedicating the Temple in East Germany that very day." Furthermore, Hofmann said he had tried to keep the church out of the transaction and, in Christensen's words, "had been keeping President Hinckley informed was all." "I called Elder Pinnock over the telephone," Christensen wrote, "and I was fortunate enough to get through to him. I briefly reviewed the facts with him." Pinnock had never heard of the McLellin collection, though he recognized McLellin's name.[29]

Writing later in his journal, Christensen summarized some of the important considerations in the McLellin transaction. He noted that Wesley Walters, whom he labeled as "an anti-Mormon antagonist," and George Smith, whom he described as "owner of Signature Books, humanist, intellectual anti-Mormon and semi-financially independent businessman," had also contacted the McLellin collection's owner. Pinnock, jotting notes about what he learned that day, also recorded Walters's and Smith's names.[30]

"Mark's concern (as shared by myself and Elder Pinnock)," Christensen wrote, "was that they would make an attempt to purchase the collection should Mark miss the funding deadline of Sunday, June 30, 1985." Christensen's journal also mentioned "some speculation in print (via the Tanner's newsletter) and considerable speculation by word of mouth" that the church had already bought the collection and had suppressed it because it contained information damaging to the church. Though the rumors about the purchase were false, Christensen noted some of the contents of the collection that could raise historical questions. These included the original of Facsimile No. 2, an affidavit from Emma Smith, the only extant copy of the Canadian copyright episode revelation, several other Mormon documents, and McLellin's journals. The Emma Smith affidavit, Christensen noted, showed "that Joseph's first religious experience with the divine was in the coming forth of the Book of Mormon." "In other words," he explained parenthetically, "she omits reference to the occurence of the First Vision." Pinnock recorded a similar list of materials.[31]

In his telephone call to Pinnock, Christensen said that Hofmann was in the process of selling *The Oath of a Freeman* to the Library of Congress for $1.5 million dollars, three-fourths of which would be paid to him on August 15. Hofmann had said he would use part of the money to purchase the McLellin collection outright and donate it to the church. Christensen wrote in his journal that after he discussed the matter briefly with Pinnock, the church leader "indicated that he could arrange for the funds within one hour and that Mark and I should come over to his office as soon as possible."[32]

Before meeting with Christensen and Hofmann, Pinnock consulted with Dallin Oaks, the member of the Quorum of the Twelve to whom Pinnock reported in his role as president of the Utah South Area of the church. Oaks's office was next door to Pinnock's in the Church Administration Building. Pinnock, who had not heard of the McLellin collection before that day, asked Oaks what he knew about it. Oaks said he knew only what had been mentioned in the press but knew who McLellin was and assumed his papers would be valuable if found. Pinnock asked Oaks if he thought the church might lend Hofmann $185,000 to purchase the collection.[33]

"I said emphatically not," Oaks later recalled. "President Hinckley was in Europe at the time of this conversation. No one else could or would approve such a transaction. I had never discussed this subject with President Hinckley. I had no idea what his views or knowledge of the matter were. Moreover, to have the church involved in the acquisition of a collection at this time would simply fuel the then current speculation reported by the press that the church already had something called the McLellin collection or was trying to acquire it in order to suppress it."[34]

The two men discussed whether the church would accept the collection as a gift. Oaks concluded it probably would, provided it was "a genuine gift from a real donor." "Now I inquired," Oaks recounted, "in the course of this conversation, if Hofmann had a million dollars receivable from the Library of Congress why wouldn't a bank simply loan him $185,000? Elder Pinnock inquired whether it would be appropriate to put him [Hofmann] in touch with banking officials. I said I saw no harm in that provided it was clearly understood by all parties that the church was not a party or a guarantor and that Hugh Pinnock was not a party or a guarantor to such a loan."[35]

When Christensen and Hofmann reached Pinnock's office at 11:25 A.M., Pinnock met Hofmann for the first time. Pinnock invited his two visitors in and had them wait while he stepped out to make some telephone calls. He first called Zions Bank but learned that its highest officials were out of town. He then phoned First Interstate Bank of Utah, on whose board of directors he served. He spoke to executive vice-president Robert J. Ward about extending Hofmann a loan for $185,000. Pinnock said he did not know much about Hofmann's financial condition but mentioned that Hofmann had a valuable document he was selling to the federal government. Hofmann, he said, would repay the loan around August 15, as soon as the sale to the government had closed. When Pinnock returned to his office, he told Christensen and Hofmann that everything had been arranged.[36]

Hofmann said he planned to fly to Texas to purchase the collection and agreed to update Pinnock and Christensen on the matter over the weekend. Pinnock offered to arrange for secure transportation of the documents by jet or armored car, but Hofmann said he would send them back to Utah by registered mail, adequately insured. He would then hold them in a safe-deposit box until he received his money from the Library of Congress and paid off the First Interstate loan, when he would then be able to donate the documents to the church.

During the meeting in Pinnock's office, the men also talked about other historical matters, including the lost 116 pages of the Book of Mormon manuscript. "Mark has been working on this for some years," Christensen recorded. They laughed that everyone seemed to have a lead on the lost pages, and Pinnock added his own story, recounting that when he had served as president of the Pennsylvania Harrisburg Mission, a woman in the area claimed to have information about the whereabouts of the pages. At about 12:45 P.M., Christensen and Hofmann left Pinnock's office.[37]

Christensen and Hofmann went together to First Interstate Bank, where they briefly met Bob Ward, who introduced them to loan officer Harvey

Tanner. Tanner issued a $185,000 loan to Hofmann at 1 percent over prime. Hofmann signed a promissory note, received the money in the form of a cashier's check, and promised to furnish the bank a copy of his contract with the Library of Congress.[38] Within a few weeks, it seemed, Hofmann would receive payment on the contract, the bank would receive its money back with interest, and the church would receive the McLellin collection.

"Ancient Mormon Manuscript Found, Sold in Texas," proclaimed the headline of a *Salt Lake Tribune* article on July 6. The article announced that Mark Hofmann had located the McLellin collection and that it contained Facsimile No. 2, "one of the most famous relics in Mormondom." Hofmann, the article reported, also said the collection contained McLellin's diaries, correspondence and affidavits from the 1830s, and a blessing from Joseph Smith, Jr., to his son Joseph Smith III. "The collection is of considerable historical value in regards to the early [Mormon] church," Hofmann reportedly said. "It contains insights into the personality of William McLellin and numerous references to Joseph Smith."

Hofmann told the reporter he could not divulge the location of the collection, the buyer's name, or the sale amount. The article cited Brent Metcalfe as saying the church did not have the collection as earlier thought and that it appeared to be owned privately. Jerry Cahill, it also noted, denied church ownership or possession of the collection, and Hofmann likewise agreed he had not sold the collection to the church. Hofmann said the documents might be made public after they had been authenticated.[39]

Though Hofmann had publicly announced his purchase, he had not yet called Hugh Pinnock as promised. When he finally spoke by phone to Pinnock on Thursday, July 11, Hofmann apologized for the delay, saying the purchase had not gone as smoothly as expected. He said he had had to make three trips in two weeks to close the deal but finally paid for the collection on Monday, July 8. Pinnock took notes as Hofmann spoke. "George Smith was *hot* on *it*," Pinnock wrote. What about the July 6 article in which Hofmann claimed to have already bought the collection? "Article appeared before collection was obtained—to get George Smith off back," Pinnock recorded. And what about the bank loan? "Going to pay off the account on Tues or Wed with 1st Interstate Bank." When would the church get to see the collection? "Church will receive when note is paid off."[40]

Despite all the trouble he had in obtaining the collection, Hofmann said he had gotten it safely back to Salt Lake City, where it was being stored in safe-deposit boxes. Noting his conversation with Hofmann in his journal, Pinnock wrote, "Things are more complicated than thought, but going well."[41]

The following day at 9:30 A.M., Hofmann visited Pinnock in his office and showed him a document he said was from the McLellin collection. It was an 1822 deed signed by several persons, including Solomon Spalding and Sidney Rigdon. Pinnock asked if he could make a photocopy of it. Hofmann consented on condition that Pinnock keep the document confidential and not distribute it. Pinnock agreed. Noting the meeting in his journal, Pinnock described the document as "interesting but not significant beyond a historical connection." He felt that though the document might prove Spalding and Rigdon knew each other, it did not prove Spalding had influenced the writing of the Book of Mormon.[42]

In the August 1985 issue of their newsletter, Jerald Tanner and Sandra Tanner ran an article about the McLellin collection that speculated on the place in Texas from which Hofmann obtained it. The July 6 newspaper article reporting the purchase had said that Hofmann had acquired McLellin's journals. J. L. Traughber, the Tanners noted, had lived in Tyler County when he wrote in a letter that he had the journals. The Tanners also reported "that Mark Hofmann did obtain a copy of the revelation to sell the copyright of the Book of Mormon as part of the McLellin collection." They also explained that the affidavits reported to be in the collection apparently included ones from Emma Smith, Martin Harris, Elizabeth Cowdery (Oliver's wife), and David Whitmer.

The Tanners also returned to their earlier discussion about Facsimile No. 2. The newspaper article about the McLellin collection had cited Brent Metcalfe as saying that the facsimile apparently was "owned by a private individual." Referring to the Stowell letter, the Tanners noted that "George Smith stated that it was his understanding that President Gordon B. Hinckley 'purchased the letter in 1983 in his own name from collector Mark Hofmann. . . .' We have no additional information to support this accusation, but if President Hinckley bought the letter in his own name, the church leaders could say that the church did not own it." They acknowledged, however, that "it is not known if the individual who holds the McLellin collection is trying to suppress it for the Mormon Church."[43]

By Monday, August 26, the date Hofmann had given for his payment from the Library of Congress had passed, but the bank had not yet received its money and church officials had seen no more of the McLellin collection. Both these facts increased Hugh Pinnock's concern about the growing complexity of the transaction. Loan officer Harvey Tanner called Pinnock about the loan, and Pinnock in turn contacted Christensen, who had been the one to introduce Hofmann to him. Christensen apparently could not reach Hofmann by phone and so wrote him a letter instead.[44]

"I have been notified by the bank," Christensen explained to Hofmann, "that they have not received any word from you since you borrowed the funds on the McLellen Collection. You will recall that you indicated that you would receive the funds from the Library of Congress by August 15.

Naturally, the bank is concerned and most interested in receiving the funds back on this Note." Christensen asked Hofmann to call Harvey Tanner at First Interstate Bank immediately. "Also," he added, "please do me the courtesy of giving me an adequate update on the status of this project."[45]

Over the next several weeks, Pinnock's journal would record both Christensen's and Hofmann's names with increasing frequency. Pinnock, however, had more reasons than just the McLellin collection for talking to Christensen. CFS Financial Corp., the business in which Christensen and Gary Sheets were heavily involved, had become insolvent. Foreseeing its dissolution and the personal bankruptcy it portended for him, Christensen quit the company in early August, braced himself for impending financial disaster, and started his own business with friend and CFS associate Randy Rigby. He also sought personal counsel from Pinnock and met with him repeatedly to discuss his problems.[46]

Sometime in this same period, Pinnock had an opportunity to inform Gordon Hinckley about what had happened on the McLellin collection transaction during Hinckley's trip to Europe. Pinnock explained the intervening events and Hofmann's expressed desire ultimately to donate the collection to the church.[47]

Meanwhile, on Wednesday, August 28, Mark Hofmann and Brent Metcalfe visited Ron Barney in the Historical Department. They discussed the Oliver Cowdery history. Metcalfe said access to the First Presidency's vault was limited to certain persons, and Hofmann said he had never been in the vault. He said he saw some items from the vault, but Francis Gibbons retrieved them and showed them to him in Gibbons's office. These statements altered Barney's earlier conclusions about Hofmann. "To me," Barney concluded in notes to himself, "Hofmann could not possibly be the 'source' for Brent Metcalfe." Barney also wrote, "Mark says he thinks the McLellin stuff will be out before long. He said that some material is circulating already."[48]

Around September 6, Mark Hofmann visited Curt A. Bench in the church-owned Deseret Book store just south of the Church Administration Building. Bench ran the store's fine and rare books department, and he had recently obtained a copy of *The Book of Common Prayer* from one of the store's corporate officers. The book had been in Deseret Book's possession since 1973, when it had been purchased along with a first edition of the Book of Mormon. Though *The Book of Common Prayer* was not a Latter-day Saint work, Bench thought it might interest Hofmann, his friend and client, because it had once belonged to Nathan Harris of Kirtland, Ohio. Bench showed Hofmann the book. Hofmann glanced at it and said he might be interested in buying it because Nathan Harris was related to Martin Harris. Hofmann left the store book in hand.[49]

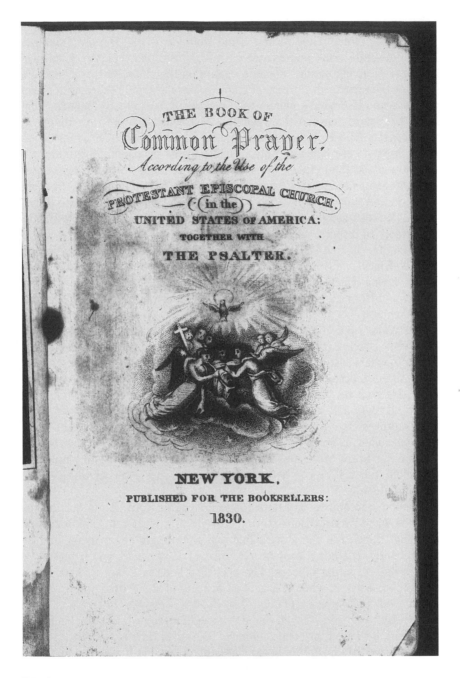

The Book of Common Prayer. (Paul L. Swensen)

On Wednesday, September 11, Hofmann returned to Deseret Book to see Bench. Hofmann said that as he was going through *The Book of Common Prayer*, he discovered some Martin Harris handwriting, which made it possible for him to resell the book for two thousand dollars. Hofmann, who had finally paid Bench fifty dollars for the volume just the previous day, now volunteered to pay Deseret Book one thousand dollars instead. The arrangement seemed fair to Bench, and he and Hofmann worked out the details for payment to be made in trade.[50]

The significance of Hofmann's new discovery became clear to Ron Barney of the Historical Department when, on the same day, Brent Metcalfe explained the new find to him. Summarizing his conversation with Metcalfe, Barney wrote, "Hofmann has purchased a volume of Nathanial Harris from Kirtland which evidently has Martin Harris' handwriting in it in several places which corresponds perfectly to the 1830 Harris to Phelps [salamander] letter."[51]

Metcalfe told Dean Jessee about the book that day too. The next day, Jessee spoke with the manager of the acquisitions section of the Historical Department's Library-Archives Division, who also told him about the volume. "Evidently," Jessee recorded, "the Church will have a chance to purchase it." A few weeks later, Jessee called Curt Bench "and asked him about the Nathan Harris prayer book and how they got it. He said D[eseret] B[ook] has had it for many years. . . . I asked him if he remembered the handwriting in the back of the book. Said he did."[52]

In January 1985 Jerald Tanner and Sandra Tanner had reported that one of Christensen's researchers claimed to find a Book of Mormon with a Martin Harris inscription. The Tanners had cautioned against accepting the inscription as proof the salamander letter was authentic. "A forgery in a book," they had asserted, "would be much easier to perpetrate than a postmarked letter, and there is always a possibility that a second forgery would be created to provide support for the first." Still, they had conceded, "if the book was known to have had this writing in it for a number of years *prior* to the discovery of the Salamander letter, it could be very important in determining the authenticity of the letter."[53] The Harris *Book of Common Prayer* appeared to meet the Tanners' criterion.

The day Hofmann offered to pay Bench a thousand dollars, Hugh Pinnock made a note of the names and telephone numbers of both Harvey Tanner and Steve Christensen. Hofmann had given First Interstate Bank a check to pay off the loan, but the check had bounced. Finally, at 9:15 A.M. on Friday, September 13, Hofmann visited Pinnock's office. Pinnock discussed the loan with him, encouraging him to repay it as quickly as possible and emphasizing the importance of maintaining good relationships with banks.[54]

Handwriting from *The Book of Common Prayer* that matched handwriting of the salamander letter. (Paul L. Swensen)

Hofmann said he was still waiting for his payment from the Library of Congress but expected to receive it soon. His assurances did not totally satisfy Pinnock, who wrote in his journal, "Mark Hofmann came in and made several semi-wild promises about the money he owes the bank but did not deliver on anything he had said. The whole situation has left me concerned and discouraged with him."[55]

Later that day, Hofmann again met with Curt Bench at Deseret Book. Bench recorded that the usually staid Hofmann was "very distraught" and "visibly nervous." He also noticed that Hofmann was being followed by someone whose presence he did not explain. Pale and shaking, Hofmann told Bench he desperately needed money. He offered Deseret Book his personal book collection, valued at $375,000, in exchange for $100,000 and a promise from him to buy the collection back for $150,000 by year's end. "He said he would do that or anything he had to to raise the $100K," Bench recorded. "He needed the $ badly."

Bench discussed the proposal with his supervisor, who said he would not want to rush into such a transaction and would have to think about it. When Bench reported the decision to Hofmann, Hofmann insisted on talking to Bench's supervisor personally. Bench took Hofmann to meet him and the stranger followed. Bench's supervisor told Hofmann he would consider the matter over the weekend and give him an answer on Monday.[56]

The next morning, a Saturday, Hofmann called Bench at home. Hofmann had regained his composure and placidly explained that he had resolved his predicament and would not need Deseret Book's help. Hours later at 11:30 P.M., Steve Christensen called Bench. Bench and Christensen knew each other because Christensen had purchased items, mostly books, through Bench at Deseret Book. Their earlier dealings had generally been during normal business hours. The late phone call signaled something unusual was on Christensen's mind.

Christensen told Bench, who he knew had dealt with Hofmann, that an unnamed general authority of the church who was on the board of a local bank wanted to know about a recent transaction in which Hofmann had paid Deseret Book one hundred thousand dollars. The bank on whose board the general authority served had found out about the check and wanted to know what was going on because Hofmann owed the bank money that he had borrowed on the church leader's recommendation. Bench recorded that Christensen told him the money "was to acquire [the] McLellin collection which was to be considered collateral" for the loan and which "would then be given to [the] Church." Bench already knew about the McLellin collection; Hofmann had told him about it in July.[57]

The check to which Christensen referred was partial payment to Deseret Book in a complex transaction involving a letter apparently written by

Joseph Smith on the day he was killed. The letter, addressed to Mormon militia general Jonathan Dunham, ordered Dunham to bring his troops to the jail where Smith and his associates were being held. Hofmann had promised the letter to Brent Ashworth but had sold it instead to Arizona medical doctor Richard Marks, much to Ashworth's disappointment. To console Ashworth, Hofmann had asked Deseret Book to buy the letter back from Marks so Hofmann could offer it to Ashworth. The check Hofmann gave Deseret Book largely covered the buy-back. Bench discreetly told Christensen about Hofmann's check, noting in his journal, however, that he "didn't identify item sold to him or seller of it to us" but "did say it wasn't part of McLellin coll[ection]."[58]

Bench wrote that Christensen told him the McLellin collection contained "2 apple crates' worth of material." Christensen also said that Hofmann was supposed to pay off his loan to the bank in mid-August, but that no one had seen the collection or any money. Hofmann had given the bank a check to repay the debt, but it had bounced. Hofmann had offered no explanations and could not be reached. The general authority was trying to forestall criminal action against Hofmann, together with the scandal and embarrassment it might cause the church.[59]

Bench told Christensen about Hofmann's attempt to raise money the day before and about his apparent success in meeting his needs from another source. Bench assumed Hofmann had been trying to raise money to pay off the bank loan and that he had apparently succeeded in getting the money he needed. Christensen told Bench he would keep him informed about the situation. He feared, however, that the circumstances could ruin Hofmann's reputation and jeopardize his ability to work with Gordon Hinckley.[60]

On Thursday, September 19, Hofmann dropped by Deseret Book again. This time he showed Bench a piece of papyrus that he offered to sell for forty thousand dollars. Hofmann said it was from the McLellin collection. Bench declined buying it, and Hofmann told him not to tell anyone about it. After what he had heard about the McLellin collection, Bench found it puzzling that Hofmann would try to sell a piece of it. "I asked if the Church wasn't supposed to have rec'd McLellin collection by now," Bench recorded.[61]

Despite Hofmann's request that he not mention it to anyone, Bench decided Christensen was entitled to know about the papyrus anyway and mentioned it to him during a telephone conversation a few days later. "That, of course, made Steve curious," Bench later recalled, "because he was wondering where the McLellin collection was and why would there be a piece offered for sale if indeed it was supposed to go to the church."[62]

By Tuesday, September 24, Hofmann still had not fulfilled his promises to pay off the bank and deliver the collection. Pinnock recorded, "We are experiencing a [number] of problems with Mark Hoffman and the McLellin collection. He has not yet paid 1st Interstate Bank." Over the past weeks as Pinnock and Christensen had talked, they had marveled at Hofmann's failure to repay his debt. Hofmann was a businessman, and they both knew that running a business well required a sound reputation and good credit. By not paying off the bank, it seemed, Hofmann was creating a host of future problems for himself.[63]

On the evening of the twenty-fourth, Steve Christensen telephoned Curt Bench at his home. Without giving out the names of Hugh Pinnock and Dallin Oaks, Christensen told Bench that a member of the First Quorum of Seventy and a member of the Quorum of Twelve were disturbed at Hofmann's apparent lack of good faith in carrying out his obligations. "They're planning to tell Pres. Hinckley tomorrow what's been going on," Bench recorded, "which could very well result in [the] Church never buying anything from Mark again."[64]

Bench also recorded that the bank had received a bad check from Hofmann and was "ready to file criminal charges." He also wrote that the "Church might have to pay bank & sue Mark or bank might sue Mark." Hofmann had promised the bank he would be in daily contact, but no one had heard from him. "Apparently," Bench wrote, the two general authorities "have concluded he's a crook. . . . Scenario could be very bad. Mark could conceivably go to jail and/or be sued. He would be blacklisted by Church [and] might lose credit & credibility [with] very important people & institutions. Church prob[ably] would never buy from him again. News might leak to newspapers which could be very embarrassing to all."

Bench noted that Christensen asked him "to contact Mark & tell him all & to contact him and G[eneral] A[uthority] who had [the] loan made & to let him know how serious this is." Christensen had been unable to reach Hofmann, and he thought Bench might be able to give Hofmann the message because he saw the document dealer more frequently.[65]

Hofmann had a reputation for being virtually impossible to reach by telephone. Bench drove to Hofmann's house, arriving around 8:30 or 9:00 P.M. Bench gave Hofmann the message, encouraged him to call the general authority to straighten out his problems before Gordon Hinckley found out about them, and also reminded him that he still owed Deseret Book some money. "He thanked me for telling him even though it was unpleasant," Bench later recalled of Hofmann's reaction. "He appreciated it, said he would take care of it[,] and I believe he indicated he would straighten it out with President Hinckley very soon."[66]

At around 7:30 the next morning, Hofmann dropped in on Hinckley. "Have no recollection of disc[u]ssing historical documents," Hinckley wrote of the meeting several weeks later. Instead, Hofmann used the meeting to tell Hinckley that church dissidents had acquired advance copies of talks to be delivered the following week in the church's world conference. Though Hinckley did not realize what was happening, Hofmann was apparently trying to reinforce the church leader's trust in him. Hinckley later discussed Hofmann's message with J. Martell Bird, managing director of the church's Security Department.[67]

On September 27, the vice-president and general counsel of First Interstate Bank of Utah wrote Hofmann about his unpaid promissory note and bounced check. The letter demanded that Hofmann pay the money due the bank within five days or face legal action.[68]

Hofmann eventually offered *The Book of Common Prayer* to the church through Glenn Rowe. Hofmann explained the book's provenance and significance to Rowe, who kept the volume with other rare and valuable items in the Historical Department's vault while he was studying it and seeking approvals for its purchase. Dean Larsen and Earl Olson, Rowe's immediate superiors in the Historical Department, eventually gave permission to buy the book, and on Thursday, October 3, the transaction was closed. In exchange for the volume, Rowe traded Hofmann three hundred canceled, five-cent Bishop's General Store House notes, an early Mormon medium of exchange with a total trade value of between six and seven hundred dollars and a retail value of roughly twice that amount.[69]

The same day, Harvey Tanner of First Interstate Bank called Hugh Pinnock about the bank loan, which was still unpaid. Late that evening, Steve Christensen located Hofmann at Pinnock's request and went with him to Pinnock's house. Christensen said to Hofmann, "You have to let Elder Pinnock know the situation."[70]

Hofmann said he was experiencing some financial problems. He owed First Interstate Bank $185,000 plus interest. The bank had written a letter to him, and he had written back, he said. The Library of Congress, however, had been unable to authenticate *The Oath of a Freeman* to its satisfaction, meaning the money he expected was not immediately forthcoming. He owed coin dealer Al Rust $160,000 in a transaction for which the McLellin collection was collateral. The collection, more valuable and controversial than originally thought, was in two large safe-deposit boxes at the Bank of Utah to which Rust held the keys. Also, he owed a doctor a lot of money on other document transactions. Thus, his debts exceeded $345,000.[71]

On the positive side, the American Antiquarian Society had offered $250,000 for the *Oath*, meaning he would be able to get at least that much out of it. Meanwhile, he had made an oral agreement to sell a private party half his interest in the *Oath* for $150,000. Also, a friend was holding a check he had gotten from Deseret Book for $20,000. Until the *Oath* sold, therefore, he had only $170,000 to cover his debts. Pinnock thought the implications were clear: Hofmann would have to sell the McLellin collection to cover his other debts. Pinnock suggested that perhaps he could find a buyer for the collection. By combining the money from the buyer with his other assets, Hofmann could repay the bank and Rust too. Rust could then release the collection to the buyer, who might eventually donate it to the church.[72]

Pinnock also counseled Hofmann that if he planned to remain in the document business, it was important that he repay the bank to protect his credit. Since Hofmann's problem was cash flow, Pinnock recommended that the document dealer obtain a line of credit at a bank for buying documents and then sit down with his creditors to work out payment plans on his other debts. Apparently enthusiastic about the plan, Hofmann volunteered to pick up the twenty-thousand-dollar check from his friend immediately. Pinnock said it was rather late at night to do something like that. Hofmann insisted his friend would understand. Hofmann and Christensen left Pinnock's house together. A little after 12:30 A.M., Christensen called Pinnock from Hofmann's car phone to say they had the check. Pinnock instructed Christensen to see that the bank got the check.[73]

On Friday, October 4, First Interstate Bank received the check, which was enough to pay the interest due to that point and to reduce the principal slightly. Bank employee Harvey Tanner called Justin Schiller and Raymond Wapner, Hofmann's New York agents, who confirmed that Hofmann would soon be receiving $150,000 for the sale of his interest in *The Oath of a Freeman* and agreed to send that sum directly to First Interstate. Meanwhile, at 9:30 that same morning, Pinnock met with his supervisor, Dallin Oaks. Pinnock went over the notes from his meeting with Hofmann and Christensen the night before. At the bottom of his notes, Pinnock had written a question about the McLellin collection that he then posed to Oaks: "Should [Hugh W. Pinnock] get friend to acquire or should Church[?]"[74]

Later, using notes he made in his meeting with Pinnock, Oaks spoke with Gordon Hinckley to pass on what Pinnock had learned. A few details, however, were lost in all the retelling. Pinnock's notes of the previous night showed he was aware that Hofmann owed $160,000 to "Rust—the coin dealer." Oaks's notes referred to the source of the $160,000 as "? lender." At the bottom of his notes, however, Oaks had captured Pinnock's key question about the McLellin collection: "Ask: Should HP get friend to acquire? or do ourselves?"[75]

Oaks later conveyed Hinckley's response back to Pinnock: The church would not buy the collection. Oaks told Pinnock it would be fine to have one of his friends buy it, provided he understood the transaction was separate and apart from the church and that the church would not buy the collection nor lend any money for its purchase.[76]

Pinnock telephoned David E. Sorensen, a Latter-day Saint businessman who had recently been asked to preside over the church's Canada Halifax Mission. Sorensen and Pinnock had been friends for many years, and Sorensen had earlier offered to contribute money for missionary support or other church needs. Sorensen later recalled that Pinnock "asked if I would listen to a matter of concern to the church and determine if I would be in a position or interested in helping."[77]

Pinnock briefly described the McLellin collection to Sorensen and explained that someone had recently obtained it from McLellin's descendants and had planned to give it to the church. Financial problems, however, had prevented him from doing so. "Therefore," Sorensen recalled, "Elder Pinnock was interested in seeing if I might purchase the collection. If so, would I consider donating it to the church at a later date." Pinnock said he understood the collection had been appraised at about $185,000 and that the current owner would sell it for that price. Pinnock also said he thought the collection might be quite valuable. However, Sorensen recounted, "He emphasized the church would not be interested in buying the collection or reimbursing anyone who purchased it."[78]

"Immediately," Sorensen recollected, "I mentioned to Elder Pinnock that my conservative intuition would make me question whether the Mc'Lellin Collection even existed since I had never heard or read of it before. And, if it did exist, was it authentic?" He told Pinnock he would buy it only if an independent third party verified its authenticity. "I mentioned I was not interested in buying a box of old newspapers," Sorensen remembered. "I told Elder Pinnock I had never been involved in buying collections, documents or artifacts."[79]

Pinnock later recalled assuring Sorensen that Steve Christensen could "verify that the collection appeared authentic and had value." Sorensen agreed that Christensen could serve as authenticator but wanted to think the matter over before deciding for certain whether to go ahead with the transaction. Sorensen later remembered saying that he would be happy to help the church if he could but wanted to "investigate the matter in a business-like way." During this first phone call, Pinnock later recalled, Sorensen did not mention anything about having his own attorney involved.[80]

"Elder Pinnock invited me to talk to Elder Dallin Oaks since he, too, was aware of the collection," Sorensen later wrote. "Elder Oaks, he added, was well-known for his background in legal matters. He would understand my concerns and discuss ways the collection may be verified and authenticated."[81]

At 11:30 A.M. that day, Steve Christensen met with Pinnock, who recorded in his journal, "Steve Christensen came in. He reports all is well. I am glad he is the person to authenticate the collection."[82] Though cautious, Sorensen had been willing to consider buying the collection. Christensen had agreed to serve as authenticator. Now they needed to find Hofmann to pass on the good news and work out the details of the plan. Locating Hofmann, however, was not always easy.

At about 2:00 P.M., Christensen went to the offices of CFS Financial Corp. to see his friend Randy Rigby, who was finishing up some projects with CFS before joining Christensen full-time in their newly formed company in the nearby Judge Building. "I could tell he was really pumped up," Rigby later recalled.

"You wouldn't believe what's going on," Christensen said excitedly.

"Why?" Rigby asked.

"Well, I've been up all night."

Rigby asked where he had been, and Christensen told him briefly about his late night meeting at Pinnock's house and his visit to the Church Office Building that morning. Christensen was hungry and asked Rigby if he wanted to go to lunch. Rigby had just gotten back from eating but agreed to go again because he could tell Christensen wanted to talk. They headed toward a cafe in the nearby Judge Building, and as they walked, Christensen talked about his involvement with the McLellin collection, which he thought made the salamander letter look tame.

"Let me put this in perspective for you," Christensen said. "To get myself in the mood for this thing, I stopped by Crossroads Mall on the way at eight o'clock last night and bought a tape of *Miami Vice*." When the two reached the Judge Building, Christensen suggested they run up to their new office on the sixth floor. "I've got to see if there's a call from Mark Hofmann," Christensen said. There was no message from Hofmann, so the pair went back downstairs to eat.[83]

As they ate, Christensen explained how he thought the McLellin collection closing would work. He would receive the collection from the seller (who Rigby assumed was Hofmann) and money from an investor. Christensen would authenticate the collection, give the money to the seller, and hold the collection on behalf of the investor until some later time, when the investor would donate it to the church. As Christensen ate, he continued to talk excitedly with Rigby about what he viewed as a great business prospect. Church officials, he said, had lost all confidence in Hofmann, who now seemed self-serving to them. Christensen said church leaders trusted him and had given the okay for them, Christensen and Rigby, to set up their own document business, for which they would furnish leads.

"Steve, I don't know anything about that stuff," Rigby said dubiously. He suggested that if there was any money to be made in such an arrangement, Christensen ought to apply it to his own financial problems. Christensen, still optimistic, insisted they split any profits as partners.[84]

An avid student of Mormon history, Christensen had described his dream of a document business in optimistic tones to Rigby. The realities were more bleak. One of Hugh Pinnock's responsibilities as a church leader was counseling people with problems. Despite the difficulties with the bank loan and closing the McLellin collection, much of the conversation between Pinnock and Christensen after June had dealt with Christensen's own problems. The impending bankruptcy of CFS and Christensen's inevitable financial ruin had left him wallowing in economic quicksand.

As Pinnock counseled Christensen about his future, Christensen proposed that he become a full-time document dealer. Pinnock replied that he thought Christensen would probably do better in the kind of financial services business in which he was already experienced, though he allowed that Christensen might do some document dealing on the side. Pinnock helped Christensen in other ways too. Though he could not recall for certain, Pinnock later said he probably did as church leaders often do in counseling sessions and placed his hands on Christensen's head, invoking a blessing of comfort from the Lord upon him that he would be able to work out his problems. Pinnock also agreed to try locating a buyer for Christensen's extensive book collection.[85]

Though Pinnock viewed Christensen's plan for document dealing as somewhat of a caprice, Christensen apparently saw it more seriously. As Hofmann gradually proved his undependability, Christensen saw a void he could fill, one that would allow him to combine vocation and avocation. While Christensen sat eating with Rigby on October 4, he may have recalled Pinnock's counsel to Hofmann the previous evening to get a line of credit for buying documents. In describing his new business concept to Rigby, Christensen suggested that church officials could arrange a line of credit for them to buy documents.[86]

When Christensen had brought Hofmann to Pinnock's office on June 28, Pinnock had mentioned having some leads on the 116 pages and an unnamed item that Pinnock later told Christensen was a seer stone.[87] As Christensen ate with Rigby on October 4, he told him Pinnock "may even know of people who have the Urim and Thummim and the 116 pages."[88]

While eating with Rigby, Christensen also said he had been talking to Pinnock about CFS. By talking to Christensen, Sheets, and others who had worked for CFS, Pinnock had learned about some of the problems the floundering company was experiencing.[89]

At 3:31 P.M., Christensen called Pinnock's office, but Pinnock was not available. Christensen told the secretary who answered that he would call back. He also left the message that he had reached Hofmann, would see him at 4:00 P.M., and would phone back to report on the meeting. At 4:40 when he called again, Pinnock was still unavailable. Christensen asked Pinnock's secretary to have the church leader return his call. He also left a message that the secretary recorded as follows: "He met with Mark Hoffman—Would like to talk with you. He said, 'We hit a home run.' "[90] Hofmann apparently liked the plan.

Meanwhile, David Sorensen decided to call Dallin Oaks as Hugh Pinnock had suggested. Oaks told Sorensen he had never seen the McLellin collection. Sorensen asked for information on McLellin, and Oaks told him that McLellin was a former member of the Quorum of the Twelve who had become an enemy to Joseph Smith and whose papers, therefore, would contain negative information about the church founder.[91]

"Elder Oaks mentioned he would like to see the collection in the hands of someone friendly to the church; someone who would consider giving the collection to the church at a future date," Sorensen recounted. "Elder Oaks indicated it would be up to the person purchasing the collection to thoroughly investigate and satisfy oneself as to its intrinsic value. He made it clear this was an arms-length transaction. The church would not be a party to the purchasing of the documents. Neither would the church make funds available for this transaction. Elder Oaks indicated there may be a security interest in the collection and this should be taken into account by the purchaser." Oaks cautioned Sorensen because he wanted to be sure he was not entering the transaction lightly. As a member of the Missionary Executive Council, Oaks felt responsible to look after the welfare of all the mission presidents of the church, including Sorensen.[92]

Sorensen suggested having the transaction handled by Salt Lake attorney David E. West, who had represented him for over twenty years. He anticipated handling the purchase much like a real estate transaction. The seller would deliver the collection to West, a third party would evaluate its authenticity, and when the collection had been verified and appraised, West would deliver money to the seller, who would warrant his title to the collection and issue a bill of sale. Contemplating this procedure, Sorensen eventually transferred $185,000 belonging to his wife and himself from a New York City bank account to West's Salt Lake City trust account.[93]

Randy Rigby was not the only person Steve Christensen tried to sell on his dream of setting up a document business. Steve's wife, Terri, also heard about it. When Steve explained the concept to her, she, like Rigby, was not especially enamored of it.

"With all you've got going on, you're going to go traipsing around the country?" she asked him in disbelief. She was less than pleased but could tell he was excited about the idea.

During the church's general conference that weekend, a church official talked about the importance of members' accepting callings to work in the church. Just as he had to Rigby, Steve had enthusiastically presented his document-business concept to Terri as something church officials wanted him to do. When Terri heard the conference talk, she felt a twinge of guilt in recalling how she had reacted to the idea when Steve told her about it. Broaching the subject again with him, she asked, "Now is this, like, an official calling?"

If Steve had said no, he might have upset Terri. Instead, he chose a gentler approach. "He never gave me a straight answer," Terri later said.[94]

David E. West first heard from Sorensen about the McLellin collection deal on Monday, October 7. "He called," West explained later that month, "and said he was going to buy the . . . papers, and he wanted to get me involved to make sure it was handled properly . . . to make sure he was getting what he was buying." Sorensen told West a man named Steve Christensen would contact him about the transaction. West learned Sorensen had two purposes for buying the collection. First, he planned to donate it to the church because the church was interested in owning the collection but not in purchasing it. Second, he wanted to obtain a tax deduction for the donation.[95]

The tax considerations dictated how the transaction should be handled. "I discussed the matter with our accountants," Sorensen later wrote, "and they advised that if one were to purchase the Mc'Lellin Collection it would be essential that legal and constructive receipt of the collection be established by the purchaser. They also advised [that] the collection should be held for at least a year before considering donating it to the church." Sorensen mentioned the accountants' advice to Oaks, Pinnock, and West. Oaks told Sorensen that whatever he wanted to do was fine; it was his transaction, and he was free to structure it as he pleased. As a lawyer, West understood the legal significance of the accountants' counsel. The collection could not be allowed to pass prematurely into the church's actual or constructive possession, or Sorensen would lose the tax benefit of the gift.[96]

Later that day, October 7, Christensen met with West in his law office to discuss details of the transaction. Christensen said that Mark Hofmann owned the collection and that he, Christensen, would authenticate and appraise it. Christensen said he had rented two safe-deposit boxes at First Interstate Bank in which to put the documents after the closing. "But I told him they weren't going into those boxes over at First Interstate,"

West recalled, "that Sorensen was entrusting these documents to me, that I would arrange for the safekeeping of the boxes. I would get my own boxes, and there wasn't anybody in this world that was going to have a key to that box except me and Sorensen."

West felt it was his duty as a lawyer to eliminate all potential risk in the transaction for his client and to ensure that Sorensen had possession of the documents for the period required by the tax laws. He told Christensen he trusted him, but the last thing he wanted to happen "is to have Sorensen come back from his mission in two years, go look in his box and not find anything there or something because someone else has had access to it, even though it's you and you're an honest guy."[97]

West's candor surprised Christensen. "He was a little bit uncomfortable with that, actually," West would later recall. "I mean he wanted, he expected, to get the stuff and be the person to have control of it so he could be reviewing it. But I told him that we weren't going to do that."[98] Christensen apparently interpreted West's reaction as evidence someone did not trust him. If church officials did not trust him, his dream of a document business would shrivel and die. When Pinnock arrived at his office Monday afternoon, Christensen was waiting for him and reviewed his earlier meeting with West and the difficulties he thought West was causing.

"Then," Pinnock wrote, "Steve Christensen did a very strange thing. He turned over to me photographs of a [number] of documents he has collected through the years. He said, 'I have been quite a liberal in the past.' He implied that he is doing that which he is doing to show he can be trusted—which we already knew."[99]

The photographs Christensen turned over to Pinnock were ones taken of the Joseph Smith Egyptian papyri at the request of Ed Ashment, who had been an employee of the church's Translation Division. Don Schmidt had granted permission for the photographs to be taken because he tacitly assumed that the project related to official translation work for the church. In fact, it was a private project that Christensen had helped to underwrite. After Schmidt had retired, church officials had learned the project was not official. Schmidt's successor, Glenn Rowe, had phoned Ashment to ask about the project and had learned about Christensen's role in financing it.

"I called Steve Christensen who has the negatives in a bank vault," Rowe had recorded in March 1985, "and also asked him to please not duplicate them without permission. He said [that] at the time the project was done four color sets were made and one black and white. One color and one black and white set went to Ed Ashment; one set was to come to us; one color set went to Brent Metcalfe; and he personally kept one color set and the negatives. Since Brent M. and Ed. A. now work for George Smith and not Steve Christensen, George Smith asked for a set. For $6,000

Steve allowed George Smith to borrow his negatives. George Smith now has a set of negatives and a set of photographs." When Rowe had spoken with him, Christensen had been apologetic, saying he had been told the matter was discussed in detail with Schmidt.[100]

When Christensen turned the photographs over to Pinnock, he also showed him a piece of papyrus pressed between two pieces of plastic held together by screws. Christensen said the piece came from the McLellin collection. Pinnock told him he ought to put it in a safe-deposit box. Christensen agreed and later put it in a box at First Interstate Bank.[101]

Anxious to close the deal, Pinnock sided with Christensen in viewing West's requirements as hindering the transaction. "Dave West became very possessive over the whole transaction," Pinnock wrote in his journal, "which seems to be injuring more than helping." Pinnock spoke to Oaks and brought him up to date on what had been happening. Oaks suggested Pinnock discuss the matter with Sorensen. Pinnock did so and found Sorensen "most cooperative."[102]

Unlike Pinnock and Christensen, Oaks was pleased to hear about the steps West had outlined for closing the transaction. Oaks wanted Sorensen to be well represented in the transaction, and the conditions West had described to Christensen showed Oaks that West was doing his job. "I was pleased that West was being hard-nosed," Oaks later recalled, "since this meant he was protecting David Sorenson, who I thought needed protection. I remember telling Hugh Pinnock to be patient with a lawyer who had to protect his client."[103]

Yet not knowing West personally, Oaks remained unsure exactly how far West's expertise extended. Still concerned about Sorensen's welfare, Oaks sat down and prepared a suggested bill of sale for the parties in which he listed the representations and warranties of each. As a former law professor, Oaks knew the kind of language to include in the draft. One paragraph in the bill of sale warranted "that no document or paper or other thing of value in this Collection has been copied by Seller, by any person under his direction or with his consent, or by any other person whatsoever during the time that Seller has owned any interest in the Collection or had it in his possession or under his control or partial control."

Under the terms of the bill of sale, the seller also warranted that he had not removed or withheld anything from the collection; that he owned "a 100 percent interest in the Collection, without any security interests outstanding in any other person"; that he "has full authority to sell the Collection"; and that "to the best of Seller's knowledge and belief, the documents and papers in the Collection are genuine and what they purport to be."

Oaks did not want to replace West as Sorensen's lawyer, but he wanted Sorensen to be protected and hoped his draft bill of sale would remind West of the kinds of clauses to include in the final document. He gave the document to his secretary and had her deliver it to West's office. Later he would say the precaution had been unnecessary. West, he learned, was an excellent lawyer and did not need any reminders.[104]

Pinnock hoped the transaction would be completed on October 7, but it wasn't. Hofmann said he had tried three times to get Al Rust's signature to release the collection but was unable to do so. Without Rust's approval, Hofmann could not gain access to the safe-deposit box where the collection was kept, and Rust was reportedly on vacation in Oregon and thus unavailable.[105]

On Tuesday, October 8, at 9:00 A.M., Steve Christensen met with David West at his law office to discuss the McLellin transaction again. West and Christensen spoke to Sorensen by phone about the deal. Sorensen later recalled that Christensen "felt that I was maybe a little too meticulous about how the money was going to be disbursed." Sorensen again described the plan he and West had established for carrying out the transaction, telling Christensen, as he later recalled, that "there was no way I was going to release those funds without it."[106]

Thus, the procedure for closing the deal was finalized. Hofmann would deliver the documents and Christensen would evaluate them. If Christensen found them to be in order, West would then disburse the money, put the documents in a safe-deposit box, and mail all the keys to Sorensen. During the telephone conversation, Christensen told Sorensen that he already had one or two pieces from the collection in his possession, that he was satisfied the collection was authentic and valuable, and that Sorensen would be doing the church a great favor by securing the collection "in friendly hands." Later in the day, Hugh Pinnock, whose other church responsibilities kept him in meetings virtually the whole day, received an oral report of the three-way conversation.[107]

Like most days, Wednesday proved extremely busy for Pinnock. At 8:20 A.M., while Pinnock was in an unrelated meeting, his secretary took a telephone call from Hofmann. The secretary left a note for Pinnock: "Mark Hoffman will be here at 10:30 this morning." Christensen called fifteen minutes after Hofmann. "Steve Christensen called," the secretary noted. "He has a question about Thursday & the money. He will call again." In the middle of his busy morning, Pinnock met with Hofmann. "Mark Hoffman came in," the church leader wrote in his journal. "I brought him up to date and then reported to [Dallin H. Oaks]. Everything is progressing towards a successful conclusion to this whole issue tomorrow."[108]

In the late morning, Pinnock and Oaks met to examine the papyrus photographs Christensen had given Pinnock two days earlier. The photographs were transferred to the Historical Department vault for safekeeping. Early the next morning, Pinnock spoke to Christensen about them. Christensen told how he had paid for the photographs to be taken. He also explained that George Smith, "a bit of [a] rebel," had commissioned Ed Ashment, a former employee of the church's Translation Division, to write a book about the Book of Abraham. Christensen told Pinnock he had given the photographs to him for the church. He also said that the only other known pieces of Joseph Smith papyri were three pieces in the McLellin collection.[109]

After Pinnock spoke to Christensen, he talked by phone to Sorensen about the collection. The call was interrupted by a request from Gordon Hinckley for Pinnock to come down to his office. Pinnock went down, and Hinckley asked him to take his place at the investiture of a local college president. The two men also discussed Mark Hofmann, and Pinnock brought Hinckley up to date on what he had learned from Christensen about the Book of Abraham materials. Later in the day, he also brought Oaks up to date.[110]

Despite efforts to finalize the deal, it dragged on. Rust reportedly was still out of town, making it impossible to retrieve the documents. Without the documents, no money would change hands.[111]

Meanwhile, Hofmann was feeling financial pressure from another source and needed evidence that the $185,000 payment from Sorensen for the McLellin collection was forthcoming. Christensen initially asked Sorensen's lawyer, David E. West, if he would write out a check for that amount and allow him, Steve Christensen, to hold it. West felt he simply could not do that. "Will you write a check and you hold it," West remembered Christensen suggesting next, "so that I can at least represent then that the check is in hand." West agreed and, at Christensen's request, wrote out a check payable both to Hofmann and Christensen. West then filed the check away pending the closing on the collection.[112]

Christensen later said that because of a real estate transaction involving Hofmann, he needed a letter certifying that the money would be paid. David E. West had left on vacation, and so his son David C. West (who worked for the same law firm) gave Christensen a letter on the firm's stationery addressed to whom it may concern and certifying that the firm was holding $185,000 in trust for the purchase of documents. Christensen added and signed his own note at the bottom of the certificate: "This is to certify that the funds will be available Monday, October 14, 1985 to enable me to purchase some documents owned by Mr. Mark Hofmann."[113]

Like David E. West, Hugh Pinnock had also planned to take the day off on Friday, October 11. He decided not to, however, "because of the Mark Hoffman situation" and other business. His responsibility as a church leader kept him inordinately busy, and the McLellin transaction had become a distracting nuisance. "There are times when there is simply too much going on for a day away to be comfortable," he observed in his journal. Instead of vacationing, he spent most of the day in meetings. Late in the morning as he walked through the foyer of the Church Administration Building, he noticed Mark Hofmann waiting outside Gordon Hinckley's door. "Don't know why," Pinnock wrote in his journal.[114]

The reason had nothing to do with the McLellin collection. Hofmann visited Hinckley to offer the church some of the Kinderhook plates, which he did not own but said he could obtain. When Hofmann offered Hinckley the plates, the church leader vaguely recalled learning that the plates were considered bogus. "There stirred in the back of my mind," he later wrote, "a faint recollection of these having been shown to be fraudulent back in Nauvoo days. Told him I saw no reason why we should purchase them."[115]

At 2:25 P.M., Steve Christensen tried calling Hugh Pinnock, but he was tied up in a meeting. Christensen told Pinnock's secretary he would call again in fifteen to twenty minutes. Christensen also left a message. The secretary recorded, "Friend is back in town—'Game has started again.' " Pinnock interpreted the note in his journal: "Steve Christensen reported that Rust came back from Oregon."[116]

For a time, it seemed the McLellin transaction might close that week after all. Christensen, however, had a hard time finding Hofmann. At 4:30 P.M., Christensen called Pinnock's office. "He is still looking," Pinnock wrote in his journal. Eventually, time ran out. "Couldn't reach Hoffman," Pinnock wrote, "so papers will be closed out next week."[117]

Initially, Monday seemed a likely day for concluding the transaction. Monday was Columbus Day, however, and the banks were closed. The closing was finally set for 10:00 A.M. on Tuesday, October 15, 1985. Almost no one could imagine the horror that day would bring.[118]

Part Two

The man in whom you have trusted has sought to destroy you.
—Doctrine and Covenants 10:6

7

The Bombings

"Randy Rigby on 2146. A[n] emergency!!" the note read. Hugh Pinnock had just arrived at his office Tuesday morning, October 15, 1985. When his secretary handed the note to him, he was on another line and did not recognize the caller's name. He answered the blinking extension anyway.[1]

"This is Elder Pinnock."

"This is Randy Rigby," the caller would later remember saying. "You don't know me, but I'm Steve Christensen's partner, and I just came from our office, and Steve has been either severely injured or killed by a bomb." Rigby said Christensen had told him about a document deal involving Pinnock. Rigby said he thought the bombing might relate to the deal.[2]

Word of the bombing stunned Pinnock. "Steve is dead!!!" he scrawled on the note paper in front of him sometime that morning when he learned that Christensen had in fact died. Pinnock would later say the news filled him with the same emotion he felt at the passing of a close relative. "I liked him a great deal," he would explain, "and felt that we had a close association."[3]

Pinnock was also taken aback by Rigby's suggestion that the bombing might be tied to the McLellin collection. Pinnock knew from Christensen, Gary Sheets, and others about some of the problems CFS Financial Corp. had been having, problems that might anger some of the company's investors. Pinnock told Rigby the bombings were undoubtedly connected to CFS.[4]

The flood of emotions that engulfed Pinnock included fear. If Steve Christensen had been a target, Gary Sheets would be too.[5]

Dallin Oaks would recall Pinnock bursting into his adjacent office that morning "flushed and excited." Pinnock recorded in his journal that after telling Oaks about the tragedy, he "still couldn't believe" what he had heard. Minutes later, Pinnock received another note written on a preprinted telephone message sheet. *"Emergency,"* it read. Mac Christensen, Steve's

father, had called. Pinnock's secretary had checked the box beside the
words "Please call" and added "*now*" in her own hand. Pinnock phoned
Mac, who also told him of the bombing.[6]

Soon Gary Sheets called too. Pinnock told Sheets he felt the bombing
stemmed from CFS's problems. "If they're after Steve, they're probably
after you," he would recall saying. But Sheets discounted the danger. "I
warned Gary that I felt it was a business problem," Pinnock wrote in his
journal, "but he said he didn't think so." For a time, Pinnock wondered if
the bombing might have something to do with the salamander letter that
Christensen had bought and later given to the church.[7]

Still, despite Sheets's protests, the CFS connection seemed the most
rational explanation, and before Pinnock left to speak at a funeral later
that morning, he asked his secretary to call a long-time friend who had
also worked for CFS to warn him to be careful.[8] As Pinnock drove to the
funeral, he heard a radio announcer report a second explosion, this one on
Naniloa Drive, the street on which Sheets lived. The report validated Pinnock's earlier impressions that Sheets too was in danger. Pinnock continued
on to the funeral and spoke as scheduled. As the funeral was concluding,
his secretary telephoned. Pinnock excused himself to take the call. Another
bomb had gone off, the secretary said, this one at Gary Sheets's house.
Kathy Sheets, Gary's wife, was dead. Pinnock had known Kathy even longer
than he had Gary. In a matter of hours, he had lost two friends to bombs.[9]

As soon as he could after the funeral, Pinnock rushed to the local sheriff's
office, where a distraught Gary Sheets was in protective custody. "He
doesn't understand fully what has transpired," Pinnock would write in his
journal. Later in the day, Pinnock drove to a local church leader's home,
where he met and prayed with grieving members of the Sheets family
before returning to the Church Administration Building.[10]

At about 2:45 P.M., while Pinnock was still away, Mark Hofmann approached a security desk in the Church Administration Building. He told
the attending officer he had an appointment to see Pinnock. The officer
called Pinnock's office and spoke to his secretary, who asked him to have
Hofmann wait near the desk. The secretary then walked next door to Dallin
Oaks's office and asked his secretary if Oaks, as Pinnock's supervisor, would
see Hofmann in Pinnock's absence.

Oaks assumed Christensen's death had prompted Hofmann to seek advice on closing the McLellin transaction, and so he agreed to see him.
Pinnock's secretary called the security desk and told the officer that Oaks
would see Hofmann. A week later, Oaks would dictate a memorandum
recording the details of the brief meeting.[11]

When Hofmann arrived at Oaks's office at about 2:50 P.M., the two men
met for the first time. Oaks told Hofmann that Pinnock had kept him

Steven F. Christensen (1954–85). (Ravell Call/*Deseret News*)

Kathleen Webb Sheets (1935–85). (Garry Bryant/*Deseret News*)

informed about the McLellin collection. The two expressed shock at the bombings that had killed Steve Christensen and Kathy Sheets earlier that day. Oaks asked Hofmann about the purpose of his visit. Hofmann said he thought bombing investigators might want to question him. He worried about what to tell them. Oaks told him to tell the truth. Oaks was unaware of any connection between Sheets and Hofmann or church documents. To him, the bombings seemed connected to CFS.[12]

"But why would the police want to question you?" he asked Hofmann, describing the apparent tie between the bombings and Sheets's and Christensen's business dealings. "Their business activities don't have anything to do with you, do they?"

Hofmann said no.

Oaks asked Hofmann if he thought the bombings related to his association with Christensen.

Again Hofmann answered no.

"Do you know anyone in your documents business who would enforce his contracts with bombs?" Oaks asked.

When Hofmann once again replied no, Oaks said, "Well, then, what do you have to worry about? The police probably won't question you, and if they do, just tell them the truth."

Even about the McLellin collection deal? Hofmann wanted to know.

Oaks said that as far as he knew, Hofmann's activities with the McLellin collection, though confidential, were just part of an ordinary commercial transaction and had nothing to do with the bombing investigation. Police probably would not ask him about the deal. If they did, he should answer truthfully and completely.

Oaks asked Hofmann if he still intended to proceed with the closing on the collection. Hofmann said he planned to go to New York the next day but would be willing to stay in Salt Lake to close the deal. Oaks told him he ought to get in touch with David E. West, Sorensen's attorney, who would doubtless wonder how Christensen's death would affect the transaction. West and his client would have to decide if they wanted to go ahead with the deal and who would replace Christensen as authenticator. Thus, Oaks reminded Hofmann, they might need some extra time to arrange for the closing. Hofmann said he would get in touch with West. Oaks thanked Hofmann for his work in discovering church documents and for his willingness to sell the McLellin collection to someone "friendly" to the church.[13]

As Hofmann left Oaks's office, Hugh Pinnock's secretary called out to the document dealer, but he walked on as though he did not hear her. Proceeding downstairs, he left the Church Administration Building at 3:05 P.M. and exited into the adjacent underground parking lot just as Pinnock arrived back from his visit with the Sheets family. Meeting briefly in the parking lot, the two men discussed the apparent connection between the bombings and CFS. Hofmann told Pinnock he would be going to New York to get some money to pay off the bank loan. They talked briefly about closing the McLellin transaction, and in a telephone conversation later that day, they agreed Don Schmidt should replace Christensen to authenticate the documents.[14]

Throughout the day, J. Martell Bird, managing director of the church Security Department, received telephone calls about the bombings from the Salt Lake City Police Department, the FBI, and general and local church leaders. Both bombing victims had been members of the church. Bird wrote, "It appears the motive lies in the fact that Christensen and Gary Sheets were two of the top management of Consolidated Financial Services (CFS) a company declared insolvent just last week." He noted that other CFS employees who were members of the church were in hiding, "thinking that they too might be on the list 'to go!' " One such man had walked unannounced into Bird's office. "Needless to say," Bird wrote, "he was concerned about the safety of his family and his own welfare. He made it very clear that he would have his family out of Utah this evening."[15]

The bombings provoked several bomb threats in the Salt Lake area, keeping law enforcement agencies busy investigating hoaxes. Pranksters also focused their mischief on the church. Bird recorded, "We had reports of as many as nine telephone calls concerning alleged bombs in the area of Church headquarters! We kept our K-9 dogs busy all day."[16]

Over in the east wing of the Church Office Building, the news of Steve Christensen's and Kathy Sheets's deaths rolled through the Historical Department like successive shock waves. Several employees knew Christensen personally or had heard him speak. He had occasionally spent time doing research in the department, and his connection to the salamander letter was well known. Kathy Sheets's name drew blank stares. That she was the wife of Steve Christensen's business associate seemed to confirm a connection between the bombings and CFS business problems. In the midst of the excitement, however, an anonymous caller phoned Glenn Rowe to ask for Mark Hofmann's address.[17]

At about 3:45 P.M., Gordon Hinckley, Dallin Oaks, and Hugh Pinnock met in Hinckley's office to discuss the bombing tragedy. They also wondered how Christensen's death might affect the McLellin collection transaction. "We called [David E. Sorensen]," Pinnock wrote in his journal, "hoping to tie down the details on the collection transfer with Mark Hoffman." Sorensen did not know Don Schmidt and asked about his qualifications. Oaks had not been the one to suggest Schmidt but knew him and thus was able to tell Sorensen about him.[18]

Sorensen's wife, Verla, who knew Steve Christensen's parents well, wrote in her journal, "Dallin Oaks called David several times again. Hugh called. Mac Christensen's son & Gary Sheets wife were killed by bombs in [Salt Lake City]. Apalling!"[19]

The bombings also unsettled attorney David E. West, who had connections with both bombing victims. Steve Christensen was supposed to have met with him to conclude the McLellin transaction, and West's son had dated one of Kathy Sheets's daughters. West phoned Sorensen to discuss the impact of the bombings on the proposed closing.[20]

Sorensen called West back to say that Oaks had assured him the bombings had nothing to do with the McLellin deal, that they seemed tied to CFS, and that there appeared to be no reason not to proceed with the transaction. Later in the day, Sorensen called West back and passed on the recommendation that Don Schmidt replace Christensen as authenticator in the deal.[21]

That evening, newspapers took up the question of motive for the murders. One article quoted a police lieutenant at the scene of the first bombing who said, "We have absolutely no idea on the motive." Another article dwelt on Christensen's love of documents and his purchase and donation of the salamander letter, but it pointed to CFS as "the link" between the two bombings.[22]

By day's end, police had developed two theories on the motives for the murders. "The first and most likely," the *Washington Post* reported, "is that a disgruntled investor or businessman hired a killer." The other possibility, it explained, "is that the murders were ordered or carried out because of the controversial 'white salamander' letter, which Christensen bought and recently turned over to the Church." Sheets, the article reported, apparently paid to help authenticate the letter.[23]

Like the police, church officials felt the CFS connection provided the most likely explanation for the bombings. Still, they took no chances. Though the violent persecution directed against the church in its earliest days had largely abated, the church continued to suffer occasional outbursts of violence, including bomb attacks, that forced church officials to take security precautions when threats were posed.[24] They recognized that if the remote possibility of a link to the salamander letter proved valid, church leaders might become the killer's next target—especially Gordon Hinckley, who had received the document on behalf of the church from Steve Christensen. Writing in his journal, Bird explained, "I recommended that President Hinckley make a change in normal patterns tonight. He will stay in the home of his daughter. . . . We have no specific threats that would involve President Hinckley—but just in case."[25]

At about 6:00 P.M., David West called Don Schmidt in Provo to ask if he would be willing to come to Salt Lake the next day to look at some material West wanted to purchase for an unnamed client. Schmidt asked what the material was. West said it was the McLellin collection. Schmidt told West he could examine the material only from the standpoint of historical content and was unable to perform scientific tests on it. West said that would be fine.[26]

On Wednesday morning, October 16, newspapers described the Christensen and Sheets bombings and again emphasized two motives. "The first is that a disgruntled investor or businessman, angry about CFS's recent financial problems, could have hired a 'hit man' to carry out the murders," explained two *Salt Lake Tribune* writers. "The bombings," they reported, "prompted police in Salt Lake, Utah and Davis counties to search the homes of other CFS officials and employees, many of whom have gone into hiding until more is learned about the killer." The other possibility was "that the murders were ordered or carried out by someone angry about the controversial 'white salamander' letter."[27]

Another *Tribune* article focused exclusively on the first motive. "The apparent targets of bombings that killed two people Tuesday were both recently involved as officers of a financially troubled Salt Lake City–based investment company," it began. The article described the company's recent financial reverses, reporting that Gary Sheets had sent a letter to investors on September 26 explaining the company's insolvency. It also reported that a disgruntled investor had filed suit against the company earlier in the month.[28]

Using wording that could only describe Mark Hofmann, another article explained, "Rumors persist that a collector, who had located several controversial early Mormon historical documents, may have had an appointment with Mr. Christensen the morning of the bomb blast. Last week, the collector supposedly received death threats."[29]

When Hugh Pinnock arrived at his office Wednesday morning, he found a message from Mark Hofmann's wife, Doralee. She said her husband had to see some other persons and would have to postpone the closing on the McLellin collection from 10:00 A.M. to 2:00 P.M. Pinnock telephoned David Sorensen to tell him about the postponement. David's wife, Verla, recorded part of the conversation in her journal: "David went to the office where he talked with Elder Pinnock about the bomb murders—they think it's the mafia. It's so terrible."[30]

Sorensen called West to tell him about the delay, but the call came too late for West to inform Schmidt, who had already left for West's office. When Schmidt arrived, West told him the meeting had been delayed to two o'clock. West also gave Schmidt an additional detail he had not mentioned earlier: the seller of the collection was Mark Hofmann. That fact piqued Schmidt's interest even further.[31]

At 2:00 P.M., Schmidt returned to West's office for the closing on the McLellin transaction and waited for Hofmann to appear. West had lined up two safe-deposit boxes at Continental Bank with the expectation that Hofmann would show up with the documents.[32]

About 2:20, West called Sorensen. "Dave, you're the one that set up this appointment," he said. "Are you sure that it was for two o'clock this afternoon?"

"Yeah, that's when it is, two o'clock," Sorensen replied. "He's supposed to be there."

"Okay, we'll just wait for a while and see what happens."[33]

Sometime after 2:00, Pinnock or Oaks spoke to Sorensen, who said the deal had not yet closed. Pinnock called Doralee Hofmann at her parents' house and asked where Mark was, explaining that he was supposed to be meeting with West and Schmidt. Doralee said she hadn't heard from her husband all day. Pinnock thought she sounded nervous.[34]

Meanwhile, West and Schmidt waited patiently at West's office for Mark to show up. Then they heard sirens.[35]

At approximately 2:40 P.M., an explosion rocked the apartment building where church security chief Martell Bird lived with his wife, Venice, a few hundred feet northwest of the Church Office Building. Martell was not

Steve Christensen's body is removed from the Judge Building, October 15, 1985. (*Deseret News*)

Kathy Sheet's body is removed from her driveway, October 15, 1985. (Howard C. Moore/*Deseret News*)

home, but Venice looked down from her window onto Second North Street, where she saw a car in flames and a man lying in the street beside it. She rushed to the telephone and dialed 911 to reach an emergency operator. When no one answered after four or five rings, she tried phoning her husband. He was out of the office, and her call was transferred to Ronald D. Francis, another Security Department employee.

Francis thanked her for the information and phoned his department's communications center to forward the information and to request that local police be notified immediately. Francis then called Jerel D. Lindley, another security officer, and together they drove to the church-owned Deseret Gym, adjacent to the scene of the explosion, where they parked before running to the smoking car.

When they arrived, a uniformed Salt Lake City police officer was already on the scene. The bleeding victim lay motionless on the lawn near the curb opposite the smoldering vehicle. Francis and Lindley assumed the man was dead, though he wasn't. A Salt Lake City police officer found a fragment of clothing containing the victim's wallet. Thumbing through the wallet for identification, the officer discovered the victim was Mark Hofmann. Learning the victim's name, Francis and Lindley drove back to the Church Administration Building. On their way, they radioed to their communications center to request that Martell Bird be located and advised of the matter.[36]

Bird was at a local barber shop when the phone call came informing him that a bomb had exploded at 50 West on Second North Street in Salt Lake City. Bird instantly realized the explosion had been near his apartment. Haircut unfinished, he raced to the bombing scene, which he found to be directly below his eleventh floor bedroom window. "As I looked upward to the eleventh floor," he wrote in his journal, "I could see my dear Venice looking down at the sickening sight—the car, the body, or man lying in the street, his clothes blown and or burned off most of his body, while paramedics labored over him to make him ready to place in the ambulance and race him to the hospital in an effort to save whatever life might be in the badly mangled body." Before long, Bird too learned the victim was Mark Hofmann. "I knew the name!" he wrote. "Hofmann is the man I have known of for some time as one interested in documents, particularly relating to the early days of the Church."[37]

Francis and Lindley arrived back at the Church Administration Building and immediately headed to Gordon Hinckley's office to report what they had learned. Francis asked Hinckley if he had heard about the bombing. He said he had. The managing director of the church's Personnel Department had telephoned from his fourteenth floor office to report that smoke was rising from the north of the Deseret Gym. Another employee in that department had heard a radio report of a car bombing on Second North Street. Francis asked Hinckley if he knew the identity of the bombing victim. He said he did not. Francis said identification found at the scene showed the victim to be Mark Hofmann.[38]

Unaware that Francis and his partner had preceded him, Bird dashed to the Church Administration Building and into Hinckley's office to describe the explosion scene and identify the victim as Mark Hofmann. The third bomb, Bird wrote, "brought into force again the 'Church document' angle for the two murders by bombs yesterday."[39]

After returning to church headquarters, Bird took a telephone call from Al Rust. Rust had asked to speak to Hinckley, who was unable to accept the call at the time. Rust identified himself and expressed concern over media reports he had just heard about Mark Hofmann being injured in an explosion near the Deseret Gym. Rust asked Bird if he had heard of the McLellin collection. Bird said he had heard "considerable" about the collection in recent days. Rust asked if the church had the collection in its vault. Bird said he had been told that Rust and Hofmann had the collection in a joint safe-deposit box. A long time ago they had had a joint box, Rust said, but the McLellin collection had never been in it.

Investigators search for clues in Mark Hofmann's bombed-out car (*above*) and nearby on the street (*p. 161*), October 16, 1985. (Tom Smart/*Deseret News*)

Rust grew very emotional about not getting an answer back from Hinckley about his earlier letter on the McLellin collection. After a few minutes, Rust calmed down somewhat and described his long relationship with Hofmann. He had known Hofmann for several years, he said, and had worked with Hofmann as a silent partner by helping him to purchase old documents and other items, which Hofmann would then resell at a profit. Rust explained that his son had gone to New York with Hofmann to buy the McLellin collection but that Hofmann had concluded the transaction without his son present and then had failed to deliver the documents to Rust's store as promised.

Despite these problems, Rust said, he admired and trusted Hofmann, had profited from several earlier transactions with him, and would probably continue dealing with him in the future. Rust pointed out that even though Hofmann had recently experienced financial troubles, he had still managed to pay Rust enough to reduce his debt to $132,000. Rust said he had written Hinckley because Hofmann had told him Hinckley intended to buy the McLellin collection for the church. Hofmann had also told him not to mention the planned purchase to anyone.

"Had President Hinckley communicated with me and answered some of my questions," Rust lamented, "perhaps all this could have been averted." Bird assured Rust that whether Hinckley replied was irrelevant to the bombings. He said he hadn't seen Rust's letter but would look into the matter. Rust said Hofmann was supposed to have visited him in his store that afternoon and that because he and Hofmann had done so much business together, the news of Hofmann's being bombed made him fear for his own safety. Bird said he did not know enough about the bombings to be sure Rust was in danger, but he suggested it would be prudent for Rust to take security precautions for himself and his family for a few days.[40]

Bird followed his own advice. Shortly after Hofmann was injured, the church Security Department placed its K-9 services staff on alert and summoned the K-9 supervisor and his partner to the Church Administration Building to conduct an exterior inspection for bombs. Other Security Department personnel visually surveyed the interior of the building. Later, Bird asked his K-9 crew to sweep the church headquarters area for bombs. Two K-9 officers were dispatched to Hugh Pinnock's house, where they inspected the exterior of his home, his vehicles, and his mailbox.[41]

Despite the previous day's bombings, the Historical Department was conducting business as usual on Wednesday until Hofmann's car blew up. Almost immediately, radio, newspaper, and television reporters began telephoning the department for information. "The motives had now shifted from business to Church documents," Glenn Rowe wrote in his journal, "and the shock and fear went through all who were even remotely associated with documents. We had a bomb squad and dogs in the department."[42]

As the dogs searched the Historical Department, some employees tried to relieve nervous tension with humor. "So what does the dog do if it has a bomb?" they joked among themselves. "Pick it up and shake it?" Still, no one thought it funny when someone reported an unclaimed briefcase had been found under an unused desk in the department's library. The anxiety eased when the bomb squad determined the briefcase did not contain explosives.[43]

Shortly after Hofmann was injured, Dean Larsen, executive director of the Historical Department, called into his office employees who had dealt with Hofmann and told them the bombings seemed tied to the Mormon historical community. The department office journal noted the third bomb victim was "Mark Hofmann, a dealer in historical documents . . . who sold the Martin Harris letter to Christensen and Sheets." The third bomb, it explained, added to the two of the previous day, "caused fear in the minds of all persons involved with the Martin Harris letter transaction." Though the third bomb established a connection between the bombings and historical documents, the motive for the Tuesday bombings was still not clear, it continued. "The Historical Department was placed under securities supervision and searches made for any bombs that might have been planted in the east wing."[44]

Fear of the unknown and the uncertain gripped many department employees. Returning home that evening, Ron Barney, who had handled many Hofmann documents as an acquisitions specialist for the department, drove past the police barricades around Hofmann's bombed car. "I was frightened. I was really frightened," he later recalled. "And when I went home, I was concerned about the welfare of my family."[45]

Wednesday's bombing brought Tuesday's into sharper focus for those involved with the McLellin collection. "Today the bombings took a shocking turn," Dallin Oaks wrote in his journal. "Mark Hoffman, document collector, was injured when a bomb went off in his car. This focusses the bombings on Church history document collection contacts, rather than on Steve Christensen's failing business."[46]

Oaks heard about Wednesday's bombing from Richard Lindsay of the church's Public Communications Department. Hofmann's smoldering vehicle was visible from Lindsay's office high in the Church Office Building tower.

Oaks's experience as a lawyer and judge made him sensitive to investigators' need for any information that might help solve a crime, and he now sensed a possible connection between the McLellin deal and the bombings. He phoned Gordon Hinckley, who agreed Oaks should contact law enforcement agencies to tell them what he knew about Christensen's and Hofmann's connection with the McLellin transaction. Oaks immediately called Martell Bird and requested that he arrange a meeting with investigators.[47]

Oaks also called his wife to tell her a mad bomber seemed to be targeting church people with ties to historical documents. He had spoken to Hofmann just the day before and was worried he too might be a target. He felt safe in the Church Administration Building but worried that his wife, like Kathy Sheets, might become a victim. He told her not to pick up any packages or go anywhere in her car. Oaks also told Hugh Pinnock about the bombing. "And when I talked to Hugh about it," Oaks later recalled, "Hugh was frightened for his own safety."[48]

South of Salt Lake City in Utah County, home of Brigham Young University, the campus police, city police, and county sheriffs cooperated in searching the homes and offices of persons associated with the bombing victims, CFS, and the salamander letter. The campus police also inspected the university's archives.[49]

Late in the day, a bomb threat prompted Martell Bird to order an evacuation of all the downtown church buildings except the Salt Lake Temple. A careful search of the complex took several hours but turned up no bombs. Bird would return home weary that night.[50]

Meanwhile, just after 4:00 P.M., the Salt Lake County Sheriff's Office received a report of another explosion, this one near Hugh Pinnock's house in the southeast section of the Salt Lake Valley. The sheriff's office dispatched several officers to investigate, but they found no evidence of a bomb.[51]

An hour later, two FBI agents and a local police officer responded to Dallin Oaks's request through Bird for an interview. When the officers arrived, Oaks was in his office meeting with some local church leaders on an unrelated matter. He left the local leaders in his office and took investigators to the adjacent office of another general authority, who was absent at the time.

As the law enforcement officers listened, Oaks rehearsed the McLellin collection transaction from Pinnock's first meeting with Hofmann and Christensen to earlier that day when the deal was scheduled to close in David West's office. Oaks mentioned that Hofmann had borrowed money to buy the collection. He described how Hofmann had originally promised to donate the collection but later told Pinnock that debts would prevent him from doing so. Hofmann had said the collection was in a bank vault shared with a man who had loaned him money for the collection.

Oaks said the church did not intend to buy the documents but was interested in them because McLellin had been an early church leader who had apostatized and reportedly taken papers and other items from Joseph Smith's home. Oaks reported Pinnock's proposal that someone buy the collection and donate it to the church. He told the investigators he did not feel at liberty to provide the potential buyer's name but that they could get it from West, who was the buyer's attorney.

The buyer, Oaks said, had wanted assurance the documents were genuine, and Oaks had told him he should find someone to authenticate them. Pinnock had recommended Steve Christensen, and the buyer had agreed. West had received the money to complete the purchase, but Hofmann had been hard to reach. The transaction had been scheduled to close October 14, but the banks were closed, and so the closing had been postponed to the next day. Oaks said that when Pinnock learned Christensen had been killed, he came to Oaks's office quite upset. The bombing of Kathy Sheets convinced them the bombings related to Christensen's and Sheets's business. Oaks told the officers about his brief visit with Hofmann the previous day and about the rescheduling of the McLellin closing to that day in West's office. As the interview ended, Oaks recommended that the officers also talk to Pinnock.[52]

For Hugh Pinnock, the third bomb brought fear and puzzlement. "Each hour I feel like I understand less," he wrote in his journal. In the absence of solid answers, rumors about the bombings flourished throughout the Salt Lake Valley and beyond. Some rumors pegged the injured Hofmann as the bomber. Pinnock recorded in his journal a rumor that suggested Hofmann may have been on his way to kill a close friend of Gary Sheets when he was injured. The rumor, later discounted, arose because Sheets's friend had an office near where the third bomb exploded. Pinnock also wrote, "We thought the problem with Kathy Sheets and Steve Christensen was business related; but now we don't know. I don't seem to know anything. Maybe it deals with Mormon artifacts."

Pinnock had discussed the case with Gordon Hinckley, Dallin Oaks, and others, but no one had certain answers to the many questions the bombings posed. "No one seems to know anything now that Hoffman was almost killed," Pinnock wrote. "At first we thought he was but later reports confirmed that he was severely injured." Referring to his wife and children, Pinnock wrote, "I am worried about Anne, the kids and my own safety because of Kathy being killed. Dumb telephone calls. Today & tonight are [a] nightmare."[53]

One telephone call to the Pinnock home that night seemed especially odd. The caller, a stranger to Hugh Pinnock, identified himself as Shannon Flynn. Flynn turned out to be the friend from whom Hofmann and Christensen picked up the twenty-thousand-dollar check after their meeting with Pinnock during the night of October 3. Flynn recited a garbled account of the First Interstate Bank loan and told Pinnock he thought Mark Hofmann was innocent.[54]

Despite specious rumors alleging a church role in the killings, official church response to the bombings was initially restrained as spokesmen declined to comment on the case. An official response ultimately came in the form of a news release issued by Richard Lindsay. It read, "We extend our heartfelt sympathies to the families and associates of the bombing victims. We are deeply saddened by these tragic acts and deplore such violence. It is our fervent hope and prayer that those responsible will be quickly apprehended and that justice will be served. To this end, we pledge our fullest cooperation with city, county and federal authorities in the investigation."[55]

8

In the Aftermath

"Victim of Third Bombing Is Suspect in Others That Killed Two in S.L.," blared the headline of the *Salt Lake Tribune* on Thursday morning, October 17, 1985. The article identified Mark Hofmann as prime suspect in the Christensen and Sheets murders and quoted Salt Lake City Police Chief Bud Willoughby as saying investigators had sought to question Hofmann even before he was injured because he was connected with the salamander letter and matched the description of a man seen carrying a package to Steve Christensen's office just before Christensen died. According to the article, federal charges would likely be filed against Hofmann Thursday morning, revenge was a possible motive for the killings, up to three additional persons may have been targeted for death, and investigators did not rule out co-conspirators in the case. Because the salamander letter seemed to link the three bombing victims, a related article reprinted the letter's full text.[1]

The *Washington Post* reported that police were reviewing several leads in the case, "including the possibility that some of the documents distributed by Hofmann were forgeries or that there were financial problems between Hofmann and the victims."[2]

That morning, Hugh Pinnock attended a board meeting at First Interstate Bank, where the loan to Hofmann was briefly discussed amid other business. A few minutes into the meeting, Pinnock was called back to his office for an interview with the FBI agents who had met with Dallin Oaks the day before. For the next hour and a half, Pinnock related what he knew about the case.[3]

He said he had known Steve Christensen and his father, Mac, for a long time and had known Gary Sheets since high school. He explained how Steve had telephoned him and had then brought Hofmann to see him about the McLellin collection, which Hofmann planned to donate to the church after being paid by the Library of Congress for *The Oath of a Freeman*. He recounted his conversation with Oaks about the collection and Oaks's feeling that the church would accept it as a donation but would not be willing to buy it. Pinnock also explained to the agents how he had then sent Hofmann to First Interstate Bank for the loan.

Pinnock next described the problems he and Christensen had had with Hofmann. He said Hofmann went to Texas to buy the collection but did not phone him to say he had it until ten days to two weeks later. Eventually, Pinnock said, the bank informed him that Hofmann was delinquent on the loan. Pinnock said he told Christensen to contact Hofmann about the matter. Hofmann later explained he was having financial problems. He made an appointment with the bank but did not show up. Later, he visited Pinnock's office to assure the church leader he was financially sound.

Pinnock said he again instructed Christensen to talk to Hofmann about the loan. Pinnock also told the agents about the evening meeting at his house in which Hofmann had sketched his financial problems and had mentioned that he had twenty thousand dollars he had received from Deseret Book. Pinnock said he had learned that Hofmann had received money for several projects but had neglected to pay off the bank loan. He suggested that Hofmann use the twenty thousand dollars from Deseret Book to apply to the loan. Christensen later called to say he had the check in hand.

Pinnock explained the trouble Hofmann was having in selling *The Oath of a Freeman*. Hofmann, he said, eventually found someone to buy a half-interest in the document for $150,000. Hofmann notified the bank about the sale of the half-interest, and the bank confirmed that Hofmann would in fact receive the $150,000. Pinnock described how he had tried to find a private buyer for the McLellin collection so Hofmann could use the proceeds to repay the bank loan. He also told the agents that David Sorensen was to have been the buyer but did not want to acquire the collection until it had been authenticated. Christensen, he said, was to have authenticated the documents. Pinnock also related what he had heard about Al Rust's financial interest in the collection.

Pinnock described his thoughts and activities on the day of the bombings, including his brief conversation with Hofmann when he ran into him in the parking lot after returning from seeing Gary Sheets. He said that Hofmann told him he had been meeting with Dallin Oaks. Pinnock explained how Don Schmidt had replaced Christensen as authenticator in the deal. He rehearsed events of October 16 too, including the morning message from Hofmann's wife, his later call to her, and the telephone conversation with Sorensen.

He also gave the agents other information, including details about his relationship with Steve Christensen. He told them Christensen had been a bishop in the church, that he had experienced financial problems that a bishop in the church, that he had experienced financial problems that eventually became desperate, and that he had come to him for counsel. Apparently in response to a question about whether Christensen had received a calling or blessing to acquire documents for the church, Pinnock told the agents that as a church leader, he frequently blessed people to comfort them in times of trial and may have given Christensen such a blessing, but it would not have been for the purpose of having him acquire documents. Pinnock said Christensen had asked him to help find someone to buy his extensive book collection. He checked around for a buyer but could not find one.[4]

When the lengthy interview ended, Pinnock felt satisfied he had reported all the relevant information he had. "I told them everything I know," he recorded in his journal.[5]

At about 10:00 that same morning, Shannon Flynn, the man who had telephoned Pinnock the night before, showed up unannounced at the Church Administration Building. He marched through the front doors, walked straight to the security desk, and said, "I need to see President Hinckley."

The security officer suggested Flynn speak instead to someone from the Security Department.

"I don't want to talk to anybody from security," Flynn answered.

The security officer remained firm, and Flynn eventually relented. He was escorted to a security office, where he rehearsed to his bewildered listeners a distorted story about church officials, Mark Hofmann, and the McLellin collection. Flynn said he had an appointment with police but needed to speak with church officials first. The members of the First Presidency and Quorum of the Twelve were in their weekly meetings in the Salt Lake Temple. The security officers decided to interrupt.[6]

Like other church officials, Dallin Oaks had frequent travel assignments, necessitated by the demands of a growing church membership worldwide. At 10:00 A.M., when the First Presidency joined a meeting with the Quorum of the Twelve, Oaks asked if he should cancel an assigned trip to England that weekend because of the bombing investigation. Gordon Hinckley agreed it would probably be best if he stayed in town.

In the meeting, Hinckley and Oaks recounted what they knew about Hofmann's and Christensen's involvement with the McLellin collection. Later, church security interrupted with the message about Shannon Flynn's request to see Hinckley. Hinckley did not know Flynn and said he had no desire to talk to him. He suggested Oaks might talk to him if he wished. Oaks agreed to see him and left the meeting.[7]

Before Oaks arrived at the security office, Flynn asked the security officers to call Salt Lake City police detective Don Bell, whom Flynn said he had been scheduled to meet at 10:30 that morning. One of the security officers in the room picked up the phone and dialed the police department. Church Security Department officials had long maintained good relations with local law enforcement officials, and the security officer apparently expected Bell would be pleased to hear from him. He wasn't. The security officer explained to Bell that Flynn was at the Church Administration Building and was about to meet with Oaks. Bell felt church officials were disrupting his investigation and responded angrily. Flynn, who overheard the conversation, thought it "readily apparent" that Bell "was using some profanity."[8]

Recalling Bell's reaction to the security officer's call, Flynn later said some investigators distrusted church officials. "They knew that there was a great church collusion at that time, which was readily apparent by me being hidden inside . . . that great granite vault [the Church Administration Building]. . . . They were ready to storm the building if necessary. And so the fellow assured him that was not necessary."[9]

Bell later explained that from his view at the time, it appeared church officials were "running their own investigation. Shannon Flynn is in their office being interviewed, and I don't know why. Why would the LDS Church call Shannon Flynn down to their office and interview him? I mean, why would they do that? See, I never put it in perspective that maybe Shannon Flynn went to the LDS Church," and not vice versa.[10]

Unaware of this episode with police, Oaks, who did not know Flynn, recruited security officers and a stenographer to accompany him and then met with Flynn in the security office. He first asked Flynn if he was a member of the church. When Flynn said yes, Oaks felt obligated to speak to him.

Flynn said he had associated with Hofmann for several months and that Hofmann had told him some details of his business transactions. "The police want to talk to me," he said, "because they found a check which was made out to me from Deseret Book last week and that check was endorsed over to Mark Hofmann. I had sold some things to Deseret Book for Mark. Mark and Steven Christensen came to my home at 12:30 in the evening and they were quite nervous because the loan at First Interstate Bank had been called due on demand. Mark needed the $20,000 from Deseret Book to pay towards the loan."

Flynn said the $185,000 loan was unsecured and that Hofmann obtained it "with nothing more than a signature." He was aware of Hofmann's financial condition, he said, and felt Hofmann could not have gotten a loan for that amount without some help.

"Do you know anything about why he got that loan?" Oaks asked.

"I understand why he got it," Flynn said. "I was involved with this. During the weeks before, he had purchased the M'Lellin Collection. He needed those funds to get that collection. He had tried to get money from other people. One of the partners I know. I went to Arizona with him, trying to arrange for money."

"Have you seen the M'Lellin Collection?" Oaks asked, "First hand?"

Flynn said all he knew was what Hofmann had told him, though he had seen "a part, a papyrus." Flynn said Hofmann told him he had spoken with Gordon Hinckley by phone about the collection several months earlier when Hinckley was in France, and that he had also telephoned Francis Gibbons twice about the collection when Hinckley was out of town. "He told me President Hinckley had arranged the loan for him at the First Interstate Bank. Plus, he specifically said someone had helped him."

Oaks asked Flynn to describe his relationship with Hofmann. Flynn said he and Hofmann were "partners, not in business but in specifics." Oaks asked if he was a partner with Hofmann in the McLellin collection. Flynn said he was not, but he said Hofmann told him Hinckley "was nervous to have it" because church critics were close to locating it in Texas.

Flynn said he and Hofmann flew to Arizona to try raising money to buy the papers. "We came back empty-handed," he said. "Mark went to speak with President Hinckley," Flynn asserted, "and within days Mark came away with the money from the bank."

"The plan was he was going to donate the collection to the Church," Flynn said. "He could have made it if the other deal would have materialized but it went sour."

"The Library of Congress deal?" Oaks asked, referring to *The Oath of a Freeman.*

"Yes," Flynn answered. "He was supposed to receive all the money up-front. Instead he received a small portion of the total amount and he was to receive the rest over eighteen months. So he got some money but the rest wasn't coming." Consequently, he said, Hinckley had arranged for Hofmann to borrow money from the bank.

Knowing that Hinckley had nothing to do with the loan, Oaks asked Flynn, "What do you know about it?"

Flynn claimed he had waited outside in his car while Hofmann went to Hinckley's office. At 11:00 A.M., he said, Hofmann went to the bank and found the loan had been arranged.

"Had the note gone to maturity?" Oaks asked.

"No, it was called due on demand," Flynn said. "Several banking regulations had been broken in making that loan."

"That is your judgment?"

"Obviously he was persuaded by President Hinckley."

"Did he say 'President Hinckley'?" Oaks asked, again focusing on misinformation in Flynn's account.

"Yes," Flynn insisted, again recounting Hofmann's attempts to raise money and the visit from Hofmann and Christensen to pick up the twenty-thousand-dollar check.

Knowing it was Pinnock, not Hinckley, who had helped arrange the loan, Oaks asked, "Was anyone else's name mentioned in connection with obtaining this loan?"

"No," Flynn said.

"Where did that money go?"

"To the First Interstate Bank," Flynn answered, apparently assuming the question referred to the twenty-thousand-dollar check.

Oaks then asked, "How can we be of help to you?"

"I want to find what posture I need to take," Flynn answered. "The whole room is falling down."

Oaks then gave Flynn two points of advice. The first he explained and illustrated by his own example: "As soon as I learned that Mark Hofmann had been the object of a bomb, I knew that I had some facts that would help the police. Within sixty minutes of the incident I talked to two F.B.I. agents. I told them everything I knew about it. The Church is going to cooperate fully and it has absolutely nothing to hide. Sometimes there are some confidential transactions but this is a murder investigation. Confidentiality is set aside. We will cooperate fully. You will not do anything favorable by assuming that you need to cover up." Recognizing the inaccuracy of many of the details Flynn had told him, Oaks next counseled Flynn to distinguish between what he actually knew and what others had told him. "Mark Hofmann," he said frankly, "has told you some things that are not true."

Again emphasizing the importance of cooperating in the murder investigation, Oaks said, "The Church has nothing to hide in this transaction. . . . We have great concern for the lives that have been lost. You tell the police what you know. Let them draw the conclusions."

Flynn left the brief interview and headed for the police station to see Don Bell.[11]

Summing up the interview with Flynn in his journal that evening, Oaks wrote, "I told him to tell the truth, to tell everything he knew or which had been reported to him, and not to fear any embarassment to anyone, since the truth would win out and the Church had nothing to hide. Mark H. had apparently told him many lies about Church involvement or direction and he feared disclosing this."[12]

About the time Flynn was leaving to see Bell, Bell dialed a church operator and asked to speak to Hugh Pinnock. Pinnock was unavailable, so Bell left a message. Learning that Bell had called, Martell Bird telephoned him. The previous day, Bird had arranged for a police officer to interview

Dallin Oaks and assumed Bell would know who he was. Bird gave Bell his name and asked if he could be of any help in answering questions for Pinnock.

"Now what concern is this of yours?" Bell asked, unaware of who Bird was.

"I'm with church security," Bird replied.

Hearing church security mentioned, Bell exploded, accusing church security of interfering with his homicide investigation. "I was not what you'd call real polite," Bell later recalled of the conversation. In fact, he said, "no question about it," he was "very angry."

"No, you can't help me," he told Bird, "and I'd just appreciate it if you wouldn't help me and if you would take my phone message and give it right back to [Pinnock's] secretary and that's the way I'd like it to be."[13]

Bird had placed the call on his office speaker phone with church security officer Ron Francis present. Francis recalled that Bird was merely trying to find out if the message was urgent enough to interrupt what Pinnock was doing. "Detective Bell was hostile and belligerent in his attitude toward Brother Bird," Francis later recorded. "His conversation was laced with profanity and basically consisted of his shouting demands into the telephone." Bird, he said, "could not get through to Don Bell during the . . . conversation because of Bell's non-stop berating of Brother Bird, the Church in general, and Elder Pinnock."

Bird had spent many years with the FBI before becoming head of church security and had formed his own opinion about what constituted appropriate behavior for law enforcement officials. Appalled at Bell's deportment, Bird reported it to Salt Lake City Police Chief Bud Willoughby. "Brother Bird explained," Francis recalled, "that we at Church Security were cooperating fully with all the law enforcement officers and that Detective Bell's obvious hostility towards the Church was fully manifested in his recent loud, demanding, and profane telephone conversation with Brother Bird. . . . Chief Willoughby agreed with Brother Bird that Detective Bell's manners left something to be desired and apologized."[14]

Though offended by Bell's response, Bird wanted to cooperate with police and so did as Bell had instructed and got the message to Pinnock. Within minutes, Pinnock called Bell, who later recalled that the church leader was "very pleasant on the phone."

"I got your message," Pinnock said. "You can come over anytime you want."

"Are you available now?" Bell asked.

"Absolutely," Pinnock answered.

"I'm on my way."[15]

Bell arrived at Pinnock's office only a few minutes after the FBI agents finished interviewing him.[16] Pinnock chatted briefly with Bell about how tragic the bombings were and explained that he knew family members of both murder victims. Bell then began asking questions, and Pinnock briefly reiterated what he had just told the FBI.[17] Bell did not remain long, however, spending only about a third of the time interviewing the church leader that federal investigators had.[18]

Writing about the events of the day in his journal, Pinnock recorded that he told the FBI agents all he knew about the case. "A little later," he wrote, referring to Bell, "a man from the S[alt] L[ake] Police force came in and I told him the same." Bell's suspicious demeanor, however, apparently puzzled Pinnock. "Nothing to hide," he wrote. "I just don't understand."

What Pinnock did not know frightened him. Hofmann was the police's prime suspect, but no one had proved his guilt or even arrested him. And what about the possibilities of co-conspirators mentioned in the media? "If the mystery person would kill Kathy Sheets then what about Anne and kids," Pinnock wondered in his journal. "I think about them all the time."[19]

Pinnock was not the only one to worry. Late in the afternoon, Martell Bird again received a telephone call from Al Rust. Rust said he had expected Bird to call or visit him the previous evening. His family members feared for their safety. Bird said he had not meant to imply he would be back in touch with Rust that soon, and he apologized for any inconvenience or concern he may have caused. Rust asked for an immediate meeting with Gordon Hinckley. Bird said he could not make an appointment for Hinckley but would ask about arranging one.[20]

After another fitful night of sleep, Hugh Pinnock arose Friday morning, October 18, and insisted on starting each car before allowing his wife or children to drive them. With the killer still on the loose, car bombs loomed as a constant threat.[21]

At 8:00 A.M., the church's Special Affairs Committee met. The committee, which was responsible for overseeing media relations, considered several matters that day, one of which was recent media coverage of the bombings. Playing up Hofmann's connection to the church, some news stories had drawn unwarranted conclusions about the church and its leaders, implying they were involved in criminal activity or might even be responsible for the bombings. During the meeting, Dallin Oaks urged that the church make a public statement about its relationship to Hofmann. The committee accepted his recommendation and assigned Oaks and Richard Lindsay to prepare a news release.[22]

At 10:00 A.M., Brent Ward, United States Attorney for Utah, telephoned Hugh Pinnock's office to suggest that the church allow the FBI to test the salamander letter "on the chance," Ward recorded in his journal, "that it may be a forgery and may be part of the motive for the bombings." Pinnock was not in the office at the time, having planned to attend Steve Christensen's funeral but being pulled away into unscheduled meetings instead. Ward left a message for him.[23]

Meanwhile, Martell Bird tried to decide how to handle Al Rust's repeated requests to meet with Hinckley. "Realizing President Hinckley's heavy work schedule," Bird wrote, "and with his permission, I arranged with Elder Dallin H. Oaks to afford some time to listening to Brother Rust." The request caught Oaks at an inconvenient time because he was busy drafting the press release, but he agreed to meet with Rust because he felt the coin dealer "needed to be briefed and calmed."[24]

Oaks asked his secretary to call Rust. She was a coin collector and so knew Rust, having visited his coin shop perhaps a dozen times herself. She found it a bit unusual to talk to Rust about something other than coins. "Brother Rust," she said, "could you come up? Brother Oaks would like to speak to you."

"Sure," the coin dealer responded, "I can be there in thirty minutes."

"Well, could you come right now? Brother Oaks has an appointment in thirty minutes and he'd like to visit with you."

"Sure."[25]

At about 11:10 A.M., Rust arrived at Oaks's office, where he met with Oaks and Bird, joined later by two other church security officers. Rust repeated what he had told Bird earlier. He also said that after Hofmann had bought the McLellin collection, he had told Rust he would be reselling it to the church through Hinckley. As time passed, Rust said, he began to worry because of the size of his investment, but Hofmann had assured him that if the church did not buy the collection soon, he would sell other documents to repay him. Later, however, Hofmann had told Rust he intended to donate rather than sell the collection to the church, repaying Rust's investment from the proceeds of a separate deal with the Library of Congress.

Then in September, Rust continued, Hofmann had approached him and asked to borrow more money, saying he was in financial trouble. Rust had told Hofmann he wanted to help but could not loan any more money and needed his previous investment returned so he could meet his business needs. In mid-September, Hofmann had approached him again, this time at a coin show. By then, Hofmann's financial problems appeared critical, Rust said. He and Hofmann had tried to devise a way to resolve Hofmann's problems, but Rust would not agree to put any more money into Hofmann's ventures.

Rust said that Hofmann, despite his financial problems, had sold some other materials during the late summer and early fall and had reduced what he owed Rust to $132,000. The events of the past few days, however, seemed to convince Rust that Hofmann no longer deserved his trust. "It appears that I have been betrayed by Mark Hofmann," Rust said.

When Rust finished his account, Bird told him that Hinckley had received his letter of June 11 but had been promised the next day by Hofmann that he would repay Rust soon. Seeing the problem was about to be resolved, Hinckley had decided not to interject himself further into the matter.

"I think I understand what has happened," Rust remarked. Hofmann had called him from New York the day after he had written his letter and had assured him he would soon have his money. While they were on the phone together, Rust had told Hofmann he had written to Hinckley about the matter. Rust said the news had upset Hofmann, who had told Rust he made a big mistake and should have kept the deal completely confidential.

Hearing Rust recount his story, Oaks gave him the same advice he had given to Shannon Flynn: be open and frank in talking to investigators. Bird recorded, "He told Brother Rust that he should tell the truth in every instance, and that he should not be worried at all about the Church, because when the facts all come out, the Church will have no need to be embarrassed, that nothing has been done by the Church or agents for the Church which has been dishonest or illegal in any way." Oaks told Rust that he and Pinnock had already told investigators what they knew, and he should do the same. He then recounted in detail for Rust his own involvement in the case.

"In concluding this period with Brother Rust," Bird recorded, "Elder Oaks again emphasized that at no time did President Gordon B. Hinckley of the First Presidency or any representative of the Church express their intention to purchase the 'M'Lellin Collection' or to finance the purchase. He said that the only discussion by Mark Hofmann on that point by any Church official was that if there was such a collection, and if the purchaser so desired, the Church would be pleased to receive the collection as a donation."

After hearing Oaks's explanation, Rust said it looked as if Hofmann had deceived him and many others. He guessed he would probably lose the rest of the money Hofmann owed him. Bird recorded that Rust seemed satisfied with the interview and seemed to understand why Hinckley had not answered his letter.[26]

When Rust left, Hugh Pinnock went into Oaks's office and returned Brent Ward's call. After Ward explained why he had called, Pinnock handed the phone to Oaks, whom Ward knew because his and Oaks's daughters had had violin training together. Oaks told Ward he thought turning the letter over to the FBI would be in the church's best interests but that he wanted to discuss the matter with others before acting. He told Ward he would call him back. At around 1:00 P.M., Oaks phoned Ward back to say he had just emerged from a meeting with other church leaders in which Ward's request was approved. Hinckley, Oaks said, wanted to release the letter directly to Ward. Oaks told Ward he would call him again later about turning the letter over and about issuing a church press release on the transaction.[27]

Later that afternoon, Pinnock attended Kathy Sheets's funeral, where he was among those who spoke. After returning from the funeral, he wrote a letter to Steve Christensen's widow, Terri, apologizing for a last-minute meeting that had kept him from Steve's funeral earlier that day. "Several times Steve came in just to talk about his life, the future, and business experiences," he wrote. "We became quite close friends."

Several people had asked him what Steve was doing associating with Hofmann. "I guess none of us knows," he wrote, "but since Steve brought him to my office, where I met Hoffman for the first time, your husband has been honorable and true to his word in every way." Referring to an earlier phone call, he wrote, "Thank you for calling me the other day in order to ask me the questions that you asked. Several of us have talked with law enforcement people. We want them to know whatever is relevant." Pinnock concluded the letter by expressing his concern for her and inviting her to call any time if she had questions.[28]

At 3:30 P.M., Gordon Hinckley and several members of the Twelve, including Dallin Oaks, met to discuss the proposed news release Oaks had been assigned to write earlier that day. They agreed their statement ought to mention Brent Ward's request to have the salamander letter tested. After the meeting, Hinckley asked Francis Gibbons to retrieve the salamander letter from the First Presidency's vault and prepare a receipt for it so it could be taken for testing.[29]

At 4:15 P.M., Oaks called Ward and told him the salamander letter would be ready to pick up at 4:30. Ward suggested the transaction be postponed until Monday, when it could be added to other evidence gathered by investigators to be taken back to the laboratory in Washington, D.C. As a courtesy, Oaks read the church's proposed press release to Ward, which included reference to the church's turning the document over to him, and Ward accepted the wording. Oaks then called Hinckley to tell him the transaction had been postponed. Hinckley had Gibbons put the document away.[30]

After he hung up from talking with Oaks, Brent Ward prepared a letter to the special agent in charge of the local FBI office asking that the salamander letter be analyzed. The agent called Bird and told him he was pleased to have the FBI laboratory test the document and would be by to pick it up on Monday.[31]

The Wednesday bombing of Hofmann had prompted Gordon Hinckley to begin asking questions about the extent of Hofmann's dealings with the church. By the end of the week, Francis Gibbons had prepared a report on all dealings with Hofmann mentioned in minutes of the First Presidency and Quorum of the Twelve, and Glenn Rowe had prepared a list of all the documents that the Historical Department knew had been acquired from Hofmann. Rowe's list included forty items or groups of items located as of October 18. Rowe explained the list might not be complete and that it also did not include printed items that may have come through Hofmann.[32]

Friday evening's *Deseret News,* while recounting other details about the ongoing investigation, published an article about Hofmann's attempts to sell *The Oath of a Freeman* to the Library of Congress. The article quoted the chief of the Rare Book and Special Collections Division of the Library of Congress, who confirmed that the document had been offered to the library but had been declined for "confidential reasons." The chief also reportedly said, "We had no information to say that it wasn't genuine. On the basis of what looking we did, we believed that it was genuine."[33]

During the early stages of their investigation, local investigators in Utah devoted little attention to issues of genuineness. Despite the FBI's interest in testing the salamander letter, examining documents to pursue a forgery theory was not a high priority for the police. "Salt Lake Police Lt. Nick Paloukos said it isn't very important to detectives right now whether the documents are forgeries or not," the *Deseret News* reported that evening. "The focus of the entire investigation is proving the actual elements of the murders, securing homicide complaints and collecting enough evidence to obtain murder convictions."

"We're not really looking into that (forgery) aspect right now," the lieutenant said. "We're trying to put a homicide together. As far as forgeries or authenticities, we don't know anything about it."[34]

On Saturday, October 19, the church issued its news release announcing it would turn over the salamander letter to the FBI on Monday for testing. "From the outset of this investigation," the release noted, "the Church has cooperated fully with federal, state, and local law enforcement officials, responding to every inquiry and request. The Church will continue to co-operate with law enforcement officials to bring to light any facts that may contribute to this investigation." The release also clarified that Hofmann had represented himself to the church as a document dealer and had never been an employee or agent of the church. Over the years, the release noted, Hofmann had sold, loaned, or donated several documents to the church, including the Anthon transcript, the Joseph Smith III blessing, the salamander letter, and the Stowell letter, all of which had already been published.

"From time to time," the release explained, "Mark William Hofmann has also contacted various Church officials to propose that he give or sell to the Church various other documents or artifacts, including the so-called William M'Lellin Collection. So far as we have been able to determine, no Church officials or personnel have ever seen the 'M'Lellin Collection,' nor has it been purchased by the Church, directly or indirectly." The release explained the church's revealed instruction to collect historical materials and expressed confidence "that the divine origins and destiny of the Church will be affirmed and sustained by the continuing disclosure of relevant historical data on the early Church and its leadership." It concluded by again expressing church leaders' sympathy for the families affected by the bombings.[35]

The release provided additional information for reporters who were already churning out story after story about the case. "Lawyer Silences Bomb Suspect," the headlines of one article had announced earlier that morning in the *Salt Lake Tribune*. Late Thursday night, it reported, Hofmann had asked to give police a "statement," but before detectives could arrive with a tape recorder, someone, perhaps a hospital nurse, phoned Hofmann's defense attorney, Ronald J. Yengich, who kept detectives from talking to his client. The nurse apparently remained in Hofmann's room as he and Yengich talked, and detectives then sought to interview her. After a hearing, however, a judge barred detectives from forcing her to talk, ruling that her presence was justified by her position and that therefore what she overheard was protected by the attorney-client privilege.[36]

Though Hofmann's aborted statement made headline news, church officials focused on a development that occurred later in the day. A television reporter called Glenn Rowe to ask what he knew about Shannon Flynn. "Shortly after that," Rowe wrote, "they announced he had been arrested."[37]

In a search of Flynn's home, investigators had found an Uzi machine gun. A special agent for the U.S. Treasury Department's Bureau of Alcohol, Tobacco, and Firearms talked to reporters about Flynn. "We are considering him a suspect in the bombing investigation," he said. "The bureau is planning to seek a complaint charging him with weapons violations." Meanwhile, Flynn's attorney announced that his client "categorically denies" involvement in the murders.[38]

Rowe was not the only one listening to the news when the announcement of Flynn's arrest was made. Hinckley heard the report and was surprised to hear of Flynn's arrest. "I do not know Shannon Flynn," he recorded in a file memo. "I have never met him. He tried to see me last Thursday and I would not see him but asked Dallin Oaks to talk with him if he cared to do so."[39]

Oaks spent Saturday at home, working in his yard, tying up tree limbs, cleaning out his garage, and preparing his home for winter. Late in the afternoon, Hinckley called to tell him about Flynn's arrest. Noting the call that evening in his journal, Oaks expressed his relief. "I had felt sure there was someone else in addition to Hoffman," he wrote.[40]

Hugh Pinnock spent part of his day visiting with Terri Christensen and other of Steve's family members. They seemed concerned that Steve might have been involved in some kind of wrongdoing. "I testified to them that Steve had not done anything that could be considered wrong as I had delt with him," Pinnock wrote. "I also discussed how our relationship had become one of friendship and helpfulness. . . . I hope it put their minds to rest."[41]

In the evening, Pinnock called Hinckley, explaining that Mike Carter, a reporter for the *Salt Lake Tribune,* had called him for information to use in the Sunday morning edition of the paper. "Hugh asked whether it would be all right to call Carter and give him the facts," Hinckley wrote. "I told him that if he [Carter] didn't have the facts that he had better give them to him, that I saw no reason why he should not give them to him."[42]

It was also Saturday evening that Pinnock learned of Flynn's arrest. Though Pinnock did not know Flynn personally, he wrote in his journal, "I am quite sure he is the person who called last Wednesday saying Mark Hoffman was innocent." News of Flynn's arrest helped reduce Pinnock's concerns for his family's safety. "I slept a little better," he wrote Sunday, "now that I am not as worried for the kids and Anne's safety. It has been a very uncomfortable week."[43]

Sunday morning's *Salt Lake Tribune* reported Flynn's arrest and also discounted rumors that documents found in Hofmann's car were the long-sought McLellin collection. Salt Lake Police Chief Bud Willoughby said it was "an absolute fact" that police had searched the evidence and "not found one single document that can be linked to the M'Lellin papers." "In fact," he added, "no one can say they've ever seen the M'Lellin papers."

To Willoughby, forgery remained a possible motive in the case. "We will not discount forgery as being involved," he said. "We are still looking at that as a probability." The newspaper noted that the church was allowing the salamander letter to be taken to the FBI laboratory for authentication. It reported that several other documents from Hofmann's home and car would also be sent to the FBI laboratory for testing. Willoughby reportedly "praised the church for its cooperation" in the investigation.

Not all investigators agreed with Willoughby's focus on forgery. According to the newspaper, task force detectives felt fraud, not forgery, underlay the murders. "Some police officials believe that the documents—whatever they are—are legitimate," the paper reported, but "that Mr.

Hofmann, in dire financial straights, was selling the same set of documents to various investors or was splitting up the whole collection and selling the portions as the whole."

Hofmann's track record had apparently convinced many investigators that his finds were authentic. "Hofmann has an extremely good reputation all around the country," one investigator said. "People seek him out for documents. I don't think the ones in the past have been forgeries."[44]

That afternoon, the *Deseret News* reported similar stories and also noted that the salamander letter "no longer appears to be a motive for the murders." Early media reports had focused on the letter and had inaccurately accused church officials of trying to buy and suppress it, when in fact they had declined buying it when it was offered to them and had published it after Christensen gave it to them. "The LDS Church has been put into a precarious position on the questioning of that document," Willoughby reportedly said. "Very frankly, people are beating up on them. I don't think that's fair. That was a donated document."[45]

At about 2:30 Sunday afternoon, Willoughby called Ron Francis of church security at home to ask for information about several individuals, including Hofmann and Flynn. "When the police officers searched Flynn's residence," Francis recorded, "they found a large amount of guns, black powder, ends of pipe, various terrorist books, pamphlets, and other materials. The police have a suspect who remembers Flynn and Hofmann coming in the 'Cosmic Aeroplane Books' store and purchasing the *Anarchist's Cookbook*, which gives precise instructions with illustration on the method of manufacturing pipe bombs. Witnesses have also reported that Flynn and Hofmann have bought explosives in Richfield and have on several previous occasions built pipe bombs for practice and exploded them in the desert."[46]

On Monday, October 21, Mike Carter's *Salt Lake Tribune* article for which Pinnock had furnished information ran under the headline "LDS Official Secured Hofmann Loan." The article cited "sources close to the investigation," who obviously had passed on information they had received from Pinnock and others. "When first contacted," Carter wrote, "Elder Pinnock declined to comment on the transaction, stating that police had asked he not talk about the incident. He said he contacted officers Sunday, however, and was given the OK."

The article quoted Pinnock describing how Christensen had brought Hofmann to his office and had told him Hofmann wanted to donate the McLellin collection to the church. "They came to me as a banker," Pinnock reportedly said, "not as a representative of the church." Relying on Christensen's word and Hofmann's statement that the Library of Congress would be paying him a lot of money for a valuable document, Pinnock then called the bank, Carter reported.

"Sources stressed that there was no wrongdoing on Elder Pinnock's part" nor on the part of the bank, the article said, but it also quoted an unnamed investigator who said bank officials agreed the loan transaction "wasn't normally the way things are done." It also noted that a loan officer at the bank refused to answer questions without legal counsel. Relying on information from detectives, the reporter asserted that the loan was called back early because of publicity about the McLellin collection and thus "caused or contributed to a financial crisis on the part of Mr. Hofmann and may lead investigators to a motive in the homicides."

Referring to Pinnock's brief encounter with Hofmann in the church parking lot on October 15, Carter wrote, "Investigators also said that Elder Pinnock reported meeting and having a conversation with Mr. Hofmann, the topic of which was not disclosed, the morning after Mr. Christensen had been killed." After mentioning that church officials had earlier acknowledged Oaks's brief interview with Hofmann, Carter returned to the meeting between Pinnock and Hofmann. He wrote that it "took place in the secure parking lot beneath the church office building, leading detectives to believe that Mr. Hofmann had a closer contact with the hierarchy in the church than has previously been disclosed." The article also quoted friends of Hofmann as saying he "did regular business" with Hinckley.[47]

Though the article contained elements of truth, church officials felt its inaccuracies and tone conveyed a distorted view of their roles in the case. "Today, Monday, October 21st," Hinckley wrote, "after seeing what the *Tribune* had done with the story, I was disgusted. They are not interested in finding a solution to the murders. They are interested only in trying to make the Church look suspect." To clarify his role in the case, Pinnock drafted a statement of his own later in the day. "Dallin Oaks, Hugh Pinnock and Brother Lindsay came to my office," Hinckley wrote, "and read a statement which Hugh had prepared giving the facts on the loan that was made by First Interstate Bank to Mark Hofmann."[48]

The statement, issued to the press that day, read as follows:

Following the tragic bombings of last week, I reported the following information to law enforcement officers.

On the last Friday in June of this year a friend of mine, Steven F. Christensen, called, mentioning he had something important to talk to me about. He came to my office. With him was Mark W. Hofmann. I had neither met nor talked with Mr. Hofmann before that afternoon.

Mr. Christensen explained that Mark Hofmann had made a down payment on some early Church documents known as the M'Lellin Collection. I was not familiar with the collection nor of any value it might have.

After having its potential value explained, and inasmuch as Mr. Hofmann had reported he was going to receive a substantial payment from the Library of Congress on the sale of a paper he had found, titled, "The Oath of a Free Man," which was reportedly the first printed document in America, I called two banks. My contacts at the first bank I attempted to reach were out of town at a management seminar, so I called First Interstate Bank, an institution which I serve as a director. The bank inquired about the security of the loan and also the necessity of making the loan as quickly as it was being negotiated. I explained that Mr. Hofmann had advised me that he had an option which was running out and the money was needed to pay for some valuable documents.

The next I heard about the 30-day loan was when it was past due. A vice president called me mentioning that Mr. Hofmann had gone beyond the date when he should have paid off the loan. I called Steven Christensen and he began working with Mr. Hofmann in order to get the bank loan paid.

I have never seen the M'Lellin Collection.

Until last week I assumed there was a collection and that it was valuable.

I have been informed that several weeks ago Mr. Hofmann brought the interest on the loan up to date and made a partial payment to First Interstate Bank. I have further been informed that First Interstate Bank contacted the Library of Congress and also contacted a document dealer in New York substantiating that Mark Hofmann would be receiving the means to pay off the loan.

I have found Mr. Christensen to be honorable and open in all dealings.

When Steven Christensen approached me on June 28 he stated it was because of the career I had had in business before being called as a General Authority that led him to believe I might find a party to lend the needed funds. He apparently knew that I have never had any responsibility for obtaining historic documents for the Church. I had never received any query in reference to historical documents before that time.

I have never had any reason to believe that Mark Hofmann was either an agent or an employee of the Church. The last time I saw Mr. Hofmann was last Tuesday afternoon, October 15, 1985. As I was parking my car he was leaving the first level of the Church parking lot. Our conversation revolved around the tragedy where two fine people had been killed that morning. Mark Hofmann and I did not have a meeting during last week. Our conversation lasted approximately 30 seconds.

The above facts were reported to law enforcement officers during the morning of Thursday, October 17, 1985.

Our thoughts and prayers have been with the families of all affected parties and we pray the Lord's protecting hand will be with them.[49]

"Today is a difficult day," Hugh Pinnock recorded in his journal on the day he released his statement. "Almost as painful as any I have ever known." The distorted news accounts hurt church leaders deeply as they struggled to balance the competing factors governing their release of information. On the one hand, church officials wanted to tell the media all they knew. "We have felt that the church should communicate all that it knows to the press," Pinnock wrote.[50]

Yet when church officials spoke, reporters anxious for stories sometimes misinterpreted their statements, and the distortions were repeated and further embellished through the media chain. Church leaders also wished to avoid making public statements that might unduly condemn Hofmann or any other suspect in the public mind and thus prejudice the administration of justice. Before becoming a general authority of the church the previous year, Dallin Oaks had been a justice of the Utah Supreme Court and had written court opinions about the impact publicity could have on a defendant's rights.

"An accused can be denied a fair trial," he had written in one opinion, "where the process of news-gathering is allowed such a free rein that it intrudes into every aspect of a trial and creates a 'carnival atmosphere' and where the publicity is so weighted against the defendant and so extreme in its impact that members of the jury are encouraged to form strong preconceived views of his guilt."[51]

With such opinions fresh in his mind, Oaks encouraged church officials to avoid public statements that would prejudice the public's views and thus taint a jury verdict should the bomber be apprehended and brought to trial. Thus, when media pressure forced them to make a statement like the one Pinnock issued, it was worded to avoid prejudicing the case, though the result sometimes left church leaders open to additional speculation and criticism.[52]

"The papers & TV are portraying me (by innuendo) as a sinister directing force," Oaks lamented in his journal, "because of the admission that I had met with Hoffman on the day of the first two bombings. I have remained silent, cheerfully, under the strategy that we would not give all the facts until charges were filed. But it is a little disquieting to think about what my friends and just casual observers are suspecting or concluding from this one-sided, leering or sneering publicity."[53]

Church officials continued to learn about the bombing case and about Hofmann. The day Pinnock issued his release, he learned that police felt one of the bombs had been designed for him.[54]

The same day, a church security officer returned a telephone call from a man who had gone to junior high school and high school with Hofmann. The man said he was calling to volunteer information he thought might be useful to the church. When he and Hofmann were thirteen or fourteen years old, he said, Hofmann showed him an electroplating set in his basement and told him he had used it to change the mint mark on an old dime that had been worth only about two dollars until the mark had been added. He had then sent the altered coin to an appraiser, who had certified it as an authentic rare coin. The appraiser had charged Hofmann two or three hundred dollars, a sum representing 2 percent of the appraised value of the coin. The caller also said Hofmann excelled in chemistry and physics and had made his own nitroglycerine at age ten. Later, he said, Hofmann was injured in an explosion that left a scar on his neck. The information seemed material to the criminal investigation of Hofmann, and so Ron Francis of church security once again telephoned police to pass the information on to them.[55]

The same day, another man wrote to Dallin Oaks explaining how someone could forge a document like the salamander letter using modern technology. He described how computers could be used to prepare handwriting samples that could then be copied on a light table using specially selected writing materials, which in turn could be artifically aged in such a way that there would be no evidence of forgery. Oaks gave the letter to his secretary and asked her to make copies, including one to Martell Bird "for his info. & sharing if he thinks appropriate."[56]

Though publicly silent on the issue of Hofmann's guilt, church officials continually passed information to law enforcement agencies and cooperated in the investigation. That day, October 21, they turned the salamander letter over to the FBI for testing. The FBI wanted other handwriting samples, so the church provided the Grandin contract and two documents that had not come through Hofmann.[57]

The special agent in charge of the local FBI office issued a statement explaining that Salt Lake City Police Chief Bud Willoughby and U.S. Attorney Brent Ward had requested the FBI to conduct tests on the documents. He said the FBI would coordinate its analysis with the Bureau of Alcohol, Tobacco, and Firearms. "The FBI will conduct various scientific examinations based on the evidence submitted," he explained, promising, "The evidence will receive expeditious handling, and the appropriate law enforcement authorities will be advised of the results."[58]

Reporters devoured the statement, just as they had every scrap of information they could find about the case. That afternoon, one newspaper article described the media frenzy the case had engendered: "Reporters from the three national television networks, the Denver Post, the Chicago Tribune, the Dallas Morning News, and People and Time magazines swarmed to create a carnival-type atmosphere during a press conference called to announce progress in the case."[59]

Nationwide interest in the case created intense competition among the media, making the already tough job of news reporting even tougher. Though many media stories about the bombing case proved to be both accurate and timely, one segment of the media or another reported erroneous information about even basic elements of the case, especially in the early stages of the investigation when reliable information was hard to come by but deadlines would not wait.

For example, the second bombing victim, Kathy Sheets, was erroneously described as a man,[60] Steve Christensen's wife,[61] "the wife of a church historian,"[62] a co-purchaser of the salamander letter,[63] a person "involved in the public debate" over the letter,[64] someone "who had dealings with Hofmann,"[65] or a person who was "linked to controversial research on the origin of the Mormon church."[66] According to one report, she died three hours before Steve Christensen.[67] According to another, they both died in the same blast.[68]

Similarly, church officials' roles were misconstrued. Many news reports were couched in ambiguous terms that stopped short of accusing them of ordering the bombings yet allowed for the possibility. One story began, "Bombings, killings, connected to the Mormon Church? What in the world is going on in Utah?"[69] Focusing on the salamander letter, which it said bombing victim Steve Christensen had "produced," another sensationally asserted that "Church leaders were enraged over the letter and labeled it blasphemous."[70] One station reported that "one of the church's biggest critics says that the letter was embarrassing to the Mormon Church, and that's why the bombings happened."[71] Yet another referred to "the Mormon Connection" in the killings. "Police," the station reported, "say Mark Hofmann, who has been charged with murder, met with church officials just before those bombings and $90,000 in money orders were found in Hofmann's car after it exploded injuring him."[72]

On October 21, when the *Salt Lake Tribune* ran Mike Carter's article on the bank loan, the insinuations of criminal activity by church leaders intensified. One station reported that the *Tribune* had come up with "what it calls some new leads in those Utah bombings that killed two people. The paper says that a high official from the Mormon Church met with the prime suspect the same day the two bombings took place." The station then mentioned that Hugh Pinnock also "helped suspect Mark Hofmann secure a $185,000 loan."[73] Another station ran a similar story, adding that Pinnock was not suspected of wrongdoing "at this time."[74] Yet another reported that Pinnock "may now be connected to those bombings that killed two people last week." Citing the *Tribune* account, the station noted the seemingly sinister detail that Pinnock met with Hofmann "in a parking garage on Tuesday of last week, the day of the bombings." By adding that "Pinnock, though, is not being questioned," the station may have left some listeners to speculate that church officials were wielding influence to evade prosecution.[75]

In an article published the same day, a media watchdog who had been monitoring the case commented about the reporting of it. "Last week's Salt Lake bomb deaths and the confusion and hysterics they generated likely will be the year's major local story," he wrote. "The reporting of them already has brought up some ethical questions and will spawn others for a long time to come." He described the case as a "sensational story . . . built on a number of prime news elements: bizarre and public violence, well-known people, intrigue, money, religion, suspense." Then he observed, "The tendency of the media working on such a story is to go overboard, head first."[76]

9

Deep Concern

After a committee meeting on Tuesday, October 22, Dallin Oaks sat talking about the media coverage of the bombing case with James E. Faust, a fellow member of the Quorum of the Twelve. "Jim Faust & I shared our deep concern," Oaks wrote of the discussion in his journal, "about the cumulative impact of the one-sided publicity about the Church's role in the bombings (implications of coverup and secret deals to get the papers)." The two men voiced their concerns to David B. Haight, a member of the Twelve who chaired the Special Affairs Committee, and also to church spokesman Richard Lindsay. The men decided they would recommend to Gordon Hinckley that the church hold a news conference to clarify the matter. Haight, Faust, and Oaks called on Hinckley, who received their recommendation and said he would call a special meeting of the Quorum of the Twelve at 4:30 P.M. to discuss it.[1]

At 3:15 P.M., Hinckley called Martell Bird into his office and, as Bird later recorded, told him "that Elders Haight, Faust and Oaks had contacted him urging a news conference be held immediately to set the record straight and dispel feelings of doubt and concern among members of the Church in all parts of the world as to the actions of Church leaders as portrayed by the news media." Bird told Hinckley that he "had little or no feeling that the news media would be objective or fair to the Church" and that he "had a long standing aversion to the media and the trying of a case in the papers, TV, radio, while the formal investigation is underway." Bird said he "understood the keen concern that some members of the Church would have about many of the media disclosures concerning the Church and the innuendos casting some question upon some Church leaders," but he "concluded that at best holding a press conference would be dangerous but perhaps worthwhile for members of the Church worldwide." Hinckley told Bird about the meeting he had called with the Twelve to discuss the matter and invited him to attend.

At 4:30, the meeting began with prayer. Then followed an in-depth and frank discussion of what the church leaders knew about the case. "It became clear," Bird wrote, "that involvement of President Hinckley was minimal and [that he was] entirely innocent of the innuendos and some allegations that have been voiced by the generally unfriendly press." Oaks's and Pinnock's roles in the case were also detailed, and Bird was invited to express his feelings. When all the facts had been aired, a vote was called on whether to hold a news conference. The result, Bird recorded, was a "unanimous decision to hold a press conference at 9 A.M. tomorrow."[2]

Anticipating the decision, Oaks had spent part of the day preparing a memorandum that described his brief meeting with Hofmann on October 15. Referring to Hofmann's demeanor in the meeting, Oaks wrote, "He appeared to be very nervous." Oaks showed a copy of the memorandum to Faust, who before his call as a general authority of the church had been president of the Utah State Bar. Oaks felt Faust could provide a critical perspective because he had legal training and was not personally involved in the events described in the memo.

Faust suggested Oaks strike the sentence about Hofmann's appearing nervous. It was important that the church's public stance toward Hofmann be strictly neutral so as not to prejudice the public toward him and thus impede the administration of justice. The sentence about Hofmann's nervousness seemed to stray beyond the line of neutrality. Oaks had already informed law enforcement officials about Hofmann's nervousness and so did not need to include it in his public statement for their sake. He saw the wisdom in Faust's counsel and struck out the sentence before the final draft was typed.[3]

Oaks's memo pointed out that he had met with investigators on October 16 and had apprised them of what he "had been told or knew about Hofmann, Steven Christensen, and the McLellin Collection." The memorandum also described Oaks's limited relationship with Steve Christensen. "To the best of my recollection," he wrote, "I have met Steven Christensen only once. He was standing in Elder Pinnock's office sometime last summer when I stepped in to deliver a message to Elder Pinnock. I shook hands with Christensen on that occasion. We had no other conversation other than an informal greeting."[4]

Besides drafting this statement, Oaks also prepared a letter for Shannon Flynn's attorney, James N. Barber, to accompany a secretary's transcript of Oaks's meeting with Flynn on October 17. "The secretary's notes have just been transcribed," Oaks wrote to Barber, "and after reviewing them, it seems to me that I should share this transcript with the police and with his counsel." Oaks also notified Barber that he might inform the media about the advice he had given Flynn at the end of their interview.[5]

With the help of church security, Oaks sent copies of the just-completed transcript of Flynn's interview to the heads of the Salt Lake City Police Department, the Salt Lake County Sheriff's Office, the FBI, and the Bureau of Alcohol, Tobacco, and Firearms, all of which were investigating the case and were invited to the press conference. Oaks then spent the evening preparing his remarks for the next morning.[6]

At around 11:00 P.M., Barber called church headquarters and spoke to a security officer. The officer called Martell Bird at home and gave him Barber's number, which Bird then dialed. Barber thanked Bird for the transcript of the interview between his client and Oaks, and, in Bird's words, "felt he should offer a thought, hopefully to assist the Church in keeping its good name and the impeccable position maintained during the past week relating to the ongoing investigation into the murders."[7] During Flynn's interview with Oaks, Flynn had said Hofmann told him that Hinckley had arranged the First Interstate loan. Knowing Hinckley had nothing to do with it, Oaks had questioned Flynn on this point during the interview.[8]

In the late-night telephone call with Bird, Barber referred to that part of the interview. "Mr. Bar[b]er said," Bird wrote, that "he is concerned about what Elder Oaks told Flynn and that if the Church makes the announcement that President Hinckley did not refer Mark Hofmann to Elder Pinnock for the purpose of obtaining a loan (bank loan) for Hofmann the effort may backfire to the embarrassment and detriment of the Church." Barber conceded that Flynn's testimony on that point was hearsay, but he felt it could be corroborated by other sources. He told Bird to make this point clear to Hinckley and Oaks before the press conference the next day. Through his participation in the 4:30 meeting that day, Bird had learned that Hinckley had nothing to do with the loan. "I told Bar[b]er," Bird wrote in his journal, "that I would convey the message to Elder Oaks and that he could rest assured that the truth and only the truth would be made available to the news media tomorrow morning."[9]

On Wednesday morning, October 23, dozens of reporters signed in to attend the news conference. They represented television and radio stations, as well as newspaper and magazine publishers. Major wire services were represented, as were CBS and the BBC.[10] At 9:00 A.M., the conference began in the auditorium of the Church Office Building. Richard Lindsay introduced Hinckley, Oaks, and Pinnock and explained that the first two men would give statements and then all three would answer questions. Pinnock, Lindsay said, had issued a statement to the press two days earlier, and copies of it were available for those interested. He pointed out that the conference would end at about 9:40 to give the participants a chance to travel to the church's new genealogical building, which was being dedicated at 10:00.

LDS news conference, October 23, 1985. *From left to right:* Dallin H. Oaks, Gordon B. Hinckley, Hugh W. Pinnock. (Don Grayston/*Deseret News*)

Hinckley then began his statement, welcoming those present and expressing sympathy for the families and associates of the bombing victims. "That such tragedies could occur here," he said, "is beyond our comprehension." He then explained the purpose of the press conference, which was "to respond, insofar as we are knowledgeable and to the extent answers will not jeopardize legal processes, to questions, speculations, and innuendos that have arisen consequent to those tragic acts."

"Throughout the investigation," he continued, "the church and its officers have cooperated with law enforcement officials responding to every inquiry and request. We will continue to do so." He noted the church's revealed instructions to collect materials pertaining to its history. "The acquisition of historic documents is not new to us," he observed. "It has been going on for more than a century and a half." In fulfilling this collection mandate, he said, church officials had followed generally accepted procedures, "which have been legal and ethical in every respect insofar as we have been able to determine."

He next reviewed his association with Mark Hofmann. He said they first met in April 1980 when Hofmann, then still a student at Utah State University, brought the Anthon transcript to the church. Later, the church Historical Department traded other items to Hofmann for it. They met again, he said, on March 17, 1981, when Historical Department personnel brought Hofmann and the Joseph Smith III blessing to his office. He described how the LDS Church acquired the blessing and traded it to the RLDS Church.

"Since that time," he continued, "Mr. Hofmann has sold various documents to the church, as well as, we understand, to other purchasers having an interest in the early history of the church." Relying on the data furnished to him earlier by Francis Gibbons and Glenn Rowe, Hinckley then reported that the church had "acquired by purchase, donation, or trade forty-some documents, some of relatively little importance, and some of some significance," including the salamander and Stowell letters. "I acquired the latter two items for the church," he said, "and made the decision to make them public. They were widely publicized."

He observed that he had served as an adviser to the Historical Department for many years and was deeply interested in church history, having written a small book on the subject that had been published in many editions and widely distributed. Before that he had produced a long series of church history dramatizations for radio. "In the course of these efforts," he said, "I necessarily did extensive research in the history of the church."

He then described receiving the salamander letter on behalf of the church from its donor, Steve Christensen. At the request of civil authorities, he noted, the letter had been turned over to the FBI for testing.

Next, Hinckley delineated the extent of his meetings with Christensen and Hofmann. "While I had received a letter earlier indicating Mr. Christensen's desire to donate the document to the church after research on it had been completed," he said, "I have no recollection, nor any record of his ever having been in my office until the day he presented it to the church. Nor has he been in my office since then."[11]

"Mr. Hofmann has come to my office occasionally, certainly not frequently," he said. "Many people come to see me. Many from many areas across the world, about scores of matters. I have tried to maintain a reasonable open-door policy and have met and talked with many hundreds, if not thousands."

Turning to events immediately preceding the bombings, he explained Al Rust's letter to him about the McLellin collection, which was followed the next day by a visit from Hofmann. "I had never heard of the McLellin collection," Hinckley said, and he asked Hofmann what was in it. Hofmann described its contents and said he wanted to donate it to the church. "There was no discussion of our purchasing it," Hinckley noted.

Hinckley asked Hofmann if he had repaid Rust for the money he advanced to make possible the purchase of the collection. "He indicated that he would do so," Hinckley said, "and I told him that when he had settled his account with Mr. Rust, then we could discuss the matter of his making a contribution of the so-called McLellin collection to the church."

"I have never seen any such collection," Hinckley continued, "and know nothing about it beyond that. I have no recollection of ever meeting Mr. Rust, nor have I met Mr. Shannon Flynn." Shortly after Hofmann's visit, Hinckley went to Europe on church business.

"More recently," he said, "Mr. Hofmann called and asked my secretary if he could see me. I was under pressure for time, but agreed that I would see him for a few minutes. He came in. I have no recollection of discussing the so-called McLellin papers with him." Instead, Hofmann wanted to discuss the Kinderhook plates. "But I saw no reason why we should have them and so indicated to him. That is the last time I saw Mark W. Hofmann."[12]

Hinckley concluded his statement by saying that although Hofmann had been in his office a few times, he did not recall meeting the document dealer any other place. Hinckley then turned to Dallin Oaks for his statement.

"I welcome this opportunity," Oaks said, "to share what I know about what appeared to be a normal, though confidential, commercial transaction. With the benefit of hindsight, and in the feverish context of a murder investigation, and in the glare and innuendo of publicity accompanying the recent investigations, a normal though confidential proposed commercial transaction has been made to appear sinister and underhanded. My own contact with it has been seen as mysterious and questionable. I therefore welcome this opportunity to set the public record straight." A week earlier, he explained, he had told the FBI and local police all he knew about the case, as had Hugh Pinnock the following morning. "Now it is timely and desirable to make this public explanation, a week later."

Oaks described his role as a member of the Quorum of the Twelve in overseeing the work of Pinnock, who was president of the Utah South Area and who thus reported to him frequently on a wide variety of church matters. Because of this reporting relationship, Pinnock had immediately advised Oaks of the meeting he held with Christensen and Hofmann in June. "I will note here," Oaks paused to explain, "that from the outset, with a few exceptions that I will identify later, including my meeting with Mark Hofmann last week, all my information about this subject was received in brief reports from Elder Pinnock, communicated in the context of the multitude of matters of church business on which we regularly met." Oaks then proceeded to summarize the information he had received in these meetings.

He explained how Pinnock had approached him about Hofmann's sudden need for money to purchase the McLellin collection. "Elder Pinnock asked me," he related, "if I thought the church would loan Mark Hofmann 185,000 [dollars] for this purpose. I said, emphatically not." Oaks felt the only person who could approve such a transaction was Hinckley, who was then in Europe and whose views on the matter were unknown.

"Moreover," Oaks explained, "to have the church involved in the acquisition of a collection at this time would simply fuel the then current speculation reported by the press that the church already had something called the McLellin collection or was trying to acquire it in order to suppress it." Oaks told Pinnock he did not want the church involved "even indirectly" in acquiring the collection. They then talked about whether the church would accept the collection as a gift. "It was my judgment," Oaks said, "that the church probably would at some future time, but in that event it had to be a genuine gift from a real donor."

Pinnock had earlier explained that Hofmann said the Library of Congress owed him $1 million on a document contract. "Now I inquired, in the course of this conversation," Oaks said, "if Hofmann had a million dollars receivable from the Library of Congress why wouldn't a bank simply loan him $185,000?" Pinnock asked Oaks if it would be appropriate to introduce Hofmann to banking officials. "I said I saw no harm in that," Oaks continued, "provided it was clearly understood by all parties that the church was not a party or a guarantor and that Hugh Pinnock was not a party or a guarantor to such a loan."

In July when Hinckley returned from his trip, Oaks reported the incident to him. "He was interested in what had happened," Oaks said, "but he gave me no assignment. He gave no direction on it, he simply received the information." Over the summer, Pinnock updated Oaks on the matter, relying primarily on information about Hofmann provided by Christensen. In this way, said Oaks, he learned that the bank lent Hofmann money and that Hofmann reported buying the collection in Texas and storing it in a Salt Lake safe-deposit box. Later, he learned Hofmann had not paid the loan when it matured.

"Hofmann later admitted," Oaks continued, "that his Library of Congress receivable was not worth a million dollars at that point, and therefore, he really wasn't in a position to give the McLellin collection to the church. Mark Hofmann at that point said or implied he would have to sell the collection entirely or a piece at a time."

When Pinnock reported this information to Oaks, he mentioned knowing a couple of persons who might buy the collection and asked Oaks if there was any harm in drawing the collection's availability to their attention. "I said no," Oaks explained, "I didn't see any harm in calling its availability to their attention, but we must stress to them that the church was not involved as a purchaser or as a guarantor. We should also caution that none of us had seen the collection, so we had no knowledge of its authenticity or of its value."

Pinnock had seen a letter and piece of papyrus that were reportedly from the collection, the former shown to him by Hofmann, the latter by

Christensen. "But there was no evidence," Oaks said, "that either of these documents was part of the McLellin collection or had anything to do with McLellin, apart from Mark Hofmann's assertions."

Oaks later learned that Pinnock had contacted an interested buyer who wished to remain anonymous and who wanted the collection evaluated to be certain it was worth the $185,000 asking price. Christensen agreed to evaluate it before the transaction closed.

"Sometime about the time of October conference," Oaks said, "the potential buyer phoned me. This was my first direct information about this matter other than what Elder Pinnock had told me from time to time. The potential buyer wanted to know what I knew about the McLellin collection and whether it was worth the price. He also asked whether the church would be interested in receiving it as a gift at some future time if he purchased it and later saw fit to give it."

"I said I supposed so," Oaks explained, "but I stressed again that whether he bought it was his decision and the church would not finance it in any way and we had no information to guarantee its genuineness or its value." Oaks said the buyer later asked his attorney in Salt Lake City to handle the transaction. The attorney had a check for $185,000 that he was holding until the transaction closed.

Hofmann had informed Pinnock that Alvin Rust had the key to the safe-deposit box containing the collection and was holding it as security for his advance to Hofmann. Rust was to be repaid from the sale proceeds of the McLellin collection. "All of this sounded very regular," Oaks explained, "and is the kind of thing taken care of routinely in a closing." The closing was delayed because Rust was out of town, he said, and was then scheduled for Tuesday, October 15.

On that morning, Steve Christensen and Kathy Sheets died. Oaks said he had never heard of Kathy or Gary Sheets before this time. In the afternoon, Oaks said, Hofmann came to church headquarters and asked to see Pinnock, who was absent. Oaks agreed to see him instead and met with him for about ten minutes.

"Normally what goes on in a conversation between a general authority and a member of the church is confidential," Oaks said, but he had decided to make an exception because of the conversation's possible relevance to a murder investigation and because of the "week of innuendo and suspicion about what went on in that meeting." A week earlier, he pointed out, he had shared all this information with police. (Though Oaks did not say so, the public had learned about his meeting with Hofmann only because Oaks had volunteered the information to investigators, who in turn had told the media.)

At this point, Oaks distributed copies of the memorandum he had written about his meeting with Hofmann. He said he would not take the time to read it aloud but invited questions on it later. "I will just say here," he summarized, "for the benefit of those who are on the electronic media, that Hofmann came to my office and said he thought the police would question him. What should he say when they questioned him?"

"And I said, 'You should simply tell them the truth. You don't have any reason to believe that this bombing has anything to do with you, do you? And simply tell them the truth.' And then, when he seemed to be questioning whether we should tell them about the McLellin collection, I said, 'Look. That's been handled on a confidential basis, but there's a murder investigation underway. You should tell the police everything you know and answer every question—and I intend to do the same.' "

Oaks then reiterated that he had contacted law-enforcement personnel the next day when he learned Hofmann had been injured by a bomb, that he had told them what he knew, and that Pinnock had done the same the next morning.

On Thursday, Oaks said, Shannon Flynn showed up at the church offices and asked to speak to Hinckley. Oaks agreed to see him and did so in the presence of others, including a stenographer who recorded the interview. Oaks said he had given transcripts of the interview to investigators and Flynn's attorney. "In brief," Oaks summarized, "Flynn wanted to know what he should say if he was questioned, and I told him to tell the truth, just as I had told Hofmann." Oaks also described his Friday meeting with Al Rust and the similar advice he gave to him.

Oaks then concluded his statement, and Richard Lindsay opened the floor to questions. The first questioner asked Oaks for the name of the person who was to buy the McLellin collection. Oaks answered, "He wished to remain anonymous and the police are aware of his identity and I think it would not be ethical for me to make it [public] except to say that he is a person who is a member of the church."

The next questioner asked Hinckley if it were true Pinnock had found the 116 lost pages of the Book of Mormon manuscript, "or at least counterfeit copies?" Hinckley smiled and said he hadn't heard that. He referred the question to Pinnock, who said he had heard rumors about the lost pages while serving as a church mission president in Pennsylvania, and that rumors continue to circulate from time to time, but that he did not know such papers had ever actually been found.

Regarding the Stowell letter, a reporter asked, "Why wasn't Don Schmidt, the church archivist, informed when the church purchased the 1825 letter? And why was Dean Jessee—Why did Dean Jessee, the state's and Mormondom's foremost authority on the handwriting of Joseph Smith—

How come he found out about that letter after the church released the letter, and who authenticated that letter?"

Hinckley answered, "I don't know why Don Schmidt wasn't advised. The head of the Historical Department knew about it. But I don't know why Don Schmidt wasn't advised." Richard Lindsay pointed out that the head of the Historical Department at that time was Durham, and Hinckley added, "Yes, and he's no longer with us, unfortunately."

The next questioner asserted that Rust's letter had stated the church was going to buy the collection for three hundred thousand dollars. Then she asked Hinckley, "At that time did you realize that Hofmann was at least telling people that the church has agreed to buy the letter for three hundred thousand dollars?"

Hinckley answered, "Alvin Rust delivered a letter to me in which he said something, but I don't know that he said what you indicate he has said to have said."

The reporter rephrased her question: "Were you aware at any time that Mr. Hofmann was telling people that the church had agreed to pay three hundred thousand dollars for the letter?"

"No, I was not," Hinckley answered.

The next questioner posed a related question, asking Hinckley if he went through Rust's letter before the bombings or attempted to answer Rust's concerns about the sale of the McLellin collection.

Hinckley said he did not respond to Rust because Hofmann had come to him the next day and had promised to settle the matter. Hinckley noted he had Rust's letter with him but would not read it because he considered it confidential. "But to answer your question specifically," he continued, "there is no indication in this letter of our purchasing . . . the so-called McLellin collection." He said the letter dealt more with Rust's arrangement with Hofmann and with the trip Rust's son and Hofmann made to acquire the collection, and that Rust then wrote, "I still have no idea what is going on."

"In that regard," the reporter asked, "when he said he had no idea what is going on, did it concern you at all at that time that perhaps something funny was going on concerning the McLellin collection or at least the attempted acquisition of this collection?"

Hinckley answered, "Well, I always had some doubt about the McLellin collection because I had asked our Historical Department what they had on McLellin and they had one or two little items but knew nothing so far as they were able to tell me of any so-called McLellin collection."

The next reporter prefaced her question with a statement. "We have been told by the attorney who was working on the sale to the private purchaser for $185,000 that Steven Christensen was facilitating that negotiation. I'd like to ask if any one of you heard from Mr. Christensen that something had gone awry, that there was something wrong with either the documents or the deal that concerned him?"

Hinckley replied, "I had never heard anything, no."

"Nor had I," Pinnock added. "That was—Mr. Christensen and I talked several times about that and there was no suspicion ever communicated that there was not a McLellin collection." Pinnock's response reflected the fact that he and Christensen had discussed Hofmann's business problems and his failure to repay the loan but did not doubt the existence of the McLellin collection.

Oaks said, "Nor had I. I had no communications with Steve Christensen, and I had never heard that."

The next questioner mentioned the loans from First Interstate Bank and from Rust and asked Pinnock when he learned two loans were made to purchase the same documents.

At first, Pinnock answered, all he knew was that Hofmann needed money to add to his down payment for the McLellin collection. Later, he was told Hofmann had pledged the collection to Rust as security for what he understood was a different document transaction.

The next questioner referred to the *Los Angeles Times* article on the Oliver Cowdery history. The article had relied on a secret source who claimed access to the First Presidency's vault, and the questioner asked Hinckley who the source was and whether it was Hofmann.

Alluding to Francis Gibbons, Hinckley said only one man had the combination to the vault, and that without going through that person, even he himself could not get into it. Hinckley also affirmed "without any equivocation" that during his tenure in the First Presidency, Hofmann had never had access to the vault.

The next questioner asked Pinnock if he knew whether Hofmann ever paid any money toward the bank loan. "Yes," Pinnock answered, "he obtained a payment of twenty thousand dollars which he took down to First Interstate Bank, brought the interest up to date, and reduced the principal by a small amount."

The questioner then added, "The historians from the church evidently don't know that much about the McLellin collection. Was there anything in your knowledge that would have made them worth the amount he was asking for?"

Pinnock said he had not heard of the collection before either but assumed it would be valuable because it was supposed to contain numerous old documents, and it was common knowledge that some old documents were being sold for large sums at that time.

Asked if he had known that the RLDS Church owned a few McLellin materials, Pinnock answered, "No."

The next question posed was, "Do you believe that the McLellin papers exist at all, and if so, are you still interested in purchasing them?"

Oaks asked, "May I handle that?" Giving the reporter a second chance, he said, "Your question assumes that the church is interested in purchasing them and I stated flatly the church was not. Would you like to rephrase your question?"

The reporter then asked, "Do you believe they exist?"

Oaks, the most sensitive of the three church leaders to the legal issues the case presented, knew that a yes or no answer could jeopardize the legal process by swaying public opinion for or against Hofmann. He responded, "What I believe about the existence or nonexistence of the McLellin collection is really quite beside the point."

The reporter turned to Pinnock. "Do you feel it is proper," he asked, "for a high-ranking official of the LDS Church to help secure a loan for any member of the church as has been reported that you did . . . for one Mark Hofmann?"

"When they came in that Friday afternoon," Pinnock answered, "and when at that time I called two banks, I had not thought it improper. I was calling on what I thought was a legitimate transaction." Pinnock added that people sometimes approach church officials to ask questions, "but we would certainly not use our office for a favor for someone that was inappropriate."

"Would you do so again?" the reporter asked.

"No," he replied.

Another reporter then asked Pinnock what collateral he thought was securing the loan and if the church had agreed to pay off the loan to the bank. Pinnock answered that Hofmann had said payment on *The Oath of a Freeman* was imminent and would be used to pay off the loan. "Second," Pinnock said, "I would be sure that the church would not pay off any indebtedness that someone else would have at a bank."

"I can tell you this," Hinckley quickly added on the issue of repayment, "that . . . I have not been questioned on that matter, nor has any response been given, nor would we so respond."

The forty minutes allotted for the news conference had almost elapsed, and Richard Lindsay said, "We have time for two more quick questions."

A reporter asked if any of the church leaders had received threats that might be connected to the bombings. "Not to my knowledge," Hinckley and Oaks each answered.

"No," said Pinnock.

The reporter then asked Hinckley if he had ever bought documents from Hofmann for himself personally and if any payments to Hofmann had been

made in cash. The question revived the theory George Smith had pop-
ularized that Hinckley had bought the Josiah Stowell letter personally so
church officials could claim the church had not bought it.

"The payments were made by check," Hinckley clarified, "and they are
fully authenticated, receipted for, on two occasions. Two items. Nothing
like the figures that you have been hearing today. Relatively small." Asked
what the two items were, Hinckley said one was the Stowell letter and he
could not remember the other (which was the Grandin printing contract).
When questioned about the price of the letter, Hinckley said, "Well, I don't
know that I'm going to tell you the price, but I'm going to tell you that it
was nothing like the kind of figures that you've talked about this morning.
Nothing like that."

Richard Lindsay asked for one final question from someone who had not
yet posed one. A reporter from KBYU, a station at Brigham Young University, asked, "Why is the church so intent on getting the papers? Is it
to secure them in the right hands so that they are not taken advantage of
and make the church look bad? And where does the money come to purchase
these letters?"

Oaks recognized part of the question as something he had already answered repeatedly. "May I take the first part of that?" he asked Hinckley.

"Yes," Hinckley replied, "go ahead."

Oaks then repeated the answer he gave when the question was asked
earlier in the conference: "I thought it was clear from my statement that
the church was very intent on *not* getting the papers, so that there would
be no misunderstanding about this. Could you rephrase that question?"

The reporter directed his question away from the McLellin collection
and instead toward "letters in the past, like the blessing that Joseph gave
to his son and other letters."

Hinckley then answered by returning full circle to where he had begun
his remarks. From the day the church was organized, he said, it has had
a revealed mandate to collect historical materials, "to keep a record of
that which is said concerning the church, that which is for and that which
is against."

"If this goes on," he quipped, "we will have to find a lot more room to
house all the newspaper clippings."

"But we have a mandate," he continued more seriously. "We would
suppose the institution for which you work keeps a history, a corporate
history. We have an obligation to keep a history of the church and we regard
that very seriously. We are going over to dedicate the new genealogical
building. . . . It's essentially a historical library. It has cost a very handsome
sum and it's a beautiful archive. The finest in the world and the purpose
of it is historical—historical research."

On that note, the news conference, which had run four minutes over, came to an end, and the church leaders left for the dedication.[13]

Though church officials generally felt good about the news conference, it had not gone flawlessly. Some of the reporters' questions, like the one about the Stowell letter, had not been easy to answer. Also, because the conference had been hastily called, the church leaders were not exceptionally well prepared for it, and some of their answers suffered accordingly. Hinckley, for example, had carried Al Rust's letter to the conference with him but had not taken adequate time to review its contents. Thus, he was caught off guard when reporters began asking specific questions about its contents.

When one reporter asked him if Rust's letter had said the church would agree to buy the McLellin collection for three hundred thousand dollars, Hinckley was not clear on what the letter said. "Alvin Rust delivered a letter to me in which he said something," he replied, "but I don't know that he said what you indicate he has said to have said." In fact, Rust's letter had not mentioned the three-hundred-thousand-dollar figure or any other price.

In response to a later question, Hinckley had volunteered that "there is no indication in this letter of our purchasing . . . the so-called McLellin collection." He said the letter dealt more with Rust's arrangement with Hofmann and with the trip Rust's son and Hofmann made to acquire the collection. Though most of the letter did in fact deal with the matters Hinckley recollected, one portion expressed Rust's belief that the church had bought the collection.

Meanwhile, the mere mention of Rust's letter had caught Pinnock off guard. Until the news conference, he had never heard of it. When Hinckley had received the letter, he had not had any reason to tell Pinnock or Oaks about it since neither then had any contact with Hofmann nor any responsibility for acquiring historical documents. Oaks had not learned of the letter until the interview he had with Rust the Friday before the news conference.[14]

Hinckley had also confused another point. Referring to the church's acquisition of the Joseph Smith III blessing, he said he had met Hofmann on March 17, 1981, when Historical Department personnel brought the document and Hofmann to his office. In fact, they did not meet on that date. They did meet in 1981, but the focus of the meeting was the Bullock-Young document, not the Joseph Smith III blessing, though the two were sufficiently related to make confusing them easy.

In preparing for the news conference, Hinckley had relied on excerpts furnished him by Francis Gibbons from the minutes of the First Presidency and Quorum of the Twelve. The excerpts did not mention the Bullock-

Young letter but did include information about the March 17, 1981, meeting in which Hinckley, Historical Department administrators, and the First Presidency had discussed the Joseph Smith III blessing. Hofmann had not been present at the meeting, but Hinckley, recalling a 1981 meeting with Hofmann, incorrectly assumed he had been.[15]

After the news conference, Pinnock wrote letters to Steve Christensen's father, Mac, and widow, Terri. In the letters, he affirmed that so far as he knew, Steve had done nothing improper in dealing with Hofmann. Because Hofmann's dealings had come under suspicion, some persons had apparently suspected Steve too of wrongdoing because he had associated with Hofmann. Pinnock, however, defended Steve.

To Terri, he wrote that Steve seemed to conduct himself in an "honorable manner." He assured Mac, "I have already reported to you and Terri my knowledge that nothing within my observations have led me to believe that he did anything in any way inappropriate." Pinnock enclosed a copy of his publicly issued statement with both letters and noted especially his testimony on the second page of the statement that he had "found Mr. Christensen to be honorable and open in all dealings."[16]

That evening, Dallin Oaks, who had canceled an assigned trip to England the preceding week because of the bombings and was preparing to go on another assignment to South America that weekend, described in his journal the attention given to the press conference by the media. "The national news media gave this top coverage," he wrote. "I heard myself on the CBS world news at noon. Now this is done, I can go to So. America with a light heart. It will be great to get back to the spiritual ministry."[17]

At Wednesday's news conference, Hinckley, Oaks, and Pinnock had all reaffirmed their understanding of the loan Hofmann received from First Interstate Bank. When Pinnock told Oaks that Hofmann needed money, Oaks had suggested to him that Hofmann simply borrow from a bank using *The Oath of a Freeman* receivable as collateral. Pinnock had referred Hofmann to First Interstate Bank because he believed Hofmann had a large receivable from the Library of Congress. When a news conference reporter had asked if the church agreed to repay the loan, Pinnock had responded he was "sure that the church would not pay off any indebtedness that someone else would have at a bank." Hinckley had been in Europe when the loan was made but assumed from what he heard later that the loan was a private transaction between Hofmann and the bank. When the reporter suggested the church had agreed to repay the loan, Hinckley declared the church had not agreed, and would not agree, to pay it.[18]

These statements apparently surprised some officials at the bank, who had seen the loan from their perspective as being guaranteed either by

Pinnock personally or by the church. Thursday morning, October 24, the bank chairman telephoned Pinnock and voiced this view.[19]

"I was called out of the temple meeting this morning by Hugh Pinnock, who informed me that First Interstate Bank was asking him to pay the balance of the loan he had helped Mark Hofmann obtain," Oaks recorded in his journal that day. "By assignment, I delayed our departure [to South America] for two hours . . . so I could confer with Hugh Pinnock, assisting him with a public announcement, and conferring with others."[20]

At 11:00 A.M., Oaks and Pinnock met to discuss the matter. Pinnock explained the telephone call he had received. Though he had not signed any kind of loan agreement, bank officials said the only reason they made the loan was that Pinnock had asked for it. Sometime during Pinnock's interaction with the bank, one of its officials had asked about security for the loan. At the time, Pinnock believed Hofmann would soon receive money from the Library of Congress and said that that money would be used for repayment. He felt no concern about additional security because he was convinced Hofmann had valuable assets and would quickly repay his indebtedness.

While assuring bank officials, Pinnock recalled, he may have said something like "We have lots of assets," or even "I've got assets—[the] Church has assets. You'll be paid." These statements, whatever they may have been, meant little to him at the time because he was convinced Hofmann was both financially sound and morally upright. Later, when Christensen and Hofmann visited Pinnock at his home and explained that Hofmann was encountering financial difficulties, it became clear the assumption of financial soundness was inaccurate.

At that point, Pinnock arranged for David Sorensen to purchase the McLellin collection, thereby providing funds to repay the bank. Sorensen agreed to do so and eventually wired the funds to his attorney's account pending the closing of the transaction. Thus, the funds were available, and though Pinnock's initial assumptions about Hofmann's financial soundness proved inaccurate, the bank would still have been repaid had Hofmann delivered the McLellin collection.[21]

The bombings had halted the transaction, however, and no one could be sure the collection even existed. Suddenly, Hofmann could not be relied on in any way to repay the loan. Thus, Pinnock's earlier assurances took on new meaning, and bank officials looked to him to make good on his word.

"My honor means more than anything," he told Oaks. "I will pay it."[22]

Pinnock telephoned Bob Ward, the bank vice-president whom he had originally called about the loan, and asked for the loan balance. Ward told him it was $171,243.76, of which $170,215.47 represented principal and $1,028.29 interest. Pinnock thanked him, hung up, and did some figuring.

Pinnock had been a successful insurance executive before he entered full-time church service. For him, as for many full-time church officials, the call to service had meant a large reduction in lifetime income and diminished opportunities for accumulating additional wealth. Thus, the assets he had acquired before becoming a general authority would be hard to replace. Pinnock owned some shares of stock that represented nearly all his liquid assets. It did not take him long to calculate the impact the loan repayment would have on his resources. "That will wipe out our liquidity completely," he wrote.

He telephoned the bank chairman who called him that morning and told him he would be in the next day to pay off the loan. Then he called his attorney, he recorded, "and asked him to help me think through the situation." He conferred with other acquaintances too. "Most people, it appears, think I am wrong," he wrote in his journal. Hofmann had signed the loan agreement and received the money. Pinnock had not. Still, he felt morally responsible for the bank's loss. After recording that he had decided to pay off Hofmann's debt, Pinnock wrote of the obligation, "It is mine alone & I know that within my heart."[23]

Recording his feelings about Pinnock that day, Oaks wrote, "My heart ached for him."

At 3:00 P.M., Oaks finally left for South America, laying over for the night at an airport hotel in Dallas. After arriving in Dallas, Oaks telephoned Pinnock and, as he recorded in his journal, "found him brave as he conferred with his family and supervised the liquidation of his securities in order to raise the funds, about $180,000." Again recording his feelings, Oaks wrote, "I feel so bad for a good brother who acted solely out of a motive to help the Church, but did so in such a way that he now feels that he has a moral (though not a legal) obligation to pay the loan."[24]

Though repayment of the loan dominated Pinnock's mind that day, it was not the only matter to occupy his attention. Church leaders continued to wonder about the mystery that surrounded the bombing case, including the question of a motive for the killings and the possibility of document forgery. Pinnock wrote, "We keep talking of that which is going on & I feel progressively more unknowledgable—where are the answers?"[25]

Friday morning at 9:00, Pinnock went to First Interstate Bank and repaid the loan. The same day, he issued a statement through the church's Public Communications Department. The statement briefly reviewed the circumstances leading to the loan. "I was not a party to the loan," the statement observed, "but as a result of my referral the bank made the loan to Mr.

Hofmann. I am convinced that the bank would not have made the loan to Mr. Hofmann were it not for my assurance that it was a safe loan."[26]

The bank chairman who had called Pinnock told him the bank was being criticized for extending the loan, and Pinnock hoped his repayment and statement would alleviate the criticism.[27] He included a sentence in his statement to help the bank. "In my dealings over a number of years with First Interstate Bank," the sentence read, "I have found them to be sound and skillful bankers." "Although I am not legally obligated to the bank," Pinnock's statement continued, "I feel morally and ethically responsible to make certain the bank does not suffer any loss as a result of the loan to Mr. Hofmann. Accordingly, today I have paid to the bank the balance of all principal and interest owing on the obligation."

The statement's final two sentences reinforced declarations made at the Wednesday press conference that the church itself had not and would not repay the loan: "Such payment has been made exclusively from my personal resources. No funds or other resources of the Church have been or will be used, either directly or indirectly, to satisfy the loan."[28]

During the day, Hinckley called Pinnock and said, "When you are free please drop down to see me." At 2:00 P.M., Pinnock went to Hinckley's office. The two men embraced. "He felt sorry," Pinnock wrote, "that we were going through these problems. He said, 'We just don't know what to do.' "[29] Despite the hardship on Pinnock personally, the church could not use funds entrusted to it to pay Hofmann's debt.

With the debt paid, one issue in the Hofmann case was resolved. But bigger issues remained. Who killed Steve Christensen and Kathy Sheets? Was it Mark Hofmann, as police sources apparently believed? If so, why? Were some of Hofmann's "discoveries" actually forgeries? If so, how many and which ones? Saturday morning, October 26, the *Salt Lake Tribune* reported that investigators "continued to search for a viable motive that could explain the murders."[30]

On Monday morning, October 28, Gordon Hinckley called Martell Bird into his office to share the latest information he had heard on the case. He told Bird that investigators had learned Hofmann obtained $300,000 from a group of investors, apparently to buy the McLellin collection. "That makes $300,000, $185,000, $185,000, and $150,000," Bird wrote in his journal. "We are now aware Hofmann had sold the idea to four parties for $820,000! All this without anyone known to have seen the alleged documents!"[31]

On Tuesday, October 29, the *Salt Lake Tribune* reported that detectives planned to send Kenneth Rendell the papyrus fragments they thought had been represented by Hofmann as coming from the McLellin collection. They theorized that Christensen, who was supposed to authenticate the collection, might have told Hofmann he was going to have Rendell authenticate the papyri, thus leading Hofmann to murder him to prevent a scam from being uncovered. Yet the theory had a gaping hole: "Police have said there apparently is no link between Mr. Sheets and the documents deal."[32]

That same day at the Church Office Building, Pinnock had several conversations about the papyri photographs Christensen had given him on October 7. On October 22, Pinnock had told Salt Lake City police detective Ken Farnsworth about the photographs, as well as about the actual papyrus fragment Christensen had shown him. The investigators had shown special interest in the papyrus fragment. After a discussion about the photographs with Gordon Hinckley, however, Pinnock wrote they had "decided they did not have special significance."[33]

Further south at Brigham Young University, Historical Department adviser Boyd K. Packer of the Quorum of the Twelve addressed those gathered for the dedication of the Crabtree Technology Building. During his speech he alluded to the bombing tragedy. "In this drama," he said, "some one, for some reason, has taken two lives. The victims, and perhaps the villain, are members of the Church." Referring to distorted reports about the case, he said, "These tragic events are cast in such a light by the media that the faith of some is being challenged, and of a few, beyond the breaking point. That is a tragedy in itself."

"A few are cast in starring roles in this heartbreaking tragedy," he continued. "We may not know until the final scene is worked out who will be unveiled as the villain. Until then, as always, we support the forces of law and order, and due process. We lend our encouragement to them."[34]

That afternoon, the *Deseret News* reported that a local toy store manager claimed Hofmann bought forty feet of rocket fuse from him on October 3. The purchase stuck in his mind, he said, because most model rocket hobbyists typically bought much smaller lengths. "You're not going to launch rockets, are you?" the manager had asked jovially.

"No," Hofmann had answered.

"Oh," the manager joked, "you're going to make bombs."

"Yeah," Hofmann reportedly laughed.[35]

The next day, the same writer reported that Kenneth Rendell had seen a reproduction of a papyrus fragment Hofmann represented to Ed Ashment as coming from the McLellin collection. Rendell identified the fragment as being cut from a larger piece of papyrus he had sent Hofmann on consignment. "The removal of the drawing from the larger piece of papyrus," Rendell said, "is further indication of fraudulent intent."[36]

"Hofmann Charged with Firearms Violation," the *Salt Lake Tribune* announced Friday morning, November 1. Just hours after the hospital released him the previous day, federal prosecutors filed charges against Hofmann for possession of an unregistered machine gun taken earlier from

Shannon Flynn's home. According to the article, Flynn testified Hofmann gave him money for the firearm, which had been converted from semi- to fully automatic at Hofmann's house. A search of Hofmann's home turned up parts to the weapon.

The article also reported that a man named Thomas R. Wilding, on behalf of a group of investors, had lent Hofmann three hundred thousand dollars in May for the purchase of documents, none of a religious nature. The loans matured October 14, the paper reported, just one day before Christensen and Sheets were bombed.[37]

During the day at church headquarters, Martell Bird talked to Hugh Pinnock and then Dean Larsen about again offering police the photographs that Christensen had given Pinnock on October 7 and that Pinnock had turned over to the Historical Department two days later. Both church leaders agreed to the proposal.[38]

Saturday morning, the *Salt Lake Tribune* ran an article on *The Oath of a Freeman*, describing it as potentially one of the century's most important document discoveries. "Spokesmen for The Library of Congress, Washington, D.C., and the American Antiquarian Society in Massachusetts said preliminary examinations show the 17th century document was printed during the era in which it was purported to be printed," the article reported, adding, however, that neither institution had bought the document.[39]

"The bombings are still the topic of the day," wrote Glenn Rowe on Monday, November 4. Like most of the public interested in the bombing case, church officials could do little more than wait for investigators to conclude their work. Tuesday morning, the *Salt Lake Tribune* reported that laboratory tests on the bomb parts provided some "promising" results for investigators, who were, however, still far from filing homicide charges. What they lacked, the article said, is a "viable motive for the death of Kathleen Sheets, or the intended murder of her husband."[40]

But that evening, the *Deseret News* quoted Salt Lake County Sheriff Pete Hayward as saying, "Our primary concern is to establish a motive (for the killings), and we think we know what that motive is." Although Hayward refused to describe the motive, he said, "This whole idea of forgery or fraud or extortion is secondary to the murder investigation."[41]

Though church leaders followed news accounts of the investigation, the burdens of running a worldwide church occupied their foremost attention. Tuesday evening, November 5, President Spencer W. Kimball passed away following a prolonged period of ill health. Over the next several days, many of the church leaders planned and participated in Kimball's funeral and the reorganization in leadership that followed it. In the reorganization, Dallin Oaks replaced Gordon Hinckley as an adviser to the Historical Department with Boyd Packer.[42]

The morning after Kimball's death, Police Chief Bud Willoughby called the church Security Department to ask if church security officers had been following Hofmann when his car exploded. Security officer Ron Francis, who handled the call, reported it to Martell Bird, who in his journal described the entire idea as "ridiculous." Bird telephoned Willoughby and assured him his information was incorrect.[43]

That afternoon, two agents from the Bureau of Alcohol, Tobacco, and Firearms visited Bird and posed the same question. Once again, Bird tried to dispel the rumor, which apparently originated when someone noticed the church security officers who rushed to the scene of the third bombing shortly after Hofmann was injured. Bird explained how the officers became aware of the bombing, but he wrote that one of the agents "didn't seem completely satisfied." He offered to let them talk to any of his personnel if they wished.[44]

On November 7, the *Salt Lake Tribune* reported that a federal grand jury indictment of Hofmann for possession of an unregistered machine gun had superseded the complaint filed the previous week. The article went on to discuss the still puzzling question of a motive for the murders, reiterating the theory that Hofmann killed Christensen because he feared Christensen would expose Hofmann's fraud in trying to sell the McLellin collection, papers that apparently did not exist. The article also said detectives felt Hofmann planted the Sheets bomb to divert investigators toward CFS. The tentativeness of this theory became apparent from the next sentence, however, in which the reporter wrote, "Investigators also continue to look into the possibility that Mr. Hofmann may have believed Mr. Sheets was to be made aware of the apparent documents fraud."[45]

Later that day the *Deseret News* reported, "At least four different individuals or groups apparently gave unknown hundreds of thousands of dollars to Mark Hofmann to purchase a Charles Dickens manuscript, 'The Haunted Man.'" One investor said the deal in which he had invested was scheduled to close October 15, the day Christensen and Sheets died.[46] The news story added to mounting evidence that Hofmann had been double dealing.

The next day, the Salt Lake newspapers reported that investigators suspected other conspirators in the bombing case. Finding a motive for the Sheets killing remained a major hurdle. "No matter how many different angles you look at this case from, there is just no reason to kill Mrs. Sheets, or her husband for that matter," an unnamed detective told one reporter. "It just doesn't make sense."[47]

The following week, the *Salt Lake Tribune* again noted that the motive for the Sheets killing continued to puzzle investigators. "While it has been nearly a month since Mr. Christensen and Mrs. Sheets died in separate

pipe-bomb explosions," the *Tribune* pointed out, "detectives and prosecutors continue to struggle with a case scenario which would explain the
motives in the killings."[48]

On November 18, the *Tribune* published an article about "the missing
key strong enough to tie a suspect or suspects to the deaths of Steven F.
Christensen and Kathleen Sheets so murder charges can be filed." The
article said pressure to file charges in the case had exacerbated the usual
friction between competing investigative agencies, as well as between detectives and prosecuting attorneys. "There is some fear among [local]
investigators," the article read, "that the federal agents will beat the city
and county to the punch and seek indictments for violations of federal
statutes regulating the manufacture of explosive devices." Local prosecutors, on the other hand, feared premature filing would invite "a preliminary hearing within the mandated 10-day time period and prosecutors may
risk having the case thrown out of court."[49]

On November 19, Hugh Pinnock noted a major news story announced
by broadcast news services that evening. "Mark Hofmann, it was reported,
passed a polygraph test," the church leader wrote in his journal.[50] Next
morning, the *Salt Lake Tribune* confirmed that a "world-renowned polygraph expert" verified the results of the examination, in which Hofmann
denied planting the bombs that killed Christensen and Sheets. The newspaper also reported that Shannon Flynn passed a polygraph test.

The article further announced that a federal grand jury would soon begin
hearing testimony about the bombing murders. Federal prosecutors could
not charge Hofmann with murder because "federal statutes deal only with
the making of explosive devices, not homicide," the article explained. On
the other hand, it observed, "federal prosecutors would not have to show
any motive for the killings, which has been the thorn in the side of local
investigators since the murders occurred."[51]

That evening the *Deseret News* reported that police had searched a
vacant canyon home Hofmann considered buying and had discovered "significant evidence" related to the bombing case. The evidence led police to
believe that the house may have been the site where the bombs were
constructed. "We found what we've been looking for all along," one investigator said. The article observed that the evidence seemed to contradict
the polygraph results announced earlier by Hofmann's attorneys.[52]

At the November 21 meeting of the board of directors of First Interstate
Bank of Utah, the board deliberated on several matters of business, including the loan the bank had made to Mark Hofmann. Later in the meeting
the board would discuss the "policy and procedures regarding director
referral of business prospects," but as it "discussed in detail the Hofmann
loan," it "found no violation of policy or law."[53]

The following morning, the *Salt Lake Tribune* ran an article about the federal grand jury's investigation of the bombing case. The article raised potential questions of double jeopardy for Hofmann if both federal and state cases proceeded to trial. It quoted Salt Lake County Attorney Ted Cannon as saying he was aware of the issue but that federal and local authorities had been cooperating "so we don't botch up each other." Asked if the federal grand jury's investigation was a rehearsal of the county's homicide case, Cannon laughingly responded, "All I can say to that is, 'What case?' " Cannon's remark punctuated prosecutors' apparent frustration that despite weeks of investigation, they had been unable to find the catalyst to solidify their other evidence and provide a motive for the killings.[54]

Like other members of the public, church officials watched with interest as the investigation continued, hoping it would soon solve the mystery behind the brutal killings, as well as resolve questions about fraud and forgery. Over the past several weeks, they had responded to requests from law enforcement agencies at both the federal and local level and had repeatedly volunteered information that had not been requested because they thought it might prove useful in the investigation.[55]

On Wednesday, November 27, the FBI requested additional information from the church to assist in the ongoing evaluation of the salamander letter. In the afternoon, two FBI agents met with Earl Olson and Glenn Rowe to ask questions about *The Book of Common Prayer*, which Hofmann had sold to the church in October before the bombings. The agents were interested in the handwriting attributed to Martin Harris that Hofmann said he found in the book. They asked if the church had other samples of Harris's handwriting. Olson offered what signatures the church had, but because all were from Martin Harris's later life, the agents said they were not interested in them. Olson and Rowe agreed to let the agents take the prayer book for examination, and they did so, leaving a receipt for it.[56]

As those affected by the bombings waited for law enforcement officials to complete their investigation, the aftershocks of the bombings continued to be felt. That evening, the day before Thanksgiving, found Brent and Charlene Ashworth in a Salt Lake hospital room wondering what to be thankful for. To help themselves relax after the strained days following the bombings, they had traveled to California, leaving their children with relatives. The vacation was interrupted by the tragic news that their son Sammy had been struck by a car while riding his bicycle on Sunday. Brent later said that had they been home, he and Charlene would not have allowed their children to ride their bicycles on the Sabbath.

Now, three-and-a-half weeks later, Sammy lay hospitalized, and the Ashworths' lives had collapsed in the aftermath of the bombings. Brent walked out of the hospital room with a visiting friend, leaving Charlene at Sammy's bedside. The telephone rang, and Charlene picked it up.[57]

"Can I speak with Brent Ashworth?" a voice inquired.

"Well, this is Charlene Ashworth."

"Is this Sam's mother?"

"Yes."[58]

"This is Gordon Hinckley from Salt Lake. I just want you to know that we're very concerned about you and your family and that our love and prayers are with you."

Recalling the impact of the phone call on his family, Brent Ashworth later said that it "turned our Thanksgiving the next day into a real Thanksgiving—which it wouldn't have been."[59]

On Thanksgiving Day, the *Salt Lake Tribune* surprised readers by reporting it had located "what may be the McLellin collection." The article cautiously explained that though "it has not been substantiated that these are the same documents referred to by Mr. Hofmann, the collection located by The Tribune in Texas apparently is the same one alluded to in other Mormon historical papers." The owner of the collection said it had been with his family for over a century, the article continued. "He said he has never heard of Mr. Hofmann, and he is unaware of any document dealers contacting other family members."

The article described the collection as containing three small McLellin journals from the 1830s, as well as numerous copies of letters from early church members. The author of the article commented that investigators had believed Hofmann was "trying to sell nonexistent documents to several different buyers." She added, "The existence of such a collection could force investigators to alter that theory."[60]

An article in that evening's *Deseret News,* however, found investigators clinging even stronger to their theory. A police source commenting on the papers the *Tribune* had discovered said, "If they are the McLellin papers and if the statements (of the owner) made to the media are true, it just proves our point that . . . Hofmann never had the papers. The guy who says he has the papers says that he has never heard of Hofmann."[61]

Investigators were clearly feeling public pressure to charge Hofmann. Another *Tribune* article once again examined the growing rift between local police and prosecutors over whether enough evidence existed to file charges. City police and county sheriff's office investigators maintained that "except for follow-up work and unforeseen leads" in the case, their work was basically done. "They are tired of taking the heat from the media, and claim the ball is now in the court of County Attorney Ted L. Cannon and his prosecutors to file charges in the killings," the article said. Prosecuting attorneys, on the other hand, apparently felt investigators had yet to come up with enough evidence to succeed in court.

Referring to the tension that often exists between police and prosecutors on the issue of sufficient evidence, Cannon said, "What we have here is a magnification of the screening tension. That's when the officer says, 'I have a good case,' and the attorney says, 'It's not good enough. It's not to my standards.' " The key issue, the article explained, was the motive in the case. No one had solid proof of why anyone would kill Kathy Sheets, nor could anyone reasonably explain the bomb that injured Hofmann.[62]

Investigators badly needed a break, one that would crack the case wide open. Soon they would get it.

10

The Focus Shifts

In early December 1985, *Utah Holiday* magazine published a provocative article in which George J. Throckmorton, described as the state's only practicing forensic document examiner, and other experts challenged basic assumptions that underlay the salamander letter's claim to be authentic. Previous tests conducted on the letter had focused on paper, ink, and handwriting. The paper and ink had been found to be consistent with those used during the early nineteenth century, but, the article pointed out, paper and ink with the right composition could easily be acquired or manufactured and then artificially aged. Handwriting analysis simply compared one sample of handwriting against another, yet for the salamander letter, little Martin Harris handwriting existed to compare. The article chided police for not consulting Throckmorton about the case, but by the time it was published, Throckmorton had taken the initiative to contact them and was soon added to the investigative team. His help came at a critical time.[1]

"They just can't do anything," the December 1 *Salt Lake Tribune* quoted one investigator as saying. "They" were the prosecutors, the lawyers who had to decide if evidence justified charging Hofmann (or anyone else) with the bombing murders. The frustrated investigator claimed the case was "solid," but the article cited "sources close to the investigation" who revealed problems with the collected evidence. Though it had been widely reported that Hofmann was seen buying forty feet of rocket fuse, investigators had to concede they did not have a positive identification of Hofmann as the purchaser, and that in any case, laboratory examinations of the bomb fragments established that the killer had used electric rocket igniters, not fuses. Detectives also had to abandon earlier theories that linked the bombs to two blasting caps picked up by Shannon Flynn the previous winter. "Those blasting caps . . . apparently were fuse detonated," the article reported, "and in no way have been connected to the bombs that went off last month, sources said."[2]

Contrary to early rumors, as time went on, it became apparent that although Flynn and Hofmann had possessed a machine gun together, Flynn had nothing to do with the bombings.[3]

On December 2, the *Salt Lake Tribune* reported that the "McLellin collection" discovered in Texas consisted of just three small manuscript books thought to have been written by McLellin and "more than 500 pages of handwritten material that owners of the papers say are the interpretive work of J.L. Traughber, a 19th century confidante of McLellin." Traughber's son, Otis, who owned the documents, "said family members lost other material, and his father recorded that still other documents were given away or burned by McLellin's widow." Thus, the article concluded, "There is no single 'McLellin Collection,' at least in Traughber's possession."[4]

"Texas Papers Not Quite 'McLellin Collection,'" read the headline to the *Deseret News* article on the subject that afternoon. The article quoted a state government archivist who said of the collection, "It really should be called the Traughber collection, because the bulk of the material is (J.L.) Traughber's notes on McLellin." The article reported that the collection apparently did not contain McLellin's journals, as had been expected, nor any other material from the 1830s.[5]

Immediately after the bombings, investigators had shown great interest in talking to church officials about the case. Though church officials continued to cooperate with them in the ensuing weeks, investigators' interest in the church seemed to dwindle as the investigation lingered on. On the afternoon of December 2, church officials noticed a sudden resurgence in interest. At 3:40 P.M., Gordon Hinckley telephoned the Historical Department to pass on a request received from the county attorney's office for high-quality photographs of several documents.[6]

Twenty minutes later, a detective from the Salt Lake City Police Department met with church security officer Ron Francis, who had hurried to the scene after Hofmann had been bombed. Francis wrote of the detective, "He asked if I were aware that Mark Hofmann was escorted out of the First Security Bank Building on Main Street by two men and if those two men might have been Church Security officers. I stated that I had no knowledge whatsoever of the incident at First Security Bank." The detective also asked if church security had tailed Hofmann on October 15 and 16, a rumor Security Department officials had repeatedly disavowed. Francis explained to the detective that neither he nor anyone else in his department had followed Hofmann and that he did not even know who Hofmann was until after his car exploded.

The police detective said suspicious vehicles had been seen driving past the Christensen residence on the day Steve Christensen died. He asked if anyone from church security had driven by that day. "I stated that to the best of my knowledge," Francis wrote, "no one from Church Security was at the Christensen residence on that day or any other day for that matter!" The detective then requested descriptions of vehicles used by the Security Department, which Francis immediately provided.[7]

As the police detective was interviewing Francis in the Church Administration Building, a second investigator was interviewing another church security officer in the adjacent Church Office Building high rise. The investigator identified herself as an agent from the San Francisco office of the Bureau of Alcohol, Tobacco, and Firearms. She said she had been assigned to work with Salt Lake City police detectives on the case and began asking questions similar to those posed by the police detective. When she asked the security officer how he learned Hofmann had been bombed, he explained he had learned about it by watching television. "She asked," he would write, "if anyone in the Security Department had Mark Hoffman under surveillance. I told her that ou[r] department doesn't do those type of things. . . . She said she knew of a time that Mark Hoffman was escorted out of a First Security Bank by two security officers. She wanted to know what section of our department would do that. I again explained that we don't do those things."[8]

Just minutes after this interview began, Ken Farnsworth and Jim Bell, detectives from the Salt Lake City Police Department, met with Hugh Pinnock in his office, remaining there about half an hour. Farnsworth later recalled that Bell said little in the interview. "He just went with me," Farnsworth said. "I was the one that knew all of the background on it, and we needed to tell Elder Pinnock . . . what his role would be for us as a witness in the Hofmann case." Steve Christensen was dead and so could not testify. The detectives wanted Pinnock to take Christensen's place. Farnsworth recalled telling Pinnock that "he would be the person who would be representing everything that Steve knew about the case that he had common knowledge of." And the most important part of this role would be "to show the motive for killing Steve Christensen." "Mark Hofmann had a reason to kill Steve Christensen," Farnsworth remembered saying. "We're trying to find out why."

The detectives had a theory they hoped Pinnock would confirm. They believed Hofmann killed Steve Christensen to relieve pressure Christensen was putting on him. They wanted Pinnock to take the stand and testify of the pressure Hofmann was under when Christensen died. Farnsworth and Bell told Pinnock that when they returned to interview him Friday, they expected him to be prepared to talk all about Mark Hofmann and the document dealer's relationship with Steve Christensen.[9]

The detectives' request disturbed Pinnock. They wanted him to advocate their theory, but he did not agree with it. As he had told the police and

FBI just after the bombings, he and Christensen had pressured Hofmann to repay the bank loan. Pinnock felt, however, that the pressure had ended the night of October 3 when he offered to find a buyer for the McLellin collection and thus opened the way for Hofmann to pay off his debts. From Pinnock's point of view, all that stood between Hofmann and financial freedom was closing the sale of the McLellin collection, something Christensen was helping Hofmann facilitate. It simply didn't make sense for Hofmann to kill him.[10]

"I gathered documents for police," wrote Glenn Rowe about his activities on December 3. When Gordon Hinckley had called the previous day, he had given the Historical Department a list of several documents requested by the county attorney's office. Now Rowe had to locate the documents and bring them together so investigators could examine them.[11]

At a December 3 meeting, the First Presidency reviewed the county's request, which sought several items that could be traced to Hofmann, as well as handwriting samples of Joseph Smith, Martin Harris, Lucy Mack Smith, and Thomas Bullock. The First Presidency assigned Francis Gibbons to work with church counsel Wilford W. Kirton, Jr., in complying with the request. Kirton spoke with Salt Lake County Attorney Ted Cannon about the matter, agreeing to be helpful but expressing concern for the security of the documents.[12]

The next day, Cannon wrote Kirton, thanking him for the church's cooperation in the investigation and suggesting procedures to govern his staff in their use of the church documents, which considered as a whole were worth a small fortune. Cannon proposed the documents be picked up by George Throckmorton and by Michael P. George, a detective in the county attorney's office. They would provide a receipt and take the documents immediately to a safe-deposit box, where they would remain except when being tested. Only a few persons would be permitted to handle them, and Cannon promised they would conduct no destructive tests. Cannon assured Kirton that the investigators were interested primarily in the documents' physical characteristics, not their contents, and that they would not discuss the contents with the media.

Acknowledging that the church's provision of the documents was voluntary, Cannon agreed to subpoena the documents formally should investigators determine they would need them as evidence at trial. If they decided they did not need the documents, they would return the originals and all copies. Cannon hoped that a similar arrangement might be made for any other documents local investigators might decide they needed later. He explained that his team would negotiate directly with federal investigators for access to documents they had obtained from church officials.

Attached to Cannon's letter was an amended list of requested materials. The list omitted documents then in federal possession but contained other blanket statements, including a request for "any other letter, document, book, journal, manuscript or papyrus purporting to be in the handwriting of an early church figure, acquired from or through Mark W. Hofmann."[13]

On December 5 at 9:00 A.M., Glenn Rowe and Earl Olson of the Historical Department, along with Kirton, met with George Throckmorton, Mike George, and Deputy County Attorney Robert L. Stott. Stott explained the need for investigators to examine the originals of documents in church possession. Then he turned to Throckmorton and asked him which documents he needed. Throckmorton's list substantially paralleled the one in Cannon's letter.[14]

Kirton again expressed concern about how the documents would be handled. He asked that the documents not leave the building unless accompanied by a church representative. No one doubted the authenticity of the sample documents the county had requested, and in Kirton's view, even the questioned documents needed to be treated as though they were genuine until they were shown to be otherwise. Though he had not been instructed to do so, Kirton also expressed concern that the contents of the documents not be publicized. He assumed that because the documents were archival, they were confidential. Because the investigators' interest was in the documents' physical properties and not their content, he saw no reason why they should publicize their content.[15]

The request to keep the documents confidential bothered Throckmorton, who thought Kirton was being unreasonable. The investigators had brought with them a copy of Dean Jessee's *Personal Writings of Joseph Smith,* which contained published copies of many of the requested documents. Throckmorton opened the book to show Kirton photographs of them. Archivist Glenn Rowe intervened to explain that the documents were not confidential, that many of them had been published in church periodicals and elsewhere, and that he could see no reason for investigators not to examine them. Kirton conceded but requested that any copies made from the documents be returned after the investigation.[16]

Throckmorton said investigators wanted to take both photographs and photocopies of the documents. They would make notes on the photocopies so as not to damage the originals. He promised that tests on the documents would all be nondestructive. He asked for a room in the Church Office Building in which to carry out his examination but said the documents would also have to be taken to a laboratory for examination, and he did not want a church representative to be present during the laboratory analysis. The group agreed that Rowe would locate the documents and that Throckmorton would then decide which ones he wanted to take.[17]

After the meeting, Throckmorton asked Rowe if he could talk with the archives conservators, whose responsibilities included washing and deacidifying documents to preserve them. The conservator with whom Throckmorton spoke later recalled, "He asked about inks feathering when a document was washed—giving a light discoloration around each letter. Such questions as treatment methods and chemicals we use were discussed."[18]

Glenn Rowe spent much of his morning after the meeting retrieving documents for Throckmorton. When Throckmorton finished talking to conservators, he wanted to take several of the documents Rowe had located to the state crime lab, not for full analysis but just to be photographed. In keeping with the agreement made at the meeting earlier that day, a church library employee went with him.[19]

When they arrived at the lab and the church employee got out of the car, the two folders of documents he had been carrying slipped from his hand and fell to the ground. Though most remained protected in the folders, three or four touched the ground, much to his mortification. He quickly gathered them up as Throckmorton ribbed him about being sent to protect the documents, only to let them fall to the ground. "I was busy picking them up and only said 'I know,' " the employee later remembered saying. "It was a very embarrassing moment for me." When he inspected the documents, however, he found them undamaged.

The men went indoors, where they met a man who helped them photograph the documents. The library employee opened a folder and handed the Anthon transcript to the investigators. They handled it very delicately as they photographed it. Throckmorton assumed it was probably genuine. When they had finished photographing it, they moved to the next document. After several hours, they finished their task, and Throckmorton drove the church employee and the documents back to the Church Office Building.[20]

The next day, December 6, Throckmorton went back to the Church Office Building, where he looked up Richard Lindsay, who had formerly been the president of Throckmorton's stake (a church unit comparable to a diocese). Lindsay invited him in, and the two conversed congenially. Lindsay asked Throckmorton what he could do for him, and Throckmorton explained he was involved in the Hofmann investigation. Lindsay was surprised, saying he thought Throckmorton was still working as security director at a local hospital.

Throckmorton described some of his background in examining documents and asked Lindsay if he could arrange for one of the general authorities to give him a special blessing to help him in examining the Hofmann documents. Church members needing comfort or counsel often sought such blessings, which involved having a person in authority lay his hands on the recipient's head and pronounce whatever promises, counsel, or exhortation he felt inspired to give.[21]

Lindsay told Throckmorton to put his request in writing and agreed to have it considered. Throckmorton sat down later that day and wrote Lindsay a letter. He sensed that the examination he was conducting might affect not just his local congregation but the entire church and its interpretation of history. Thus, he wanted the opportunity to receive a blessing from one of the general authorities. For what he considered obvious legal reasons, he requested that the blessing be given by a general authority who was not involved in the investigation.[22]

Lindsay later took Throckmorton's request to church leaders, who decided they could not grant it. Throckmorton would obviously play a key role in the investigation, and a blessing by a general authority might be misinterpreted as an attempt to influence the legal process, something the leaders were determined not to do. Relaying their response, Lindsay told Throckmorton to seek a blessing from his local church authorities, who would not be viewed as having the same influence.[23]

That same day, Throckmorton went to the Church Administration Building to pick up the Josiah Stowell letter. Consistent with the earlier agreement, a church employee accompanied Throckmorton to the state crime lab, where the document was photographed. Throckmorton also spent time in the Historical Department with Glenn Rowe, who was spending much of his time carrying out his assignment to gather documents for the investigators.[24]

At about 1:30 P.M., Ken Farnsworth of the Salt Lake City Police Department, Mike George of the county attorney's office, and Steven F. Clark of the FBI entered the Church Administration Building. They had come to interview Hugh Pinnock but learned that Dallin Oaks was available too. They had not planned to interview him, but since he was available, they decided to ask him what time Hofmann had visited him on October 15. A bus driver had said he saw Hofmann on October 15 up a canyon near some property Hofmann had considered buying. Investigators theorized Hofmann had used the property to build bombs, and they wanted to use the bus driver's testimony as proof Hofmann had been there that day. Yet they also knew Hofmann had been in Oaks's office, and they wanted to make sure they did not have Hofmann in two places at the same time.

The three investigators proceeded to Oaks's office, where they shook hands and chatted briefly with him. Hugh Pinnock and church legal counsel Oscar W. McConkie, Jr., were also present. In response to the question of what time Hofmann had visited Oaks on October 15, investigators received a copy of the portion of the building visitor log that recorded Hofmann's arrival and departure. To the investigators' consternation, the log showed

Hofmann was in the building at the same time the bus driver supposedly saw him up the canyon. Summarizing the meeting with Oaks, Mike George said, "Oaks happened to be there, and we had the one question for him, and he was gracious enough . . . to give us his time and answer the question and . . . get the information from the security desk. And that's all we wanted it for—till we got it and we wished we didn't have it."[25]

Investigators appreciated Oaks's making himself available to them, but they had no interest in talking to him further. "We didn't have any intention of interviewing him," Farnsworth later recalled. "We needed Elder Pinnock. Elder Pinnock dealt with Hofmann. We already had Elder Oaks's statement about his only contact with Mark Hofmann and his perception of all the things that had happened." After investigators received a copy of the log entry, they left Oaks in his office and went next door to Pinnock's to begin their scheduled interview.[26]

Using extracts from his journal, Pinnock detailed his association with Steve Christensen and Mark Hofmann from June 28, when they both came to his office, through the time of the bombings. The detectives had prepared sheets of questions to ask, and as Pinnock spoke, they interrupted occasionally to pose them. Farnsworth asked most of the questions, though Mike George also asked many. Farnsworth recalled about the interview that "there would be diversions in the middle of it where we'd go off on a tangent, and then we'd get back with the journal."[27]

Despite the tangents, Pinnock managed to read the detectives most of his relevant journal entries, which described meetings, telephone calls, and related events during the period in which they were interested. He also answered their questions and volunteered other information he felt might be useful. When they asked, for example, about the documents the church had acquired from Hofmann, Pinnock said he doubted the salamander letter was authentic because research by LDS Institute instructor Rhett James had concluded that the language of the letter did not match Martin Harris's. After the two-and-a-half-hour interview, Pinnock wrote about the meeting in his journal. "I reviewed the Christensen-Hofmann situation until about 4[:]30," he recorded. "[Dallin H. Oaks] called asking how things went. I felt quite well. Willing, open communications."[28]

Church legal counsel Oscar McConkie left the meeting with the same feeling. McConkie saw his role as seeing "that no unfair advantage was taken of Elder Pinnock in any of the interrogations." He was satisfied with the investigators' conduct. "It was a very friendly meeting," he later recalled. "All officers were polite and asked all the questions they wanted to ask. There were no restrictions on any questions. Elder Pinnock was relaxed and answered all of the questions to the best of his ability."[29]

Pinnock and McConkie were not alone in feeling good about the interview. Mike George said that "when we came out of this interview, I'd say most of the investigators—and we talked about it afterwards—felt good about it, you know, and I felt good about it." Yet, though generally satisfied with the interview, Farnsworth and George did not believe everything Pinnock told them. "I don't think he was being truthful," George would later say.

The day Christensen first brought Hofmann to Pinnock's office, Pinnock had gone to Oaks to ask if the church would be interested in buying the McLellin collection. During his interview with investigators, Pinnock said that Oaks had told him the church would not be interested in buying the collection. When George recorded this statement in his notes, he put a question mark beside it. Later, when asked to recall the interview, George remained distrustful. "I don't believe that," he said. "I believe if you look at the evidence of the case and what transpired during that time period, they were obviously interested." Asked if he meant interested in owning the collection or interested in purchasing it, George responded, "Purchasing."

George had apparently not realized that if the church had wanted to buy the McLellin collection at the time, it could have done so, assuming the collection really existed. Church officials had wanted the collection, and the church had had the means to purchase it outright without assistance. But they had made a conscious decision not to buy it, and that decision had led to the bank loan and ultimately to the involvement of David Sorensen.

During the interview, detectives also asked Pinnock if Christensen was called on a special mission to acquire documents for the church. During September, Pinnock said, he had discussed Christensen's business and future dealings with him, but Christensen had never been given a church calling to procure documents. George, who had learned how Christensen described his document-business proposal to his wife and business partner, again interpreted Pinnock's response as a lie. "I don't believe that at all," he said. "I think Steve was looking at this as possibly or potentially maybe becoming his calling in life."[30]

When investigators interviewed Pinnock, they inevitably came around to motive, the one element they lacked to make a solid murder case. They asked Pinnock what pressures he or Christensen had placed on Hofmann. "Placed on normal business pressures," George wrote in his notes, recording Pinnock's response. They asked Pinnock to describe what Hofmann was like near the time of the bombings, apparently hoping he would say Hofmann appeared desperate or irrational. Yet in Pinnock's presence, Hofmann had always seemed in control of himself. Certainly his cash-flow problems showed he lacked financial acumen. Pinnock answered that Hofmann appeared steady and benign, though not very sophisticated.

Detectives had hoped for more. They wanted to prove friction and distrust between Christensen and Hofmann that was strong enough to make Hofmann murder, and Pinnock would not tell them what they wanted to hear. He had already recounted for them the difficulty in getting Hofmann to repay the bank loan. Still, however unsophisticated Hofmann might be in handling his finances, he was the premier document dealer in his field. Pinnock told investigators that Hofmann's reputation was good. In his presence, Hofmann and Christensen had seemed friendly toward one another. "The relationship between Steve & Mark was very friendly and not marked with frustration," George recorded.[31]

That response too frustrated investigators. Mike George recalled, "I didn't believe that Pinnock felt that Mark's reputation was good during this time period that he was dealing with him." George gave basically two reasons for not believing the church leader. First, he said the difficulties in getting Hofmann to repay the bank loan and close the collection deal showed Hofmann's reputation was not good. Yet Pinnock had already described those difficulties and felt that despite them, Hofmann's reputation as a finder of historical documents was untarnished. The other reason George gave was that "there was talk about people confronting Mark in the bank lobby of the First Interstate Bank." At the time he was interviewing Pinnock, he thought church employees had been the ones confronting Hofmann. Later, he learned the incident involved unrelated persons.[32]

Detective Ken Farnsworth shared George's frustration. Farnsworth said the responses upset him because Pinnock "wouldn't make Hofmann a bad guy—never did at any time ever." Farnsworth's own notes from the interview record Pinnock as saying that although there was pressure on Hofmann because of the loan, Hofmann was much more dependable and reliable after October 3. Pinnock had acknowledged the problems he and Christensen had with Hofmann before the October 3 meeting at Pinnock's house, but the murders occurred after that date, when the pressure on Hofmann, from Pinnock's point of view, had seemed to let up.[33]

For his part, Pinnock finished the interview confused. After the bombs had gone off, he had begun to question whether the McLellin collection existed. After his interview that day with detectives, however, he recorded in his journal, "Detective Farnsworth showed me a remarkable letter where [Steven F. Christensen] had communicated to [David E. Sorensen] that the McLellin collection is worth 250,000–300,000 and that he had seen it. Does the collection really exist. Probably—or why would he had written the letter?" Actually, the letter Farnsworth showed Pinnock was prepared by Christensen in anticipation of the closing that never occurred. The letter, never sent, was in Christensen's office the day he was killed.[34]

On December 9, Glenn Rowe recorded in his journal that Gordon Hinckley called to ask whether he or the Historical Department had purchased the Grandin printing contract. Francis Gibbons had furnished Hinckley with two excerpts about the document from the minutes of the First Presidency, but the minutes were ambiguous on who had purchased the document. Rowe told him that as best he could determine, the Historical Department had actually acquired the document, with the First Presidency simply providing the funds for the purchase.[35]

Hinckley called about the printing contract because he was preparing for an interview later that day with investigators. Although he could recall highlights of his association with Hofmann, many details had faded amid the myriad of other activities that had occupied his mind during the years since Hofmann first approached the church with his documents. The seventy-five-year-old leader had been among the busiest of church officials during those years. For most of that time, he had been a member of the First Presidency, and other members of the Presidency had at times been incapacitated by age or illness, leaving him principally responsible for operating the burgeoning international church.[36]

Late in the afternoon on December 9, Hinckley met with Ken Farnsworth, Mike George, and church general counsel Wilford Kirton. During the interview, Hinckley chronologically recounted his association with Mark Hofmann and Steven Christensen. Much of this information he had already made public during the October 23 news conference, but he provided a few additional details.[37]

At the press conference, Hinckley had said Hofmann "sold various documents to the church," specifically mentioning the Anthon transcript, the Joseph Smith III blessing, the salamander letter, and the Stowell letter. During his interview with investigators, Hinckley also mentioned the acquisition of the letter from David Whitmer to Walter Conrad, which, he pointed out, Hofmann wanted to trade for two blank pages from the original Book of Mormon manuscript, a copy of A Book of Commandments, or fifteen thousand dollars cash. He said the Historical Department negotiated a purchase of the document for ten thousand dollars.

At the press conference, Hinckley had declined giving specific information on how much had been paid for the documents he purchased from Hofmann directly for the church. He had answered simply that the payments had been made by check, that they were receipted, and that the prices did not approach the six-digit figures being bandied about in the news conference. During his interview with investigators, however, Hinckley said he negotiated the purchase of the Stowell letter directly from Hofmann for fifteen thousand dollars after it had been authenticated in New York by Charles Hamilton.[38]

During the press conference, Hinckley had said that when Hofmann visited him in June to propose donating the McLellin collection, Hofmann had said it contained "various letters, some affidavits and related items." Hinckley told Farnsworth and George that Hofmann said it contained Facsimile No. 2, affidavits, and journal writings.[39] Hinckley also told investigators about the visit he had from Hofmann on September 26 at about 7:30 A.M. During that visit, he said, Hofmann told him of persons who had obtained copies of talks for the upcoming general conference of the church.[40]

During his interview with Farnsworth and George, Hinckley reiterated that the last time he saw Hofmann was in October, when Hofmann told him he thought the Kinderhook plates were available. Hinckley said he told Hofmann the plates were a fraud perpetrated against Joseph Smith and declined Hofmann's offer to try to acquire them for the church.[41]

Just as they had not believed everything Pinnock told them, the investigators distrusted some of Hinckley's responses too. For example, when Hinckley said the Joseph Smith III blessing was secured by the Historical Department, Mike George wrote "???" next to the statement. Later, he said, "At that point, I had a question mark about that, but I think we ultimately resolved that the Historical Department in fact bought that one."[42]

When Hinckley told investigators he had never heard of the McLellin collection before June 1985, George again questioned the statement. George later said he "found it hard to believe that he'd never heard of the McLellin collection if he was head of the history department when everybody else seemed to know what was going on." George, who was not a Latter-day Saint, wrongly assumed that existence of a McLellin collection had been common knowledge among historically minded church officials before Hofmann claimed to have found it. In reality, few persons connected with the Historical Department knew such a collection was supposed to exist before Hofmann came along. Don Schmidt was among the few who did. Hinckley, who advised but did not work in the department, was not.[43]

During the interview, Hinckley also answered questions from the investigators. Hofmann had apparently boasted that he was very close to Hinckley and that the church leader even called him at home on occasion. The investigators asked Hinckley if he had ever telephoned Hofmann's home. Hinckley said he could not recall doing so personally but thought his secretary might have Hofmann's numbers.[44]

The investigators doubted that answer too. Mike George later explained, "The people we were talking to at that time—and I even think ultimately with Hofmann— . . . said that he was receiving . . . calls at his home from Hinckley."[45] However, investigators' information about a close relationship between Hofmann and Hinckley came largely from Hofmann's friends, who had gotten their information from Hofmann. Though investigators assumed they were weighing Hinckley's word against that of several independent witnesses, they were really weighing the church leader's word against Hofmann's.[46]

In response to other questions, Hinckley said he knew of no dealings between Hofmann and general authorities of the church beyond those already mentioned. Mike George later explained that "what we were talking about at that time was other dealings involving Hofmann in regards to documents being sold to members of the First Presidency." When Hinckley said he knew of no others, George did not believe him.[47]

Hinckley answered based on his recollections, supplemented by information provided him by Francis Gibbons and Glenn Rowe. Two pieces of information had eluded the church officials, however, in their attempts to reconstruct Hofmann's dealings with the church. They recalled that the Grandin printing contract had been purchased by the Historical Department using funds provided by the First Presidency. Later research would convince them, however, that the transaction itself was closed in Hinckley's office.

The other elusive item was the Bullock-Young letter. Hofmann had given it free to Hinckley for the church, meaning no financial records had been maintained on the document. In the more than four years that had elapsed since the gift, Hinckley had forgotten about it, assuming his 1981 meeting with Hofmann had dealt with the Joseph Smith III blessing, which was actually acquired by the Historical Department. Later, Gibbons would rediscover the Bullock-Young letter and bring it to Hinckley's attention, but on December 9, 1985, when George and Farnsworth interviewed him, the document had been forgotten.[48]

In response to questioning, Hinckley also said he was not aware that anyone had purchased the Facsimile No. 2 papyrus from the McLellin collection. In fact, church officials had not purchased any papyri, but investigators had heard rumors that they had. Earlier, Hofmann had shown Pinnock the Spalding-Rigdon contract that likewise purported to be from the McLellin collection. When investigators asked Hinckley about it, he could not recall that Pinnock ever showed it to him. The investigators knew when the First Interstate Bank loan had occurred, but they asked Hinckley when Pinnock had told him about it. Hinckley had been in Europe when the loan was made and answered that he could not recall for sure when he had been told. The detectives asked Hinckley if he was aware of any veiled threats made to Hofmann. He was not.[49]

The investigators asked Hinckley if Hofmann had told him the McLellin collection was explosive. Hinckley said he had not. Referring later to this response, George said, "And I've got some problems with that."[50] Yet other evidence tended to support Hinckley's statement. Hinckley had written a file memo to record what Hofmann told him on June 12, 1985, when he first offered to give the McLellin collection to the church. The memorandum noted that the collection contained Facsimile 2, "journals and diaries, some affidavits, and quite a number of things," but mentioned nothing about its being explosive.[51]

Well before the bombings, Hofmann had also mentioned the McLellin collection to Glenn Rowe, who had expressed particular interest in McLellin's journals. "I asked if they contained more information like the 'Salamander' letter," Rowe later recorded. "He said that they were quite tame and didn't contain much new information."[52] Al Rust recalled that in April 1985, he asked Hofmann about the contents of the McLellin collection and learned it contained Facsimile 2, letters from Joseph Smith, and other material. "Now, is this a controversial collection?" he remembered asking Hofmann. "Is it an anti-Mormon collection or anything of this sort?" Rust said Hofmann answered, "No, it isn't."[53]

Still anxious to find a motive for the murders, investigators extrapolated from what Christensen's wife and business partner had told them about his hopes to establish a document business. They assumed that Hinckley and others had met with Christensen to request that he replace Hofmann as an agent for the church to collect documents. In his December 9 interview, Hinckley told them that nothing he ever said should have led Hofmann to believe he was an agent for the church and that Christensen had come to his office only once, which was when he delivered the salamander letter.[54]

Hinckley's answers frustrated Farnsworth and George. Anxious to find a motive for the killings, they had come to the meeting with theories that Hinckley's answers were not confirming. Farnsworth later said he stopped asking questions in the interview because he was "purple" and "wouldn't have said anything nice from that moment on; so Mike George conducted the rest of the interview." "Knows nothing about nothing," George wrote at the bottom of his own notes, venting his own emotions.[55]

The following afternoon, December 10, 1985, Mark Hofmann entered the church Historical Department library, pushed in a wheelchair by his wife, Doralee, and accompanied by Shannon Flynn, whose T-shirt read, "My lawyer can beat up your lawyer." Their appearance caused a stir. The trio said hello to the library staff, though Doralee and Shannon did most of the talking, Mark's hearing still suffering from the bomb explosion. Mark asked Doralee to wheel him over to look at a book or magazine. After staying only five or ten minutes, the group left. During the brief visit, Flynn explained to a staff member that Hofmann was "bedlogged" and needed to get out of the house. Flynn had suggested they visit the library. As the group left the Historical Department, Doralee drolly apologized to a staff member for visiting, saying she hoped the visit had not jeopardized the staff members' jobs.[56]

On the evening of December 11, the Historical Department held its annual Christmas party. At the party, Dallin Oaks had his first opportunity to address the department since being appointed one of its advisers. During his address, he commented on the stress the bombings had created for the department's employees. "Now, these aren't easy times for any of us," he said. "History is hot. So are documents. They are both so hot that the strands of a murder investigation thread through this department. I know that because a strand looped through my office, quite by accident. I am uncomfortable with you. It is not easy to be the object of daily slander and innuendo."

In his talk, Oaks compared and contrasted the Historical Department and other historical institutions. Of the bombing investigation, he said, "We are like others in that we must cooperate fully in an investigation and tell the truth on all matters material to that investigation." But, he added, "we are quite unlike others in that I hope each one of us is praying fervently— as I am praying—that the police will solve these terrible crimes, which vex our community and give our enemies the occasion to slander us on a daily basis."[57]

The following day, December 12, local newspapers reported that Doralee Hofmann had successfully passed a polygraph test, strengthening Mark's alibi that he had been home at the time someone placed the bombs that killed Christensen and Sheets. The test cast additional doubt on the belief that Mark was the murderer. "The evidence police have been strongly relying on in that belief," the *Salt Lake Tribune* reported, "hinges mostly on eyewitness accounts at the Judge Building," where three persons identified Hofmann as being present the morning of the murders. "One of those witnesses, however," the article pointed out, "has been 'tainted' by being exposed to videotape of Mr. Hofmann by a local television station prior to being able to pick him out in either a lineup or a group of photographs, according to police and prosecutors."

Circumstantial evidence connecting Hofmann to the killings included a high school letter jacket found in Hofmann's home that resembled the one seen on the man witnesses saw at the Judge Building. Another witness claimed to have seen a van in the Sheetses' neighborhood a few hours before Kathy Sheets died. The van was similar to one Hofmann drove. Laboratory tests had detected similarities among the bombs but had failed to connect Hofmann to the actual bomb construction.

On balance, the evidence was enough to confirm investigators' suspicions that Hofmann was the killer but not enough to convince a jury of Hofmann's guilt beyond a reasonable doubt. The inevitable consequence of the distinction was more tension between investigators and prosecutors. "Detectives maintain their investigations are almost complete and that both homicide cases against Hofmann are solid," a *Deseret News* story read. "They say prosecutors are dragging their feet in filing criminal charges." The *Tribune* account, while noting detectives' claims of a solid case, explained, "Prosecutors have said that they do not believe, at this point, that police have given them enough evidence on which they could file a murder case."[58]

The next day, December 13, Glenn Rowe worked to collect documents for investigators. On December 16, a Monday, George Throckmorton began moving equipment into a locked conference room furnished for him in the Historical Department. The room would permit examiners to study the documents owned by the church and yet would reduce concerns about the security of the documents that church officials might have had if the documents had been permitted to leave the building.[59]

The next day, Throckmorton returned to the Church Office Building bringing with him William J. Flynn (no relation to Shannon), a document examiner from Arizona who was not of the LDS faith. Earlier, Glenn Rowe had spoken to Throckmorton about who would be examining the documents. Throckmorton, Rowe noted in a letter to Dallin Oaks, "is a member of the Church. He has indicated that they are bringing in at least one, if not more than one, investigator from out of state who is not a member so that their conclusion may not be questioned as biased."[60]

In addition to Throckmorton and Flynn, county attorney's office representatives and church counsel Wilford Kirton also arrived to discuss the procedures that would be followed. In the privacy of their makeshift laboratory, Throckmorton and Flynn then began to examine the documents from the church, as well as some documents brought by Richard Howard, RLDS Church historian, who also arrived that day.[61]

The next day, a Wednesday, Throckmorton and Flynn gave the Josiah Stowell letter back to Rowe, who returned it to the First Presidency's Office, which had lent it to Rowe the previous day so the document examiners could study it. The examiners carried on their work quietly behind closed doors, speaking little to church employees except when they needed documents or information about them.[62]

The examiners returned Thursday and Friday too, continuing their work behind closed doors and saying nothing of their findings to church employees. Friday, Throckmorton and Flynn concluded their preliminary examination. The Historical Department Office Journal recorded the events of the week, noting the forensic specialists' work in examining documents.

It also recorded, "The examiners have withheld any results of their investigation pending a presentation of the findings in court."[63]

Though the examiners did not share their findings with church officials, newspaper accounts soon suggested that the examination had provided additional evidence to the beleaguered investigators. On Sunday, December 22, the *Deseret News* described the past week's examination of documents and added, "Sources in the Salt Lake County attorney's office and the Salt Lake City Police Department confirmed that, in addition to Hofmann being their prime suspect in bombings that killed two people last October, they are considering fraud and/or forgery charges against him."[64]

When the county attorney's office and the church originally entered into a voluntary agreement to allow the church's documents to be examined, prosecutors said that if their examination showed documents would be needed at trial, they would subpoena them. Referring to church counsel Wilford Kirton, Deputy County Attorney Bob Stott later said, "Kirton thought it was best that we subpoena. That made it look, I guess, from his standpoint that the church was cooperating but it wasn't being overly cooperative, you know, to the point that they were trying to . . . help or hurt Mark Hofmann."[65]

On December 27, the county attorney's office prepared subpoenas to be sent to the church requesting delivery of fifty-four documents. The subpoenas would signal to church officials that the examiners' work had paid off and perhaps provided a motive for murder.[66] Later that day, the *Deseret News* printed an article showing that others had received the same signal. "A lawyer for bombing suspect Mark Hofmann," the article began, "said he expects murder charges to be filed against the Mormon document dealer sometime soon after the first of the year."[67]

An account in the next morning's *Salt Lake Tribune,* however, diluted the suggestion. It reported that Salt Lake County Sheriff Pete Hayward, frustrated at the failure to file charges, planned to seek a grand jury investigation of the case. The article also reported that Ted Cannon, the county attorney, did not intend to file charges until after the first of the year, perhaps weeks after. It said that though the county attorney's office was now "pinpointing forgery as well as fraud as a possible motive for the killings," the investigation still had "failed to turn up a single piece of physical evidence actually linking Mr. Hofmann to the construction of the bombs."[68]

On December 30, Cannon wrote Wilford Kirton, thanking him for church authorities' cooperation. Reiterating the terms agreed upon four weeks earlier, the county attorney assured church officials that the documents being subpoenaed would be kept physically safe, that their contents would not be released to anyone, and that only experts would be allowed to examine them.[69]

On the final day of 1985, Pete Hayward made good on his promise and appeared before the fourteen judges of Utah's Third District Court to request that they impanel a grand jury to investigate the bombings. Investigators and prosecutors, who had long been on the hot seat, felt the heat rise even further.[70]

As 1986 began, the Utah media named the bombing case the top local news story of 1985. But the case was far from over. "Although police named Hofmann as the prime suspect in the case, he has been charged only with possession of a machine gun," the *Deseret News* noted. "However, investigation and speculation continue."[71]

On January 2, Wilford Kirton delivered to Glenn Rowe one of the two December 27 subpoenas received from the county attorney's office. The subpoena requested fifty-four documents, most not especially significant, but a few both important and valuable. Among them were irreplaceable documents of unquestioned age and authenticity that the county wished to use for comparison purposes. The request prompted a meeting between Dean Larsen, executive director of the Historical Department, and his department's advisers, Boyd Packer and Dallin Oaks. Rowe recorded in his journal that Oaks expressed concern about the subpoena "because of the value and condition of the documents."[72]

The church was legally entitled to challenge the subpoena if it seemed illegal or unreasonable, and to church officials, the legal justification and reasonableness of the request seemed far from clear. The county attorney's letter of December 30 had not shown with certainty that the fragile documents were yet needed for any kind of trial. In fact, the county had not filed charges against anyone in the case. If investigators wished to continue examining the documents, church officials felt, why not continue with the earlier arrangements under which the documents could both be studied and protected?[73]

As church officials considered whether to challenge the subpoena, Rowe spent January 2 and 3 gathering the requested items together in case they should decide to turn the documents over as requested. On the third, George Throckmorton returned to the Historical Department, where he spoke to Rowe and once again visited the department's conservation laboratory to speak with a conservator. Throckmorton asked questions about the methods the department used to deacidify documents. In the course of the discussion, the conservator lent Throckmorton a spray can of fluid often used in deacidifying documents.[74]

In midafternoon on the third, a meeting was held to discuss the county's request for documents. Present at the meeting were Gordon Hinckley,

Boyd Packer, Dallin Oaks, Dean Larsen, Francis Gibbons, and Wilford Kirton. Recording the gist of the meeting, Oaks wrote, "The County Attorney has subpoenaed 55 documents for preparation of the bombing case, all of which have been examined at the Church Office Bldg by state document examiners, but which they now want in their sole possession. About a dozen of these are irreplaceable documents, like Joseph Smith's first known letter and the so-called Anthon manuscript. Most are trivial documents acquired from Mark Hoffman." The group decided "to resist the subpoena as to the dozen, for reasons of value and fragility, but to produce the rest as requested."[75]

Both subpoenas had ordered the church to turn over the Stowell letter, which investigators had already examined. During the afternoon meeting in Hinckley's office, Gibbons turned the letter over to Larsen. According to a memorandum Gibbons made of the meeting, Larsen was to "make this letter available to the Salt Lake County Attorney in connection with an investigation he is conducting into the recent bombing deaths."[76]

The same day, the *Salt Lake Tribune* published an article reporting the results of additional attempts by the newspaper to locate the McLellin collection. The newspaper's earlier discovery in Texas turned out to be less than scholars had hoped, and the whereabouts of McLellin's journals and other papers remained a mystery. The newspaper began contacting other McLellin descendants in hopes of finding the materials, but the article reported that none knew of any extant documents. One said that whatever documents had remained probably burned during a house fire earlier in the century.

The article also cast doubt on Hofmann's assertion that the collection contained the Facsimile No. 2 papyrus. Relying on information furnished by a Brigham Young University professor, the paper reported that neither Joseph Smith nor William McLellin ever mentioned McLellin's having the papyrus and that other historical evidence showed Smith had it long after the date on which others had assumed McLellin might have stolen it.[77]

On Monday, January 6, 1986, church and county officials met in Dean Larsen's office to discuss the subpoenas that had been issued for church documents. Ted Cannon, Bob Stott, and George Throckmorton attended from the county attorney's office. Representing the church were Oaks, Larsen, Rowe, Kirton, and Earl Olson. The meeting resulted in a compromise. Church officials agreed to turn over all but five of the requested items to the county. The remaining five items would be delivered to and picked up from the state crime lab by a Historical Department employee each day they were needed and returned to the Historical Department vault each evening for safekeeping.[78]

The five were the Anthon transcript, the Stowell letter, Joseph Smith's
first letter book, his diary for 1835 to 1836, and a group of four handwritten
white notes. The Anthon transcript and Stowell letter were considered the
two oldest known Mormon manuscripts. The white notes were extremely
rare and valuable from a numismatic standpoint. The Smith letter book
and diary, two items of unquestioned authenticity, had been in the church's
possession for a century and a half and were considered among the most
priceless of church documents. The letter book contained Joseph Smith's
1832 history, which included the earliest account of Joseph Smith's First
Vision (the only one in the church founder's own hand). The diary contained
the second earliest account of the vision. Both volumes were in fragile
condition.[79]

Church and county officials agreed to earmark the five items for special
handling "because they were very old and fragile, but more importantly,
irreplaceable as potentially important documents of Church history." Thus,
church officials wished to retain custody while permitting investigators to
study the documents. Even so, they agreed to relinquish custody if ultimately required to do so by the county attorney's office or a court.[80] County
officials said they expected to conclude their evaluation of all the documents
in about two weeks, but they did not discuss the conclusions to which their
studies were leading. The Historical Department Office Journal recorded,
"No indication has been received from the forensic examiners as to whether
some of these materials are forgeries."[81]

Also during the meeting, Ted Cannon asked if the church had made
public all of the documents it had received from Hofmann. Larsen responded
that to the best of his knowledge, it had. Cannon then asked if the church
could be certain no other documents had been planted in its collections.
He said Hofmann's attorneys might try to assert in court that the church
had acquired pieces of the McLellin collection and was sequestering them.[82]

Glenn Rowe spent much of the rest of the day gathering materials to
turn over to the county. The county's request was not the only one oc-
cupying his attention. An FBI representative also called that day and asked
if the church owned a document with a Palmyra, New York, postmark that
had not come through Mark Hofmann. The salamander letter, which the
FBI was still examining, bore a Palmyra postmark, and the FBI apparently
needed another one for comparison. Rowe was unable to find one for the
period the FBI wanted.[83]

The following day, January 7, Rowe also spent "working on things for
the SL Co. Attorney and the FBI." At 9:00 A.M., Rowe and two other
department administrators met with their executive director, Dean Larsen,
in a routine administration meeting. The minutes of the meeting noted the
request from the FBI that Rowe had received the previous day. "The county

attorney," the minutes added, "has also requested permission to use the Thomas Bullock document that was loaned to the RLDS Church in their verification of the Joseph Smith, III blessing. This was a copy of Thomas Bullock's patriarchal blessing written with his own hand. It was agreed that this may be used by the county attorney."

Also, according to the minutes of the meeting, "Elder Larsen indicated he will meet with key people of the Historical Department and take whatever steps are necessary to help identify all materials which have been received from Mark Hofmann. The key people will be counseled to be aware of any materials that might be planted in the Historical Department by Mark Hofmann or his associates, and that they should be aware of anything which Hofmann might leave or give to any Historical Department employee."[84]

Newspaper accounts that day showed that a gulf remained between police detectives and county prosecutors. The *Deseret News* quoted Bud Willoughby as saying that police had gone as far as they could in the case, that it was "absolutely winnable," and that the county attorney's office now had to decide whether or not to file charges in the case.[85]

Ted Cannon responded, "This whole thing will bear fruit or not fairly soon." He said his staff members were divided in their approach to the case. Some felt investigators had gathered enough evidence to get the case through a preliminary hearing. They were willing to file charges, trusting that other evidence would roll in between the preliminary hearing and the trial. Others wanted to be sure they were completely ready for trial before filing charges.[86]

On January 8, detective Mike George of the county attorney's office visited Glenn Rowe to ask questions. The county also sent Rowe a subpoena requesting six more documents, including the Bible in which the Anthon transcript had reportedly been discovered and several Thomas Bullock items that were apparently needed for handwriting comparisons. With all the other demands the case imposed on him, Rowe wrote in his journal, "It is a full-time job keeping up on this whole affair."[87]

Also on January 8, Francis Gibbons transferred to Dean Larsen the original and a typescript of the Bullock-Young letter, which Gibbons had rediscovered. "The original letter," Gibbons explained in a memorandum, "and the typescript were given to the Church by Mark W. Hofmann on September 4, 1981. There was no consideration given for the letter or the typescript." Earlier searches for Hofmann documents in the First Presidency's possession had relied on entries in the indexed minutes of the First Presidency and Quorum of the Twelve. Because the Bullock-Young letter was never mentioned in the minutes, it was overlooked until Gibbons happened across it.[88]

The rediscovery of the letter put church officials in an awkward position. Because the letter had been forgotten, it had not been mentioned in the church's news conference or in previous interviews with investigators. Undoubtedly, its discovery would subject church officials to ridicule. Despite the likelihood of criticism, however, Hinckley directed Gibbons to turn the letter over to investigators. In his memorandum to Larsen, Francis Gibbons wrote, "The brethren understand you will make this letter available to the Salt Lake County Attorney under a subpoena which has been served on the Church to produce all documents in its possession received from Mark W. Hofmann, and in accordance with procedures which have been worked out between the Church General Counsel and the County Attorney."[89]

On January 6, 1986, Glenn Rowe had handed Dallin Oaks an eighteen-page list of legal documents from Hancock County, Illinois, asking him to review them to see if he recognized any of them as documents he had used a decade earlier when doing research in Hancock County for a book he had coauthored. In their continuing search for documents that might have come from Hofmann, employees of the Historical Department had discovered some items from Hofmann in a group of uncatalogued legal documents that had been growing in size over the years.

For decades, such legal documents had been offered for sale by manuscript dealers. After circulating among dealers and collectors, some had ended up at the Historical Department. Some church archivists examining the documents began to wonder if the items had been properly obtained from the local courthouses or other repositories where they had apparently originated. Harboring doubts, the archivist in charge of assigning manuscript collections for cataloguing began in the late 1970s to set aside such documents in an uncatalogued collection pending the day when the ownership questions could be resolved. When the search for Hofmann documents led to this collection, archivists decided the time had come to raise the issue.[90]

On January 8, Oaks wrote a memorandum to Rowe about the legal documents. He listed those he remembered using during his Hancock County research. "Many of the papers," he wrote, "have probably been stolen from the office of the clerk of the circuit court in Carthage, Illinois. I say 'probably' because I do not think it is the practice of the custodians of official records to give away such papers or to sell them on the common market." Oaks said that the "obvious question" raised by the documents was "whether the Church can legitimately purchase papers that it knows to have been stolen." He argued against acquiring such materials in the future. "As long as we are involved in purchasing records that are known to have been stolen," he wrote, "don't we create an incentive for further thefts and make such wrongs profitable?" He suggested the matter be taken up at a future meeting of the Historical Department advisers.[91]

For the next several days, church employees carried materials to and from the state crime lab as earlier agreed, working through the weekend to meet the needs of examiners. On Saturday, January 11, a *Salt Lake Tribune* editorial noted the tension between investigators and prosecutors in the case. "If the evidence is so strong, why aren't murder charges filed?" the editorial asked rhetorically. "It isn't unusual for police to be more persuaded by signs of guilt than prosecuting attorneys. The county attorney's office claims just such a difference of opinion exists. And Mr. Cannon is obliged to hesitate as long as his prosecutors tell him they haven't enough evidence to make murder charges stick." Admittedly, the county attorney could bow to pressure and order his staff to file charges, it said, but then he would merely be "indulging politics."[92] Early the next week, however, newspapers began to report that charges would be filed soon, perhaps by the end of the week.[93]

On Tuesday, January 14, the county requested several more documents and a seal from the church. Most of the items did not come to the church through Hofmann but were apparently intended for use as exemplars in doing comparisons with documents that had passed through the dealer's hands. The church also continued to shuttle documents to the state crime lab. Even if investigators were ready to file charges, as the newspapers had suggested, they obviously were not finished with their investigation.[94]

On Wednesday, January 15, church spokesman Jerry Cahill wrote a memorandum to his supervisor, Richard Lindsay, summarizing the press reports and media inquiries about church historical documents in recent months. In the memo, Cahill pointed out that the October 23 news conference had informed the public that the church acquired some forty items from Hofmann. To date, however, only four had been publicly identified. Cahill implied that public speculation would continue until more information about the acquired items was released. Cahill's memorandum set in motion efforts by church officials to make a list of the documents public.[95]

Writing in his journal, Glenn Rowe described the day as one he "would prefer to not remember." Dallin Oaks had wanted to release a list of the forty-odd documents to the media. Rowe expressed concern about the original list of documents. When he prepared the list, he had explained it might not be complete and that further searching might turn up more documents. After he had passed on the list, his staff had in fact discovered additional legal documents from Hofmann. "In fact," Rowe wrote in his journal, "by mistake an additional box was found this day. Then all heck broke loose and we are accused of incompetence because we couldn't find all documents from Mark Hofmann, and cannot swear that we are now positive we have them all. Elder Oaks, Bro. Kirton and Earl [Olson] seemed quite unhappy. I was at the end of my rope."[96]

Besides trying to prepare a list of Hofmann documents, Rowe also began preparing a list of the church's cash transactions with Hofmann. The list would ultimately be helpful in dispelling exaggerated accounts of how much money the church had paid Hofmann for documents over the years.[97]

The following day, January 16, archivists located further Hofmann documents in the Historical Department's collections. One archivist noted in his journal, "We spent most of the morning poring over acquisition forms looking for those bearing the donor's name as Mark W. Hofmann. That procedure netted some previously undetected documents that Mr. Throckmorton wanted to see." Glenn Rowe recorded, "We continued to search [for] materials. We finally feel quite comfortable that we have located all material from Mark Hofmann." Also that day, Rowe received a telephone call from a television reporter who asked if he knew when the FBI intended to return the materials the church had lent.[98]

Describing the day in his journal, Oaks recorded that he was working with the Historical Department and the Public Communications Department on a press release about the documents the church received from Hofmann. The release, he wrote, was intended "to counteract the public inuendo that the church has acquired some damaging documents and suppressed them." Regarding the bombing case, he wrote, "Still no charges filed, but the prosecutor is making noises like he will do so in the next few days."[99]

Meanwhile, public pressure to file charges in the case increased. An article in the morning's *Salt Lake Tribune* reiterated that prosecutors differed in their opinions of the strength of the case, and that the police were still working on the motive for the killings. "Without physical evidence to tie the bombs directly to Mr. Hofmann—and apparently there is none—motive and opportunity will be paramount to any case presented in court," the article said. That evening, the *Deseret News* printed an article in which Shannon Flynn was quoted as saying he thought investigators' interest in LDS documents was irrelevant to the killings and, in his words, "an exercise in futility."[100]

On Friday morning, January 17, the FBI finally returned to the church the salamander letter, *The Book of Common Prayer*, the Grandin contract, and two comparison documents it had borrowed. The agents who returned the documents offered no explanation of what they had learned from their examination or why it had taken them so long. Salt Lake City police officers Ken Farnsworth and Jim Bell also visited the Historical Department, and the FBI agents, police detectives, and church officials sat down together to complete paperwork immediately transferring possession of the returned documents to local investigators for their examination.[101]

A church security officer visited with Dean Larsen, executive director of the Historical Department, about the items returned by the FBI and picked up by local investigators. Reporting to his supervisor about the visit, the officer wrote, "Elder Larsen . . . said he inquired of the F.B.I. representatives as to their findings concerning these documents. He was told by the F.B.I. that a report of findings would be submitted to the Salt Lake County Attorney's Office and that the Church would only be able to find out what these findings are during the course of the Mark Hofmann trial.

"Elder Larsen also told me," the officer continued, "that of the 40 documents having already been placed in the hands of the Salt Lake County Attorney's Office by the Church, that 10 were still in their possession. Elder Larsen also told me that from the jist of the conversations between the F.B.I. and County Attorney representatives he felt the subpoenaed documents and those still being held by the County Attorney's Office were fraudulant, but had no proof of this."[102]

Also on January 17, a church archivist once again carried documents to the state crime lab and waited while investigators conducted their examination. When evening came, the examiners had not finished studying the materials. Dean Larsen authorized leaving the documents at the lab over the weekend without bringing them back to the vault each night as earlier agreed.[103]

Also that day, Oaks met with Hinckley to discuss the church's earlier proposed news release. As Oaks took notes, Hinckley recounted the meetings he remembered having with Hofmann. Every detail Hinckley recalled had already been given to investigators. Oaks asked about rumors alleging that Hinckley had purchased the McLellin collection and Kinderhook plates (or at least a translation of them) from Hofmann. "No substance," Oaks recorded in his notes.[104]

The weekend came and went, and on Monday, January 20, Glenn Rowe went to the state crime lab to retrieve the documents left the previous Friday. When he got there, he was told he had to leave several of the most valuable items for "chain of evidence" reasons. The retained documents were apparently ones the prosecutors would use in court, where they would be required to trace their custody of the documents from the time they first entered their possession. Returning to church headquarters, Rowe went into a meeting with Gordon Hinckley, Dallin Oaks, and Richard Lindsay to discuss the content of the proposed news release about documents acquired by the church from Hofmann. By the end of the meeting, they had still not decided to issue it.[105]

On Tuesday, January 21, Hinckley, Oaks, Lindsay, Rowe, Dean Larsen, and Wilford Kirton all met to discuss the release again. They agreed it should not be issued because it would create more questions than it would answer, because it might unduly influence the bombing investigation, and because it might make it appear the church had chosen sides against Hofmann in the case. "I was quite relieved," Rowe wrote in his journal. After being chastised earlier for being unable to locate all the documents his department had acquired from Hofmann, Rowe was hesitant to release any lists purporting to be definitive. "The time has been well spent anyway," Oaks recorded. "We now have reliable information to issue later, as needed."[106]

The next day, Rowe inventoried the materials being retained by the investigators. He also met with county detective Mike George to answer questions. They discussed the Grandin contract, as well as the Bullock-Young, salamander, and Stowell letters. Describing the interview in his journal, Rowe wrote that George "seemed quite pleased that we have been so helpful and cooperative. We also have been manipulated by a few who have attempted to alter history[,] he said."[107]

That same afternoon, Boyd Packer, Dallin Oaks, Dean Larsen, and Earl Olson met in their regular monthly meeting to discuss Historical Department matters. Richard E. Turley, Jr., a young Salt Lake attorney, was also present in the meeting. Turley, a life long student of church history, had recently been appointed to replace Olson, who was scheduled to retire a few weeks later after fifty-two years of church service. In the meeting, several items were discussed, one of which was the legal documents the church had acquired from Hofmann. According to the minutes of the meeting, "Elder Oaks pointed out that there are two boxes of legal documents which are being held in the Historical Department temporarily with no finalization of their disposal, and the question was raised as to whether legal title of these can be procured if there was a possibility that they were stolen from the appropriate legal custodian." The group decided the issue merited further attention.[108]

On Thursday, January 23, all but thirteen of the documents from the state crime lab were returned to the church. The next day, Hinckley, Oaks, and Kirton met to discuss a request from the county attorney's office to have investigators carry the retained documents to eastern experts for examination. On January 27, Packer and Oaks, the Historical Department's advisers, wrote to the First Presidency about the request, recommending that a church security officer accompany the detectives who were to take the documents east. They offered this recommendation despite the "legitimate concern that the public perception could be that the Church is taking one side or another in this investigation." Though they had sought to avoid such perceptions, protecting the irreplaceable documents was paramount, and in the long run, they felt, the public would understand the church's position.[109]

Late the following afternoon, January 28, after Packer and Oaks had delivered their letter to the First Presidency, they returned a telephone call from Kirton. To their dismay, Kirton told the two church leaders that he had been informed the documents had already been taken to New York. Reporting this new information to Hinckley, Packer wrote, "We will discuss the implications of this after you have had a chance to consider the letters. The principles outlined in the letter still seem valid to us."[110]

At 8:50 A.M. on Friday, January 31, Deputy County Attorneys Bob Stott and David Biggs, together with Detective Ken Farnsworth, visited Hugh Pinnock, who was joined by church counsel Oscar McConkie. The prosecutors and detective interviewed the church leader until midafternoon about his association with Christensen and Hofmann.[111]

At the beginning of the interview, they told Pinnock they planned to call him as a witness when they tried Hofmann. They said they thought the McLellin collection would play a key role in the case, and they anticipated that Hofmann would raise two defenses. The first was that the church had acquired materials it was holding back. The second was that the church and the county attorney's office were in collusion. They said they wanted to review Pinnock's testimony with him, retracing all the ground they had covered in earlier interviews. Consequently, Pinnock once again began a chronological recitation of his association with Hofmann and Christensen, leading up to the mid-October bombings.[112]

Pinnock again went over his journal entries, supplementing them with recollections. As he spoke, his visitors interrupted to ask questions and add occasional insights from their investigation. When Pinnock described the Spalding-Rigdon document that Hofmann allowed him to copy the previous July 14, his visitors said the document was originally dated 1792 and then altered to 1822. Also, they said, the Spalding who purportedly signed the document died in 1816, making it impossible for him to have signed it six years later. Furthermore, they said, he preferred spelling his name "Spaulding."[113]

Later in the interview, they told Pinnock that Hofmann spent the First Interstate loan money the day he borrowed it, and not on the McLellin collection. They said he gave $125,000 of the amount to Al Rust and $60,000 to another creditor. Pinnock had remained uncertain about whether the collection really existed. This new information convinced him it did not. After the interview, he would write in his journal, "I learned in this meeting that Hofmann used the $185,000 that he got on 6–28–85 to pay off Rust & someone else—no McLellin collection."[114]

During the interview, Pinnock again told investigators about the papyrus photographs Christensen had turned over to him on October 7, 1985. After their interview with Pinnock, the investigators would finally visit Glenn Rowe in the Historical Department to see the photographs. But the main purpose for their interview had not yet been accomplished.[115]

"Motive for murder?" wrote Oscar McConkie at the end of his notes from the meeting. The motive for the bombings continued to elude investigators, and as the lengthy interview drew to a close, they converged on motive, hoping once again that Pinnock would back their theory: that the pressure he had exerted on Hofmann through Christensen prompted the document dealer to murder.[116]

Pinnock, however, remained unconvinced.[117]

Though satisfied with much of what they had been told, Stott, Biggs, and Farnsworth left the interview frustrated that Pinnock would not support their theory.[118]

In trying to persuade Pinnock that he and Christensen had pressured Hofmann to murder, the three law enforcement officials had exerted considerable pressure of their own on the church leader. Writing in his journal later, Pinnock described the meeting as "the most uncomfortable experience I have had for a long period."[119]

11

The Malefactor Charged

On the morning of February 4, 1986, Salt Lake City police informed Martell Bird that Mark Hofmann had been arrested and twenty-eight criminal counts filed against him. Grouped into four cases, the charges included two capital murder counts for the deaths of Steve Christensen and Kathy Sheets, three "infernal machine" counts for the bombings, thirteen counts of theft by deception, and ten counts of communications fraud. Bird recorded in his journal that police told him Throckmorton had found the salamander letter to be a forgery. "I suppose from the local findings," he continued, that "all the documents examined which the Church acquired from Hofmann are fraudulent! I wonder how that will compare with the findings of the FBI laboratory wh[ich] previously examined some of the same documents that Throckmorton has examined and [from which he has] drawn his 'state of the art' conclusions?"[1]

At noon, a local news program included an interview with Bud Willoughby, who was asked about earlier statements police had made regarding prosecutors' delay in filing charges. Willoughby said hindsight had convinced him the case was complex and that prosecutors were right in emphasizing the need to prepare the case adequately for trial. "In order to do that," he said, "we've got to have all the information we possibly can." "So, you know," he said, "I'm not going to throw any stones at a glass house, because I live in a glass house, and I think if there's any criticism we've got to take it on the chin like anyone else. But I do think we did our job, and we did it professionally. And I think that now it's in the hands of the County Attorney's Office and the courts, and I have full confidence that it will come out the right way."[2]

The information filed in one of the four cases against Hofmann repeatedly listed the church as a victim of theft by deception. One count, however, named Gordon Hinckley as the victim in a transaction that occurred "on or about January 11, 1983." To church officials, it was apparent the count

Foreground: Defense attorney Ronald J. Yengich (*left*) and Deputy County Attorneys Robert L. Stott (*center*) and David L. Biggs (*right*) arrive for arraignment, February 4, 1986. (Ravell Call/*Deseret News*)

pertained to Hofmann's sale of the Josiah Stowell letter. Before the bombings, George Smith and others had inaccurately surmised that Hinckley bought the letter with his own funds, when in fact he had bought it for the church using a church-issued check drawn on a church bank account. This error led them to accuse Hinckley of purchasing the letter privately so he could deny the church had bought it.[3]

By naming Hinckley as a private victim rather than as an agent for the church, prosecutors perpetuated the earlier errors and their uncomplimentary implications. Reporters scouring the publicly available documents filed in the case immediately observed and reported that the church and Hinckley had been listed separately as victims. They would continue to note the distinction over the next several days.[4]

That evening, the *Deseret News* carried a lengthy article on the charges against Hofmann. "At the crux of the police investigation," the article explained, "is the investigators' determined belief that Hofmann has been dealing in forged or altered documents. In fact investigators claim to have recovered evidence that irrefutably confirms Hofmann was perpetrating sophisticated forgeries and frauds." "Still," the article noted, "most of the evidence against Hofmann is circumstantial, and even police admit there are some puzzling problems with their case." Hofmann, his wife, and associates had all passed polygraph tests, and though tests confirmed a similarity in the bombs, "anticipated evidentiary breakthroughs directly linking Hofmann to those bombs never materialized."[5]

Following the filing of charges, church officials who were asked for public comment explained in simple terms that they could not discuss the matter. "The investigation and prosecution of these matters are in the hands of the appropriate legal authorities," Richard Lindsay explained. "Further comment by us would be inappropriate."[6]

Church officials also tried to maintain an open mind about Hofmann's guilt or innocence. The charges made it clear that investigators felt some Hofmann documents were forged. Yet investigators had kept most of their evidence to themselves, and nationally known document experts had previously declared some of the items authentic. With experts disagreeing on the genuineness of the documents, church officials felt it prudent to protect them as though they were irreplaceable remnants of the past. Thus, they worried about the county's decision to take the documents out of state in apparent violation of their earlier agreement, and they consulted with church counsel Wilford Kirton on how best to register a complaint. Kirton voiced church officials' concerns to Ted Cannon, who told him the dual-custody agreement was off and that the county now considered itself to have sole custody of the documents.

Kirton responded to Cannon in writing, reviewing the circumstances leading to the joint-custody arrangements and reiterating the church officials' concerns about the safekeeping of its documents. "Without disputing your prosecutor's rights in the documents," Kirton wrote, "we are deeply concerned that you ignore the Church's rights to protect the integrity of its property. The Church has tried in every way to cooperate with representatives of your office in completing your investigation. It is very disappointed that the arrangements we made in good faith with your office have not been honored." He requested that the county continue to honor the earlier agreement.[7]

On Wednesday, February 5, Utah Fifth Circuit Court Judge Paul G. Grant ordered the release of prosecutors' probable cause statements, which gave reasons why the charges against Hofmann were filed. The probable cause statement describing Hofmann's alleged theft by deception from the church named several documents obtained from Hofmann between 1980 and 1985, explaining that all of them had been made available to George Throckmorton, who had "done extensive scientific analysis on all of the documents . . . and ha[d] concluded that none are authentic."[8]

The next day, newspapers reviewed the probable cause statements, focusing on Throckmorton's conclusions of forgery. A *Salt Lake Tribune* article described the Stowell letter purchase and again drew unsavory conclusions from it. "Early press releases from the church said the LDS Church purchased the letter," the article reported. "However President Hinckley is named in the complaint as a separate victim apart from the church, indicating he apparently used personal funds despite the earlier statements."9

Around 3:30 that afternoon, Martell Bird received a call to meet with Hinckley, who had spent time earlier that day in his regular Thursday temple meetings with other church leaders. Describing his visit with Hinckley, Bird wrote, "President Hinckley had a long meeting in the temple and some discussion about the 'private victim' label afforded President Hinckley . . . in today's paper. He was very upset." Bud Willoughby had tried phoning Hinckley earlier in the day when the church leader was in the temple and thus unavailable. Bird later recorded that he and Hinckley "both felt it would be best if President Hinckley doesn't talk with Willoughby in view of the recent developments in the Mark W. Hofmann case."

Instead, Bird, who had not been named in the documents charging Hofmann, volunteered to return the call. He located the police chief at his home. "Bud said he called President Hinckley just to ask 'how is he doing!' " Bird wrote of their conversation. "I said he is fine and if I could help in any way I would be pleased to do so." Bird then told Willoughby that the two investigators who had interviewed Hinckley "had misunderstood and that one count of the information was faulty when it listed President Hinckley as a 'private victim' of Hofmann." Willoughby said he would have the investigators call Bird to discuss the matter.10

Meanwhile, church officials learned more about the investigators' case as they listened to radio and television broadcasts and read the newspapers. Dallin Oaks, who viewed the case with his extensive legal background, began to wonder about the adequacy of the murder case against Hofmann and about whether, even at this late date, the prosecution had filed its charges prematurely. "I hope the prosecution has more evidence on the murder charges than the newspaper speculation has hinted," he confided in his journal.11

Some media reports also cast doubt on the adequacy of the fraud charges, which were tied to accusations of forgery. "There are conflicting reports tonight about the authenticity of the so-called Salamander Letter," one television station reported. "The F.B.I. apparently has reported that there is no evidence that it's a fake. But a local authenticator, George Throckmorton, . . . has concluded otherwise on the basis of some kind of new test unknown to experts in the rest of the country."12

The FBI had compared the salamander letter and Grandin contract with documents of undisputed origin and had concluded that the inks on both were "consistent with an 'Iron Gall' type . . . which was common in the 1800s." The report, however, added a caveat: "It should be noted that the chemical and instrumental analyses of the inks on the submitted documents only shows that these inks are similar to inks used in the questioned time period. No information was developed as to when the inks were actually applied to these documents." The conclusion based on ink analysis, there-fore, was that "there is no evidence to suggest that these documents were prepared at a time other than their reported dates."

The postmark on the salamander letter was found to be so "indistinct" that "a definite conclusion was not reached [on] whether the . . . postmark was or was not made with the same device used to produce" the genuine samples.

The FBI also evaluated the Martin Harris handwriting on the salamander letter and the Harris signature on the Grandin contract. "These writings appear to have been normally written," the report explained, "and no evidence was observed which would indicate forgery or an attempt to copy or simulate the writing of another." The writing was also compared with other purported samples of Harris's rare handwriting. "Although lack of sufficient known signatures and writing prevented a definite conclusion," the report observed, "similarities were observed which indicate these writ-ings were probably written by the same person."[13]

Other information, however, began to emerge supporting local investi-gators' claims of forgery. "Much more information is coming up on the Hofmann trials," Glenn Rowe wrote in his journal. "Kenneth Rendell says the documents are, many of them, obvious forgeries."[14] Rendell said he had examined several documents shown to him by investigators and had concluded that all but the salamander letter were clearly forgeries. Of the salamander letter, which he had earlier helped to evaluate, he said, "There's nothing to show it was forged—but that is not to say it is real."[15]

Besides questioning the adequacy of the murder evidence, Dallin Oaks also wrote in his journal about the media's portrayal of the church's in-volvement in the case. "The inference in the newspapers," he wrote, "is that the Church was victimized to the extent of perhaps $500,000. I wish we had issued that press release so the true, nominal, figure would be public knowledge, along with the contents of several documents not yet released, which sound sinister and are actually quite benign."[16]

The next day, February 7, Martell Bird received a telephone call from a captain in the Salt Lake City Police Department. "I explained my con-cerns," Bird recorded, "that President Hinckley had been listed as a 'pri-vate victim' in the Mark W. Hofmann matter—which is not true[—]and that if called as a witness President Hinckley would testify to the contrary which would make the investigating officers look foolish and could have a material effect on the case." The captain said he would discuss the matter with officer Ken Farnsworth and then call him back.[17]

When Hofmann was charged, attorneys requested he be held without bail on the capital murder counts. Friday, February 7, marked the last day of a hearing to decide if Hofmann should be released on bail. The hearing gave the public another opportunity to view some of the evidence investigators had gathered. It also gave them a chance to hear Hofmann's attorney Ronald Yengich denigrate the case as "circumstantial . . . at best." Ultimately, the judge decided to release Hofmann on $250,000 bail. He then scheduled the next round of legal proceedings, the preliminary hearing, to begin April 14.[18]

On Monday, February 10, Martell Bird phoned Wilford Kirton and talked to him for an hour about the Hofmann case and investigators' erroneous description of Gordon Hinckley as a private victim. Kirton told Bird that Hinckley had called him in Baltimore the previous Friday to discuss the matter. Kirton said that after talking to Hinckley, he had called Ted Cannon and suggested he do something to correct the mistake. Kirton said, however, that Cannon seemed unwilling to do anything about the error and told him to have the church's Public Communications Department issue a statement instead.

Later Monday, Hinckley telephoned Bird to ask his opinion. "President Hinckley called me," Bird wrote, and "wanted my feelings about his writing Ted Cannon to deny being a 'private victim' of Hofmann and get the record straight. I told President Hinckley I agreed[;] however, I felt he should get Bill Kirton's thoughts or better still have Bill Kirton write such a letter. He agreed."[19]

Kirton wrote to Cannon later that day, again pointing out the error and explaining, "If President Hinckley were required to testify at a trial of this matter, he would contradict this allegation." Kirton reiterated that "President Hinckley never at any time in conversation with Mr. Hoffman purported to acquire any document for himself nor did he intend to acquire any of the presently questioned documents for himself. His negotiations with Mr. Hoffman were in his representative capacity, acting for and in behalf of the Church. We are at a loss to understand how the investigators who have spoken with President Hinckley could have reached the conclusion set forth."[20]

On February 13, Cannon wrote to Kirton. He said he reviewed the information used in filing the disputed count and found it ambiguous on whether Hinckley was acting individually or as an agent of the church. Cannon said he then talked to a detective who had interviewed Hinckley.

Although he had not recorded it in his notes, the detective recalled that Hinckley had implied he was acting for the church when he bought the Stowell letter. Cannon said this new information convinced him that the prosecutors would have done better to name the church as the victim instead of Hinckley. He apologized for the trouble the mistake caused and said he expected to correct the error "in due course."[21]

Because of word-processing problems and a change in secretaries, Cannon did not send the letter until several days later after he had drafted another one to Kirton. The second letter, dated February 18, responded to Kirton's letter of February 4 regarding custody of the church's documents. Cannon acknowledged that his office had entered into a joint custody agreement with church officials. But he felt the agreement was unusual because no other institution or collector had asked for a similar arrangement, even though they too had concerns about their documents, and because he could have demanded sole custody of the documents through the subpoena power granted by statute to county attorneys. He admitted the church could have resisted the subpoena, but he did not think doing so would have benefited it or investigators.[22]

Cannon said there was nothing wrong with the joint custody arrangement when it was made, but that the pace of the investigation had picked up after the preliminary analysis, requiring that the documents be transported out of Utah. Cannon recalled having assured Kirton that the documents would be treated as if they were real, even though investigators suspected they were not. He remembered Kirton telling him that a member of the First Presidency had reluctantly consented to the arrangements. Thus, Cannon said he was surprised when Kirton protested the move.

He assured Kirton that investigators shared the church's interest in protecting the documents from being changed, switched, or destroyed. Cannon also said his team and church officials had a common interest in preventing charges of collaboration or inappropriate influence in the case. Cannon reminded Kirton that he had offered to meet personally with church officials to assuage their fears, even though some persons might then unjustly accuse him and his office of colluding with the church, a charge that was already being rumored and that he expected Hofmann's attorneys to use to divert attention away from their client.

Church officials had declined his offer, however, and given the conjectures of collaboration, Cannon said they had made the right decision. Still, he felt such a meeting might have prevented the misunderstandings that had arisen. Cannon said he had spoken to some of his staff about the church's concern that someone might try to alter or switch the documents. The prosecutors felt confident someone would make such a claim with the suggestion that it was the church that had switched or changed them. Such accusations were more likely to be made, he wrote, if the county were to continue returning the documents each day as originally agreed. Thus, county officials had decided to enforce the provision of their earlier agreement that allowed them to take full custody of the documents if ultimately necessary.[23]

About the time Cannon sent his letters, the relationship between investigators and church officials became even more formal as church officials began exercising extreme caution to avoid any familiarity with investigators that might be interpreted as undue influence. On February 18, someone from the county attorney's office called Glenn Rowe to request a list of everything Hofmann and two of his associates had used over the past five years. Rowe asked for a subpoena. When Mike George delivered one the next day, the county's request had expanded to "any records, check out slips, logs, cards, or other documentation of visits to the LDS Church Historical Archives and the documents, books, catalogs, letters, information, etc" that Hofmann and five others had used since 1975. Rowe was given until February 28 to comply. He began compiling lists of some of the requested material but was instructed by his supervisors that thereafter all information provided to law enforcement agencies was to be funneled through the Historical Department's advisers, Boyd Packer and Dallin Oaks.[24]

The next day, February 20, a county investigator delivered a subpoena to the church's Missionary Department asking for missionary records pertaining to Hofmann and one of his associates. At the direction of Packer and Oaks, the department gathered the records together and forwarded them to church counsel Wilford Kirton, asking him to review them and send them to the county attorney's office before the February 28 deadline specified in the subpoena.[25]

Unlike many old historical records, library circulation records and missionary records dealt with living individuals and thus raised issues of privacy that were hot topics among legal scholars, librarians, and archivists across the United States.[26] Church officials felt a responsibility to comply with the subpoenas while at the same time fulfilling their legal and ethical responsibility to safeguard the privacy of living individuals. Thus, in responding to requests for information, officials sometimes removed or masked information not specifically required by the investigators. When Kirton received the missionary records, he reviewed them and eliminated portions not required by the subpoena. As a result, investigators received the information they needed for their investigation, but the integrity of the records was preserved to the maximum extent possible. On February 27, Kirton sent the screened materials on to the county.[27]

Responding to the February 19 subpoena, Glenn Rowe and his staff had prepared a typed list of materials used in the Historical Department by Hofmann and others. The list alone was ninety-nine typed pages long but did not satisfy investigators. On February 27, Rowe recorded in his journal that the county attorney's office called him and "now wants copies of everything Mark H. used or to see and read it all." In line with his earlier instructions, Rowe told the caller to put his request in writing and to submit it to the church's legal counsel.[28]

The next morning, Dallin Oaks telephoned Rowe for more information about the request in anticipation of a formal demand from the county through church counsel. Rowe described the burden the request imposed on the Historical Department and the risks it posed to the 261 books and manuscripts involved. Oaks, in turn, wrote to Thomas Monson of the First Presidency about the request. "It would be a very large burden and risk for the Church to produce 261 books and manuscripts, or to copy them," Oaks observed. He also doubted that investigators really needed all they were seeking. He recommended that the church go to court to resist the subpoena, even though "our differences with the County Attorney would then become public." After drafting the letter, Oaks received a telephone call from his fellow Historical Department adviser, Boyd Packer, who was on church business in Florida with Gordon Hinckley. Hinckley and Packer both backed Oaks's recommendation.[29]

That evening, Oaks recorded in his journal, "Today I worked on . . . the County Attorney's request for more documents to use in prosecuting Hoffman. The Church must be cooperative, but it cannot be a joint participant in the prosecution. It is a fine line to walk."[30]

March 1986 brought a startling discovery. Historical Department personnel seeking information about William McLellin had contacted Dean Jessee. Though Jessee was no longer employed by the Historical Department, he remained an unrivaled expert on some of its holdings. Jessee visited the department and explained to Glenn Rowe that he had found some interesting information about McLellin in his research files. Jessee's notes referred to correspondence in the department's uncatalogued Joseph F. Smith collection. The correspondence mentioned McLellin's diaries and other belongings. Following Jessee's lead, Rowe and his staff searched the collection and located letters that amazed church officials.[31]

The first letter had been written by J. L. Traughber of Doucette, Texas, the father of the man located by the *Salt Lake Tribune* the previous November. Dated January 13, 1908, and addressed to the librarian of the church, the letter explained that Traughber had an original copy of A Book of Commandments. Traughber said he obtained the book in 1884 from McLellin's widow. When the church's press had been destroyed by anti-

Mormons in 1833 as the book was being printed, a boy had gathered up uncut sheets for the book from the street and had given them to McLellin, who later had them bound. "I thought you might like to have this book," Traughber wrote, "either for the Church Library or for The Museum of the Church." Given the rarity of the book, Traughber's offer was significant.

But what Traughber offered next was even rarer. He wrote, "I also have the Journal, in part, of Elder W. E. McLellin for the years 1831, 2, 3, 4, 5, 6." Traughber said he had tried to get more of the journal from McLellin's widow, but she had refused to give them up "as she said she did not want some things to be known." Traughber said he also had some manuscript books that McLellin had written. He wanted all these materials preserved and offered to sell them for fifty dollars.[32]

On January 18, 1908, President Joseph F. Smith and his counselors wrote to President Samuel O. Bennion of the Central States Mission. The Presidency forwarded Traughber's letter and instructed Bennion on how to handle the offer: "While we have studiously avoided expressing any particular desire on our part to purchase the things mentioned by Mr. Traughber, we desire *you* to know that we would like very much to possess McClellan's Journal, if for no other reason than to prevent the writings of this unfortunate and erratic man, whose attitude after his apostasy was inimical to the Prophet Joseph Smith, from falling into unfriendly hands; and for this reason alone, we feel quite willing to pay the price asked for these things, but at the same time you may be able to purchase them for less money. We suggest that you satisfy yourself that the Journal is the original and not a copy." The Presidency also suggested that Bennion contact McLellin's widow to obtain the rest of the journals, even if their acquisition were to cost another fifty dollars.

The letter to Bennion mentioned an interview Joseph F. Smith and another church leader had had with McLellin in 1878, when McLellin had told them he had writings he wished to publish. The Presidency wrote Bennion that the manuscripts to which Traughber referred might be the same ones McLellin had mentioned in 1878. "We hope they are," the First Presidency wrote, "as it would be an act of mercy on our part to purchase them, and thus prevent them from being published by unfriendly hands to the injury of innocent people."[33]

Rowe and his staff also found a February 12, 1908, response from Bennion to the First Presidency. Bennion reported that he had returned from Doucette, where he had acquired the proffered materials from Traughber. "This man is endeavoring to get the rest of the McLellin journal," Bennion wrote, "and also to get the rest of the manuscript copy, of which I got only a part." Bennion also said he had acquired a copy of McLellin's periodical the *Ensign of Liberty.* He said he would send all the acquired items to the First Presidency that day by registered mail.[34]

Rowe had kept his new supervisor, Richard Turley, informed about Jessee's clue and the letters to which it led. Turley told Dean Larsen about the letters, and Larsen informed Packer and Oaks, who in turn contacted the First Presidency. When Gordon Hinckley learned of the letters, he asked Francis Gibbons if the First Presidency's vault contained the items the letters mentioned. Gibbons searched the vault. Hinckley and the other church officials then learned, to their astonishment, that the church had owned McLellin's journals and manuscripts all along.[35]

The journals, spanning most of the period when McLellin was active in the church, revealed a man deeply dedicated to his religion. McLellin endured hardship and persecution as he preached the gospel revealed through Joseph Smith. McLellin's faith was evident in his unflinching recording of a revelation Smith received in 1831 in which McLellin was chastised for his shortcomings. "Commit not adultery—" the revelation had read in part, "a temptation with which thou hast been troubled."[36]

The little manuscript books, on the other hand, typified the later McLellin, an avowed enemy of the church. In content they resembled many of McLellin's other writings, including letters owned by the RLDS Church, articles in the *Ensign of Liberty,* and the materials that the *Salt Lake Tribune* had discovered in Texas.[37]

Like the materials the *Tribune* had discovered, the McLellin items found in church possession were not the McLellin collection touted by Hofmann. Absent, for example, were affidavits from early church members, Facsimile No. 2 from the Book of Abraham, and the Canadian copyright revelation. Unlike the *Tribune*'s discovery, however, the church's McLellin materials included a key item from the collection Hofmann claimed to have bought. That item, McLellin's early journals, confirmed to church officials that Hofmann was a fraud.[38]

The discovered documents did not fall within any of the subpoenas issued to the church, and thus officials were not legally obligated to mention them to anyone. Still, it was apparent they were relevant to the case, and those involved in the discovery felt the documents' existence should be revealed. Yet disclosing them would not come without cost. Church officials had sought to dispel the notion that they were buying documents to hide them. Disclosure of the newly discovered McLellin materials, however, would reinforce notions of church suppression because those documents had in fact been bought at the direction of the First Presidency and locked away nearly eight decades earlier, eventually to be forgotten.

Yet that was in an earlier age, an age in which the church was emerging from a battered infancy, loath to supply its enemies the rods with which to beat it. This was a new age, not free of persecution and eager critics by any means, but one in which a stronger, more mature church stood a better chance of defending itself. Alluding in his journal to the day's re-markable discovery, Oaks wrote, "Today [Boyd K. Packer] & I learned that the Church has some documents that have been unknown until now, but will be of great interest when they are revealed, as they should be prior to the Hoffman trial (in my opinion)."[39]

What church officials did not know was that there would be no trial.

In early March, a trial for Hofmann seemed likely. Hofmann's attorneys continued to proclaim their client's innocence, though investigative sources maintained they had proof he was guilty. In the actual trial, prosecutors would have to prove Hofmann's guilt beyond a reasonable doubt. But in the preliminary hearing, in which a judge would decide whether Hofmann should be bound over for trial, they need only convince the judge that there was "probable cause to believe that the crime charged has been committed and that the defendant has committed it." If the prosecution's evidence was as strong as some sources had hinted, the preliminary hearing would almost certainly result in Hofmann's being bound over for trial. Because a prelim-inary hearing was not a trial to determine ultimate guilt or innocence, state law would allow prosecutors to try again if they failed during the first hearing to prove probable cause.[40]

According to the newspapers, however, prosecutors had resisted pres-sure to file charges against Hofmann until they had enough evidence to build a strong case against him. Their recent decision to charge Hofmann suggested they now had the evidence they needed. Yet their investigation clearly had not ended. On March 4, Glenn Rowe received a subpoena to provide investigators an 1835 hymnal in which a page had been tipped in. Two days later, Rowe delivered the hymnal to Wilford Kirton for delivery to investigators. In turning the hymnal over to investigators, Kirton ex-plained that the volume was worth more than thirty-five thousand dollars and had been on display in the church's museum. He requested that the hymnal be examined as quickly as possible and then returned to the church so it could again be put on display.[41]

Meanwhile, Hofmann's sometime partner Shannon Flynn pleaded guilty in federal court to possession of an unregistered machine gun, parts of which had been found in a search of Hofmann's home. Hofmann still faced a similar federal charge in addition to the numerous charges filed at the state level.[42]

The cautious distance being kept between church headquarters and investigators meant church officials remained largely unaware of the di-rection the investigation was taking, except to the extent they could piece together clues from media reports, subpoenas, and other sources. On

March 5, church legal counsel complied with yet another subpoena, this one for records about one of Hofmann's close associates.[43]

Church officials had even fewer clues about the direction Hofmann's defense would take. On March 12, an investigator hired by defense attorney Ron Yengich telephoned Hugh Pinnock's office. He left a message with Pinnock's secretary that he wanted to meet with Pinnock and Oaks. Pinnock took the message to Oaks's office and left it with his secretary, who noted that Pinnock would not return the call until he had spoken to Oaks. When Oaks got the message, he discussed the request with Packer. Both felt that in the spirit of fairness to both sides in the case, they should comply with requests from the defense too. Oaks referred the matter to Wilford Kirton, and the defense detective later interviewed Pinnock. Near the end of the month, Ron Yengich also interviewed Pinnock, who gave Yengich the same information he had given the prosecution. After the interview, investigators for the prosecution called Pinnock and wanted to know what Yengich had said.[44]

Church officials had more historical matters to worry about than just those clearly associated with the bombing investigation. The Oliver Cowdery history remained a mystery, one they were determined to solve. Historical Department employees continued their research on the whereabouts of the manuscript. Unlike the McLellin research, which (thanks to Dean Jessee's tip) eventually turned up some long-lost materials, research into the whereabouts of the Cowdery history consistently led to dead ends. A preliminary report dated March 6 tentatively confirmed the earlier conclusion that the church did not own the history.[45]

Church officials had talked for years about improving security in the Historical Department. The church's irreplaceable collections, long treasured for their informational value, had increased in monetary value over the years and provided a tempting target for thieves. Church officials had resisted upgrading security, however, because archives patrons had generally proved to be honest, and known thefts and mutilations of historical materials had been rare. Moreover, they felt patrons might interpret any changes in security as a signal of mistrust.

In archives and libraries around the country, however, the vulnerability of books and documents to theft, arson, mutilation, and other crimes had prompted unprecedented measures to enhance security in order to prevent losses before they occurred, thereby preserving collections for succeeding generations.[46] Church officials had observed these changes but had taken little action themselves until after the bombings. When prosecutors suggested Hofmann or someone else could have violated the integrity of the church's collections by planting forged documents in them, Historical Department administrators and advisers resolved to join the professional trend toward improving security.

Through church archivists' contacts with other professional archivists around the country, the Historical Department hired a consultant from the National Archives who was nationally recognized as an expert in archival security. During March 1986, the consultant visited the department, taught seminars, and provided a report to department management recommending numerous changes to improve security. Many of these recommendations would be implemented over the next several months.[47]

In mid-March, however, church officials' attention was quickly drawn back to the investigation. On March 17, Glenn Rowe received a subpoena. With the emphasis on maintaining distance between the church and investigators, the receipt of subpoenas had become a fairly common occurrence for church officials. But this one was different. It did not order Rowe to provide books or documents. It ordered him to appear as a witness at the preliminary hearing.[48] Rowe was not alone. The next morning, Hugh Pinnock stopped by Dallin Oaks's office and left a message with the secretary that he too had received one. "Then immediately after he came in," the secretary wrote in a note to Oaks, "Bill Kirton called asking if you had received a subpoena. I told him no, but that Elder Pinnock had." Gordon Hinckley also received one.[49]

Before the preliminary hearing, Hinckley received a visit from prosecutors Bob Stott and David Biggs. Church counsel Wilford Kirton also attended the meeting. Stott later said he and Biggs scheduled the appointment "because President Hinckley was going to be a witness and like every witness in the case, we interviewed him in advance. President Hinckley was no exception."[50]

Cordial was a term Biggs would later use to describe the first part of the interview with Hinckley. Biggs remembered that Hinckley first asked if they were members of the church. Biggs said he answered that he was a member, though not a particularly good one.[51] Stott did not recall that question but remembered that Hinckley asked if he were related to another Stott the church leader knew. Stott felt Hinckley was trying to establish a rapport with them.[52]

Biggs recalled that they told Hinckley why they were there, and then Kirton began to do most of the talking. Eventually, however, the prosecutors explained that they needed to talk to Hinckley so they could find out what his relationship had been with Hofmann. Hofmann had claimed a close relationship with the church leader, telling people that he had Hinckley's private numbers and could get hold of him day or night, in the country or out. Prosecutors wanted to know when, where, and how many times Hinckley had met with Hofmann and with Christensen.[53]

Hinckley said he had met about half a dozen times with Hofmann, but he could not recall any information about those meetings beyond what he had told investigators earlier. His answers frustrated both Stott and Biggs. "President Hinckley was very little help, extremely little help," Stott later said. "His memory of the occasions was very poor."[54]

The prosecutors then asked Hinckley if he had a journal that he could use to refresh his recollection and provide them with more details. Stott later recalled that Hinckley said he did not have a "Day-Timer," diary, or journal. Biggs recalled that Hinckley said he did not keep his journal on a daily basis. Biggs said they then asked him if he could have his secretary go through the journal to see what it might contain. Biggs remembered that Hinckley either said it did not exist or would not have the information prosecutors wanted.[55]

"When the inquiry concerning Mark Hoffman was in progress," Hinckley later wrote, "I was interviewed by a number of investigators and I recall that one asked whether I kept a detailed journal. I responded that I was an erratic and inconsistent journal keeper and that my secretary reminds me quite frequently of blanks in that record; further, that I do not ordinarily make detailed records of visits or conversations. I do not keep a 'Daytimer.' "[56]

Biggs later said this response bothered him because the church had long advocated keeping journals.[57] Biggs did not realize how differently various church leaders interpreted the admonition to keep journals. Some kept detailed daily records. Others made only occasional notations about significant events in their lives. Boyd Packer, then senior adviser to the Historical Department, considered the record of his life to be primarily his published talks, the books he had written, his family history records, and the minutes of meetings he had attended. He did not keep a daily record of his life. Some other general authorities also did not.

Bruce McConkie, in his influential *Mormon Doctrine,* had acknowledged the importance of record keeping but had declared that "there is no particular obligation to keep a daily *journal* or diary."[58] In doing so, he had relied on long-time church historian Joseph Fielding Smith, who, discoursing on the duty of church members to keep records, had reflected, "Is it necessary for each one of us individually to keep a daily journal? I would say not."[59]

Often, church officials who maintained a daily or near daily record omitted detailed information about conversations and office visits because these were considered routine or confidential or were simply too numerous to record. Many also omitted detailed information from the meetings of councils and committees, both because the meetings were intended to be confidential and because the details were generally recorded by secretaries in the form of minutes. Though he kept a journal, Hinckley had been forced to turn to Francis Gibbons when trying to reconstruct for investigators the meetings he had with Hofmann.[60]

To prepare Hinckley to be a witness, the prosecutors questioned him about specific meetings he had with Hofmann. They began with the Josiah Stowell letter, Biggs remembered. "He was the only person who had contact with Mark Hofmann concerning the buying of the Stowell letter," Stott recalled. "He was the only one that could testify as to what went on, and that was one of our charges. So he was an essential witness in that respect."[61]

Hinckley explained how Hofmann had offered the document and how he had purchased it and had it placed in the First Presidency's vault. During an earlier interview with investigators, Hinckley had described how much the church paid for the Stowell letter. By this later interview with prosecutors, however, Hinckley had forgotten the precise amount. The prosecutors tossed out a figure, and Hinckley said it sounded about right.

Hinckley had mentioned the First Presidency's vault, and the prosecutors asked questions about it. They told Hinckley that Hofmann had bragged to some of his friends that he had access to the vault. Hinckley said that was impossible. Only Francis Gibbons had the combination. (Gibbons later said the only time he could remember Hofmann coming to his office was on February 23, 1981, when Hofmann showed him the Joseph Smith III blessing).[62]

The prosecutors then asked Hinckley about specific items Hofmann claimed to have offered the church or said the church had in its possession. As they listed items, Hinckley said there was no substance to any of them until they came to the Kinderhook plates. Hinckley then said that Hofmann had offered some of the plates to the church but had been turned down.[63]

The prosecutors asked Hinckley about the Oliver Cowdery history that someone had claimed the church owned. Biggs recalled that Hinckley said he had not seen it and felt it was not his concern. As the interview continued, both Kirton and Hinckley tried to get the prosecutors to understand the size and scope of the church and the responsibilities imposed on Hinckley during the past few years when some other members of the First Presidency had been disabled by age or illness.[64]

Because Hinckley was so busy, Kirton suggested to the prosecutors that they postpone calling him as a witness until the trial itself rather than using him at the preliminary hearing. Hinckley added that he would prefer not to testify. Kirton's suggestion riled Stott, who thought the attorney was being paternalistic. "How old is he?" Stott later asked, recalling the incident. "Anyway, the old experienced lawyer going to tell the young lawyer how to handle the case. I became very incensed at that because there was no one with more experience in criminal matters in the state than me, and he doesn't know a thing about criminal law. And he's saying, 'Why don't we do it this way? Why don't we save President Hinckley for the trial and don't use him at the prelim.?' I got a little upset at that, him trying to tell me how to run my case. And so I just told him, 'I'm in charge. I need President Hinckley. And he'll testify.' "[65]

Neither Biggs nor Stott found it unusual that Hinckley would not want to testify. Biggs later observed that white-collar crime victims often felt that way, and he did not find that sentiment inappropriate or unethical. "I wouldn't want to do it either," he said. "But every witness I interviewed said that." No one was anxious to testify.[66]

Stott said, "Obviously, President Hinckley's an extremely busy person. I mean, we're used to that. In most of our cases, we ha[ve] people who don't want to testify for business reasons, for schedule reasons, whatever." Stott recalled that prosecutors expected the preliminary hearing to run three weeks and that they would not be able to tell Hinckley in advance specifically what day he would testify. At best, they could narrow down the date to a three-day period. "And of course, they wanted to be more sure, and we couldn't be more sure."

"Kirton let it be known explicitly, 'Is there some way we could get along without President Hinckley?' " Stott recalled. " 'Is there some way that he could have a deposition or whatever it takes?' "[67]

Stott told Kirton the only way the prosecution would consent to have Hinckley not testify at the preliminary hearing would be for the defense to agree to stipulate to what the prosecution wanted Hinckley to testify about if he were present: that he bought the Stowell letter from Hofmann on a certain date for a given price. Kirton and Hinckley asked Stott if he would broach the subject with the defense, and he agreed to do so.[68]

In late March 1986, the Special Affairs Committee proposed that the church issue a press release listing all the documents it had acquired from Hofmann and how much was paid for them. "Such a press release was considered last winter," the proposal read, "but it was thought inadvisable since Hofmann had not been formally charged." Since Hofmann had now been charged, it seemed appropriate to go forward with the release. On the afternoon of March 26, in a meeting between Historical Department administrators and their advisers, Dallin Oaks requested that the Historical Department begin preparing such a statement. "For transactions handled on an exchange basis," the minutes recorded, "the Department should estimate the value of the items exchanged."[69]

The next day, Bob Stott called Glenn Rowe to help pin down the date in 1984 when the church purchased Deseret Currency Association notes from Hofmann's associate Lyn Jacobs. Ordinarily, Rowe would have requested a subpoena in order to keep relations with investigators formal. But he knew he did not have the information they wanted and simply referred the prosecutor to Don Schmidt, who, having retired from church employment, did not need to worry about maintaining his distance.

Later, Schmidt called Rowe. "He doesn't remember the date nor what we traded," Rowe recorded in his journal. "I told him we have no record of the transaction." Many acquisitions from Hofmann had involved trading duplicate materials from the church's collection. Schmidt, who had carried out most of the trades, had not taken the time to record them. Thus, later that day when Rowe's supervisors passed on the assignment received the previous day from Oaks, Rowe foresaw the difficulty in fulfilling it. "In the afternoon," he wrote, "we also were told to put together a cost estimate of everything we got from Mark. 90% of that must come from Don's memory of what he traded, and he doesn't remember. I will go down Monday to spend the morning with him."[70]

The following day, Friday, March 28, Stott phoned Rowe again about Deseret Currency Association notes. This time, however, he asked to see them. "I could not help," Rowe recorded in his journal, "because of the policy to have him go through the Church Attorney etc." Rowe spent much of the rest of the day trying to figure out values on documents traded with Hofmann.[71]

As previously arranged, Rowe met with Don Schmidt on Monday, March 31, to tap his memory of transactions with Hofmann. The time that had elapsed since the trades, combined with the comparative insignificance of many of the transactions, left Schmidt with little recollection of them. "Spent a few hours with Don Schmidt trying to put a value on all documents from Mark," Rowe wrote. "A real guessing game."[72]

On Tuesday, April 1, Rowe finished his list of documents and values. The figures on trade values were based on considerable guessing. Still, Rowe was surprised to learn that the total estimated value of all documents, including those few for which cash was paid, fell below $150,000. "A far cry from the half million or million being talked about," he wrote.[73]

The same day, Bob Stott called Rowe to ask about more items. As a result of the conversation, Rowe received a subpoena on April 2 for documents that included Deseret Currency, Spanish Fork Co-op notes, and records of Historical Department transactions. Church officials soon furnished the requested materials, for which Stott signed a three-page receipt detailing the items obtained and agreeing to return them to the Historical Department after legal proceedings in the case had ended.[74]

Also on April 2, Rowe met with Dallin Oaks and Richard Turley to discuss the old legal documents acquired from Hofmann. Though it was not completely clear whether the documents had been removed improperly from their original repositories or legally deaccessioned, it seemed a prudent course to attempt returning them to the courthouses or document repositories from which they might have been taken. Before carrying out the plan, however, church officials asked county investigators if they would object. The investigators accepted the plan, saying the legal documents were not material to their case. Over the next several days, Rowe and Turley returned legal documents to several repositories by mail or in person.[75]

On April 2, Rowe also issued a memorandum to other Historical Department employees about contacts with the media. "In anticipation of the upcoming hearings and trial," he wrote, "please be aware and cautious of making comments which might be taken by others as 'news worthy' or 'inside scoop.' We need to be certain that only accurate, non-partisan information is released through the proper channels at the appropriate time and place." Thereafter, he directed, no statements were to be made to reporters without specific approval.[76]

On Friday, April 4, the Salt Lake County Attorney's Office filed four additional theft-by-deception counts against Hofmann. Named as victims of the crimes were Al Rust, Brent Ashworth, Shannon Flynn, and Deseret Book. The new charges signaled that investigators' efforts were yielding new evidence of wrongdoing.[77]

One week later, the church issued a press release explaining the discovery and return of the legal documents and listing forty-eight other documents known to have been obtained from Hofmann. "All of the 48 documents and the later-discovered court documents have been made available to law enforcement officials," the statement noted. The release also reported that the church had paid out a total of $57,100 in cash for seven of the documents, and that it had traded duplicate materials for the other items, "the total value of which is undetermined." The statement on the undetermined value of traded items was added after an appraisal from a Deseret Book employee arrived at a total differing by about thirty thousand dollars from the estimate Rowe had made with Schmidt's help.[78]

The release was an effort by church officials to answer the public's questions about the extent of the church's dealings with Hofmann, while at the same time not prejudicing the pending case. To assure the balance was not upset, the general authorities and public affairs staff were instructed not to comment on the news release but to let it speak for itself. Church officials most familiar with the case felt convinced Hofmann was guilty of at least some crimes. They had said all they could publicly about the case and had elaborated further for investigators, all in a way intended to preserve the integrity of the legal system. Now they would wait to see how well the system operated.[79]

They would not wait long. On Monday, April 14, 1986, the preliminary hearing would begin.

12

Probable Cause

"For the record, gentlemen, would you introduce yourselves and your representation," requested Judge Paul G. Grant of Utah's Fifth Circuit Court at the beginning of the preliminary hearing.

"Your honor, Robert Stott for the state along with Mr. David Biggs and Gerry D'Elia," responded the prosecution.

"Ronald Yengich on behalf of the defendant, Mark Hofmann, who is present. Bradley Rich assisting in this matter," answered the defense.

"We will now proceed in the case of State of Utah vs. Mark Hofmann," Judge Grant declared. After a few preliminaries, the court gave the prosecution permission to call witnesses. Prosecutor Gerry D'Elia began by calling Bruce L. Passey to the stand.[1]

Passey testified that he and his father were jewelers who worked in the Judge Building, where Steve Christensen had his office. At about 6:45 A.M. on October 15, 1985, Bruce arrived at the Judge Building and waited in the lobby for his father. Perhaps a minute later, a man entered wearing a green letter jacket and carrying a brown box addressed in a dark marker ink to Steve Christensen. The man walked to the elevators, pushed a button, and waited. Meanwhile, Bruce's father arrived.[2]

An elevator eventually came, and the three men boarded it. The Passeys exited on the third floor, and the man in the letter jacket continued up in the elevator, apparently destined for the fifth floor. A little after 8:00 A.M., the Passeys heard the explosion that killed Christensen. Two days later, a detective showed Bruce a jacket, which he identified as the one worn by the stranger who rode the elevator with him.[3]

"Now," D'Elia asked, "with respect to the person that you saw in the elevator and in the foyer of the Judge Building in the lobby on October 15, 1985, are you able to recognize that person again?"

"Yes," Passey answered.

"For the record, would you indicate where that person is seated and point out the person and tell us what the person is dressed in?"

"He is sitting next to Mr. Yengich wearing glasses and a blue suit." Passey had described Mark Hofmann.[4]

D'Elia asked Passey if he was shown photographs on October 17, the day he identified the letter jacket. Passey said he was given a stack of eight or nine photographs.

"Would you just describe to the court what happened while you went through those photographs?" D'Elia requested.

"I was looking through the pictures," Passey testified, "and the one photo that I picked is—just gave me a real strong feeling in my stomach, made me feel uneasy." Passey said he initialed the picture. It was a driver's license photograph of Mark Hofmann.[5]

A few days after the bombing, investigators showed Passey some writing on a piece of cardboard. He testified that it was like the writing he saw on the box carried by the man in the elevator.[6]

When defense counsel Ron Yengich cross-examined Passey, he focused on inconsistencies in the state's evidence about Passey's identification of the sleeve color of the letter jacket. He also identified differences between Hofmann's features and those of a composite figure prepared with Passey's input just after Christensen's death. Moreover, he tried to establish that Passey's identification of Hofmann had been influenced by media reports and that the stack of photographs from which Passey picked Hofmann was unduly suggestive.[7]

For the prosecution's second witness, D'Elia called Janet McDermott, whose office was directly across from Christensen's in the Judge Building. McDermott said that when she arrived at her office between 6:45 and 6:50 on the morning of October 15, she noticed a cardboard box in front of the door to Christensen's office. She also noticed a strange man in the hall.

"Right in front of my office," she testified, "I stopped and put my briefcase down and probably my purse, got out my keys, and then bent down in front of the box to pick it up, because Steve and I are often not in our offices on a regular basis every day, and if there is something out there in the doorway, we will take it for one another, so that it does not get taken by someone else."

Then she noticed the first name on the box was written "Steve," not "Steven," in black marker ink. "That's the only reason I didn't pick up the box," McDermott said. "It appeared personal. Anything that I had ever taken of Steven's always said Steven. It was always business-related."

So she stood back up and went into her own office, bolting the door behind her because of the stranger who was alone with her on the floor at that early hour. She went about her business, then left her office briefly just before 8:00 A.M. to feed her parking meter. When she returned a short time later, the package was still there.

She went back into her office, made a phone call or two, and then gathered up her belongings to leave. As she was about to lock her door, she remembered she needed to dial a number to forward her phone calls. She went back inside her office, and as she was dialing the number, she heard an explosion.

"Simultaneous with the sound," she said, "parts of my wall came in."

"When you say parts of your wall, that would consist of what, plaster?" asked D'Elia.

"Yes, plaster. There was broken glass. I had a picture on the opposite window or opposite wall that was shattered, and there was a shock from the phone. I dropped the phone. The plaster came in on my leg."

She thought someone had been shot. Frightened, she crouched by her desk, positioning herself so it was between her and the door. "I was very scared," she said. "I thought that if there was somebody out in the hallway, that they would know for sure that I was there."

Judge Paul G. Grant of Utah's Fifth Circuit Court meets with prosecution and defense during the preliminary hearing. (*Deseret News*)

She heard the recorded voice of a telephone operator asking her to hang up and dial again. Then she heard "a very high-pitched crying," like "a little child dying." Something, perhaps a fire alarm, made her think the building was on fire, that she had to hurry out or be trapped. She grabbed her belongings and threw open her door.

There in front of her lay Steve Christensen.[8]

After additional questions from both prosecution and defense, Mc-Dermott was dismissed, and the prosecution called a woman who worked for Thomas Wilding and others at Summit Financial Concepts. She knew Mark Hofmann, she testified, from his business dealings with her bosses. Between 9:00 and 9:30 A.M. on October 15, she saw Hofmann at her office. He was wearing a green letter jacket. Hofmann asked her if Wilding was in. He wasn't. Hofmann had been to their office many times before, she recalled, but he usually had an appointment. This time he didn't.[9]

After Yengich's cross-examination, D'Elia called Gary Sheets, who described his family, especially his deceased wife. "I think Kathy was one of the most loved individuals I have ever seen," he said. "Everyone in the neighborhood loved her. She had a great number of friends. She was a

Gerry D'Elia (*left*) confers with fellow prosecutors David L. Biggs (*center*) and Robert L. Stott (*right*). (*Deseret News*)

Defense attorney Bradley P. Rich (*left*) consults with partner Ronald J. Yengich (*center*) as Mark Hofmann (*right*) looks on. (Tom Smart/*Deseret News*)

great wife, a great companion, a super mother, a great grandmother." She had a "great sense of humor, great wit," Sheets said. "I used to tell people the best job of selling I ever did was to convince Kathy to marry me. She was just an outstanding person."

Sheets described his morning on October 15, recounting how he learned of Christensen's death and then of his wife's.

"How would you term your five-year relationship with Steve Christensen?" D'Elia asked.

"Steve was the most outstanding, brightest, most intelligent young man I have ever met in my life, and I loved him like a son. He was—we were business partners, associates, and great friends. There was just a lot of love that existed between us."

Sheets described how Christensen left the company. He also told briefly what he knew about the purchase and authentication of the salamander letter. The hearing then adjourned for the day.[10]

Hugh Pinnock had tried to remain as compassionate toward Hofmann as he could throughout the months following the bombing, giving the document dealer the benefit of the doubt and refusing to condemn him despite

repeated pleas of investigators. After the first day of the preliminary hearing, however, the church leader began to relinquish hope for the man. "The
Hoffman hearing began today," he wrote in his journal. "They seem to be
presenting a strong case against him. What a tragedy. When I think of the
lives he has eternally injured it becomes even more pathetic."[11]

By 9:00 the next morning, April 15, Jerry Cahill of the church's Public
Communications Department had read the voluminous local newspaper reports of the first day of the hearing and had summarized their contents in
a memorandum to Richard Lindsay that could then be passed on to other
interested officials. He would continue to file such reports throughout the
preliminary hearing.[12]

As Cahill finished his memorandum, the second day of the preliminary
hearing began with Yengich cross-examining Gary Sheets in an attempt to
develop other theories on who committed the murders. Yengich drew out
the fact that some CFS investors were disgruntled and that 60 percent of
Sheets's clients were from Las Vegas.[13] Sheets was followed on the witness
stand by a thirteen-year-old neighbor, who testified that he saw a gold
Toyota Wonderwagon in their neighborhood late at night on October 14.
He had never seen the van before but noted it because strange vehicles
rarely entered the secluded area in which they lived.[14] Another neighbor
testified she had heard a loud noise at around 9:40 A.M. on October 15.
"My impression at that point was that I was hearing the sound of falling
lumber," she said. She later learned that it was the explosion that killed
Kathy Sheets.[15]

Next, a detective from the Salt Lake County Sheriff's Office testified.
During part of his testimony, he described how investigators searching
Hofmann's home had discovered a letter jacket, inside out, lying on the
floor of a closet.[16]

The detective was followed on the witness stand by Bradley Robert
Christensen (no relation to Steve), a passerby in his twenties who rushed
to Hofmann's side after the bomb exploded in the document dealer's car
on October 16. Christensen said he saw Hofmann approach his car, open
it up, and lean over inside of it. After Christensen had passed by, he heard
an explosion. "It sounded to me like a car back firing and a gun shot
combined," he said. "Double that sound." The explosion briefly startled
him as he turned to search for its source. "I could see the debris and a
haze of smoke. I—things were flying. I looked and about that time I could
see an individual laying on the ground right next to the car." Christensen
said he ran to Hofmann's side.

"Did you notice any wounds?" D'Elia asked.

"Yes, I did."

"Where?"

"I noticed that he had a gaping hole in his knee and that a finger had been blown off and the bone was exposed. There was a gash in the head. I could see powder burns, what seemed, to me, to be powder burns. Those are the immediate ones that I noticed. And there was a wound in the chest also." Fearing Hofmann might have a back injury, Christensen hesitated to move him until the flames from Hofmann's burning car became so intense that he and two other rescuers felt compelled to move him across the street. As they administered first aid to Hofmann, Christensen took out a container of consecrated oil he carried with him. "And I, of course, got somebody else who is L.D.S. to [anoint] him," Christensen explained, "and then I commanded him to live and that proper medical help would get there quickly."

"And did it?" D'Elia asked.

"It certainly did," Christensen answered.

Later in his direct examination, D'Elia asked Christensen if he saw Hofmann do anything before he opened his car door.

"I believe vaguely I remember him quickly going to his trunk, opening it up," Christensen said.[17]

When Ron Yengich cross-examined Christensen, he focused on differences between the young man's earlier statements to police and the testimony he had just given to the court about such details as how much time elapsed between the time he saw Hofmann and the time the explosion occurred. Yengich also questioned Christensen on whether he had seen Hofmann get into the trunk of his car.

"I said I possibly, I vaguely remember," Christensen answered.[18]

The final witness of the day was a Radio Shack employee, who testified that on Monday, October 7, 1985, she had sold a mercury switch, two C-cell battery packs, and a package of lamps to a man who identified himself as Mike Hansen.[19]

The first witness on Wednesday, April 16, 1986, was a Salt Lake City police officer who had been at the hospital on October 16, 1985, when the injured Hofmann arrived by ambulance. Later, Hofmann's father, Bill, also arrived. The officer overheard a conversation between the father and son. Mark told his father that when he opened his car door, an unknown object began to fall out of the car. "He reached for the object and he didn't really remember anything after that."

"Fall out of the car?" D'Elia asked.

"Yes."

"Do you recall that as being the exact words?"

"Yes," the officer affirmed.[20]

On cross-examination, Yengich established that before Hofmann's father arrived at the hospital, the officer had been informed that Mark was a suspect in the case.

"Did you Mirandize him at any time?" Yengich asked.

"No, I did not," the officer admitted. He also acknowledged that he was present during the time that police detective Jim Bell interviewed Hofmann.

"Did Jim Bell . . . apprise Mr. Hofmann of his rights before he asked him any questions?" Yengich inquired.

"I don't remember," the officer replied.[21] Yengich's questions aimed at whether the information gathered by the two police officers would be admissible during trial.

Jim Bell was the next witness to take the stand. Bell testified that police seized a copper Toyota van belonging to Hofmann. He also described the scene of the Steve Christensen bombing, including some of the bomb parts found there. They included pipe shrapnel, pieces of C-cell batteries and battery packs, and a mercury switch.[22]

Bell also described the hospital interview he conducted with Hofmann. Bell asked Hofmann to describe what he had been doing that day. Hofmann provided details of his morning's activities up to breakfast. Then, Bell testified, "things started to become a little evasive about where he'd been." Bell pressed him for details, but Hofmann remained evasive. Bell asked Hofmann to describe events just before his car exploded. Hofmann said that when he opened his car, a package fell from the seat onto the floor of the car. As he reached for it, it exploded.[23]

Bell left the hospital and went to the scene of Hofmann's car explosion, where he passed on Hofmann's story to federal bomb expert Jerry Andrew Taylor. Bell did not elaborate on his conversation with Taylor, but he testified that it changed his opinion of Hofmann immediately. Earlier, he said, he had considered Hofmann as "totally a victim." Thereafter, he would consider Hofmann the prime suspect in the bombings.[24]

Bell also testified that a search of the trunk of Hofmann's car yielded a black marker, rubber gloves, a piece of pipe, numerous documents, and some brown wrapping paper.[25]

The next morning, Bell testified, he returned to the hospital and read Hofmann his Miranda rights. Hofmann agreed to talk, and Bell questioned him further about his earlier story. "Then," Bell testified, "I asked him if he was the one that planted the bombs and killed the two people, and he said he didn't, he didn't do it."

"What occurred at that time, if anything?" D'Elia queried.

"At that time," Bell said, "I explained to him that I was fairly confident that he was the person responsible and informed him that we'd located a green jacket in his house and there was never any reply after that because that set off the medical alarms." When the alarms went off, the hospital staff asked Bell to leave.[26]

The next day, Bell said, he participated in a daytime warrant search of Hofmann's home. During the search, investigators discovered an envelope lying on top of a box in a basement bedroom. The envelope bore the name "Mike Hansen." Asked why investigators seized the envelope, Bell answered, "Because prior to going in there, we'd heard of M. Hansen who had purchased the mercury switch and the battery pack and that's Mike Hansen and that's why it was taken."[27]

Bell also testified that he went to the address written on the Radio Shack receipt issued to Mike Hansen. "And what did you find?" D'Elia asked.

"I found a vacant field and a parking lot," Bell replied.[28]

Later in his testimony, Bell explained that the Mike Hansen envelope seized at Hofmann's home also bore the address of Utah Engraving. Detectives later visited that business and discovered a negative for an unsigned Jim Bridger note.[29]

The final testimony of the day was given by Jerry Taylor, the federal bomb expert whose opinion had changed Bell's view of Hofmann. Taylor testified in detail about the makeup of the three bombs that killed Christensen and Sheets and injured Hofmann. He deduced that one person built all three bombs and "that the same person that made the devices positioned the devices." He also testified that the battery packs and mercury switches recovered from the bombing scenes proved to be the same types as were sold at Radio Shack.[30]

When the prosecution questioned Taylor about the bomb that exploded in Hofmann's car, Taylor said the bomb exploded just below the highest level of the console next to the driver's seat. D'Elia asked if the bomb could have fallen to the ground or to the floorboard of the car before exploding. "The box did not explode on the floor," Taylor said. The physical evidence showed the explosion occurred at the console level.[31] Taylor's testimony directly contradicted the story Hofmann told Jim Bell in the hospital. Now it was clear why Bell's earlier conversation with Taylor had changed his opinion of Hofmann.

D'Elia also asked Taylor how twelve-volt lamps purchased with the battery packs and mercury switch from Radio Shack might fit into a bomb-building scheme. Taylor said the lamps could be used by the bomb's builder to test the circuitry of the bomb.[32]

While Taylor and others had been testifying that day, most church officials continued their usual routines but learned of developments at the hearing through news reports. "The Pre-trial hearing goes on with very little new," Glenn Rowe wrote in his journal, "but bits and pieces of tidbits which look badly for Mark."[33]

On Thursday morning, April 17, Taylor continued his testimony. Again trying to develop other theories for the killings, Yengich questioned Taylor about the possible connection between the deadly pipe bombs and the Mafia. Taylor testified, "A bomb such as that was never used in any mob activity that I know of."[34]

A short while later, D'Elia asked Taylor why the Mafia would not use pipe bombs. Taylor answered, "The pipe bomb, even though it's an instrument that can cause death, doesn't have near the effectiveness of five or six sticks of dynamite that the Mafia like to use. When you use five or six sticks of dynamite you don't have to worry about the victim living or the vehicle, if it's in a vehicle, being damaged. It's blown out over a block, block and a half, and half the victim won't be recovered. It's a sure thing."[35]

Taylor was followed by several employees of local engraving companies, whose testimony combined to help connect the name *Mike Hansen* with Mark Hofmann and to show that Hofmann had ordered printing plates or stamps for items that he later represented and sold as authentic historical materials. One order was for a plate used to print the last page of the incomplete Emma Smith hymnal that Lyn Jacobs acquired from the church and sold to Hofmann, who added the missing page and sold it to Brent Ashworth. Another order was for four stamps that would later prove to have been used in printing Spanish Fork Co-op notes.[36]

Later that day, the testimony of an examiner from the state crime lab further identified Hansen with Hofmann. The examiner testified he found a latent fingerprint from Hofmann on a Mike Hansen order form from one of the printing companies.[37]

Shannon Flynn also testified, connecting Hofmann to several Jim Bridger notes, as well as a purported Betsy Ross letter. Later that day, the prosecution noted that the Betsy Ross letter, dated 1807, bore the name of William B. Smith as postmaster. Records from the National Archives proved Smith was not appointed until 1834.

Flynn's testimony confirmed that Hofmann was driving a Toyota van late in the evening on October 14, 1985. Prosecutor David Biggs, who was examining Flynn, also referred to an earlier statement Flynn had made to investigators about discussing gunpowder with Hofmann. Biggs pointed out that Flynn had said Hofmann told him on the evening of October 14 that he needed to buy some Coca-Cola to help him stay awake that night.[38]

The final witness of the day was Don Schmidt, whose testimony continued the following morning. Schmidt answered questions about Hofmann's transactions with the church and about the significance and value of some of the items the church acquired from Hofmann. He also explained how he had traded the incomplete Emma Smith hymnal to Lyn Jacobs.[39]

Schmidt testified that Hofmann mentioned the McLellin collection to him around the last week in June 1985, several month's after Schmidt's retirement. Hofmann described the collection to him, said it was in a Texas bank vault, and implied he would be purchasing it soon for about $185,000. In early October, Schmidt said, Hofmann told him the collection had been sold. Schmidt also described how he came to be involved in the McLellin transaction that was supposed to close on the day Hofmann was injured.[40]

Following Schmidt on Friday was an employee from a Denver engraving company who testified that a Mike Hansen placed an order for plates of Deseret Currency Association notes in denominations from one to one hundred dollars. The church had purchased several such notes.[41]

The next witness, an orthodontist, testified to loaning Hofmann ninety thousand dollars in 1985. As collateral for some of this amount, he received from Hofmann a copy of Jack London's *Call of the Wild* that contained an Austin Lewis address stamp and a handwritten inscription by London.[42] Other witnesses had earlier testified that a Mike Hansen had ordered a printing plate of the inscription from one company and a stamp of the address from another company.[43] The order form for the stamp was the one on which a latent fingerprint from Hofmann had been discovered.[44]

The next witness was the Arizona businessman Wilford A. Cardon, who had been president of the church mission in which Shannon Flynn once served. Cardon described his purchase of an interest in the Betsy Ross letter, which he was later told had been traded for sixteen Jim Bridger notes. He also testified of other interactions with Hofmann, including a transaction in which he invested $110,000 in a Charles Dickens manuscript that Hofmann and Flynn were acquiring. Referring to the money invested, prosecutor David Biggs asked, "Have you received that back?"

"No," Cardon answered.[45]

In June 1985, Cardon testified, Hofmann and Flynn visited him to request that he put up $185,000 to buy the McLellin collection. He said Hofmann claimed the collection would then be given to Gordon Hinckley to handle and that "it was important that the Church not purchase the documents outright or that they not be donated to the Church but that they be put in the Church's possession for safekeeping."[46]

Biggs asked Cardon if he responded to Hofmann's statement.

"Yes," he said, "my response to that was that based on my association with the General Authorities of the Church, that isn't the way they generally did things and if that really indeed was the desire of President Hinckley, that I would request that he contact me personally and so state that desire." Later, Cardon said, Hofmann tried phoning Hinckley but learned he had left for Germany. Cardon and his partner agreed with Hofmann that Hinckley should contact them directly if he really wanted the collection purchased.

"Did you ever, within the next days or weeks after that, receive a call from President Hinckley?" Biggs asked.

"No," Cardon answered.[47]

In September, he asked Hofmann if he had completed the McLellin transaction. Hofmann said he had. "Well, where is it now?" Cardon had asked.

"It's been deposited with the First Presidency," Hofmann had claimed.[48]

That same month, Hofmann also offered him part interest in a second copy of *The Oath of a Freeman,* claiming that it was in even better condition than the first, which he said was being purchased jointly by the Library of Congress and the American Antiquarian Society. Cardon, whom Hofmann had already told about the first *Oath,* was surprised that two would exist and declined the offer.[49]

The next witness was the Arizona physician Richard Marks. Marks testified of his transactions with Hofmann, including his purchase of the Dunham letter from Hofmann for $20,000. Marks later resold the letter to Deseret Book for $90,000, part of which he received in trade in the form of a complete set of Deseret Currency Association notes. Later, he learned that Hofmann had bought the letter from Deseret Book for $110,000. Marks also said he bought a set of Spanish Fork Co-op notes from Hofmann.[50]

Among the many documents Marks acquired from Hofmann was a handwritten copy of the lyrics to a favorite LDS hymn, purportedly in the handwriting of its author.[51] Though Marks did not say so, he had lent the document for display at the church's museum several months earlier.[52]

The final witness of the day was Glenn Rowe, who testified about two letters he had acquired from Hofmann for the church. Rowe explained what items had been traded for the letters and how much they were worth. He also testified briefly about a seal, impressions of which had been found on some Hofmann documents.

"Let me ask you this," prosecutor Bob Stott then said. "On October the 3rd of 1985, did you have an occasion to come into possession of what is called a *Book of Common Prayer?*"

"Yes."

After Rowe described the acquisition, Stott asked about Hofmann, "Did he explain to you what the book was or what significance it had?"

"Yes."

"What did he tell you?"

"It was a Nathan Harris prayer book and it had Nathan Harris's signature in the front of it and some handwriting in the back of the book that would appear to have been similar to that of the Martin Harris letter of 1830."

Later in the questioning, Stott asked Rowe to hold up the book and show the judge the handwriting he had mentioned. "What did he relate that to, for clarification?" Stott asked.

"Being similar handwriting to that of the Martin Harris 1830 letter."

"Is that the one that's commonly known as the Salamander letter?"
"Yes."

Stott later asked Rowe if the writing added value to the book. "Well, yes," Rowe replied, "that was the definite primary interest, the handwriting being similar." When Stott had finished asking about the book and moving for the introduction of an exhibit into evidence, the day's and week's proceedings concluded.[53]

Like other members of the public, church officials listening to news accounts of the first week of the hearing found themselves more and more convinced that Hofmann was guilty, and they wondered how the document dealer could have deceived persons so effectively. "Watched news," Hugh Pinnock wrote in his journal during the week. "It seems that Hofmann has left a trail of evidence. The only effective manner to understand this situation is to realize that M[ark] H[ofmann] was well considered before 10–17 or 18th even though he fooled us all. M[ark] H[ofmann] did not internalize the gospel."[54]

On Monday, April 21, the preliminary hearing resumed with defense counsel Brad Rich cross-examining Rowe about his dealings with Hofmann and about church procedures in acquiring documents. Rich also spent considerable time questioning Rowe about what items the church had turned over to the prosecution for examination and which ones the prosecutors had retained in their possession.[55]

Next to take the stand was Al Rust, who testified about his numerous transactions with Hofmann. Rust described his acquisition of Spanish Fork Co-op notes, Deseret Currency Association notes, and white notes from Hofmann. He also explained how he helped Hofmann finance the purchase of the Joseph Smith III blessing and the Lucy Mack Smith letter.[56]

Rust described at length his investment in the McLellin collection, recounting how his son and Hofmann went to New York and how Hofmann claimed to have purchased the collection and sent it back to Salt Lake. During the first week of May, Hofmann told Rust that he had sold the collection to the church for three hundred thousand dollars but that payment would be delayed a couple of weeks and that the entire transaction had to be kept strictly confidential.[57]

"Did he explain why it had to be kept so secret?" Stott asked.

"He said that the church would like to have time to examine the collection, that it had a lot of material in it and if word got out that the church had it, they would be bombarded by inquiries and other people wanting to investigate and seek out the collection," Rust replied.

Stott then inquired, "At any time, either before or after this phone call, did he ever indicate that there was anything of a controversial or embarrassing nature about these documents?"

"No," Rust answered. "I even questioned. I remember asking him about this when he mentioned the secrecy and he said, 'Well, it isn't because of the controversy or anti-Mormon material. It is just that the church would like to keep it confidential and I promised them, as I sold it, that we would do that.' "[58]

In June, Rust said, Hofmann told him the church had decided not to buy the collection, but that a Texas buyer had agreed to purchase it and donate it to the church. In August, however, Hofmann told him the Texas buyer had backed out. "I have decided that I will purchase the collection and I will donate it to the L.D.S. church," Hofmann told Rust.

Rust felt he owned the collection because of his large investment in it, and he asked how Hofmann could donate it when he did not own it. "I can't afford to donate it to the L.D.S. church," Rust told him. Hofmann answered that he would be receiving more than a million dollars by September 1 from the Library of Congress for *The Oath of a Freeman* and that when he received his money, he would repay Rust's investment plus a profit and then donate the collection to the church.[59]

During the latter part of August, Hofmann gave Rust a large check, but it bounced. On September 12, Rust testified, Hofmann approached him at a local coin show. Rust said Hofmann was "very distraught, very upset. I had never seen Mark under the trauma of his behavior like that. He was desperate, kind of."[60]

Rust followed Hofmann to the foyer, where Hofmann threw his hands in the air and exclaimed, "I'm losing everything. I'm losing my home. I'm losing my car. They are coming to lock my house down."

Rust responded, "Well, wait a minute, Mark, calm down. What's going on?"

"I have a bank foreclosing on me for $185,000," Hofmann said. "And I've got to raise some money to stop them from taking my home and everything that I have."

At the time, Rust still believed in Hofmann and tried to be understanding, but he told Hofmann he could not give him any more money. "I don't know what you are doing owing a bank $185,000 and owing me," Rust said to him. Later that day, though, Rust agreed to withdraw Hofmann's bounced check from collection until November 1 to allow Hofmann to work through his difficulties.

On Saturday, October 12, Rust said, Hofmann approached him again. This time he said a mission president was going to buy the collection but was willing to pay only $185,000 for it. Hofmann said he was anxious to get the matter resolved and so would accept that amount and repay Rust. He told Rust the mission president would be in Salt Lake City the following week and that he would likely be able to repay Rust on Wednesday or Thursday.

At noon on Monday, October 14, Hofmann called Rust and said, "I need to see you. It is very urgent."

"Well," Rust answered, "I'm going to be here all afternoon. Come in any time." Hofmann never showed up.[61]

During cross-examination, Rust provided additional details about his dealings with Hofmann. He also described his letter to Gordon Hinckley and his meeting with Dallin Oaks after the bombings.[62] On redirect examination, Stott referred to two checks Hofmann had given Rust in the summer of 1985, one for $125,000 and another for $40,000. He handed Rust an exhibit to refresh his recollection on the date the checks changed hands.

After Rust had looked at the exhibit, Stott asked, "What date would that be?"

"It would have been June twenty-eighth," Rust answered.[63] June 28 was the day Hofmann borrowed the money from First Interstate Bank.

When Rust completed his testimony, Hugh Pinnock took the witness stand. Stott referred to Pinnock's June 28, 1985, meeting in which Christensen introduced Hofmann. "Had you known Steve Christensen prior to this?" he asked.

"Yes."

"And how well did you know him?"

"Fairly well," Pinnock replied.[64]

Pinnock recounted Hofmann's need for money to exercise an option to buy the McLellin collection.

"Did he tell you some other people were interested in it?" Stott asked.
"Yes."

"Did he give you any name?"

"A George Smith from San Francisco, I think," Pinnock said. "And another name I can't remember."[65]

Hofmann told Pinnock he needed $185,000, that he would repay the amount from money owed him by the Library of Congress on *The Oath of a Freeman*, and that he intended to donate the McLellin collection to the church. Pinnock said he conferred with Dallin Oaks and asked if the church would lend Hofmann the money he needed. Oaks said no. They talked about the reported value of *The Oath of a Freeman* and "agreed that that would perhaps be something that a bank would lend money on."[66]

Pinnock explained the loan from First Interstate Bank and Hofmann's later claim to have purchased the McLellin collection and to have stored it in a bank safe-deposit box. He said Hofmann showed him the Spalding-

Rigdon document and allowed him to make a copy of it but told him to keep it confidential. He later gave a copy of the copy to investigators.[67]

Pinnock also described a mid-September meeting in which he talked to Hofmann about repaying the loan, which was then overdue. He next recounted the October 3 evening meeting at his home when Hofmann explained his financial difficulties and disclosed to him for the first time Rust's interest in the collection. Then Pinnock related the events leading up to the day Hofmann was injured, as well as his own repayment of Hofmann's bank loan.[68]

Stott asked Pinnock, "Did you ever possess, obtain, or buy the McLellin collection?"

"No."

Referring to the Spalding-Rigdon document, Stott continued, "Did you ever, besides this one document, did you ever have the McLellin collection in your possession?"

"No."

"To your knowledge, did any authority in the L.D.S. church ever obtain or possess the McLellin collection?"

"No," Pinnock answered. (He had not been told about the McLellin materials discovered the previous month.)

"To your knowledge did any third parties ever possess or obtain the McLellin collection?"

"No. Not that I know of."[69]

During cross-examination, defense attorney Brad Rich asked Pinnock if he had given Christensen "a blessing of some sort . . . immediately prior to his death?"

"Oh no," Pinnock answered, trying to negate the story that Christensen had been called to be a document agent for the church.

"How about in any period over the several weeks before his death?" Rich continued.

"In August or September," Pinnock recalled, "we talked on a number of occasions and we are often called to give blessings. And during that period of time we talked about what his occupation would be. He was concerned about past business difficulties. And I would suspect that during that time I gave him a blessing."

"You would suspect that?"

"Well, it is something that we do often."

"And what would the substance of that blessing have been?"

"Well, blessing him that he would work through the difficulties that he was confronted with."

"The business difficulties we are talking about?"

"Yes."[70]

When Pinnock had finished testifying, investigator Richard W. Forbes of the Salt Lake County Attorney's Office took the stand to testify about the contents of Steve Christensen's two safe-deposit boxes. When the boxes were opened on October 17, 1985, he said, one was empty. The other "contained what appeared to be papyrus with Egyptian-type hieroglyphics and figures on it."[71]

Forbes was the last witness of the day, but the hearing continued a few minutes as the court and the attorneys discussed several housekeeping matters. Ron Yengich explained that he had reviewed a list of potential witnesses compiled by the prosecution. Yengich told the judge he thought the prosecution and defense might reach agreements that would eliminate the need for seven witnesses on the list to testify. One of those witnesses, he said, was Gordon Hinckley, whose testimony could possibly be handled by stipulation.[72]

Dallin Oaks had not attended any of the hearing but had kept informed about the proceedings from press accounts and the Cahill summaries. Although he had become convinced after the bombings that Hofmann was guilty of some wrongdoing, he had earlier confided in his journal that he hoped the prosecution had a better case on the murder charges than had been reported in the media. By the evening of April 21, however, his doubts had withered. Summing up what he had heard about the hearings, Oaks wrote, "The evidence against Hofmann has been very damning."[73]

"Tell us where you were and who, if anyone, brought that document to your attention," Bob Stott instructed witness Steven G. Barnett the following morning after showing him the Spalding-Rigdon document.

"I was at my desk in the rare book room and Mark Hofmann brought it to me," said Barnett, who was the rare and used book buyer of Cosmic Aeroplane Books, a Salt Lake City bookstore. Hofmann offered the document to the store for two thousand dollars. Barnett said he would like to research the document, and Hofmann left it with him.[74]

That evening, Barnett testified, he learned that the Solomon Spalding familiar to Latter-day Saints had died several years before the date on the document. Barnett assumed the document was authentic but that the signature of Spalding belonged to a different man of the same name. He bought the document from Hofmann for a reduced price because of its Rigdon signature. Hofmann also sold Barnett other items, including two Jim Bridger notes, one for himself and one for his store.[75]

Next to take the stand was Kenneth Rendell, the Massachusetts dealer who had been engaged before the bombings to evaluate the authenticity of the salamander letter. Rendell said he considered about half a dozen factors in his evaluation, one of which was the letter's provenance. "I consider who is bringing the document to me, what are the present circumstances, who has it," he said.

"What were the circumstances in your consideration at that time?" Gerry D'Elia asked.

"Well," Rendell replied, "the person that I had known for five years, a person that I had every reason to believe was reputable and honest."

"This, again, being Mark Hofmann?"

"Yes. I had no suspicions whatsoever in that regard."[76] Rendell then detailed the steps he had taken to evaluate the letter, pointing out that he "dealt with the question of authenticity but . . . did not determine it to be genuine." Summing up his conclusions, Rendell said, "I could find no evidence of forgery and I saw no reason to believe it would be a forgery."[77]

After the bombings, however, Rendell had been shown the letter again, this time with several other documents, including major documents the church received from Hofmann. When he examined them, Rendell saw signs of forgery in all except the salamander letter, which did not appear on its face to be forged. Rendell noted, however, that the paper and ink analysis on the letter had been farmed out to other experts.[78]

D'Elia asked Rendell how his opinion of the salamander letter would be affected if an expert were to question the authenticity of the letter's ink. Rendell said his opinion would change "if a person of substantial reputation found something wrong with the ink."[79]

Rendell also testified that his office sent Hofmann two pieces of papyrus on consignment in mid-September 1985. Hofmann neither paid for nor returned them, he said. When D'Elia showed him a piece of papyrus, Rendell said the exhibit was only a segment of one of the pieces he had sent Hofmann. Later, he testified that cutting up papyrus reduces its commercial value.[80]

Rendell also explained that Hofmann called his office on October 1, 1985. During that call, he told Hofmann he planned to be in Jackson, Wyoming, around October 20 and thought he would stop in Salt Lake en route to visit collectors like Brent Ashworth. He asked Hofmann if he too would be in town then. Hofmann said he would and asked Rendell to be sure to let him know when he came.[81]

Hofmann later called Rendell's office and spoke to his assistant. As a result of Hofmann's call, a memo was circulated in the office about the papyri Hofmann had borrowed. "It basically said," Rendell testified, "that Mark Hofmann had called and he wanted to make certain that we understood that this transaction was to be considered very confidential and no information given out to anyone about the transaction."[82]

The next witness was Curt Bench of Deseret Book. Bob Stott handed Bench the *Book of Common Prayer* Bench had sold to Hofmann. Stott asked

Bench to turn to the writing in the back of the book that appeared to be in the same hand as that of the salamander letter. Stott asked Bench if he could remember whether the writing was in the book when he got it.

"I can't identify it as being there," Bench replied. "It seems when I first saw the book there was some writing in the back but I couldn't identify it. It was not striking in any way so it does not come to memory."[83]

Bench explained how he had shown the book to Hofmann, who offered to buy it for fifty dollars and then took it with him. Later, Hofmann returned to Deseret Book and talked to Bench about the volume.

"What did he tell you about the book?" Stott asked.

"That it had some Martin Harris handwriting," Bench said, "and that he had been able to sell it for $2,000 and would offer us a thousand for it instead of the $50."

"Is that the first time he told [you] that the book contained the Martin Harris handwriting?" Stott inquired.

"Yes," Bench replied.[84]

Bench testified about Hofmann's desperate attempt to raise money on September 13, 1985, and about his later offer to sell a piece of papyrus he said was from the McLellin collection. Bench further described his discussion with Steve Christensen about these events.[85]

He also detailed his later conversation with Christensen on September 24. Bench said Christensen told him that two unnamed general authorities, "a member of the First Quorum of Seventy and an apostle," were disturbed that Hofmann had defaulted on his loan, bounced a repayment check, and failed to keep the bank informed as he had promised. "They were quite upset over this," Bench testified, "and said some very serious things could happen as a result of that not being taken care of. They were interested in Steve getting ahold of Mark and letting him know the seriousness of the situation so that he could take care of it."

"Did he mention what some of these serious things were that could occur?" Stott probed.

"Steve told me that various things could occur if Mark didn't make good," Bench said. "Some of them were he would certainly lose his credibility and credit with the Church and with President Hinckley, that criminal action could be taken, that he could conceivably go to jail, he could also be sued by the bank or even by the Church if the Church was sued. He could lose his membership in the Church."

Bench also testified that Christensen told him the two general authorities planned to report Hofmann's behavior to Gordon Hinckley the next morning. "He wanted me to tell Mark," Bench said, "that if he didn't want them to see President Hinckley then he had better get in touch with him that night or that morning, the next morning, and work something out."[86]

After Bench related how he had passed Christensen's message to Hofmann, Stott asked, "When Mr. Christensen called you did he mention the McLellin collection?"

"Yes," Bench answered, recounting how Christensen had earlier described the collection as collateral for the bank loan, though "no one had seen any merchandise from that or any money."

"So from what Mr. Steve Christensen told you," Stott inferred, "the Church didn't have the McLellin collection, is that correct?"

"That's correct."[87]

Stott later turned Bench's attention to January 9, 1985. On that day, Bench bought a Jim Bridger note for Deseret Book from Brent Ashworth, who in turn had acquired it from Hofmann. Bench could not recall ever seeing such a note before that date. Yet on October 2, Shannon Flynn offered the store another one, along with five white notes, all of which had belonged to Hofmann. The next day, Deseret Book gave Flynn a twenty-thousand-dollar check for the items. Bench further said his store bought a full set of eight Deseret Currency Association notes from Hofmann for eighteen thousand dollars in October. Bench also testified about the Dunham letter transaction.[88]

On cross-examination, Brad Rich asked Bench to elaborate on his earlier testimony. Referring to the September 24 conversation in which Christensen had listed possible consequences of Hofmann's failure to repay the bank loan, Rich asked, "Is it your impression, having heard this list from Mr. Christensen earlier in the day, that that was a threat from Mr. Christensen or simply a matter of fact recitation of the possible consequences of Mark's act?"

"It was a recitation of the possible consequences," Bench affirmed. "He didn't do it in a threatening manner but indicated that it would almost certainly happen if things did not get taken care of."

"He wasn't threatening personally to have those things visited upon Mark if he didn't follow through?"

"No. No."

"He was just telling you what would happen?" Rich queried.

"Or could happen," Bench corrected.

"Or could happen if Mark didn't see to it that that loan was paid?" Rich restated.

"That's correct," agreed Bench.[89]

The next witness to take the stand was Lyn Jacobs, Hofmann's friend and occasional business associate. Jacobs testified that he was going to school at Harvard in the fall of 1983 and had agreed with Hofmann to look up dealers of stampless covers, old letters that were folded to form an envelope and were sent without adhesive stamps. Hofmann was especially interested in stampless covers bearing postmarks from places associated with the church's early history.

Around mid-November, Jacobs said, he called Hofmann and gave him the names of dealers who might have such items. Later that month, Hofmann called Jacobs back, and, in Jacobs's words, "mentioned that basically one of those dealers had panned out or, in other words, had been successful."

Bob Stott asked, "Did he tell you whether or not he had picked something up?"

"Something to that effect."

"What did he say?"

"Well, he read to me the Martin Harris [salamander] letter."[90] Though Jacobs felt he had aided in the letter's discovery and had become one of its owners, Hofmann, not he, first had possession of it. Stott drove the point home. "Prior to the telephone conversation, the first conversation in November, had you ever heard anything of a so-called Martin Harris letter?"

"Never before."

"Had you ever seen anything such as that that he read over the phone to you?"

"I had not."

"It is my understanding [that] at that time you were not the person who located the letter in the sense of going to a place and picking it up or purchasing it, is that correct?"

"That is correct."[91]

Jacobs testified that Hofmann did not want the publicity the letter would generate and so transferred complete ownership to him, with the understanding that Hofmann would receive the bulk of the proceeds when Jacobs had sold it. Jacobs then described their unsuccessful attempts to market the document to the church and to Brent Ashworth, followed by the sale of the document to Steve Christensen.[92]

"During this period of time or thereabout," Stott inquired, "did you have occasion to tell people that it was—that you were the one who located the item, and purchased the item and that Mr. Hofmann was brought in to help you market the item?"

"Unfortunately that is correct," Jacobs admitted.

"And you are doing this under Mr. Hofmann's instructions?"

"Not instructions, under his request—not his request that I fabricate a story but at his request that I took full responsibility for the document. That was my decision to fabricate a story several months later."[93]

Stott next showed Jacobs the hymnal he had acquired in a trade with the church through Don Schmidt. The church owned another copy of the hymnal that was in better condition but was missing its last printed page.

Schmidt had offered to trade Jacobs the copy that was in poorer condition, provided he could first remove the last printed page to replace the one missing in the otherwise better copy. Jacobs had agreed.[94]

Later, Jacobs spoke to Hofmann about the hymnal, and Hofmann agreed to look for a genuine final page to replace the one removed by Schmidt. Eventually, Hofmann came up with such a page, claiming to have obtained it from an elderly woman who had an original hymnal and was willing to part with the page for about a thousand dollars. Jacobs was willing to pay the requested amount because a complete copy of the rare volume was worth considerably more than one missing its final page.[95]

Referring to the final page Hofmann had obtained, Stott asked Jacobs, "Did he ever tell you [at] that time or any other time that that was a modern printing?"

"He certainly did not."

"Did he ever tell you that he had had a plate made of that particular page?"

"I had never heard such a thing."

"So he didn't tell you that, is that correct?"

"Of course he didn't."[96]

Later, Stott examined Jacobs about Deseret Currency Association notes that had been purchased by Rust and by the church. Jacobs said he participated in the marketing, not the original discovery, of the notes. "I have never been involved in obtaining any of them," he explained.

"Well, didn't you have a source back east?" Stott pressed, alluding to a story about the origin of the notes.

"No, Mark Hofmann had a source back east," Jacobs said.

"Didn't he come back east with you and there was a little old lady or something and you were the one who had the source and he had to work through you and you had to go get them?"

"That is not correct." Jacobs repeated a different story Hofmann had told him about the source of the notes.

"So you had nothing to do with that acquisition, is that correct?" Stott asked.

"I did not," Jacobs confirmed. "I just simply knew what he told me about it."[97]

Stott next turned to *The Oath of a Freeman.* "Have you ever heard of a second copy of the Oath of a Freeman?" he asked.

"I have heard of people talking about it and rumors about it, yes," Jacobs answered.

"Have you ever seen that copy of that second Oath of a Freeman?"

"I have not."

"Have you ever had possession of it?"

"I have not."

"Was that document ever yours?"

"Never."

"Did Mark Hofmann obtain that document from you?"

"He did not."

"Or through you?"

"He did not."

"Did there ever come a time that you received any money from Mr. Mark Hofmann, specifically $142,000 or whatever, in payment of that item?"

"I have never received any money in conjunction with that document or any other entitled the Oath of a Freeman."

"You never had a proprietary interest in any Oath of a Freeman?"

"I haven't," Jacobs said. "That's all his business."

"Thank you," Stott said. "That's all the questions I have." The significance of Stott's questions would become apparent later in the hearing. When the prosecutor finished his examination, Tuesday's proceedings ended, with the expectation that the hearing would continue Thursday, April 24.[98]

Thursday, however, defense attorneys asked that proceedings be postponed because Hofmann had fallen, fracturing the kneecap on the leg injured in the bomb explosion. Hofmann was scheduled for surgery that afternoon, they said. Pain and medication would prevent him from adequately assisting in his own defense as guaranteed by the Constitution.

Bob Stott represented the prosecution in concurring with the request. "We don't want to proceed where surgery is necessary that might affect the substantial rights of the defendant," he said. Judge Grant then continued the hearing to May 5. The delay did not please him, but he justified it, saying the postponement "is the wiser course of action to take rather than facing the possibility of having to repeat this hearing."[99]

When the preliminary hearing resumed May 5, Al Rust's son testified about the trip he took with Hofmann to acquire a McLellin collection that he never saw.[100] He was followed on the stand by Deseret Book employee Wade Lillywhite, who testified about repeated attempts by Hofmann to raise large sums of money as late as October 14, 1985, by trying to sell or borrow against several documents, including papyrus he said was from the McLellin collection.[101]

Lillywhite said that on September 30, he met Hofmann and Thomas Wilding at a local bank, where he was shown several valuable items kept in a safe-deposit box.[102] Defense counsel Brad Rich asked about the connection between Hofmann and Wilding. "Mr. Wilding," Lillywhite said, "was the one who came in with Mark, if I recall correctly, on September

13th when Mark was attempting to obtain a loan from Deseret Book Company." Wilding, then, was the unexplained stranger accompanying Hofmann the day he implored Curt Bench for a loan.

At the September 30 meeting, Lillywhite testified, "I inquired as to who he was and what his role was in the whole thing. He indicated that he represented a client or clients who had a fiduciary interest in the collateral."[103]

The next witness, who described himself as "an income property finance mortgage broker," testified about a meeting he had with Christensen on October 10 at Christensen's office in the Judge Building. During the meeting, Hofmann walked into the office unannounced. Christensen did not introduce Hofmann but excused himself momentarily to talk with him briefly in another room. The witness said he could hear them talking but could not distinguish what was being said.

"Did there come a time," Bob Stott asked, "when you heard any of the words that were said?"

"Yes," the witness answered. "At that time I heard Steve raise his voice and say, 'You can't hide that.' " A few minutes later, the two men emerged from the room.

"What happened then?" Stott inquired.

"Both of them were so—had a somber look on their faces. Mr. Hofmann left the office." Christensen did not tell the witness what had transpired in the meeting.[104]

The next witness, an engraving company employee who had testified earlier, explained that a Mike Harris ordered and picked up a printing plate on March 8, 1985. Investigators had recognized that a telephone number listed on the receipt for the order matched an unlisted number Mark Hofmann had at the time. As they eventually discovered, the ordered plate bore the title *The Oath of a Freeman* but contained a text identical to a post–Civil War hymn titled "Give Thanks, All Ye People."[105]

The employee also testified that a Mike Hansen ordered another plate titled *The Oath of a Freeman* on March 25, 1985. All the wording on the plate matched the *Oath* Hofmann offered to the Library of Congress and the American Antiquarian Society, except that the plate also bore the words "This 'Quaker Catichism' was printed opposite the title-page in the 1653 edition of Cotton's book. Enlarged."

"Now," David Biggs began, "based on your 40 years in the engraving business, is there any way or multiple ways, if you know, of eradicating that particular piece of writing that I just read to you?"

"Oh, yes," the witness replied. "It would be easily sawed off, or it could be filed off or cut off with a knife, you know, with a number of strokes."[106]

The final witness of the day was police detective Jim Bell, who was asked to identify an exhibit. "This is a piece of paper," he said, "which was a Walden Books receipt that was located up at 200 North Main Street in the papers that belonged to Mr. Mark Hofmann that were on the street and the total is for 50 cents." The receipt, Bell said, bore a time and date of 2:30 P.M. on October 16, 1985, which was the Wednesday on which the bomb exploded in Hofmann's car.

"Now, as to that particular document," Biggs asked, "have you personally gone to Walden Books in the Crossroads Mall and walked from Walden Books . . . to where Mr. Hofmann's car was parked up on Second North?"

"Yes."

"How much time, approximately, did it take you?"

"Seven to 8 minutes."

"And based upon information that you have received of the calls in of an explosion on Second North on October 16th, 1985, what was the time?"

"2:41 P.M. on the 16th is when it came into our dispatch office."[107]

Bell also testified about another receipt, this one found in a search of Hofmann's van. It was from Argosy Book Store in New York, the place where Hofmann claimed to have bought *The Oath of a Freeman*. The receipt listed items purchased, including the *Oath*, which the receipt showed cost twenty-five dollars. More important, however, the receipt was dated March 13, 1985, five days after the man with Hofmann's telephone number picked up a plate he had ordered of the hymn that had been retitled *The Oath of a Freeman*. Bell's testimony suggested that Hofmann printed a copy of the retitled hymn, planted it in the bookstore, and then purchased it in order to create a provenance for the *Oath* that he later created with the March 25 plate.

Bell further testified that a copy of Charles Hamilton's book *Great Forgers and Famous Fakes* was taken from Hofmann's house during a search on October 18, 1985, and that the original of the Betsy Ross letter was found in a basement room during the same search.[108]

The testimony given by witnesses that day was reported as usual in the next morning's *Salt Lake Tribune*. The *Tribune* also reported that defense attorneys were scheduled to meet that morning with Gordon Hinckley "to see if a stipulation to his testimony could be reached in order to prevent the necessity of calling President Hinckley as a witness." The primary relevance of Hinckley's testimony for the purpose of the hearing was implied in the next sentence, which read, "President Hinckley is named as a victim of theft by deception in a complaint alleging that a letter he purchased allegedly authored by church founder Joseph Smith is a forgery." Hofmann's counsel also wanted to discuss another matter. "The defense," the newspaper reported, "would like to ask President Hinckley about the church leader's role in pressuring Mr. Hofmann to pay back an overdue $185,000 bank loan arranged by another church elder."[109]

Before the preliminary hearing that morning, May 6, Ron Yengich met with Hinckley and church counsel Wilford Kirton. Yengich asked Hinckley several questions about his dealings with Hofmann over the years. "He asked specifically," Hinckley wrote, "about the acquisition of the Joseph Smith-Josiah Stowell letter. I told him that I bought this in behalf of the Church, that it was paid for by a Church check, and that Mark Hofmann had issued a receipt to the Church for it. He questioned whether I had bought anything on my own account, and I told him that I had not bought anything from Mark Hofmann on my own account."

Yengich also asked about the McLellin collection. Hinckley explained Hofmann's visit to him after his receipt of Rust's letter. Hinckley said he had never heard of the collection, and Hofmann told him it included "letters, diaries, affidavits, and the Facsimile 2." The visit, Hinckley explained, came when he was "preparing to leave for Europe and was under great pressure to get ready." He said he told Hofmann "to clear up his problem with Alvin Rust and we would then consider his donating the so-called McLellin collection to the Church."

Yengich asked Hinckley when he had next discussed the collection with Hofmann. "I told him," Hinckley recorded, "that I had no remembrance of discussing it further with Mark Hofmann, but that when I returned from Europe and subsequent to this Hugh Pinnock and Dallin Oaks had talked with me. I could not fix the dates of these conversations."

Hinckley also told Yengich about the meeting in which Hofmann offered to sell some of the Kinderhook plates. Hinckley said he had vaguely recalled that the plates had been shown to be fraudulent and thus had declined the offer. He also told Yengich that he may have seen Hofmann one other time, but he had no clear recollection of the occasion.

Yengich asked Hinckley about his association with Steve Christensen. "I told him," Hinckley recorded, "that the only time Mr. Christensen had been in my office was the occasion when he presented to me in behalf of the Church the Martin Harris-W.W. Phelps letter. I had met him informally and casually some time before this at a luncheon where I sat at the same table and he introduced himself by telling me that he was Mac's son. Other than these two occasions I have no recollection of ever being with him."

Yengich also asked Hinckley about his attitude toward Hofmann. "I responded," Hinckley recorded, "that I had seen him only in my office, that my attitude was cordial, that we dealt on a basis of trust, that I regarded him as a returned missionary, a member of the Church with whom we could deal on the basis of trust just as we have to deal with others such as doctors and lawyers on the basis of trust."

Yengich then asked Hinckley about the notion that he was quite close to Hofmann. "I told him that I felt there was no basis for any such conclusion," Hinckley wrote recounting his answer, "that I treated him cordially as I try to treat everyone who comes to my office and that large numbers of people over the years do come to my office. It has been my policy always to try to have them feeling better when they left than when they came in."

Yengich told Hinckley he wanted to question him on one or two other matters but had to get to court.[110]

When the preliminary hearing resumed later that morning, Thomas R. Wilding took the witness stand. Wilding, whose business was investments and insurance, said he met Mark Hofmann around 1980 when he sold Hofmann and his wife some medical insurance. In 1985, Wilding's group of investors began funding deals with Hofmann that promised a high rate of return. In March, they invested $22,500 in the purchase of eighteen rare books. In April, they were told the books had been sold and their investment had doubled. Hofmann returned their initial investment plus half the profit and said the remainder was going into another investment.[111]

In May, they added $160,000 to that investment, which was supposed to help purchase a Charles Dickens manuscript titled "The Haunted Man." Hofmann told the investors that the manuscript would take a few months to sell. In September, Hofmann told them the manuscript had been sold, yielding a 66 percent gain. Payment on the investment was due October 16, 1985, he said.[112]

Meanwhile, in August, they gave Hofmann $23,600 to purchase some Brigham Young papers and artifacts at auction. In September, Hofmann told them the items had been sold at a 42 percent gain. He said payment on the investment was available to them, but he also offered what he described as the best investment opportunity he had yet provided them. It was a chance to invest in a second copy of *The Oath of a Freeman*, the first copy of which, he said, had been sold to the Library of Congress for $1 million.

Hofmann felt the second copy would fetch $1.5 million. Hofmann said he found the first copy in a New York bookstore. The second copy, he said, would be purchased from a Boston dealer named Lyn Jacobs, who was willing to part with it for $500,000 because he had held it for a year and would realize a major gain on his investment.[113]

For the earlier investments, Hofmann had provided collateral and signed personal guarantees. On one of them, the Charles Dickens manuscript, the investors had contacted New York dealer Justin Schiller for assurance that the document existed. On *The Oath of a Freeman* investment, Hofmann also agreed to pledge collateral, though he never finished delivering it all.[114]

Hofmann told the investors that Schiller had helped market the first copy of the *Oath*, and they phoned him to ask about the history and value of the document, though Hofmann cautioned them not to refer to the second copy, with which, he said, Schiller was not involved. The telephone call convinced the investors of the second *Oath*'s value, and they gave Hofmann $173,870 in additional money on September 12.[115]

On that same day, Wilding said, Hofmann and he went to First Interstate Bank with an investor named Sid Jensen (Wilding's brother-in-law) to purchase some cashier's checks and exchange some money.[116] Wilding and Jensen, then, were the two men in the bank with Hofmann that investigators earlier had wrongly assumed to be church security officers.

While they were in the lobby of the bank, Wilding testified, loan officer Harvey Tanner approached Hofmann, took him aside, and talked with him. Tanner seemed "a little bit upset," Wilding said.

"What happened after that discussion between the defendant and Harvey Tanner?" Biggs asked.

"Mr. Tanner left," Wilding said, "and I asked Mark about it. I asked him what it was about, why would an officer of a bank pull him aside and talk to him like that. Mr. Hofmann said there was no problem, that there was a small loan that he was a cosigner on with the bank and that it would be taken care of."[117]

Later that day, however, Jensen visited Wilding in his office. Jensen was "extremely nervous, anxious and upset." He had talked to Wilding's partner and had discovered some inconsistencies in Hofmann's story. Wilding and Jensen then met with the partner to discuss the matter. The partner said he understood that the loan from First Interstate Bank was not small and that Hofmann had not been just a cosigner as he had claimed.

Hofmann had given Jensen the airline and flight number for the plane he would be taking to New York that day to buy the *Oath*. The men called the airlines and found no flight leaving at the time Hofmann had given them. Thinking Hofmann may have taken a different flight, they drove to the airport, where they learned that all flights to New York had left. They then drove through the airport parking lot but failed to find Hofmann's car.

"What did you do then, if anything?" Biggs asked.

"Well, we attempted to call Mr. Hofmann several times [but] could not get any response. We went by his home. His car was not there. Ultimately late that night, Mr. Jensen had to go pick up his wife and family and return home."

"And what did you do?"

"Laid awake all night."[118]

The next morning at 5:30, Wilding pulled his truck in front of the Hofmann house and waited. At 6:30, his partner joined the vigil. At about 7:30, they went to the door and knocked. Hofmann's wife, Doralee, answered. "What's going on?" she asked.

"We just need to talk with your husband for a little while," they said.

Mark was in the shower at the time. When he finished and emerged to meet them, he asked, "What's the big deal?"

"We'll tell you what the big deal is," they said. "There's a lot of things that don't jibe that you've been telling us and we need to get them straight."

"No problem," Hofmann said. "I can explain everything."

"You were supposed to be in New York," they challenged. "What's the deal?"

Hofmann said he wasn't able to go as scheduled but would be going that day and taking his son with him.

Wilding and his partner said, "There's enough inconsistencies and problems here that there's no way we want to invest this money. We want it back."

"Fine," Hofmann said. "Let's go to the bank and get it. I'll meet you at my bank at 10 o'clock."

"No, I'll wait here and go with you," Wilding insisted.

When they arrived at the bank, Hofmann's account yielded only about eighteen thousand dollars, a tenth of what they had given him just the day before. Wilding asked where the rest of the money was. Hofmann gave ambiguous answers but promised to return the money. "Let's go get it," Wilding ordered.[119]

Wilding testified that he accompanied Hofmann from place to place as the document dealer tried raising money on that Friday, September 13. They visited Al Rust at a coin show, where Wilding remained in the background but kept his eye on Hofmann as he pleaded with Rust. They went to Deseret Book twice but both times came away penniless. Other attempts also proved futile.[120]

At about 6:30 that evening, they went back to Wilding's office, where they met Sid Jensen. For the next two hours, the men interrogated Hofmann, who explained he had already sent the rest of the money east. Hofmann claimed that their money had already been spent to purchase the *Oath*, but he said he would find other investors to replace them and would have their money back to them by Tuesday, September 17.[121]

Biggs asked Wilding, "Was there any frustration on your part or Mr. Jensen's part concerning the inability of Mr. Hofmann to return your money during that day?"

"Certainly," Wilding said. "There was a large amount of money at risk there, a lot of people involved, so there was a great deal of frustration."

"What was Mr. Hofmann, the defendant's, attitude during the first hour of that meeting?" Biggs continued.

"I would say almost a detached arrogance."

"And what, if anything, did that cause in yourself and Mr. Jensen?"

"It caused great concern," Wilding acknowledged. "It caused more emotional and—it caused me a great concern, and it caused Mr. Jensen anger."

"Did Mr. Jensen do anything at that meeting because of that anger?"

"Yes, he did."

"What?"

"He slugged Mr. Hofmann."[122]

Through the rest of September and into October, Wilding worked with Hofmann in several attempts to gain repayment of all the money Wilding's group had invested with Hofmann. Wilding's detailed testimony about these attempts dovetailed with earlier testimony about Hofmann's money-raising efforts in September and October. Under the direction of Wilding's attorney, Hofmann signed agreements that converted the investments and owed profits into loans totaling $455,155, much of which Hofmann was obligated to repay on October 16.[123]

In October, Wilding testified, Hofmann said he would be selling to the church several boxes of miscellany he had gathered over the years and that Steve Christensen would be acting as the agent. The price would be $185,000. Hofmann offered to use most of this amount as partial repayment to Wilding's investors. Sid Jensen said he wanted the entire amount to go to them, and Hofmann agreed. Asked why the church would pay so much for a hodgepodge of materials, Hofmann said that he had so much of it (he needed his van to deliver it all) that the church was willing to pay the price. The deal was supposed to close Friday, October 11. Hofmann agreed to meet Wilding at 8:30 that morning.

"Mr. Hofmann didn't show up," Wilding said. "I was obviously concerned and distraught and attempted to call him several times on his car phone and no answer, no response. At approximately 11:30, Mr. Hofmann called me, and I asked him if he had any money from the transaction."

"No," Hofmann had replied, "but I have something else that I think will suffice for over the weekend."[124]

Soon Hofmann was at Wilding's office, where he tossed a letter on the desk. "This is to show you that everything is in order, that that transaction is going to, in fact, take place," Hofmann said. The October 10 letter was from David C. West addressed to Whom It May Concern certifying that $185,000 was being held for documents the firm would be buying for an undisclosed client in a transaction in which Christensen would serve as agent.[125]

Hofmann and Wilding went in to meet with Wilding's lawyer, who said, "Well, I know Steve Christensen. Why don't we just give him a call and verify this."

"What was the defendant's response to that?" Biggs asked.

"Extremely reluctant to do that," Wilding answered. "In fact, he said, if you call him, let me talk to him and you listen." Hofmann said he was concerned a call might upset the deal. The lawyer said he would give Hofmann some time. "But I think it was quite apparent in that discussion," Wilding said, "that shortly, we'd call Mr. Christensen if things didn't happen."[126]

Hofmann told them they would have the money on Monday, October 14, but it turned out to be Columbus Day, so they agreed to meet the next day. On the fifteenth, Wilding returned to his office in the late morning to find Hofmann meeting with the attorney. It was then he learned that Christensen had been killed.

"Mr. Hofmann was sitting in the chair to my left," Wilding recalled of the meeting. Hofmann, he said, "seemed upset, almost—breathing very heavily, almost to the point of overventilating, so to speak." During the meeting Wilding noticed that Hofmann appeared to have showered and shaved very recently.[127]

After the noon recess of the court, Wilding's testimony was interrupted briefly while another witness testified. The witness, an elderly woman, had owned *The Book of Common Prayer* that Hofmann later sold to the church through Glenn Rowe because it contained handwriting matching that of the salamander letter. The woman testified that she married a member of the Harris family in 1936 and the same year acquired the book from her mother-in-law. She held onto it until 1973, when she loaned it to a book dealer, who died shortly thereafter. The dealer's son, apparently unaware that his father did not own the volume, sold it to Deseret Book.

Biggs handed the book to the woman and asked her to examine it. She identified signatures in the front of the book. Biggs then had her turn to the writing in the back of the book. He asked if the writing had been there when she received the book from her mother-in-law. She testified that it had not.

During cross-examination, Brad Rich asked, "Do you recall looking at the rear of the book specifically?"

"Yes," she answered. "Because once we saw those in the front, we were curious."

"To see if there was anything else," Rich said, finishing her sentence. "And you would have leafed through the book to see if there was anything there," he suggested.

"Yes," she affirmed.[128]

When the woman stepped down from the witness stand, Wilding resumed his place there. Rich cross-examined him, and then Biggs asked if any penalties were to be imposed on Hofmann if he did not meet his financial obligations by a certain date. Wilding acknowledged that Hofmann had agreed to penalties.

"And what penalties were agreed upon?" Biggs asked.

Wilding said Hofmann was to pay two thousand dollars a day on each of two agreements he had signed, for a total of four thousand dollars daily. "You need to remember," Wilding pointed out, "that he had promised for several months to return money and with very little success."

Referring to the penalties, Biggs asked, "When did they start to accrue, after what day?"

Wilding checked some written materials and answered that the penalties were to begin after October 14.[129]

When Rich again cross-examined Wilding, he tried to establish that Wilding and his associates had pressured Hofmann. "You had put some pressure on Mr. Hofmann, had you not?" he asked.

"Well, what do you mean by pressure?" Wilding countered. "Obviously on the night of the 13th, there was some physical contact."

"Okay," Rich responded. "And in addition to that, there was some psychological contact, as well, was there not?"

"Well," Wilding said, "contact to keep in touch with us. That's right, sure. If you had several hundred thousand dollars, I think you'd keep in contact."

"I understand your motivation," Rich said. "You've explained that at great length here this afternoon. What I'm asking you is something slightly different and let me rephrase it more carefully. You had, during the course of these negotiations prior to the signing of these various documents, put significant pressure on Mr. Hofmann to pay you back, had you not?"

"Significant pressure to perform what he had agreed to perform, correct," Wilding answered.

"I take it that's a yes," Rich commented.

Biggs objected, "Your Honor, that's argumentative in form."

"You may answer," ruled the court.

Wilding answered, "I don't consider it to be significant pressure, no. I consider it to be trying to solve a problem which obviously had occurred. I think it would have been significant pressure if we had taken him to the police or something because at that time it started to be a real concern. And maybe that's what should have happened."

"Or broken his legs or run over him with a car," Rich said. "We can all agree that those are significant forms of pressure."[130]

"Objection your honor . . . ," interrupted Biggs, only to be interrupted himself by the voice of Mac Christensen, Steve's father, who interjected, "Or bombed him!"

". . . That's argumentative in form," the prosecutor finished.

"It's argumentative," Judge Grant ruled. Then, raising his voice because of the outburst from the audience, he added tensely, "Am I hearing multiple voices or is that an echo or what? I'm not sure who I'm looking at. I'm hearing multiple voices."

The courtroom audience was silent, and eventually Rich began again. "You had, had you not, threatened Mr. Hofmann over a period of weeks with what would happen if he did not get you the money?"

"Threatened that he ought to go to the police," Wilding answered. "If you call that a threat, I guess so."

"Well, and you had used or Mr. Jensen had used what we can characterize as some fairly stern language on him in your presence and had struck him at least once?"

"We already went over that. Yes."

"And that you had insisted that Mr. Hofmann contact you daily?"

"That's right."

"Had insisted that radical changes be made in the conditions and terms of any contractual agreements between you?"

"Under his agreement, sure."

"And under those circumstances, he agreed?"

"Yeah," Wilding concurred. "But there was not undue pressure."

"Well," Rich responded, "I'm asking you what that pressure was. And it's for someone else to decide what's due or undue."[131]

After Wilding finished testifying, Biggs called Brent Ashworth. Ashworth testified of his numerous transactions with Hofmann beginning in 1981. Among the many items Ashworth acquired from Hofmann was a hymnal. Ashworth paid Hofmann about ten thousand dollars for the book, half in cash and half in trade. Ashworth identified the hymnal mentioned earlier in the hearing as the one he bought from Hofmann.[132]

Biggs had Ashworth turn to the last page of the hymnal. He then asked, "When Mr. Hofmann gave you that in November 1984, was that last page in there?"

"Yes," Ashworth said. "The book was complete."

"There were no missing pages?" Biggs inquired.

"No missing pages," Ashworth assured him.

"Mr. Hofmann never told you that there were missing pages."

"No."

"He never told you that he had had a plate made[,] printed up the last page of that book and added it to the book."

"No."

"If he told you that, would you have paid $10,000 for it?"

"No. I wouldn't have," Ashworth said. "In fact, the $10,000 price at that time seemed to be kind of an over payment." Ashworth also said Hofmann told him the book came from the McLellin collection.[133]

Ashworth mentioned the McLellin collection in other parts of his testimony too. He said, for example, that on September 23, 1985, Hofmann showed him a piece of papyrus, describing it as coming from the McLellin collection, the rest of which had been sold to a Salt Lake businessman. Ashworth was thrilled to see and hold the piece but told Hofmann he knew nothing about papyrus. "The only person I know that does is Ken Rendell, who is an old friend of mine, and I'd known Ken for 15 years or more," Ashworth said.

"What was Mr. Hofmann's response to that, if any?" Biggs asked.

"He didn't really say anything that I recall to that," Ashworth replied.[134]

An especially intriguing part of Ashworth's testimony was what he said about his pattern of meeting with Hofmann. "We usually visited on Wednesdays," he said. "I'd go by his home in the morning and sometimes meet him later on in the day at the Crossroads Mall." Later, he testified, "Sometimes when we had to complete transactions, we would meet at our spot. That's what we both called it, which was down in the Crossroads Mall." Even later in his testimony, he elaborated further, explaining that "our usual spot . . . was in the open area just around from the Walden bookstore in the Crossroads Mall."[135]

According to Jim Bell's earlier testimony, a receipt found "in the papers that belonged to Mr. Mark Hofmann that were on the street" showed that someone had been at Waldenbooks (a seven- or eight-minute walk from Hofmann's car) just eleven minutes before a police dispatcher received word of the third bomb on Wednesday, October 16, 1985.[136]

After the preliminary hearing, Ashworth would say that October 16, 1985, "was the only day I'd really, you know, for a year or so broken my pattern on Wednesday." Instead of going to the Crossroads Mall in Salt Lake City, he had stayed in Provo.[137] Consequently, he would say that "I've been unable to rule myself out as the third bombing victim."[138]

When the prosecution finished its examination of Ashworth, it was well after 5:00 P.M. The judge asked the defense counsel, "Shall we have Mr. Ashworth come back then about 2 o'clock tomorrow afternoon for cross-examination? Is that an agreeable time?"

Brad Rich answered, "That's fine," but then he added, "We may be able to make some other arrangements on that, your Honor."

Ron Yengich joined in. "Your Honor, we have previously discussed a personal situation with Mr. Ashworth. And so he does not have to return, we will pass cross-examination on Mr. Ashworth. He has indicated that at a later date, he will feel free to talk to us."[139]

The personal situation to which Yengich referred was the recent death of Ashworth's son Sammy, the boy who was struck by a car while his parents were away, escaping the pressures the bombings had exerted on their lives. Ashworth's appearance at the hearing had fallen after the boy's death but before his funeral.[140]

Dallin Oaks picked up the *Salt Lake Tribune* on May 7 and began to read its summary of the previous day's preliminary hearing proceedings. Thomas Wilding's testimony, the article explained, showed Christensen was about to discover that Hofmann planned to use the McLellin transaction proceeds to repay Wilding's investors rather than the First Interstate Bank loan. "Earlier testimony," the article continued, "indicated the Church of Jesus Christ of Latter-day Saints had threatened Mr. Hofmann with both criminal prosecution and excommunication if that obligation was not met." The assertion that church officials had threatened Hofmann with criminal penalties or church discipline bothered Oaks, who marked the statement in his copy of the newspaper and filed it for future reference.[141]

Later that day, church officials and other members of the public finally got a clear view of what document experts George Throckmorton and Bill Flynn had been doing during their repeated examinations. Flynn, a document analyst for the Arizona state crime lab in Phoenix, was the day's first witness at the preliminary hearing.[142]

Bob Stott asked Flynn several questions about his background and credentials. Flynn's responses to these inquiries established for the record that he was a well-qualified forensic document examiner.[143]

In December 1985 when the authenticity of the documents had become an important focus of the case, investigators had anticipated that court testimony challenging the documents' authenticity would itself be challenged. When the county had accepted George Throckmorton as part of the investigative team, Throckmorton, a devout Latter-day Saint, had insisted that another expert also be retained whose testimony could not be challenged on religious grounds.[144]

Thus, Flynn, a non-Mormon, was also added to the team. To eliminate doubts listeners might harbor about Flynn's objectivity, Stott asked Flynn at the hearing, "Are you a member of either the LDS Church or the Reorganized LDS Church?"

"No, I'm not," Flynn answered.[145]

Flynn testified in detail about the documents he had examined. The paper, he said, seemed consistent with the time period in which the documents were purportedly written. The ink was a different matter.

"With respect to the ink," Stott asked, "did you find any peculiar or abnormal characteristics associated with any of the documents?"

Indeed he had. "On many of the documents," Flynn testified, "there appeared a microscopic cracking on the surface of the ink."

"Besides the cracking," Stott inquired, "were there any other characteristics?"

"Yes," Flynn confirmed. "Under ultraviolet examination, on several of the questioned documents, there was a one directional running of the inks or a constituent part of the inks as if they had been wet."

"Were you able to determine if there had been any additions on the documents, any additional applications of ink?"

"Yes. On several of the documents, there were inks that were not consistent with the body of the document. That is to say, that data had been added to the document with a different ink."

"Now, besides these characteristics, was there anything common about the documents that you found these characteristics on?"

"Yes," Flynn answered.

"What was that?"

"These anomalies that I spoke of, all occurred on documents that had been dealt by the defendant in this case, Mark Hofmann."[146]

At Stott's request, Flynn then listed the documents, which included major documents the church had acquired from Hofmann, as well as many of Hofmann's other notable finds.[147]

Besides examining documents from Hofmann, Flynn had looked at many other documents for comparison. All told, he had studied about 461 documents during his work on the case. Stott asked him, "Besides these particular ones that you've mentioned associated with Mr. Mark Hofmann, were there any other documents of the 461 or so that you examined that exhibit these characteristics?"

"No," Flynn answered.[148]

Flynn said the inks used on the questioned documents were iron gallotannic inks, inks of a type that had been used for hundreds of years, including during the period in which most of the documents purported to have been written. "These are very simple inks," he said. "I made some of these inks in my kitchen sink, to give you some idea. There's not a lot of technology involved in forming the iron gallotannic inks."

Flynn testified that a formula for iron gallotannic ink appeared in Charles Hamilton's book on fakes and forgeries, a copy of which had been seized during a search of Hofmann's home. He also testified that ingredients for the inks were readily available to the average person.[149]

Flynn said he also tried to figure out how the ink could be artificially aged and why the ink cracked on the Hofmann documents. From his reading, he learned that iron gallotannic ink could be artificially aged by exposing it to ammonia. "After I read that," Flynn said, "I made iron gallotannic inks of various types myself and exposed them to ammonia, both ammonia and sodium hydroxide, and found that it did indeed artificially age the inks." But these chemicals did not cause the cracking characteristic of the Hofmann documents.

Flynn then experimented with ink formulas, adding the kinds of ingredients that historically had been used to improve viscosity and to act as a preservative. Common among such additives were sugars and gums. "When I mixed the iron gallotannic inks and added either the sugars or the gum arabic and then artificially aged them with the sodium hydroxide, I got exactly the same phenomenon that I described in the examination of the questioned documents," he said. "The ink both artificially aged and cracked."[150]

After Flynn explained the chemistry behind the cracking phenomenon, Stott asked if conservation measures taken by archivists to preserve the documents could have caused what he observed. Flynn explained that he obtained "typical fixing compounds" used by archival conservators and used them in his experimentation. "Those typical archival preservatives were used on the inks that I made and on some of the older documents that were not in question. And in no instance did we find those archival treatments to affect the ink and crack the surface."[151]

"In your experimentation," Stott asked, "as far as applying the ammonia [to] the different kinds of documents, did you apply the ammonia solutions you're talking about to legitimate 19th Century documents?"

"I did," Flynn replied.

"And what was the result of that?"

"It did not crack."

"It only cracked when you applied it to new writing?"

"Fresh ink, that's right."

"And did you also apply it to new writing on say old paper? Does that have any [e]ffect on it?"

"The new writing on old paper would crack when the ammonia was applied. That's fresh ink on old paper."[152]

Stott later questioned Flynn about specific documents he had examined. Beginning with the Josiah Stowell letter, Flynn discussed individual documents, pointing out cracking of ink, unidirectional running of the ink (suggesting the document had been hung to dry), handwriting problems, and other characteristics that seemed abnormal to him. His conclusion regarding the Stowell letter was echoed time and time again as he was asked his conclusions about the authenticity of other documents: "I don't believe it was a genuine document of that era."[153]

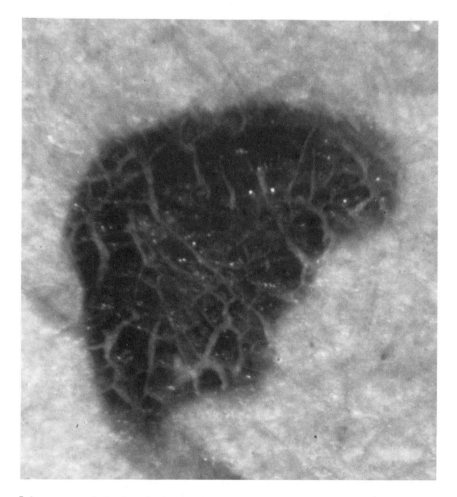

Ink on one of the handwritten white notes, magnified to show alligator-skin cracking. (George J. Throckmorton)

When he came to *The Book of Common Prayer,* Flynn testified that the handwriting in the back of the book was done by the same hand that wrote the salamander letter, a document he had just declared a forgery. The paper in the back of the prayer book appeared authentic, he said, but the writing was added later.[154]

The Anthon transcript did not display the cracking characteristic of other Hofmann documents. "And do you have an explanation," Stott asked, "as to why perhaps there would not be cracking there that was on some of the others?"

Ultraviolet close-up of Joseph Smith III blessing showing one-directional running of the ink. (George J. Throckmorton)

"Yes," Flynn answered. "There was no sugar or gum added to that ink."[155] But there were other signs of forgery. The uneven browning of the paper suggested the document had been heated to age it artificially. Moreover, the Bible in which the document was supposedly found did not display the characteristics that would be expected if the document had in fact remained folded between its pages for decades. Iron gallotannic ink is highly acidic, Flynn pointed out.

"If the document had been in intimate contact with the pages of this Bible over a prolonged period of time," he said, "I would have expected the characters themselves, which are made up of the iron gallotannate ink, to transfer on to the pages themselves. The highly acidic ink would have burned the pages in the forms of the letter[s] themselves, the characters which comprise the ink. In fact, that did not happen."[156]

Hofmann had claimed the Bible once belonged to an early relative of Joseph Smith named Samuel Smith, whose signature appeared in the book.

Stott asked Flynn about the signature. Flynn said the signature differed from other writing in the Bible and, unlike the other writing, exhibited the cracking characteristic of Hofmann documents.

"Did you notice anything else," Stott asked, "as far as around the signature area, the paper?"

"Yes," Flynn replied. "There was an area around the signature Samuel Smith that had been bleached out. What it appears is that there had been a different signature at that location or writing that had been bleached out and the name Samuel Smith written on top."[157]

The Spalding-Rigdon document that Hofmann had shown Hugh Pinnock also showed signs of tampering. "The Solomon Spaulding and Sidney Rigdon signatures that appear on that document were written with a different ink than the other text of the document and the other signatures that appear on the document," Flynn said. Also, the date on the document had been changed from 1722 to 1822.[158]

Abnormal characteristics were not limited to Mormon documents. Flynn testified of other documents too, such as the Betsy Ross letter. "And can you tell us the results of your examination?" Stott inquired.

"Yes," Flynn said. "The name Ross is written in a different ink, in my opinion, than the signature Betsy appearing on that document. It's also— the name Ross, in my opinion, is also in a different handwriting than the rest of the text on that document."

And what about the date?

"It had been altered from November the 24th, 1837, to November 24th, 1807."[159]

When Flynn had finished going over the manuscript documents individually, Stott listed them and asked Flynn, "Is it your opinion after examining all of these articles that they are not genuine articles of the time that they purportedly were written?"

"Yes," he affirmed. "That is my opinion."[160]

The subject then turned from manuscripts to printed materials. Flynn said he had compared the negative of *The Oath of a Freeman* to one of the two *Oath*s Hofmann had claimed were genuine. The negative, Flynn concluded, was used to make the printed document, not vice versa. How could he tell? He looked for microscopic flaws on the negative that resulted from the film developing. He found matching flaws on the printed document. A zinc plate created from the negative would duplicate the flaws, he said, which would then be transferred to paper in the printing process. If the negative had been created from the printed copy, the flaws would not have been captured by the film. "We're talking about microscopic flaws that would not be resolvable by a camera lens," he explained.[161]

During cross-examination, Brad Rich hammered at Flynn's credentials vis-à-vis the case. Flynn admitted he was not a theoretical chemist. "I have a year of college chemistry. That's all," he said. Also, 99 percent of his experience was with modern documents, not old ones, he conceded.[162]

Questioning brought out that Flynn had worked little in the past with iron gallotannic ink. Summing up what his questioning had revealed, Rich asked, "It would have been just a handful of times that you've worked with iron gallotannic inks?"

"Yes," Flynn said.

"Have you ever attempted to synthesize such an ink before?"

"Never."[163]

Rich continued to pick at Flynn's credentials later in the day. Flynn said he had not seen cracking in any of the documents he had examined for the case except those that came through Hofmann. Rich asked, "And you hadn't had any other—you hadn't had enough experience with other documents of antiquity independent of this comparison to identify that as being unusual."

"Yeah," Flynn said. "I had probably only examined 25 or so documents of antiquity prior to this case."

"Have you ever testified in a court about documents of antiquity?"

"No."[164]

Rich also tried to downplay the significance of the ink-cracking phenomenon. For example, on the David Whitmer to Walter Conrad letter, he asked Flynn, "On what basis have you pronounced it a forgery?"

"The ink is cracked, indeed," Flynn said.

"Is there anything else about this?"

"That was all, the cracked ink."

"Nothing strange about the paper. No other analysis, that we haven't talked about, that has been done on it. The cracked ink, bogus document, as simple as that."

"Did you want me to answer your question?" Flynn asked.

"Yes."

"The paper is genuine," Flynn said. "I'm convinced the paper is genuine. Outside of that, I couldn't do very much more."[165]

Near the end of the day's proceedings, Rich asked Flynn, "Has anyone ever testified in court so far as you know about this ink cracking phenomena?"

"I've found no references in the literature to the ink cracking phenomenon in the thousands of pages, literally thousands of pages that I've read," Flynn answered. "Nor have any of the modern forensic experts that I've talked to discussed the ink cracking phenomenon."

"Then I take it that it has never been used as the test for the legitimacy or illegitimacy of a document before?"

"As far as I know, it has not," Flynn agreed. "Remember that the research on iron gallotannic ink came to a screeching halt in the 40's, because most modern forensic documents are not written with iron gallotannic ink. And so a lot of the modern analytical techniques that could have been applied had the ink still been applicable have never been used."

A short while later, Rich asked, "Then I take it, that you're the first expert ever to use this particular test in a courtroom, so far as you know, to claim a particular document to be a forgery?"

"Yes," Flynn said. "I may well be the only expert that has seen artificially aged gallotannic ink."[166]

Rich then raised what could prove to be an important issue if Hofmann were bound over for trial: "Do you have an opinion as to who wrote these things? Is it or could it have been the same author?"

Flynn did not name the documents' author but said, "I believe that if indeed the writings are forgeries, a fair degree of calligraphic skills would have been required to do it, but not an insurmountable degree of calligraphic skills." In fact, the documents that Flynn himself had created looked "fairly capable," he said, "and I'm not a real good writer."[167]

On Monday, May 12, George Throckmorton took the stand, corroborating what Flynn had said earlier and adding further details about specific documents, including some not mentioned in Flynn's testimony. Throckmorton said he had examined 688 documents written with iron gallotannic ink, 21 of which exhibited cracking.

"Out of the twenty-one or so that you have exhibited with the cracking effect, where, to your knowledge, did those documents come from?" asked Gerry D'Elia.

"All of them were purported to me as coming through Mark Hofmann," Throckmorton answered.[168]

Some of the Spanish Fork Co-op notes, he testified, included impressions made from the same stamps that created the proofs found at a local engraving company. The inks used in making the impressions proved to be indistinguishable from modern stamp-pad inks. The notes also fluoresced under ultraviolet light, proving that modern pigments or whiteners had been added to the paper used to print them.[169]

Throckmorton testified that one set of Spanish Fork notes bore letters matching those missing from sheets of rub-off letters found in Hofmann's home. He also concluded that negatives of Deseret Currency were used to produce plates from which several notes admitted into evidence were printed.[170]

When questioned about the Emma Smith hymnal, Throckmorton testified that a negative found at an engraving company was used to create the plate from which the text on the final page of the hymnal was printed.[171]

With Throckmorton on the stand, D'Elia continued to throw out questions about documents as though he were tossing clay pigeons for shooting practice. As each document became a target, Throckmorton took careful aim and fired, in some cases nicking, in most cases blowing apart, its credibility with a blast of research data. From the Anthon transcript to *The Oath of a Freeman,* Throckmorton proved to be a crack shot.[172]

When the defense finally got its chance to shoot at Throckmorton, its first shot was aimed at his religious beliefs. "Mr. Throckmorton, you are still under oath," Brad Rich adjured. "Are you familiar with a document known as the Book of Mormon?"

"The Book of Mormon?" Throckmorton echoed.

"Yes."

"Yes, sir."

"Do you have a particular belief about from whence that volume came?"

"I do."

"Can you tell us what that is?"

D'Elia, a non-Mormon, objected, seeking to truncate the defense's line of questioning. "I realize that we do have a potential cross-examination point with respect as to the religion of Mr. Throckmorton and I think that his religious bias, simply stated, would be sufficient for the record."

Rich responded that the salamander letter was one of the "central difficulties with these documents." He added, "And certainly a belief in the origin of The Book of Mormon that is inconsistent with the involvement of a salamander gives a power of motivation for bias, and anybody who believes an inconsistent scheme for that volume being produced. It's as simple as that. I don't intend to belabor the point but I'm entitled to that much."

"You may answer," the judge ruled.

"What was the question?" Throckmorton asked.

"Can you tell me," Rich paraphrased, "what your beliefs are vis a vis the origin of The Book of Mormon?"

Throckmorton answered, "I believe my beliefs would be what would be considered the conservative point of view for a member of the Mormon faith and that is that The Book of Mormon was translated from the plates that were given to Joseph Smith."

"And who gave those plates to Joseph Smith?"

"That would have been Moroni, the Angel Moroni, as he is called."

"An angel," Rich repeated. "Do you believe that either a salamander or a toad was involved in any way in that process?"

"I don't believe so."[173]

After several more questions directed at Throckmorton's religious convictions, the defense turned its attention to Throckmorton's professional credentials, asking questions aimed at proving Throckmorton had little experience dealing with nineteenth-century documents. This line of questioning gradually dissolved into a minute review of documents discussed earlier.[174]

On May 13, the final day of testimony in the hearing, the defense took its opportunity to cross-examine police detective Jim Bell. Toward the end of the cross-examination, Ron Yengich asked Bell what evidence he had of a motive for Hofmann to kill Christensen. The question sparked an objection from the prosecution that was followed by arguments on both sides about whether Bell should be permitted to answer the question. Finally, the judge ruled that Bell should recite facts related to motive but not provide his conclusions on the subject.[175]

With these instructions, Bell then testified as follows, relying on the statement of Curt Bench: "It's my understanding that Mr. Christensen had gotten the information through additional people to Mr. Hofmann that if he couldn't produce the McLellin Collection . . . he would make sure that he would be charged criminally, that he would be charged civilly, that he would be excommunicated from the Church, and that he would no longer be dealing in Mormon documents, which is—basically has been his livelihood, and if he removes Mr. Christensen, that's one thing he removes is that threat." Bell also said he understood that Christensen might have tried reaching Kenneth Rendell to discuss the papyrus fragment, thereby learning its true origins. Christensen's death removed this possibility. Under questioning, however, Bell conceded this latter information was conjecture.[176]

Kathy Sheets was killed, Bell said, to lead investigators away from the real motive for the Christensen murder.[177]

When Bell finished his testimony, David Biggs read two stipulations into the record.[178] The first dealt with Justin Schiller, the New York book dealer with whom Hofmann frequently dealt. Yengich pointed out that the stipulation was "only for the purposes of this hearing and only to represent what he would say if he were called to testify at this hearing."

According to the stipulation, Schiller and Hofmann did not have an agreement for the purchase of eighteen rare books from Europe as represented by Hofmann. Schiller acted as Hofmann's agent in purchasing the Charles Dickens "Haunted Man" manuscript, but none of the money came from Thomas Wilding's group. In fact, most of it came from Schiller and his partner Raymond Wapner. Hofmann, the stipulation said, never bought out Schiller's portion, nor was the manuscript ever sold to any investors as claimed by Hofmann. Schiller and Hofmann "owned the Oath of a Freeman in a 50–50 partnership."[179]

The defense agreed to the second stipulation under the same terms as the first. The second stipulation, which Biggs noted was "prepared and signed by Mr. Yengich and Mr. Stott," identified Gordon Hinckley and stated that he met with Hofmann sometime between January 11 and 14, 1983, when Hofmann sold the Josiah Stowell letter to Hinckley "in his role as a representative for the Church of Jesus Christ of Latter-day Saints," representing that the letter was authentic. With this stipulation, the prosecution finally corrected the "private victim" error perpetuated by the charging documents. The stipulation also described the church's purchase of the Grandin contract, "represented by Mark W. Hofmann to be an authentic document." Finally, it stated that Hinckley "has never seen nor possessed nor has any knowledge of the whereabouts of a document or a group of documents known as the McLellin Collection."[180]

The prosecution had prepared the stipulation, received the defense's approval of it, and then read it into the record without Hinckley ever seeing it.[181] Had he reviewed it, Hinckley could have revised the stipulation to reflect the church's discovery of McLellin materials in its possession. Yet those materials, like the McLellin documents discovered in Texas by the *Salt Lake Tribune,* were not the composite McLellin collection Hofmann had described. Hofmann's McLellin collection had never been seen by anyone—nor could it be—because it did not exist.

The following morning, the *Salt Lake Tribune* summarized Jim Bell's testimony on motive. Although Bell had not used Gordon Hinckley's name, the newspaper reported that Bell said Hofmann killed Christensen because he "was a 'threat' to Mr. Hofmann in that he had told Deseret Book employee Curt Bench that high authorities in the Church of Jesus Christ of Latter-day Saints—including President Gordon B. Hinckley, the first counselor to then-President Spencer W. Kimball—had threatened Mr. Hofmann with criminal, civil and ecclesiastical punishments unless he made good on an overdue $185,000 loan arranged by Elder Hugh Pinnock, a member of the church's First Quorum of the Seventy."[182]

Jerry Cahill of the church's Public Communications Department used the *Tribune* article to prepare a summary of the previous day's hearing. In one sentence, he summarized Bell's purported statement that church authorities, including Hinckley, had threatened Hofmann. Hinckley, who received a copy of the summary, read the sentence disapprovingly. Having neither threatened Hofmann nor intended that others should do so, he wrote "No" next to the sentence and underlined it.[183]

On Tuesday, May 20, Bob Stott delivered the prosecution's closing argument in the case, summarizing the evidence presented during the hearing to show how the elements of the charged crimes had been proved. Near the end of his two-hour speech, he zeroed in on motive. During the second week of October 1985, Stott said, Hofmann was under "severe, unrelenting pressure." He owed the Wilding group nearly $500,000 and he had signed notes obligating himself to pay $4,000 a day in interest if the sum was not repaid. He owed Al Rust $132,000. And Steve Christensen, Stott said, was pressuring Hofmann to repay the First Interstate Bank loan.

At the same time, Stott noted, Hofmann experienced the fear of exposure. "He was obviously double-dealing on the nonexistent McLellin collection, and he was desperately trying to keep the different parties apart." Hofmann was also trying to keep Schiller and Wilding apart, lest Schiller discover there were *two* copies of *The Oath of a Freeman*. Hofmann had shown Rendell's papyrus to several persons, and Hofmann had to keep information about the papyrus from getting to Rendell, who was planning to visit Utah. "So he had the fear of Kenneth Rendell coming [and] talking with people," Stott explained, reminding the court that Rendell knew both Christensen and Ashworth. If any of Hofmann's fears were realized, Stott said, his reputation and business would be ruined and he would be unable to pay off his obligations.

"Well, what was the center of all of this pressure?" Stott asked rhetorically. "It was Steve Christensen," he answered. Then he explained why. Wilding's attorney threatened to call Christensen "to tell Steve about all the problems he was having, and all the money that was owed." Christensen was pressuring Hofmann on the bank loan. And Christensen knew Rendell, who had authenticated the salamander letter for him and thus would likely contact Christensen when he arrived in Salt Lake City. "So how did Mark Hofmann bear this unbearable, unrelenting pressure?" Stott asked. "Well, he had to get rid of Steve Christensen." Christensen's death would not solve all Hofmann's problems, but it would buy him some time, and "the only thing a con artist ever wants is time."

Elsewhere in his speech, Stott moved to dismiss one of the communications fraud charges because the alleged act occurred before the effective date of the statute on which the count was based. Later, he moved to dismiss another count because prosecutors felt that the alleged misrepresentation really pertained to one of the other crimes already charged. Stott also asked that the count dealing with the Stowell letter be amended to show that the church, not Hinckley as an individual, had acquired the document. These motions were all eventually granted.[184]

The following day, May 21, Ron Yengich gave the defense's closing argument, focusing on inconsistencies and other weaknesses in the prosecution's case. Much of his argument was taken up with motive, the subject that had plagued investigators from the beginning of the investigation and promised to become a key issue at trial. The prosecution, Yengich charged, had been unable to find a convincing motive that would tie the three bombings together. Referring to Stott's speech of the previous day, Yengich said, "Intriguingly, Mrs. Sheets's death . . . was glossed over, if discussed at all, by Mr. Stott."

Yengich said the prosecution tried to tie the three bombings together using Jerry Taylor, the federal bomb expert who testified that the three bombs were similar. Yet, Yengich asserted, the only similarity among the bombs was that they were pipe bombs. He went on to point out differences among the three devices.

Yengich said the prosecution's other reason for suspecting Mark Hofmann to be the bomber was the direct testimony of Bruce Passey and the hearsay testimony of his father. Bruce's testimony may have been tainted through conversations with his father, whose testimony was contaminated by television videotapes of Hofmann before he had a chance to participate in a formal police lineup. Also, the police composite drawing prepared with Bruce's input was "generically the same as many of us in the courtroom," Yengich argued, and lacked any feature that would be "substantially consistent with the identity of Mr. Hofmann." Moreover, Yengich pointed out, Bruce could not remember Hofmann wearing glasses, and he gave the wrong color for the sleeves of the letter jacket Hofmann was supposedly wearing.

Janet McDermott, who supposedly saw Hofmann, gave a somewhat different description of the bomber, Yengich noted, pointing out that "she also said Mr. Stott's physical characteristics were similar" to the bomber's. In fact, Yengich contended, "the description would fit, again, a number of us in this courtroom."

Yengich pointed out that the young neighbor who said he had seen a van that matched Hofmann's was unable to recall the "unusual antenna" on Hofmann's van, a characteristic that would distinguish it from other similar vans. Yengich also said he gave the wrong color for the van.

Detective Bell had testified that Hofmann said the bomb package exploded on the floor of the car, whereas Jerry Taylor had concluded it actually exploded at the console level. This contradiction was supposed to be evidence that Hofmann was the bomber. But, Yengich countered, the contradictory statement by Hofmann was given while he was hospitalized after being injured by a bomb, and it was unreasonable to conclude "that Mr. Hofmann's inability to go through a thorough cross-examination under those circumstances . . . is indicative of his guilt."

Furthermore, Yengich charged, prosecution witness Brad Christensen "changed his testimony considerably, and he changed it to dovetail with the theory of Mr. Taylor, upon whom the prosecution really hangs their hat in the bombing."

Yengich hammered at other problems with the evidence and then returned to the crucial issue in the case: "But Mr. Stott recognizes that there is a problem in this case, . . . good prosecutor that he is. And what is it? Well, what is the motive for Mr. Hofmann to perform all of these vile acts?"

Reviewing some of Stott's arguments of the previous day, Yengich then commented, "Mr. Stott says, 'Steve Christensen was the center of all [Hofmann's] problems,' and I say to the court that that's bull. Steve Christensen was helping Mark. They had been friends." Even if there had been tension between them, Yengich argued, Christensen's death did not promise to relieve Hofmann of any difficulties. Stott had argued that Hofmann wanted to buy time. But, Yengich responded, Stott's argument did not make sense because "killing any of the participants in this particular scheme, to use the prosecution's argument, not only would not buy time but would focus an inquiry, a police inquiry, on all of the participants involved."

"I suggest to the court that this case . . . , as far as homicide is concerned, is based on all *maybes*," Yengich said. " 'Maybe' this was going to happen. Maybe it wasn't. But a case based on *maybes* is no case at all, and the bombings in fact bought no one additional time."

"They do not tell us anything," Yengich also said, "about the Sheets death or any reason based on evidence for the death of Gary Sheets or his wife. Nothing." Yengich concluded by asking the court to dismiss the murder and infernal device counts.[185]

On Thursday, May 22, 1986, Judge Paul Grant issued his findings. "Because of the widespread public interest in these matters," his statement began, "the court would remind all that it is not determining the guilt of the defendant but simply assessing the adequacy of the state's evidence to further proceed in these cases." He then declared that the court had found probable cause that the crimes alleged had been committed and that Hofmann had committed them.[186]

13

Plea, Sentencing, and Interviews

When the curtain closed on the preliminary hearing, church officials, like other members of the public, anticipated a long intermission before the next acts began in the legal drama. While waiting for the curtain to rise again, they continued to cooperate with investigators and prosecutors gathering evidence in the case. Meanwhile, however, two other issues also occupied their attention.[1]

The first grew out of the preliminary hearing. Deseret Book employee Curt Bench had testified that Steve Christensen told him of two unnamed general authorities who wanted Christensen to warn Hofmann of consequences that might follow if Hofmann did not repay the First Interstate Bank loan. Media accounts of Bench's testimony identified the general authorities as Hugh Pinnock, Dallin Oaks, and even Gordon Hinckley. Church officials read the accounts and became concerned about correcting what to them were obvious errors.[2]

Contrary to media reports, Bench had not said in his testimony that Hinckley issued any warnings. Bench had said Christensen described the two general authorities as "a member of the First Quorum of Seventy and an apostle." He also said Christensen explained "that these general authorities were going to tell President Hinckley" about Hofmann's perfidy and that Hinckley would therefore lose faith in the document dealer. That portion of Bench's testimony showed that Hinckley was not involved in issuing any warnings. Nevertheless, as happened repeatedly during retellings of stories about the case, reporters and others imputed the warnings to Hinckley.[3]

Oaks was convinced that he too had never said what was attributed to him. He had met Christensen only once, and that meeting consisted merely of a handshake and a formal exchange of greetings.[4]

During the summer and early fall of 1985, Pinnock had met with Christensen repeatedly. Much of the time in these meetings was spent discussing Christensen's employment difficulties. It may have been in one of their conversations about Hofmann, however, that the list of consequences Bench mentioned had its origin.

After the bombings, Pinnock was surprised to learn what Christensen had told Bench. He racked his brain to figure out what he might have said to lead Christensen to suggest a list of consequences that could follow from Hofmann's nonpayment of the loan. In his discussions with Christensen, Pinnock recalled, they might have discussed the problems a person could get into by not paying off debts, but he would not have intended what he said as a threat to be communicated to Hofmann.[5]

At the October 23 news conference, Pinnock had told reporters that he and Christensen had discussed several times the problems that had arisen in trying to close the McLellin deal, though they had never doubted the collection existed. Over a year later, as church officials considered issuing a statement denying any threats of excommunication, Pinnock told Oaks that Christensen might have said something like, "What if he's conning us?" to which he might have replied, "Yeah, that could lead to a [church] court." As Oaks recorded, Pinnock "couldn't deny that this [was] said to [Steve Christensen] though doesn't recall. Nothing to do with bank loan!"[6]

Whatever the case, Christensen apparently wished to infuse some seriousness into Hofmann and used the earlier conversations as a basis for his statement to Bench. Christensen undoubtedly knew Pinnock reported to Oaks and so alluded to Oaks when conveying impressions gained in conversations with Pinnock.

Still, Hinckley was confident he had made no threats. Oaks knew he had not either. And Pinnock felt he had not intended anything he said to be a threat. Oaks obtained a transcript of Bench's testimony through the church's legal counsel. He then sent portions of it to Hinckley, proposing that the church issue a short statement to correct the misperception.[7]

On and off over the next several weeks, church officials considered making a statement, but they waited until court proceedings against Hofmann had concluded.[8] By then, Oaks had decided to address the subject during a Brigham Young University symposium on church history and recent forgeries. In his talk, Oaks explained, "These allegations of threats of excommunication were not answered at the time they were made because the case was still pending, and it was deemed undesirable to make out-of-court comments on the testimony of various witnesses."

Then he expressed church officials' views on the subject. "Now, I am authorized to say in behalf of Elder Hugh W. Pinnock that he made no threat of excommunication or other Church discipline against Hofmann in his discussions about the payment of the loan," Oaks said. "I am also authorized to say in behalf of President Gordon B. Hinckley, and I likewise say for myself, that neither of us ever discussed the possibility of Church discipline of Hofmann with Hofmann or his associates or with anyone else. As far as we can determine, no Church official ever made any threats of excommunication against Hofmann for non-payment of debts, directly or indirectly."[9]

Besides worrying about the alleged threats of excommunication, church officials also spent the months after the preliminary hearing trying to put to rest the rumor that they were suppressing a history written by Oliver Cowdery. For over a year since Brent Metcalfe had first publicized the rumor, they had tried to locate the volume in the church's vast collections but had been unable to do so. All the while, Metcalfe refused to reveal the name of his secret source who claimed to have seen the volume in church possession. After exhaustive research, church officials finally resolved to go public with their conclusions. On October 16, 1986, one year to the day after Hofmann's car exploded, the church issued a statement categorically denying ownership of the Cowdery history. An early history found in the First Presidency's vault was determined not to be the long-lost history. Furthermore, it contained nothing about salamanders or Alvin Smith's purported role in discovering the golden plates. (The history, later published by Dean Jessee, also proved not to be in Cowdery's hand.)[10]

The day after church officials denied having the Cowdery history, the *Salt Lake Tribune* published an article in which Metcalfe confirmed what church officials suspected but had been unable to prove: the secret source of rumors about the Cowdery history was none other than Mark Hofmann. Metcalfe said it was he who had arranged a meeting between Hofmann and the *Los Angeles Times* that led to that paper's story on the purported history. Despite Metcalfe's disclosure, it would be many months before the *Times* would acknowledge Hofmann as the story's source and apologize that "in retrospect, it's clear we erred in publishing it without verifying Hofmann's story with another source."[11]

With the Oliver Cowdery history rumor laid to rest, church officials waited for the next act in the legal drama to begin. Like other members of the public, they heard and read of rumors suggesting that plea negotiations might be going on backstage.[12] Yet investigators continued to request evidence from the church, suggesting an equal likelihood Hofmann would be tried.[13]

The five cases against Hofmann that had been combined for the preliminary hearing became separate again when Hofmann was bound over for trial.[14] Eventually, the first trial was scheduled to begin March 2, 1987, with other trials to follow.[15] Prosecutors sought to have the trials consolidated, but their motion was denied.[16]

Meanwhile, rumors of a plea bargain continued. On October 14, 1986, a *Salt Lake Tribune* writer relying on unnamed sources speculated that a plea would have to include the homicides to be acceptable to the prosecution. "And," the reporter continued, "it is doubtful that the prosecutors involved would take any plea that didn't include at least some explanation of the alleged forgeries, thefts and frauds with which Mr. Hofmann is charged."[17]

In December, both sides filed motions in the case, which appeared to be proceeding toward trial despite the ever-present rumors of plea negotiations.[18] In late December, however, rumors of a potential plea agreement intensified.

On Tuesday morning, December 30, the *Salt Lake Tribune* reported that plea negotiations were underway and speculated on what the terms of the agreement might be. On the rationale for the plea, the article explained, "Most police and attorneys involved in the case have said that the 32-year-old Mr. Hofmann is an unlikely candidate for the death penalty, given his young age, his lack of prior criminal history and that he has a family."[19]

That afternoon, the *Deseret News* reported information furnished by Gerry D'Elia, who had recently resigned from the county attorney's office after being transferred from the Hofmann case by the new county attorney, David Yocom. According to the article, "D'Elia suggested that if a plea bargain were offered, it might include reducing the two capital homicide charges to second-degree homicide counts, punishable by indeterminate sentences of five years to life," which "could be imposed consecutively or concurrently."

The article cited unnamed proponents of such a deal as saying it would benefit the state because Hofmann would likely not receive the death penalty anyway and because the agreement would "save the expense of a lengthy trial and would guarantee that Hofmann would spend prison time." Opponents, on the other hand, felt a plea bargain would leave unanswered questions about the reasons for the Sheets murder and about the document forgeries.[20]

January 1987 brought with it media reports exemplifying the mixed public reaction that nearly always follows announcements about plea bargains, long a controversial aspect of the criminal justice system in the United States.[21]

Then on Wednesday, January 21, a Salt Lake television station reported that a plea agreement had been reached and that Hofmann would enter his guilty plea at a hearing scheduled for the following day. Other news sources repeated the story. Reportedly, Hofmann would plead guilty to second-degree murder in the death of Christensen and manslaughter in the death of Sheets. He was also expected to plead guilty to at least one charge of theft by deception and one of communications fraud. The Thursday hearing was canceled, however, reportedly in reaction to the publicity.[22]

On Friday, January 23, 1987, Mark W. Hofmann finally entered the courtroom to admit his guilt and be sentenced. Under the terms of the plea agreement, dated January 7, Hofmann pleaded guilty to second-degree murder in the deaths of both Steve Christensen and Kathy Sheets, with the prosecution agreeing it would "specifically not oppose, at the time of sentencing, a defense motion . . . to reduce [the Sheets homicide] to the next lowest category of offense, a Second Degree Felony pursuant to the Court's authority."

Hofmann also agreed to plead guilty to one count of theft by deception in obtaining money from Al Rust for the purported purchase of the McLellin collection and to another count of theft by deception in the sale of the salamander letter to Steve Christensen. Under the agreement, all other charges were dropped, including the federal machine gun charge, and New York authorities would not prosecute Hofmann for *The Oath of a Freeman*.[23]

Mark Hofmann, standing between his attorneys, pleads guilty as family members of bombing victims look on. (Don Grayston/*Deseret News*)

Another provision of the agreement, which apparently had already been met, permitted prosecutors to ask Hofmann, through his attorney, to "communicate the circumstances of four charged offenses, to be selected by the prosecution attorneys." The agreement also provided that "if the prosecuting attorneys are satisfied with the information provided by the defendant to the four selected charges, the prosecution will not request of the trial judge, at the time of sentencing, consecutive prison time on the four guilty pleas . . . and will not object to concurrent sentences," though the prosecution would insist "that a prison commitment be imposed on each of the four charges pled to."

In what would later prove to be the most controversial of the provisions, Hofmann agreed to meet with the prosecuting attorneys within thirty days of his commitment to prison to "answer, truthfully and completely, all questions said attorneys may have on any or all of the charged offenses . . . and the surrounding circumstances of those offenses and any other related activities." An incentive for complying with this term was also provided: "If the prosecuting attorneys are satisfied with the defendant's responses to all questions and believe the defendant has been totally open, forthright, and honest, said attorneys will represent that conclusion to the Board of Pardons of the State of Utah and make no further recommendation. If, on the other hand, the prosecuting attorneys feel the defendant has not fulfilled this part of the plea agreement, said prosecuting attorneys will be free to make any recommendation to the Board of Pardons they feel is necessary and consistent with the ends of justice." This arrangement aimed at removing fears that a plea bargain would reduce the amount of information the public would receive about the nature and extent of Hofmann's criminal activities.[24]

In approving the plea agreement, Utah Third District Court Judge Kenneth Rigtrup explained that lead prosecutor Bob Stott was experienced in trying capital murder cases and thus "well qualified to evaluate, in the light of public interest, the advantages and disadvantages to the public of going to trial." Rigtrup's own review of the preliminary hearing transcripts convinced him that "there's been a reasonable public trial of the case already." The judge found "that there's a substantial rational basis for the plea bargain, and the Court's approval is justified." Later, referring to the families of the murder victims, the judge also pointed out that "although there may be some disagreement with what the ultimate resolution is in this case, . . . the victims have generally expressed an interest in bringing this matter to an early resolution" and "have a real and substantial desire to close this chapter of their lives."[25]

After Hofmann pleaded guilty, Rigtrup sentenced him to one term of five years to life in prison and three terms of one to fifteen years, at the same time expressing an opinion he hoped would carry weight with the Board of Pardons: "Due to the indiscriminate nature of the killings and the types of devices employed . . . I want you to serve the rest of your natural life in the Utah State Prison."[26]

Later that day, after church officials learned of the agreement, spokesman Richard Lindsay issued a statement explaining that church officials were victims of Hofmann's crimes but had not been consulted on the plea agreement.[27] The statement also expressed sympathy and hope. "On behalf of The Church of Jesus Christ of Latter-day Saints, its leaders and members," Lindsay said, "we extend again our heartfelt sympathies to the families and associates of all whose lives have been so deeply affected by the bombings and related events of the past months. It is our hope that the healing process may now be hastened for those who have suffered from these tragedies."[28]

Though prosecutors chose not to consult church officials before entering a plea agreement, as the time for Hofmann's prison interviews drew near, George Throckmorton approached Glenn Rowe to ask if the church had any questions it wished to pose to Hofmann. As a key document expert in the case, Throckmorton expected to be able to examine Hofmann about the forgeries during the interviews. Rowe took Throckmorton's question to his supervisors in the Historical Department, who slated it for discussion at their regular meeting with Boyd Packer and Dallin Oaks. Still wary of reducing the distance between the church and law enforcement officials, the group "determined that Brother Rowe's answer to Mr. Throckmorton should simply be that we hope the questioning will bring out the truth about all the documents, including those on the list furnished to the prosecution during the investigation."[29] Church officials hoped Hofmann would tell the truth. They also worried he would not. Hofmann had injured the church repeatedly with his deceit, and his promise to tell all seemed as much an opportunity to further injure his victims as to help them.[30]

Though the prosecutors' questioning of Hofmann began within the thirty-day period specified in the plea agreement, it did not end until May.[31] Early that month, Richard Lindsay wrote a memorandum to several church leaders, including Gordon Hinckley and Dallin Oaks, explaining an offer received from the county attorney's office. The memo explained that Bob Stott "has advised the Church Legal Department that the follow-up debriefing with Mark Hofmann will probably be completed in about two weeks," although "it would be several weeks (4–6) after that before a comprehensive public report is issued." Stott added, Lindsay said, that when the interviews were completed, county officials "would be willing to brief a Church-designated representative of any additional information revealed in the Hofmann interviews that was not disclosed in the earlier process of discovery that led to the plea-bargained sentence."[32]

Church officials felt that the church, as a victim of Hofmann's crimes, deserved a preview of the information that would shortly thereafter become public. Before accepting Stott's offer, however, they wanted to be certain the church was not receiving preferential treatment. After learning the same offer was being extended to other victims of Hofmann's crimes, they agreed to accept it. Hinckley suggested the church be represented in the meeting by its own legal counsel and representatives from the Historical and Public Communications departments.[33]

As church officials awaited their briefing, newspaper accounts signaled that not all had gone well in prosecutors' interviews with Hofmann. In asking questions of Hofmann, prosecutors had proceeded chronologically, beginning with Hofmann's early crimes and moving to the time of the bombings. When they reached the murders, Hofmann began to balk, refusing to speak to a police investigator and demanding a change in his confinement.[34]

On July 30, 1987, one day before copies of the prison interview transcript were released to the general public, church officials finally got their chance to meet with County Attorney David Yocom and his deputies Bob Stott and David Biggs to receive a copy of the transcript and ask questions. The meeting was held in a conference room at the office of the church's general counsel, represented at the meeting by Oscar McConkie. Other church representatives at the meeting were Richard Lindsay and Jerry Cahill from the Public Communications Department and Richard Turley of the Historical Department, who spent much of the rest of the day studying the transcripts.[35]

The transcripts proved generally tedious reading, occasionally interrupted by interesting details. At the beginning of the first day of interviews, Bob Stott had explained how the interviews would proceed. "We'll go to the Anthon Transcript," he said, "and go from there in kind of chronological order," which "might be the easiest way for everybody to look at it."[36]

Stott spent nearly the entire first session asking Hofmann about the Anthon transcript and the Bible in which he claimed to have found it. Hofmann admitted having bought the Bible in England while he was serving as a missionary. Under questioning, he described in detail how he had altered the Bible and forged the Anthon transcript.[37]

"Did you think about what you were going to do and then go out and do it," Stott asked, "or did you kind of experiment along the way or what?"

"I had already previously played with the inks," Hofmann answered. "I had a couple methods of oxidizing the ink. I had recipes concerning the manufacture of the proper ink. I had handwriting samples of Joseph Smith which I had acquired from various books or whatnot, Xerox copies of his letters or whatnot. I knew that I could obtain the proper paper."[38]

Hofmann said later in the session that he stole the paper from the library of the LDS Institute of Religion near the Utah State University campus, the very place he took the transcript after claiming to have discovered it. The paper was an end sheet of a book on biblical history printed around 1830 in the United States.[39]

Stott also spent nearly the entire second session discussing the Anthon transcript and Bible, though Hofmann mentioned that the Stowell letter too was a forgery and hinted he had also forged Daniel Boone's writing. Responding to questions about the Anthon transcript, Hofmann explained how he staged its discovery and then established a provenance for it. He said he began by telling people the Bible came from a man named White, a name he chose because he felt its commonness would make it difficult to verify. He added a first name after he visited Carthage to talk to Dorothy Dean.[40]

Later in the second session, Stott talked to Hofmann about the way he acted around the persons to whom he first showed the Anthon transcript. Stott wanted to know if he had planned how he would react to their responses or if he just went "with the flow."

Hofmann replied, "I think that's what I did is just more or less go with the flow, as you say."

"Is that something you thought you could handle pretty easily," Stott continued, "kind of acting somewhat ignorant of what was going on and amaturish?"

In responding, Hofmann said, "I think I have that ability in my personality. I obviously do for the number of frauds that have been committed, you know as far as, I don't think I give myself away very easily as far as I can look someone in the eye and lie, for example."[41]

In the first two interview sessions, Bob Stott and David Biggs had represented the prosecution and Ron Yengich the defense. At the third session, Yengich's partner Brad Rich replaced him. Yet again, the interview began with the Anthon transcript, and Stott asked Hofmann about taking it to church headquarters for examination. "How did you feel," he inquired, "about going down and presenting it to the so-called Church scholars and experts?"

"I believed that it would pass their inspection as far as being in Joseph Smith's handwriting," Hofmann said, "and as far as how I felt, probably a combination of emotions. There was, of course, a little bit of fear involved since, of course, it was a forged document. There was some excitement involved, a feeling of duping them, I guess."

"I think this is a[s] good time as any to ask," Stott ventured, "what were your feelings at this time generally to start out, say with your faith?"

"Well," Hofmann answered, "previous to this I had lost faith in the Mormon Church."

"Do you want to tell us when or was it a gradual thing?"

"Right around the age of 14," Hofmann replied. "Therefore, I wasn't or I had no fear as far as—" He hesitated. "This is something that I guess Ron wants to be here when I start talking about." But then he continued, "Well, I will finish what I was saying."

Rich interrupted, "We are very close to an area that I know Ron wants to be here [to discuss] but I think you can finish this."

"I wasn't fearful of the Church inspiration detecting the forgery," Hofmann finished. "That's all I was going to say."

"Let me ask you this," Stott continued. "It's another question related to this issue. What was your feeling about Mormon history and specifically early Mormon history with Joseph Smith at this time? Did you have some perceptions or—"

"Yes," Hofmann concurred.

"Some things you wanted to do with Mormon history?"

"I won't go so far as to say I wanted to change Mormon history," Hofmann began. Then he backtracked. "Let me take that back. Maybe I did. I believed that the documents that I created could have been a part of Mormon history. I'm speaking specifically, for example, of the magic-related items. The 1825 Stoal Letter, the so-called Salamander Letter. In effect, I guess, the questions I asked myself in deciding on a forgery[,] one of the questions was, what could have been? I had a concept of Church history and I followed that concept."[42]

Hofmann went on to explain how taking the Anthon transcript to church headquarters allowed him to meet Homer Durham, then Gordon Hinckley and Boyd Packer.

"First time you met them?" Biggs asked.

"Yes," Hofmann affirmed. "And then [they] introduced us to the first presidency, but this is the point where we don't want to discuss the Church until Ron is here."[43]

By balking when asked to talk about high-ranking church officials, Hofmann breached his agreement to "answer, truthfully and completely, all questions . . . on any or all of the charged offenses . . . and the surrounding circumstances of those offenses and any other related activities." To facilitate his forgery and fraud schemes, Hofmann had circulated inaccurate stories about church officials and his associations with them. By avoiding questions about church leaders in his prison interviews, Hofmann left many of the inaccuracies uncorrected.[44]

Though there were tangents during the third prison session, Stott continued to ask questions about the Anthon transcript and Bible. Finally, he asked Hofmann, "Do you have anything else on the Anthon transcript you think we ought to ask you?"

"Simply that it's a crude forgery," Hofmann answered, "and shouldn't have fooled the people that it did, in my opinion."[45] Just moments earlier, however, he had acclaimed the forgery's excellence, saying he had "hoped the Church would carry on some tests because I felt confident it would pass."[46]

Eventually, the discussion moved on to the Joseph Smith III blessing, a forgery Hofmann said was aimed partially at the "rewriting of Mormon history" but was "mostly money motivated." In passing, he admitted forging the "White Notes and the associated material." He also acknowledged starting a rumor that the church already had a copy of the Joseph Smith III blessing in its possession. The session ended with a discussion of how Hofmann tried to create a credible provenance for the blessing document.[47]

At the fourth session, just Biggs, Rich, and Hofmann were present. With Stott and Yengich gone, Biggs altered the chronological approach to asking questions. "What I would like to do in their absence," he said, "if it is all right with everyone, is to go to a different area basically because it happens to be my area, and see if we can't get a lot of the printed material done."[48]

Biggs then asked about the seal used to emboss the white notes. Hofmann admitted he made it and that he had earlier made himself a notary seal. Next Biggs asked about the Spanish Fork Co-op notes, and Hofmann described how he made them. During an in-depth description of how he created Deseret Currency, Hofmann admitted destroying a set of plates for the currency after the bombings when the hospital released him to go home. "I went in the room, in my office," he said, "and whatever incriminating evidence that wasn't already taken [by investigators] I put in a bag and probably that same night is when I built a fire." Under further questioning, Hofmann admitted burning the negative used to print a postmark for another purported Joseph Smith letter.[49]

Hofmann described techniques he may have used to print and tip in the final page of the Emma Smith hymnal that went to Brent Ashworth. He explained that he was not exactly sure what method he had used to tip in the page. "I don't remember specifically doing this work," he said, "as opposed to the dozens or possibly hundreds of other pages that I've t[ip]ped in."[50]

After skipping over two other items because Rich wanted to wait until Yengich was present, Biggs moved on to *The Oath of a Freeman*. Hofmann described with obvious relish what was probably his most ambitious fake. He went to the Argosy Book Store in New York and planted the hymn he had retitled *The Oath of a Freeman* so that he could buy it, obtain a receipt with the title on it, and thereby establish a credible provenance for the *Oath* he would later print and try to sell.

He went to great lengths to make sure the latter *Oath* would deceive. He stole seventeenth-century paper from a book in the Brigham Young University library. He burned the paper, catching the carbon in a glass tube chimney. He then mixed the carbon with a specially prepared linseed oil, using a seventeenth-century ink recipe. He also made a solution of tannic acid by boiling a leather binding from the same time period in distilled water "until it turned a nice brown color." He added the solution to the carbon and linseed oil mixture, along with ordinary beeswax. He then had an ink he felt would pass a carbon 14 dating test. He had a zinc printing plate made from artwork he produced to match the printing of the period. To disguise the modern qualities of the plate, he used a small drill with a "fine grinding tip stone" to wear down some of the letters. Then he went over the whole plate with iron wool.

He took special care in selecting the right paper on which to print the document. He studied a genuine copy of the Bay Psalm Book (*The Whole Booke of Psalmes*, 1640), another early work printed by the man known to have printed the genuine lost *Oath*. Hofmann then stole a piece of paper that matched that of the Bay Psalm Book and had been manufactured near the time when the *Oath* was supposed to have been printed. Finally, he rolled his homemade ink on the plate, placed the paper on top of it, put a piece of felt and a copper plate over it, and pressed the pile with a C clamp.[51]

At the fifth interview session, Biggs continued to ask questions about the *Oath*. Investigator Mike George of the county attorney's office accompanied Biggs to the interview, even though Yengich had earlier refused to allow anyone other than "prosecuting attorneys" (the term used in the plea agreement) to sit in. But Yengich was still absent.

"We ought to say," Brad Rich explained on the record, "Mike George is here, in direct contravention to the instructions of Mr. Yengich, on his good behavior and if this appears in the Trib [*Salt Lake Tribune*] tomorrow morning, Yengich will have us both killed."

After an off-the-record discussion, Biggs launched into his questioning. He and George had brought with them two volumes of the *Niles National Register* from which blank pages had been removed. Hofmann said he had used blank sheets from the periodical for the salamander letter, the Lucy Mack Smith letter, and the Stowell letter, though he had no precise recollection of the specific volumes the two men showed him.[52]

A little later in the interview, Hofmann explained the intricate work he had done to come up with the text, the lettering, and the border for the

Oath. "By the time I forged the Oath," he added, "I considered myself a pretty good forger. I thought I had a pretty good knowledge of different techniques that would be used in analyzing it."

Biggs asked Hofmann if he had ever looked at handwritten or printed material with a microscope under ultraviolet light.

"Yes," Hofmann replied, "I have. I've studied that. You will be interested to know that I also, even before the preliminary hearing, spoke to Ron [Yengich] about my fears as far as the cracking was concerned."

"Oh really?" Biggs asked. "You had seen that cracking before yourself?"

"Yes, although I didn't know the cause of it until the preliminary hearing as far as the gum arabic and undoubtedly when somebody reads this transcript they'll keep gum arabic out of the formula."[53]

In a subsequent session, however, Hofmann would claim he had actually been "experimenting . . . in not putting the gum arabic in the ink" on some notes created before the bombings and "was surprised at the preliminary hearing that there was still some cracking."[54]

As the fifth interview continued, Hofmann explained other details about the *Oath* and how he had used New York dealers Schiller and Wapner to try to market it to the Library of Congress and the American Antiquarian Society. Biggs asked Hofmann if he had been concerned that his story about finding the *Oath* in the Argosy Book Store might not prove satisfactory.

"No," Hofmann answered. "I had afterwards gone to Argosy Bookstore with a Xerox of the Oath and the receipt and talked to the lady who had allegedly sold it to me. Interestingly, she claimed to have recognized the Oath and I felt like that source was, or that provenance was secure as far as that's where I obtained it. She informed me that there would be no way for Argosy Bookstore to discover where they had received it since they purchased large collections and thousands of items at a time and so I felt no one would know the source other than Argosy Bookstore. But I felt like Argosy Bookstore would acknowledge that this was the source where I had purchased it."

Hofmann also said that when he told the woman that he thought the *Oath* was valuable, she did not seem overwrought about it. Hofmann recalled that "she said, that's nice, or something like that" and "made some comment about that other people had found some pretty valuable things there before."[55]

Biggs mentioned a letter from the American Antiquarian Society requesting that the *Oath* undergo cyclotron testing. "Did it concern you," Biggs asked Hofmann, "that it may be tested by cyclotron method?"

"No."

"Why not?"

"Because I felt that the document would pass," Hofmann said. "Incidentally," he added, "I never heard. Did it or didn't it?"

"Well," Biggs explained, "it depends on who you talk to. If you talk to Schiller and Wapner, it passed. But if you talk to the people who actually did the tests, they were not that positive about it."

"I'm sure when you called them," Rich interjected, "they were backing up as far as they could."

"Yes," Hofmann maintained, "I'm sure if it wasn't for the other suspicion, i.e. the bombings, etc., I believe it would have passed very well."[56]

Biggs referred to a letter from the American Antiquarian Society to Raymond Wapner expressing interest in buying the *Oath* provided specific conditions were met. The conditions included the provision of certain proofs, a drastic reduction in price, and the approval of the society's council at its October 15 meeting.

"Hypothetically," Biggs asked Hofmann, "if the American Antiquarian Society had been able to and did vote to purchase your Oath on October 15, 1985 for about a million dollars, what would that have done to the financial hole that you dug yourself into by that time?"

"It would have relieved me from it," Hofmann said. "Hence, I guess you want me to say the bombings would not have taken place."

"I don't want you to say that unless it is true," Biggs replied.

"I'll say it," Hofmann said, "since it's true."[57]

Under questioning, Hofmann acknowledged that the second *Oath* he printed and later gave to Wilding was not as sophisticated as the first. He did not take nearly as much care in manufacturing the ink for it and did not think it would pass a cyclotron test.[58]

After yet more discussion, Biggs asked George and Rich if they had other questions about the *Oath*. Neither did. "Mark," Biggs asked Hofmann, "anything else that should be said concerning the Oath of the Freeman?"

"I never went in to the other aging techniques other than the oxidizing the ink on the back," Hofmann said, referring to a forged inscription he had penned on the back of the first *Oath*. "Did you want me to go into anything else?"

"Certainly," Biggs answered.

Hofmann recited a list of techniques he used to age the first *Oath*. "I created foxing markings on it," he said. "I folded it repeatedly. I browned the edges of the document. I browned the entire document. I believe that I waterstained it."

"How did you create the foxing?" Rich asked with apparent interest.

"With a fungus, a red fungus."

"How did you learn how to do that?" Biggs asked.

"Just asking myself what causes this on a genuine old document and trying to imitate it," Hofmann replied. "Foxing is caused by fungus."[59]

Later in the interview, Biggs and George questioned Hofmann about how he made the Jim Bridger notes. Then at the end of the day's session, George showed Hofmann an old book investigators had gotten from the University of Utah library. "The reason I show you this," George said, "is there are many areas throughout the book where letters and words have been carved out from the typing. Did you ever do that?"

"I remember the book," Hofmann said, "because of the end sheet paper but I do not remember, I cannot imagine why I would have done that. For a couple of reasons. I did not actually cut out of books. I cut out of Xeroxes which I made of books and I can't think of . . . any item I would have cut those out to use it for."

"That means," Rich said, "there is another forger out there."[60]

Stott, Biggs, and Yengich were present at the sixth session with Hofmann when the discussion reverted back to the Joseph Smith III blessing. Stott asked Hofmann if he wanted to correct anything he had said in the past about that transaction.

"There's probably a lot that I could say," Hofmann began, "but let me just leave it at the Reorganized Church and Mr. Howard acted honorably during the negotiation process. Which statement somewhat contradicts my previous writings or talking, as you describe it. I'll just leave it at that."

"Let's make something clear, all right," Yengich interjected, "just so the public is going to have access to it. You have avoided giving your impressions of people and institutions, is that right?"

"Yes, that's correct," Hofmann concurred.

"And as I understand it, the reason is that your feeling is that those are just your own conclusions and they may or may not be valid?" the defense lawyer suggested. "Is that a fair statement, because they are just your conclusions[,] right?"

"That's right," Hofmann said. "And there's no need to cause embarrassment."

"Okay," Yengich said, "I just wanted that clear."[61]

Shortly thereafter, *The Oath of a Freeman* came up again, and Biggs asked Hofmann if there were any other techniques used on the first *Oath* that they had not already discussed. Hofmann said he had used turpentine in the ink formula to make it conform to early ink recipes. "Any other techniques used?" Biggs inquired.

"Yes," Hofmann said, "there was other techniques in aging of the paper. I believe that there is a, what appears to be a book worm's hole through the document. When it is folded it goes through two pages."

"How did you accomplish that?" Biggs asked.

"That's a strange story," Hofmann began. "We had some bags of wheat down in our basement which were in a type of paper bags which we found little bugs had eaten through and I took, I thought that was interest[ing] so I took what looked like a little fly and put it in a notebook and came by a couple days later and it ate through a few pages. So I thought it was rather convincing, so I believe that that document has bookworm holes in it."

"How did you do that?" Biggs asked again.

"That's a new one on me," Yengich admitted.

Hofmann began again. "I believe I took a bug and stuck it in a book. Put the Oath—" He hesitated. "I've just changed my story. I don't believe that that was used on this particular document. The reason being—"

"It was an interesting story," Biggs commented.

"Is that true?" Yengich queried. "You did do that? It's not a story in the Grimms Fairy [Tales] I take it?"

Hofmann did not answer the question directly. Instead he said, "What document did I do that on?"

"Answer my question," Yengich directed his client. "It is not a story in the Grimms Fairy [Tales]? You actually did do that with a document; is that right?"

"Yes," Hofmann assured them. "I'm thinking I wouldn't have done it on that document since the next day I took it to New York and I wouldn't have been able to leave the bug on it for a couple days."

"What document has bookworm holes in it?" Biggs asked.

"Tell me if you ever find a document with bookworm holes in it," Hofmann said. "I'll be interested to see. It's probably a printed document, as I remember. I believe it would have been a printed document."[62]

Eventually, the discussion turned to the Bullock-Young letter. Hofmann described how he forged and aged it. Near the end of the session, Bob Stott asked Hofmann, "Why did you create that document, and what did you do with it?"

Hofmann said he forged it "to give validity" to the Joseph Smith III blessing. "What I did with it, I gave it to President Hinkley."

Stott asked Hofmann if he gave it to the church leader before or after the blessing document transaction.

"It would have been afterwards, probably," Hofmann answered. "I believe, guess, a week afterwards maybe. Maybe two weeks. I don't know, maybe even less." In fact, it had been six months later.

Shortly after Hofmann gave this answer, the session drew to a close. Referring to Hofmann, Yengich asked Stott and Biggs, "Are you satisfied with the answers that he gave you today, as far as you know?"

"Up to the last part," Biggs replied.[63]

In the seventh session, Stott returned to the Bullock-Young document and asked Hofmann, "To refresh our memory again, can you put somewhere, a date on when you did that?"

Hofmann answered, "I would guess it would have been within one or two weeks after the Church acquired the Joseph Smith, 3rd Blessing and donated it, or traded it, to the Reorganized Church."[64]

The prosecutors did not challenge Hofmann's statement further. Police detective Ken Farnsworth, like other members of the investigative team who were excluded from the interviews under Yengich's strict interpretation of the plea agreement, was periodically debriefed by the prosecutors so he could help point out inconsistencies in Hofmann's statements and suggest further avenues for questioning. Farnsworth would later observe that the questioners intentionally "did not counter him [Hofmann] when they realized that he was probably lying or distorting something." He said the team's strategy was "not to be confrontational and shut off the interviews because of his temperament, but to get as much as was possible out of him realizing he'd be lying all the way along." After gently pumping him for most of the interviews, they would then "deal with the hard issues toward the end."[65]

"What was your purpose for giving it to the President?" Stott asked next about the Bullock-Young document.

"Probably the greatest purpose in my mind was to demonstrate to him my concern for the Church, or in other words, possibly, a potentially embarrassing document would not fall into hands that might use it against the Church. And to prepare him for future dealings as far as if my true interest and intent was for the welfare of the Church."[66]

During the remaining sessions, Hofmann admitted forging many documents pertaining to the church's history, including some, though not all, of those acquired from him by the church. Most of the items he conceded to be forgeries had already been discredited at the preliminary hearing. When the Josiah Stowell letter was discussed, Biggs asked Hofmann, "What did President Hinkley tell you relative to this document?"

"He told me," Hofmann answered, "that for the time being, or in other words, without giving a date as far as how long this would be in effect, that the Council of the Twelve and the First Presidency and Elder Durham would be the only ones to know about this document."

"Did he tell you anyone else would ever know about the document?"

"I guess I should include his secretary. Oh—"

"Well, go ahead."

"Francis Gibbons."

"Did he say no one would ever know about this document other than those people?"

"No."

Under further questioning, Hofmann said Hinckley asked him if his wife or anyone else knew about the document. "I told him that no one else within the Church knew about it," Hofmann said. "I left open the possibility that someone out of the Church [did]. Obviously, I claimed to have acquired it from someone outside of the Church." Later, Hofmann explained, Hinckley asked him if Charles Hamilton was the source, but Hofmann said he would neither confirm nor deny the suggestion.[67]

Hofmann also acknowledged being paid for the document by a check drawn on a church account. He said he agreed with Hinckley not to discuss the document with others but did so anyway.[68]

The eighth session began with Hofmann describing how he had aged *The Oath of a Freeman* using ozone. In an earlier session, Hofmann had briefly described the technique, and when Biggs returned to the subject to begin the eighth session, Hofmann responded, "Yes, you keep bringing it up. That must be mysterious."[69]

Later, when Hofmann began answering questions about the Grandin contract, he mentioned a characteristic of the contract that had convinced historians the document was authentic. "There's an impression," he said, "that appears to have been made . . . with uninked type which was actually an uninked plate which I had manufactured of E. B. Grandin's ad for various printed items."

"How did that get on there and why?" Stott asked.

"I embossed it on there," Hofmann replied, "more to make the paper appear to be a piece of scrap paper which was still good enough to be used from the Grandin work shop or printing office."

"Was this to be something like a watermark or trademark or something or what?"

"No, it would have been when Grandin was setting up type, it would have either looked like another piece of paper was on top of this and received the—, well, this document also received the impression but the other would have received the ink, the paper on top of it. Either that or it was a dry run through the press as Grandin was setting the type. In other words, to make it appear like it came from the Grandin work shop."[70]

Among the documents considered during the ninth interview session was the salamander letter, which Hofmann had already admitted in his plea to be a forgery. Stott questioned Hofmann about the story that Alvin Smith, not Joseph, discovered the Book of Mormon gold plates.

"Is there anything to that story?" Stott asked.

"No."

"Is that all a creation of yours?"

"That's pure creation."[71]

Under further questioning, Hofmann said he also shared the story with John Dart of the *Los Angeles Times* after Brent Metcalfe contacted Dart to tell him that "an inside source named Limy" wanted to talk about materials from the First Presidency's vault.

"Dart flew into Salt Lake," Hofmann said. "Metcalf and he, myself had lunch one afternoon at—, I can't think of the name of the restaurant. At a sandwich shop of some sort, hamburger place. We then went to a park where we sat down at a table, picnic table, and I told him this fabrication. It is purely made up. It's not based on anything I saw in the First Presidency's office or elsewhere."

"My next question," Stott asked, "would be, had you ever seen anything or ever been invited in to the First Presidency's vault?"

"No," Hofmann answered. "I saw some materials from the First Presidency's vault and looked in to the First Presidency's vault but I've never set foot into the vault."

"Some things were brought out and showed to you?"

"Right."

"What were those things? Anything relating to anything we've talked about?"

"No," Hofmann said. "If there is a characteristic—I'm getting philosophical now. There is a characteristic of human nature that if something is unknown, people imagine the worst. That's basically how it is with the First Presidency's vault. People imagine that everything is in there and that [it] is being kept in there to cover it up by the Church or whatever, which I don't believe is true but people like to imagine all kinds of interesting skeletons in the closet."[72]

Hofmann then admitted making up the rumors about the Oliver Cowdery history.

"Why did you make the story up?" Stott asked.

"For a couple of reasons. First of all, I remember distinctly when I did make it up we were eating at Wendy's. Indigestion, perhaps. And I first talked about it actually out of amusement. It wasn't anything I had previously thought of, I just kind of evolved into it, to keep them interested. One thing about Metcalf is he's always interested in these little hidden rumors or truths or whatever. And I noticed I could throw out a little thing to wet his appetite and he would always be after me for more and more information. So I would just make it up as we went along."[73]

Though Hofmann said the history was something he had not "previously thought of," Metcalfe would remember the situation differently. He recalled approaching Hofmann in early 1984 about Joseph Fielding Smith's statements on what some persons assumed to be the Cowdery history. At that time, Hofmann said he had heard nothing about the history. Hofmann discussed the subject with him a second time in 1985 before the meal at Crown Burger (not Wendy's) in which Hofmann mentioned it a third time.[74]

Hofmann also told those present for the ninth prison session that the other reason he created the Oliver Cowdery history rumor was to validate the salamander letter by claiming that the Cowdery history also referred to a salamander. "One forged idea to validate another forged idea," he explained.

Stott asked Hofmann if he had been aware that the rumors about an Oliver Cowdery history were causing "considerable embarrassment to the LDS authorities."

"Yes," Hofmann affirmed.

"But you went along with it to the point of giving an interview. What were your feelings during this time? Why were you doing that?"

"As far as my feelings, there was actually a mixture of emotions. One of which was amusement for the whole idea. As far as the embarrassment to the Church, it is true that it was embarrassing but I was also interested to see how the Church would react to the situation."[75]

Among the forgeries Hofmann talked about during his tenth prison session with prosecutors was the Betsy Ross letter, which Hofmann used to defraud Wilford Cardon. "Did you have this letter prepared and ready to obtain money from someone," Biggs asked, "or did you go to him and then—"

"No," Hofmann interrupted, "the document was forged actually some time after obtaining the money from him just to send him a copy of what the document looks like."

"Did he request that, some verification that the letter existed?" Biggs inquired.

"I don't believe that he did," Hofmann said. "I think I just did it. I think, as I remember, Shanon Flynn suggested that would be a nice thing [to] do, he would appreciate it or whatever. We let him see what it looked like or something."

"Why keep it?"

"As an oversight."[76]

Later, the discussion turned to Hofmann's defrauding of the Wilding group, with whom he had had several transactions. "Your first transaction," Biggs stated, "I think was for 18 rare books. You told them you could purchase them for a certain amount of money and sell them for about twice that amount of money?"

"Yes," Hofmann admitted.

"Did you ever have 18 rare books?"

"No."

"Did you ever purchase 18 rare books with the money they gave you."

"No."[77]

A similar exchange occurred when Biggs asked about the second Wilding transaction, which was supposed to have involved papers of Brigham Young. "Was there any Brigham Young papers you were going to purchase with the new money they gave you?" Biggs inquired.

"No," Hofmann replied.

"Did you ever purchase any Brigham Young papers with the money they gave you?"

"No."[78]

Biggs's line of questioning had brought out Hofmann's pattern of obtaining money for materials that did not exist. It was the same pattern that became evident with the McLellin collection fraud, to which the discussion soon led.

Stott asked Hofmann how he was able to put off repaying Al Rust as long as he had. Hofmann said that his "plan wasn't to put him off that long but it just worked that way, just kept on going." Hofmann said that at first he thought he would repay Rust using proceeds from *The Oath of a Freeman,* "but then when that didn't happen, I approached the Church, . . . President Hinkley specifically." Hofmann said he "was feeling him out as far as the possibility of getting money from the Church to make the purchase."[79]

Al Rust, however, would suggest a different reason why Hofmann had gone to Hinckley. Dropping Hinckley's name, Hofmann had told Rust that the church had the McLellin collection, planned to buy it, but was slow in paying. Rust was paying interest on the money he borrowed for the collection and became frustrated when Hofmann kept putting him off. Finally, Rust decided to tackle the problem directly. "And I wrote a letter to President Hinckley," he said. "And what happened was, I made the mistake of telling Hofmann this."

Hofmann said he was in New York at the time. Rust broke the news to him by phone, adding, "We need to just sit down, the three of us, and hash it out. There's no problem, but I'd like to just get it all straightened out because I just can't keep carrying this note, Mark." Rust remembered the document dealer's reaction. "Oh, he got upset. 'Why did you do that?' he said. 'I told you you shouldn't do anything.' And I said, 'Well, it should work out all right.' He hung up on me. . . . But I know now that he immediately made arrangements and got on an airplane and flew back to Salt Lake City. And the very next day he was in President Hinckley's office."[80]

Hinckley later observed that before this visit from Hofmann, he "had never heard of the McLellin collection."[81] Hinckley dictated a memorandum immediately after the visit recording that Hofmann's first inquiry was "if I had received a letter from Alvin Rust." When Hinckley said he had, Hofmann launched into a long history of the McLellin collection and how he had gone "East and got the papers." Hinckley added parenthetically, "I suppose it was East, he stated that he had flown in from New York today."[82] Rust's and Hinckley's accounts thus suggest Hofmann had not planned to talk to Hinckley about the collection until Rust wrote his letter.[83]

Hofmann's pattern was to obtain money from investors, use it for his own purposes, and then repay it with interest, all without producing the materials in which they had supposedly invested.[84] During the eighth prison interview session, Hofmann had attempted to rationalize his frauds by telling prosecutors he did not really intend to defraud his victims. "It was more to use their money when I needed it," he said, "and then pay them back with interest to make it worth their while, which is something that for years has taken place in my transactions with Al Rust, for example." In fact, he said, "There were dozens of times when I used Rust's money for bogus transactions and paid him back with interest."[85]

Hofmann likely had the same approach in mind when he borrowed from Rust for the McLellin collection. If *The Oath of a Freeman* had sold, Hofmann could have paid Rust, telling him the church had bought the collection in a confidential deal. By swearing Rust to secrecy, Hofmann would have kept church officials from learning they had supposedly purchased the collection. And by not actually offering it to the church, Hofmann would not have had to manufacture it or show it to anyone.

The McLellin collection described by Hofmann was so large and complex that it is doubtful Hofmann intended to deliver it to Rust or anyone else. Had he been able to forge it, Hofmann might have delivered the collection to David West on October 15, using the money received to relieve debts, and most important, sparing the lives of Steve Christensen and Kathy Sheets. But Hofmann had promised more than he could deliver.

Rust's letter to Hinckley complicated Hofmann's scheme. Then, Hofmann not only had to repay Rust but he had to conceive a way to explain to Hinckley why he had told Rust the church planned to buy the collection, when in fact he had never even mentioned it to the church leader. Perhaps, as Hofmann told prosecutors in the tenth session, he really did intend at that point to ask Hinckley about "the possibility of getting money from the Church to make the purchase." Hinckley's file memorandum, however, written immediately after Hofmann met with him, does not mention that the document dealer made the suggestion.[86]

Another possibility is that Hofmann used the meeting to explain away Rust's letter by saying he had not told church officials about the McLellin collection because he intended to give, not sell, it to the church. Hinckley's memorandum records that Hofmann told the church leader he had already figured out how to repay Rust. "Mark indicated," Hinckley wrote, "that he is borrowing money from Chase Manhattan Bank using some of his inventory of historic materials as collateral. He will pay Rust all that is due Rust and get in the clear with him. He stated that he would then contribute the McLellin papers to the Church, either to the Historian's Office or he would deliver them to me."[87]

In either case, the consequence was the same. When Hofmann left the interview, Hinckley not only expected that Hofmann would resolve his problems with Rust (without church funds) but that Hofmann would then donate the collection to the church. In the tenth prison session, however, Hofmann told prosecutors that Hinckley had told him that "if things got real desperate or if I needed to get some money to let him know."[88]

Yet Hofmann did not go back to Hinckley for money, even though he became desperate. Instead, he went to others, including Steve Christensen, who took him to Hugh Pinnock. Why Hofmann did not approach Hinckley directly may be explained by another sentence in Hinckley's memo. "We concluded our conversation," Hinckley wrote, "by again saying that when he was all in the clear with Rust, that he could then get in touch with me and we could talk about his making this contribution." Hofmann could not approach Hinckley again about the collection until he had resolved matters with Rust.[89]

Hinckley's statements in the October 23, 1985, news conference and in meetings with investigators reflected the gist of his file memo.[90] Thus, prosecutors were aware of the discrepancy between what the church leader had said and what Hofmann told them at the prison. Stott asked Hofmann, "Was there an idea . . . conveyed here that the collection would be sold to the Church or donated to the Church?"

Hofmann obliquely answered, "The idea was to prevent it from falling in to the enemy's hands."[91]

Stott broached a related subject. "What did you tell him about what it contained and what the enemy was doing?" the prosecutor asked.

"Not too much," Hofmann answered. "How can I put this?"

"Put it honestly," Yengich counseled.

"Well, of course," Hofmann continued, "I basically told him that I could tell him what my fears were concerning its getting in to the enemy's hands, or whatever. And that I would, if he wanted to know, if he asked the questions or whatever, this was a previous technique or thing that we had done." Hofmann was stammering. "I guess its almost a way of protecting him from knowing something he doesn't want to know. And his interest wasn't so much in having the Church obtain it as having it going someplace where—" He started again. "In fact, I would almost say he almost didn't want the Church to obtain it, he just wanted to make sure it did not fall into the enemy's hands, which was good since I knew I didn't have it, I knew the Church couldn't obtain it."[92]

"Did you tell him what was contained in the letters?" Stott again inquired.

"I don't believe I gave him any details," Hofmann replied.[93]

Hinckley's file memorandum showed that Hofmann told him specifically that it contained Facsimile No. 2, journals, and affidavits. Hinckley had given these details to investigators in an interview.[94]

When Stott asked Hofmann to "put a time or date" on the meeting they were discussing, Hofmann once again did not answer the question directly. "Let's see, it was also, this was, I believe the reason why." Hofmann was stammering again. "See, sometime after this transaction with Rust we were talking about, he, Rust wrote a letter to the Church or to President Hinkley and made some comment about that he wanted to get his money for the McClellin Collection which he understood the Church was acquiring or whatever, and this whole conversation which took place beforehand with Hinkley pretty much prepared him or set him up for that. Therefore, I don't think it really raised any question in Hinkley's mind or whatever."[95]

Hofmann's one meeting with Hinckley had turned into two. "So Hinkley had already been told by you there was a Salt Lake investor?" Stott asked.

"Right," Hofmann answered, "and he was anxious to get his money."

"That was Rust?"

"Right."[96]

Hinckley said he had not heard of the McLellin collection until Rust's letter arrived. His file memo of the meeting he had with Hofmann after getting Rust's letter corroborated this statement by recording that Hofmann recounted the history of the collection to him on that occasion, something that would have been unnecessary had they discussed it earlier.[97]

Stott asked Hofmann, "Did you subsequently talk with President Hinkley about the letter with Al Rust?"

"Did I talk to him about the letter?" Hofmann echoed. "I remember doing that at a later time, after he got back from East Germany or wherever he was."[98] In actuality, the discussion occurred June 12 before Hinckley went to Europe.[99]

"Did he ask you why in the world does Al Rust say we've got the collection?" Stott inquired.

"No, he didn't say anything about that," Hofmann answered.

"Did you try to explain that?"

"No. I actually had not seen the letter. I just knew something, Al Rust told me about its contents."

"Wasn't that a problem that Al Rust was saying that, you know, I understand the Church has it and, of course, the Church knew they didn't have it?"

"Yes, no," Hofmann began, "that didn't raise a problem in my mind because I knew that Hinkley knew that I was protecting the collection from Rust and anyone else as far as where it was. He knew I had previously told him that I had the material in a safe deposit box in Salt Lake City and that—" He started again. "See, Hinkley, his concern was that if this disgruntled investor, he wanted to make sure he didn't reach the point where he would make public or try to obtain the collection. The actual meeting that I had with him was more to—" He tried again. "The idea I had when I went to Arizona to talk to Carden was that he would obtain phone confirmation, telephone confirmation from President Hinkley that it would be nice of him to buy out this other investor named Al Rust or whatever. Although I didn't realize that he wouldn't be available, that he would be, that he was out of the country."[100]

A little later, Biggs asked Hofmann, "Was it the understanding that Mr. Carden was going to pay off Rust's interest in the collection?"

"That was the understanding which I left Hinkley with," Hofmann answered.[101]

Hinckley's June 12 file memo mentioned nothing about Cardon. Instead, it recorded that Hofmann had said he would repay Rust using a loan from Chase Manhattan Bank.[102]

Even later in the session, Hofmann said Hinckley "wasn't so concerned, especially when he found out other people knew about this material, to actually obtain it, as to just see that the right people got it. In other words, it wasn't until Pinock entered the picture and I needed to add—" He faltered. "I didn't go into—" He tried again. "With Pinock I needed to sound more straight as far as the Church would actually end up with it. That's what was that whole idea as far as the Church actually taking possession of it. We didn't discuss the Church would take possession of it when I spoke with President Hinkley."[103]

Contrary to Hofmann's assertions, Hinckley's file memo showed that Hinckley both knew that others were aware of the collection and yet expected the church to take possession of it. Hinckley wrote that Hofmann "was disturbed over Rust because Rust had failed to keep confidences concerning these papers." Hofmann had also implied that Rust was responsible for a "leak which had led to newspaper baiting to try to get the Church to disclose that we had bought them," when in fact the church had not bought them. Despite Hofmann's claims about Rust (which were spurious), Hinckley anticipated that Hofmann would "contribute the McLellin collection to the Church" once he had obtained his Chase Manhattan loan and repaid Rust.[104]

Near the close of the tenth prison session, Stott was asking most of the questions. Biggs, however, posed the final query. "I have one question," he said, "and I have to ask it because I may be hit by a bus tomorrow. One of the pieces of Papyrus you cut up and we have one little piece of it."

"Right," Hofmann acknowledged.

"Where are the other pieces?" Biggs finished.

"Mostly destroyed."[105]

With that answer, the session ended.

Biggs was not hit by a bus, but he never questioned Hofmann again. Neither did Stott. Twelve days later, when the two prosecutors returned to the prison to meet with Hofmann, they brought police detective Jim Bell with them. Stott and Biggs had anticipated that the next session with Hofmann would bring them to the point in the chronology at which the murders occurred. Because detectives Ken Farnsworth and Jim Bell were the real murder experts, Stott and Biggs had prevailed on Yengich to allow one of them to attend the next session so he could conduct the questioning on that subject.[106]

When they arrived at the prison, however, Hofmann refused to talk. Yengich went on the record to explain why: "Mr. Hofmann has indicated to me, as his counsel, that he does not desire Mr. Bell in the room to conduct this questioning. That he is prepared to answer questions, as he was before, by Mr. Biggs and Mr. Stott and it is my understanding that is not satisfactory to the prosecution." Yengich said Hofmann refused to let Bell in the interview because he wanted to protest "his present housing situation" at the prison.

Stott did some protesting of his own. "It is our position," he argued, "that we had an arrangement for several days to the effect that Jim Bell would be present and would lead the interrogation concerning the homicides. That if Mr. Hofmann wants to abrogate that agreement, that we will not proceed with the interrogation unless that agreement is lived up to." Stott also observed that the county attorney's office had nothing to do with Hofmann's housing and would not interfere with prison officials.

"Could I point out something," Biggs added, "and that is that the prosecution, we believe, has complied with all of the conditions of the [plea] agreement and we do not believe Mr. Hofmann has complied by refusing to talk about the homicides in the presence of a police officer and investigator, Detective Bell." Biggs then delivered an ultimatum: "And these particular interviews with Mr. Hofmann, as far as the prosecution is concerned, have ended unless and until Detective Bell is allowed to question Mr. Hofmann concerning his homicides."

"And it is my position, for the record," Yengich countered, "that although I have no personal objection to Mr. Bell asking the questions, that nowhere does it state that Detective Bell has to be present, number one.

And number two, Mr. Hofmann is prepared to proceed today and answer whatever questions Mr. Biggs and Mr. Stott want to ask."

After another exchange between Biggs and Yengich, Stott intervened, telling Yengich to work out the problem with his client, but adding, "Our position is unless he wants to change, we're through and we'll report to the Board [of Pardons] what happened and we're through."

"He doesn't go to the Board for quite a while," Yengich said, "so I'll talk to him." On that note, the meeting ended.[107]

Further efforts to meet with Hofmann failed.[108]

Two years later, detective Ken Farnsworth would still ponder what he might ask Hofmann if he were finally given the chance. "I don't know what I'd want to ask him," Farnsworth would say, though acknowledging he "really would like to see him write." Referring to Hofmann, Farnsworth would say he was "convinced that if his lips are moving he's lying. . . . So I'm really not interested in asking him anything 'cause I—then I just got to sit and sort the puzzle out and find out which part of it might be true— what he's trying to do with me—'cause he's manipulating just instantly."[109]

Denied the opportunity to further question Hofmann as they wished, Stott and Biggs attempted to satisfy the public's curiosity about the murders by compiling notes they had taken during three test interviews they had conducted with Hofmann before the plea agreement. They added their compiled notes to the interview transcript as a supplement.

The notes showed Hofmann had been interested in explosives since his youth. Hofmann told the prosecutors he had variously contemplated killing himself, Thomas Wilding, Brent Ashworth, and Steve Christensen but had not settled on his precise targets until the morning of October 15. He said he packed nails around Christensen's bomb to make it more lethal. Hofmann described purchasing bomb components, testing a prototype, building the bombs, and placing them. He said the second bomb was a diversion not necessarily meant to kill.

"Hofmann said the thing that attracted him to bombs as a means of killing was that he didn't have to be there at the time of the killings," the prosecutors wrote. "He didn't think he could pull the trigger on someone if he faced them, but he could do it if he didn't have to be around."

Hofmann said he tried calling the Sheets residence on the morning of the first bombings to warn whoever answered not to touch the bomb in the driveway, but nobody answered. He also said he regretted setting the bomb for Christensen and called Christensen's office to warn him about it. When Christensen's answering machine came on, he hung up.

Doralee Hofmann had maintained that her husband was home when the bombs were reportedly placed. Mark guessed she passed her polygraph test because he had been home when she awoke both during the night and in the morning. "Also," the prosecutors noted, "his young son had told her that his dad had been downstairs all the time." Thus, Mark "said she had no idea that he had left the house that night."

Mark Hofmann claimed the third bomb was a suicide attempt. "He also admitted," the summary explained, "that he had placed a number of inconsequential papers in the car so that people would think that the McLellin Collection, which did not exist, was blown up in the explosion and fire."

Much of the rest of the supplement summarized information about documents that came out in the interview transcripts. There were a few added details. Hofmann said he sold dealer Kenneth Rendell a forged Daniel Boone letter. Hofmann also claimed he had sold more than half a million dollars in forgeries to dealer Charles Hamilton, the man who had written the book about famous fakes and forgeries and had authenticated the Josiah Stowell letter. The supplement concluded, "Hofmann had prior experience with forensic scientist[s] and knew that he could get his forgeries past the scrutiny of any expert or test available."[110]

When the transcripts of the sessions were released to the public, many persons expressed skepticism about their contents. "No one is certain Hofmann is telling the truth in these transcripts," the *Salt Lake Tribune* commented at the beginning of a long article reporting highlights of the two volumes.[111] An editorial in the *Deseret News* asked, "Is the complete story finally out?" It then answered, "Categorically—no." The transcript left "the impression that even in custody Hofmann was manipulating" by "often describ[ing] matters in a way that makes him look as good as possible under the circumstances. Even in cold print, he comes across as showing no emotion—except sarcasm—and striving to avoid any display of weakness." The editorial recommended reading the transcripts "with a generous measure of caution."[112]

Charles Hamilton would describe Hofmann's "confessions" as "worthless and nothing more than traps for fools."[113] Al Rust responded, "It's all a farce. I was waiting for a complete confession, but we have nothing; absolutely nothing."[114] George Throckmorton advised "anyone who reads the transcripts not to believe this habitual liar."[115] David Biggs said he thought it "ridiculous" that Hofmann claimed he called Christensen to warn him when Christensen would have had to set the bomb off to enter his office and answer his phone.[116] Brent Ashworth, who had good reason to believe the third bomb was intended for him, doubted Hofmann's claim that it was a suicide attempt. "You have to have a conscience to want to kill yourself," Ashworth said. "And I wouldn't credit him with that."[117]

In January 1988, prosecutors released a letter directed to the Board of Pardons. Referring to the plea agreement provision requiring Hofmann to answer queries about his crimes "truthfully and completely," Bob Stott reported, "Hofmann has not complied with that provision." Stott pointed to statements in the transcript that were not credible and referred to Hofmann's life as full of "deceit, fraud and treachery." He declared to the board, "Only natural life [in prison] will begin to adequately punish Hofmann and insure that no one will be tricked, harmed or murdered by him again."[118]

On January 29, the board met to decide the killer's fate. Victoria Palacios, who chaired the board, began by briefly describing Hofmann's crimes. When she reached the Christensen bombing, she said, "October 15, 1985, you planted a bomb in the doorway of Steve Christensen's office because you didn't want a scheduled meeting to take place between the victim and some others. The bomb in fact killed Mr. Christensen. Had the meeting taken place, . . . it is my understanding that possessive buyers would have . . . learned that you in fact had two copies of *The Oath of a Freeman,* and . . . that would lead to the discovery of the fact that they were forged, and potentially to the discovery of other forgeries." The Sheets bombing, she said, was intended as a diversion.

When Palacios finished reviewing the crimes, she asked Hofmann if he cared "to make any corrections to the record or to elaborate." He did not. Members of the board then asked Hofmann several questions before going

Mark Hofmann and Doralee Hofmann at Board of Pardons hearing, January 29, 1988. (*Deseret News*)

into executive session to vote. Twenty-seven minutes later, they emerged. Under the board's normal guidelines, Hofmann might have been eligible for parole in seven years. But Hofmann's "large number of victims," "callous disregard for life," and intent "to cover other criminal activities" called for an exception. Palacios pronounced the board's decision. "By a majority vote," she said, "the board has decided you should serve natural life in prison, Mr. Hofmann. Do you wish to comment?"

"No thanks."[119]

Conclusion

Church officials declined to offer judgment "on the amount, the size of the penalty and the period of incarceration" to which Mark Hofmann was sentenced for his offenses. Instead, they expressed thanks to those who had solved the crimes and sympathy for those affected by them. After Hofmann pleaded guilty, Gordon Hinckley said publicly that church officials were "grateful there has been a resolution of the problem, but at the same time we sense the tremendous tragedy to the lives of the families." He also issued a plea. "We earnestly and sincerely hope," he said, that "the healing process will begin immediately and . . . where there is great sorrow today there may be comfort."[1]

For many, Hofmann's conviction only partly salved the wounds he opened. Yet some who survived found forgiveness a healing balm. "I've always been an eye-for-an-eye person, but with eight children and 12 grandchildren I needed to forgive," said Steve Christensen's father, Mac. He did not want his family to live in an environment of hatred or bitterness. "When you forgive," he said, "you have peace of mind." Mac asked the community to be kind to Hofmann's family. He paved the way with his own example. After Mark Hofmann pleaded guilty and left the courtroom in January 1987, Mac approached Mark's father, Bill. They embraced. "I told him our love was with his family," Mac later said. "He cried. He didn't have to say he was sorry for what his son had done to my son. I knew he was."[2]

"Who knows why some sons grow up and get their circuits crossed?" Gary Sheets asked with a similar sentiment of charity toward Hofmann's family. "You can't blame that on the family."[3]

"It was a total hell to live through the first few months," Terri Christensen said of the period after her husband's murder. "There were many nights that both the boys and I went to sleep crying." Terri gave birth to Steve's and her fourth son three months after the bombings. The child,

His hands bound, Mark Hofmann arrives at the Utah State Prison, January 23, 1987. (*Deseret News*)

whose cesarean birth was timed to coincide with what would have been Steve's thirty-second birthday, was named Steven F. Christensen, Jr.[4]

"Of course I have had periods of anger, and hate even," Terri acknowledged. Still, she added, "To sit and blame or hate someone else, or to have all those other feelings that are contrary to peace and happiness—I'm just not willing to succumb to them." She also saw meaning in her husband's death. "Steve served a purpose in the way he died. At least that's how I have to look at it," she said. "His death and the things he discovered about Mark Hofmann were in service to the Mormon Church. Believing that may not convince anyone else, but it helps me to make sense out of it."[5]

Meanwhile, Steve Christensen's massive collection of books, pamphlets, serials, and miscellany was purchased by a friend of the Christensen family and ultimately donated to Brigham Young University, where some of the 9,953 items were used to replace or upgrade titles already in the university's library. Others, including volumes dealing with the Middle East, were sent to the university's new center in Jerusalem, Israel. Added to each volume was a bookplate that read, "In Memory of Steve Christensen."[6]

Like those affected by the murders, many of Hofmann's fraud and forgery victims proved compassionate in the end. "I have mostly pity for him," Brent Ashworth said of Hofmann. "I think he's given up a great deal. I just feel very badly for his family, and for those that lost loved ones."[7]

Al Rust survived Hofmann's crimes with quiet resiliency. For a period following the bombings, he struggled with his emotions, wondering why Gordon Hinckley had not responded to his letter about the McLellin collection. "It wasn't until I heard the facts that I was able to adjust my feelings," he later said, "because I was basing a lot on what was unknown." When he learned how Hofmann assured Hinckley that his debt to Rust would be quickly repaid, Rust asked himself how he would have reacted had Hinckley written him questioning Hofmann. He decided he would have asked Hofmann about the matter and would have dropped it had Hofmann assured him the matter would be quickly resolved. "I would have done the same thing that President Hinckley did," Rust concluded, adding, "And I'm not near as busy as he is."

Still, the specter of Hofmann continued to haunt him. Walking down the street or sitting in a restaurant, Rust would occasionally see someone with features like Hofmann's and then find himself looking twice to be certain the person was not really the forger-bomber. "I hope that I never actually see him," Rust said.[8]

Of Hofmann's immediate friends, Shannon Flynn was among the most severely affected by Hofmann's treachery. Flynn and Hofmann had possessed an illegal machine gun together, but early rumors of Flynn's being a co-conspirator in the bombings and fraud were not substantiated. Flynn entered into an agreement for pretrial diversion and ultimately had the machine gun charge dismissed.[9]

"Surprisingly enough," one television reporter commented, "Flynn and Rust say they don't hate Hofmann. They say hate only festers inside you. Instead, they said they're putting Hofmann behind them and going on with their lives." They expressed their concern, however, for the families of the victims and of Mark Hofmann, "who," the reporter noted, "will never be able to put it behind them."[10]

Doralee Hofmann supported her husband throughout the criminal proceedings, including the Board of Pardons hearing. After the hearing, prison informants told corrections officials that Mark had bragged of plans to harm members of the pardons board. Mark also sent his wife several letters containing anagrams which, when decoded by FBI cryptologists, proved to contain sketchy information about two members of the board and George Throckmorton. The discovery aroused further fear that Mark might be plotting revenge. Doralee turned the letters over to authorities when asked.[11]

While investigating the alleged threats, investigators spent three hours shaking down Hofmann's cell, hoping to find a key to the encrypted messages. Instead, they found a piece of prison stationery on either side of which Hofmann had written lists of historical figures whose autographs he had purportedly forged. The front of the sheet listed persons prominent in Mormon or Utah history, ranging from Joseph Smith, Jr., Brigham Young, and Eliza R. Snow to recent church presidents David O. McKay and Spencer W. Kimball. The back of the sheet listed non-LDS historical and literary figures from John Milton, Myles Standish, and Paul Revere to Mark Twain and Emily Dickinson.[12]

In August 1988, Doralee Hofmann filed for divorce from Mark, citing "irreconcilable differences." She sought child support for their four children, including one conceived and born after the bombings when she had faithfully defended her husband's innocence, and she asked for half of Mark's prison wages as alimony. Doralee also asked the judge to restore her maiden name. Mark signed a waiver and consent form, allowing the uncontested divorce to become final in ninety days.[13]

A few weeks later, Mark nearly died from an overdose of antidepressants. Doctors saved his life, but lying in one place too long had cut off the circulation to his right arm, necessitating repeated surgery. Reaction to the overdose incident varied among investigators, prosecutors, and victims. "We were saddened to learn of the latest tragedy in the life of Mark W. Hofmann," the church's First Presidency observed. "On behalf of The Church of Jesus Christ of Latter-day Saints, we express our deepest sympathy and condolences to his family and loved ones who now, more than ever, will need the support of loving friends."[14]

The following year, after Hofmann had returned to a somewhat normal prison routine, detective Ken Farnsworth heard a rumor he later confirmed with prison officials: Hofmann's new cell mate was none other than Dan Lafferty. Dan and his brother Ron were Mormon excommunicants who combined profligacy with religious extremism. After being expelled from the church, they came to believe God wanted them to kill their Mormon sister-in-law, who opposed their fanaticism, and her baby daughter. The year before Hofmann set his bombs, Dan and Ron entered their sister-in-law's home, beating and strangling her before cutting open her throat. She died pleading for them to spare her fifteen-month-old daughter, who stood crying in a crib. After helping murder the mother, Dan walked into the puzzled child's room, clutched her by the head, and slashed her throat.[15]

"You know, somebody's got a good sense of humor out at the prison," Farnsworth said after confirming that Hofmann and Dan Lafferty were housed together. Farnsworth found poetic justice in the match: Hofmann, the murderous atheist, sharing a cell with Lafferty, the murderous zealot.[16]

In August 1990, Hofmann managed to effect a change in his housing. A prison guard passing out lunch trays found him semiconscious. After prison medical personnel failed to rouse him, Hofmann was flown to the University of Utah Medical Center, where doctors pumping his stomach found he had once again overdosed on antidepressants. Before long, however, he was sent to the prison infirmary to convalesce.[17] "He does not appear to have suffered any long-term effects from the overdose," a corrections official announced. "The prognosis for complete recovery is good." Addressing whether Hofmann would be put back with Lafferty, the official said, "We will still consider putting him back in his same cell or we may do something else. At this point we just don't know."[18] Later, however, Hofmann was transferred to a medium-security dormitory.[19]

Hofmann's second overdose, with its sense of déjà vu, engendered a milder public reaction than had his first. A few weeks after Hofmann had once again returned to prison, Utah State University archivist Jeff Simmonds made a comment that perhaps paralleled the feelings of other Hofmann victims. "I don't think Mark can stand the greyness down there," Simmonds said. "I think every once in a while, when life gets too boring, he's going to try something like this."[20]

Meanwhile, church officials too moved forward with their lives. In their efforts to heal the wounds of the Hofmann era, they voluntarily returned the Book of Commandments that the RLDS Church had traded to them in 1981 for the Joseph Smith III blessing. RLDS officials had not requested the volume, recognizing that the agreement under which they parted with it placed on their shoulders the responsibility for authenticating the blessing document. Answering a question at a symposium called to discuss the Hofmann case, RLDS Church historian Richard Howard had noted the agreement, affirming, "A deal's a deal."[21]

LDS officials returned the book anyway in a gesture of goodwill. In a December 1987 article, Howard noted the volume had been returned. He also reported that investigators told him that had they evaluated the Joseph Smith III blessing in 1981, they would not have detected it as a forgery. "Only when all the Hofmann documents were assembled and analyzed together and compared with authentic documents of the same period—in ways and with new technologies unknown six years ago—did the patterns of duplicity begin to appear," he wrote.[22]

While deploring Hofmann's crimes, LDS officials resolved to learn from them as they carried out their mission to document the church's history. "When it comes to naivete in the face of malevolence," Dallin Oaks reflected, "there is blame enough to go around. We all need to be more cautious. In terms of our long-run interests in Church history, we now have the basis, and I hope we will have the will, to clear away the Hofmann residue of lies and innuendo."[23]

Editors of the church's *Ensign* magazine ran a notice for readers, listing the Hofmann forgeries that had appeared over the years in that publication. Historical Department officials determined to reduce the backlog of uncatalogued historical collections that had earlier made it difficult for them to deny possession of the nonexistent Cowdery history. By fall of 1989, four years after the bombings, department employees had completed a preliminary computerized cataloguing entry for nearly every archival collection in the department's massive holdings.[24]

The Hofmann case underscored another fact: competition among collectors and collecting institutions for the right to own historical materials drives up prices and provides incentives to forgers. Recognizing this fact, church archivists resolved that they would minimize their purchases of manuscripts, instead encouraging owners of such materials to donate them.

One interesting donation they received after Hofmann went to prison came from the family of Thomas Bullock. Hofmann earlier claimed to have found a Bullock collection in Coalville, Utah, where Bullock had died. Hofmann said the collection had yielded the Joseph Smith III blessing, white notes, the Bullock-Young letter, and other items, all of which later proved to be forgeries. In March 1990, Bullock descendants from Coalville donated a real Bullock collection to the Historical Department. (A Thomas Bullock journal and other Bullock materials had also been donated to Brigham Young University in 1987.)[25]

The collection's contents were nothing like what Hofmann had described. The largest single group of items in the collection was made up of early church songs and poems, a few of them printed, but most in manuscript form. Ironically, considering what Hofmann had claimed was in the collection, one handwritten set of verses contained the following lines:

> For the keys of the kingdom the lord hath confer'd
> On his servents the Twelve being duly prepar'd
> . . . .
>
> Wel go yes wel go where the saints will rejoice
> Again for to hear a Prophets known voice
> Even Brighams the head of the kingdom below
> Who wears Josephs Mantle as the Faithful do know[26]

The collection was catalogued and made available to the public.

Both by examining documents themselves and submitting them to outside experts for analysis, church officials also began taking advantage of the new forgery detection techniques developed by forensic examiners in the case. The Historical Department refined its acquisition procedures, carefully documenting all manuscripts received and giving greater emphasis than ever to provenance. Most of all, perhaps, church officials developed increased skepticism toward accepting new and startling document discoveries.

Yet to them, skepticism must never fully displace trust. In the search for causes that allowed Hofmann to dupe his many victims, trust loomed largest of all. Nationwide, the Hofmann case and other instances of fraud, theft, and forgery had threatened the survival of trust in institutions that value history.

The March 1988 issue of *American Libraries* carried an article by a former president of Chicago's renowned Newberry Library. Titled "An End to Innocence," the article deplored the tragedy of book theft in terms acutely applicable to the Hofmann case. "The real victim," the article lamented, "is trust—that fragile net that for so long and so lovingly has held the library, its staff, the scholarly user, the book collector, and the bookseller together. . . . The most terrible loss occasioned by book thefts, therefore, is in the fullest sense spiritual. Trust is replaced by mistrust. This is a moral tragedy. It is so acidic, so destructive, and it is becoming so pervasive that it may well destroy what we most desire to defend."[27]

The following year, well-known bookseller W. Thomas Taylor would say, "The very worst thing that could come out of the mess of forgeries and thefts that afflicts our little world these days is that we might . . .

behave toward each other with cynicism and mistrust. I do not wish to continue making decisions predicated upon the possible dishonesty of the people I deal with. The strongest case I can make for dealing severely with those few who betray our trust is that it makes it safer to deal with the rest of the world with a measure of faith."[28]

Similarly, church officials recognized the spiritual tragedy of abandoning all trust. "Ministers of the gospel function best in an atmosphere of trust and love," Dallin Oaks observed. "In that kind of atmosphere, they fail to detect a few deceivers, but that is the price they pay to increase their effectiveness in counseling, comforting, and blessing the hundreds of honest and sincere people they see. It is better for a Church leader to be occasionally disappointed than to be constantly suspicious."[29]

"The church by its nature is not going to change its basic philosophy of trusting individuals," church spokesman Richard Lindsay said. "In the long run that probably pays off."[30]

In the short run, the church lost the money it had paid and the genuine items it had traded for Hofmann's forgeries. Ironically, however, publicity surrounding the case made Hofmann's forgeries intriguing to collectors.[31] Dealer Charles Hamilton went so far as to say of Hofmann, "His forgeries will be treasured in times to come." Referring to the certificate on which church officials had relied in buying the Stowell letter, Hamilton added, "I, myself, would pay a substantial sum for the opportunity to take my authentication back and eat it."[32]

Despite the forgeries' interest to collectors, church officials declined to part with those the church owned. Though not what they purported to be on their face, Hofmann's documents were important artifacts of the church's recent history. As one journalist wrote, "Mark Hofmann has become a part of the history of The Church of Jesus Christ of Latter-day Saints, a history he attempted to change through forgery, deceit and murder."[33]

Though more modern in its methods, Hofmann's attempt to alter the church's past reflected efforts the church had faced throughout its history. Some believers would see it as the shadow of a scheme spun in 1828. That year, one of Joseph Smith's revelations recorded that "wicked men" took the first 116 manuscript pages of the Book of Mormon, planning "to alter the words" Smith had dictated, with the intent to "destroy him, and also the work."[34]

Had Hofmann's deceit gone undetected, he could have completed a project he had long ago conceived: the forgery of the stolen and unpublished 116 pages. As was his pattern before forging important documents, he had let people know he was hunting the lost manuscript. By the time of the bombings, he had honed his skills to the needed level. He had hired a friend to catalogue all the words in the Book of Mormon, and in what amounted to product testing, he had successfully sold or traded what he claimed to be manuscript pieces of the published portion of the Book of Mormon.[35]

Hofmann knew how to find the right paper and make the right ink, and before the bombings, he had laid the groundwork for authenticating the handwriting. Martin Harris had been scribe for the 116 unpublished pages, and the only accepted exemplars of Harris's writing beyond a few genuine signatures were to be found in the salamander letter and other Hofmann forgeries. With time and patience, Hofmann could indeed have consummated his scheme. In 1988, he conceded to detective Michael George that this had, in fact, been his object.[36]

In Joseph Smith's revelation about the lost 116 pages, those who planned to alter the manuscript were said to have "laid a cunning plan, thinking to destroy the work of God." The revelation, however, foretold that their fate would be "to catch themselves in their own snare."[37] Believers and unbelievers alike could sense both justice and irony in the fact that Hofmann's own bomb curtailed his criminal career.

En route to his ensnarement, Hofmann snatched the lives of innocent human beings and bereaved their families. He exploited even the love of his own family. He violated the trust of friends, colleagues, historians, archivists, collectors, investors, and journalists. And seeking to alter perceptions of its past, he spurned the church he once had served and those who yet served in it, adding them to the list of his many victims.

Appendix: Suspect Items Acquired by the LDS Church

In April 1986, officials of the Church of Jesus Christ of Latter-day Saints issued a press release describing forty-eight specific items acquired directly from Mark Hofmann. The salamander letter, it noted, had come from Hofmann indirectly through Steve Christensen. The release also explained that Hofmann had given the church hundreds of legal documents ("complaints, summonses, subpoenas, indentures, notices, and the like"). As announced in the press release, many of these legal documents were being given to the repositories where they may originally have been filed.[1]

The list that follows includes all documents mentioned in the 1986 release (though numbered differently), as well as additional items once in Hofmann's hands that were acquired by church officials from persons other than Hofmann or were inadvertently missed by Historical Department staff members in their 1985–86 attempts to locate Hofmann materials in church possession. The items are listed by approximate date of acquisition, with undatable items appearing at the end. The listing is meant to be exhaustive, though given the extent of Hofmann's forging and counterfeiting, it is possible other church-owned materials, especially early Mormon scrip, may eventually be identified as having come from Hofmann.

Many of the listed items are clearly forgeries; others are not. Researchers working with any of them need to be aware of the Hofmann link in the chain of possession, with its attendant possibility of alteration or complete forgery.

Most of the listed items are legal or government documents. As explained in chapter 10, archivists generally did not catalogue these materials because of doubts about title to the documents. In 1986, church representatives offered the documents to the courthouses or other government repositories where they may have originated decades earlier. Although most repositories accepted the materials, for various reasons some either ignored or refused the offer to have the items returned.[2]

In addition to the items listed below that have been in church possession, there are numerous other church-related forgeries that remain in the hands

BOX 250
DRAPER, UTAH 84020

Mormon and Mormon-Related Autographs that I Forged:

Elijah Able	Thomas B. Marsh	Solomon Spaulding
David R. Atchison	Edward Partridge	Josiah Stowell
Sampson Avard	David W. Patten	John Tanner
Israel Barlow	Orson Pratt	John Taylor
John H. Beadle	Parley P. Pratt	Moses Thatcher
John C. Bennett	William B. Preston	Louis Vasquez
Samuel Brannan	Charles C. Rich	David Whitmer
James Bridger	Willard Richards	Peter Whitmer
Thomas Bullock	Sidney Rigdon	Newel K. Whitney
George Q. Cannon	Orrin Porter Rockwell	Frederick G. Williams
Hiram B. Clawson	Thomas C. Sharp	Wilford Woodruff
William Clayton	James Sloan	Brigham Young
Oliver Cowdery	Bathsheba W. Smith	Zina D. Young
Martin Harris	Emma Smith	
William H. Hooper	George A. Smith	Butch Cassidy
Oliver Huntington	Hyrum Smith	Jonathan Dunham
Orson Hyde	Joseph Smith, Sr.	
Heber C. Kimball	Joseph Smith, Jr.	
Spencer W. Kimball	Joseph F. Smith	
William Law	Lucy Mack Smith	
John D. Lee	William Smith	
David O. McKay	Eliza R. Snow	
William Marks	Lorenzo Snow	

List discovered in search of Mark Hofmann's cell, 1988. (Jennifer Larson/ Paul L. Swensen)

of other institutions or private individuals. When investigators shook down Hofmann's cell in 1988, they found a sheet of paper on which Hofmann had listed the historical figures whose autographs he had forged. One side of the sheet listed the following figures prominent in Mormon or Utah history: Elijah Able, David R. Atchison, Sampson Avard, Israel Barlow, John H. Beadle, John C. Bennett, Samuel Brannan, James Bridger, Thomas Bullock, George Q. Cannon, Butch Cassidy, Hiram B. Clawson, William Clayton, Oliver Cowdery, Jonathan Dunham, Martin Harris, William H. Hooper, Oliver Huntington, Orson Hyde, Heber C. Kimball, Spencer W. Kimball, William Law, John D. Lee, David O. McKay, William Marks, Thomas B. Marsh, Edward Partridge, David W. Patten, Orson Pratt, William B. Preston, Charles C. Rich, Willard Richards, Sidney Rigdon, Orrin Porter Rockwell, Thomas C. Sharp, James Sloan, Bathsheba W. Smith, Emma Smith, George A. Smith, Hyrum Smith, Joseph F. Smith, Joseph Smith, Jr., Joseph Smith, Sr., Lucy Mack Smith, William Smith, Eliza R. Snow, Lorenzo Snow, Solomon Spalding, Josiah Stowell, John Tanner, John Taylor, Moses Thatcher, Louis Vasquez, David Whitmer, Peter Whitmer, Newel K. Whitney, Frederick G. Williams, Wilford Woodruff, Brigham Young, and Zina D. Young.[3] Many of these names appear in the documents described below, though considering Hofmann's record of deception, it is difficult to place unwavering trust in his list of forged autographs or, for that matter, in any of the other Hofmann admissions cited in the notes that follow.

The other side of the sheet discovered in Hofmann's cell bore the names of John Adams, John Quincy Adams, William H. Bonney (Billy the Kid), Daniel Boone, John Brown, Emily Dickinson, Button Gwinnett, Nathan Hale, John Hancock, Andrew Jackson, Francis Scott Key, Abraham Lincoln, Jack London, Thomas Lynch, Jr., John Milton, William C. Quantrill, Paul Revere, Betsy Ross, Haym Salomon, Myles Standish, Mark Twain, George Washington, and Martha Washington.[4] None of these names appear in the church-owned documents.

Thus, the list below, though the most extensive ever published, represents only a fraction of the documents that passed through Hofmann's hands. It is hoped that in the future other institutions and individuals will publish similar lists of their Hofmann-related holdings. Some collectors, of course, may be unaware that their documents came from Hofmann; others may be unwilling to admit it. For these reasons, it is unlikely that a complete list of Hofmann documents will ever be compiled.

APRIL 22 (POSSESSION), OCTOBER 13 (OWNERSHIP), 1980[5]

1. *Anthon Transcript*:[6] Described in chapter 2. First published in 1980.[7] Hofmann admitted forging it.[8]

2. *King James Bible (Cambridge, 1668):* Described in chapter 2. Photographs of title page and pages bearing initials and Samuel Smith signature were published in 1980.[9] Hofmann admitted lying about the Bible's provenance, forging the initials and Samuel Smith signature, placing the Anthon transcript in the Bible, and staging the transcript's discovery.[10]

Between February 13 and July 29, 1980[11]

3. *Presidential Campaign Token of Joseph Smith:* Brass token purportedly used during 1844 United States presidential campaign of Joseph Smith, Jr.[12] Photographs of the token were first published in 1980.[13] Hofmann admitted manufacturing the token.[14]

Between July 9, 1980, and February 1984[15]

4. *Joseph Smith to Maria and Sarah Lawrence, June 23, 1844:* Appeared to be later copy of previously unknown letter from Joseph Smith to two plural wives.[16] First published in 1984.[17] In interviews with prosecutors, Hofmann balked at answering whether he had forged the letter.[18] In 1988, however, he admitted to Mike George that he had.[19]

March 2, 1981

5. *Joseph Smith III Blessing:* Described in chapter 3. Photographs of the blessing were published in 1981.[20] Hofmann admitted forging the document.[21]

Late March? 1981[22]

White Notes: Described in chapter 4. Copies of the notes were first published in 1983.[23] Hofmann admitting forging them.[24]

    6. *Fifty-Cent Note, No. 18, Jan. 2, 1849*
    7. *One-Dollar Note, No. 143, Jan. 9, 1849*
    8. *Three-Dollar Note, No. 15, Jan. 2, 1849*
    9. *Five-Dollar Note, No. 97, Jan. 5, 1849*

March-April 1981[25]

Items Related to White Notes: Shortly after the white note transaction, Hofmann offered the church a small folder in which the notes were purportedly found, as well as an explanation (in what appeared to be Thomas Bullock's hand) of the letters on the seal used to emboss the notes.[26] Photographs of both were published in 1984.[27] Hofmann has acknowledged both items to be forgeries.[28]

    10. *White Note Folder*
    11. *Explanation of Letters on Seal of Quorum of the Twelve*

White notes and items related to them. (Paul L. Swensen)

JUNE 3, 1981[29]

12. *David McKenzie Notebook:* A 3¼-inch-by-5¼-inch notebook containing notes purportedly kept by David McKenzie, engraver of Deseret Currency. In his 1984 book on Mormon money, Al Rust quoted the notebook, in which appeared the numismatically important inscription "Burned all $10 & $20 Deseret Currency."[30] In 1988, George Throckmorton examined

the notebook and found that though the notebook "may be of early origin," it had been tainted with forged entries.[31] In 1990, Hofmann acknowledged to Rust that he had forged the entry Rust quoted.[32]

JUNE 9, 1981[33]

13. *Robert Gilmore to George and Ruth McFadden, Feb. 2, 1835:* Letter written by non-Mormon relating family information and mentioning influx of New Yorkers into the area of Warren County, Illinois. No LDS content. Steve Barnett recalls owning this letter in the early 1970s, suggesting that Hofmann probably did not forge it.[34]

14. *Robert Gilmore to John M. Richey & Ann & Children, July 6, 1844:* Letter written from Warren County, Illinois, describing death of Joseph Smith and related events. Hofmann described this item in detail in his one (and apparently only) sales catalog, *Mormon Manuscripts List #1,* issued in 1981.[35] The church acquired a photcopy of the letter in 1973, suggesting it is not a Hofmann forgery.[36]

15. *George A. Smith to Brigham Young, July 30, 1853:* Letter from Corn Creek (later Kanosh), Utah Territory, reporting activities of Southern Military Department of the Nauvoo Legion at beginning of the Walker War. Listed in Hofmann's *Mormon Manuscripts List #1.*[37]

16. *Capias (Daviess County, Mo., Cir. Ct. issued May 30, 1839):* Writ commanding sheriff to take Joseph Smith and others into custody to answer indictment for riot. Listed in Hofmann's *Mormon Manuscripts List #1.*[38]

17. *Jacob Hamblin, Bond, Dec. 22, 1868:* Binds Hamblin in penal sum of one thousand dollars to faithfully perform duties as collector and treasurer of Santa Clara School District, Washington County, Utah Territory. Listed in Hofmann's *Mormon Manuscripts List #1.*[39]

AUGUST 18, 1981[40]

18. *Ernest Young to Willard Young, May 26, 1872:* Letter from one son of Brigham Young to another (his half-brother) discussing property given them by their father and touching other topics, such as erection of telegraph poles down middle of Salt Lake City streets. George Throckmorton noted several factors (e.g., cutting along folds, ink quality, modern stains) that call the letter's authenticity into question.[41]

SEPTEMBER 4, 1981[42]

19. *Thomas Bullock to Brigham Young, Jan. 27, 1865:* Described in chapter 4. Mentioned in press release of April 11, 1986.[43] Hofmann admitted forging the letter.[44]

20. *Luman Gibbs Certificate, Mar. 11, 1838:* Seven-line document certifying that Luman Gibbs "is a worthy member of the Church of Latter Day Saints in good standing and is duly authorized to preach the gospel." Acquired because it bore purported signatures of Thomas B. Marsh and David W. Patten, "Presidents pro tem of the Church in Missouri." George Throckmorton concluded that it was "not genuine" because, for example, "the paper and ink have indications of artificial aging techniques."[46]

21. *Thomas Vickers Diary:* Diary of unnamed missionary for April 1883 to January 1884 describing work in Virginia and West Virginia and including list of persons baptized. The cataloguer identified author as Thomas Vickers by looking at journal of a person mentioned in it. George Throckmorton examined the Vickers diary but felt no certain conclusion could be reached about its authenticity.[47]

22. *Penciled Essay on Joseph Smith:* Titled "Joseph Smith the Prophet," this manuscript essay by an unnamed author uses scriptures and other published sources to show that Joseph Smith was called of God.

23. *Penciled History of Brigham Young:* Titled simply "Brigham Young," this brief account, in apparently the same hand as item 22, admiringly chronicles life of Brigham Young from birth in 1801 until the Utah War.

24. *Peter Sinclair Diary:* Covers Sinclair's life from January 1856 to March 1862, giving account of his activities in the Salt Lake Valley, including service in the Nauvoo Legion around the Utah War and work in Big Cottonwood Canyon. Also includes poetry and genealogy.

OCTOBER 7, 1981[48]

25. *Isaac Galland Promissory Note:* Recto obligates "I. Galland" to pay $504.26 plus interest to County of Hancock, Illinois, from September 11, 1837, until paid. Verso bears notation "Oblige Joseph Smith Trustee in Trust for the Church of Jesus Christ of Latter Day Saints. Nauvoo December 14th 1841," which is signed, "I Garland his agent."[49] During bombing investigation in December 1985, George Throckmorton found recto of document to be normal but discovered areas around words on verso that exhibited blue haze under ultraviolet light. The ink used to write those words displayed abnormal cracking under a microscope. These findings led to the detection of forgery in several Hofmann documents, leading Throckmorton to label the partially forged Galland document his "Rosetta Stone."[50]

26. *Photograph of Joseph Smith III and Others:* Mounted photographic print of Thomas Nutt, R. J. Anthony, Robert M. Elvin, Levi Anthony, and Joseph Smith III, all of the RLDS Church, circa 1890. On the mount board below the print are what appear to be signatures of the pictured persons. The RLDS Church owns two touched-up prints of the same photograph, one of which is signed.[51]

Front (*top*) and back (*bottom*) of the Isaac Galland note, which forensic expert George J. Throckmorton would later call his Rosetta stone. (George J. Throckmorton)

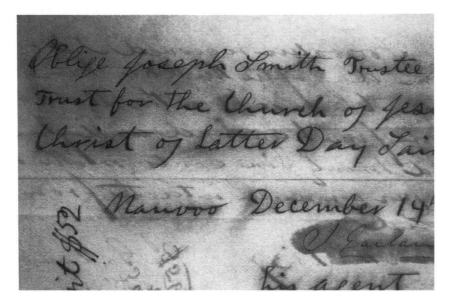

Ultraviolet close-up of Galland note showing ink bleeding. (George J. Throck-morton)

OCTOBER 30, 1981[52]

27. *Oliver B. Huntington, "Guide to Carson":* Journal of unnamed author for September to November 1854 giving account of expedition under government auspices to explore a new route between Salt Lake City and Carson Valley. Includes maps and record of distances traveled.[53] The cataloguer identified the author as Oliver B. Huntington. Although Huntington's name appears on Hofmann's list of forged autographs, the church had owned a photographic reproduction of the journal since at least 1973, suggesting it is not a Hofmann forgery.[54]

NOVEMBER 9, 1981[55]

28. *Testimony of Adam Black, State v. Daily (Daviess County, Mo., Committing Ct. filed Sept. 18, 1838):* Incomplete manuscript of testimony of Judge Adam Black of Daviess County, Missouri, given before two J.P.'s acting as committing court in case involving confrontation between Judge Black and several Mormons. The complete testimony was published in 1841.[56]

BETWEEN JANUARY 15, 1982, AND FEBRUARY 1983[57]

Spanish Fork Co-operative Institution Notes: Described in chapter 4. Copies of all four church-owned notes were published in 1983.[58] George Throckmorton examined the four notes and concluded none were genuine.[59] Hofmann admitted forging them.[60]

29. *Ten-Cent Note, No. 49, n.d.*
30. *Twenty-Five-Cent Note, No. 31, n.d.*
31. *Fifty-Cent Note, No. 92, n.d.*
32. *One-Dollar Note, No. 62, n.d.*

OCTOBER 1, 1982[61]

33. *Joseph Cain Certificate:* Letter written by Willard Richards, signed by Brigham Young, and dated February 13, 1846, certifying that Joseph Cain is an elder of the church in good standing and recommending him "to the fellowship & confidence of the Saints among whom his lot may be cast." The church had already catalogued a photocopy of the document that it acquired in 1980 from Ralph Bailey, who recalled obtaining the original from Tivoli Galleries in Salt Lake City and eventually trading it to Brent Ashworth. Ashworth, in turn, remembered trading it to Hofmann. Tivoli Galleries has no records to extend the provenance back further.[62] George Throckmorton has raised questions about the ink, paper, handwriting, embossing, and folding of the document.[63]

OCTOBER 19, 1982[64]

34. *Defendants' Answer, Burr v. Young (Utah 3d Dist. Ct. subscribed Aug. 12, 1859):* Signed by defendant James Ferguson, this document responds to a complaint filed against Brigham Young and others by David H. Burr, a territorial surveyor accused by church officials of malfeasance. Listed in Hofmann's *Mormon Manuscripts List #1*.[65]
35. *Praecipe, Babbitt v. Law (Hancock County, Ill., Cir. Ct. filed Sept. 1, 1845):* Almon W. Babbitt, guardian for the heirs of Edward Lawrence, asks court clerk to issue summonses for William Law, J. W. Coolidge, and Mary Smith.
36. *Declaration, Smith v. Street (Hancock County, Ill., Cir. Ct. filed May 8, 1844):* Document in which Joseph Smith and others seek to recover money owed them by the defendants.

OCTOBER 20, 1982[66]

37. *David Whitmer to Walter Conrad, Apr. 2, 1873:* Described in chapter 4. Color photograph published in December 1983.[67] Hofmann acknowledged the letter to be a forgery.[68]

JANUARY 11, 1983[69]

38. *Wilford Woodruff Valentine, Feb. 14, 1837:* Valentine from Wilford Woodruff (church president from 1889 to 1898) to Phoebe Carter (his future wife). Cataloguing entry for this document does not list Hofmann as doc-

ument's source.[70] Hofmann's counsel, however, referred to document during preliminary hearing.[71] Published for first time herein. Brent Ashworth later told Glenn Rowe that Hofmann had once offered the valentine (or one like it) to him but had never delivered it.[72] George Throckmorton examined document and found hazing, clamp marks, and ink cracks characteristic of Hofmann forgeries.[73]

JANUARY 14, 1983[74]

39. *Joseph Smith, Jr., to Josiah Stowell, June 18, 1825:* Described in chapter 4. Published in May 1985.[75] Hofmann admitted forging it.[76]

Wilford Woodruff valentine. (Paul L. Swensen)

JANUARY 17, 1983[77]

40. *Father to Ann E., Apr. 22, 1893:* Letter on First Presidency letterhead thought to have been written by John Daniel Thompson McAllister to his wife Ann Eliza Wells McAllister. Discusses family matters, Wilford Woodruff's health, and importance of not finding fault with others. George Throckmorton examined the document and raised questions about the ink, handwriting, and other characteristics of it.[78]

41. *J. D. T. McCallister, Memorandum, June 28, 1902:* Terse, penciled message on stationery of Temple View Home, Box B, Manti, Utah, noting that Joseph F. Smith and others would pass through the following Monday and would need carriage to and from the temple, where they would have dinner.

MARCH 4, 1983[79]

42. *Grandin Contract:* Described in chapter 4. Color photograph published in December 1983.[80] Hofmann acknowledged forging it.[81]

JUNE 17, 1983[82]

43. *The Book of Mormon (Palmyra, N.Y., 1830):* On June 17, 1983, the church Historical Department issued a check to Hofmann for an item described on the check carbon simply as "First Edition Book of Mormon, 1830."[83] Church officials have been unable to determine which of the church's many copies of this book came from Hofmann.[84]

JUNE 27, 1983[85]

44. *Unidentified Joseph Smith Holograph, 1840:* On June 27, 1983, the Historical Department issued a check to Hofmann for an item described on the check carbon simply as "Joseph Smith Holograph, 1840."[86] Church officials have been unable to identify precisely what this item was, although the price paid (two thousand dollars) suggests it probably consisted of little more than a receipt, promissory note, or pay order.[87]

SEPTEMBER 29, 1983[88]

45. *Letter to Hyram Smith, postmarked May 25, [1838]:* Unsigned letter from Far West, Missouri, thought to be in Joseph Smith, Jr.'s, hand. Text reads, "Verily thus Saith the Lord unto Hyram Smith if he will come strateaway to Far West and inquire of his brother it Shall be Shown him how that he may be freed from det and obtain a grate treasure in the earth even so Amen." Photograph published in February 1984.[89] Hofmann acknowledged forging it.[90]

OCTOBER 24, 1983[91]

46. *Mary [Lightner] to Edna Rawlings, Oct. 17, 1894:* Short, rather bland, letter signed "Mary" and sent from Provo, Utah. Though the letter has no LDS content, Don Schmidt apparently obtained it for the church's collection under the assumption it had been written by a plural wife of Joseph Smith named Mary Elizabeth Rollins Lightner.[92] This assumption was aided by the addition of the words "Mary Lightner / Recd Oct 22," written vertically across the front left-hand edge of the envelope in a dark ink. The archivist who catalogued the letter on July 10, 1984, concluded that Mary Elizabeth Rollins Lightner would not have been living in Provo at the time and that the letter's author was probably a teenage girl with a similar name.[93] George Throckmorton raised questions about the handwriting, ink, and postmarks on the letter but was unable to identify any factors that were "conclusive enough to state positively that the document is forged."[94]

47. *Church Trustee Promissory Note, Apr. 27, 1847:* Note signed by Almon W. Babbitt, Joseph L. Heywood, and John S. Fullmer, trustees for the church, promising to pay Amos Davis $403.94 on or before the next July 15. The verso bears an August 24, 1847, note in which Amos Davis endorses the note to Elvira M. Davis, as well as a court clerk's filing notation.

OCTOBER 27, 1983[95]

48. *Subpoena, City of Nauvoo v. Davis (Nauvoo, Ill., Mun. Ct. issued Nov. 30, 1842):* Commands city marshall to summon George Stevens, [blank] Gilbert, Hyrum Smith, and Ira S. Miles to appear as witnesses in court. Signed by James Sloan, clerk of the court.

49. *[George?] Farri[ngton?] to William L. Marcy, postmarked Feb. 8, [1824]:* Stampless cover letter that has been trimmed substantially, deleting most of the original text and part of the signature, and leaving a mostly blank piece of paper to which have been added penciled notations about land transactions in the vicinity of Palmyra, New York. One notation reads, "1820 Joseph Smith—Manchester."

50. *Alfred Cumming to Francis H. Wootton, Jan. 24, 1861:* Letter from governor of Utah Territory to territorial secretary, listing "Acts, Memorials and Resolutions . . . disapproved by me."

51. *Administrators Bond, Estate of Parley P. Pratt, Oct. 5, 1866:* Shakily written document in which Parley P. Pratt (Jr.) and Alma Pratt bind themselves in the penal sum of ten thousand dollars to properly administer the estate of their late father, Parley P. Pratt, with John Van Cott and W. W. Phelps acting as sureties.

52. *Permanent Injunction, Kimball v. Ivans (Henderson County, Ill., Cir. Ct. issued Apr. 1849):* Final order decreeing that the defendants (Charles Ivans, James Ivans, William Law, Wilson Law, Robert D. Foster, Charles

A. Foster, Chauncey L. Higbee, Francis M. Higbee, and James Ward) be perpetually enjoined from collecting judgment against the complainant (Hiram Kimball) and others (Daniel Spencer, Edward Hunter, Orson Spencer, Joseph W. Coolidge, John Taylor, and Alpheus Cutler). In 1986, a copy of the document was sent to the clerk of the court, who found his office had on file the judgment in the case and thus did not need the document returned.[96]

53. *Probate Petition, In re Estate of Young (Salt Lake County P. Ct. filed July 17, 1882):* A petition signed July 15, 1882, by Brigham Young (Jr.) and filed two days later seeking the admission to probate of Mary Ann Angell Young's will and the issuance of related orders and documents.

54. *Bond, Young v. Cannon (Utah 3d Dist. Ct. sworn July 12, 1879):* Bond filed by George Q. Cannon as principal and John Sharp and O. P. Arnold as sureties obligating Cannon to appear in court two days later to answer a charge of "contempt in disobeying an order of the Court in this action for the delivery of property to the Receiver herein." Cannon was one of the executors of Brigham Young's estate. In *Brigham Young: American Moses,* Leonard Arrington wrote, "Considering his long history of promoting anti-Mormon causes, it was no surprise to the church and the executors that on July 12, 1879, Judge Jacob S. Boreman adjudged the executors . . . in contempt of court."[97]

NOVEMBER 17, 1983[98]

On this date, Hofmann gave the Historical Department a large group of materials consisting mostly of legal documents.

55. *Orrin Porter Rockwell Receipt, Aug. 1, 1870:* Rockwell, signing with an *X* as "his mark," acknowledges he "received of E. Mayhew forty dollars in draft on Wells Fargo and Co." Bears a two-cent U.S. revenue stamp. George Throckmorton examined the receipt and wrote, "This receipt is not genuine. The paper and ink have been artificially aged, and the ink is not consistent with genuine ink of that time period. The handwriting is consistent with one of Mark Hofmann's handwriting styles. The stamp has been glued to the paper using a glue that appears to be of modern origin."[99]

56. *H. E. Bowring, Note, Dec. 25, 1868:* Note scrawled in pencil instructing "Bro Williams" to "Please let the bearer have fifty cents in tickets."

57. *Moses Thatcher to William B. Preston, Aug. 2, 1893:* Letter from a member of the Quorum of Twelve to the church's Presiding Bishop discussing deeds to land in Mexico.

58. *Salt Lake Theatre Corporation Receipt, Aug. 31, 1874:* Receipt written on printed blank and signed by Harry Horsley acknowledging receipt of $3.25 for working as an actor.

Daily Telegraph Pay Orders, 1865: Two pay orders from the office of the *Daily Telegraph* signed by Thomas G. Webber and requesting that the "D. D. [Deseret Dramatic] Association" pay out specific sums in tickets and charge them to the *Telegraph* office.

 59. *No. 609, Feb. 9, 1865:* Payable to bearer in amount of $2.00.

 60. *No. 685, Feb. 28, 1865:* Payable to S. A. Kenner in amount of $1.25.

 61. *C. R. Savage Receipt, Nov. 15, 1894:* Receipt signed by Savage, a prominent Utah photographer, acknowledging that John M. Cannon paid ten dollars for photographs.

 62. *Albert E. Bowen to Preston Robinson, n.d.:* Typed memorandum from member of Quorum of Twelve to a manager of the *Deseret News.* Stapled to front of memo is an undated newspaper article titled "Mayor Clarifies City Dads' Stand on Peddling Proposal," which mentions that the mayor of Provo, Utah, is C. W. Love. Love was mayor from 1950 to 1953.[100] A photograph on the reverse side of the article shows soldiers in the Korean War, which spanned the same years. Bowen writes to Robinson, "I am depending on you now to keep track of this matter and watch developments." Robinson has added in pencil, "Clyde—and I am depending on you."

 63. *Transcript, People v. Foster (Hancock County [city unspecified], Ill., J.P. Ct. filed in Hancock Cir. Ct. Apr. 15, 1844):* Appeal transcript of case in which "Esqr. [Daniel?] Wells," relying on affidavit of J. P. Green, issued warrant against R. D. Foster on charge of gaming. Foster found guilty in jury trial before Isaac Higbee, J.P. Foster appeals. Witnesses included F. M. Higbee and William Smith.

Dodd v. Flint:

 64. *Procedendo, Dodd v. Flint (Hancock County, Ill., Cir. Ct. issued Oct. 21, 1831):* Informs Hazen Bedel, acting J.P., that appeal of William Flint was dismissed; commands Bedel to proceed in collecting judgment.

 65. *Notice, Dodd v. Flint (Hancock County, Ill., Cir. Ct. issued May 2, 1832):* Notifies John Thomas II "that Dr. Isaac Garland disputes the note Given by him to Thomas Kinney and pleads a want of consideration as the note was sold by yourself and Mr Kinney to Andrew Vance."

 66. *Deposition of Isaac Galland, Ralston & Berry v. White (Hancock County, Ill., Cir. Ct. subscribed Apr. 29, 1836):* Galland, co-defendant in the suit, explains why another defendant is absent. Galland signs his name "I. Galland," but the text of the deposition gives his name as "Isaac Garland."

Doyle v. Moffit:

 67. *Summons, Doyle v. Moffit (Hancock County, Ill., Cir. Ct. issued Sept. 9, 1837):* Commands sheriff to summon John Moffit.

 68. *Summons, Doyle v. Moffit (Hancock County, Ill., Cir. Ct. issued Sept. 9, 1837):* Commands sheriff to summon Davidson Hibbard, Abraham Elwell, and [blank] Warrenton.

69. *Witness Affidavit, Doyle v. Moffit (Hancock County, Ill., Cir. Ct. subscribed Sept. 29, 1837):* James Moffitt and George A. MClellan "claim 5 days each as a witness in the case."

70. *Summons, Chandler v. Dedman (Hancock County, Ill., Cir. Ct. issued July 22, 1837):* Commands sheriff to summon defendant.

71. *Lease Indenture, May 1, 1838:* Document in which William Ayers leases buildings in Warsaw, Illinois, to Richard Ellis and John Browning for three years to use as a public tavern.

Brown v. Hamilton:

72. *Supersedeas, Brown v. Hamilton (Hancock County, Ill., Cir. Ct. issued Nov. 18, 1837):* Commands J.P. and constable not to proceed further in the case until it has been resolved on appeal.

73. *Summons, Brown v. Hamilton (Hancock County, Ill., Cir. Ct. issued Nov. 18, 1837):* Commands sheriff to summon victorious plaintiff to court when appeal is heard.

Warner v. Hine:

74. *Subpoena, Warner v. Hine (Warsaw, Ill., J.P. Ct. issued Sept. 18, 1839):* Commands Ephraim Warner and Joshua Cole to appear before A. H. Worthen, J.P., on September 28.

75. *Subpoena, Warner v. Hine (Warsaw, Ill., J.P. Ct. issued Sept. 20, 1839):* Commands Samuel Dobyns and others to appear before A. H. Worthen on September 28.

Tucker v. Sperry:

76. *Subpoena, Tucker v. Sperry (Augusta, Ill., J.P. Ct. issued Oct. 23, 1839):* Commands Alvin G. Bacon and others to appear before David Catlin, J.P., on November 2.

77. *Subpoena, Tucker v. Sperry (Augusta, Ill., J.P. Ct. issued Oct. 30, 1839):* Commands Benjamin Bacon and others to appear before David Catlin, J.P., on November 2.

78. *Praecipe, Marsh v. Galland (Hancock County, Ill., Cir. Ct. submitted Aug. 28, 1839):* Plaintiff's counsel asks clerk to issue summons. Isaac Galland is first defendant listed.

79. *Bond, State v. Deaves (Hancock County, Ill., Cir. Ct. subscribed Sept. 16, 1840):* Bond for two hundred dollars to guarantee appearance of Thomas Deaves in court to answer indictment for selling liquor without a license.

80. *Praecipe, Hendricks v. Orrill (La Harpe, Ill., J.P. Ct. subscribed July 1, 1840):* Notifies constable that subscriber, S. Humphreys, will "attend before" L. R. Chaffin of La Harpe on July 7 and asks constable to certify the plaintiff so he will be present.

81. *Witness Affidavit, Lofton v. Perkins (Hancock County, Ill., Cir. Ct. subscribed May 11, 1841):* Nathan Lincoln attests to spending five days as witness for plaintiff.

Black v. Stanton:
    82. *Witness Affidavit, Black v. Stanton (Hancock County, Ill., Cir. Ct. subscribed Oct. 15, 1841):* Sylvester Meguire attests to spending nine days as witness for defendant.
    83. *Witness Affidavit, Black v. Stanton (Hancock County, Ill., Cir. Ct. subscribed Oct. 16, 1841):* Jacob Mendenhall attests to spending eight days as witness for defendant.

84. *Settlement Agreement, Shearer v. Newberry ([Hancock County, Ill., Cir. Ct.?] subscribed Oct. 5, 1841):* The body of this simple document reads, "This case by agreement of the parties is dismissed at plaintiff's costs."
85. *John J. Hicok Deposition, Oct. 30, 1841:* Document signed by L. R. Chaffin, J.P., and deponent in which latter expresses belief that John Broomfield stole a pair of shoes from a storehouse in La Harpe, Illinois.

Osser v. Chapman: David H. Osser sues Dellmore Chapman in plea of assumpsit.
    86. *Subpoena, Osser v. Chapman (Carthage, Ill., J.P. Ct. issued Feb. 28, 1840):* Commands E. G. Haggard and others to appear before Samuel Cans, J.P., on February 29.
    87. *Venire, Osser v. Chapman (Carthage, Ill., J.P. Ct. issued Feb. 29, 1840):* Commands constable to summon six jurors unrelated to parties to appear before J.P.
    88. *Subpoena, Osser v. Chapman (Hancock County, Ill., Cir. Ct. issued Apr. 24, 1841):* Commands sheriff to summon Noah Packard and Noah Packard, Jr., to appear in court
    89. *Subpoena, Osser v. Chapman (Hancock County, Ill., Cir. Ct. issued Sept. 20, 1841):* Commands sheriff to summon three witnesses.

90. *Subpoena, Brannen v. Wilson (Hancock County, Ill., Cir. Ct. issued Sept. 20, 1841):* Commands sheriff to summon James Moore and others to appear in court.
91. *Subpoena, Finley v. Williams (Hancock County [city unspecified], Ill., J.P. Ct. issued Jan. 7, 1841):* Commands constable to summon defendant to appear January 16 at the office of the J.P., whose name, though difficult to read, appears to be John F. Callison.
92. *Subpoena, Dunlap v. Humphreys (Hancock County, Ill., Cir. Ct. issued Sept. 15, 1841):* Commands sheriff of McDonough County to summon John Gardner and Joseph Atwater to court.
93. *Witness Affidavit, Alton v. Beebe (Hancock County, Ill., Cir. Ct. subscribed May 13, 1842):* Stephen G. Ferris attests to spending five days as witness for defendant.

Hamilton v. Sampson:
    94. *Appeal Bond, Hamilton v. Sampson (Hancock County, Ill., Cir. Ct. subscribed Mar. 11, 1842):* Subscribers bind themselves to "pay and satisfy whatever judgment may be rendered by the Circuit Court" when it considers a case taken on appeal from a J.P. court.

95. *Witness Affidavit, Hamilton v. Sampson (Hancock County, Ill., Cir. Ct. subscribed May 13, 184[2]):* Marvin M. Hamilton attests to spending nine days as witness for plaintiff.

96. *Levy Order, Ivins v. Samuel ([Nauvoo], Ill., J.P. Ct. issued Sept. 30, 1842):* Commands constable to pay successful plaintiff from goods and chattels of defendant. Issued by E. Robinson, J.P. Inscription on verso records that execution was enjoined pending further action in the case.

97. *Trial Transcript, People v. Robertson (Warsaw, Ill., J.P. Ct. subscribed Jan. 7, 1842):* Records proceedings before Thomas C. Sharp in assault-and-battery case.

98. *Hancock County, Illinois, Marriage Certificate, Aug. 14, 1843:* Certifies that Moses Jared, "Minister of the Gospel," joined Horace H. Wilcox and Olivia Richardson in marriage on August 13, 1843.

99. *Witness Affidavit, Dayly v. Eley (Hancock County, Ill., Cir. Ct. subscribed May 25, 1844):* Robert Ayers attests to spending five days as witness for plaintiff.

100. *Notice of Sheriff's Sale, Nov. 12, 1844:* Sheriff M. R. Deming announces that parcel of real estate will be sold December 2 pursuant to a writ of fieri facias issued by Hancock County Circuit Court.

101. *Judgment Transcript, People v. Hackley (Hancock County [city unspecified], Ill., J.P. Ct. subscribed Feb. 16, 1844):* E. A. Bedell, J.P., records judgment rendered three days earlier.

Ralston v. Cahoon:

102. *Transcript, Ralston v. Cahoon (Hancock County [city unspecified], Ill., J.P. Ct. prepared Mar. 31, 1846):* E. A. Bedell, J.P., summarizes proceedings in case from parties' first appearance before him on October 25, 1844, until transcript was prepared.

103. *Assignment of Judgment, Ralston v. Cahoon (Hancock County [city unspecified], Ill., J.P. Ct. subscribed Mar. 31, 1846):* Assignee of successful plantiffs agrees to assign judgment once more to yet another person.

104. *Subpoena, People v. Elliot (Nauvoo, Ill., J.P. Ct. issued Feb. 11, 1845):* Commands E. A. Bedell to appear "forthwith" in the office of Aaron Johnson, the issuing J.P.

Olney v. Spencer:

105. *Praecipe for Summons, Olney v. Spencer (Hancock County, Ill., Cir. Ct. filed June 11, 1845):* Plaintiff's counsel asks that summonses be issued. Defendants include Daniel Spencer, Edward Hunter, Hiram Kimball, Orson Spencer, Joseph W. Coolidge, John Taylor, and Alpheus Cutler.

106. *Praecipe for Execution, Olney v. Spencer (Hancock County, Ill., Cir. Ct. filed Sept. 28, 1846):* Plaintiff's counsel makes the terse request, "Issue execution."

Smith v. Kimball:

107. *Summons to Appellee, Smith v. Kimball (Hancock County, Ill., Cir. Ct. issued Oct. 22, 1846):* Commands sheriff to summon appellee to circuit court.

108. *Injunction, Smith v. Kimball (Hancock County, Ill., Cir. Ct. issued Oct. 22, 1846):* Enjoins execution of J.P.'s judgment pending resolution of appeal.

109. *Attachment Bond, J. P. Eddy & Co. v. Yearsley (Hancock County, Ill., Cir. Ct. filed May 6, 1846):* Obligates plaintiffs to pay defendant $920 unless suit succeeds or unless they pay whatever damages court awards for wrongfully attaching property.

110. *Attachment Bond, Beach & Eddy v. Yearsley (Hancock County, Ill., Cir. Ct. filed May 6, 1846):* Obligates plaintiffs to pay defendant $1604.14 unless suit succeeds or unless they pay whatever damages court awards for wrongfully attaching property.

Kimball v. Rich:

111. *"Copy of notes & account sued on," Kimball v. Rich ([Hancock County, Ill., Cir. Ct.] filed May 20, 1846):* Transcribes text of financial documents (including item 112 below) that form basis of suit.

112. *Account Sheet, Kimball v. Rich ([Hancock County, Ill., Cir. Ct.] filed Apr. 17, 1847):* Shows total debt of $12.50 owed by Charles C. Rich to Hiram Kimball for transactions on November 23 and 24, 1845.

113. *Jury Verdict, Kimball v. Rich (Hancock County, Ill., Cir. Ct. filed Apr. 17, 1847):* The body of this document reads, "We the jury assess the Plaintiffs Damages at forty six Dollars and fifty Eight cents."

114. *Praecipe, Spencer v. Foster (Hancock County, Ill., Cir. Ct. filed Mar. 9, 1846):* Request by attorneys to issue writ of execution directed to sheriff.

115. *Praecipe, Kimball v. Foster ([Hancock County, Ill., Cir. Ct.] filed June 24, 1986):* Plaintiff asks clerk to issue alias writ of execution directed to sheriff.

116. *Witness Affidavit, Marsh v. Chandler (Hancock County, Ill., Cir. Ct. subscribed Sept. 17, 1847):* John D. Millen attests to spending one day as witness for defendant.

117. *Praecipe, Cowen ex rel. Backenstos v. Gates (Hancock County, Ill., Cir. Ct. submitted May 19, 1847):* Plaintiff's counsel asks clerk to issue writ of execution directed to sheriff.

118. *Praecipe, Bullock v. Gates (Hancock County, Ill., Cir. Ct. filed June 5, 1847):* Plaintiff's counsel asks clerk to issue writ of execution directed to sheriff.

Conger v. McBride:

119. *Praecipe and Affidavit, McBride v. Conger (Warren County, Ill.,*

Cir. Ct. [May term] 1847): This document contains two separate but related items on a single sheet. The first asks the clerk to issue a capias ad respondendum. In the second, McBride attests to sustaining damages because Conger breached a covenant. McBride also attests "that the benefit of whatever judgement said deponent may obtain in said case will be in danger of being lost unless said defendant be held to bail."

120. *Affidavit, Conger v. McBride (Warren County, Ill., Cir. Ct. subscribed May 3, 1847):* McBride attests "that said Conger is unable to pay the costs of this suit as deponent verily believes."

121. *Praecipe, Conger v. McBride (Warren County, Ill., Cir. Ct. submitted [May term] 1847):* McBride asks clerk to issue subpoenas for witnesses.

Mulhern v. Benbow:

122. *Praecipe, Mulhern v. Benbow (Hancock County, Ill., Cir. Ct. filed Apr. 8, 1847):* Plaintiffs' counsel asks clerk to issue subpoenas for witnesses.

123. *Subpoena, Mulhern v. Benbow (Hancock County, Ill., Cir. Ct. issued Apr. 8, 1847):* Commands sheriff to summon witnesses to appear in court.

124. *Agreement to Change Venue, Mulhern v. Benbow (Hancock County, Ill., Cir. Ct. filed Apr. 12, 1847):* The parties (represented by their attorneys) agree to have the case tried at the October term of the Adams County Circuit Court.

125. *Settlement Notice, Mulhern v. Benbow (Hancock County, Ill., Cir. Ct. written Aug. 1847):* Plaintiffs' counsel informs court clerk that case has been settled and asks him not to issue writ of execution in another case.

126. *Praecipe, Davis v. Foster (Hancock County, Ill., Cir. Ct. filed Feb. 25, 1847):* Attorney for second-generation assignee of Davis asks court clerk to issue writ of fieri facias.

Kelly v. Clark:

127. *Praecipe, Kelly v. Clark (Hancock County, Ill., Cir. Ct. filed Feb. 4, 1848):* Plaintiff's counsel asks clerk to issue summons for defendants directed to sheriff.

128. *Plea, Kelly v. Clark (Hancock County, Ill., Cir. Ct. filed Sept. 18, 1848):* Defendants deny they are indebted to plaintiff as alleged.

129. *Demurrer to Plea No. 1, Kelly v. Clark (Hancock County, Ill., Cir. Ct. filed Sept. 18, 1848):* Plaintiff maintains defendants' plea is insufficient, that he is not bound to answer it, "and this he is ready to verify; whereupon he prays judgment and his debt and damages to be adjudged to him."

130. *Praecipe, Kelly v. Clark (Hancock County, Ill., Cir. Ct. filed Mar. 25, 1850):* Plaintiff's counsel asks clerk to issue writ of scire facias.
131. *Scire Facias, Kelly v. Clark (Hancock County, Ill., Cir. Ct. issued Mar. 25, 1850):* Commands sheriff to summon defendants to court "to show cause if any they have why the said John Kelly ought not to have execution against them."
132. *Subpoena, Kelly v. Clark (Hancock County, Ill., Cir. Ct. issued Apr. 3, 1850):* Commands sheriff of Adams County to summon witness.
133. *Demurrer, Kelly v. Clark (Hancock County, Ill., Cir. Ct. filed Apr. 17, 1850):* Defendants respond that facts stated in scire facias are legally insufficient to entitle plaintiff to judgment.
134. *Amended Scire Facias, Kelly v. Clark (Hancock County, Ill., Cir. Ct. issued July 31, 1850):* Commands county sheriff to summon defendants to appear before court to answer why plaintiff "ought not to have his execution against them of the debt and damages and costs" that court records show they owe him.
135. *Pleas 1 & 2, Kelly v. Clark (Hancock County, Ill., Cir. Ct. filed Sept. 16, 1850):* Defendant Clark pleads (apparently in the alternative) that (1) there is no record showing that plaintiff recovered a judgment against him and (2) he paid the judgment.
136. *Replication to Pleas 1 & 2, Kelly v. Clark (Hancock County, Ill., Cir. Ct. filed Sept. 18, 1850):* Plaintiff responds to Clark's pleas, maintaining (1) "that there is such a record of the said recovery" and (2) that Clark did not pay it.
137. *Affidavit for Continuance, Kelly v. Clark (Hancock County, Ill., Cir. Ct. filed Sept. 19, 1850):* Clark seeks continuance on grounds that two key witnesses have moved to California and that their depositions cannot be obtained before the next term of the court.
138. *Subpoena, Kelly v. Clark (Hancock County, Ill., Cir. Ct. issued June 2, 1851):* Commands sheriff to summon James Irwin to court immediately.
139. *Praecipe, Kelly v. Clark (Hancock County, Ill., Cir. Ct. subscribed Aug. 29, 1851):* Asks clerk to issue writ of execution directed to sheriff.

Bidamon v. Phipps:
140. *Transcript of Proceedings, Bidamon v. Phipps (Nauvoo, Ill., J.P. Ct. filed Mar. 23, 1848):* Transcript of case proceedings prepared by J.P., probably for use on appeal to circuit court.
141. *Praecipe, Bidamon v. Phipps ([Hancock County, Ill., Cir. Ct.] filed June 24, 1848):* Attorney for plaintiff asks clerk to issue writ of execution.

Kelly v. Mulholland:
142. *Affidavit in Attachment, Kelly v. Mulholland (Hancock County, Ill., Cir. Ct. subscribed June 27, 1848):* Plaintiff attests that nonresident defendant owes him money on unpaid promissory note.

143. *Attachment Bond, Kelly v. Mulholland (Hancock County, Ill., Cir. Ct. filed June 29, 1848):* Obligates plaintiff and sureties to pay defendant $440 unless suit succeeds or unless they pay whatever damages court awards for wrongfully attaching property.

144. *Praecipe, Kelly v. Mulholland (Hancock County, Ill., Cir. Ct. filed June 29, 1848):* Plaintiff's counsel asks clerk to issue writ of attachment directed to sheriff.

145. *Praecipe, Kelly v. Mulholland (Hancock County, Ill., Cir. Ct. filed Nov. 2, 1848):* Plaintiff's counsel asks clerk to issue writ of execution directed to sheriff.

146. *Letters of Administration, Kelly v. Mulholland (Hancock County, Ill., Cir. Ct. issued Aug. 4, 1851):* Appoints administrator for estate of plaintiff, who has died.

147. *Praecipe, Kelly v. Mulholland (Hancock County, Ill., Cir. Ct. subscribed Nov. 14, 1851):* Asks court to "Please file Letters of Administration & *Record* & Issue Execution to Sheriff in Case of *Kelly v. Mulholland.*" Attached to item 146.

148. *Praecipe, Wilcox v. Robison (Hancock County, Ill., Cir. Ct. filed May 17, 1848):* Asks clerk to issue writ of execution directed to sheriff.

149. *Amos Davis, Promissory Note, May 1, 1848:* Note signed by Amos Davis of Nauvoo, Illinois, promising to pay $784.99 to James McClintock and Co. six months after date of note. Filed in Hancock County, Illinois, Circuit Court on Oct. 10, 1853.

150. *Execution, People v. Fulliam (Hancock County [city unspecified], Ill., J P. Ct. issued Sept. 16, 1848):* This writ of execution, issued by a J.P., was later returned uncollected and filed in the circuit court.

Riter v. Hall: Franklin Hall owes a debt to Benjamin Riter.
151. *Interrogatories, Riter v. Hall (Hancock County, Ill., Cir. Ct. filed Sept. 21, 1849):* Interrogatives directed by plaintiff's counsel to Samuel B. Elliott, purported debtor of defendant.

152. *Answers to Interrogatories, Riter v. Hall (Hancock County, Ill., Cir. Ct. filed Apr. 15, 1850):* Samuel B. Elliott responds to interrogatories.

Riter v. Elliot: Benjamin Riter sues Samuel B. Elliott, Elbridge G. Hall, and Sylvanus B. Hayden, seeking to garnish Franklin Hall's property, which is purportedly under defendants' control.
153. *Answer, Riter v. Elliott (Hancock County, Ill., Cir. Ct. filed Apr. 17, 1850):* Plaintiff's counsel responds that Elliott has not divulged all of Hall's property under his control.

154. *Subpoena, Riter v. Elliott (Hancock County, Ill., Cir. Ct. issued Apr. 22, 1850):* Commands sheriff to summon witness for plaintiff.

155. *Deposition Notice, Riter v. Elliott (Hancock County, Ill., Cir. Ct. filed July 13, 1850):* Defendants inform plaintiff of intent to obtain de-

dimus potestatem to commission Cincinnati J.P. to depose three witnesses. Includes list of proposed questions.

156. *Affidavit, Riter v. Elliott (Hancock County, Ill., Cir. Ct. subscribed Sept. 17, 1850):* Affidavit apparently to support motion for continuance on grounds that depositions of nonresident witnesses had not yet been returned.

157. *Dedimus Potestatem and Depositions, Riter v. Elliott (Hancock County, Ill., Cir. Ct. written July to Sept. 1850):* Bundle of materials including dedimus potestatem obtained by defendants and depositions of two Cincinnati witnesses.

158. *Praecipe, Riter v. Elliott (Hancock County, Ill., Cir. Ct. filed Sept. 18, 1850):* Defendants' counsel asks clerk to issue subpoena for C. E. Yates.

159. *Subpoena, Riter v. Elliott (Hancock County, Ill., Cir. Ct. issued Sept. 18, 1850):* Commands sheriff to summon C. E. Yates as witness for defendants.

160. *Plaintiff's Jury Instruction, Riter v. Elliott (Hancock County, Ill., Cir. Ct. filed Sept. 18, 1850):* Jury instruction proposed by plaintiff and given by court.

161. *Defendant's Jury Instructions, Riter v. Elliott (Hancock County, Ill., Cir. Ct. filed Sept. 18, 1850):* Several instructions proposed by defendants. Notation by each instruction indicates whether each was given or refused.

162. *Witness Affidavit, Riter v. Elliott (Hancock County, Ill., Cir. Ct. subscribed Sept. 18, 1850):* W. M. Cosgrove attests to spending three days as witness for plaintiff.

163. *Witness Affidavit, Riter v. Elliott (Hancock County, Ill., Cir. Ct. subscribed Sept. 18, 1850):* John B. Downing attests to spending two days as witness for plaintiff.

164. *Witness Affidavit, Riter v. Elliott (Hancock County, Ill., Cir. Ct. subscribed Sept. 18, 1850):* W. S. Hathaway attests to spending one day as witness for defendants.

165. *Witness Affidavit, Riter v. Elliott (Hancock County, Ill., Cir. Ct. subscribed Sept. 19, 1850):* C. E. Yates attests to spending one day as witness for defendants.

166. *Praecipe, Riter v. Elliott (Hancock County, Ill., Cir. Ct. filed Oct. 2, 1850):* Plaintiff's counsel asks clerk to issue writ of execution.

167. *Judgment and Sale Documents, Riter v. Elliott (Hancock County, Ill., Cir. Ct. 1852):* Court decides that Samuel B. Elliott transferred real estate to Charles H. Elliott with intent to defraud creditors. Appoints special master as commissioner to liquidate property. Includes copies of deeds conveying property to new buyers.

168. *"Personal attach of Edmunds ending process":* Undated document containing no court or clerk filing information; lists demands and goods delivered. Others documents in this group show that George Edmunds, Jr., was plaintiff's attorney.

Riter v. McLennan: Benjamin Riter, who is owed a debt by Franklin Hall, seeks to collect from William McLennan, who purportedly is indebted to Hall.

169. *Praecipe, Riter v. McLennan (Hancock County, Ill., Cir. Ct. filed Dec. 28, 1849):* Requests issuance of an "alias garnishee in this case against the firm of Morrill & McLennan to be served on *McLennan* only." The named firm, which had dissolved, purportedly had held the property of Hall. This document also requests issuance of a writ of execution "against Hall & to Sell property attached."

170. *Garnishee Summons, Riter v. McLennan (Hancock County, Ill., Cir. Ct. filed Mar. 8, 1850):* Commands sheriff to summon defendant to court.

171. *Interrogatories, Riter v. McLennan (Hancock County, Ill., Cir. Ct. filed Apr. 3, 1850):* Interrogatories directed to McLennan.

172. *Answers to Interrogatories, Riter v. McLennan (Hancock County, Ill., Cir. Ct. subscribed Apr. 15, 1850):* McLennan responds to interrogatories.

173. *Subpoena, Riter v. McLennan (Hancock County, Ill., Cir. Ct. issued Apr. 16, 1850):* Commands sheriff to summon Milton M. Morrill to court.

174. *Subpoena, Riter v. McLennan (Hancock County, Ill., Cir. Ct. issued Apr. 18, 1850):* Commands sheriff to summon John Downing to court "forthwith."

175. *Affidavit, Riter v. McLennan (Hancock County, Ill., Cir. Ct. subscribed Apr. 18, 1850):* McLennan maintains that a material witness, Stephen T. Cary, was presently in Pottawatomie County, Iowa, and that he "has not had time to procure the testimony of said Cary upon the trial of this cause." McLennan says witness will prove he owes nothing to Hall.

176. *Witness Affidavit, Riter v. McLennan (Hancock County, Ill., Cir. Ct. subscribed Apr. 26, 1850):* M. M. Morrill attests to spending three days as witness for plaintiff.

177. *Amended Answer, Riter v. McLennan (Hancock County, Ill., Cir. Ct. filed Sept. 17, 1850):* Contains defendant's amended answer to plaintiff's complaint. Plaintiff's response is written at the end of it.

178. *Plaintiff's Proposed Jury Instructions, Riter v. McLennan (Hancock County, Ill., Cir. Ct. filed Sept. 17, 1850):* Contains two instructions that plaintiff proposed the judge give the jury. Both were refused.

179. *Plaintiff's Jury Instruction No. 1, Riter v. McLennan (Hancock County, Ill., Cir. Ct. filed Sept. 17, 1850):* Contains plaintiff's first jury instruction, amended. Marked "given."

180. *Plaintiff's Jury Instruction No. 2, Riter v. McLennan (Hancock County, Ill., Cir. Ct. filed Sept. 17, 1850):* Contains plaintiff's second jury instruction, amended. Marked "given."

181. *Plaintiff's Jury Instruction No. 4, Riter v. McLennan (Hancock County, Ill., Cir. Ct. filed Sept. 17, 1850):* Contains plaintiff's fourth jury instruction. Marked "given."

182. *Defendant's Jury Instruction No. 3, Riter v. McLennan (Hancock County, Ill., Cir. Ct. filed Sept. 17, 1850):* Contains defendant's third jury instruction. Marked "given."

183. *Defendant's Jury Instruction No. 4, Riter v. McLennan (Hancock County, Ill., Cir. Ct. filed Sept. 17, 1850):* Contains defendant's fourth jury instruction. Marked "given."

184. *Witness Affidavit, Riter v. McLennan (Hancock County, Ill., Cir. Ct. subscribed Sept. 18, 1850):* John B. Downing attests to spending one day as witness for plaintiff.

185. *Witness Affidavit, Riter v. McLennan (Hancock County, Ill., Cir. Ct. subscribed Sept. 18, 1850):* W. M. Cosgrove attests to spending twenty-one days as witness for plaintiff.

186. *"Reasons for new trial," Riter v. McLennan (Hancock County, Ill., Cir. Ct. filed Sept. 19, 1850):* Lists four reasons defendant believes he should have new trial.

187. *"Reasons for new trial," Riter v. McLennan (Hancock County, Ill., Cir. Ct. filed Sept. 19, 1850):* Lists fifth reason defendant believes he should have new trial.

188. *Praecipe, Riter v. McLennan (Hancock County, Ill., Cir. Ct. filed Oct. 1, 1850):* Plaintiff's counsel asks clerk to issue writ of execution but does not specify to whom it should be directed.

189. *Praecipe, Riter v. McLennan (Hancock County, Ill., Cir. Ct. filed Mar. 13, 1851):* Plaintiff's counsel asks clerk to issue writ of execution directed to sheriff.

Hall v. McLennan: Franklin Hall sues W. McLennan, garnishee of Israel S. Clapp.

190. *Amended Answers to Interrogatories, Hall v. McLennan (Hancock County, Ill., Cir. Ct. filed Apr. 17, 1850):* Defendant responds to plaintiff's questions. Plaintiff pens statement at end alleging that defendant has not divulged all of Clapp's property under his control.

191. *Receipt, Hall v. McLennan (Hancock County, Ill., Cir. Ct. filed June 15, 1850):* Plaintiff acknowledges receiving payment in full from defendant for all claims against him in the suit.

Riter v. Morrill: Benjamin Riter sues M. M. Morrill in garnishment dispute over property purportedly belonging to Franklin Hall.

192. *Answer, Riter v. Morrill (Hancock County, Ill., Cir. Ct. filed Sept. 18, 1850):* Lengthy document in which defendant answers plaintiff's complaint. At end of document, plaintiff adds claim that defendant has not disclosed all property he is holding for Franklin Hall.

193. *Witness Affidavit, Riter v. Morrill (Hancock County, Ill., Cir. Ct. subscribed Sept. 18, 1850):* John B. Downing attests to spending two days as witness for plaintiff.

194. *Witness Affidavit, Riter v. Morrill (Hancock County, Ill., Cir. Ct. subscribed Sept. 18, 1850):* W. M. Cosgrove attests to spending three days as witness for plaintiff.

195. *Subpoena, Riter v. Morrill (Hancock County, Ill., Cir. Ct. issued Sept. 4, 1850):* Commands sheriff to summon three witnesses for plaintiff.

196. *Praecipe, Riter v. Morrill (Hancock County, Ill., Cir. Ct. filed Oct. 2, 1850):* Plaintiff's counsel asks clerk to issue writ of execution.

197. *Praecipe, Riter v. Morrill (Hancock County, Ill., Cir. Ct. filed Feb. 8, 1851):* Plaintiff himself asks clerk to issue writ of execution.

198. *Praecipe, Riter v. Morrill (Hancock County, Ill., Cir. Ct. filed Aug. 16, 1852):* Plaintiff's counsel asks clerk to issue writ of execution.

Hall v. Piggott: A. G. Hall sues Jabez J. Piggott for debt before Nauvoo, Illinois, J.P. Reuben Bourne.

199. *Affidavit, Hall v. Piggott (Nauvoo, Ill., J.P. Ct. subscribed Dec. 4, 1850):* Plaintiff's counsel seeks writ of attachment, averring that defendant owes plaintiff money but has left state and is about to remove his property too.

200. *Bond for Costs, Hall v. Piggott (Nauvoo, Ill., J.P. Ct. subscribed Dec. 4, 1850):* Plaintiff's counsel binds himself to pay court costs.

201. *Attachment Bond, Hall v. Piggott (Nauvoo, Ill., J.P. Ct. approved Dec. 4, 1850):* Plaintiff's sureties agree to pay defendant damages if court rules they have wrongfully attached his property.

202. *Writ of Attachment, Hall v. Piggott (Nauvoo, Ill., J.P. Ct. issued Dec. 4, 1850):* Bourne orders that constable attach enough of defendant's property to satisfy debt.

203. *Attachment Notice, Hall v. Piggott (Nauvoo, Ill., J.P. Ct. subscribed Dec. 10, 1850):* Writ of attachment was returnable before Bourne on December 10. On that date, defendant had not been served with writ because he could not be found. As a result, this notice was posted at three locations to notify defendant that if he did not appear before Bourne on December 20 at noon, a default judgment would be entered against him and his property sold to satisfy it.

204. *Plea in Abatement and Demurrer, Hall v. Piggott (Nauvoo, Ill., J.P. Ct. subscribed Dec. 20, 1850):* A. S. Kingsley represents himself as defendant's agent and maintains that defendant has not left the state and is not removing his property from it. On the same document, plaintiff's counsel has penned a demurrer. Bourne added the notation, "Demurrer sustained plea in abatement overruled."

205. *Appeal Bond, Hall v. Piggott (Hancock County, Ill., Cir. Ct. filed Dec. 21, 1850):* A. S. Kingsley, as agent for defendant and his sureties, files bond to allow them to appeal Bourne's decision.

206. *Summons to Appellee, Hall v. Piggott (Hancock County, Ill., Cir. Ct. issued Dec. 21, 1850):* Commands sheriff to summon appellee to appear in court. Summons returned unserved.

207. *Injunction, Hall v. Piggott (Hancock County, Ill., Cir. Ct. issued Dec. 25, 1850):* Enjoins execution of Bourne's judgment pending resolution of appeal.

208. *Transcript, Hall v. Piggott (Nauvoo, Ill., J.P. Ct. certified Dec. 30, 1850):* Transcript prepared by Bourne for defendant's appeal.

209. *Summons to Appellee, Hall v. Piggott (Hancock County, Ill., Cir. Ct. issued Apr. 28, 1851):* Commands sheriff to summon appellee to court ("as you have before been Commanded"). Service accepted by plaintiff's counsel.

210. *Praecipe, Hall v. Piggott (Hancock County, Ill., Cir. Ct. filed May 8, 1851):* Plaintiff's agent asks clerk to issue subpoenas for five witnesses.

211. *Subpoena, Hall v. Piggott (Hancock County, Ill., Cir. Ct. issued May 8, 1851):* Commands sheriff to summon four witnesses for plaintiff.

212. *Praecipe, Hall v. Piggott (Hancock County, Ill., Cir. Ct. filed May 29, 1851):* Defendant's counsel asks clerk to issue subpoenas for five witnesses.

213. *Subpoena, Hall v. Piggott (Hancock County, Ill., Cir. Ct. issued May 29, 1851):* Commands sheriff to summon four witnesses for defendant.

214. *Subpoena, Hall v. Piggott (Hancock County, Ill., Cir. Ct. issued May 29, 1851):* Commands sheriff to summon one more witness for defendant.

215. *Motion to Dismiss Appeal, Hall v. Piggott (Hancock County, Ill., Cir. Ct. filed June 3, 1851):* Plaintiff's counsel moves to dismiss defendant's appeal on grounds that no appeal bond is on file.

216. *Affidavit, Hall v. Piggott (Hancock County, Ill., Cir. Ct. subscribed June 4, 1851):* Plaintiff's counsel avers that A. S. Kingsley had no authority to sign appeal bond for defendant.

217. *Witness Affidavit, Hall v. Piggott (Hancock County, Ill., Cir. Ct. subscribed June 12, 1851):* N. S. Holcomb attests to spending two days as witness for plaintiff.

218. *Witness Affidavit, Hall v. Piggott (Hancock County, Ill., Cir. Ct. subscribed June 7, 1851):* John Kelly attests to spending three days as witness for plaintiff.

219. *Witness Affidavit, Hall v. Piggott (Hancock County, Ill., Cir. Ct. subscribed June 7, 1851):* Thomas Kelly attests to spending three days as witness for plaintiff.

220. *Witness Affidavit, Hall v. Piggott (Hancock County, Ill., Cir. Ct. subscribed June 7, 1851):* Albert Stow attests to spending four days as witness for defendant.

221. *Witness Affidavit, Hall v. Piggott (Hancock County, Ill., Cir. Ct. subscribed June 9, 1851):* B. Whitfield attests to spending four days as witness for defendant.

222. *Procedendo, Hall v. Piggott (Hancock County, Ill., Cir. Ct. issued June 10, 1851):* Commands Bourne to "proceed in such manner according to the Law of the land, as you may see proper, any other writ to the contrary, in any thing, notwithstanding."

Prentice v. Piggott: Frederick R. Prentice sues Jabez J. Piggott for debt before Reuben Bourne, a J.P. in Nauvoo, Illinois. Later heard before John McNamee, a Nauvoo J.P., on a change of venue. Prentice prevails. Piggott appeals to Hancock County Circuit Court.

223. *Affidavit, Prentice v. Piggott (Nauvoo, Ill., J.P. Ct. subscribed Dec. 4, 1850):* Plaintiff's counsel seeks writ of attachment from Bourne, averring that defendant owes plaintiff money but has left state and is about to remove his property too.

224. *Attachment Bond, Prentice v. Piggott (Nauvoo, Ill., J.P. Ct. approved Dec. 4, 1850):* Plaintiff's sureties agree to pay defendant damages if court rules they have wrongfully attached his property. Approved by Bourne.

225. *Writ of Attachment, Prentice v. Piggott (Nauvoo, Ill., J.P. Ct. issued Dec. 4, 1850):* Bourne orders that constable attach enough of defendant's property to satisfy debt.

226. *Affidavit for Continuance, Prentice v. Piggott (Nauvoo, Ill., J.P. Ct. subscribed Dec. 20, 1850):* Plaintiff's counsel seeks thirty-day continuance from Bourne on grounds that material witness is unavailable.

227. *Transcript, Prentice v. Piggott (Nauvoo, Ill., J.P. Ct. attested Dec. 20, 1851):* Transcript made by Bourne as part of change of venue in the case.

228. *Jury Warrant, Prentice v. Piggott (Nauvoo, Ill., J.P. Ct. issued Dec. 20, 1850):* McNamee commands constable to summon "Six lawful men of your county" to serve as jurors.

229. *Affidavit, Prentice v. Piggott (Nauvoo, Ill., J.P. Ct. subscribed Jan. 18, 1851):* Affidavit presented to McNamee to support a plea of abatement. Defendant's counsel avers that defendant has not fled state but was merely absent temporarily on business and did not intend to remove property from state.

230. *Subpoena, Prentice v. Piggott (Nauvoo, Ill., J.P. Ct. issued Jan. 18, 1851):* Commands three witnesses to appear before McNamee.

231. *Jury Warrant, Prentice v. Piggott (Nauvoo, Ill., J.P. Ct. issued Jan. 20, 1851):* McNamee commands constable to summon "Six lawful men of your County" to serve as jurors.

232. *Subpoena, Prentice v. Piggott (Nauvoo, Ill., J.P. Ct. issued Jan. 21, 1851):* Commands four witnesses to appear before McNamee.

233. *Subpoena, Prentice v. Piggott (Nauvoo, Ill., J.P. Ct. issued Jan. 22, 1851):* Commands seven witnesses to appear before McNamee.

234. *Injunction, Prentice v. Piggott (Hancock County, Ill., Cir. Ct. issued Jan. 25, 1851):* Enjoins execution of McNamee's judgment pending resolution of appeal.

235. *Summons to Appellee, Prentice v. Piggott (Hancock County, Ill., Cir. Ct. issued Jan. 25, 1851):* Commands sheriff to summon appellee to court.

236. *Transcript, Prentice v. Piggott (Nauvoo, Ill., J.P. Ct. filed Feb. 5, 1851):* Appeal transcript prepared by McNamee.

237. *Praecipe, Prentice v. Piggott (Hancock County, Ill., Cir. Ct. filed May 8, 1851):* Plaintiff's agent asks clerk to issue subpoenas for five witnesses.

238. *Subpoena, Prentice v. Piggott (Hancock County, Ill., Cir. Ct. issued May 8, 1851):* Commands sheriff to summon four witnesses for plaintiff.

239. *Subpoena, Prentice v. Piggott (Hancock County, Ill., Cir. Ct. issued May 8, 1851):* Commands sheriff to summon one witness for plaintiff.

240. *Praecipe, Prentice v. Piggott (Hancock County, Ill., Cir. Ct. filed May 29, 1851):* Defendant's counsel asks clerk to issue subpoenas for five witnesses.

241. *Subpoena, Prentice v. Piggott (Hancock County, Ill., Cir. Ct. issued May 29, 1851):* Commands sheriff to summon four witnesses for defendant.

242. *Subpoena, Prentice v. Piggott (Hancock County, Ill., Cir. Ct. issued May 29, 1851):* Commands sheriff to summon one witness for defendant.

243. *Motion to Dismiss Appeal, Prentice v. Piggott (Hancock County, Ill., Cir. Ct. filed June 3, 1851):* Plaintiff's counsel moves to dismiss defendant's appeal on grounds that no appeal bond is on file.

244. *Affidavit, Prentice v. Piggott (Hancock County, Ill., Cir. Ct. subscribed June 4, 1851):* Plaintiff's counsel avers that A. S. Kingsley had no authority to sign appeal bond for defendant.

245. *Witness Affidavit, Prentice v. Piggott (Hancock County, Ill., Cir. Ct. subscribed June 7, 1851):* John Kelly attests to spending three days as witness for plaintiff.

246. *Witness Affidavit, Prentice v. Piggott (Hancock County, Ill., Cir. Ct. subscribed June 7, 1851):* Thomas Kelly attests to spending three days as witness for plaintiff.

247. *Witness Affidavit, Prentice v. Piggott (Hancock County, Ill., Cir. Ct. subscribed June 7, 1851):* Albert Stow attests to spending four days as witness for defendant.

248. *Witness Affidavit, Prentice v. Piggott (Hancock County, Ill., Cir. Ct. subscribed June 9, 1851):* B. Whitfield attests to spending four days as witness for defendant.

249. *Procedendo, Prentice v. Piggott (Hancock County, Ill., Cir. Ct. issued June 10, 1851):* Commands McNamee to "proceed in such manner according to the Law of the land, as you may see proper, any other writ to the contrary, in any thing, notwithstanding."

250. *Witness Affidavit, Prentice v. Piggott (Hancock County, Ill., Cir. Ct. subscribed June 12, 1851):* N. S. Holcomb attests to spending two days as witness for plaintiff.

251. *Documents Pertaining to Court Costs, Prentice v. Piggott (Hancock County, Ill., Cir. Ct. filed Oct. 12, 1851, and supplemented Mar. 3,*

1852): This bundle of sheets contains notes pertaining to costs in the case that were incurred below the circuit court level.

Cases brought by Kellys against Kimballs:

252. *Transcript, [John] Kelly ex rel. [I. Z.] Kelly v. Kimball (Hancock County, Ill., Cir. Ct. filed July 6, 1849)*: Appeal transcript of assumpsit action brought before J.P. on promissory note for $65.37 signed by Hiram Kimball and Phineas Kimball.

253. *Transcript, [John] Kelly ex rel. [Robert] Kelly v. Kimball (Hancock County, Ill., Cir. Ct. filed July 6, 1849)*: Appeal transcript of assumpsit action brought before J.P. on promissory note for $80 signed by Hiram Kimball and Phineas Kimball and assigned to Robert Kelly.

254. *Transcript, [John] Kelly v. Kimball (Hancock County, Ill., Cir. Ct. filed July 6, 1849)*: Appeal transcript of assumpsit action brought before J.P. on promissory note for $80 signed by Hiram Kimball and Phineas Kimball.

255. *Summons to Appellee, [John] Kelly ex rel. [I. Z.] Kelly v. Kimball (Hancock County, Ill., Cir. Ct. issued July 6, 1849)*: Commands sheriff to summon appellee to court.

256. *Summons to Appellee, [John] Kelly v. Kimball (Hancock County, Ill., Cir. Ct. issued July 6, 1849)*: Commands sheriff to summon appellee to court.

257. *Scire Facias, [John] Kelly v. Kimball (Hancock County, Ill., Cir. Ct. issued July 19, 1849)*: Commands sheriff to summon Hiram Kimball to court to "show cause if any he have" why a judgment rendered on April 18, 1849, in a case against Phineas Kimball should not be executed against Hiram (who had been impleaded).

258. *Praecipe, [Robert] Kelly v. Kimball (Hancock County, Ill., Cir. Ct. filed Dec. 7, 1849)*: Plaintiff's counsel asks clerk to issue writ of execution.

259. *Praecipe, [John] Kelly [Jr.] v. Kimball (Hancock County, Ill., Cir. Ct. filed Dec. 7, 1849)*: Plaintiff's counsel asks clerk to issue writ of execution directed to sheriff.

260. *Praecipe, [John] Kelly v. Kimball (Hancock County, Ill., Cir. Ct. filed Dec. 7, 1849)*: Plaintiff's counsel asks clerk to issue writ of execution.

261. *Praecipe, [John] Kelly ex rel. "&c" v. Kimball (Hancock County, Ill., Cir. Ct. filed Mar. 25, 1850)*: Plaintiff personally requests, "Clerk will issue an alias Ex [alias writ of execution] in the above cause." John Kelly filed more than one case on behalf of another person, but the use of "&c" in the clerk's filing notation on this document and the one immediately below makes it impossible to determine which praecipe goes with which case.

262. *Praecipe, [John] Kelly ex rel. "&c" v. Kimball (Hancock County, Ill., Cir. Ct. filed Mar. 25, 1850)*: Plaintiff personally requests, "Issue alias Exn [alias writ of execution] in above case."

263. *Praecipe, [John] Kelly v. Kimball (Hancock County, Ill., Cir. Ct. filed Mar. 25, 1850):* Plaintiff personally asks clerk to issue alias writ of execution.
264. *Praecipe, [John] Kelly v. Kimball (Hancock County, Ill., Cir. Ct. filed July 13, 1850):* Plaintiff personally asks clerk to issue pluries writ of execution.
265. *Praecipe, [John] Kelly ex rel. "&c" v. Kimball (Hancock County, Ill., Cir. Ct. filed July 13, 1850):* Plaintiff personally asks clerk to issue pluries writ of execution in one of the cases in which Kelly sues on behalf of another person.
266. *Praecipe, [John] Kelly v. Kimball (Hancock County, Ill., Cir. Ct. filed Oct. 16, 1850):* Plaintiff's counsel asks clerk to issue venditioni exponas.
267. *Praecipe, [John] Kelly ex rel. "&c" v. Kimball (Hancock County, Ill., Cir. Ct. filed Oct. 16, 1850):* Plaintiff's counsel asks clerk to issue venditioni exponas.

Datin v. Kimball:
268. *Transcript, Datin v. Kimball (Hancock County, Ill., Cir. Ct. filed June 5, 1849):* Appeal transcript prepared by J.P.
269. *Summons to Appellee, Datin v. Kimball (Hancock County, Ill., Cir. Ct. issued June 5, 1849):* Commands sheriff to summon appellee to court.

Kingsley v. Kimball: A. S. Kingsley, treasurer of Nauvoo school district number three, sued Hiram Kimball, Almon W. Babbitt, and Thomas H. Owens. Defendants lost before J.P. and appealed to circuit court.
270. *Summons to Appellee, Kingsley v. Kimball (Hancock County, Ill., Cir. Ct. issued June 5, 1849):* Commands sheriff to summon appellee to court.
271. *Praecipe, Kingsley v. Kimball (Hancock County, Ill., Cir. Ct. filed Oct. 23, 1849):* Plaintiff's counsel asks clerk to issue writ of execution. Apparently, defendants lost appeal.

Herot v. Kimball: Pierre Herot successfully sued Hiram Kimball before J.P. Kimball appealed to circuit court.
272. *Transcript, Herot v. Kimball (Hancock County, Ill., Cir. Ct. filed June 5, 1849):* Appeal transcript prepared by J.P.
273. *Summons to Appellee, Herot v. Kimball (Hancock County, Ill., Cir. Ct. issued June 5, 1849):* Commands sheriff to summon appellee to court.
274. *Praecipe, Herot v. Kimball (Hancock County, Ill., Cir. Ct. filed Nov. 5, 1849):* Plaintiff's counsel asks clerk to issue writ of execution. Kimball apparently lost appeal.

Warren & Skinner v. Wells: Calvin A. Warren and Amos C. Skinner as partners sue Daniel Wells on unpaid promissory note later assigned to them.

275. *Declaration, Warren & Skinner v. Wells (Hancock County, Ill., Cir. Ct. filed Mar. 23, 1849):* Plaintiffs initiate action against defendant in circuit court.

276. *Praecipe, Warren & Skinner v. Wells (Hancock County, Ill., Cir. Ct. filed Mar. 23, 1849):* Plaintiffs ask clerk to issue summons.

277. *Summons, Warren & Skinner v. Wells (Hancock County, Ill., Cir. Ct. issued Mar. 23, 1849):* Commands coroner to summon defendant to court.

Hibbard v. Hilderbrand: Davidson Hibbard sued Michael Hilderbrand and Francis Loftin before J.P. Defendants lost and appealed.

278. *Praecipe, Hibbard v. Hilderbrand (Hancock County, Ill., Cir. Ct. filed July 21, 1849):* Plaintiff's counsel asks clerk to issue summons.

279. *Summons, Hibbard v. Hilderbrand (Hancock County, Ill., Cir. Ct. issued July 21, 1849):* Commands sheriff to summon defendants to court.

280. *Declaration, Hibbard v. Hilderbrand (Hancock County, Ill., Cir. Ct. filed Sept. 3, 1849):* Plaintiff complains that although defendants filed an appeal bond, they have not paid the money due him.

281. *Demurrer, Hibbard v. Hilderbrand (Hancock County, Ill., Cir. Ct. filed Sept. 19, 1849):* Defendants maintain that allegations in plaintiff's declaration "are not sufficient in law" to maintain action against them.

Ammidown Bowman & Co. v. Kimball: Holmes Ammidown, Joseph H. Bowman, George B. Nickols, and Abell W. Conant as partners sue Hiram Kimball on promissory note signed in Boston.

282. *Declaration, Bond, and Praecipe, Ammidown Bowman & Co. v. Kimball (Hancock County, Ill., Cir. Ct. filed Feb. 19, 1849):* This document contains the declaration by which the plaintiffs initiate suit against defendant, a security commitment from the plaintiffs to pay costs in the case, and a praecipe requesting issuance of summons against defendant.

283. *Summons, Ammidown Bowman & Co. v. Kimball (Hancock County, Ill., Cir. Ct. issued Feb. 19, 1849):* Commands sheriff to summon defendant to court.

284. *Praecipe, Ammidown Bowman & Co. v. Kimball (Hancock County, Ill., Cir. Ct. filed Apr. 16, 1850):* Plaintiffs' counsel asks clerk to issue writ of execution on the judgment obtained.

285. *Continuance Agreement, Ammidown Bowman & Co. v. Kimball (Hancock County, Ill., Cir. Ct. filed Apr. 19, 1849):* Parties agree to continue case until next term to give them time to settle their dispute by adjusting offsetting claims. If claims not offset by then, plaintiff is to receive judgment.

Smith Murphy & Co. v. Furness: Solomon Smith, James Murphy, and David Murphy as partners sue James E. Furness and John C. Bidamon for four thousand dollars. The documents are not consistent in the order in which they list the two defendants' names.

 286. *Bond, Smith Murphy & Co. v. Furness (Hancock County, Ill., Cir. Ct. filed Mar. 28, 1849):* Plaintiffs' counsel binds himself to pay court costs.

 287. *Praecipe, Smith Murphy & Co. v. Furness (Hancock County, Ill., Cir. Ct. filed Mar. 28, 1849):* Plaintiffs' counsel asks clerk to issue summonses for defendants.

 288. *Summons, Smith Murphy & Co. v. Furness (Hancock County, Ill., Cir. Ct. issued Mar. 28, 1849):* Commands sheriff of Adams County to summon the two defendants. Neither could be found.

 289. *Summons, Smith Murphy & Co. v. Furness (Hancock County, Ill., Cir. Ct. issued Mar. 28, 1849):* Commands coroner to summon defendants to court. Bidamon, but not Furness, is eventually served by acting sheriff and his deputy.

 290. *Praecipe, Smith Murphy & Co. v. Bidamon (Hancock County, Ill., Cir. Ct. filed Mar. 21, 1850):* Plaintiffs' counsel asks clerk to issue writ of execution against Bidamon.

 291. *Praecipe, Smith Murphy & Co. v. Bidamon (Hancock County, Ill., Cir. Ct. filed Oct. 31, 1850):* Plaintiff's counsel asks clerk to issue alias writ of execution.

 292. *Praecipe, Smith Murphy & Co. v. Bidamon (Hancock County, Ill., Cir. Ct. filed May. 22, 1852):* Plaintiffs' counsel again asks clerk to issue writ of execution against Bidamon.

293. *Summons to Appellee, Loomis v. Bidamon (Hancock County, Ill., Cir. Ct. issued June 7, 1849):* R. H. Loomis successfully sued L. C. Bidamon before a J.P., and Bidamon appealed. This writ commands sheriff to summon the appellee.

294. *Transcript, Smith v. Rollosson (Hancock County, Ill., Cir. Ct. filed Sept. 25, 1849):* Appeal transcript of case in which Francis Smith sued William H. Rollosson and Francis M. Higbee for debt. Rollosson could not be found. Judgment entered against Higbee, who appealed.

City of Nauvoo v. Vrooman: City of Nauvoo sues David W. Vrooman for debt. Mayor hears case and rules against defendant. Defendant appeals to circuit court.

 295. *Injunction, City of Nauvoo v. Vrooman (Hancock County, Ill., Cir. Ct. issued Sept. 12, 1849):* Enjoins execution of mayor's judgment pending resolution of appeal.

 296. *Summons to Appellee, City of Nauvoo v. Vrooman (Hancock County, Ill., Cir. Ct. issued Sept. 12, 1849):* Commands sheriff to summon to court the mayor and clerk of City of Nauvoo, appellee.

297. *Praecipe, City of Nauvoo v. Vrooman (Hancock County, Ill., Cir. Ct. filed Mar. 28, 1850):* Plaintiff's counsel asks clerk to issue subpoena for three witnesses.

298. *Subpoena, City of Nauvoo v. Vrooman (Hancock County, Ill., Cir. Ct. issued Mar. 28, 1850):* Commands sheriff to summon three witnesses for plaintiff.

Miller ex rel. Vancourt v. Reimbold: Anton Miller, for the use of Benjamin P. Vancourt, sues Peter Reimbold for debt.

299. *Praecipe and Bond for Costs, Miller ex rel. Vancourt v. Reimbold (Hancock County, Ill., Cir. Ct. filed Sept. 26, 1850):* Plaintiff's counsel asks clerk to issue summons and binds himself to pay costs of action.

300. *Summons, Miller ex rel. Vancourt v. Reimbold (Hancock County, Ill., Cir. Ct. issued Sept. 26, 1850):* Commands sheriff to summon defendant to court.

301. *Declaration, Pleas, and Demurrers, Miller ex rel. Vancourt v. Reimbold (Hancock County, Ill., Cir. Ct. filed May-June 1851):* Bundle of documents that include some of the pleadings in the case.

302. *Pleas, Miller ex rel. Vancourt v. Reimbold (Hancock County, Ill., Cir. Ct. filed June 5, 1851):* Contains defendant's pleas number one through four.

303. *Replications, Miller ex rel. Vancourt v. Reimbold (Hancock County, Ill., Cir. Ct. filed June 12, 1851):* Plaintiff responds to three of defendant's pleas.

304. *Praecipe, Miller ex rel. Vancourt v. Reimbold (Hancock County, Ill., Cir. Ct. filed June 17, 1851):* Plaintiff's counsel asks clerk to issue writ of execution.

Moore, Heyl & Co. v. Davis: Partnership of Marmaduke Moore, Theodore C. Heyl, and Francis Heyl sues Amos Davis for debt.

305. *Declaration, Moore, Heyl & Co. v. Davis (Hancock County, Ill., Cir. Ct. filed Feb. 20, 1850):* Plaintiffs initiate suit.

306. *Praecipe, Moore, Heyl & Co. v. Davis (Hancock County, Ill., Cir. Ct. filed May 4, 1850):* Plaintiff's counsel asks clerk to issue writ of execution.

307. *Praecipe, Moore, Heyl & Co. v. Davis (Hancock County, Ill., Cir. Ct. filed Nov. 29, 1850):* Plaintiff's counsel asks sheriff to have clerk issue writ of execution.

308. *Settlement Receipt, Moore, Heyl & Co. v. Davis (Hancock County, Ill., Cir. Ct. filed Oct. 7, 1852):* Plaintiffs accept part payment of judgment as full satisfaction and discharge defendant's obligation.

Wood & Oliver v. Davis: The partnership of Charles L. Wood and George L. Oliver sues Amos Davis for debt.

309. *Declaration, Wood & Oliver v. Davis (Hancock County, Ill., Cir. Ct. filed Apr. 17, 1850):* Plaintiff partnership initiates suit.
310. *Praecipe, Wood & Oliver v. Davis (Hancock County, Ill., Cir. Ct. filed June 7, 1850):* Plaintiff's counsel asks clerk to issue writ of execution.
311. *Praecipe, Wood & Oliver v. Davis (Hancock County, Ill., Cir. Ct. filed Sept. 23, 1850):* Plaintiff's counsel asks clerk to issue alias writ of execution.
312. *Receipt, Wood & Oliver v. Davis (Hancock County, Ill., Cir. Ct. filed Oct. 7, 1852):* Plaintiff compromises, accepts payment, and discharges defendant's obligation.

313. *Summons, Mix v. Rollosson (Hancock County, Ill., Cir. Ct. issued June 17, 1850):* Commands sheriff to summon defendants William H. Rollosson and Francis M. Higbee to court to answer complaint of Phelps Mix.
314. *Recognizance Bond, State v. Crain (Hancock County, Ill., Cir. Ct. filed June 2, 1851):* Defendant Joseph I. Crain, charged with assault, and William F. Crain agree to pay state $250 if Joseph does not appear in court to answer charge.
315. *Praecipe, People v. Bedell (Hancock County, Ill., Cir. Ct. filed Jan. 29, 1852):* E. A. Bedell asks clerk to issue subpoenas for witnesses; also to copy indictments from another case and send to lawyers in nearby Quincy.

Lifleman v. Austin: Conrad Lifleman sues William H. Austin and Theodore Martin.
316. *Subpoena, Lifleman v. Austin (Hancock County, Ill., Cir. Ct. issued Feb. 21, 1853):* Commands sheriff to summon witness for defendants.
317. *Witness Affidavit, Lifleman v. Austin (Hancock County, Ill., Cir. Ct. subscribed June 11, 1853):* P. S. Emmons attests to spending three days as witness for defendants.

Kingsley v. Warsaw & R.R.R.: William R. Kingsley sues Warsaw & Rockford Rail Road Co. for debt.
318. *Praecipe and Bond for Costs, Kingsley v. Warsaw & R.R.R. (Hancock County, Ill., Cir. Ct. filed May 1, 1857):* Plaintiff's counsel asks clerk to issue summons directed to sheriff of Henderson County and binds himself to pay court costs.
319. *Summons, Kingsley v. Warsaw & R.R.R. (Hancock County, Ill., Cir. Ct. issued May 1, 1857):* Commands sheriff to summon defendant railroad to appear in court.
320. *Declaration and Bond for Costs, Kingsley v. Warsaw & R.R.R. (Hancock County, Ill., Cir. Ct. filed May 12, 1857):* Plaintiff initiates suit, and his counsel binds himself to pay court costs.
321. *"Copy of writings sued on," Kingsley v. Warsaw & R.R.R. (Hancock County, Ill., Cir. Ct. filed May 12, 1857):* Contains copies "of the

evidences of indebtedness and account upon which this suit is brought." Includes several instruments of indebtedness from the railroad, each titled "President's Warrant." Other such warrants were filed later.

322. *Praecipe, Kingsley v. Warsaw & R.R.R. (Hancock County, Ill., Cir. Ct. filed Oct. 5, 1857):* Plaintiff's counsel asks clerk to issue subpoenas for two witnesses.

323. *Subpoena, Kingsley v. Warsaw & R.R.R. (Hancock County, Ill., Cir. Ct. filed Oct. 6, 1857):* Commands county sheriff to summon two witnesses.

324. *Plea, Kingsley v. Warsaw & R.R.R. (Hancock County, Ill., Cir. Ct. filed Oct. 8, 1857):* Defendants' counsel asserts "that they did not undertake nor promise in manner and form as the said plaintiff hath above herein declared against them."

325. *President's Warrant No. 346, Kingsley v. Warsaw & R.R.R. (Hancock County, Ill., Cir. Ct. filed Oct. 12, 1857):* Dated Aug. 30, 1855; payable to plaintiff or order for $85.97.

326. *President's Warrant No. 386, Kingsley v. Warsaw & R.R.R. (Hancock County, Ill., Cir. Ct. filed Oct. 12, 1857):* Dated Feb. [19?], 1856; payable to plaintiff or order for $1,315.

327. *President's Warrant No. 387, Kingsley v. Warsaw & R.R.R. (Hancock County, Ill., Cir. Ct. filed Oct. 12, 1857):* Dated Feb. [19?], 1856; payable to plaintiff or order for $168.10.

328. *President's Warrant No. 396, Kingsley v. Warsaw & R.R.R. (Hancock County, Ill., Cir. Ct. filed Oct. 12, 1857):* Dated Apr. 10, 1856; payable to plaintiff or order for $86.95.

329. *President's Warrant No. 397, Kingsley v. Warsaw & R.R.R. (Hancock County, Ill., Cir. Ct. filed Oct. 12, 1857):* Dated Apr. 10, 1856; payable to plaintiff or order for $254.78.

330. *President's Warrant No. 398, Kingsley v. Warsaw & R.R.R. (Hancock County, Ill., Cir. Ct. filed Oct. 12, 1857):* Dated April 10, 1856; payable to plaintiff or order for $238.35.

331. *President's Warrant No. 415, Kingsley v. Warsaw & R.R.R. (Hancock County, Ill., Cir. Ct. filed Oct. 12, 1857):* Dated Apr. 11, 1856; payable to plaintiff or order for $145.34.

332. *Witness Affidavit, Kingsley v. Warsaw & R.R.R. (Hancock County, Ill., Cir. Ct. subscribed Oct. 12, 1857):* John G. Fonda attests to spending one day as witness for plaintiff.

333. *Witness Affidavit, Kingsley v. Warsaw & R.R.R. (Hancock County, Ill., Cir. Ct. subscribed Oct. 12, 1857):* William Wise attests to spending one day as witness for plaintiff.

334. *Praecipe, Kingsley v. Warsaw & R.R.R. (Hancock County, Ill., Cir. Ct. filed Nov. 2, 1857):* Plaintiff's counsel asks clerk to issue writ of execution directed to sheriff of Rock Island County.

Lynn v. Warsaw & R.R.R.: James J. Lynn sues Warsaw & Rockford Rail Road
Co. for debt.

335. *Declaration and Praecipe, Lynn v. Warsaw & R.R.R. (Hancock
     County, Ill., Cir. Ct. filed May 12, 1857):* Initiates suit and asks
     clerk to issue summons.

336. *Summons, Lynn v. Warsaw & R.R.R. (Hancock County, Ill., Cir. Ct.
     issued May 12, 1857):* Commands sheriff to summon defendant rail-
     road to court.

337. *Plea, Lynn v. Warsaw & R.R.R. (Hancock County, Ill., Cir. Ct. filed
     Oct. 8, 1857):* Defendants' counsel asserts "that they did not un-
     dertake nor promise in manner and form as the said plaintiff hath
     above herein declared against them."

338. *Subpoena, Lynn v. Warsaw & R.R.R. (Hancock County, Ill., Cir. Ct.
     issued Oct. 10, 1857):* Commands sheriff to summon two witnesses.

339. *President's Warrant No. 394, Lynn v. Warsaw & R.R.R. (Hancock
     County, Ill., Cir. Ct. filed Oct. 12, 1857):* Dated Apr. 10, 1856;
     payable to plaintiff or order for $13.10.

340. *President's Warrant No. 438, Lynn v. Warsaw & R.R.R. (Hancock
     County, Ill., Cir. Ct. filed Oct. 12, 1857):* Dated Sept. 10, 1856;
     payable to plaintiff or order for $325.50.

341. *Witness Affidavit, Lynn v. Warsaw & R.R.R. (Hancock County, Ill.,
     Cir. Ct. subscribed Oct. 12, 1857):* John G. Fonda attests to spending
     one day as witness for plaintiff.

342. *Witness Affidavit, Lynn v. Warsaw & R.R.R. (Hancock County, Ill.,
     Cir. Ct. subscribed Oct. 12, 1857):* William Wise attests to spending
     one day as witness for plaintiff.

343. *Praecipe, Lynn v. Warsaw & R.R.R. (Hancock County, Ill., Cir. Ct.
     filed Nov. 2, 1857):* Plaintiff's counsel asks clerk to issue writ of
     execution directed to sheriff of Rock Island County.

344. *Jury Verdict, Case Unknown (Hancock County, Ill., Cir. Ct. filed Feb. 5,
     1857):* This statement, signed by five jurors, reads, "We the Jury find
     for the Plaintiff And Sustain the Attatchment."

345. *Subpoena Duces Tecum Directed to Thomas Reid, Allison v. City of Ham-
     ilton (Hancock County, Ill., Cir. Ct. issued June 2, 1859):* Alexander
     Allison sues City of Hamilton, Illinois, as garnishee. Commands sheriff to
     summon clerk of defendant city to bring with him various papers "in
     refference to a bridge or other matter."

Cabeen v. City of Warsaw: Thomas B. Cabeen sues City of Warsaw, Illinois,
to recover debts owed by City of Warsaw to Warsaw & Rockford Rail Road
Co. and later assigned to him.

346. *Praecipe, Cabeen v. City of Warsaw (Hancock County, Ill., Cir. Ct.
     filed May 16, 1864):* Asks clerk to issue summons directed to sheriff.

347. *Summons, Cabeen v. City of Warsaw (Hancock County, Ill., Cir. Ct.
     issued May 16, 1864):* Commands sheriff to summon defendant.
     Bears fifty-cent U.S. revenue stamp.

348. *Declaration, Cabeen v. City of Warsaw (Hancock County, Ill., Cir. Ct. filed May 20, 1864):* Lengthy document initiating suit and containing copies of pertinent debt instruments.

349. *Subpoena, Cabeen v. City of Warsaw (Hancock County, Ill., Cir. Ct. issued Sept. 14, 1864):* Commands sheriff to summon four witnesses for plaintiff.

350. *Subpoena, Cabeen v. City of Warsaw (Hancock County, Ill., Cir. Ct. issued Sept. 14, 1864):* Commands sheriff to summon witness for defendant.

351. *Demurrer, Cabeen v. City of Warsaw (Hancock County, Ill., Cir. Ct. filed Oct. 5, 1864):* Defendant maintains that matters alleged in plaintiff's declaration "are not sufficient in law for the said plaintiff to have or maintain his aforesaid action."

352. *Pleas 1 & 2, Cabeen v. City of Warsaw (Hancock County, Ill., Cir. Ct. filed Oct. 6, 1864):* Contains defendant's answers to two wrongs alleged by plaintiff.

353. *Witness Affidavit, Cabeen v. City of Warsaw (Hancock County, Ill., Cir. Ct. subscribed Oct. 6, 1864):* John E. Johnston attests to spending two days as witness for plaintiff.

354. *Witness Affidavit, Cabeen v. City of Warsaw (Hancock County, Ill., Cir. Ct. subscribed Oct. 6, 1864):* E. E. Lane attests to spending three days as witness for plaintiff.

355. *Agreement, Cabeen v. City of Warsaw (Hancock County, Ill., Cir. Ct. filed Oct. 10, 1865):* Contains terms of settlement between the parties in the case and the related case of *Frick v. City of Warsaw.* Thomas B. Cabeen and George A. Frick were partners.

356. *Affidavit, Ford v. Thomas (Peoria County, Ill., Cir. Ct. filed July 25, 1839):* Affidavit signed by Thomas W. Ford justifying continuance on grounds that material witness is unavailable. Witness will prove that defendant cut a trench through property without permission.

357. *Complaint, Wright v. Condit (Warren County, Ill., Cir. Ct. filed Feb. 10, 1840):* Samuel G. Wright initiates suit against Timothy C. Condit for failure to pay debt secured by mortgage. Wright asks that Condit be required to pay the debt in a short time or, if he is unable to do so, that the mortgaged premises be sold and the proceeds used for the same purpose. Complaint is signed for Wright "by his attorney, O H Browning *pr* W Bushnell."

358. *Subpoena, Benson v. Bogard (Ray County, Mo., Cir. Ct. issued June 8, 1838):* Commands James Durfee to appear in court as witness for defendants, Samuel and Alexander Bogard, who are being sued by Benjamin Benson.

Singletary v. Singletary: Emory Singletary seeks divorce from Catharine Singletary. Oliver Cowdery's and Lyman Cowdery's law firm, Cowdery and Cowdery, represents the complainant.[101]

359. *Praecipe, Singletary v. Singletary (Walworth County, Wis., Dist. Ct. filed June 4, 1847):* Complainant's counsel asks clerk to issue subpoena.

360. *Subpoena, Singletary v. Singletary (Walworth County, Wis., Dist. Ct. issued June 4, 1847):* Commands defendant to appear in court.

Martin v. Raleigh: John Martin sues John Raleigh for conversion. All three documents in case are signed by Lyman Cowdery.

361. *Declaration, Martin v. Raleigh (Walworth County, Wis., J.P. Ct. filed in Dist. Ct. July 28, 1847):* Initiates suit.

362. *Praecipe, Martin v. Raleigh (Walworth County, Wis., Dist. Ct. filed July 17, 1847):* Plaintiff's counsel asks clerk to issue writ of certiorari.

363. *Praecipe, Martin v. Raleigh (Walworth County, Wis., Dist. Ct. filed July 17, 1847):* Plaintiff's counsel asks clerk to issue a writ but does not specify what kind.

Goetschius v. Slocum: George W. Goetschius[102] sues Job Slocum for slander.

364. *Praecipe, Goetschius v. Slocum (Walworth County, Wis., Dist. Ct. filed May 28, 1847):* Plantiff's counsel, Cowdery & Cowdery & Kelsey, asks clerk to issue capias.

365. *Capias, Goetschius v. Slocum (Walworth County, Wis., Dist. Ct. issued May 28, 1847):* Commands sheriff to take defendant into custody to assure his appearance in court. Lists Cowdery & Cowdery & Kelsey as attorneys for plaintiff.

366. *Certificate of Transfer, executed July 31, 1848:* Lyman Cowdery certifies that pursuant to bankruptcy act, insolvent debtor George Goetschius had transferred all except exempt portions of his estate to Cowdery "for the benefit of all his creditors." A probate judge witnessed execution of the document.

Martin v. Storms: John Martin sues Winslow P. Storms and Clarissa M. Postle, the administrators of the estate of Charles S. Postle, over a purported mortgage. The following five items bear name of Lyman Cowdery, one of defendants' attorneys.

367. *Affidavit, Martin v. Storms (Walworth County, Wis., Cir. Ct. subscribed Oct. 3, 1848):* Affiant Lyman Cowdery justifies continuance on grounds that material witness is "lying dangerously ill."

368. *Stipulation, Martin v. Storms (Walworth County, Wis., Cir. Ct. filed June 6, 1849):* Parties agree to continue case and to allow plaintiff to file amended declaration.

369. *Amended Plea, Martin v. Storms (Walworth County, Wis., Cir. Ct. filed Oct. 13, 1849):* Responds to plaintiff's amended declaration.

370. *Demurrer, Martin v. Storms (Walworth County, Wis., Cir. Ct. filed Oct. 13, 1849):* Defendants maintain that matters alleged in plaintiff's declaration "are not sufficient in law for the said plaintiff to have or maintain his aforesaid action."

371. *Trial Notice, Martin v. Storms (Walworth County, Wis., Cir. Ct. filed May 8, 1850):* Plaintiff's counsel informs defendants' of upcoming trial.

372. *Foreclosure Certificate, Buckley v. Croswell (Walworth County, Wis., Cir. Ct. subscribed Aug. 10, 1848):* Sheriff's report to court on sale of property at public auction in case in which Thomas T. Buckley sued Caleb Croswell, Edwin Croswell, and Sherman Croswell. Includes copy of published notice of sale.

373. *Publication Affidavit, Harrison v. Hampton (Walworth County, Wis., Dist. Ct. filed May 22, 1848):* Attests that attached printed notice (which lists "O. Cowdery" as plaintiff's attorney) was published in newspaper for six successive weeks.

374. *Summons, Robertson v. Hopkins (Walworth County, Wis., Dist. Ct. issued Apr. 7, 1848):* Commands defendant to appear in court. Lyman Cowdery signs as plaintiff's attorney.

375. *Publication Affidavit, Gaylord v. Smith (Walworth County, Wis., Dist. Ct. subscribed Feb. 17, 1848):* Attests that attached printed notice was published in newspaper for six successive weeks.

Ambler v. Jones: Lyman Cowdery represents complainant in property dispute.

376. *Bill of Foreclosure, Ambler v. Jones (Walworth County, Wis., Cir. Ct. filed Feb. 9, 1852):* Complainant seeks sale of mortgaged property and correction of mistaken property description.

377. *Subpoena, Ambler v. Jones (Walworth County, Wis., Cir. Ct. issued Feb. 9, 1852):* Commands defendant to appear in court.

378. *Affidavit and Order, Ambler v. Jones (Walworth County, Wis., Cir. Ct. filed Feb. 20, 1852):* Complainant's solicitor attests that subpoena for defendant could not be served because defendant had moved to California. Court orders that complainant publish notice in newspaper and that defendant appear within three months or default.

379. *Motion to Amend, Ambler v. Jones (Walworth County, Wis., Cir. Ct. filed May 28, 1852):* Complainant seeks to amend original complaint.

Forrest v. Brown:

380. *Affidavit, Forrest v. Brown (Walworth County, Wis., Cir. Ct. subscribed May 21, 1855):* Defendant-appellant's affidavit to support continuance on ground that plaintiff-appellee's counsel had assured him he was going to let the matter drop, thereby causing plaintiff-appellant not to summon witnesses. Sworn before Lyman Cowdery, J.P.

381. *Affidavit and Notice of Motion, Forrest v. Brown (Walworth County, Wis., Cir. Ct. filed Oct. 1, 1855):* Defendant-appellant attests to plaintiff-appellee's failure to follow certain court rules. Defendant-appellant's attorney, Lyman Cowdery, provides copy of affidavit to plaintiff-appellee's attorney and notifies him of intention to move

"that this Cause be stricken from the Calendar, and that judgment be rendered in favor of the Defendant, with Costs."

DECEMBER 6, 1983[103]

On December 6, 1983, Don Schmidt acquired several other documents from Hofmann for the church.

382. *Foreclosure Certificate, Phelps v. Law (Hancock County, Ill., Cir. Ct. filed May 22, 1846):* Apparently, W. W. Phelps successfully sued Wilson Law. Sheriff J. B. Backenstos, by his deputy, reports that he sold a piece of Law's property to William Backenstos at public sale authorized by fee bill.

383. *Declaration, Ritter v. Icarian Community (Hancock County, Ill., Cir. Ct. filed Sept. 22, 1856):* George Ritter sues Icarian Community to collect on debt instruments signed by community's president, Etienne Cabet, at Nauvoo, Illinois.

384. *Writ of Replevin, Icarian Community v. Cabet (Hancock County, Ill., Cir. Ct. filed Dec. 12, 1856):* Commands sheriff to replevy five books belonging to Icarian Community that Etienne Cabet and Edward Vogel have wrongfully detained and also to summon Cabet and Vogel to court to answer claim of damages for the detention.

385. *Motion to Reinstate Indictment, People v. Foster (n.p., n.d.):* Seeks to reinstate indictment against Robert D. Foster for embezzling school funds while serving as school commissioner. Reason given for reinstating indictment is that conditions for striking indictment from books were not met.

386. *Plea and Demurrer, McIntire v. Robinson (Hancock County, Ill., Cir. Ct. filed May 20, 1845):* Defendant Ebenezer Robinson sold plaintiff George McIntire a debt instrument signed by John A. Forges. Plaintiff now sues defendant to collect on instrument. Defendant, through attorney A. W. Babbitt, maintains that plaintiff's declaration is inaccurate and that plaintiff has not tried with due diligence to collect directly from Forges. Plaintiff responds that defendant's pleas "are insufficient in law to bar the p[lain]tiff of his action."

387. *Transcript, Butterfield v. Mills (Nauvoo, Ill., Mayor's Ct. certified Sept. 5, 1843):* Transcript prepared by clerk W. W. Phelps for defendant's appeal to circuit court in debt action.

388. *Executors Bond, Estate of Horrocks (Great Salt Lake County, Utah, P. Ct. filed Aug. 6, 1866):* The principals, Edwin D. Woolley and George Goddard, together with their sureties, William S. Godbe and Frederick A. Mitchell, bind themselves in the penal sum of ten thousand dollars to faithfully serve as executors of Peter Horrocks's will. Subscribed before E. Smith, probate judge.[104]

389. *Inventory and Appraisement Bill, Estate of Sharkey (Salt Lake City [court unspecified] filed Sept. 24, 1868):* Bill prepared and signed by H. W.

Lawrence and W. S. Godbe inventorying and appraising property of Robert C. Sharkey.

390. *Administrator's Receipt, Estate of Cannon ([Court unspecified], subscribed May 5, 1898):* George Q. Cannon acknowledges receipt of $3,784 from John M. Cannon, administrator of Abraham H. Cannon's estate, and agrees to return any amount that exceeds what court later decides he warrants.

391. *Deseret Agricultural & Manufacturing Society, Diploma, 1st Class:* Awarded to James Wells of Great Salt Lake City for best cutlery in 1856 annual exhibition. Signed by Edward Hunter and Robert L. Campbell. Judges included W. H. Hooper and John R. Winder. George Throckmorton raised doubts about its authenticity based on the ink, the print quality, and the seal.[105]

392. *Reed Smoot to George J. Kelly, Feb. 1, 1917:* Typed letter on letterhead of United States Senate Committee on Expenditures in the Interior Department discussing H.R. 18984.[106]

JANUARY 9, 1984

On January 9, 1984, Don Schmidt acquired six additional items from Hofmann for the church.[107]

393. *Publication Affidavit, McIntire v. Robinson (Hancock County, Ill., Cir. Ct. filed May 19, 1845):* John Taylor, "per E. Smith," attests that attached printed notice was published in *Nauvoo Neighbor* newspaper for four consecutive weeks.

394. *Certificate of Recording, Caldwell County Clerk's Office, July 25, 1837:* This sealed document certifies that a deed from Edward Partridge to George Bebee was recorded in the clerk's office.

395. *John Smith, Patriarchal Blessing, July 11, 1845:* Transcript of blessing pronounced in Nauvoo, Illinois, by John Smith upon the head of Reuben Atwood, born May 25, 1797. A copy of this item was already in the church's collection.[108]

396. *George F. Gibbs to Frank Y. Taylor, Feb. 19, 1909:* Typed letter from secretary of the First Presidency to president of the Granite Stake informing him that two church leaders, Heber J. Grant and Hyrum M. Smith, would be attending the stake's upcoming conference.

397. *Sarah [Farr Smith] to My Dear Children, Mar. 8, 1894:* Letter apparently written to George Albert Smith (who would become the church's eighth president in 1945) and his wife, Lucy, by his mother on stationery of the Southern States Mission. George Throckmorton examined the letter and found that the letterhead was created with a rubber stamp and that there were inconsistencies in the ink and handwriting.[109]

398. *John W. Taylor to O. C. Bebee, Dec. 18, 1906:* Copy of letter written from Colonia Juarez, Chihuahua, Mexico, regarding financial matters involving Zions Savings Bank & Trust Co. of Salt Lake City. This copy includes a penciled note to "Bro Cannon" from Taylor, observing in part,

"Please write me and let me know how things look, is it wise for me to
come to S.L. now. Please send me a newsy letter and oblige."

APRIL 17, 1984

On April 17, 1984, Don Schmidt acquired several more items from Hofmann
for the church.[110]

Thomas Gregg materials: The following items deal with early Illinois journalist
Thomas Gregg. Some relate to Gregg's book *The Prophet of Palmyra.*[111]

399. *Thomas Gregg to Manager of the Nauvoo Independent, Dec. 18[91?]:*
Letter in which Gregg announces intent to reprint the *Nauvoo Expositor* newspaper and solicits an order for several hundred copies.

400. *"Early County Historian to Be Honored," Hancock County Journal
Pilot, May 28, 1975:* Newspaper article about a memorial to honor
Gregg.

401. *Program for Gregg Memorial Dedication Service, May 30, 1975:*
Program for service at which Gregg memorial was unveiled.

402. *Prophet of Palmyra!:* This small, undated broadside advertises
Gregg's book. Includes excerpts from book reviews and letters from
readers.

403. *The Prophet of Palmyra:* This handbill promotes Gregg's book and
includes fewer but lengthier testimonials than item 402.

404. *Unsigned, Undated Note about Gregg's Book:* Written on back of
printed sheet from "The Ring-Free Oil Co. of Nauvoo," this penciled
note in its entirety reads, "From Gregg's History which are scarce
and hard to see, Bot copy from Gregg's daug. Miss *Stella* Gregg
who lived at Plymouth, and died in St. Louis a few years ago. Some
of the articles of historical nature ought to be worth saving by students of history."

405. *Certificate of Proof of Will, In re Estate of Young (Salt Lake County,
Utah, P. Ct. filed July 17, 1882):* Certificate proving will of Mary
Ann Angell Young, who died June 27, 1882. Will itself is attached.
Certificate is signed by Elias Smith.

406. *David Whitmer, Deed of Manumission, July 26, 1849:* Document
by which Whitmer frees "My Negro Man Slave Carter alias Carter
Thornton."

407. *Directors Bond, Deseret Mining Stock Association, Oct. 17, 1873:*
Document in which Wilford Woodruff, Jacob Weiler, William H. H.
Sharp, John Needham, John M. Bernhisel, and others bind themselves
to execute their association responsibilities faithfully.

408. *Uncut Copy of Times and Seasons 2, no. 15 (June 1, 1841):* This
issue of the early Nauvoo, Illinois, periodical includes extracts from
a Joseph Smith revelation of January 19, 1841.[112] In this copy, someone has made manuscript corrections to the revelation. The signature "Joseph Smith" appears on the front, and following the corrections someone has written "Pr John Taylor."

Francis M. Lyman Postcards: Fifteen postcards from Mormon apostle Francis M. Lyman to family members from 1901 to 1905.

409. *Francis M. Lyman to Louisa M. Lyman, July 11, 1901:* Sent from Milan, Italy. Mentions travel to and from Switzerland.

410. *Francis M. Lyman to Louisa M. Lyman, Feb. 6, 1902:* Sent from Marseilles, France. Mentions he will soon depart for Egypt and the Holy Land.

411. *Francis M. Lyman to Louisa M. Lyman, Feb. 15, 1902:* Sent from Cario, Egypt. Briefly mentions stay in Egypt and plans to visit Beirut, Jaffa, and Jerusalem.

412. *Francis M. Lyman to Louisa M. Lyman, Apr. 20, 1902:* Sent from Rome. Mentions arrival in Rome the night before.

413. *Francis M. Lyman to Louisa M. Lyman, Apr. 22, 1902:* Sent from Rome. Reports, "I saw Pope Leo 13. today in the Vatican."

414. *Francis M. Lyman to Louisa M. Lyman, Apr. 23, 1902:* Sent from Rome. Message reads, "God Bless you from your Son affectionately."

415. *Francis M. Lyman to Miss Coombs, Apr. 24, 1902:* Sent from Rome. Message reads, "This is a kind greeting from your affectionate uncle."

416. *Francis M. Lyman to Lyman Coombs, Apr. 24, 1902:* Sent from Rome. Message reads, "This is a kindly greeting from your affectionate uncle. Be a good boy and dont you lose that knife."

417. *Francis M. Lyman to Louisa M. Lyman, Aug. 16, 1902:* Sent from Paris. Reports that he left Liverpool for London and then Paris to meet Senator Thomas Kearns. He plans next to go to Berlin and then Rotterdam before returning to Liverpool.

418. *Francis M. Lyman to Louisa M. Lyman, Oct. 29, 1902:* Sent from Liverpool. Reports he is well and happy and wishes his family the same.

419. *Francis M. Lyman to Louisa M. Lyman, Aug. 6, 1903:* Written from St. Petersburg. Report that he and his companion plan to spend three days in St. Petersburg and then travel to Moscow, Warsaw, Holland, and Liverpool.

420. *Francis M. Lyman to Louisa M. Lyman, Aug. 9, 1903:* Written in Moscow. Sends greetings "from central European Russia" and plans to go to Warsaw next day.

421. *Francis M. Lyman to Louisa M. Lyman, Postmarked Received in Salt Lake City on Aug. 18, 1903:* Written from Abo, Finland. Mentions he had arrived from Stockholm earlier that day and would be leaving for St. Petersburg that evening. Plans to spend ten days in Russia.

422. *Francis M. Lyman to Louisa M. Lyman, Jan. 15, 1904:* Postmarked Queenstown (Ireland?). "One day nearer home. Rough night but all Sunshine as we pass Queenstown."

423. *Francis M. Lyman to Louisa M. Lyman, n.d.:* Postcard commem-
     orating dedication of Joseph Smith monument at Sharon, Vermont,
     Dec. 23, 1905. No stamp or postmark.

424. *Lorenzo Snow to Mrs. Pritcher, Sept. [1?], 1869:* Written from Brigham
     City, Utah Territory, by Lorenzo Snow, who would become the church's
     fifth president in 1898. Addressed to Polly Prichard (also spelled Prit-
     chard or Pritcher), Snow's mother-in-law in Ohio, the letter introduced
     his daughter and her husband. Before Hofmann had the letter, it was
     owned by Indiana dealer Rick Grunder, who later explained that he bought
     it on June 25, 1983, from an Akron, Ohio, dealer and offered it for sale
     in one of his catalogues later that year.[113]

425. *"He himeni no Pack me Molen," Jan. 1, 1877:* Hawaiian song written
     for LDS missionaries Ward Eaton Pack and Simpson Montgomery Molen.
     On the back of the document is the date January 1, 1877. Molen's journal
     (which the church owns) mentions a song composed for the two mis-
     sionaries on that date but gives only the first line, which differs from that
     of the poem acquired from Hofmann.[114] George Throckmorton discovered
     two chemically different inks on the paper, one of which resembled inks
     of Hofmann manufacture. He also felt the handwriting was similar to that
     of some known Hofmann forgeries.[115]

426. *Director's Bond, Zion's Co-operative Mercantile Institution, Oct. 6, 1882:*
     Document in which John Taylor as principal, with James Jack and H. K.
     Whitney as sureties, binds himself to faithfully execute his office as di-
     rector of Zion's Co-operative Mercantile Institution. Witnessed by George
     Reynolds and D. L. Daniels. Approved and filed by E. Smith.

MAY 18 TO SEPTEMBER 28, 1984[116]

Deseret Currency Association Notes: Mentioned in chapter 5. The Deseret
Currency Association, organized in 1858, issued both typeset and engraved
notes.[117] Though typeset notes were known to have been issued in one-, two-,
three-, five-, ten-, twenty-, fifty-, and one-hundred-dollar denominations, late
twentieth-century collectors had located copies of only the three smallest denominations.[118] Using genuine copies of these three and composing his own
artwork for the others, Hofmann printed all eight denominations.[119] Photographs of the ten-, twenty-, fifty-, and one-hundred-dollar notes purchased by
the church were published in 1984.[120] The rest were published in 1988.[121] For
a time, church officials were uncertain whether the one-, two-, and three-dollar
notes in their possession came from Hofmann or were genuine.[122] In 1988,
George Throckmorton examined a full set of notes owned by the church,
concluding that the one- and two-dollar notes were genuine but that the higher
notes were all counterfeit.[123]

427. *Three-Dollar Note:* Series A, No. 891, Feb. 20, 1858.

428. *Five-Dollar Note:* Series B, No. 716, Apr. 22, 1858.

429. *Ten-Dollar Note:* Series B, No. 360, Apr. 8, 1858.

Deseret Currency Association notes. (Paul L. Swensen)

430. *Twenty-Dollar Note:* Series A, No. 941, Feb. 17, 1858.
431. *Fifty-Dollar Note:* Series A, No. 64, Feb. 22?, 1858.
432. *One-Hundred-Dollar Note:* Series A, No. 85, Feb. 26, 1858.

SOMETIME IN 1984?

433. *The Latter-day Saints' Emigrants' Guide (St. Louis, 1848):* Around 1984, Hofmann apparently traded to the church through Don Schmidt a copy of *The Latter-day Saints' Emigrants' Guide,* a publication to guide travelers to the valley of the Great Salt Lake. Schmidt later returned the item to Hofmann because it appeared to be a later printing, not an original. Investigators eventually discovered that Hofmann had ordered printing plates for the *Emigrants' Guide* from a Kansas City company in June 1984.[124]

APRIL 12, 1985[125]

434. *Martin Harris to W. W. Phelps, Oct. 23, 1830 ("Salamander Letter"):* Described in chapter 5. Text first published in full in 1985.[126] Hofmann admitted forging it.[127]

APRIL 16, 1985

On April 16, 1985, Glenn N. Rowe wrote acquired two items from Hofmann for the church.[128]

435. *Peter and David Whitmer to Byram Green and Bithel Todd, Aug. 12, 1828:* Recommends Warren Dodge as "honest & upright both in business & in private society." Significant because it bore signature of early church figure Peter Whitmer, whose handwriting was otherwise unattested.[129] Hofmann sold the letter to Brent Ashworth in 1982 and then bought it back in April 1985 (with a check that bounced), just before he sold it to Rowe.[130] Hofmann admitted forging it.[131]

436. *Susan [Hough Conrad Wilkinson] to [Mary] Woolley, Aug. 5, 1844:* Expresses sorrow for deaths of Joseph Smith and Hyrum Smith and nervousness over present situation. "I feel tempted to write something but I dare not," she writes from Cincinnati. "If brother Kimball had passed this way I could have trusted one by him such as I would like to write but it is not so." The letter was part of a collection of Woolley papers that Brent Ashworth obtained from Al Rust, who reportedly obtained it from Woolley family members. Ashworth later traded it to Hofmann, who traded it to the church.[132] George Throckmorton examined it in 1987 and wrote, "No indication of forgery could be detected, neither could the tests determine the authenticity of the letter."[133]

OCTOBER 3, 1985[134]

437. *Book of Common Prayer (New York, 1830):* Described in chapter 6. A photograph of the book taken in March 1979 was published in 1983.[135] A photograph of the forged inscription in the book was published in 1986.[136] Hofmann acknowledged forging handwriting in it that matched that of salamander letter.[137]

ACQUISITION DATE UNKNOWN

438. *Book of Mormon Manuscript Fragments:* Hofmann is known to have peddled purported fragments of Joseph Smith's original dictation copy of the Book of Mormon. Don Schmidt has confirmed that two groups of fragments in church possession came from Hofmann. The first contains the text for 2 Nephi 4:6–11 on one side and 2 Nephi 4:18–26 on the other side. The second is made up of many small torn pieces of paper and is labeled "Unidentified fragments of Chaps. 3, 4, 5, of II Nephi."[138]

439. *John Murdock Certificate, Feb. 10, 1838:* Printed form (with handwritten name and signatures) certifying that Murdock is an elder of the church in good standing. Signed by Thomas B. Marsh and David W. Patten, "presidents, pro tempore."[139] Ink on the document exhibits the alligator-

skin cracking characteristic of many Hofmann forgeries. In 1990, Hofmann acknowledged forging the certificate.[140]

440. *Bank of Monroe Five-Dollar Note, Series B, No. 4566, Feb. 1, 1836:* Bears the signature of Oliver Cowdery. Al Rust published a photograph of this item in 1984.[141] In 1990, Hofmann admitted he had altered the serial number and date on the note and had forged the Cowdery signature.[142]

441. *Kirtland Safety Society Three-Dollar Note, No. 4, Jan. 3, 1837:* The words "BANK," "Cashr.," and "Pres." are crossed out on this unique note, which is payable to Orson Pratt and signed "J. Smith Jr. Treas." and "S. Rigdon Sec." Harry Campbell published a copy of the note in 1983, and Al Rust published it in 1984.[143] In 1990, Hofmann admitted creating the note from an uncut sheet of Kirtland notes.[144]

442. *Nauvoo Agricultural and Manufacturing Association Stock Certificate, No. 35, Mar. 4, 1841:* Entitles bearer to one share of capital stock at $50. Signed by Sidney Rigdon, Joseph Smith, and William Law. Don Schmidt has confirmed that this item came from Hofmann.[145] George Throckmorton examined the note in 1988 and reported that it exhibited "ultra-violet smearing of the ink, microscopic cracking of iron-gall ink, and poor printing procedures," leading him to believe it was a forgery.[146] In 1990, Hofmann informed Al Rust that the similar certificate illustrated in Rust's book was forged.[147]

443. *Nauvoo City One-Dollar Scrip Note (Variety 2), No. 119, Jan. 1, 1842:* Genuine notes bear the signature of either John C. Bennett or Joseph Smith as mayor. This note in church possession bears a crossed-out signature of Bennett over which a Joseph Smith signature has been added. The inks used in the handwriting on the note differ in tone from that of other Nauvoo City notes in church possession, and the printing lacks details. In 1990, Hofmann informed Al Rust that although the Nauvoo City notes illustrated in Rust's book were genuine, counterfeit notes with both Bennett's and Smith's signatures existed. The church's note no. 119 is undoubtedly one of these. A similar note acquired from Hofmann by Richard Marks was described during the Hofmann preliminary hearing.[148]

444. *Maid of Iowa Note, No. 58, May 24, 1843:* Entitles Sarah M. Kimball to cross the Mississippi River on board the steamboat *Maid of Iowa*. Bears signatures of Joseph Smith, Emma Smith, and Dan Jones. Don Schmidt has confirmed that this item came from Hofmann.[149]

445. *"Do Your Duty" Token, 1846:* In his 1984 book on Mormon coin and currency, Al Rust provided photographs and descriptions of two brass tokens each bearing the inscriptions "Do Your Duty" and "Union Is Strength." "The inscriptions relate to the Mormon Church," Rust wrote, "so it is probable the token was struck by the Church or by a member of the Church; but there is no hard evidence to substantiate this." The second token is identical to the first but bears the initials *PH*, suggesting that Mormon Peter Haws struck them. Both tokens pictured by Rust

belong to the church, but only the second came from Hofmann.[150] In February 1980, Hofmann told Dan Bachman that the second token, combined with the 1844 Presidential token, proved that the "Do Your Duty" tokens were of Latter-day Saint origin.[151] After his imprisonment, Hofmann acknowledged that the *PH* had been added to the second token.[152]

Notes

Documenting recent history from unpublished sources can be problematic. Most style manuals dictate that source notes on unpublished materials should list the institution in which the materials are found so other researchers will know where to locate them. This provision works well when dealing with noncurrent records that have been placed in archives or manuscript repositories. The documents of recent history, however, may take decades to wend their way into these facilities.

In the notes that follow, I list the locations of unpublished documents only if they have found their ultimate resting place in archives or manuscript repositories or if they are being held by governmental entities (such as law enforcement agencies and courts) whose files are so carefully ordered as to make specific source locations useful to researchers. The location of most other cited materials should be obvious but may change, as so often happens with materials in private possession and corporate materials not yet formally accessioned by archives. Thus, for example, copies of written correspondence will usually be found in the possession of their senders or recipients or (frequently) both but may someday pass into the hands of heirs or private collectors. I personally hope most will end up in archival institutions, where they may be preserved for future generations.

For brevity in the notes, I have omitted the names of interviewers in all cases in which I conducted the interview being cited. If I did not conduct the interview, I give the interviewer's name. Also, because of the sometimes hazy distinction between modern letters and memoranda, I do not distinguish between the two when citing written correspondence unless lack of other information (such as the name of sender or recipient) might make readers wonder if correspondence is being cited. Though some persons distinguish among diaries, journals, "Day-Timers," and other records with dated entries, I have found these distinctions unimportant for source citations in this book and use the term *journal* to encompass all these sources, even when entries in the records are sporadic.

The notes that follow serve two purposes. First, they allow the interested reader to understand the source for the information that appears in the text of each chapter. All dialogue in the text, for example, comes directly from the sources cited, and the notes allow the reader to determine whether the dialogue represents a contemporaneous transcription or a participant's later recollection. Second, the notes serve tacitly to acknowledge many—though by no means all—of the persons who cooperated toward the completion of this book. To all who assisted, I offer my sincere thanks. Most of all, I wish to thank my wife, Shirley, and our children, who gave up nights, weekends, holidays, and vacations to help make this book possible.

Introduction

1. This history, the manuscript of which is found in the Historical Department of the Church of Jesus Christ of Latter-day Saints (hereafter abbreviated HDC), has been edited and published as Joseph Smith, *History of the Church of Jesus Christ of Latter-day Saints*, 2d ed., 7 vols., ed. B. H. Roberts (Salt Lake City: Deseret Book, 1948–53).

The canonized portions of this history are most conveniently found in a section titled "Joseph Smith—History" in *The Pearl of Great Price: A Selection from the Revelations, Translations, and Narrations of Joseph Smith, First Prophet, Seer, and Revelator to the Church of Jesus Christ of Latter-day Saints* (Salt Lake City: Church of Jesus Christ of Latter-day Saints, 1981), 47–58. Scholarly editions of the canonized text include Dean C. Jessee, ed., *The Papers of Joseph Smith*, vol. 1 (Salt Lake City: Deseret Book, 1989), 231–32, 267–86, 288–92; Dean C. Jessee, ed., *The Personal Writings of Joseph Smith* (Salt Lake City: Deseret Book, 1984), 196–209. On the canonization, see H. Donl Peterson, *The Pearl of Great Price: A History and Commentary* (Salt Lake City: Deseret Book, 1987), 6–24; James R. Clark, "Our Pearl of Great Price: From Mission Pamphlet to Standard Work," *Ensign* 6 (Aug. 1976): 13–17.

On the nature of this history, see Dean C. Jessee, "The Writing of Joseph Smith's History," *Brigham Young University Studies* 11 (Summer 1971): 439–73; Dean C. Jessee, "The Reliability of Joseph Smith's History," *Journal of Mormon History* 3 (1976): 23–46; Howard Clair Searle, "Early Mormon Historiography: Writing the History of the Mormons, 1830–1858" (Ph.D. diss., University of California, Los Angeles, 1979), 190–336; Howard C. Searle, "Authorship of the History of Joseph Smith: A Review Essay," *Brigham Young University Studies* 21 (Winter 1981): 101–22; Howard C. Searle, "Willard Richards as Historian," *Brigham Young University Studies* 31 (Spring 1991): 41–62; Leonard J. Arrington, "The Writing of Latter-day Saint History: Problems, Accomplishments, and Admonitions," *Dialogue* 14 (Autumn 1981): 121–22; Davis Bitton and Leonard J. Arrington, *Mormons and Their Historians*

(Salt Lake City: University of Utah Press, 1988), 7–14, 19–23, 75–76; Richard Lloyd Anderson, "Editing the Prophet: Dean C. Jessee's *The Personal Writings of Joseph Smith*," *Journal of Mormon History* 11 (1984): 115–17; "I Have a Question," *Ensign* 15 (July 1985): 15–17; David J. Whittaker, "Historians and the Mormon Experience: A Sesquicentennial Perspective," in *The Eighth Annual Sidney B. Sperry Symposium: A Sesquicentennial Look at Church History* (Provo, Utah: Brigham Young University, 1980), 293–327; Jessee, *Personal Writings of Joseph Smith*, xiii–xix, 196–211, 665–67; Jessee, *Papers of Joseph Smith* 1:xxiv–xxxii, 230–386; James B. Allen, *Trials of Discipleship: The Story of William Clayton, a Mormon* (Urbana: University of Illinois Press, 1987), 106 nn. 8, 11, 115–20, 186 n. 20; Dean Jessee, "Howard Coray's Recollections of Joseph Smith," *Brigham Young University Studies* 17 (Spring 1977): 343–46; Jerald F. Simon, "Thomas Bullock as an Early Mormon Historian," *Brigham Young University Studies* 30 (Winter 1990): 76–79; Dean C. Jessee, "The Early Accounts of Joseph Smith's First Vision," *Brigham Young University Studies* 9 (Spring 1969): 275–76, 286–94; Richard L. Anderson, "New Data for Revising the Missouri 'Documentary History,' " *Brigham Young University Studies* 14 (Summer 1974): 488–501; Kenneth W. Godfrey, "The Zelph Story," *Brigham Young University Studies* 29 (Spring 1989): 31–56; Dean C. Jessee, "Return to Carthage: Writing the History of Joseph Smith's Martyrdom," *Journal of Mormon History* 8 (1981): 3–19; Dean C. Jessee, "Priceless Words and Fallible Memories: Joseph Smith as Seen in the Effort to Preserve His Discourses," *Brigham Young University Studies* 31 (Spring 1991): 22–23, 27–33.

Some anti-Mormons, most notably Jerald Tanner and Sandra Tanner, have charged the compilers and publishers of the history with deliberately falsifying portions of it. See, e.g., *Changes in Joseph Smith's History* (Salt Lake City: Modern Microfilm, [1965?]) and *Falsification of Joseph Smith's History* (Salt Lake City: Modern Microfilm, 1971). Some scholars have responded by pointing out that the bulk of the critics' claims fall into the historical fallacy of presentism. "To charge early Mormon historians with deliberated distortion of their history without considering the times in which they wrote, is to criticize previous generations for disobeying rules that did not then exist." Dean C. Jessee, *Has Mormon History Been Deliberately Falsified?* (Salt Lake City: Mormon Miscellaneous, 1982), 7. Others have noted that although the history may not meet modern standards of scholarly historical writing, it fits comfortably into the genre of written religious history. "I believe the vision of the critics is so narrow they do not see that their standard is so rigid that by it all religions which have produced a written history stand condemned, including their own Bible-centered religion." Van Hale, "Writing Religious History: Comparing the *History of the Church* with the Synoptic Gospels," in *Restoration Studies III* (Independence, Mo.: Herald House, 1986), 134.

2. "Joseph Smith—History" 1:5–15; Smith, *History of the Church* 1:2–5; Jessee, *Papers of Joseph Smith* 1:269–72; Jessee, *Personal Writings of Joseph Smith*, 197–99. The New Testament passage was James 1:5.

3. "Joseph Smith—History" 1:15–19; Smith, *History of the Church* 1:5–6; Jessee, *Papers of Joseph Smith* 1:272–73; Jessee, *Personal Writings of Joseph Smith,* 199–200.

Other accounts of this vision may be found in Jessee, *Papers of Joseph Smith* 1:5–7, 125–27, 389–91, 404–9, 429–30, 444, 448–49, 461; Jessee, *Personal Writings of Joseph Smith,* 4–6, 75–76, 199–200, 213; Milton V. Backman, Jr., *Joseph Smith's First Vision,* 2d ed. (Salt Lake City: Bookcraft, 1980). See also Richard L. Bushman, *Joseph Smith and the Beginnings of Mormonism* (Urbana: University of Illinois Press, 1984), 53–59; James B. Allen, "Eight Contemporary Accounts of Joseph Smith's First Vision," *Improvement Era* 73 (Apr. 1970): 4–13; Jessee, "The Early Accounts of Joseph Smith's First Vision," 275–94; Milton V. Backman, Jr., "Awakenings in the Burned-over District: New Light on the Historical Setting of the First Vision," *Brigham Young University Studies* 9 (Spring 1969): 301–20; Richard Lloyd Anderson, "Circumstantial Confirmation of the First Vision through Reminiscences," *Brigham Young University Studies* 9 (Spring 1969): 373–404; James B. Allen, "The Significance of Joseph Smith's 'First Vision' in Mormon Thought," *Dialogue* 1 (Autumn 1966): 29–45.

4. "Joseph Smith—History" 1:30, 33–35; Smith, *History of the Church* 1:11–12; Jessee, *Papers of Joseph Smith* 1:276–78; Jessee, *Personal Writings of Joseph Smith,* 202–3.

Other accounts of this vision may be found in Jessee, *Papers of Joseph Smith* 1:7–8, 50–54, 73–74, 127–28, 392–94, 408–15, 430–31, 449–50; Jessee, *Personal Writings of Joseph Smith,* 6–7, 76, 213–14. See also Bushman, *Joseph Smith,* 61–62.

5. "Joseph Smith—History" 1:50–53; Smith, *History of the Church* 1:15–16; Jessee, *Papers of Joseph Smith* 1:281–82; Jessee, *Personal Writings of Joseph Smith,* 206.

Other accounts of finding the plates may be found in Jessee, *Papers of Joseph Smith* 1:8–9, 74–91, 128, 394–99, 414–21; Jessee, *Personal Writings of Joseph Smith,* 7, 76–77. See also Bushman, *Joseph Smith,* 63, 73.

6. "Joseph Smith—History" 1:59–61; Smith, *History of the Church* 1:18–19; Jessee, *Papers of Joseph Smith* 1:283–84; Jessee, *Personal Writings of Joseph Smith,* 207–8.

7. Stanley B. Kimball, "The Anthon Transcript: People, Primary Sources, and Problems," *Brigham Young University Studies* 10 (Spring 1970): 325–52; Smith, *History of the Church* 1:19–20; "Joseph Smith—History" 1:61–65; Jessee, *Papers of Joseph Smith* 1:9, 284–86, 400–401; Jessee, *Personal Writings of Joseph Smith,* 7–8, 208–10; "Testimonies of Oliver Cowdery and Martin Harris," *Millennial Star* 21 (1859): 545–46; E. D. Howe, *Mormonism Unvailed* (Painesville, Ohio: E. D. Howe, 1834), 269–73; John A. Clark, *Gleanings by the Way* (Philadelphia: W. J. and J. K. Simon, 1842), 232–38; B. H. Roberts, *A Comprehensive History of the Church of Jesus Christ of Latter-day Saints,* 6 vols. (Provo, Utah: Brigham Young University Press, 1965), 1:99–109; Bushman, *Joseph Smith,* 85–90.

8. Smith, *History of the Church* 1:20–21; Jessee, *Papers of Joseph Smith* 1:286; Jessee, *Personal Writings of Joseph Smith*, 210; Bushman, *Joseph Smith*, 89–93.

9. Smith, *History of the Church* 1:32; "Joseph Smith—History" 1:66; Jessee, *Papers of Joseph Smith* 1:288; Bushman, *Joseph Smith*, 96–97.

10. Smith, *History of the Church* 1:32–33, 48–49; Jessee, *Papers of Joseph Smith* 1:288, 293; Bushman, *Joseph Smith*, 102–3.

11. Smith, *History of the Church* 1:49, 52–53; Jessee, *Papers of Joseph Smith* 1:293–95; Bushman, *Joseph Smith*, 103–5.

12. "The Testimony of Three Witnesses," in *The Book of Mormon* (Palmyra, N.Y.: E. B. Grandin, 1830), 589; Smith, *History of the Church* 1:53–57; Jessee, *Papers of Joseph Smith* 1:295–98; Bushman, *Joseph Smith*, 105–7.

13. Pomeroy Tucker, *Origin, Rise, and Progress of Mormonism* (New York: D. Appleton, 1867), 4, 50–53; Bushman, *Joseph Smith*, 107–8; Smith, *History of the Church* 1:71; Jessee, *Papers of Joseph Smith* 1:300; "The Book of Mormon," *Wayne Sentinel*, Mar. 26, 1830.

14. Smith, *History of the Church* 1:74–80, 2:62–63, 3:23–24; Jessee, *Papers of Joseph Smith* 1:241–44, 302–4; Bushman, *Joseph Smith*, 143–49; *The Doctrine and Covenants of the Church of Jesus Christ of Latter-day Saints* (Salt Lake City: Church of Jesus Christ of Latter-day Saints, 1981), 20:1, 115:3–4; "The Saints," *The Evening and the Morning Star* 2, no. 20 (May 1834): 158–59; "Communicated," *The Evening and the Morning Star* 2, no. 20 (May 1834): 160; Russell M. Nelson, " 'Thus Shall My Church Be Called,' " *Ensign* 20 (May 1990): 16–18; Gordon B. Hinckley, "*Mormon* Should Mean 'More Good,' " *Ensign* 20 (Nov. 1990): 51–54.

15. Doctrine and Covenants (1981) secs. 18, 20, 27, 81, 84, 90, 102, 107, 112, 124; D. Michael Quinn, "The Evolution of the Presiding Quorums of the LDS Church," *Journal of Mormon History* 1 (1974): 21–38; *Deseret News 1980 Church Almanac* (Salt Lake City: Deseret News, 1980), 67–121.

16. Smith, *History of the Church* 1:78; Doctrine and Covenants (1981) secs. 21, 47, 69, 85, 123, 127, 128.

Chapter 1: Alterations of the Past

1. "Preface" in *The Book of Mormon* (1830), iii.

2. Parley P. Pratt, *Mormonism Unveiled: Zion's Watchman Unmasked* (New York: Parley P. Pratt, 1838), 40–42; A. S. Hayden, *Early History of the Disciples in the Western Reserve, Ohio* (Cincinnati: Chase and Hall, 1876), 191–95, 209–16; Henry K. Shaw, *Buckeye Disciples: A History of the Disciples of Christ in Ohio* (St. Louis: Christian Board of Publication, 1952), 79–82; Roberts, *Comprehensive History* 1:222–23, 225–26; Heman C. Smith, "Biography of Sidney Rigdon," *Journal of History* 3, no. 1 (Jan. 1910): 3–20.

3. "To the Public," *Painesville Telegraph*, Jan. 31, Feb. 7, 1834; Howe, *Mormonism Unvailed*.

4. Howe, *Mormonism Unvailed*, 100, 103–4, 278–90. For biographical information on Spalding, see Charles H. Whittier and Stephen W. Stathis, "The Enigma of Solomon Spalding," *Dialogue* 10 (Autumn 1977): 70–73.

5. Pratt, *Mormonism Unveiled,* 42; Benjamin Winchester, *The Origin of the Spaulding Story* (Philadelphia: Brown, Bicking, and Guilbert, 1840), 3–21; Benjamin Winchester, *Plain Facts Shewing the Origin of the Spaulding Story . . . Re-published by George J. Adams* (Bedford, England: C. B. Merry, 1841), 26–27; Lester E. Bush, Jr., "The Spalding Theory: Then and Now," *Dialogue* 10 (Autumn 1977): 40–69.

6. Bush, "The Spalding Theory: Then and Now," 42–43, 53–57. The diverse group of scholars who have rejected the Spalding theory include Fawn M. Brodie, *No Man Knows My History* (New York: Alfred A. Knopf, 1945), 419–33; Whitney R. Cross, *The Burned-over District* (Ithaca, N.Y.: Cornell University Press, 1950), 144; Thomas F. O'Dea, *The Mormons* (Chicago: University of Chicago Press, 1957), 23–24; Marvin S. Hill, "The Shaping of the Mormon Mind in New England and New York," *Brigham Young University Studies* 9 (Spring 1969): 352; Bushman, *Joseph Smith,* 126–27, 191, 231.

Another popular explanation of the origin of the Book of Mormon has been that Joseph Smith plagiarized Ethan Smith's *View of the Hebrews* or similar works appearing before the Book of Mormon. "But it would be a mistake to see the book as an imitation of these earlier works," Richard L. Bushman has explained. "Nor is there evidence of heavy borrowing from *View of the Hebrews,* as some critics have said. Comparison of the two works reveals too many fundamental differences." *Joseph Smith,* 134–35.

7. Stanley B. Kimball, "Kinderhook Plates Brought to Joseph Smith Appear to Be a Nineteenth-Century Hoax," *Ensign* 11 (Aug. 1981): 66–74; Allen, *Trials of Discipleship,* 117–18.

8. Dallin H. Oaks and Marvin S. Hill, *Carthage Conspiracy: The Trial of the Accused Assassins of Joseph Smith* (Urbana: University of Illinois Press, 1975), 90. Daniels signed a simpler and more reliable affidavit on July 4, 1844, but as B. H. Roberts noted, "He enlarged his affidavit to a sensational pamphlet detailing many miraculous occurrences in connection with the martyrdom which discredited him as a witness and did much towards making the [trial of the] murderers of the Prophet farcical." Smith, *History of the Church* 7:163.

9. William M. Daniels, *A Correct Account of the Murder of Generals Joseph and Hyrum Smith, at Carthage, on the 27th Day of June, 1844* (Nauvoo, Ill.: John Taylor, 1845), 15. Daniels's testimony has been excerpted or reprinted several times. See, e.g., Lyman O. Littlefield, *The Martyrs; A Sketch of the Lives and a Full Account of the Martyrdom of Joseph and Hyrum Smith* (Salt Lake City: Juvenile Instructor Office, 1882), 71–86; *Nauvoo Classics,* Mormon Collector Series, vol. 3 (Salt Lake City: Mormon Heritage, 1976).

10. Oaks and Hill, *Carthage Conspiracy,* 127–28, 133–34. The typesetter, Lyman O. Littlefield, would later insist that the sensational details came from Daniels. Littlefield, *The Martyrs,* 71. N. B. Lundwall, comp., *The Fate of the Persecutors of the Prophet Joseph Smith* (Salt Lake City: Bookcraft, 1952), 226–33, excerpts the Daniels testimony from *The Martyrs,* together with other material that superficially seems to support it. As Oaks and Hill point out, however, this material merely consists of "hearsay or secondhand accounts apparently relying on" the Daniels-Littlefield account, 96 n. 60. On the extent

of Littlefield's contribution to the original Daniels pamphlet, see Oaks and Hill, *Carthage Conspiracy*, 139 n. 52, 168, 187 n. 31.

11. Jessee, "Return to Carthage," 14–19.

12. Roberts, *Comprehensive History* 2:325 n. 14.

13. Ibid. 2:332–33.

14. The two general authorities were John Taylor and Willard Richards. Taylor's account appeared first in *The Doctrine and Covenants of the Church of Jesus Christ of Latter Day Saints*, 2d ed. (Nauvoo, Ill.: John Taylor, 1844), 444–45. On the attribution of this account to Taylor, see Robert J. Woodford, "The Historical Development of the Doctrine and Covenants" (Ph.D. diss., Brigham Young University, 1974), 1794. Richards's account was first published as "Two Minutes in Jail," *Nauvoo Neighbor*, July 24, 1844.

15. Roberts, *Comprehensive History* 2:334.

16. Copies of this purported letter from William Web to Mr. Editor can be found in Ms 5053, HDC; Edward Stevenson, Journal, vol. 36, pp. 47–52, HDC; Littlefield, *The Martyrs*, 87–90.

17. Roberts, *Comprehensive History* 2:334. The earliest and most complete description of the letter's provenance is James Wareham to A. M. Musser, Mar. 18, 1867, Edward Hunter Collection, HDC.

18. Jessee, "Return to Carthage," 15 n. 26.

19. Roger Van Noord, *King of Beaver Island: The Life and Assassination of James Jesse Strang* (Urbana: University of Illinois Press, 1988), 7–11, 39; Richard E. Bennett, *Mormons at the Missouri, 1846–1852* (Norman: University of Oklahoma Press, 1987), 18–20, 40, 64–65, 90, 144, 159, 162, 206, 226, 233, 238–39, 250; Richard E. Bennett, " 'A Samaritan Had Passed By,' " *Illinois Historical Journal* 82 (Spring 1989): 13–15; Lawrence Foster, "James J. Strang: The Prophet Who Failed," *Church History* 50 (June 1981): 183–86; William D. Russell, "King James Strang: Joseph Smith's Successor?" in *The Restoration Movement: Essays in Mormon History*, ed. F. Mark McKiernan, Alma R. Blair, Paul M. Edwards (Lawrence, Kans.: Coronado, 1973), 231–56; John Quist, "John E. Page: An Apostle of Uncertainty," *Journal of Mormon History* 12 (1985): 57–63.

20. Van Noord, *King of Beaver Island*, 53–54; Charles Eberstadt, "A Letter That Founded a Kingdom," *Autograph Collectors' Journal* 3, no. 1 (Oct. 1950): 3–4.

21. Van Noord, *King of Beaver Island*, 54–56, 274; Robert P. Weeks, "A Utopian Kingdom in the American Grain," *Wisconsin Magazine of History* 61 (Autumn 1977): 7–9; Foster, "James J. Strang," 185; Eberstadt, "Letter That Founded a Kingdom," 4–5; Quist, "John E. Page," 57 n. 19.

22. Van Noord, *King of Beaver Island*, 17–20. Forgery was used more than once in support of Strang's cause. Strang's *Voree Herald* 1, no. 7 (July 1846), published a document, purportedly signed by members of Joseph Smith's family, certifying that they "do believe in the appointment of J. J. Strang." Katharine Salisbury, a sister of Joseph Smith, did not learn about the certificate until decades later. Then in a published disclaimer she wrote, "I now in truth declare that I never signed my name to such certificate or document; neither

did I give my consent for anyone to sign it." She doubted most other Smith family members had signed it either. "So," she concluded, "I say the whole thing was a forgery. Whoever the perpetrator was, his acts will surely be revealed sometime, as justice will prevail." "Testimony of Katharine Salisbury," *Saints' Herald* 46 (1899): 261.

23. Donald Q. Cannon and Lyndon W. Cook, *Far West Record: Minutes of the Church of Jesus Christ of Latter-day Saints, 1830–1844* (Salt Lake City: Deseret Book, 1983), 162–71.

24. The reprint was incorporated in R. B. Neal, *Oliver Cowdery's Defence and Renunciation*, Anti-Mormon Tracts no. 9 (Grayson, Ky.: Ashland Independent, 1906), 3–9.

25. See, e.g., Roberts, *Comprehensive History* 1:163; Heman C. Smith, "Oliver Cowdery's Defense," *Saints' Herald* 54 (1907): 229–37; R. B. Neal, *Oliver Cowdery's Defense*, "Sword of Laban" Leaflets, 2d series, no. 11 (Grayson, Ky.: American Anti-Mormon Association, [1908–11]); *"Second Elder" Oliver Cowdery's Renunciation of Mormonism and His "Defence" for So Doing* (Cleveland, Ohio: Utah Gospel Mission, 1927), 1–7; Hal Hougey, *Oliver Cowdery and the Book of Mormon* (Concord, Calif.: Pacific, 1963), 14–19.

26. Charles A. Davies, "Question Time," *Saints' Herald* 111 (1964): 457; Jerald Tanner and Sandra Tanner, *A Critical Look: A Study of the Overstreet "Confession" and the Cowdery "Defense"* (Salt Lake City: Modern Microfilm, 1967), 7–31; Richard Lloyd Anderson, "The Second Witness of Priesthood Restoration," *Improvement Era* 71 (Sept. 1968): 20–22; Chad J. Flake, ed., *A Mormon Bibliography, 1830–1930* (Salt Lake City: University of Utah Press, 1978), 182, 455; Richard Lloyd Anderson, "I Have a Question," *Ensign* 17 (Apr. 1987): 23–25; "Mormon and Anti-Mormon Forgeries," *Salt Lake City Messenger*, no. 73 (Oct. 1989): 5–15.

27. Reuben Miller, Journal, Oct. 21, Nov., 1848, HDC; Reuben Miller to Henry Sabey, Nov. 16, 1848, Ms 88, HDC; George A. Smith to Orson Pratt, Oct. 20, 31, 1848, as printed in *Millennial Star* 11 (1849): 12–14; Richard Lloyd Anderson, "The Second Witness on Priesthood Succession," *Improvement Era* 71 (Nov. 1968): 18–20; Richard Lloyd Anderson, "The Scribe as a Witness," *Improvement Era* 72 (Jan. 1969): 57–59.

28. "A Confession of Oliver Overstreet: The Overstreet Letter," Ms 845 #1, HDC.

29. *"Second Elder" Oliver Cowdery's Renunciation*, 16.

30. Anderson, "I Have a Question," 23; Anderson, "The Scribe as a Witness," 57–59; Anderson, "Second Witness on Priesthood Succession," 18–20; Richard Lloyd Anderson, "Reuben Miller, Recorder of Oliver Cowdery's Reaffirmations," *Brigham Young University Studies* 8 (Spring 1968): 277; Tanner and Tanner, *A Critical Look*, 1–6; Daniel B. Richards, Affidavit, July 8, 1930, Ms 845 #2, HDC; "Mormon and Anti-Mormon Forgeries," 6–15.

31. Wilford Woodruff, Journal, June 15, 1878, HDC. Several copies of the vision, including the one copied by the Historian's Office clerk and one in Woodruff's hand, are in Ms 4244, HDC. The clerk who made the Historian's

Office copy was John Jacques. Historian's Office Journal, vol. 36, entry of June 15, 1878, HDC.

32. See, e.g., Matthias F. Cowley, *Wilford Woodruff: Fourth President of the Church of Jesus Christ of Latter-day Saints* (Salt Lake City: Deseret News, 1909), 505; Robert W. Smith and Elisabeth A. Smith, comps., *Scriptural and Secular Prophecies Pertaining to the "Last Days,"* 2d ed. (Salt Lake City: Pyramid, 1932), 114–16; Duane S. Crowther, *Inspired Prophetic Warnings* (Bountiful, Utah: Horizon, 1987), 193–96; Blaine Yorgason and Brenton Yorgason, *Spiritual Survival in the Last Days* (Salt Lake City: Deseret Book, 1990), 44–48.

33. Woodruff, Journal, June 15, 1878; Ms 4244, fd. 1, HDC. Some persons apparently attributed the vision to Woodruff because an incomplete copy in his hand exists in the Historical Department collections. See Ms 4244, fd. 1, HDC. For the reasons already noted, however, it appears that Woodruff simply made this copy from someone else's. Because of his well-known connection with the publication of the Book of Mormon in French, John Taylor has been suggested as the author of the vision. See, e.g., Anthony E. Larson, *And the Earth Shall Reel To and Fro* (Orem, Utah: Zedek Books, 1983), 169–74. On the date the vision was purportedly received, Taylor was the church's senior apostle and would soon become its president. Though Taylor oversaw the translation of the French Book of Mormon, his French was limited, and the actual translation work was carried out by others working under him. See Curtis Edwin Bolton, Journal, July 5, 1850, to Jan. 19, 1852, HDC; Samuel W. Taylor, *The Kingdom or Nothing: The Life of John Taylor, Militant Mormon* (New York: Macmillan, 1976), 147–48, 152–53, 155–56; Davis Bitton, "Bertrand's Contribution," *Church News,* Dec. 16, 1978; Francis M. Gibbons, *John Taylor: Mormon Philosopher, Prophet of God* (Salt Lake City: Deseret Book, 1985), 121–22; L. R. Jacobs, *Mormon Non-English Scriptures, Hymnals, and Periodicals, 1830–1986: A Descriptive Bibliography* (Ithaca, N.Y.: L. R. Jacobs, 1986), entry 136B. The fact that persons close to Taylor in the church leadership vehemently denounced the vision as fraudulent casts doubt on Taylor's authorship.

34. Copies attributed to Joseph F. Smith are found in Ms 4244, fds. 2–3, HDC.

35. "A Fraud," *Deseret Evening News,* Nov. 17, 1880; "A Fraud," *Millennial Star* 42 (1880): 810.

36. Jacob Spori, "True and False Theosophy," *Juvenile Instructor* 28 (1893): 673–74; J. Sporri, "Wahre und falsche Theosophie," *Der Stern* 25 (1893): 374–75.

37. Rulon S. Wells, "A Fraudulent Prophecy Exposed," *Improvement Era* 11 (Jan. 1908): 161–64. The best scholarly assessment of the purported prophecy is Paul B. Pixton, " 'Play It Again, Sam': The Remarkable 'Prophecy' of Samuel Lutz, Alias Christophilus Gratianus, Reconsidered," *Brigham Young University Studies* 25 (Summer 1985): 27–46.

38. James E. Talmage, "The 'Michigan Relics': A Story of Forgery and Deception," *Deseret Museum Bulletin,* n.s. no. 2, Sept. 6, 1911; "Archaeological Finds Declared Spurious," *Deseret Evening News,* Aug. 5, 1911. A useful

survey of the Michigan relics and the controversy they engendered is John Cumming, "Humbugs of the First Water: The Soper Frauds," *Michigan History* 63, no. 2 (Mar.–Apr. 1979): 31–43. Not all Latter-day Saints have been as certain as Talmage that the relics are bogus. See, e.g., Leonard D. Carter, comp., "Report: Historical Background of the Soper-Savage Collection of Inscriptions and Drawings" (Center for Religious Studies, Brigham Young University, 1977).

39. Talmage, "The 'Michigan Relics,' " 20, 22.

40. Ibid., 22, 24.

41. *Eighty-ninth Semi-annual Conference of the Church of Jesus Christ of Latter-day Saints* (Salt Lake City: Deseret News, [1918]), 54–55.

42. Ibid., 57.

43. See copy stamped October 18, 1918, in Ms 4244, fd. 3, HDC.

44. See copy stamped April 29, 1918, in Ms 4244, fd. 3, HDC.

45. *One-Hundred and First Annual Conference of the Church of Jesus Christ of Latter-day Saints* (Salt Lake City: Church of Jesus Christ of Latter-day Saints, [1931]), 68–69.

46. "The Coming of the Great White Chief," Ms 3337, HDC; Norman C. Pierce, *The Great White Chief and the Indian Messiah* (Salt Lake City: Norman C. Pierce, 1971), v.

47. Spencer W. Kimball, " 'The Coming of the Great White Chief,' " *Church News*, May 16, 1953.

48. "Avoid Publication of Mythical Story," *Priesthood Bulletin* 2, no. 1 (Jan.–Feb. 1966): 1.

49. Ray T. Matheny, "An Analysis of the Padilla Gold Plates," *Brigham Young University Studies* 19 (Fall 1978): 21–22, 33.

50. "Gold Plates from Mexico," *University Archaeological Society Newsletter*, no. 78, Jan. 17, 1962, 4.

51. Matheny, "Analysis of the Padilla Gold Plates," 21, 40. Other comparable examples could be cited of forged inscriptions that seem aimed at a Mormon audience. See, e.g., William James Adams, Jr., and Ray T. Matheny, "Archaeological and Cryptological Analyses of the Manti Inscriptions," *Utah Historical Quarterly* 44 (Spring 1976): 133–40, in which some bogus inscriptions were found to be made up in substantial part from the brands of Utah cattle ranchers.

52. Russell Chandler, "Book of Mormon Challenged Anew," *Los Angeles Times*, June 25, 1977; Edward E. Plowman, "Who Really Wrote the Book of Mormon?" *Christianity Today*, July 8, 1977, 32–34; "Mormon Mystery," *Time*, July 11, 1977, 69.

53. Chandler, "Book of Mormon Challenged Anew."

54. Ibid.; "LDS Aides Deny Theory," *Salt Lake Tribune*, June 26, 1977; "Expert Avoids Opinion," *Deseret News*, June 29, 1977; Russell Chandler, "Added Support Seen for Challenge to Mormon Text," *Los Angeles Times*, June 30, 1977.

55. "LDS Aides Deny Theory."

56. Roger Bennett, "LDS Refute Book of Mormon Pirating Claim," *Herald Journal* (Logan, Utah), June 29, 1977.

57. "Theory Merits Little LDS 'Faith,' " *Salt Lake Tribune*, June 29, 1977.

58. Clark Lobb, "Handwriting Expert Quits Book of Mormon Case," *Salt Lake Tribune*, July 9, 1977.

59. John Dart, "Manuscript Handwriting Spalding's, Expert Vows," *Salt Lake Tribune*, Sept. 9, 1977; "Church Defends Book's Origin," *Salt Lake Tribune*, Sept. 9, 1977; Russell Chandler, "Expert Changes View on Book of Mormon," *Los Angeles Times*, Sept. 24, 1977.

60. "Novelist Theory Disputed," *Deseret News*, Sept. 24, 1977.

61. Dean C. Jessee, " 'Spalding Theory' Re-examined," *Church News*, Aug. 20, 1977; John Dart, "LDS Offers 'Most Detailed' Response to Book of Mormon Scribe Challenge," *Salt Lake Tribune*, Aug. 20, 1977; "Expert's Report Quells Attack on Authenticity of the Book of Mormon," *Church News*, Oct. 15, 1977.

62. John Dart, "Mormons Reply in Text Author Dispute," *Los Angeles Times*, Aug. 20, 1977.

63. Edward E. Plowman, "Mormon Manuscript Claims: Another Look," *Christianity Today*, Oct. 21, 1977, 38–39; Jerald Tanner and Sandra Tanner, *Did Spalding Write the Book of Mormon?* (Salt Lake City: Modern Microfilm, 1977), 1.

Despite serious objections from the Tanners and others, the three researchers, Wayne L. Cowdrey, Howard A. Davis, and Donald R. Scales, went ahead with their original plan to publish *Who Really Wrote the Book of Mormon?* (Santa Ana, Calif.: Vision House, 1977). "After reading this book carefully," the Tanners wrote, "we must report that our feelings have not changed. In fact, we are more convinced than ever that we made the right decision. The evidence against the new Spalding theory now seems to be overwhelming, and the California researchers' failure to come to grips with some of the basic criticisms leads us to the conclusion that they have no real answers to the objections." *An Examination of "Who Really Wrote the Book of Mormon?"* (Salt Lake City: Modern Microfilm, 1978), 18.

64. *Deseret News 1980 Church Almanac*, 5–6, 244–52.

65. Gordon B. Hinckley, "150-Year Drama: A Personal View of Our History," *Ensign* 10 (Apr. 1980): 10–14.

Chapter 2: The Anthon Transcript

1. Office of Salt Lake County Attorney, *Mark Hofmann Interviews* (Salt Lake City: Office of Salt Lake County Attorney, 1987), 93–95; Mark William Hofmann, "Finding the Joseph Smith Document," *Ensign* 10 (July 1980): 73; Danel W. Bachman, "Sealed in a Book: Preliminary Observations on the Newly Found 'Anthon Transcript,' " *Brigham Young University Studies* 20 (Summer 1980): 325, 327; Danel W. Bachman, "A Look at the Newly Discovered Joseph Smith Manuscript," *Ensign* 10 (July 1980): 69; Mark W. Hofmann, Affidavit, Apr. 25, 1980.

2. A. J. Simmonds, "A Historian's Dream," *Herald Journal/Valley* (Logan, Utah), May 5, 1980; A. J. Simmonds, Affidavit, May 27, 1980; Hofmann, "Finding the Joseph Smith Document," 73; *Mark Hofmann Interviews*, 95–97; A. J. Simmonds, Telephone Interview, Aug. 13, 1990.

3. Richard P. Howard, "Prologue to the Sesquicentennial: 150 Years Ago This Month," *Saints Herald* 125 (1978): 176; John L. Sorenson, "The Book of Mormon as a MesoAmerican Codex," *Newsletter and Proceedings of the Society for Early Historic Archaeology*, no. 139 (Dec. 1976): 2–3; Bachman, "Sealed in a Book," 331–40. See also Introduction, note 7.

4. Simmonds, "A Historian's Dream."

5. Danel W. Bachman, Journal, Feb. 13, Apr. 17, 1980; Danel W. Bachman, Interview, July 27, 1989. The relative was James P. Mitchell.

6. Bachman, Interview, July 27, 1989; Bachman, Journal, Apr. 17, 1980; *Mark Hofmann Interviews*, 16; Lucy [Mack] Smith, *Biographical Sketches of Joseph Smith the Prophet and His Progenitors for Many Generations* (Liverpool: Orson Pratt, 1853), 38. The spelling of Joseph Smith's sister's name varies. I have used "Katharine" throughout my text, following the rationale given in Richard Lloyd Anderson, "What Were Joseph Smith's Sisters Like, and What Happened to Them after the Martyrdom?" *Ensign* 9 (Mar. 1979): 45.

7. Bachman, Interview, July 27, 1989.

8. Bachman, Journal, Apr. 17, 1980; Bachman, Interview, July 27, 1989; Hofmann, "Finding the Joseph Smith Document," 73; Dean C. Jessee, Journal, Apr. 17, 1980; Dean C. Jessee, Interview, Feb. 10, 1989. "There is no greater authority on early Mormon handwriting than Dean Jessee." Richard Lloyd Anderson, "Editing the Prophet: Dean C. Jessee's *The Personal Writings of Joseph Smith*," *Journal of Mormon History* 11 (1984): 114.

9. Bachman, Journal, Apr. 18, 1980.

10. Bachman, Interview, July 27, 1989; Bachman, "Newly Discovered," 71; Bachman, "Sealed in a Book," 327; Hofmann, "Finding the Joseph Smith Document," 73; Jessee, Interview, Feb. 10, 1989; Jessee, Journal, Apr. 18, 1980.

11. Bachman, Interview, July 27, 1989.

12. Jessee, Journal, Apr. 18, 1980.

13. Jessee, Journal, Apr. 19, 1980; Bachman, Journal, Apr. 19, 21, 1980; Leonard J. Arrington, Interview, Mar. 21, 1989. The other person Bachman said he told about the document was Richard W. Sadler.

14. Jessee, Journal, Apr. 21, 1980; Bachman, Journal, Apr. 21, 1980; Arrington, Interview, Mar. 21, 1989.

15. Arrington, Interview, Mar. 21, 1989.

16. "Three New General Authorities Called," *Church News*, Apr. 2, 1977; Lynne Hollstein, "Experiences in Church Are Most Prized," *Church News*, Apr. 16, 1977; "Historical Dept. Gets New Director," *Church News*, May 14, 1977.

17. Arrington, Interview, Mar. 21, 1989.

18. Gordon B. Hinckley, Interview, Apr. 26, 1989; Wendell J. Ashton, "Gordon B. Hinckley of the Quorum of the Twelve," *Improvement Era* 64 (Dec. 1961): 983; Historical Department Office Journal, Feb. 8, Mar. 15, 1978. The

Historical Department Office Journal is a sporadic log of activities in the LDS Church Historical Department. During the time period covered by the case, entries in the journal were made under the supervision of Earl E. Olson, the department's assistant managing director.

19. Jessee, Journal, Apr. 22, 1980.

20. Bachman, Journal, Apr. 22, 1980; Bachman, Interview, July 27, 1989; Jessee, Journal, Apr. 22, 1980.

21. Eudora Durham and George Homer Durham II, Interview, Mar. 20, 1989; George Homer Durham II, Telephone Interview, Aug. 31, 1989. The boarder's name was Dolores Isom.

22. Jessee, Journal, Apr. 22, 1980; Bachman, Journal, Apr. 22, 1980; Videotape, LDS Press Conference, Oct. 23, 1985, HDC.

23. Bachman, Journal, Apr. 22, 1980; Bachman, Interview, July 27, 1989.

24. Jessee, Journal, Apr. 22, 1980.

25. Bachman, Journal, Apr. 22, 1980; Jessee, Journal, Apr. 22, 1980; Spencer W. Kimball, Journal, Apr. 22, 1980; Marion G. Romney, Journal, Apr. 22, 1980. D. Arthur Haycock (Kimball's secretary) and F. Michael Watson (assistant secretary to the First Presidency) were also present. "LDS Scholars Study Joseph Smith Transcript," *Deseret News*, Apr. 28, 1980; Arrington, Interview, Mar. 21, 1989.

26. N. Eldon Tanner, Journal, Apr. 22, 1980.

27. Historical Department Acquisition Sheet 80–157; Bachman, Journal, Apr. 22, 1980; Bachman, "Sealed in a Book," 327, 330.

28. Jessee, Journal, Apr. 23, 1980; G. Homer Durham to Mark W. Hofmann, Apr. 23, 1980. Janet Brigham, in "Original Copy of Gold Plate Characters Discovered," *Ensign* 10 (June 1980): 76, notes, "Brother Jessee says that the newly found document has yet to be examined by linguists."

29. First Presidency and Quorum of Twelve, Minutes, Apr. 24, 1980.

30. Jerry P. Cahill, "Newly Discovered Transcript May Be 1828 Example of Joseph Smith's Writing," Press Release, Church of Jesus Christ of Latter-day Saints, Apr. 28, 1980.

31. Mark W. Hofmann to G. Homer Durham, Apr. 25, 1980. A date stamp on the letter shows it was received April 28.

32. G. Homer Durham to Mark W. Hofmann, Apr. 29, 1980.

33. G. Homer Durham to Donald T. Schmidt, Apr. 30, 1980; Bachman, Interview, July 27, 1989. The expert named in Durham's memorandum was Sherman Young.

34. Jessee, Journal, Apr. 29, 1980.

35. Dale D. Heaps, "Research on Document Given to Us by Mark W. Hofmann," Apr. 30, 1980. The conservation scientist in Pittsburgh was Robert Feller.

36. Jessee, Journal, May 13, 1980. The journal does not identify the Library of Congress employee by name.

37. John L. Sorenson to G. Homer Durham, May 6, 1980; see also Reporter's Transcript of Preliminary Hearing, vol. 4 at 210, State v. Hofmann,

Nos. 860003035, 860003041, 860003044, 860003045, 860020193 (Utah 5th Cir. Ct. heard Apr. 14 to May 22, 1986) (hereafter "Preliminary Hearing").

38. As quoted in John L. Sorenson, Form Letter, [1980].

39. Bachman, Journal, May 5, 29, 1980; Richard P. Lindsay to Special Affairs Committee, May 14, 1980; Kenneth W. Godfrey, Journal, May 30, 1980; Richard P. Lindsay to G. Homer Durham, June 9, 1980; Historical Department Advisers Meeting Minutes, June 11, 1980, June 12, Aug. 12, 27, 1981; "Scholar Says Mormon Document May Be Too Brief for Translation," *Ogden Standard-Examiner*, July 9, 1980; John W. Welch to Friends, Nov. 1980; "Toward a Translation of the Anthon Transcript," *Foundation for Ancient Research and Mormon Studies Newsletter* (hereafter *FARMS Newsletter*) (July 1981): 2–3; "Anthon Transcript Studied," *FARMS Newsletter* (Nov. 1981): 2–3; "Anthon Transcript," *FARMS Newsletter* (Apr. 1982): 3; Earl E. Olson, Memorandum, June 11, 1981; John L. Sorenson, Form Letters, July 17, Aug. 11, 18, 1981; Earl E. Olson to John L. Sorenson, Aug. 13, Sept. 1, 1981, Apr. 16, 1982; John L. Sorenson to Earl Olson, Aug. 22, 1981, Apr. 12, 1982; John L. Sorenson to Donald T. Schmidt, Sept. 2, 1981; John L. Sorenson, Interview, May 3, 1989; Godfrey, Interview, July 27, 1989. The Harvard professor emeritus was Barry Fell.

40. Bachman, "Newly Discovered," 69–73; Bachman, "Sealed in a Book," 321–45.

41. Infrared and Ultraviolet Photographs of Anthon Transcript, Taken June 4, 1980; *Mark Hofmann Interviews*, 124–25; "Preliminary Hearing," 4:210–12; Historical Department, Library-Archives Managers Meeting Minutes, May 22, June 5, 1980.

42. Historical Department Advisers Meeting Minutes, June 11, 1980.

43. Hofmann, Affidavit, Apr. 25, 1980. A copy of this affidavit sent to Durham bears a May 29 date stamp.

44. Mark W. Hofmann to Jay Todd, May 27, 1980. See also *Mark Hofmann Interviews*, 100.

45. Jessee, Journal, May 23, 1980; Jay M. Todd, Interview, May 5, 1989; *Mark Hofmann Interviews*, 120.

46. Noel R. Barton, Telephone Notes, June 4, 1980; Dorothy Dean, Affidavit, July 29, 1980; *Mark Hofmann Interviews*, 121. Cf. Jessee, Journal, June 4, 1980: "Noel Barton . . . said he had made contact with two daughters of Mary Hancock but neither knew anything about the bible. They never knew of it in the Smith family, nor did they think their mother would have sold it to anyone." The relative Barton spoke with who remembered seeing a Bible was Winfield Salisbury, Sr.

47. Untitled Loan Agreement between the Historical Department and Mark W. Hofmann, June 19, 1980.

48. Dean, Affidavit, July 29, 1980; Mary Dean Hancock, Sales Record, Entry for Aug. 13, 1954, attached to Dean, Affidavit, July 29, 1980; Bachman, "Sealed in a Book," 325 n. 9; *Mark Hofmann Interviews*, 116–19; Dorothy Dean to Glen L. Rowe, July 22, 1989.

49. Jessee, Journal, July 2, 9, 1980. On August 7, Jessee recorded, "Mark Hofmann was in today with affidavits showing the provenance of the bible in which he found the Anthon Ms. He says he paid $325 for the bible, and he finally divulged that he had purchased it from an Ansel White here in SLC."

50. Barton, Telephone Notes, June 23, 30, July 10, 1980; Noel R. Barton to Jay M. Todd, June 30, 1980; Donald T. Schmidt, Handwritten Note, July 2, 1980, inscribed on Untitled Loan Agreement between the Historical Department and Mark W. Hofmann, June 19, 1980; *Mark Hofmann Interviews,* 120–21.

51. Barton to Todd, June 30, 1980; Noel R. Barton to Vital Statistics Section, California Department of Health, Sept. 9, 1980; Ansel J. White Death Certificate, Certified Copy Issued Nov. 17, 1980, attached to Barton to California Department of Health; Ms. Zito to Noel Barton, Nov. 29, 1980, enclosing "Ansel White Passes Away," *Lodi News Sentinel,* Jan. 7, 1952; [Noel R. Barton] to Jay M. Todd, Retained Manuscript Copy, [Nov.? 1980]; *Mark Hofmann Interviews,* 120–22.

52. Jessee, Interview, Feb. 10, 1989; Dorothy Dean to Noel Barton, July 25, 1980.

53. Hofmann, Affidavit, Apr. 25, 1980; Simmonds, Affidavit, May 27, 1980; Dean, Affidavit, July 29, 1980 (postmarked Aug. 1); Jeffrey P. Salt, Affidavit, Apr. 28, 1980; *Mark Hofmann Interviews,* 122–23.

54. Donald T. Schmidt to Earl E. Olson, Aug. 13, 1980; Historical Department Advisers Meeting Minutes, Aug. 13, 1980.

55. Mark W. Hofmann to Donald Schmidt, Aug. 28, 1980.

56. Donald T. Schmidt to Mark W. Hofmann, Sept. 2, 1980.

57. Mark W. Hofmann to Donald T. Schmidt, Sept. 26, 1980; Wilfrid Clark to Donald T. Schmidt, Sept. 19, 1980; Peter Crawley to Whom It May Concern, Sept. 19, 1980.

58. Donald T. Schmidt, "Conversation with Mark Hofmann," Oct. 9, 1980.

59. Donald T. Schmidt, "Notes Concerning the Anthon Transcript," [Oct. 1980]; Historical Department Acquisition Sheet 80–402; "Preliminary Hearing," 4:160–61, 215–16, 218, 5:94–95; *Mark Hofmann Interviews,* 296–97; Historical Department Office Journal, Oct. 13, 1980; Godfrey, in his Journal, Apr. 24, 1980, calls the Anthon transcript, if authentic, "the oldest church manuscript in existence"; Brigham, in "Original Copy," writes, "If authentic, the one sheet of paper is the oldest known Latter-day Saint document and the oldest known sample of Joseph Smith's handwriting," 74.

Chapter 3: The Joseph Smith III Blessing

1. "Behind the Scenes: The Joseph Smith III Blessing," *Sunstone Review* 2, no. 8 (Aug. 1982): 1; *Mark Hofmann Interviews,* 150–51. On when Hofmann first showed Schmidt the document, see Jessee, Journal, Feb. 20 (Hofmann showed blessing to Jessee), Feb. 25, 1981 (Hofmann said he had offered it to Schmidt); Donald T. Schmidt, Personal Engagement Notebook, Feb. 24 ("saw Doc[ument]"), Feb. 27–28, 1981 ("saw Mark" on both days); Historical De-

partment Office Journal, Mar. 2, 1981 (Hofmann brought document to department "one week ago"); G. Homer Durham, Journal, Mar. 20, 1981 (Hofmann "brought it to Donald T. Schmidt Monday, February 23"); Melvin L. Bashore, Journal, Mar. 25, 1981 (Schmidt "knew of the document's existence as early as 20 Feb."); "Preliminary Hearing," 4:222–23 (Schmidt saw first a copy, later the original).

2. Jessee, *Personal Writings of Joseph Smith*, 565–66.

3. Ibid., 694. For detailed information on Bullock's scribal activities, see Simon, "Thomas Bullock as an Early Mormon Historian," 71–88.

4. Inez Smith Davis, *The Story of the Church*, 6th ed. (Independence, Mo.: Herald House, 1959), 362, 400–414, 450–53.

5. Roger D. Launius conveniently collects the reminiscences of these blessings in *Joseph Smith III: Pragmatic Prophet* (Urbana: University of Illinois Press, 1988), 9–10, 15–16, 27 nn. 35–36, 31–32, 46 n. 5. D. Michael Quinn describes difficulties with the reminiscences in "Joseph Smith III's 1844 Blessing and the Mormons of Utah," *John Whitmer Historical Association Journal* 1 (1981): 14–15, 21.

6. See, e.g., Reorganized Church of Jesus Christ of Latter Day Saints, *The Successor in the Prophetic Office and Presidency of the Church*, rev. ed. (Plano, Ill.: Herald Book and Job Office, n.d.); B. H. Roberts, *Succession in the Presidency of the Church of Jesus Christ of Latter-day Saints* (Salt Lake City: Deseret News, 1894), 49–85; Elbert A. Smith, *Corner Stones of the Utah Church* ([Lamoni, Iowa]: Reorganized Church of Jesus Christ of Latter Day Saints, [1920?]), 16–19; Heman C. Smith, *True Succession in Church Presidency of the Church of Jesus Christ of Latter Day Saints* (Lamoni, Iowa: Reorganized Church of Jesus Christ of Latter Day Saints, 1900), 36–66; Joseph F. Smith, Jr., *Origin of the "Reorganized" Church/The Question of Succession* (Salt Lake City: Skelton, 1907), 53–65.

7. Examples of goodwill and cooperation between the churches include "A S.L. Visitor," *Church News*, Mar. 18, 1967; "Document Copies Traded: Church, RLDS Exchange Historic Papers," *Church News*, Nov. 30, 1974; "It's a Time of Rebirth, Church Historians Told at Y. Conference," *Deseret News*, Apr. 12, 1975; "LDS, RLDS Plan Series," *Deseret News*, Oct. 20, 1978.

8. "Behind the Scenes," 1; "Preliminary Hearing," 4:162–63, 222–23; Donald T. Schmidt, Interview, Feb. 8, 1989; Susan Oman and Peggy Fletcher, "From the Editors," *Sunstone* 6, no. 2 (Mar.-Apr. 1981): 2.

9. Peter Crawley, "A Bibliography of the Church of Jesus Christ of Latter-day Saints in New York, Ohio, and Missouri," *Brigham Young University Studies* 12 (Summer 1972): 480–86; Jessee, Journal, Feb. 27, 1981 ("Don said he thought the Book of Commandments was too high a price").

10. Jessee, Journal, Feb. 20, 1981.

11. Jessee, Journal, Feb. 23, 1981; Jessee, *Personal Writings of Joseph Smith*, 691. Many portions of the Book of the Law of the Lord have been published or cited. See, e.g., Jessee, *Personal Writings of Joseph Smith*, 525–28, 530–37, 690–91; Allen, *Trials of Discipleship*, 118, 120; Andrew F. Ehat and Lyndon W. Cook, *The Words of Joseph Smith* (Provo, Utah: Religious

Studies Center, Brigham Young University, 1980), 61, 91 n. 3, 388 n. 2, 406 n. 5.

12. Francis M. Gibbons, Interviews, Apr. 6, Oct. 25, 1989; Francis M. Gibbons to Gordon B. Hinckley, Sept. 11, 1984; Doctrine and Covenants (1981) 26:2, 28:13, 107:22. To Gibbons's best recollection, this was the only meeting he ever had with Hofmann.

13. Richard P. Howard to Mark W. Hofmann, Mar. 9, 1981; "Behind the Scenes," 1. The archivist was L. Madelon Brunson.

14. Howard to Hofmann, Mar. 9, 1981; "Behind the Scenes," 6. The assistant commissioner was Grant McMurray.

15. Richard P. Howard, "The Joseph Smith III Blessing-Designation: The Story of the LDS-RLDS Exchange," *Saints Herald* 128 (1981): 220.

16. Howard to Hofmann, Mar. 9, 1981; "Behind the Scenes," 6.

17. Jessee, Journal, Feb. 26, 1981. Howard later said that Jessee's summary of what he said about the RLDS position on lineal descent was worded more strongly than the statement he actually made during the conversation. Richard P. Howard, Interview, June 21, 1990.

18. Jessee, Journal, Feb. 27, 1981; Durham, Journal, Mar. 20, 1981.

19. M[arjorie] G[older] to [Gordon B.] Hinckley, Feb. 27, 1981; Durham, Journal, Mar. 20, 1981; Jessee, Journal, Feb. 27, 1981. The other son mentioned in the phone message was David Hyrum Smith, who actually was not born until after his father's death. Regarding promises to David Hyrum Smith, see D. Michael Quinn, "The Mormon Succession Crisis of 1844," *Brigham Young University Studies* 16 (1976): 229–30; Quinn, "Joseph Smith III's 1844 Blessing," 16–17.

20. Jessee, Journal, Feb. 27, 1981; The Church of Jesus Christ of Latter-day Saints, *My Kingdom Shall Roll Forth*, 2d ed. (Salt Lake City: Church of Jesus Christ of Latter-day Saints, 1980), 10–15; Leonard J. Arrington and Ronald K. Esplin, "The Role of the Council of the Twelve during Brigham Young's Presidency of the Church of Jesus Christ of Latter-day Saints," Task Papers in LDS History, No. 31, Dec. 1979, 11–13, HDC.

21. Jessee, Journal, Feb. 27, 1981; Durham, Journal, Mar. 20, 1981; Donald T. Schmidt, Two-Page Memorandum of Events for Feb. 27, 28, Mar. 2, 3, 1981 (hereafter cited as Schmidt, Two-Page Memorandum).

22. Jessee, Journal, Feb. 27, 1981; Durham, Journal, Mar. 20, 1981; Schmidt, Two-Page Memorandum; Historical Department Office Journal, Mar. 2, 1981.

23. G. Homer Durham to Whom It May Concern, Mar. 4, 1981; Durham, Journal, Mar. 20, 1981; Schmidt, Two-Page Memorandum; Historical Department Office Journal, Mar. 2, 1981; Jessee, Interview, Feb. 10, 1989; Jessee, Journal, Feb. 27, 1981.

24. Schmidt, Two-Page Memorandum; Donald T. Schmidt, Telephone Note, [Feb. 27, 1981]; "Behind the Scenes," 6; Durham, Journal, Mar. 20, 1981; Schmidt, Interview, Feb. 8, 1989.

25. Schmidt, Two-Page Memorandum; "Preliminary Hearing," 4:224. Howard later observed that contrary to Hofmann's assertions, RLDS officials

did not offer to fly him to Independence. Howard also said he never even considered bringing a copy of A Book of Commandments with him when he came to Salt Lake City to meet Hofmann. Howard, Interview, June 21, 1990.

26. Schmidt, Two-Page Memorandum.

27. Schmidt, Two-Page Memorandum; Durham, Journal, Mar. 20, 1981.

28. Durham, Journal, Mar. 20, 1981; Jessee, Journal, Mar. 2, 1981.

29. Jessee, Journal, Mar. 2, 1981.

30. Buddy Youngreen, Interview, Feb. 17, 1989. Youngreen was present for Hofmann's 9:00 A.M. meeting with Howard; he overheard and recorded Jessee's statement.

31. Schmidt, Two-Page Memorandum; Durham to Whom It May Concern, Mar. 4, 1981; Durham, Journal, Mar. 20, 1981.

32. "Behind the Scenes," 7.

33. Youngreen, Interview, Feb. 17, 1989; Howard to Hofmann, Mar. 9, 1981. The LDS historian was D. Michael Quinn, who according to Youngreen's notes, felt the original blessing would have been in the hand of William Clayton. On the reasons for Bullock's dismissal from the Historian's Office, see sources cited in Simon, "Thomas Bullock," 88 n. 67.

34. Jessee, Journal, Mar. 2, 1981.

35. Howard to Hofmann, Mar. 9, 1981. The Kansas City handwriting expert was Charles C. Scott.

36. Historical Department Office Journal, Mar. 2, 1981; Earl E. Olson, "From the Memory of Earl E. Olson," 1988.

37. Schmidt, Two-Page Memorandum; Historical Department Acquisition Sheet 81–84; Historical Department Advisers Meeting Minutes, Mar. 11, 1981; [Gordon B. Hinckley], Memorandum, Mar. 11, 1981; *Mark Hofmann Interviews*, 296–98; "Preliminary Hearing," 4:164–65, 225–27.

38. Schmidt, Two-Page Memorandum.

39. G[older] to Hinckley, Feb. 27, 1981.

40. "Behind the Scenes," 7; Howard to Hofmann, Mar. 9, 1981; Howard, "Joseph Smith III Blessing-Designation," 220; Richard P. Howard, "The Joseph Smith III Document Is Authentic," *Saints Herald* 128 (1981): 374. The president of the RLDS Church with whom Howard met was Wallace B. Smith.

41. Howard, "Joseph Smith III Blessing-Designation," 220; Howard to Hofmann, Mar. 9, 1981; Howard, "Document Is Authentic," 374; "Behind the Scenes," 7. The reporter who called Howard was Lorie Winder, associate editor of *Sunstone* magazine.

42. Howard, "Joseph Smith III Blessing-Designation," 220; "Behind the Scenes," 7; Howard to Hofmann, Mar. 9, 1981.

43. Richard P. Howard to Donald T. Schmidt, Mar. 9, 1981.

44. Leonard J. Arrington to Gordon B. Hinckley, Mar. 9, 1981.

45. Historical Department Advisers Meeting Minutes, Mar. 11, 1981; Gordon B. Hinckley to Leonard J. Arrington, Mar. 12, 1981.

46. Glenn N. Rowe, Journal, Mar. 12, 16, 1981. According to Rowe's journal, the critic was Michael Marquardt. On Marquardt's knowledge of the Joseph Smith III blessing, see *Mark Hofmann Interviews*, 298–300.

47. Howard to Hofmann, Mar. 9, 1981; "Behind the Scenes," 7.

48. Howard to Hofmann, Mar. 9, 1981; Howard, "Joseph Smith III Blessing-Designation," 220. A reproduction of the receipt for the blessing copy Hofmann lent to Howard on March 2 is attached to Mark W. Hofmann to Richard P. Howard, Apr. 6, 1981.

49. Donald T. Schmidt, Three-Page Memorandum, Mar. 19, 1981.

50. Durham, Journal, Mar. 20, 1981.

51. Schmidt, Three-Page Memorandum, Mar. 19, 1981; G. Homer Durham to Gordon B. Hinckley, Mar. 16, 1981; Durham, Journal, Mar. 20, 1981.

52. Durham, Journal, Mar. 20, 1981; Schmidt, Three-Page Memorandum, Mar. 19, 1981.

53. Durham to Hinckley, Mar. 16, 1981; Durham, Journal, Mar. 20, 1981.

54. Earl E. Olson, "Phone call to Richard Howard, 12:20 P.M. 13 March 1981 by Earl E. Olson," 1981; Howard, "Joseph Smith III Blessing-Designation," 220; Durham to Hinckley, Mar. 16, 1981.

55. First Presidency, Minutes, Mar. 17, 1981. The other secretary present was D. Arthur Haycock.

56. First Presidency, Minutes, Mar. 17, 1981. As anticipated, the Tanners eventually did use the blessing document. See Jerald Tanner and Sandra Tanner, *Joseph Smith's Successor: An Important New Document Comes to Light* (Salt Lake City: Modern Microfilm, 1981); "Joseph as a Prophet," *Salt Lake City Messenger*, no. 46 (Oct. 1981): 9–11.

57. First Presidency, Minutes, Mar. 17, 1981.

58. Tanner, Journal, Mar. 17, 1981.

59. "Conditional Transmittal Agreement," Mar. 19, 1981.

60. Videotape, LDS-RLDS Press Conference, Mar. 19, 1981, HDC.

61. Howard, "Joseph Smith III Blessing-Designation," 231.

62. Bruce R. McConkie, "Answer to the Hoffman Document," attached to Bruce R. McConkie to [Gordon B. Hinckley], [Mar.? 1981].

63. *Official Report of the One Hundred Fifty-first Annual General Conference of the Church of Jesus Christ of Latter-day Saints* (Salt Lake City: Church of Jesus Christ of Latter-day Saints, 1981), 24–28; Gordon B. Hinckley, "The Joseph Smith III Document and the Keys of the Kingdom," *Ensign* 11 (May 1981): 20–22.

64. Renee Murray, "For Release Monday, May 18, 1981—10:00 A.M.," Press Release, Reorganized Church of Jesus Christ of Latter Day Saints; Donald T. Schmidt to Richard Howard, Mar. 24, 1981; Richard P. Howard to Donald T. Schmidt, Apr. 2, 28, May 15, 1981; Donald T. Schmidt to Grant McMurray, Apr. [day illegible], 1981; Howard, "Document Is Authentic," 374–75.

65. Albert W. Somerford to Richard P. Howard, Apr. 30, 1981; Howard, "Document Is Authentic," 374–75; James R. Dibowski to Richard P. Howard, May 7, 1981; Murray, "For Release Monday."

66. James R. Dibowski to Richard P. Howard, Apr. 11, May 7, 1981; Somerford to Howard, Apr. 30, 1981; Richard P. Howard to Donald T. Schmidt, May 15, 1981; Howard, "Document Is Authentic," 374–75; Reorganized Church of Jesus Christ of Latter Day Saints, *For He Shall Be My Successor*

([Independence, Mo.]: Reorganized Church of Jesus Christ of Latter Day Saints, 1981), [4–5].

67. Somerford to Howard, Apr. 30, 1981.

68. Skip Palenik to Richard P. Howard, May 15, 1981; Howard, "Document Is Authentic," 375; Reorganized Church, *For He Shall Be My Successor*, [5].

69. Howard to Schmidt, May 15, 1981; G. Homer Durham to Gordon B. Hinckley and Boyd K. Packer, May 19, 1981; Donald T. Schmidt to Richard P. Howard, June [day illegible], 1981.

70. Hofmann to Howard, Apr. 6, 1981.

71. Richard P. Howard to Mark Hofmann, Apr. 13, 1981.

72. Alan Bullock, Affidavit, Mar. 28, 1981; Howard to Schmidt, May 15, 1981; Jessee, Journal, Mar. 30, 1981; "Preliminary Hearing," 4:194–95, 5:5, 95–96; *Mark Hofmann Interviews*, 169. LDS Church Historical Department employee Ronald O. Barney recalled that Homer Durham asked him to try tracking down Alan Bullock in April 1981. He tried contacting several Bullock family members but was unsuccessful in locating the source for the Joseph Smith III blessing. Ron Barney to Rick Turley, June 1, 1990. Among those with whom Barney spoke was Albert S. Bullock of Salt Lake City and E. Gerald Bullock of Coalville, Utah, the community from which Hofmann said the document came. According to a report Barney made, Albert "said that he has given everything that he had to the historical department." Gerald, Barney noted, "is recovering from a heart attack and is just now getting up and about. He said that there is more material. He doesn't remember right off hand any specifics but he sounded like he might be quite cooperative." Barney asked Gerald if he could call later when he was feeling better, and the convalescing man agreed. Barney also found a reference in the church records to an Alan Lee Bullock who was born in Tacoma, Washington, and who had a father with the same name. Ronald O. Barney to Earl E. Olson, Apr. 14, 1981. A few months later before Barney got around to meeting with him, Gerald Bullock died. Barney to Turley, June 1, 1990. See also "Preliminary Hearing," 5:4–5; Schmidt, Interview, Feb. 8, 1989.

73. Hofmann to Howard, Apr. 6, 1981; Schmidt to Howard, June [day illegible], 1981; "Preliminary Hearing," 5:5; *Mark Hofmann Interviews*, 172.

74. Howard, "Document Is Authentic," 374–75.

75. Richard P. Howard, "Revisionist History and the Document Diggers," *Dialogue* 19 (Winter 1986): 65; Helen T. Gray, "Mormon Document Naming Smith Leader Is Ruled Authentic," *Kansas City Times*, May 16, 1981; "Museum Renovation Features Document," *Saints Herald* 128 (1981): 349.

76. Resolution G–4, in *Saints Herald* 129 (1982): 81; Office of the [RLDS] First Presidency, "A Transcript of the Legislative Sessions, the 1982 World Conference," Mar. 28 to Apr. 4, 1982, 265–68; Reorganized Church of Jesus Christ of Latter Day Saints, *World Conference Bulletin*, Apr. 4, 1982, 365; Reorganized Church of Jesus Christ of Latter Day Saints, *Book of Doctrine and Covenants* (Independence, Mo.: Herald House, 1984), appendix G. Howard, "Document Diggers," 67, notes that placement of a document in the historical

appendix of the RLDS Doctrine and Covenants "carries with it non-binding status, in terms of church policy and doctrine."

The action placing the blessing document in the appendix was later rescinded. Office of the [RLDS] First Presidency, "A Transcript of the Legislative Sessions, the 1988 World Conference," Apr. 9–17, 1988, 205; Reorganized Church of Jesus Christ of Latter Day Saints, *World Conference Bulletin,* Apr. 9, 1988, 240.

Chapter 4: On the Trail

1. Godfrey, Journal, Apr. 13, 1981. Jeffrey E. Keller, "Making a Buck off Church History," *7th East Press,* Sept. 28, 1982, quotes Hofmann as saying, "I made the transition from collector to dealer with the discovery of the Anthon manuscript."

2. See, e.g., Franklin D. Richards, Journal, May 12, 1880, HDC; Charles C. Richards, Address delivered in Hawthorne Ward, Sugar House Stake, Apr. 20, 1947, HDC.

3. Historical Department Advisers Meeting Minutes, June 12, 1981.

4. Dean C. Jessee, "The Original Book of Mormon Manuscript," *Brigham Young University Studies* 10 (Spring 1970): 264–65, 267–69; Margery W. Ward, ed., *Register of the Papers of Frederick Kesler (1816–1899)* (Salt Lake City: University of Utah Libraries, 1977), 1, 33–34, 44, 83.

5. Historical Department Advisers Meeting Minutes, June 12, 1981. Hofmann later said he sold the half page to another buyer and purposefully did not give church historians a copy because "of course, that would make the document less valuable." Keller, "Making a Buck off Church History"; see also "Hunting for LDS Documents: An Interview with Mark Hofmann," *Sunstone Review* 2, no. 9 (Sept. 1982): 17.

6. "A Report of the Historical Department of the Church of Jesus Christ of Latter-day Saints," Dec. 31, 1980; Donald T. Schmidt, Memorandum, Oct. 20, 1982 ("Hofmann would prefer to have items for trade [rather] than cash"); Donald T. Schmidt to Richard E. Turley, Jr., Apr. 26, 1991.

7. Historical Department, "Public Services Statistical Report for the Year 1981"; Schmidt, Interview, Feb. 8, 1989; Ronald O. Barney, Interview, Feb. 16, 1989.

8. "Brigham Young's Daily Transactions in Gold Dust," Ms 1234, box 75, fd. 4, HDC; Thomas Bullock, Journal, Dec. 28–31, 1848, Jan. 1–5, 7, 9–12, 15–19, 1849, HDC; History of the Church, Jan. 1849, Ms 100/102, vol. 19, 1, HDC; Hubert Howe Bancroft, *History of Utah* (San Francisco: History Co., 1890), 290–91; Feramorz Y. Fox, "Hard Money and Currency in Utah," *Deseret News,* Church Department, Aug. 17, 1940; Sheridan L. McGarry, *Mormon Money* (n.p.: American Numismatic Association, 1951), 12–13; Leonard J. Arrington, *Great Basin Kingdom* (Cambridge: Harvard University Press, 1958), 56; Donald H. Kagin, *Private Gold Coins and Patterns of the United States* (New York: Arco, 1981), 185–87.

9. [Gordon B. Hinckley], Memorandum, Sept. 4, 1981; *Deseret News 1982 Church Almanac* (Salt Lake City: Deseret News, 1981), 32–33.

10. [Hinckley], Memorandum, Sept. 4, 1981.

11. See Appendix, item 19.

12. [Hinckley], Memorandum, Sept. 4, 1981.

13. Francis M. Gibbons, Handwritten Note, inscribed on [Hinckley], Memorandum, Sept. 4, 1981; Tanner, Journal, Sept. 8, 1981; Romney, Journal, Sept. 8, 1981; Kimball, Journal, Sept. 4–6, 15, 1981.

14. Examples of criticism resulting from the Joseph Smith III blessing include Tanner and Tanner, *Joseph Smith's Successor;* "I Told You So!!" *Ex-Mormons for Jesus Newsletter,* Jan.-Apr. 1981, 2; "Proof of Mormon Error," *Utah Evangel* 28, no. 5 (May 1981): 1; "The Blessing Document," *Mormonism Research Ministry* 3, no. 7 (July 1981): 1–2.

In a speech candidly describing the challenges of serving as counselor to an ailing church president, Hinckley would later say, "We postpone action when we are not fully certain of our course and do not move forward until we have the blessing of our President and that assurance which comes from the Spirit of the Lord." *Official Report of the One Hundred Sixtieth Semiannual General Conference of the Church of Jesus Christ of Latter-day Saints* (Salt Lake City: Church of Jesus Christ of Latter-day Saints, 1991), 66; " 'In . . . Counsellors There Is Safety,' " *Ensign* 20 (Nov. 1990): 51.

15. Schmidt, Interview, Feb. 8, 1989. Schmidt later said that before he bought Hofmann's notes, he was aware of the ten-cent Spanish Fork Young Men's Co-op Institution scrip note pictured in Alvin E. Rust, *Mormon and Utah Coin and Currency* (Salt Lake City: Rust Rare Coin, 1984), 155, fig. 212, which, Schmidt recalled, had been in church possession for some time. On the history of the Spanish Fork Co-operative Institution, see LaNora P. Allred, *Spanish Fork: City on the Rio De Aguas Calientes* (Spanish Fork, Utah: J-Mart, 1981), 27–169 passim; "History of Spanish Fork," *Tullidge's Quarterly Magazine* 3 (Apr. 1884): 160–61.

16. Lyn Jacobs, "Reminiscences" (1986), 5–6, 14.

17. Jacobs, "Reminiscences," 25–26; "Preliminary Hearing," 4:179–86, 5:27, 40–55, 57, 99–101, 7:259–77; *Mark Hofmann Interviews,* 224, 227; Donald T. Schmidt, Telephone Interviews with Glenn N. Rowe, Mar. 30, 1989, Jan. 28, 1991; Brent F. Ashworth, Interview, Mar. 29, 1989; Emma Smith, comp., *A Collection of Sacred Hymns, for the Church of the Latter Day Saints* (Kirtland, Ohio: F. G. Williams, 1835). On the history of the first LDS hymnal, see Michael Hicks, *Mormonism and Music: A History* (Urbana: University of Illinois Press, 1989), 10–14, 19–20.

18. B. Ashworth, Interview, Mar. 29, 1989; "Preliminary Hearing," 9:177–78.

19. B. Ashworth, Interview, Mar. 29, 1989; *1988 Guinness Book of World Records* (Toronto: Bantam Books, 1988), 207.

20. B. Ashworth, Interview, Mar. 29, 1989; "Rare Photo Profits Utah Seller," *Salt Lake Tribune,* Aug. 15, 1982.

21. Brent F. Ashworth, "The Lucy Mack Smith Letter, 23 Jan 1829" (1983); B. Ashworth, Interview, Mar. 29, 1989.

22. Dean C. Jessee, "Lucy Mack Smith's 1829 Letter to Mary Smith Pierce," *Brigham Young University Studies* 22 (Fall 1982): 460–61.

23. B. Ashworth, "Lucy Mack Smith Letter." Jessee, "Lucy Mack Smith's 1829 Letter," 456–58, suggests additional reasons why the letter was significant in Mormon history.

24. B. Ashworth, "Lucy Mack Smith Letter"; "Preliminary Hearing," 9:180–83; B. Ashworth, Interview, Mar. 29, 1989.

25. Jessee, Journal, Apr. 28, Aug. 11, 1982.

26. B. Ashworth, "Lucy Mack Smith Letter."

27. Jessee, Journal, Aug. 19, 1982; B. Ashworth, "Lucy Mack Smith Letter."

28. Jessee, "Lucy Mack Smith's 1829 Letter," 456.

29. B. Ashworth, Interview, Mar. 29, 1989; B. Ashworth, "Lucy Mack Smith Letter."

30. Charlene Ashworth, Interview, Mar. 1, 1991; B. Ashworth, Interview, Mar. 29, 1989.

31. B. Ashworth, Interview, Mar. 29, 1989; B. Ashworth, "Lucy Mack Smith Letter"; C. Ashworth, Interview, Mar. 1, 1991.

32. B. Ashworth, Interview, Mar. 29, 1989; B. Ashworth, "Lucy Mack Smith Letter."

33. B. Ashworth, "Lucy Mack Smith Letter."

34. C. Ashworth, Interview, Mar. 1, 1991.

35. Brent F. Ashworth, Journal, Aug. 21, 1982; B. Ashworth, "Lucy Mack Smith Letter."

36. First Presidency, Minutes, Aug. 23, 1982; G. Homer Durham, Memorandum, Aug. 20, 1982; B. Ashworth, "Lucy Mack Smith Letter"; B. Ashworth, Interview, Mar. 29, 1989; Tanner, Journal, Aug. 23, 1982; Romney, Journal, Aug. 24, 1982; "Jubilance at Asian Temple Ceremonies," *Church News,* Sept. 4, 1982.

37. B. Ashworth, Journal, Aug. 23, 1982; B. Ashworth, Interview, Mar. 29, 1989; C. Ashworth, Interview, Mar. 1, 1991.

38. Audiotape, LDS Press Conference, Aug. 23, 1982; Historical Department Office Journal, Aug. 23, 1982.

39. Audiotape, LDS Press Conference, Aug. 23, 1982.

40. George Raine, "LDS Church Releases 1829 Smith Letter," *Salt Lake Tribune,* Aug. 24, 1982; see also George Raine, "New Letter Said to Back Founder of Mormonism," *New York Times,* Aug. 24, 1982.

41. "Hunting for LDS Documents," 16.

42. Keller, "Making a Buck off Church History."

43. *Official Report of the One Hundred Fifty-second Semiannual General Conference of the Church of Jesus Christ of Latter-day Saints* (Salt Lake City: Church of Jesus Christ of Latter-day Saints, 1983), 73–77; Boyd K. Packer, "Scriptures," *Ensign* 12 (Nov. 1982): 51–53.

44. "Martin Harris's 1873 Letter to Walter Conrad," *Brigham Young University Studies* 23 (Winter 1983): 114–15; "Letter Reaffirms His Testimony," *Church News*, Oct. 9, 1982; "The Coming Forth of the Book of Mormon," *Ensign* 13 (Dec. 1983): 45.

45. Durham, Journal, Oct. 4, 1982; "Martin Harris's 1873 Letter," 115; First Presidency, Minutes, Oct. 5, 1982.

46. Jerry P. Cahill, "Newly Discovered Letter Confirms Testimony of Book of Mormon Witness," Press Release, Church of Jesus Christ of Latter-day Saints, Oct. 5, 1982.

47. Videotape, LDS Press Conference, Oct. 5, 1982, HDC.

48. Historical Department Office Journal, Oct. 5, 1982; First Presidency, Minutes, Oct. 5, 1982.

49. Brent F. Ashworth to G. Homer Durham, Oct. 9, 1982; G. Homer Durham to Brent F. Ashworth, Oct. 5, 1982.

50. Historical Department Advisers Meeting Minutes, Oct. 13, 1982; Mark W. Hofmann to Gordon B. Hinckley, Oct. 15, 1982 ("I first offered this item to the Church last Monday"); Appendix, item 37; "Preliminary Hearing," 4:175–76.

51. Videotape, LDS Press Conference, Oct. 5, 1982.

52. Historical Department Advisers Meeting Minutes, Oct. 13, 1982.

53. Hofmann to Hinckley, Oct. 15, 1982.

54. First Presidency, Minutes, Oct. 19, 1982.

55. Schmidt, Memorandum, Oct. 20, 1982; Historical Department Office Journal, Oct. 19, 1982; Mark W. Hofmann, Invoice, Oct. 19, 1982; Corporation of the President of The Church of Jesus Christ of Latter-day Saints, check no. 5500C68526, drawn on Zions First National Bank, Salt Lake City, Utah, Oct. 20, 1982; Earl E. Olson, Journal, Oct. 21, 1982; "Preliminary Hearing," 4:177, 5:39; *Mark Hofmann Interviews*, 415–16. The other document Hofmann mentioned to Schmidt was the church's original articles of incorporation. Hofmann said he knew who owned the document and had made an offer to purchase it.

56. Historical Department Advisers Meeting Minutes, Nov. 24, 1982.

57. "An Agreement between Mark Hofmann and the Church of Jesus Christ of Latter-day Saints," Unexecuted Draft, attached to G. Homer Durham to Gordon B. Hinckley and Boyd K. Packer, Dec. 8, 1982; Schmidt, Interview, Feb. 8, 1989. Other sources mentioning Hofmann's plans to move to New York include B. Ashworth, Interview, Mar. 29, 1989; Jacobs, "Reminiscences," 17; Shannon Flynn, Interview with Bob Swehla, Mike Fierro, and Ken Farnsworth, Oct. 18, 1985.

58. Historical Department Advisers Meeting Minutes, Nov. 24, 1982.

59. Durham to Hinckley and Packer, Dec. 8, 1982.

60. Historical Department Advisers Meeting Minutes, Dec. 22, 1982.

61. Smith, *History of the Church* 1:17; Jessee, *Papers of Joseph Smith* 1:282; Jessee, *Personal Writings of Joseph Smith*, 207.

62. See, e.g., Smith, *History of the Church* 1:93; Jessee, *Papers of Joseph Smith* 1:257, 316; Bushman, *Joseph Smith*, 64–76. On Joseph Smith and money digging, see *Brigham Young University Studies* 24 (Fall 1984), which is devoted

to the matter. (The Fall 1984 issue of *Brigham Young University Studies* actually did not appear until May 1986.)

63. Appendix, item 39.

64. Gordon Hinckley offered the following comment on nineteenth-century folk magic in an address he gave at the October 1987 general conference: "I have no doubt there was folk magic practiced in those days. Without question there were superstitions and the superstitious. I suppose there was some of this in the days when the Savior walked on the earth. There is even some in this age of so-called enlightenment. For instance, some hotels and business buildings skip the numbering of floor thirteen. Does this mean there is something wrong with the building? Of course not. Or with the builders? No.

"Similarly, the fact that there were superstitions among the people in the days of Joseph Smith is no evidence whatever that the Church came of such superstition." *Official Report of the One Hundred Fifty-seventh Semiannual General Conference of the Church of Jesus Christ of Latter-day Saints* (Salt Lake City: Church of Jesus Christ of Latter-day Saints, 1988), 66; " 'Lord, Increase Our Faith,' " *Ensign* 17 (Nov. 1987): 52; see also "Expand Faith into Certainty, Pres. Hinckley Counsels," *Deseret News*, Oct. 5, 1987.

65. *Mark Hofmann Interviews*, 352–53; "Preliminary Hearing," 5:81.

66. Gibbons, Interview, Apr. 6, 1989; *Mark Hofmann Interviews*, 353–61; Church Administration Building Daily Visitor Log, Jan. 12, 1983; "Preliminary Hearing," 12:119; John Dart, "Letter Revealing Mormon Founder's Belief in Spirits, Occult Released," *Los Angeles Times*, May 11, 1985.

67. Francis M. Gibbons to Richard C. Edgley, Jan. 12, 1983; Gibbons, Interview, Apr. 6, 1989; Corporation of the President of The Church of Jesus Christ of Latter-day Saints, check no. 0905282, drawn on Zions First National Bank, Salt Lake City, Utah, Jan. 13, 1983; Mark W. Hofmann, Bill of Sale, Jan. 14, 1983; "Preliminary Hearing," 12:119; *Mark Hofmann Interviews*, 352, 354–58. Gordon Hinckley described the "almost overwhelming burden of responsibility" he felt during this period in " 'In . . . Counsellors There Is Safety,' " 50.

68. Donald T. Schmidt to G. Homer Durham, Mar. 1, 1983; Durham, Journal, 1983, pp. 42–43; "Preliminary Hearing," 4:172–73, 5:30–33; *Mark Hofmann Interviews*, 383, 386; Gordon B. Hinckley, Interview, Dec. 15, 1989.

69. First Presidency and Quorum of Twelve, Minutes, Mar. 3, 1983; Gibbons, Interview, Apr. 6, 1989.

70. Durham, Journal, 1983, p. 42; Mark W. Hofmann, Receipt, Mar. 4, 1983; First Presidency, Minutes, Mar. 7, 1983; "Preliminary Hearing," 12:119; *Mark Hofmann Interviews*, 372, 385–86. According to the receipt signed by Hofmann, he received "check No. 0905365 of The Church of Jesus Christ of Latter-day Saints, drawn on Zions First National Bank, Salt Lake City, Utah, in the amount of $25,000."

71. See Appendix.

Chapter 5: The Salamander Letter

1. Church Administration Building Daily Visitor Log, Jan. 3, 1984; Durham, Journal, 1984, p. 6; Jacobs, "Reminiscences," 20; "Preliminary Hearing," 5:81–83, 93–94, 7:238–45; Lyn R. Jacobs, Telephone Interview with Glenn N. Rowe, Apr. 25, 1989; Lyn R. Jacobs, Telephone Interview, Apr. 28, 1989; Appendix, item 434; Andrew Jenson, *Latter-day Saint Biographical Encyclopedia*, vol. 3 (Salt Lake City: Andrew Jenson History Co., 1920), 692–97.

2. Appendix, item 434.

3. Durham, Journal, 1984, p. 6; "Preliminary Hearing," 5:82–85, 7:243–45; Schmidt, Interview, Feb. 8, 1989; Jacobs, "Reminiscences," 20; Jacobs, Telephone Interview, Apr. 28, 1989; Donald T. Schmidt to Glenn N. Rowe, Nov. 19, 1988; Shannon Flynn, Interview, July 5, 1989; *Mark Hofmann Interviews*, 475–76. On the value of ten-dollar Mormon gold pieces, see "Top 10," *Latter-day Sentinel* (Utah ed.), May 17, 1989; "1849 Mormon 'Pure Gold' \$10," *Deseret News*, Apr. 16, 1989.

4. "Preliminary Hearing," 7:245–48; Jacobs, "Reminiscences," 21; Lyn Jacobs, Interview, Jan. 25, 1991; Church Administration Building Daily Visitor Log, Jan. 3, 1984.

5. "Preliminary Hearing," 7:248–49; Jacobs, "Reminiscences," 21.

6. B. Ashworth, Interviews, Mar. 29, May 3, 1989; *Mark Hofmann Interviews*, 449.

7. B. Ashworth, Interview, May 3, 1989; Howe, *Mormonism Unvailed*, 242.

8. B. Ashworth, Interview, May 3, 1989.

9. Ed Magnuson, "Hitler's Forged Diaries," *Time*, May 16, 1983, 36–47; Kenneth Rendell, "Cracking the Case," *Newsweek*, May 16, 1983, 58–59.

10. Schmidt, Interview, Feb. 8, 1989.

11. Olson, "From the Memory of Earl E. Olson"; Kenneth C. Farnsworth, Jr., Interview, Dec. 12, 1989, relying on Farnsworth's notes of interview with Donald T. Schmidt, Dec. 30, 1985; *Mark Hofmann Interviews*, 477–80.

12. Steven F. Christensen to G. Homer Durham, Jan. 9, 1984; G. Homer Durham to Steven F. Christensen, Jan. 13, 1984; Durham, Journal, 1984, 6; Steven F. Christensen to Gordon B. Hinckley, Feb. 24, 1984; Steven F. Christensen, Journal, June 28, 1985; "Preliminary Hearing," 7:251–58; Jacobs, "Reminiscences," 22–23; *Mark Hofmann Interviews*, 432, 469.

13. Jacobs, "Reminiscences," 22; "New Institute at Y. to Assume Role of Church History Division," *Church News*, July 5, 1980; "Historians Prepare for Move to New Institute at Y.," *Church News*, July 12, 1980; "Church History Institute Established," *Brigham Young University Today* 34 (Aug. 1980): 1; Arrington, "The Writing of Latter-day Saint History," 127.

14. Christensen to Durham, Jan. 9, 1984; Durham to Christensen, Jan. 13, 1984.

15. Durham to Christensen, Jan. 13, 1984.

16. Audiotape, "Utah Considered," KUER-FM (Salt Lake City), May 16, 1985, HDC (radio interview with Brent Metcalfe); Randy Rigby, Interview, Apr. 20, 1989; Joe Robertson, Interview, Aug. 15, 1989; *Mark Hofmann*

Interviews, 450, 485; "Man Fired from LDS Post Says He's Still Faithful," *Salt Lake Tribune*, Aug. 25, 1983. As noted in the *Tribune* article, "The church has a policy against releasing the reasons for termination of employees," and thus church officials were unable to present their views on Metcalfe's departure.

17. Jessee, Journal, Jan. 7, 9, 10, 11, 1984.

18. Jessee, Journal, Jan. 17, 1984.

19. Ronald W. Walker, Journal, Jan. 18, 1984, as quoted in Ronald W. Walker, "Joseph Smith: The Palmyra Seer," *Brigham Young University Studies* 24 (Fall 1984): 461.

20. Jessee, Journal, Jan. 19, 1984.

21. Historical Department Advisers Meeting Minutes, Jan. 25, 1984.

22. First Presidency and Quorum of Twelve, Minutes, Feb. 16, 1984.

23. Richard N. Ostling to [Steven F.] Christensen, Feb. 17, 1984.

24. George D. Smith, "Joseph Smith and the Book of Mormon," *Free Inquiry* 4, no. 1 (Winter 1983–84): 21–31.

25. Jessee, Journal, Feb. 19, 1984.

26. Christensen to Hinckley, Feb. 24, 1984. The Indiana dealer and "friend to anti-Mormons" were Rick Grunder and Michael Marquardt, respectively. Grunder, however, never obtained the copy he was seeking for his customer. A copy of the letter did end up in Idaho, but it was procured directly from Christensen. Also, Hofmann later acknowledged speaking to Marquardt himself about the letter. Jacobs, "Reminiscences," 23; *Mark Hofmann Interviews*, 480–84, 487–88; Rick Grunder, Telephone Interview, Nov. 29, 1989.

27. Christensen to Hinckley, Feb. 24, 1984.

28. Gordon B. Hinckley, Memorandum, Feb. 24, 1984. Christensen made the following note of the telephone call: "2/24/84 / Pres. Gordon B. Hinckley. *1:30 p.m.* / —Don't Cave in— / —This will not embarrass the Church—." One book about the Mark Hofmann case would misinterpret this note as being one that Christensen made to himself while preparing for what the book suggests was intended to be a face-to-face meeting between Christensen and Hinckley. "In late February," the book conjectures, "Christensen was *apparently scheduled* to meet with President Gordon B. Hinckley to discuss the [salamander] letter." After quoting Christensen's note, the book adds, "But in another note, Christensen implied that the *scheduled meeting* did not take place." Linda Sillitoe and Allen D. Roberts, *Salamander* (Salt Lake City: Signature Books, 1988), 284 (italics added).

29. Jerry P. Cahill to Richard P. Lindsay, Mar. 1, 1984.

30. Richard P. Lindsay to Gordon B. Hinckley, Mar. 2, 1984.

31. Gordon B. Hinckley, Statement on Martin Harris letter to W. W. Phelps, Mar. 2, 1984.

32. Gordon B. Hinckley, Signed Typewritten Note, added to bottom of copy of Hinckley, Statement, Mar. 2, 1984.

33. Jerry P. Cahill to Richard N. Ostling, Mar. 5, 1984.

34. Jerry P. Cahill to Richard P. Lindsay, Mar. 7, 1984; Richard P. Lindsay to Gordon B. Hinckley, Mar. 7, 1984. The church representative in New York was Stephen H. Coltrin.

35. "Moroni or Salamander? Reported Find of Letter by Book of Mormon Witness," *Salt Lake City Messenger*, no. 53 (Mar. 1984): 1, 4. The Tanners' article had already run by the time Christensen issued his March 7 release. Cecelia Warner, "The 'Martin Harris Letter': Fact, Fiction . . . Fate," *Sunstone* 10, no. 1 (1985): 50.

36. Steven F. Christensen, "Letter from Martin Harris to William W. Phelps Dated October 23, 1830," Press Release, Steven F. Christensen, Mar. 7, 1984.

37. News Broadcast, KSL-TV (Salt Lake City), Mar. 16, 1984, 6:00 P.M. The news anchor for the story was Dick Nourse; the religion specialist was Duane Cardall.

38. Schmidt, Interview, Feb. 8, 1989; Jacobs, "Reminiscences," 7-8; Appendix, items 427-32. On April 22, 1986, Jacobs was asked if he had traded a full series of Deseret Currency Association notes to the church for Hofmann. "I do not remember it being a full series," he answered. "I do remember, however, that a hundred and a fifty were in it but I don't remember it being a complete series. It might have been." "Preliminary Hearing," 7:278. Later, Jacobs recalled offering the church only the one-hundred-dollar note. Jacobs, Interview, Jan. 25, 1991.

39. Ronald W. Walker to Gordon B. Hinckley, Aug. 6, 1984; Gibbons, Interview, Apr. 6, 1989. The Tanners later wrote that "by September 1984 we had obtained a typed copy of the letter purportedly written by Joseph Smith to Josiah Stowell on June 18, 1825." See the Utah Lighthouse Ministry's advertisement for *Tracking the White Salamander* in *Salt Lake Tribune*, Mar. 9, 1986.

40. Jerry P. Cahill to Richard P. Lindsay, Aug. 21, 1984; Richard P. Lindsay to Gordon B. Hinckley, Aug. 21, 1984.

41. Lindsay to Hinckley, Aug. 21, 1984.

42. Richard P. Lindsay, Interview, May 5, 1989; Jerry P. Cahill, Telephone Interview, May 4, 1989.

43. First Presidency, Minutes, Aug. 23, 1984.

44. "Statement by President Gordon B. Hinckley," Aug. 23, 1984. Though not issued at the time, the statement was later incorporated into Jerry P. Cahill, "Church Releases Text of Presumed Letter of Joseph Smith to Josiah Stowell," Press Release, Church of Jesus Christ of Latter-day Saints, May 9, 1985.

45. John Dart, "Mormons Ponder 1830 Letter Altering Idealized Image of Joseph Smith," *Los Angeles Times*, Aug. 25, 1984.

46. Jan Shipps to Rick Turley, June 13, 1991.

47. John Dart, "Joseph Smith: His Image Is Threatened," *Salt Lake Tribune*, Aug. 27, 1984; "Occult Colors History of Mormon Founder," *San Jose Mercury News*, Aug. 26, 1984; John Dart, "The Mormons and the White Salamander," *International Herald Tribune*, Aug. 28, 1984; Thomas S. Monson to [Gordon B.] Hinckley, Aug. 29, 1984.

48. Steve Eaton, "Historians Testing Authenticity of Martin Harris Letter," *Salt Lake Tribune*, Sept. 2, 1984.

49. Neal A. Maxwell to Ezra Taft Benson and the Council of the Twelve, Sept. 5, 1984.

50. *Official Report of the One Hundred Fifty-fourth Semiannual General Conference of the Church of Jesus Christ of Latter-day Saints* (Salt Lake City: Church of Jesus Christ of Latter-day Saints, 1985), 11–12 (hereafter cited as *Conference Report* [Oct. 1984]); Neal A. Maxwell, " 'Out of Obscurity,' " *Ensign* 14 (Nov. 1984): 8–11.

51. *Conference Report* (Oct. 1984): 68–69; Gordon B. Hinckley, "The Cornerstones of Our Faith," *Ensign* 14 (Nov. 1984): 52.

52. *Conference Report* (Oct. 1984): 103–5; Bruce R. McConkie, "The Caravan Moves On," *Ensign* 14 (Nov. 1984): 84–85.

53. Steven F. Christensen to Gordon B. Hinckley, Oct. 16, 1984; "Preliminary Hearing," 1:243–44; 2:25–26.

54. Christensen to Hinckley, Oct. 16, 1984.

55. Ronald L. Knighton, Interview, Nov. 14, 1989; Rigby, Interview, Apr. 20, 1989. The friend mentioned was Knighton.

56. Steven F. Christensen, Unsigned Typed Note, Oct. 17, 1984.

57. Steven F. Christensen to Gordon B. Hinckley, Feb. 26, 1985.

58. Albert H. Lyter III to Steven F. Christensen, Feb. 13, 1985; "Preliminary Hearing," 7:35. Lyter's letter has been reproduced in full in Dean C. Jessee, "New Documents and Mormon Beginnings," *Brigham Young University Studies* 24 (Fall 1984): 424.

59. Christensen to Hinckley, Feb. 26, 1985.

60. Ibid. Christensen did not give details to Hinckley but apparently had been offered sixty thousand dollars for the letter. Christensen, Journal, June 28, 1985.

61. Gordon B. Hinckley, Memorandum, Mar. 1, 1985. The date of this telephone call is also established by a note Christensen penned on a copy of Christensen to Hinckley, Feb. 26, 1985: "Pres. Hinckley Called 3 days later & Confirmed Church Wanted letter. SC."

62. Though this volume bears a 1984 copyright date, publication problems delayed its mailing to around March 1985. See "Journal of Mormon History," *Mormon History Association Newsletter,* no. 56 (Nov. 1984): 1; "Volume 11 Forthcoming," *Mormon History Association Newsletter,* no. 57 (Mar. 1985): 3.

63. Marvin S. Hill, "Richard L. Bushman—Scholar and Apologist," *Journal of Mormon History* 11 (1984): 130, 132.

64. Church Administration Building Daily Visitor Log, Apr. 12, 1985; Christensen, Journal, June 28, 1985; First Presidency, Minutes, Apr. 12, 1985. The two secretaries present were D. Arthur Haycock and F. Michael Watson; the photographer was Eldon Linschoten.

65. Kenneth W. Rendell to Mark Hofmann, Mar. 20, 1985; First Presidency, Minutes, Apr. 12, 1985. Rendell's letter has been reproduced in full in Jessee, "New Documents and Mormon Beginnings," 422–23.

66. First Presidency, Minutes, Apr. 12, 1985.

67. Spencer W. Kimball, Marion G. Romney, and Gordon B. Hinckley to Steven F. Christensen, Apr. 18, 1985.

68. John L. Hart, "Letter Sheds Light on Religious Era," *Church News,* Apr. 28, 1985.

69. "Presidency Comments on Letter's Authenticity," *Church News,* Apr. 28, 1985.

70. Dawn Tracy, "LDS Church Publishes Controversial 1830 Letter," *Salt Lake Tribune,* Apr. 28, 1985.

71. Dawn Tracy, " 'Smith' Letter Seems to Have Disappeared from View," *Salt Lake Tribune,* Apr. 29, 1985.

72. See text accompanying notes 40–42.

73. Cahill, Telephone Interview, May 4, 1989; Richard P. Lindsay and Jerry P. Cahill, Interview, May 5, 1989.

74. Jerry P. Cahill to Will Fehr, May 3, 1985.

75. "LDS Church Has Purported Smith Letter," *Salt Lake Tribune,* May 6, 1985. A similar letter to the editor of the *Deseret News* was published the previous evening. Jerry P. Cahill, "Church Has Letter to Stowell," *Deseret News,* May 5, 1985.

76. George D. Smith, "Wrong Context," *Salt Lake Tribune,* May 6, 1985.

77. On the circumstances surrounding purchase of the letter, see chapter 4, text accompanying notes 61–67.

78. Cahill, "Church Releases Text"; Dawn Tracy, "Letter Linking Joseph Smith, Magic to Be Released," *Salt Lake Tribune,* May 10, 1985; "1825 Joseph Smith Letter Is Made Public," *Deseret News,* May 10, 1985; Marjorie Hyer, "Mormon Church Stirred by Founder's Letter," *Washington Post,* May 11, 1985; "Joseph Smith Letter of 1825 Is Released by First Presidency," *Church News,* May 12, 1985.

79. Dart, "Letter Revealing Mormon Founder's Belief." Cf. Charles Hamilton's letter to Sam Pennington, n.d., published in *Maine Antique Digest,* June 1987, 3-A, in which Hamilton explains how Hofmann overcame his initial objections to the letter.

80. Richard N. Ostling, "Challenging Mormonism's Roots," *Time,* May 20, 1985, 44. The article's byline includes the note "Reported by Christine Arrington/Salt Lake City."

81. Jerry P. Cahill to Henry Anatole Grunwald, May 16, 1985. *Time* deleted Ostling's and Arrington's names when it published Cahill's letter in its June 10, 1985, issue.

82. "Two BYU Scholars Defend 'Salamander' Letter," *Deseret News,* May 3, 1985; "BYU Scholars Defend Letter," *Ogden Standard-Examiner,* May 3, 1985; "Mormon Scholars Discuss Letter about Founder of Church," *New York Times,* May 5, 1985; Steve Eaton, "Mormon Research Beneficial to Church," *Salt Lake Tribune,* May 6, 1985.

Jessee's and Walker's papers were later edited and published as Dean C. Jessee, "New Documents and Mormon Beginnings," *Brigham Young University Studies* 24 (Fall 1984): 397–428, and Ronald W. Walker, "The Persisting

Idea of American Treasure Hunting," *Brigham Young University Studies* 24 (Fall 1984): 429–59.

83. George D. Smith, "A Response to the Papers of: Dean C. Jessee, Associate Professor of History, BYU; Ronald W. Walker, Associate Professor of History, BYU," Paper delivered at the Twelfth Annual Meeting of the Mormon History Association, Kansas City, Mo., May 2, 1985, 9–10.

84. Rhett S. James to Glen Rowe, Oct. 24, 1984; Rhett S. James to Steven F. Christensen, Oct. 26, Nov. 3, 1984; Rhett S. James, "Style and Historical Content Analysis of Known and Purported Martin Harris Correspondence and Interviews" (Logan, Utah, Jan. 28, 1985); "Author Says 'Folk Magic' Letter May Be a Forgery," *Deseret News*, May 17, 1985; "Computer Indicates Harris Letter a Forgery," *Ogden Standard-Examiner*, May 17, 1985; Ronald Vern Jackson, Untitled Statement (Issued on letterhead of Accelerated Indexing Systems International, Inc., North Salt Lake, Utah, May 17, 1985); "Bishop Says Salamander Letter Declared Genuine Too Soon," *Salt Lake Tribune*, May 20, 1985; "1830 Letter Linked to Mormons Called Fake," *Deseret News*, May 25, 1985.

The most cogent arguments against the authenticity of the letter appeared in Robert B. White, "The Salamander Letter and the Detection of Forgery" (Edmonton, Alberta, June 8, 1985). White's unpublished paper was forwarded to LDS headquarters by a church educational administrator. E. Dale LeBaron to Bryan Weston, June 11, 1985.

85. Jessee, "New Documents and Mormon Beginnings," 407–12.

86. Ibid., 399–400.

87. Ibid., 402, 404. In his journal for September 3, 1985, Jessee wrote, "I learned that Don Enders [a church Historical Department employee] visited Elw[y]n Doubleday, the collector who apparently sold the Harris letter to Lyn Jacobs. Doubleday is confident the Harris letter came from one of two collectors of long standing, both of whom are deceased now. It would be difficult to trace the letter beyond that." A few weeks later, Jessee recorded a telephone conversation he had with Doubleday: "He said he does not remember the 1830 letter *per se*; but is 95% certain it was in his possession and that he sold it for $25. Said he felt like a fool when he learned how much it had been sold for. The letter was part of a large Phelps family (Oliver Phelps) collection of postal covers he obtained when Royden H. Lownesbury died in March 1982. Lownesbury had bought a lot of material in the Ithaca-Syracuse area of New York in the late 1960s, 20–25,000 New York handstamped covers. The Phelps correspondence of which the Harris letter was a part came from another collector, Ableson, in Syracuse in 1970." Jessee, Journal, Oct. 23, 1985.

88. Jessee, "New Documents and Mormon Beginnings," 404–7.

89. Steven F. Christensen to Gordon B. Hinckley, May 22, 1985. See also "An Interesting Document," *Salt Lake Daily Tribune*, Apr. 23, 1880. Nearly a year and a half earlier, Christensen and Metcalfe had anticipated the eventual acquisition of the money-digging agreement. Four days after Christensen obtained the salamander letter, Dean Jessee wrote in his journal that Brent Metcalfe "also said that prior to the completion of the project they will probably

have the original of the 1825 money digging agreement signed by Joseph, Isaac Hale, and others." Jessee, Journal, Jan. 10, 1984.

90. Gordon B. Hinckley to Steven F. Christensen, May 28, 1985.

91. F. Mark McKiernan and Roger D. Launius, eds., *An Early Latter Day Saint History: The Book of John Whitmer* (Independence, Mo.: Herald House, 1980), 25, 56; Cannon and Cook, *Far West Record*, 2, 5; Doctrine and Covenants (1981), sec. 47; Smith, *History of the Church* 1:166.

92. On attempts to locate the Cowdery history, see the following items in the Richards Family Collection, HDC: Franklin D. Richards, Journal, Oct. 15, 1889, Sept. 27, 1890; Franklin D. Richards to George Schweich, Oct. 15, 1889, Sept. 27, 1890, Jan. 31, 1896; Franklin D. Richards to Andrew Jenson, Sept. 9, 1893. See also Andrew Jenson to Franklin D. Richards, Sept. 5, 14, 1893, Ms 5020, HDC. For examples of Cowdery records in church possession, see Jessee, "The Writing of Joseph Smith's History," 440, 442, 463.

93. Joseph Fielding Smith, "History and History Recorders," *Utah Genealogical and Historical Magazine* 16 (Apr. 1925): 56; Smith, *Church History and Modern Revelation*, vol. 1 (Salt Lake City: Deseret Book, 1953), 106; Smith, *Doctrines of Salvation*, vol. 2, comp. Bruce R. McConkie (Salt Lake City: Bookcraft, 1955): 201; Jerald Tanner and Sandra Tanner, *The Case against Mormonism*, vol. 1 (N.p., n.d.), 77; Tanner and Tanner, "Mormonism and Magic," *Salt Lake City Messenger*, no. 49 (Dec. 1982): 4; Tanner and Tanner, *Mormonism, Magic, and Masonry* (Salt Lake City: Utah Lighthouse Ministry, 1983), 43, 46; " 'Salamandergate,' " *Salt Lake City Messenger*, no. 57 (June 1985): 1 (mentioning 1961 date).

94. Christensen to Hinckley, Feb. 24, 1984.

95. Gibbons to Hinckley, Sept. 11, 1984.

96. G. Homer Durham to Gordon B. Hinckley, Oct. 17, 1984; Oliver Cowdery, "Oliver Cowdery's Sketch Book," Ms 3429, HDC.

97. Leonard J. Arrington, "Oliver Cowdery's Kirtland, Ohio, 'Sketch Book,' " *Brigham Young University Studies* 12 (Summer 1972): 410–26.

98. Ronald O. Barney, Journal, May 1985.

99. Videotape, "FirstNews," KUTV Channel 2 (Salt Lake City), May 13, 1985, HDC.

100. Rowe, Journal, May 14–15, 1985; Historical Department Office Journal, Mar. 6, Sept. 28, Oct. 1, 1984.

101. Dawn Tracy, "Researcher Says LDS History Disputes Golden Plates Story," *Salt Lake Tribune*, May 15, 1985.

102. Historical Department Office Journal, Sept. 24, Oct. 4, 12, 15, 24, Nov. 30, 1981, Jan. 21, Apr. 28, 1982, Jan. 9, 10, 1985.

103. Dean L. Larsen to Gordon B. Hinckley, May 15, 1985.

104. Barney, Journal, May 15, 1985.

105. Rowe, Journal, May 16, 1985.

106. Aura Lee Johnson, "Alvin Smith Found Gold Plates, according to Historical Account," *Universe* (Brigham Young University), May 16, 1985.

107. Audiotape, "Utah Considered," KUER-FM (Salt Lake City), May 16, 1985, HDC.

108. George D. Smith, "Release Cowdery History," *Salt Lake Tribune,* May 24, 1985.

109. Jerry P. Cahill to Richard P. Lindsay, May 24, 1985.

110. Wesley P. Walters to Gordon B. Hinckley, May 28, 1985.

111. Francis M. Gibbons to Wesley P. Walters, June 4, 1985.

112. John Dart, "Mormon Origins Challenged Anew over Purported History," *Los Angeles Times,* June 13, 1985.

113. Wesley P. Walters, Handwritten Notes, June 25, 1985; Kenneth C. Farnsworth, Jr., Interview, Dec. 12, 1989, relying on notes of Farnsworth's telephone interview with Wesley P. Walters, Jan. 6, 1986; Barney, Journal, July 1, 1985; Jessee, *Papers of Joseph Smith* 1:230-64.

114. Gibbons, Interview, Apr. 6, 1989; Walters, Handwritten Notes, June 25, 1985.

Chapter 6: The McLellin Collection

1. Cannon and Cook, *Far West Record,* 14, 19, 24-25, 70, 73, 101, 123, 160-61; Smith, *History of the Church* 1:220-21, 226, 2:124, 190-91, 218, 240, 356-57, 509, 3:31-32; Doctrine and Covenants (1981) 66:1-13, 75:6-8, 90:35; Smith, *Biographical Sketches of Joseph Smith,* 184-85; Andrew Jenson, *Latter-day Saint Biographical Encyclopedia,* vol. 1 (Salt Lake City: Andrew Jenson History Co., 1901), 280; Lyndon W. Cook, *The Revelations of the Prophet Joseph Smith* (Salt Lake City: Deseret Book, 1985), 106-7.

2. Smith, *History of the Church* 3:286-88; William E. McLellin to Samuel Bennett, Mar. 15, 1845, published in *Latter Day Saint's Messenger and Advocate* (Pittsburgh) 1 (1845): 150; William E. McLellin to Orson Pratt, Apr. 29, 1854, Ms 6237, HDC; William E. McLellin to Joseph Smith III, Jan. 10, 1861, Reorganized Church of Jesus Christ of Latter Day Saints Library-Archives, Independence, Mo. (hereafter cited as RLDS Library-Archives); William E. McLellin to Joseph Smith III, July 1872, RLDS Library-Archives; Joseph F. Smith to William E. McLellin, Feb. 1, Apr. 18, 1879, Ms 1325, box 5, fd. 2, HDC; John Lowe Butler, Journal, Ms 2952, fd. 2, p. 26, HDC; Robert M. Elvin, "Book of Commandments," *Saints' Herald* 31 (1884): 563; J. L. Traughber to A. T. Schroeder, July 11, 1901, Theodore Schroeder Papers, Rare Books and Manuscripts Division, New York Public Library, Astor, Lenox, and Tilden Foundations.

3. William E. McLellin to My Dear Old Friends, Oct. 21, 1870, RLDS Library-Archives; William E. McLellin to My Old Friends, Feb. 22, 1872, RLDS Library-Archives; Joseph Fielding Smith, comp., *Life of Joseph F. Smith: Sixth President of the Church of Jesus Christ of Latter-day Saints* (Salt Lake City: Deseret Book, 1969), 239-40.

4. Traughber to Schroeder, July 11, 1901.

5. J. L. Traughber to A. T. Schroeder, Aug. 21, 1901, Theodore Schroeder Papers, Rare Books and Manuscripts Division, New York Public Library, Astor, Lenox, and Tilden Foundations.

6. A. Burt Horsley, "Theodore Schroeder Mormon Antagonist—Content and Significance of the Theodore Schroeder Collection, New York Public Library," Ms 9030, fd. 1, no. 1, HDC; Linda Sillitoe, "More Questions Raised with the Discovery of McLellin Papers in Texas," *Deseret News*, Dec. 18, 1985. The scholar who tried contacting Traughber's descendants was D. Michael Quinn.

7. Smith, *Life of Joseph F. Smith*, 240. The historians who visited McLellin were Orson Pratt and Joseph F. Smith. Manuscript sources that mention the copyright incident are cited in Bruce G. Stewart, "Hiram Page: An Historical and Sociological Analysis of an Early Mormon Prototype" (M.A. thesis, Brigham Young University, 1987), 157–59. Published sources that mention it include W. Wyl [Wilhelm Ritter von Wymetal], *Joseph Smith the Prophet, His Family and His Friends* (Salt Lake City: Tribune Printing and Publishing, 1886), 310–11; David Whitmer, *An Address to All Believers in Christ* (Richmond, Mo.: David Whitmer, 1887), 31; R. B. Neal, *That Canada Revelation*, "Sword of Laban" Leaflets, 2d series, no. 10 (Grayson, Ky.: American Anti-Mormon Association, n.d.).

8. Roberts, *Comprehensive History* 1:163–66.

9. Francis M. Gibbons, *Joseph Smith: Martyr, Prophet of God* (Salt Lake City: Deseret Book, 1977), 74–75. See also Richard Lloyd Anderson, "I Have a Question," *Ensign* 17 (Apr. 1987): 24, which accepts the incident as authentic.

10. Jeffrey R. Holland, Notes Dictated by Telephone, Aug. 9, 1984. The Tanners had repeatedly cited the purported Canadian revelation as an example of failed prophecy. See, e.g., Jerald Tanner and Sandra Tanner, *The Changing World of Mormonism* (Chicago: Moody, 1980), 417–18.

11. Barney, Journal, Jan. 17, 1985.

12. Smith, *History of the Church* 2:236; Jay M. Todd, *The Saga of the Book of Abraham* (Salt Lake City: Deseret Book, 1969); Jay M. Todd, "Egyptian Papyri Rediscovered," *Improvement Era* 71 (Jan. 1968): 12–16; Doyle L. Green, "New Light on Joseph Smith's Egyptian Papyri," *Improvement Era* 71 (Feb. 1968): 40; Jay M. Todd, "Background of the Church Historian's Fragment," ibid. 40A–40I.

13. Rowe, Journal, Jan. 23, 1985. On Facsimile No. 2, see James R. Harris, "Understanding Facsimile 2 of the Book of Abraham," *The Tenth Annual Sidney B. Sperry Symposium: The Pearl of Great Price* (Provo, Utah: Brigham Young University, 1982), 83–104; Michael Dennis Rhodes, "A Translation and Commentary of the Joseph Smith Hypocephalus," *Brigham Young University Studies* 17 (Spring 1977): 259–74.

14. "Important Find?" *Salt Lake City Messenger*, no. 55 (Jan. 1985): 15.

15. B. Ashworth, Interview, Mar. 29, 1989; Todd, Interview, May 5, 1989. In November 1983, the Tanners had noted that they had heard a rumor about a purported copy of the 116 pages but had not had an opportunity to examine the copy. "Lehi's Lost Book," *Salt Lake City Messenger*, no. 52 (Nov. 1983): 8–9.

16. B. Ashworth, Interview, Mar. 29, 1989.

17. Richard P. Lindsay to Special Affairs Committee, June 3, 1985; *Deseret News 1991–92 Church Almanac* (Salt Lake City: Deseret News, 1990), 17.

18. Lindsay to Special Affairs Committee, June 3, 1985. The reporter was Dawn Tracy of the *Salt Lake Tribune.*

19. Kathie Andrus, "Summary of Telephone Conversations between Alvin Rust and Kathie Andrus, June 11, 1985" (n.d.).

20. Alvin E. Rust to Gordon B. Hinckley, June 11, 1985.

21. Gordon B. Hinckley, Memorandum, June 12, 1985; Church Administration Building Visitor Introduction Slip, June 12, 1985.

22. See Justin G. Schiller, " 'In the Beginning . . . ': A Chronology of the 'Oath of a Freeman' Document as Offered by Schiller-Wapner," in *The Judgment of Experts*, ed. James Gilreath (Worcester, Mass.: American Antiquarian Society, 1991), 8–13; James Gilreath, "The 'Oath of a Freeman' and the Library of Congress: An Ambiguous First Impression and an Elusive Finish," ibid., 14–24; Gilreath, "Schiller-Wapner Galleries Offers the 'Oath' to the Library of Congress," ibid., 58–61; "Excerpts about the 'Oath' from the 'Mark Hofmann Interviews,' with the Office of the Salt Lake County Attorney," ibid., 190–269. As these sources explain, the Library of Congress had examined the *Oath* but had returned it to Wapner on June 14, 1985.

23. Hinckley, Memorandum, June 12, 1985.

24. First Presidency and Quorum of Twelve, Minutes, June 13, 1985.

25. Barney, Journal, June 25, 1985.

26. Christensen, Journal, June 28, 1985.

27. Christensen, Journal, June 28, 1985; "Preliminary Hearing," 1:240–42, 2:16–21, 26–27, 40–46, 6:164; Rigby, Interview, Apr. 20, 1989.

28. *Deseret News 1985 Church Almanac* (Salt Lake City: Deseret News, 1984), 31; "Preliminary Hearing," 2:27–28, 6:128, 158; Hugh W. Pinnock, Interview, Oct. 14, 1988.

29. Christensen, Journal, June 28, 1985; "Statement by Elder Hugh W. Pinnock," Press Release, Church of Jesus Christ of Latter-day Saints, Oct. 21, 1985; "Preliminary Hearing," 6:130, 133, 159, 165.

30. Christensen, Journal, June 28, 1985; Hugh W. Pinnock, Journal, June 28, 1985; "Preliminary Hearing," 6:131. *Salamander* observes, "For their part, neither Walters nor Smith knew anything but rumors about the McLellin collection," 329.

31. Christensen, Journal, June 28, 1985; Pinnock, Journal, June 28, 1985; "Preliminary Hearing," 6:130.

32. Christensen, Journal, June 28, 1985; Pinnock, Journal, June 28, 1985.

33. Dallin H. Oaks, Statement at LDS Press Conference, Oct. 23, 1985, Videotape, HDC (hereafter cited as Oaks, Statement, Oct. 23, 1985); "Preliminary Hearing," 6:133–34; Michael P. George, Handwritten Notes of Interview with Hugh W. Pinnock, Dec. 6, 1985.

34. Oaks, Statement, Oct. 23, 1985; "Preliminary Hearing," 6:134.

35. Oaks, Statement, Oct. 23, 1985.

36. Christensen, Journal, June 28, 1985; Pinnock, Journal, June 28, 1985; "Statement by Elder Hugh W. Pinnock"; "Preliminary Hearing," 6:129, 134–35, 158–59, 165–66, 179, 193; George, Handwritten Notes, Dec. 6, 1985.

37. Christensen, Journal, June 28, 1985; Pinnock, Handwritten Note on photocopy of Christensen, Journal, June 28, 1985; Pinnock, Journal, June 28, 1985.

38. Christensen, Journal, June 28, 1985; First Interstate Bank of Utah, N.A., "Floating Rate Promissory Note," signed by Mark W. Hofmann, June 28, 1985; "Preliminary Hearing," 6:167, 193.

39. Dawn Tracy, "Ancient Mormon Manuscript Found, Sold in Texas," *Salt Lake Tribune,* July 6, 1985; see also "Book of Abraham Papyrus Piece Located and Sold, Collector Says," *Deseret News,* July 7, 1985. Christensen read Tracy's article and put a copy in his journal with the note, "This is the collection referenced in my Journal Notes of June 28, 1985. Needless to say there are errors in the article." Christensen, Journal, page following entry of June 28, 1985.

40. Hugh W. Pinnock, Telephone Note, [July 11, 1985]. Despite Hofmann's assertions, Smith had heard only rumors about the McLellin collection. See note 30.

41. Pinnock, Journal, July 11, 1985; Hugh W. Pinnock, Interview with FBI, Oct. 17, 1985; "Preliminary Hearing," 6:136–37.

42. Pinnock, Journal, July 12, 1985; "Preliminary Hearing," 6:137–39, 191–92; Church Administration Building Daily Visitor Log, July 12, 1985; George, Handwritten Notes, Dec. 6, 1985.

43. "McLellin Collection," *Salt Lake City Messenger,* no. 58 (Aug. 1985): 9–11.

44. Pinnock, Journal, Aug. 26, 1985; Pinnock, Interview with FBI, Oct. 17, 1985; "Preliminary Hearing," 6:140–42.

45. Steven F. Christensen to Mark Hofmann, Aug. 26, 1985.

46. Pinnock, Journal, Aug. 28–30, Sept. 4, 6, 11, 1985; "Preliminary Hearing," 2:20–21, 45–46, 6:162–64, 188–89; Pinnock, Interview, Oct. 14, 1988; Rigby, Interview, Apr. 20, 1989.

47. "Preliminary Hearing," 6:168–72.

48. Barney, Journal, Aug. 28, 1985.

49. "Preliminary Hearing," 7:173–76, 204–7; Curt A. Bench, Interview, May 2, 1989. Nathan Harris was Martin's father. Madge Harris Tuckett and Belle Harris Wilson, *The Martin Harris Story* (Provo, Utah: Vintage Books, 1983), 178.

50. Curt A. Bench, Journal, Sept. 11, 1985; "Preliminary Hearing," 7:176–79, 207–9; Bench, Interview, May 2, 1989. The handwriting to which Hofmann referred was reproduced in Jessee, "New Documents and Mormon Beginnings," 428.

51. Barney, Journal, Sept. 11, 1985.

52. Jessee, Journal, Sept. 11–12, Oct. 21, 1985. The manager of acquisitions was Larry W. Draper. Jessee continued tracing the provenance of the volume. He reported his findings in Jessee, "New Documents and Mormon Beginnings," 406–7.

53. "The Salamander Letter," *Salt Lake City Messenger,* no. 55 (Jan. 1985): 1–2.

54. Pinnock, Journal, Sept. 11, 13, 1985; Pinnock, Interview with FBI, Oct. 17, 1985; "Preliminary Hearing," 6:140–43, 179; *Mark Hofmann Interviews,* 403.

55. Pinnock, Journal, Sept. 13, 1985; "Preliminary Hearing," 6:142.

56. Bench, Journal, Sept. 14, 1985; "Preliminary Hearing," 7:179–80, 209–10, 8:38–39, 66–67; Bench, Interview, May 2, 1989. Bench's supervisor was Ronald A. Millett.

57. Bench, Journal, Sept. 14, 1985; Bench, Interview, May 2, 1989; "Preliminary Hearing," 7:179–80, 184–87, 191, 210–11, 214, 218.

58. Bench, Journal, Sept. 14, 1985; "Preliminary Hearing," 5:199–204, 207, 210–13, 7:200–204, 223–36, 9:184–90, 202–11; *Mark Hofmann Interviews,* 387–406, 432, 516–17; B. Ashworth, Interview, Mar. 29, 1989; Bench, Interview, May 2, 1989. The Dunham letter was published in full in Jessee, *Personal Writings of Joseph Smith,* 616–18.

Referring to the Dunham letter, Hofmann reportedly wrote to Marks, "I cannot read it without feeling the helpless dispair of a man who knew that he was soon to die but who was not resigned to his fate. What a sad day in the history of the Church!" Terry Green, "Is It Joseph's Last Written Message?" *Latter-day Sentinel* (Arizona), Jan. 27, 1984. See also *Mark Hofmann Interviews,* 395–97.

59. Bench, Journal, Sept. 14, 1985; Bench, Interview, May 2, 1989; "Preliminary Hearing," 7:191.

60. Bench, Journal, Sept. 14, 1985; "Preliminary Hearing," 7:218; Bench, Interview, May 2, 1989.

61. Bench, Journal, Sept. 19, Oct. 16, 1985; Bench, Interviews, May 2, 1989, Sept. 7, 1990; "Preliminary Hearing," 7:181–83, 211–12.

62. "Preliminary Hearing," 7:183–84, 219–20; Bench, Journal, Oct. 16, 1985.

63. Pinnock, Journal, Sept. 24, 1985; Hugh W. Pinnock, Interview, May 16, 1989.

64. Bench, Journal, Sept. 24, 1985; "Preliminary Hearing," 7:187–89; Bench, Interview, May 2, 1989.

65. Bench, Journal, Sept. 24, 1985; "Preliminary Hearing," 6:180, 7:187–90, 214, 216–17; Bench, Interview, May 2, 1989.

66. "Preliminary Hearing," 7:189–92, 215–17; Bench, Interview, May 2, 1989; Bench, Journal, Sept. 24, 1985.

67. Gordon B. Hinckley, Handwritten Chronology, apparently prepared sometime between Dec. 9, 1985, and Apr. 14, 1986 (hereafter cited as Post-Bombing Chronology); Church Administration Building Daily Visitor Log, Sept. 26, 1985; J. Martell Bird, Journal, Sept. 26–27, 1985.

68. Pamela T. Greenwood to Mark W. Hofmann, Sept. 27, 1985.

69. Historical Department Administration Meeting Minutes, Oct. 2, 1985; Glenn N. Rowe, Untitled Note, Oct.-Nov. 1985, filed with *The Book of Common Prayer;* "Preliminary Hearing," 5:226–31, 6:9–11, 45–46, 96–97; Appendix, item 437. For an example of a canceled, five-cent Bishop's General Store House note, see Rust, *Mormon and Utah Coin and Currency,* 193, fig. 259.

70. "Preliminary Hearing," 6:143; Pinnock, Journal, Oct. 3, 1985; Randy Rigby, Journal, Oct. 4, 1985; George, Handwritten Notes, Dec. 6, 1985; Kenneth C. Farnsworth, Jr., Interviews, Sept. 8, Dec. 5, 1989 (citing Terri Christensen).

71. Hugh W. Pinnock, Handwritten Notes of a Meeting with Mark W. Hofmann and Steven F. Christensen, Oct. 3, 1985, 10:37 P.M.; "Preliminary Hearing," 6:143–45, 147, 181–82. The Library of Congress had returned the *Oath* to Hofmann's agents in mid-June. Gilreath, "Schiller-Wapner Galleries Offers the 'Oath,' " 61. The doctor to whom Hofmann referred was orthodontist Ralph Bailey, who had lent Hofmann ninety thousand dollars. "Preliminary Hearing," 5:127–28.

72. Pinnock, Handwritten Notes, Oct. 3, 1985; Hugh W. Pinnock, Notes Prepared for LDS Press Conference, Oct. 23, 1985; George, Handwritten Notes, Dec. 6, 1985; "Preliminary Hearing," 6:143–44, 146, 156–57. The American Antiquarian Society had offered $250,000 for the *Oath* but had returned the document to Hofmann's agents on September 11, 1985, after the agents rejected the offer. Marcus A. McCorison, "Found at Last? The 'Oath of a Freeman,' " the End of Innocence, and the American Antiquarian Society," in *The Judgment of Experts*, 69; McCorison, "The Routine Handling of Forgeries in Research Libraries: Or, Can Dishonesty Ever Be Routine?" in *Forged Documents: Proceedings of the 1989 Houston Conference*, ed. Pat Bozeman (New Castle, Del.: Oak Knoll Books, 1990), 49, 52.

Pinnock recorded that the half interest in the *Oath* was "going to be sold to Randolph Schlagel." Pinnock, Handwritten Notes, Oct. 3, 1985. Pinnock later testified that Hofmann "mentioned a Randolph or Rudolph Schlagle, or a name like that." "Preliminary Hearing," 6:144. Investigators later concluded that the name was a pseudonym for Justin Schiller, one of Hofmann's agents for selling the *Oath*. Farnsworth, Interview, Dec. 5, 1989; George, Handwritten Notes, Dec. 6, 1985. See also *Mark Hofmann Interviews*, 276–77, 366; Schiller, " 'In the Beginning,' " 10, 12; Kenneth C. Farnsworth, Jr., "The Investigation of the 1985 Mark Hofmann Forgery of the 'Oath of a Freeman,' " in *The Judgment of Experts*, 133.

73. George, Handwritten Notes, Dec. 6, 1985; Pinnock, Interview, Oct. 14, 1988; "Preliminary Hearing," 4:133–35, 151–52, 6:146–47, 177, 192–93; S. Flynn, Interview, July 5, 1989.

74. Pinnock, Handwritten Notes, Oct. 3, 1985; Pinnock, Journal, Oct. 4, 1985; Pinnock, Interview with FBI, Oct. 17, 1985; "Preliminary Hearing," 6:143–48, 177–78, 183; *Mark Hofmann Interviews*, 276–78.

75. Dallin H. Oaks, Handwritten Notes, Oct. 4, 1985.

76. Oaks, Statement, Oct. 23, 1985; "Preliminary Hearing," 6:148.

77. David E. Sorensen, Memorandum, July 22, 1986; George, Handwritten Notes, Dec. 6, 1985; "Preliminary Hearing," 6:148–49, 184–85; David E. Sorensen, Interview, Mar. 1, 1989.

78. D. Sorensen, Memorandum, July 22, 1986; D. Sorensen, Interview, Mar. 1, 1989.

79. Ibid.

80. "Preliminary Hearing," 6:149, 186; D. Sorensen, Interview, Mar. 1, 1989.

81. D. Sorensen, Memorandum, July 22, 1986; D. Sorensen, Interview, Mar. 1, 1989.

82. Pinnock, Journal, Oct. 4, 1985; "Preliminary Hearing," 6:186–87.

83. Rigby, Interview, Apr. 20, 1989; Rigby, Journal, Oct. 4, 1985. Rigby's journal records Christensen as saying that he had been meeting with Gordon Hinckley, Dallin Oaks, and Hugh Pinnock. The other contemporaneous evidence in the case, however, shows that Christensen met only with Pinnock, who earlier that day had gotten a response from Hinckley and Oaks about whether to have the church or one of his friends buy the McLellin collection. See text accompanying notes 74–76, 82.

84. Rigby, Interview, Apr. 20, 1989; Rigby, Journal, Oct. 4, 1989.

85. Hugh W. Pinnock to Dallin H. Oaks, Nov. 2, 1987; Pinnock, Interviews, Oct. 14, 1988, May 16, 1989; "Preliminary Hearing," 6:188–89. Pinnock was unable to find a buyer for the book collection.

86. Rigby, Interview, Apr. 20, 1989.

87. Christensen, Journal, June 28, 1985; Hugh W. Pinnock, Handwritten Notes made in 1986 on copy of Christensen, Journal, June 28, 1985.

88. Rigby, Interview, Apr. 20, 1989.

89. Rigby, Journal, Oct. 4, 1985; Pinnock, Interview, Feb. 15, 1989.

90. Telephone Messages for [Hugh W. Pinnock], Oct. 4, 1985, 3:31 and 4:40 P.M. The secretary who took the messages was Geneene Brady.

91. Dallin H. Oaks, Interview, Feb. 24, 1989; D. Sorensen, Memorandum, July 22, 1986.

92. D. Sorensen, Memorandum, July 22, 1986; D. Sorensen, Interview, Mar. 1, 1989; Dallin H. Oaks, Interviews, Oct. 7, 1988, Feb. 24, 1989.

93. D. Sorensen, Memorandum, July 22, 1986; D. Sorensen, Interview, Mar. 1, 1989.

94. Terri Christensen, Interview, Apr. 20, 1989.

95. Mike Carter, "McLellin Mystery Unravels a Bit," *Salt Lake Tribune*, Oct. 25, 1985.

96. D. Sorensen, Memorandum, July 22, 1986; Dallin H. Oaks to Richard E. Turley, May 26, 1989; David E. West, Interview, Apr. 19, 1989.

97. West, Interview, Apr. 19, 1989; Carter, "McLellin Mystery Unravels a Bit."

98. West, Interview, Apr. 19, 1989.

99. Pinnock, Journal, Oct. 7, 1985.

100. Glenn Rowe to [Dean L.] Larsen, Mar. 21, 1985; Bird, Journal, Oct. 29–30, 1985; Ronald D. Francis, Memoranda, Oct. 30, 31, 1985; Rowe, Journal, Feb. 5, Mar. 18, 20, 1985. George Smith maintains he did not borrow the items from Christensen. George Smith to Elizabeth G. Dulany, May 29, 1992.

101. George, Handwritten Notes, Dec. 6, 1985; Pinnock, Journal, Oct. 8, 1985; "Preliminary Hearing," 6:197–200; Richard W. Forbes, Interview, July 20, 1989; Kenneth C. Farnsworth, Jr., Interviews, Sept. 8, Oct. 6, 1989.

102. Pinnock, Journal, Oct. 7, 1985.

103. Oaks to Turley, May 26, 1989.

104. "Bill of Sale and Representations and Warranties," Unexecuted Draft, Oct. 7, 1985; Oaks, Interviews, Oct. 7, 1988, Feb. 24, Nov. 8, 1989. Under the exceptions to the warranty on no copies, someone subsequently typed in a description of the Spalding-Rigdon document Hofmann had allowed Pinnock to copy. The typeface of the description differs from that of the rest of the bill of sale but is similar to the typeface of Steve Christensen's journal.

105. Pinnock, Journal, Oct. 7, 1985; George, Handwritten Notes, Dec. 6, 1985; "Preliminary Hearing," 6:145, 150.

106. D. Sorensen, Interview, Mar. 1, 1989; Pinnock, Journal, Oct. 8, 1985; D. Sorensen, Memorandum, July 22, 1986; Kenneth C. Farnsworth, Jr., Interview, Oct. 6, 1989, relying on Steven F. Christensen's calendar for Oct. 8, 1985.

107. D. Sorensen, Interview, Mar. 1, 1989; Pinnock, Journal, Oct. 8, 1985; D. Sorensen, Memorandum, July 22, 1986.

108. Telephone Messages for [Hugh W. Pinnock], Oct. 9, 1985; Pinnock, Journal, Oct. 9, 1985; Church Administration Building Daily Visitor Log, Oct. 9, 1985; Church Administration Building Visitor Introduction Slip, Oct. 9, 1985.

109. Pinnock, Journal, Oct. 9–10, 1985; Bird, Journal, Oct. 29, Nov. 1, 1985.

110. Pinnock, Journal, Oct. 10, 1985; George, Handwritten Notes, Dec. 6, 1985; "Preliminary Hearing," 6:172, 183–84. The investiture noted was that of Charles H. Dick, who was installed as president of Westminster College in Salt Lake City on October 19, 1985. Peter Scarlet, "Westminster College Installs New President," Salt Lake Tribune, Oct. 20, 1985.

111. George, Handwritten Notes, Dec. 6, 1985.

112. West, Interview, Apr. 19, 1989.

113. Ibid.; David C. West to Whom It May Concern, Oct. 10, 1985.

114. Pinnock, Journal, Oct. 11, 1985; Church Administration Building Daily Visitor Log, Oct. 11, 1985; S. Flynn, Interview, July 5, 1989.

115. Hinckley, Post-Bombing Chronology; Gordon B. Hinckley, Statement at LDS Press Conference, Oct. 23, 1985, Videotape, HDC (hereafter cited as Hinckley, Statement, Oct. 23, 1985); Gordon B. Hinckley, Memorandum, May 6, 1986.

116. Telephone Message for [Hugh W. Pinnock], Oct. 11, 1985; Pinnock, Journal, Oct. 11, 1985; "Preliminary Hearing," 6:151.

117. Pinnock, Journal, Oct. 11, 1985; George, Handwritten Notes, Dec. 6, 1985; "Preliminary Hearing," 6:151, 187–88.

118. Dallin H. Oaks, Interview with FBI, Oct. 16, 1985; "Preliminary Hearing," 6:151; West, Interview, Apr. 19, 1989. Randy Rigby understood the deal was to close Wednesday. Rigby, Interview, Apr. 20, 1989.

Chapter 7: The Bombings

1. Telephone Message for [Hugh W. Pinnock], Oct. 15, 1985; Pinnock, Journal, Oct. 15, 1985; Pinnock, Interview, Feb. 15, 1989; Geneene Brady, Telephone Interview, Sept. 12, 1989.

2. Rigby, Interview, Apr. 20, 1989.

3. Hugh W. Pinnock, Handwritten Notes written on telephone message, Oct. 15, 1985; Pinnock, Journal, Oct. 15, 1985; Jerry Spangler, "Booby-Trapped Bombs Claim Two in S.L. Area," *Deseret News*, Oct. 15, 1985; Pinnock, Interview, Feb. 15, 1989.

4. Hugh W. Pinnock, Interview, Feb. 15, 1989; Rigby, Interview, Apr. 20, 1989; Max B. Knudson, "Bombings Punctuate Financial Firm's Troubles," *Deseret News*, Oct. 16, 1985. Gary Sheets would later say that CFS's "biggest problem" was that it had received "a negative audited financial statement . . . , which, in the syndication business, is a very serious thing," in June 1985. "And so I would say that became common knowledge with the employees and certain people in the community along in June or July of 1985." "Preliminary Hearing," 2:46.

5. Pinnock, Journal, Oct. 15, 1985; Pinnock, Interview, Feb. 15, 1989.

6. Oaks, Interview, Feb. 24, 1989; Pinnock, Journal, Oct. 15, 1985; Telephone Message for [Hugh W. Pinnock], Oct. 15, 1985.

7. Pinnock, Interview, Feb. 15, 1989; Pinnock, Journal, Oct. 15, 1985; Pinnock, Interview with FBI, Oct. 17, 1985.

8. Brady, Telephone Interview, Sept. 12, 1989. Brady did not mention who the long-time friend was.

9. Pinnock, Interview, Feb. 15, 1989; Brady, Telephone Interview, Sept. 12, 1989. The funeral Pinnock attended was for Euleta W. Burton, who passed away on October 11, 1985. See obituary in *Salt Lake Tribune*, Oct. 13, 1985.

10. Pinnock, Journal, Oct. 15, 1985; Pinnock, Interview, Feb. 15, 1989. The local church leader was David A. Burton, a counselor in the presidency of the Salt Lake Holladay South Stake. *Directory of General Authorities and Officers, 1986* (Salt Lake City: Church of Jesus Christ of Latter-day Saints, 1984), 108.

11. Mark H. Burton to Ron Francis, Dec. 6, 1985; Church Administration Building Daily Visitor Log, Oct. 15, 1985; Brady, Telephone Interview, Sept. 12, 1989; Virginia Archer, Telephone Interview, Sept. 13, 1989; Dallin H. Oaks, Memorandum, Oct. 22, 1985; Oaks, Interview, Feb. 24, 1989.

12. Oaks, Memorandum, Oct. 22, 1985; Archer, Telephone Interview, Sept. 13, 1989.

13. Oaks, Memorandum, Oct. 22, 1985.

14. Brady, Telephone Interview, Sept. 12, 1989; Church Administration Building Daily Visitor Log, Oct. 15, 1985; Ronald D. Francis to Oscar W. McConkie, Dec. 6, 1985; Pinnock, Interview with FBI, Oct. 17, 1985; "Preliminary Hearing," 6:152–53, 164, 189–91.

15. Bird, Journal, Oct. 15, 1985; J. Martell Bird, Interview with FBI, Oct. 15, 1985. CFS actually stands for Coordinated Financial Services.

16. Bird, Journal, Oct. 15, 1985; Spangler, "Booby-Trapped Bombs"; Jim Woolf and Mike Carter, "Bombs Kill Two; Police Weigh Two Motives," *Salt Lake Tribune*, Oct. 16, 1985.

17. Historical Department Office Journal, Oct. 15, 1985; Rowe, Journal, Oct. 15, 1985; Barney, Interview, Feb. 16, 1989; Glenn N. Rowe, Interview, Feb. 10, 1989; Glenn N. Rowe to Richard E. Turley, Jr., May 17, 1991.

18. Pinnock, Journal, Oct. 15, 1985; Oaks to Turley, May 26, 1989.

19. Verla Sorensen, Journal, Oct. 15, 1985; D. Sorensen, Interview, Mar. 1, 1989.

20. West, Interview, Apr. 19, 1989; V. Sorensen, Journal, Oct. 15, 1985.

21. West, Interview, Apr. 19, 1989; D. Sorensen, Interview, Mar. 1, 1989.

22. Spangler, "Booby-Trapped Bombs"; Kathy Fahy, "A Financial Consultant and History Enthusiast," *Deseret News*, Oct. 15, 1985.

23. Jim Woolf, "Package Bombs Kill Two in Salt Lake City," *Washington Post*, Oct. 15, 1985.

24. Oaks, Interview, Feb. 24, 1989; Pinnock, Interview, Feb. 15, 1989; "Preliminary Hearing," 6:190. Much actual or threatened violence against the church's members, officials, and properties never receives publicity. Examples of publicized incidents during the prior two years include "Eight Bombs Blast Two Colombian LDS Churches," *Salt Lake Tribune*, Nov. 29, 1983; "Leftists Claim Responsibility for LDS Church Bombings," *Salt Lake Tribune*, Nov. 30, 1983; "Second Boise Church Building Vandalized," *Deseret News*, June 7, 1984; "S.L. Man Charged with Vandalism," *Salt Lake Tribune*, Aug. 8, 1984; "L.A. Visitors Center Statue Damaged in Hammer Attack," *Church News*, Aug. 12, 1984; "Police Investigate Bomb Threat at Broadcast House," *Salt Lake Tribune*, Aug. 15, 1984; "Knife-wielding Man Goes on Temple Square Rampage," *Deseret News*, Sept. 30, 1984; "Search of Hotel Fails to Turn Up Bombs," *Salt Lake Tribune*, Dec. 1, 1984; "Eight LDS Buildings Damaged in Bomb Attacks," *Church News*, July 14, 1985; "Two Arrested after LDS Temple in Boise Gets a Spray-Painting," *Deseret News*, July 22, 1985; "Eight Chapels Bombed in Chile," *Ensign* 15 (Sept. 1985): 79.

25. Bird, Journal, Oct. 15, 1985.

26. "Preliminary Hearing," 4:190–91, 5:67–70; Schmidt, Interview, Feb. 8, 1989; Farnsworth, Interview, Dec. 12, 1989, relying on notes of interview with Schmidt, Dec. 30, 1985. West recalled that he might not have mentioned the name of the collection to Schmidt until the following day. West, Interview, Apr. 19, 1989.

27. Woolf and Carter, "Bombs Kill Two."

28. Steve Oberbeck, "Bombs' Targets Were Officers in Troubled Investment Firm," *Salt Lake Tribune*, Oct. 16, 1985.

29. Dawn Tracy, "LDS Link Not Ruled Out in Bomb Blasts," *Salt Lake Tribune*, Oct. 16, 1985.

30. Pinnock, Interview with FBI, Oct. 17, 1985; "Preliminary Hearing," 6:190–91; V. Sorensen, Journal, Oct. 16, 1985.

31. "Preliminary Hearing," 4:190–92, 5:67–71; West, Interview, Apr. 19, 1989.

32. "Preliminary Hearing," 4:193; West, Interview, Apr. 19, 1989; D. Sorensen, Interview, Mar. 1, 1989.

33. West, Interview, Apr. 19, 1989.

34. Pinnock, Interview with FBI, Oct. 17, 1985; Shannon Flynn, Interview with Glenn N. Rowe, July 7, 1989.

35. West, Interview, Apr. 19, 1989.

36. Ronald D. Francis, Memorandum, Oct. 16, 1985; Jerel D. Lindley, Telephone Interview, May 17, 1991.

37. Bird, Journal, Oct. 16, 1985.

38. Francis, Memorandum, Oct. 16, 1985. The managing director of the Personnel Department was J. Russell Homer.

39. Bird, Journal, Oct. 16, 1985.

40. J. Martell Bird, Memorandum, Oct. 22, 1985. Cf. "Preliminary Hearing," 6:122–23.

41. Richard T. Bretzing to Richard E. Turley, Mar. 14, 1989.

42. Rowe, Journal, Oct. 16, 1985.

43. Glenn N. Rowe, Interview, Feb. 11, 1989.

44. Historical Department Office Journal, Oct. 16, 1985; Barney, Interview, Feb. 16, 1989.

45. Barney, Interview, Feb. 16, 1989.

46. Dallin H. Oaks, Journal, Oct. 16, 1985.

47. Ibid.; Oaks, Interview, Feb. 24, 1989.

48. Oaks, Interview, Feb. 24, 1989.

49. Max Gardner, "Recent Salt Lake Bombings Prompt Utah Valley Search," *Daily Universe* (Brigham Young University), Oct. 17, 1985; Ellen Fagg and Brett DelPorto, "Bombings Shatter Area's Composure: 'It's Beginning to Seem like Lebanon,'" *Deseret News*, Oct. 17, 1985.

50. Bird, Journal, Oct. 16, 1985; Historical Department Office Journal, Oct. 16, 1985; "Temple Square Gets Telephone Threat," *Salt Lake Tribune*, Oct. 17, 1985; Fagg and DelPorto, "Bombings Shatter Area's Composure."

51. "Preliminary Hearing," 12:66–68.

52. Business Cards of FBI agents David L. Barker and E. Rhead Richards, Jr., and Salt Lake City police corporal J. I. Stoner, left with Dallin H. Oaks, Oct. 16, 1985; Oaks, Interview with FBI, Oct. 16, 1985; Investigative Information Memo #72, Case #85–98153, Oct. 17, 1985, Salt Lake City Police Department (hereafter abbreviated as SLCPD); Oaks, Memorandum, Oct. 22, 1985; Oaks, Interview, Feb. 24, 1989. Oaks's interview with investigators took place in the office of Franklin D. Richards.

One book about the case would later observe that the various agencies investigating the bombings were "evolving into a group of militias commanded by rival warlords." According to the book's author, "the Salt Lake City detectives could not fathom what the FBI agents, most of whom were Mormons, were doing on the case." The book would also claim, "Senior church officials refused to meet with the homicide investigators several times unless an FBI agent who was a returned Mormon missionary was present, even though the Bureau's only apparent jurisdiction in the case was the possible role of organized crime in the murders or possible fraud involving the operations of Gary Sheets's company, C.F.S." Robert Lindsey, *A Gathering of Saints* (New York: Simon and Schuster, 1988), 227, 230, 266–67.

Actually, the October 16, 1985, interview between Oaks and investigators is the only one known in which a general authority of the church requested the joint presence of FBI and local police. Oaks later explained that in his

previous work as a lawyer and judge, he had observed the rivalries that frequently spring up among competing investigative agencies, and to keep from
fueling the rivalry, he specifically instructed Martell Bird to have both the FBI
and the local police come see him so one group of investigators would not feel
the other had been given favored status by the church. Oaks, Interview, Feb.
24, 1989.

As far as the FBI was concerned, Salt Lake City police detective Ken Farnsworth would say that at first he "didn't know what their jurisdictional responsibility was." Later, he learned that the FBI had for some time been investigating the "UNABOM" serial bomber who had struck in several parts of the
country, giving the FBI jurisdiction (see U.S. Code citation below). The FBI
agents, he later said, would have had an immediate interest in the Salt Lake
bombing case because "there was a bombing, and it was a pipe bomb, and they
want[ed] to know if it's UNABOM." Farnsworth, Interview, Oct. 26, 1989.
(The "UNABOM" killer, credited with several explosions since 1978, remained
at large in 1991. See Mike Carter, "Revenge, Vandalism Motivate Those Who
Use Bombs," *Deseret News,* May 28, 1991.)

According to title 18 of the United State Code, "the Federal Bureau of
Investigation . . . shall have authority to conduct investigations with respect
to violations of subsection (d) . . . of section 844 of this title." Subsection 844(d)
provides penalties for "whoever transports . . . in interstate . . . commerce any
explosive with the knowledge or intent that it will be used to kill, injure, or
intimidate any individual." 18 U.S.C. §§844(d), 846 (1982 & Supp. IV 1986
[reflecting irrelevant 1984 amendments]).

On the FBI's jurisdiction in the case, see also chapter 9, note 37.

53. Pinnock, Journal, Oct. 16, 1985. The friend of Gary Sheets that Pinnock
mentioned was Dean Larsen, not to be confused with the general authority by
that name. On Sheets's friendship with Larsen, see "Preliminary Hearing,"
1:240.

54. Pinnock, Journal, Oct. 20, 1985; George, Handwritten Notes, Dec. 6,
1985; S. Flynn, Interview, July 5, 1989.

55. "News," Press Release, Church of Jesus Christ of Latter-day Saints,
Oct. 16, 1985; "LDS Leaders Saddened," *Deseret News,* Oct. 17, 1985; Dawn
Tracy, "Letter Was Only One of Hofmann's Finds," *Salt Lake Tribune,* Oct.
17, 1985; Ted Robbins, "Mormon Letter May Be Link," *USA Today,* Oct. 17,
1985.

Chapter 8: In the Aftermath

1. Jim Woolf, Mike Carter, and George A. Sorensen, "Victim of Third
Bombing Is Suspect in Others That Killed Two in S.L.," *Salt Lake Tribune,*
Oct. 17, 1985; "Here Is the Text of Original 'White Salamander' Letter," *Salt
Lake Tribune,* Oct. 17, 1985.

One book about the case would later hypothesize a church conspiracy to
block the bombing investigation. According to the theory, on October 17, 1985,
"the day after the third bombing, The Word came down from the offices of

the First Presidency." "The Word" was supposedly an "edict" commanding church officials not to cooperate with investigators. To bolster this theory, the book dismisses examples of church cooperation by telescoping them into the period before the supposed edict and claiming it was "quick, but not quite quick enough" to prevent some cooperation.

For example, it asserts that Salt Lake City police detective John Foster confronted LDS security director Martell Bird on October 16 about rumors that church security had been following Hofmann when he was bombed. "Bird denied the story adamantly," the book says. "And he was willing to cooperate with the police in any way necessary to clear himself and his colleagues." The book also claims that before the conjectured edict, Bird told Foster that Hofmann visited Gordon Hinckley on October 4, 1985, to tell him about persons who had unauthorized transcripts of upcoming conference talks. Bird's cooperation reportedly impressed police. "The next day," however, the book postulates, "The Word came down." Steven Naifeh and Gregory White Smith, *The Mormon Murders* (New York: Weidenfeld and Nicolson, 1988), 301–2.

The book says that when Foster then requested a copy of the Church Administration Building log entry for October 4, Bird called him back to say he had erred on the date of the meeting, which had actually occurred in September. Bird offered Foster a copy of the log entry for the September date. "But when Foster went to pick up the photocopy," the book maintains, "every entry except the one relating to Hofmann had been whited out. The day-timer had been copied, then expurgated, then copied again, giving the police no way to determine if relevant entries had been whited out along with irrelevant ones." It also claims, "When he asked for a photocopy of the sheet for October 4, the date originally mentioned, Bird refused." Foster, whom the book describes as "a good cop, and, like all good cops, suspicious," then reportedly concluded about Bird, "Somebody's told him to shut up, or told him that he shouldn't have ever said anything about it in the first place." Ibid., 301–3.

The evidence in the case, however, does not sustain the *Mormon Murders* hypothesis. A police report filed by Foster shows he visited Bird to talk about rumors of following Hofmann not on October 16, 1985, as the book claims, but on December 19. John Foster, Handwritten Notes, Dec. 19, 1985, attached to Investigative Information Memo #679, Case #85–98153, Nov. 30, 1985, SLCPD. Contemporary records show the meeting between Hofmann and Hinckley occurred September 26, 1985, not on October 4, as the book asserts. See chapter 6, note 67, and accompanying text. A police report filed by Foster shows he obtained a photocopy of the September meeting log on April 10, 1986, not shortly after the bombings, as the book seems to imply. And the log photocopy attached to Foster's police report has no whited-out entries. Investigative Information Memo #840, Case #85–98153, Apr. 10, 1986, SLCPD.

Though *The Mormon Murders* does not mention it, there was one Administration Building log page on which extraneous entries were whited out before being given to police. It was a page for October 15, 1985, that was furnished to investigators who asked when Hofmann met with Dallin Oaks on that day. The unmasked entry answered their question, and they did not ask to see the other entries, which had been whited out because they were irrelevant to the question and because church officials felt ethically bound to protect church visitors' privacy unless required by investigators to do otherwise. Investigative Information Memo #881, Case #85–98153, June 28, 1989, recording events of Dec. 6, 1985, SLCPD; see chapter 10, note 25, and accompanying text.

Finally, reports filed by police detectives show that church security repeatedly took initiative to provide information to police well after the edict postulated in *The Mormon Murders* supposedly came down. That church personnel would continue to volunteer data also militates against the theory that such an edict was ever issued. See, e.g., Investigative Information Memos #245, #249, #309, Case #85–98153, Oct. 21, 25, 1985, SLCPD.

2. Jim Woolf, "Police Look for Motive in Mormon Bombings," *Washington Post*, Oct. 17, 1985.

3. Pinnock, Journal, Oct. 17, 1985; Pinnock, Interview with FBI, Oct. 17, 1985.

The Mormon Murders, 296, would later assert, "The police asked to see the FBI interviews, a courtesy routinely extended to local law enforcement agencies on a confidential basis. The FBI refused." Salt Lake police detective Don Bell later acknowledged, however, that FBI agents "finally" did turn interview notes over to them. Asked when they did so, Bell checked his file and replied, "Twenty-first; twenty-first they were received by our department."

"Of October?" he was asked.

"Of October," Bell confirmed. "And this was the seventeenth. I knew it was two or three days later when we finally got their interview notes." Don Bell, Interview, Aug. 18, 1989.

Considering that the notes had to be typed and that October 19 and 20 were a Saturday and Sunday, the FBI's provision of the notes to police on October 21 would not seem to be untimely.

Salt Lake police detective Ken Farnsworth agreed that FBI officials did turn over interview notes to local investigators. Referring to the FBI, Farnsworth said, "The information they gleaned from their interviews were helpful and certainly provided a good, clean background for going to another interview and collecting other information." Kenneth C. Farnsworth, Jr., Interview, Oct. 26, 1989.

4. Pinnock, Interview with FBI, Oct. 17, 1985.

5. Pinnock, Journal, Oct. 17, 1985.

6. S. Flynn, Interview, July 5, 1989; Church Administration Building Daily Visitor Log, Oct. 17, 1985; Shannon Flynn, Interview with Dallin H. Oaks, Stenographer's Transcript, Oct. 17, 1985; Shannon Flynn, Telephone Interview, Sept. 18, 1989.

7. Oaks, Journal, Oct. 17, 1985; Gordon B. Hinckley, Memorandum, Oct. 21, 1985.

8. S. Flynn, Interview, July 5, 1989; S. Flynn, Telephone Interview, Sept. 18, 1989; Bell, Interview, Aug. 18, 1989.

9. S. Flynn, Interview, July 5, 1989.

10. Bell, Interview, Aug. 18, 1989.

11. S. Flynn, Interview with Oaks, Oct. 17, 1985; Dallin H. Oaks to Rick Turley, June 19, 1991.

12. Oaks, Journal, Oct. 17, 1985.

13. Bell, Interview, Aug. 18, 1989. Bell said the number he dialed was 531–2531, which (according to the August 1985 Salt Lake City phone directory) was the church's general information number. Pinnock's secretary later said she had no specific recollection of Bell calling. Brady, Telephone Interview, Sept. 14, 1989. An Associated Press writer would later assert, "Bell threatened to arrest . . . Martell Bird for interfering with his attempts to interview church leaders." Mike Carter, "Mormon Security Receives Cautious Praise," *Salt Lake Tribune,* Oct. 9, 1990.

14. Ronald D. Francis, Memorandum, Oct. 26, 1988.

15. Bell, Interview, Aug. 18, 1989.

16. Pinnock, Journal, Oct. 17, 1985; *Salamander,* 57 (Bell "did not know that the FBI had already interviewed . . . Pinnock").

Pursuing a church cover-up theory, *The Mormon Murders,* 246, prefaces the account of the interview by claiming that Pinnock went to see Terri Christensen "the day after the bombings," telling her "that he had come to 'collect' Steve's confidential papers on the McLellin Collection" because "the transaction was a 'private matter,' and therefore all materials relating to it should be kept under 'Church control.' " This background superficially appears to establish that Pinnock had something to hide.

Yet *The Mormon Murders* distorts important details. Pinnock visited Terri not "the day after the bombings" but on October 19, four days after Steve died. Pinnock, Journal, Oct. 19, 1985. The timing of the event is important, because to fit the book's cover-up theme, the incident had to occur before Pinnock's October 17 interview with FBI agents in which he gave them information paralleling much of what was in Steve's papers.

Calling *The Mormon Murders* depiction of this event "not true," Terri explained the actual circumstances behind Pinnock's visit. "Pinnock came to offer condolences," she said. "I voluntarily gave him a journal entry of Steve's regarding the McLellin Collection. But Pinnock didn't come to get the paper. He didn't know about it." Jan Thompson, "Victims' Families Are Hurt, Appalled: Authors Deceived Us, They Charge," *Deseret News,* Oct. 16, 1988. Moreover, Terri did not give Pinnock her dead husband's *original* journal entry. Steve had made several *copies* for his file, and, Terri explained, "It just so happened to be that we had it out, I think for the detectives. . . . So we just gave him one." T. Christensen, Interview, Apr. 20, 1989. Thus, Pinnock's visit was not intended to keep Steve's journal from investigators, nor did his acceptance of the copy hamper their access to the original.

17. Bell, Interview, Aug. 18, 1989.

The interview between Bell and Pinnock would later be described in *The Mormon Murders,* 246–50, and *Salamander,* 58–61.

The Mormon Murders describes how Bell's interview with Pinnock supposedly started:

"Elder Pinnock, this is the deal," Bell began, notebook in hand. "This is a homicide investigation. Do you know Mr. Hofmann?"

Pinnock paused and reflected for a moment. "No, I don't believe I do."

The book asserts, "Wherever dialogue appears [in the book] within quotation marks, it represents an exact transcription of a conversation as related by a participant." Only two persons participated in the interview: Pinnock and Bell. The book's authors did not interview Pinnock. *The Mormon Murders*, ix, x, 247.

The authors of both *Salamander* and *The Mormon Murders* interviewed Bell about his meeting with Pinnock, but only *The Mormon Murders* claims Pinnock denied knowing Hofmann. Asked to explain the difference between the two accounts, Bell said, "Well, there's a contradiction in what is printed. There wasn't a contradiction in what was given" by him to the two sets of authors. Bell clarified the contradiction by explaining that Pinnock's "beginning scenario was that, yes, he did meet Mark Hofmann; he never did deny knowing Mark Hofmann." Bell, Interview, Aug. 18, 1989.

In recounting Bell's interview with Pinnock, *Salamander*, 58, quotes Pinnock as saying he helped Hofmann obtain a loan for "the McLellin or McCellin—something like that—collection." *The Mormon Murders*, 248, says that Pinnock "fumbled with the pronunciation" of the McLellin collection. Neither book explains that McLellin's name was often spelled "M'Lellin" in church publications and that many church members would pronounce these variants differently, unaware that *M'* and *Mc* represent the same patronymic prefix and should be pronounced identically. (Mike Carter, "LDS Official Secured Hofmann Loan," *Salt Lake Tribune*, Oct. 21, 1985, which would first make public the details of Bell's interview with Pinnock, specifically notes that "McLellin" is "also spelled M'Lellin.")

Salamander, 60–61, recounts that Pinnock told Bell about running into Hofmann on October 15 in the church parking lot, where Hofmann said he had just come from meeting with Oaks. Bell reportedly asked, "So did Mark Hofmann know Oaks?" According to the book, Pinnock gave an explanation ending in the statement, "I don't really think he saw Elder Oaks or anybody."

When told of this account, Pinnock responded, "I never said that." Pinnock said he knew Hofmann had met with Oaks. Pinnock, Interview, Feb. 16, 1990. In view of all the evidence in the case, it seems unlikely Pinnock would deny that Hofmann met with Oaks. Oaks had already told both the FBI and the police about meeting with Hofmann and had encouraged Pinnock to tell them what he knew. Bell would later say, "I never heard Dallin Oaks's name until Hugh Pinnock told me himself [what] he had heard from Mark." Bell, Interview, Aug. 18, 1989. Had Pinnock been trying to keep Oaks's name out of the case, he likely would not have mentioned it in the first place.

According to *The Mormon Murders*, 248–49, Bell told Pinnock, "You know, we have some information that Mr. Hofmann met with President Hinckley." Pinnock then reportedly gave a speech that included the statement, "But I'm sure President Hinckley has never met this man."

When this account was brought to his attention, Pinnock labeled it "false." He said he knew Hinckley had made public announcements about documents with Hofmann in his presence. (A widely publicized photograph, released with the Anthon transcript by the church, had shown Hinckley and other church officials standing by Hofmann.) Pinnock, Interview, Feb. 16, 1990.

Salamander, 60–61, reports that Pinnock said to Bell, "Well, the thing you're going to have to learn is that when people come to this building, they say, 'I want to see the First Presidency,' or 'I want to see Elder Oaks,' but they don't. They see me or someone like me. Then they leave and tell their friends they saw President Hinckley or whoever." A similar account appears in *The Mormon Murders,* 249.

Neither book, however, explains the meaning of Pinnock's statement in the context of Bell's interview. *The Mormon Murders,* 248, observes that before Pinnock made this statement, Bell said, "You know, we have some information that Mr. Hofmann met with President Hinckley." In neither *Mormon Murders* nor *Salamander,* however, does Bell tell Pinnock exactly what the information was.

The information consisted of inaccurate stories innocently repeated over the phone to Bell by Shannon Flynn about Hofmann's association with Hinckley. Though Bell did not know it, Flynn had already phoned Pinnock and told a similar story, complete with the incorrect detail that Hinckley had arranged the bank loan for Hofmann. A later passage (253) in *The Mormon Murders* would acknowledge that "Flynn . . . knew only this cockeyed version of the story that Hofmann had fed him." The same page explains, "The allegations about Gordon Hinckley's role in the loan transaction could be easily and truthfully denied." Pinnock knew Hinckley had nothing to do with the loan and thus told Bell that persons sometimes claim to have been dealing with the First Presidency when in reality they have been dealing with someone like him. Bell, Interview, Aug. 18, 1989; S. Flynn, Interview, July 5, 1989; Pinnock, Journal, Oct. 16, 20, 1985.

Salamander, 60, explains, "Pinnock would not tell [Bell] the name of the [McLellin collection] buyer but said the attorney's name was David West, Sr. Within minutes Pinnock also mentioned the name David Sorenson, and Bell jotted it down, assuming he now knew the buyer." *The Mormon Murders,* 249, paraphrases Pinnock as saying that "the donor was a private collector in Canada."

After these books were published, Bell recounted that Pinnock had referred to Sorensen first by the descriptions "Canadian friend" or "Canadian buyer." Bell said that later in the interview, Pinnock referred to Sorensen by name, "and I immediately went back up where I had circled 'Canadian' and wrote under [it] 'Mr. Sorensen' 'cause I now had a name and I knew that I was feeling pretty good 'cause I knew he never had any intention of divulging his name, but it just kinda came out, and I said to myself, 'I know who the Canadian buyer is now.'" Yet when asked if Pinnock said he would not give him the name, Bell answered, "No, and I never asked him." Bell, Interview, Aug. 18, 1989.

For additional information on this interview, see chapter 9, note 22.

18. Pinnock, Journal, Oct. 17, 1985.

The Mormon Murders incorrectly interprets the brevity of the second interview as an attempt at cover-up. The book compounds the problem by mixing up the timing of events. After giving its account of the interview between Bell and Pinnock (see preceding note), *The Mormon Murders*, 254, asserts that Pinnock realized he would be caught lying. "Not all was lost, however," it continues. "The FBI agents who had interviewed Oaks the day before were coming to see Pinnock later that day. Pinnock didn't have to make the same mistakes a second time. And he didn't." Though mentioning some details not covered, the book observes that in the FBI interview Pinnock "not only acknowledged knowing Hofmann, he detailed most of their dealings, including the loan from First Interstate Bank. He knew how to pronounce 'McLellin.' He even gave them David Sorensen's name." The book, however, overlooks a crucial bit of information that undermines this interpretation entirely: the FBI agents met with Pinnock *before* Bell did. Pinnock, Journal, Oct. 17, 1985; *Salamander*, 57.

19. Pinnock, Journal, Oct. 17, 1985.

20. Bird, Memorandum, Oct. 22, 1985.

21. Pinnock, Journal, Oct. 18, 1985.

22. Oaks, Journal, Oct. 19, 1985; William S. Evans, Telephone Interview, May 16, 1989.

23. Brent D. Ward, Journal, Oct. 18, 1985; Pinnock, Journal, Oct. 18, 1985.

24. Bird, Memorandum, Oct. 22, 1985; Oaks, Journal, Oct. 19, 1985.

25. Alvin E. Rust, Interviews, Apr. 6, Oct. 5, 1989; Virginia Archer, Telephone Interview, Dec. 21, 1989; "Preliminary Hearing," 6:122–24.

26. Bird, Memorandum, Oct. 22, 1985; Bird, Journal, Oct. 18, 1985. The two security officers who joined the meeting later were Ron Francis and Jerel Lindley.

27. B. Ward, Journal, Oct. 18, 1985; Pinnock, Journal, Oct. 18, 1985; Bird, Journal, Oct. 18, 1985.

28. Hugh W. Pinnock to [Terri] Christensen, Oct. 18, 1985; Pinnock, Journal, Oct. 18, 1985; Kathleen Webb Sheets Funeral Program, Oct. 18, 1985. Gordon Hinckley also made himself available when Terri Christensen called the following week seeking an appointment with him. "And I got one," she later said, "but I decided not to go." T. Christensen, Interview, Apr. 20, 1989.

29. Oaks, Journal, Oct. 19, 1985; Hinckley, Memorandum, Oct. 21, 1985.

30. B. Ward, Journal, Oct. 18, 1985; Hinckley, Memorandum, Oct. 21, 1985.

31. B. Ward, Journal, Oct. 18, 1985; Bird, Journal, Oct. 18, 1985.

32. Francis M. Gibbons to [Gordon B.] Hinckley, received Oct. 18, 1985; Rowe, Journal, Oct. 18, 1985; Glenn N. Rowe, "Items Acquired from Mark Hofmann," [Oct. 18, 1985], attached to Richard P. Lindsay to Special Affairs Committee, Oct. 24, 1985.

33. Marianne Funk, "Hofmann Also Traded Important Documents of American History," *Deseret News*, Oct. 18, 1985. The Library of Congress official

quoted in the article was William Matheson. For the reasons why the library declined the offer, see *The Judgment of Experts,* 14–24, 58–61.

34. Jerry Spangler, "Police Focus on Evidence, Not Theories," *Deseret News,* Oct. 18, 1985.

35. Jerry P. Cahill, "FBI to Authenticate Martin Harris Letter in Bombing Probe," Press Release, Church of Jesus Christ of Latter-day Saints, Oct. 19, 1985.

36. Mike Carter, "Lawyer Silences Bomb Suspect," *Salt Lake Tribune,* Oct. 19, 1985.

Hofmann's attorney, Ron Yengich, had earlier instructed hospital personnel to contact him should police try to question his injured client. Petition for Extraordinary Writ at 3, Hofmann v. Conder, No. 21020 (Utah filed Nov. 27, 1985); Yengich, Interview, Sept. 20, 1989. According to the police guard on duty, the nurse went to call Hofmann's counsel and then "stated I would have to waite to talk with Hofmann that her duties came first." The officer asked "what she was trying to do and she stated something [to] the effect that she was just concerned about Hofman's rights." Affidavit, In re Investigation of Homicides of Christensen and Sheets, No. CS 85–94 (Utah 3d Dist. Ct. filed Oct. 31, 1985).

Because the nurse was represented in legal proceedings by attorney Charles Dahlquist of Kirton, McConkie, and Bushnell (the principal law firm that represents the church), some persons speculated that the church had intervened, for whatever reason, to block the nurse's testimony. See, e.g., Sillitoe and Roberts, *Salamander,* 69 (note Gerry D'Elia's reaction and his statement about standing); Naifeh and Smith, *The Mormon Murders,* 272–74; Lindsey, *A Gathering of Saints,* 220, 236.

The conjecture rested on two inaccurate assumptions. The first was that the church owned LDS Hospital, where the nurse worked. See, e.g., *A Gathering of Saints,* 220. Actually, the church had divested itself of the hospital a decade earlier. David Croft, "Church Divests Self of Hospitals," *Church News,* Sept. 14, 1974. Intermountain Health Care (IHC), which became the hospital's new owner, had "an independent board of trustees representing all facets of the community." Intermountain Health Care, *Sown in Generosity, Nurtured with Service, Growing . . .* (Salt Lake City: Intermountain Health Care, [1985]), 2.

The other inaccurate assumption was that because Dahlquist worked for Kirton, McConkie, and Bushnell, he must have been representing the church. Though the law firm counted the church among its clients, Dahlquist himself spent virtually no time on church legal matters. Instead, he spent most of his practice representing IHC. Dahlquist said he counseled the nurse not to testify in order to protect IHC from a civil suit resulting from the nurse's divulgence of information arguably protected by a lawyer-client privilege.

Dahlquist said he didn't care if the nurse testified as long as he first had a nonappealable court decision that would protect his client from suit. He told the district court judge hearing the case that he would instruct the nurse not to talk "until the matter is resolved." His position was "that the issue needs to be resolved." Reporter's Transcript of Proceedings at 6, In re Investigation of Homicides of Christensen and Sheets, No. CS 85–94 (Utah 3d Dist. Ct. Oct. 18, 1985); Charles Dahlquist, Interview, Aug. 1, 1989.

On October 30, 1985, U.S. Attorney Brent Ward tried to persuade Dahlquist to have the nurse talk. "I spent an hour with him but could not budge him," Ward wrote in his journal. Ward strongly disagreed with Dahlquist's legal position but recorded, "Dahlquist says that all we have to do is show him a case that proves that the hospital and the nurse could not be liable for damages and he will allow her to testify." Ultimately, the state supreme court held that an attorney-client privilege in fact existed. Consequently, the nurse was unable to testify without jeopardizing herself and the hospital. Brent D. Ward, Journal, Oct. 30, 1985; Hofmann v. Conder, 712 P.2d 216 (Utah 1985).

37. Rowe, Journal, Oct. 19, 1985.

38. Mike Carter, "Hofmann Associate Held in Weapons Violations," *Salt Lake Tribune,* Oct. 20, 1985. The ATF special agent was Jerry Miller. Flynn's attorney was James N. Barber.

The Mormon Murders, 294, later suggested that U.S. Attorney Brent Ward, supposedly out to please church officials, sandbagged the machine gun search. It claimed Salt Lake police detective Ken Farnsworth called Bruce Lubeck, "Ward's assistant on the case," to obtain a warrant to search Flynn's house for the weapon. Lubeck purportedly told Farnsworth to call Ward. "Then," the book claims, "Ward wouldn't give them an answer. He told them to stay off Lubeck's line for at least fifteen minutes while he discussed the case with him." Farnsworth began to wonder what was taking so long. "Something was up," the book asserts.

Then, it maintains, Lubeck unexpectedly asked Farnsworth to arrange a consent search instead. Farnsworth demanded a warrant. "But Lubeck still resisted," the book continues. "He—and Ward obviously—still wanted a consent search." Farnsworth "finally pushed" Lubeck into relenting. Farnsworth got what he wanted. "But," the book concludes, "the episode left a lot of unanswered questions in Ken Farnsworth's mind."

When Farnsworth heard the *Mormon Murders* version of this episode, he replied, "I can't remember talking to Brent Ward that night. I don't have any recollection of talking to Brent Ward. The rest of it is right. I mean, I—he did not want to give a search warrant." One reason for Lubeck's resistance, Farnsworth felt, was that "attorneys don't like to come out in the middle of the night and do search warrants." Kenneth C. Farnsworth, Jr., Interview, Feb. 21, 1990.

When Lubeck heard the Naifeh-Smith account, he said, "It's possible that I said, 'Why don't you just get a consent search as opposed to doing a search,' . . . only because it was the middle of the night." Lubeck said he felt it was often easier to perform a consent search than to get a judge's approval at odd hours, especially "when you've got someone who's cooperating," as Flynn was at the time. Bruce Lubeck, Interview, Aug. 22, 1989.

Ward's journal for the evening of the search likewise shows no evidence he spoke to Farnsworth. Ward recorded that late in the evening, he spoke by phone to ATF agent Robert Swehla, who had been interviewing Flynn, and that Swehla told him about the machine gun. "I call[ed] Bruce," Ward wrote, "and ask[ed] him to talk with Swehla about a warrant to search Flynn residence. He end[ed] up going to the office at 1:00 A.M. to draft an affidavit and search warrant for Flynn's residence and storage unit." Ward, Journal, Oct. 18, 1985.

39. Hinckley, Memorandum, Oct. 21, 1985.

40. Oaks, Journal, Oct. 19, 1985.

41. Pinnock, Journal, Oct. 19, 1985. The previous day in a letter to Terri Christensen about Steve, Pinnock wrote, "I testify to you, as I have testified to others, that he has not done anything that was inappropriate or questionable. Until this situation can be settled, there will be many questions asked; but I wanted you to know that never have I observed anything to be amiss in his life." Pinnock to [T.] Christensen, Oct. 18, 1985.

42. Hinckley, Memorandum, Oct. 21, 1985. Pinnock, Journal, Oct. 19, 1985, lists Hinckley's initials and beside them the note, "Yes, go ahead."

43. Pinnock, Journal, Oct. 20, 1985.

44. Dawn Tracy, "Hofmann Frequently Met LDS Official," *Salt Lake Tribune*, Oct. 20, 1985; Carter, "Hofmann Associate Held."

45. Marianne Funk and Ellen Fagg, "Police Arrest a Hofmann Associate after Finding Items Linked to Bombings," *Deseret News*, Oct. 20, 1985.

46. Ronald D. Francis, Memorandum, Oct. 20, 1985.

47. Carter, "LDS Official Secured Hofmann Loan."

48. Hinckley, Memorandum, Oct. 21, 1985.

49. "Statement by Elder Hugh W. Pinnock," Press Release, Church of Jesus Christ of Latter-day Saints, Oct. 21, 1985.

50. Pinnock, Journal, Oct. 21, 1985.

51. Codianna v. Morris, 660 P.2d 1101, 1111 (Utah 1983).

52. Dallin H. Oaks to Richard E. Turley, May 30, 1989.

53. Oaks, Journal, Oct. 21, 1985.

54. Pinnock, Journal, Oct. 21, 1985.

55. Larry Klenk to Ronald D. Francis, Oct. 21, 1985; Investigative Information Memo #245, Case #85–98153, Oct. 21, 1985, SLCPD. On the coin alteration, see *Mark Hofmann Interviews*, 409–10, 421.

56. R. Terance Gallagher to Dallin Oakes, Oct. 21, 1985, and Oaks's note to his secretary written on the letter.

57. FBI Receipt, signed by E. Rhead Richards, Jr., David L. Barker, Ronald D. Francis, and Glenn N. Rowe, Oct. 21, 1985; Rowe, Journal, Oct. 21, 1985; Historical Department Office Journal, Oct. 21, 1985; Gibbons, Interview, Apr. 6, 1989.

58. Brett DelPorto and Marianne Funk, "Figure in Probe of Bombings Posts Bail on Weapons Count," *Deseret News*, Oct. 22, 1985. The special agent in charge was Terry Knowles.

The Mormon Murders later tried to portray Ward as out to scuttle the investigation in order to curry church favor. "Ward's first action," the book declared, "was to help arrange to have a key piece of evidence shipped out of state" so that "by the time the police department knew enough to ask the

Church for the so-called Salamander Letter, it was already gone." Earlier, the book asserted that the church "had shipped the Salamander Letter off to the FBI so the county attorneys could *never* get their hands on it." *The Mormon Murders*, 295, 273 (italics in original).

The books authors credit Salt Lake police detectives Ken Farnsworth and Jim Bell as key sources for their book. Ibid., vii. Farnsworth was later asked if he "felt that the Church had somehow arranged to have the salamander letter taken away so that local investigators wouldn't have access to it." Farnsworth said he did not feel that way and did not remember any police officers expressing such a view. Farnsworth said his impression was that his own chief, Bud Willoughby, "was the engineer behind" sending the material to the FBI. Farnsworth, Interview, Oct. 26, 1989. Similarly, Jim Bell testified in court that FBI personnel were brought into the case "basically for the use of their lab." "Preliminary Hearing" 12:13. The contemporary newspaper article by Del-Porto and Funk cited above corroborates Willoughby's involvement.

59. Ellen Fagg and Brett DelPorto, "Loan Was Secured for Purchase by Hofmann," *Deseret News*, Oct. 21, 1985.

60. News Broadcast, KGTV Channel 10 (San Diego), Oct. 15, 1985, 6:30 P.M. Unless otherwise stated, all quotations from television news programs in this chapter rely on transcripts provided to the church in 1985 by Luce Press Clippings, 420 Lexington Ave., New York, N.Y. 10170, and are identified by the station's call letters, channel number (if applicable), and date and time of broadcast.

61. News Broadcast, WJZ Channel 13 (Baltimore), Oct. 16, 1985, 11:00 P.M.

62. News Broadcast, WTAE Channel 4 (Pittsburgh), Oct. 17, 1985, 6:00 P.M. Other stations referred to her as "the wife of a Church history buff." See, e.g., News Broadcast, WCCO Channel 4 (Minneapolis–St. Paul), Oct. 17, 1985, 5:00 P.M.; News Broadcast, KSDK Channel 5 (St. Louis), Oct. 17, 1985, 12:00 P.M.

63. "NBC News at Sunrise," Oct. 17, 1985, 5:30 A.M. See also News Broadcast, WRC Channel 4 (Washington, D.C.), Oct. 17, 1985, 6:00 P.M.; News Broadcast, KFMB Channel 8 (San Diego), Oct. 17, 1985, 4:30 P.M.

64. News Broadcast, KGO Channel 7 (San Francisco), Oct. 15, 1985, 5:00 P.M.

65. News Broadcast, KNBC Channel 4 (Los Angeles), Oct. 17, 1985, 4:00 P.M.

66. "CBS Nightwatch," Oct. 17, 1985, 1:30 A.M.

67. News Broadcast, KTSP Channel 10 (Phoenix), Oct. 17, 1985, 10:00 P.M.

68. News Broadcast, WJZ Channel 13 (Baltimore), Oct. 16, 1985, 11:00 P.M.

69. News Broadcast, KOMO Channel 4 (Seattle), Oct. 17, 1985, 5:00 P.M.

70. News Broadcast, KGTV Channel 10 (San Diego), Oct. 15, 1985, 5:00 P.M.

71. News Broadcast, KOMO Channel 4 (Seattle), Oct. 17, 1985, 11:00 P.M. The critic cited was Ed Decker. The station also noted that "the church's Seattle president though says that any connection between the bombings and the letter is far fetched."

72. News Broadcast, KPTV Channel 12 (Portland), Oct. 18, 1985, 10:00 P.M.

73. News Broadcast, WTAE Channel 4 (Pittsburgh), Oct. 21, 1985, 6:00 P.M. See also "CNN PrimeNews," Oct. 21, 1985, 6:00 P.M.; News Broadcast, KPTV Channel 12 (Portland), Oct. 21, 1985, 10:00 P.M.

74. News Broadcast, KPNX Channel 12 (Phoenix), Oct. 21, 1985, 12:00 P.M.

75. News Broadcast, KGTV Channel 10 (San Diego), Oct. 21, 1985, 11:30 A.M.

76. Milton Hollstein, "Bombings Underscore Questions of Ethics," *Deseret News,* Oct. 21, 1985.

Chapter 9: Deep Concern

1. Oaks, Journal, Oct. 23, 1985 (describing previous day's activities); Bird, Journal, Oct. 22, 1985.

2. Bird, Journal, Oct. 22, 1985.

3. Oaks, Journal, Oct. 23, 1985; Dallin H. Oaks, Memorandum Draft, Oct. 22, 1985; *Deseret News 1985 Church Almanac,* 22; Dallin H. Oaks to Richard E. Turley, May 31, 1989.

4. Oaks, Memorandum, Oct. 22, 1985. Investigators later questioned Oaks's recollection of not having any substantive conversation with Christensen. Their doubts were based on an entry they found in Steve Christensen's calendar book. Under the date of October 14, 1985, at 12:30, Christensen had written "Oaks" and a telephone number. The calendar book gave no first name, title, or other information. Detective Ken Farnsworth later explained investigators' assumption that the number was "[Dallin] Oaks's phone number at home in Provo or Orem, wherever he is. And so Steve apparently is supposed to jump all over the normal contacts that I'm aware of and make contact with Elder Oaks." Farnsworth, Interview, Oct. 6, 1989.

After the investigation ended, however, it was brought to Farnsworth's attention that the phone number appeared to have a Brigham Young University prefix. "I thought I checked that phone number," Farnsworth responded. "I can't remember specifically. I thought I checked it. But if that's a BYU thing, then I can tell you I didn't check it because I don't know that." Ibid.

Later research proved that the number was, in fact, assigned to Brigham Young University in Provo, Utah. By October 14, 1985, Dallin Oaks had moved some forty or fifty miles north to Salt Lake City. He spent his October 14 (Columbus Day) at his new residence, where he and his son-in-law Louis Ringger "removed the shingles on the garage, installed plywood & covered it with tar paper, as well as straightening the garage with a gear driven chain mechanism." Oaks, Journal, Oct. 16, 1985 (describing events of October 14). He was not near Brigham Young University that day and had no conversation with Christensen as investigators had assumed.

5. Dallin H. Oaks to James [N.] Barber, Oct. 22, 1985.

6. Bird, Journal, Oct. 22, 1985; Oaks, Journal, Oct. 23, 1985.

7. Bird, Journal, Oct. 22, 1985. According to Bird's journal, the security officer who called him was Neil Knight.

8. S. Flynn, Interview with Oaks, Oct. 17, 1985.

9. Bird, Journal, Oct. 22, 1985.

10. LDS Public Communications Department, "Working Press Who Signed In," Oct. 23, 1985.

11. Videotape, LDS Press Conference, Oct. 23, 1985. Two books about the Salt Lake bombings imply that Hinckley met with Christensen at other times too, apparently to talk about the McLellin collection. For example, *Salamander*, 350, observes, "Despite the confidentiality of the McLellin deal, a number of business associates were becoming aware that Christensen was in contact with high church leaders. One man, for instance, working with Christensen on a satellite network deal, met with Christensen and others in the Judge Building one morning only to have the meeting interrupted by a telephone call from President Hinckley. Christensen, a bishop, must have a serious problem in his ward, the businessman concluded. He guessed from the way Christensen gathered up his papers and excused himself that something was urgent."

When Salt Lake businessman Doug Snarr, who was working with Christensen on the satellite network deal, had the purported incident brought to his attention, he said that the person described could only have been he. "I was the one that interfaced with Steve, on the collapse of CFS, on all matters pursuant to SNA [Satellite Network of America]," Snarr said. "I know there was no phone call when I was there present, period. I can tell you that right now."

Snarr said that in his discussions with Christensen, "the name President Hinckley was dropped," but nothing was said about Hofmann or the McLellin transaction. On one occasion within thirty days of his death, Christensen made his only comment about possibly meeting with the church leader. Snarr said Christensen told him simply "that he'd be visiting President Hinckley." Snarr supposed the meeting might have something to do with Christensen's responsibilities as a local church leader. Snarr also said the statement was prospective, not retrospective. Douglas Snarr, Interview, Dec. 9, 1989.

Church Administration Building visitor logs show no evidence that such a meeting in fact occurred. Based on Hofmann's statements, however, Christensen may well have assumed for a while that he would meet with Hinckley. When Hofmann had informed Hinckley about the McLellin collection in June, Hinckley had told Hofmann to come back when he had resolved his problems with Rust and was ready to donate the collection. Within thirty days of Christensen's death, Hofmann finally told him about Rust's involvement in the transaction. At the same time, he might have said something about taking the collection to Hinckley when Rust was repaid. If so, Christensen may have thought for a time that he would end up meeting with Hinckley. Since the collection was never delivered, however, the meeting would not have occurred.

Detective Ken Farnsworth was one of the two principal Salt Lake City police officers who investigated the bombing case. When Farnsworth had the purported incident described in *Salamander* brought to his attention, he responded, "I didn't talk to anyone who said that." The only person he could recall interviewing who gave specific testimony about a supposed meeting between Christensen and Hinckley was Joe Robertson, business associate of Christensen and son-in-law of Kathy Sheets. Farnsworth, Interview, Oct. 6, 1989.

Both *Salamander* and *The Mormon Murders* recite the Robertson incident. *Salamander*, 329–30, explains that "sometime near" July 10, "Christensen and Hofmann were seen rushing out of Christensen's [CFS] office in a panic." Christensen approached Joe Robertson, "breathlessly" asking, "Joe, may I borrow your car? My jeep's in the shop, and I have to meet with President Hinckley." Later in the day, Christensen returned with Hofmann and gave Robertson back his keys. *The Mormon Murders*, 263–64, provides a similar account, though without ascribing a date to it.

A survey of case evidence shows that the most likely date of the incident is June 28, 1985, the day on which Hofmann and Christensen visited with Hugh Pinnock and then obtained the First Interstate Bank loan. It was a day on which Hinckley was out of town. Both Christensen's and Pinnock's journal accounts of that meeting show Christensen repeating Hofmann's statement that Hinckley already knew about the McLellin deal. Thus, it is understandable that Christensen would mention Hinckley's name when borrowing Robertson's car. Christensen, Journal, June 28, 1985; Pinnock, Journal, June 28, 1985.

Robertson later noted that Christensen did not say he had actually visited Hinckley when he returned the vehicle. Ken Farnsworth, anxious to document any meetings between Christensen and Hinckley, investigated the incident carefully, even going so far as to try to locate Christensen's car repair records that would help date Robertson's recollection. Farnsworth was unsuccessful and later said he never found any concrete evidence the two men actually met on that occasion. Robertson later said that a date of June 28 for the incident "makes sense" because when investigators asked him to narrow down the dating of the incident, he told them "sometime in June is when it occurred. And they said it couldn't have been because he [Hinckley] was out of the country." Robertson, Interview, Aug. 15, 1989; Farnsworth, Interview, Sept. 8, 1989.

Dating the Robertson incident to June 28 clarifies other evidence in the case. *Salamander*, 327, refers to a July 2 letter in which Christensen thanked Pinnock for his June 28 counsel that averted a potential crisis for the church. The tone of the letter suggests that Christensen felt his role in the McLellin transaction had ended. All other evidence indicates that Christensen did not become involved in the matter again until well into August, when Pinnock asked him to follow up with Hofmann to see that the document dealer repaid the bank loan. By then, Christensen had quit CFS, where Christensen was working when the Robertson incident occurred. The interpretation suggested by *Salamander* and *The Mormon Murders* does not adequately account for these facts.

12. Videotape, LDS Press Conference, Oct. 23, 1985. The authors of two books about the Salt Lake bombings refer to records for Hofmann's car phone that reportedly show telephone calls to Hinckley's office in October 1985 before the bombings. *Salamander*, 126, 129–30, 356; *A Gathering of Saints*, 267. Asked to comment on the records, Gordon Hinckley wrote, "A few days before the bombings Mr. Hofmann called my office and asked my secretary if he could see me. I do not know how many times he may have called in an effort to secure an appointment." The appointment Hofmann secured, Hinckley explained, was the one in which they discussed the Kinderhook plates. Gordon B. Hinckley to Dallin H. Oaks, Nov. 5, 1987.

Salamander, 129, refers to October 10 as the day on which Hofmann met with Hinckley to discuss the Kinderhook plates. The same book, 129–30, then adds, "However, the telephone record showed that the next morning Hofmann had called Hinckley's office from his mobile telephone at 7:30." *Salamander* errs, however, in setting the date of the Kinderhook meeting. It actually occurred October 11. See chapter 6, notes 114–15, and accompanying text; see also chapter 10, note 41.

Salamander, 356, observes that on October 14, 1985, "Hofmann placed two calls to Hinckley from his mobile telephone, each lasting a few minutes." *Salamander*, 130, reads, "On October 14, the day before the bombings, Hofmann had called Hinckley's office both in the morning and the afternoon, each call lasting two to three minutes." The book also notes, "It was unknown, however, if Hofmann spoke directly with Hinckley."

13. Videotape, LDS Press Conference, Oct. 23, 1985.

14. Ibid.; Hugh W. Pinnock, Handwritten Note on transcript of LDS Press Conference, Oct. 23, 1985; "Preliminary Hearing," 6:181.

15. Videotape, LDS Press Conference, Oct. 23, 1985; Gibbons to Hinckley, received Oct. 18, 1985. On October 22, 1985, Hinckley used the information from Gibbons to prepare a handwritten document he titled "Hofmann Summary," which evolved into his October 23 press conference remarks.

16. Hugh W. Pinnock to Mac Christensen, Oct. 23, 1985; Hugh W. Pinnock to Terri Christensen, Oct. 23, 1985; "Statement by Elder Hugh W. Pinnock," Press Release, Church of Jesus Christ of Latter-day Saints, Oct. 21, 1985.

17. Oaks, Journal, Oct. 23, 1985.

18. Videotape, LDS Press Conference, Oct. 23, 1985.

19. Dallin H. Oaks, Handwritten Notes, Oct. 24, 1985. The bank chairman was Leon G. Harmon.

20. Oaks, Journal, Oct. 24, 1985.

21. Oaks, Handwritten Notes, Oct. 24, 1985; "Preliminary Hearing," 6:155.

22. Oaks, Handwritten Notes, Oct. 24, 1985.

According to *Salamander*, 59, when Salt Lake police detective Don Bell interviewed Pinnock on October 17 about the loan, Pinnock said, "The church was not involved in this transaction." The book adds, "Bell noted the answer, then drew an arrow from it to the word 'lie.' " When he had this passage brought to his attention, Pinnock said Bell had quoted him accurately, but that his statement was not a lie. Hugh W. Pinnock, Interview, Feb. 16, 1990.

Bell related that as he sat listening to Pinnock say the church was not involved in the loan for the McLellin collection, he thought to himself, "You know, that really probably could be okayed as an answer, you know, because if the LDS Church's name isn't going to be on the check that's buying it, maybe the LDS Church is not purchasing it." Bell felt disposed to label Pinnock's answer a lie, however, in part because bank officials had already told him that they viewed the loan as having been authorized by the church. Bell, Interview, Aug. 18, 1989.

From Pinnock's vantage point, however, the church was not involved in the loan because Hofmann was the one who signed the promissory note, received the money, and spent it. Hofmann also was expected to pay the bank back. Moreover, Pinnock had not been authorized by his supervisors to bind the church as a guarantor. When Pinnock paid off the loan, he publicly stated that he "was not a party to the loan" but was "convinced that the bank would not have made the loan to Mr. Hofmann were it not for my assurance that it was a safe loan." "Statement from Elder Hugh W. Pinnock," Press Release, Church of Jesus Christ of Latter-day Saints, Oct. 25, 1985.

23. Pinnock, Journal, Oct. 24, 1985; "Preliminary Hearing," 6:155, 193. The attorney was Kent B. Linebaugh.

24. Oaks, Journal, Oct. 24, 1985.

25. Pinnock, Journal, Oct. 24, 1985.

26. "Statement from Elder Hugh W. Pinnock"; Pinnock, Journal, Oct. 25, 1985; First Interstate Bank of Utah, N. A., Assignment of floating rate promissory note to Hugh W. Pinnock, Oct. 25, 1985.

27. Pinnock, Journal, Oct. 25, 1985.

28. "Statement from Elder Hugh W. Pinnock."

29. Pinnock, Journal, Oct. 25, 1985.

30. Mike Carter, "Police Seeking Motive in Two Bombing Deaths," *Salt Lake Tribune*, Oct. 26, 1985.

31. Bird, Journal, Oct. 28, 1985.

32. Mike Carter, "Documents Dealer Asked to Verify Origins of Papyri," *Salt Lake Tribune*, Oct. 29, 1985.

33. Pinnock, Journal, Oct. 22, 29, 1985; Bird, Journal, Oct. 29, 1985; Farnsworth, Interview, Sept. 8, 1989. Other persons Pinnock spoke to that day about the photographs were Dean Larsen, Earl Olson, and Martell Bird.

34. Boyd K. Packer, "Dedication of the Crabtree Technology Building, Brigham Young University," Oct. 29, 1985, 5–6.

35. Brett DelPorto, "Toy Dealer Says Hofmann Bought Fuse at His Store," *Deseret News*, Oct. 29, 1985.

36. Brett DelPorto, "Papyrus Copy Linked to a Fragment Sold Hofmann," *Deseret News*, Oct. 30, 1985.

37. Mike Carter and Joan O'Brien, "Hofmann Charged with Firearms Violation," *Salt Lake Tribune*, Nov. 1, 1985.

According to Salt Lake police detective Ken Farnsworth, in September 1985 (the month before the bombings), someone in the Wilding investment group filed a complaint with the FBI against Hofmann for fraud that was, in Farnsworth's words, "on a scale that qualifies for FBI investigation." Kenneth C. Farnsworth, Jr., Interview, Oct. 26, 1989.

38. Bird, Journal, Nov. 1, 1985.

39. Dawn Tracy, "Hofmann May Have 'Find of the Century' in 1600s Document," *Salt Lake Tribune*, Nov. 2, 1985. See also Edwin McDowell, "Gallery Said to Possess First American Imprint," *New York Times*, Nov. 2, 1985.

40. Rowe, Journal, Nov. 4, 1985; Mike Carter, "Bomb-Test Results Promising, but Not Conclusive," *Salt Lake Tribune*, Nov. 5, 1985.

41. Jerry Spangler, "Firearms Agents Seek Flynn's Phone Records," *Deseret News*, Nov. 5, 1985.

42. *Deseret News 1987 Church Almanac* (Salt Lake City: Deseret News, 1986), 129; Oaks, Journal, Nov. 15, 1985; Historical Department Office Journal, Nov. 15, 1985.

43. Bird, Journal, Nov. 6, 1985; Ronald D. Francis, Memorandum, Nov. 6, 1985.

44. Bird, Journal, Nov. 6, 1985.

45. Mike Carter, "Hofmann Pleads Innocent to Gun Charge," *Salt Lake Tribune*, Nov. 7, 1985.

46. Linda Sillitoe, "Four Groups Invested in Dickens Papers," *Deseret News*, Nov. 7, 1985.

47. Jerry Spangler, "More Conspirators in Bombing Suspected," *Deseret News*, Nov. 8, 1985; Mike Carter, "Investigators Seek Co-conspirator in Utah Bombings," *Salt Lake Tribune*, Nov. 8, 1985.

48. Mike Carter, "Flynn Enters Not-Guilty Plea to Federal Firearms Charge," *Salt Lake Tribune*, Nov. 13, 1985.

49. Mike Carter, "Conflicts Hinder Bombing Probe," *Salt Lake Tribune*, Nov. 18, 1985.

50. Pinnock, Journal, Nov. 19, 1985. An example of a broadcast news statement on the subject is the news update following "Civic Dialogue," KUED Channel 7 (Salt Lake City), Nov. 19, 1985, Videotape, HDC.

51. Mike Carter, "Hofmann Not Bomber, Says Expert," *Salt Lake Tribune*, Nov. 20, 1985. The expert noted was David C. Raskin of the University of Utah. For Raskin's account of the polygraph test, see "Hofmann, Hypnosis, and the Polygraph," *Utah Bar Journal* 3, no. 9 (Nov. 1990): 7–10.

52. Jerry Spangler and Brett DelPorto, "S.L. Police Believe Canyon Home May Be Site of Bomb Construction," *Deseret News*, Nov. 20, 1985.

53. First Interstate Bank of Utah, N.A., Board of Directors Meeting Minutes, Nov. 21, 1985. The previous month, Martell Bird had recorded in his journal that "apparently a federal bank examiner made a quick audit of the

First Interstate Bank and issued the opinion that there was nothing illegal in the loan." Bird, Journal, Oct. 25, 1985.

54. Mike Carter, "U.S. Grand Jury Hears Hofmann's Friends," *Salt Lake Tribune,* Nov. 22, 1985.

55. See, e.g., Larry Klenk to Ronald D. Francis, Nov. 26, 1985; Investigative Information Memos #245, 249, 270, 304, 309, Case #85–98153, Oct. 21, 23, 25, 1985, SLCPD.

56. Claron E. Swenson to J. Martell Bird, Dec. 2, 1985; Rowe, Journal, Nov. 27, 1985; FBI Receipt, signed by Calvin C. Clegg and Glenn N. Rowe, Nov. 27, 1985.

57. B. Ashworth, Interviews, May 3, 1989, Sept. 5, 1990. Charlene remembered the call as coming on Thanksgiving Day. C. Ashworth, Interview, Mar. 1, 1991.

58. C. Ashworth, Interview, Mar. 1, 1991.

59. B. Ashworth, Interview, May 3, 1989, Sept. 5, 1990. Charlene described the phone call as "a beautiful experience" that "really helped a lot." C. Ashworth, Interview, Mar. 1, 1991.

60. Dawn Tracy, "Missing LDS Documents in Texas?" *Salt Lake Tribune,* Nov. 28, 1985.

61. "A Discovery of Documents Wouldn't Alter Bomb Probe," *Deseret News,* Nov. 28, 1985.

62. Mike Carter, "Bombing Case Now in Prosecutors' Hands, Say Police," *Salt Lake Tribune,* Nov. 28, 1985.

Chapter 10: The Focus Shifts

1. Paul Larsen, "The Chameleon and the Salamander," *Utah Holiday* 15 (Dec. 1985): 84–88; George Throckmorton, Taped Reminiscences, ca. 1988–89. Though Throckmorton formulated many of his views about the case in October 1985, telephone calls and meetings with Dean Jessee in November and December helped provide the catalyst for solidifying his conclusions. Jessee telephoned Throckmorton on November 1 while preparing to publish his earlier Mormon History Association remarks about the salamander and Stowell letters. Jessee, Journal, Nov. 1, 6, 17, 25, Dec. 3, 5, 1985.

2. Mike Carter, "Nurse's Deposition Says Police Assumed Hofmann's Guilt," *Salt Lake Tribune,* Dec. 1, 1985.

3. "Preliminary Hearing," 12:80–81.

4. Dawn Tracy, " 'LDS Papers' Found in Houston," *Salt Lake Tribune,* Dec. 2, 1985.

5. Marianne Funk, "Texas Papers Not Quite 'McLellin Collection,' " *Deseret News,* Dec. 2, 1985. The state government archivist was Jeffery O. Johnson, described in the article as "manager of the Utah State Reference Bureau."

6. [Earl E. Olson?], "Telephone call from President Hinckley, Dec. 2, 1985, at 3:40 p.m."; Rowe, Journal, Dec. 2, 1985.

7. Ronald D. Francis, Memorandum, Dec. 2, 1985. The police detective was Sam Hemingway.

8. William F. Mead, Memorandum, Dec. 2, 1985. The ATF agent was Michele Guthrie. See also Church Administration Building Daily Visitor Log, Dec. 2, 1985, which shows that the police detective and the ATF agent signed in at the same time, the latter then being directed to the Church Office Building high rise.

9. Farnsworth, Interview, Sept. 8, 1989; Church Administration Building Daily Visitor Log, Dec. 2, 1985; Pinnock, Journal, Dec. 2, 1985.

10. Hugh W. Pinnock, Interview, May 30, 1989; Pinnock, Interview with FBI, Oct. 17, 1985; Bell, Interview, Aug. 18, 1989 (says Pinnock told him on October 17, 1985, that "I called Steve Christensen, and I asked Steve Christensen if he could put some pressure on Mark Hofmann to get him to take care of this [bank loan]").

11. Rowe, Journal, Dec. 2, 1985; [Olson?], "Telephone call from President Hinckley."

12. Francis M. Gibbons to Wilford W. Kirton, Jr., Dec. 4, 1985 (describing December 3 meeting); T. L. "Ted" Cannon to Wilford W. Kirton, Jr., Dec. 4, 1985 (mentioning December 3 conversation).

13. Cannon to Kirton, Dec. 4, 1985; "Preliminary Hearing," 11:135.

14. Throckmorton, Taped Reminiscences; Michael P. George, Handwritten Notes, Dec. 5, 1985.

15. Wilford W. Kirton, Jr., Telephone Interview, Aug. 29, 1989; Throckmorton, Taped Reminiscences; George, Handwritten Notes, Dec. 5, 1985.

16. Throckmorton, Taped Reminiscences; [Salt Lake County Attorney's Office], "Documents Needed as Found in Book," in Church Historical Department internal file labeled "Dec. 2–5 1985: Request from S. L. Co. Att. Office to see documents"; George, Handwritten Notes, Dec. 5, 1985.

17. George, Handwritten Notes, Dec. 5, 1985.

18. Dale Heaps, "Recollections of the George Throckmorton Investigation," May 26, 1989; "Preliminary Hearing," 11:33–34; Throckmorton, Taped Reminiscences.

19. Rowe, Journal, Dec. 5, 1985; Throckmorton, Taped Reminiscences; Wayne A. Jacobson to Whom It May Concern, June 12, 1989. Jacobson was the library employee.

20. Jacobson to Whom It May Concern, June 12, 1989; Throckmorton, Taped Reminiscences.

21. Throckmorton, Taped Reminiscences; Richard P. Lindsay, Telephone Interview, Aug. 29, 1989; Church of Jesus Christ of Latter-day Saints, *Melchizedek Priesthood Handbook* (Salt Lake City: Church of Jesus Christ of Latter-day Saints, 1984), 29.

22. George Throckmorton to Richard Lindsay, Dec. 6, 1985; Lindsay, Telephone Interview, Aug. 29, 1989.

23. Lindsay, Telephone Interview, Aug. 29, 1989; Throckmorton, Taped Reminiscences.

24. Throckmorton, Taped Reminiscences; Gibbons, Interview, Apr. 6, 1989; Rowe, Journal, Dec. 6, 1985; John Hardy, Interview, Dec. 6, 1989. Hardy was the employee who accompanied Throckmorton to the lab.

25. Michael P. George, Interview, May 3, 1989; Church Administration Building Daily Visitor Log, Dec. 6, 1985; Church Administration Building Visitor Introduction Slip, Dec. 6, 1985; Michael P. George, Handwritten Notes, Dec. 6, 1985; Bird, Journal, Dec. 6, 1985; Farnsworth, Interview, Sept. 8, 1989; Oscar W. McConkie, Jr., Handwritten Notes, Dec. 6, 1985; Francis to O. McConkie, Dec. 6, 1985; Investigative Information Memo #881, Case #85–98153, June 28, 1989, recording events of Dec. 6, 1985, SLCPD. Cf. Investigative Information Memo #880, Case #85–98153, June 28, 1989, recording events of Dec. 5, 1985, SLCPD, which reads, "Mr. Kirton called and said we could meet with Dallin Oaks at 1345 hrs on Friday before our meeting with Hugh Pinnock."

26. Farnsworth, Interview, Sept. 8, 1989; George, Handwritten Notes, Dec. 6, 1985; Pinnock, Journal, Dec. 6, 1985; O. McConkie, Handwritten Notes, Dec. 6, 1985.

27. Farnsworth, Interview, Sept. 8, 1989; Oscar W. McConkie, Jr., to Richard Turley, Jr., Aug. 30, 1989.

28. Pinnock, Journal, Dec. 6, 1985; O. McConkie, Handwritten Notes, Dec. 6, 1985; George, Handwritten Notes, Dec. 6, 1985; Investigative Information Memo #825, Case #85–98153, Apr. 2, 1986, recording events of Dec. 6, 1985, SLCPD; O. McConkie to Turley, Aug. 30, 1989.

29. O. McConkie to Turley, Aug. 30, 1989.

30. George, Interview, May 3, 1989; George, Handwritten Notes, Dec. 6, 1985.

31. George, Handwritten Notes, Dec. 6, 1985; Farnsworth, Interview, Oct. 6, 1989; "Preliminary Hearing," 6:175–76.

32. George, Interview, May 3, 1989.

33. Farnsworth, Interviews, Sept. 8, Oct. 6, 1989, relying on Farnsworth, Notes, Dec. 6, 1985.

34. Pinnock, Journal, Dec. 6, 1985; Farnsworth, Interview, Dec. 12, 1989.

35. Rowe, Journal, Dec. 9, 1985; Francis M. Gibbons to [Gordon B.] Hinckley, received Dec. 9, 1985; Glenn Rowe to Rick Turley, Oct. 2, 1989.

36. Hinckley, Interview, Dec. 15, 1989. One interesting gauge of how busy Hinckley was during this period is his activity with respect to temple work, considered by Latter-day Saints to be one of the church's three principal missions. Extant records show that temple dedications alone took Hinckley to every continent except Antarctica during this period. "Tokyo Temple Dedication," Oct. 27–29, 1980, CR 80/2, HDC; "The Seattle Temple Dedication Services," Nov. 17–21, 1980, CR 77/3, HDC; "Jordan River Temple Dedication Services," Nov. 16–20, 1981, CR 67/3, HDC; "Jubilance at Asian Temple Ceremonies," Church News, Sept. 4, 1982; "Dallas Texas Temple Started," Church News, Jan. 30, 1983; "Atlanta Georgia Temple Dedication Services," June 1–4, 1983, CR 340/3, HDC; "Apia Samoa Temple Dedication Services," Aug. 5–7, 1983, CR 550/1, HDC; "Nuku'Alofa Tonga Temple Dedication Services," Aug. 9–11, 1983, CR 507/2, HDC; Karen Winfield, "Rites Begin Construction of New Temple near Chicago," Church News, Aug. 21, 1983; "Santiago Chile Temple Dedication Services," Sept. 15–17, 1983, CR 560/1, HDC;

"Papeete Tahiti Temple Dedication Services," Oct. 27–29, 1983, CR 1/152, HDC; "Mexico City Temple Dedication Services," Dec. 2–4, 1983, CR 79/2, HDC; Larry D. MacFarlane, "Rites Start First Temple of Eastern Rockies," *Church News*, May 27, 1984; "Boise Idaho Temple Dedication Services," May 25–30, 1984, CR 561/1, HDC; "Sydney Australia Temple Dedication Services," Sept. 20–23, 1984, CR 592/1, HDC; "Manila Philippines Temple Dedication Services," Sept. 25–27, 1984, CR 559/1, HDC; "Dallas Texas Temple Dedication Services," Oct. 19–24, 1984, CR 590/1, HDC; "Taipei Taiwan Temple Dedication Services," Nov. 17–18, 1984, CR 591/1, HDC; "Guatemala City Temple Dedication Services," Dec. 14–16, 1984, CR 556/1, HDC; "Manti Utah Temple Rededication Services," June 14–16, 1985, CR 348/42, HDC; "Freiberg DDR Temple Dedication Services," June 28–30, 1985, CR 1/151, HDC; Hal Knight, "Work 'Rolls Forward Again,'" *Church News*, July 7, 1985; "Church's Image Boosted in Sweden," *Church News*, July 7, 1985; "Stockholm Sweden Temple Dedication Services," July 2–4, 1985, CR 613/1, HDC; "Chicago Illinois Temple Dedication Services," Aug. 9–13, 1985, CR 593/1, HDC; "Johannesburg South Africa Temple Dedication Services," Aug. 24–25, 1985, CR 557/1, HDC.

37. Gordon B. Hinckley, Handwritten Notes, Dec. 9, 1985; Church Administration Building Daily Visitor Log, Dec. 9, 1985; Michael P. George, Handwritten Notes, Dec. 9, 1985; Investigative Information Memo #826, Case #85–98153, Mar. 31, 1986, recording events of Dec. 9, 1985, SLCPD; Farnsworth, Interview, Oct. 26, 1989, relying on Farnsworth, Notes, Dec. 9, 1985; "Preliminary Hearing," 12:96.

The Mormon Murders, 306, later claimed that "an FBI man tagged along" in the interview. The sources cited above, however, uniformly agree that no FBI agent was present.

38. Hinckley, Statement, Oct. 23, 1985; Hinckley, Handwritten Notes, Dec. 9, 1985; George, Handwritten Notes, Dec. 9, 1985; Investigative Information Memo #826; Farnsworth, Interview, Oct. 26, 1989.

39. Hinckley, Statement, Oct. 23, 1985; George, Handwritten Notes, Dec. 9, 1985; Investigative Information Memo #826; Farnsworth, Interview, Oct. 26, 1989.

40. Hinckley, Handwritten Notes, Dec. 9, 1985; Farnsworth, Interview, Oct. 26, 1989.

41. Hinckley, Handwritten Notes, Dec. 9, 1985; Farnsworth, Interview, Oct. 26, 1989; George, Handwritten Notes, Dec. 9, 1985.

This interview would introduce some confusion about the date on which Hofmann offered the Kinderhook plates to Hinckley. At the October 23 news conference, Hinckley had said the meeting occurred "more recently" than other meetings with the document dealer, but he had not given a specific date. Videotape, LDS Press Conference, Oct. 23, 1985. In preparing for the December 9 interview with Hinckley, Farnsworth had prepared a question that read, "Mark told another individual that he had sold the Kinderhook plates to you on 10–10 of '85. Is that true?" Farnsworth, Interview, Oct. 26, 1989, relying on Farnsworth, Notes, Dec. 9, 1985.

George's notes suggest that Farnsworth never got around to asking his question because Hinckley brought up the plates himself while recounting his various meetings with Hofmann, including the one in which he declined Hofmann's offer on the plates. George's notes record that Hinckley said he met with Hofmann to discuss the plates "in October." George, Handwritten Notes, Dec. 9, 1985.

The actual date of the meeting was October 11. See chapter 6, notes 114–15, and accompanying text. *Salamander*, 128–29, however, mistakenly adopts the October 10 date as having come from Hinckley.

42. George, Handwritten Notes, Dec. 9, 1985; George, Interview, May 3, 1989.

43. George, Interview, May 3, 1989; George, Handwritten Notes, Dec. 9, 1985; Investigative Information Memo #826; Farnsworth, Interview, Oct. 26, 1989.

44. George, Handwritten Notes, Dec. 9, 1985.

45. George, Interview, May 3, 1989.

46. See, e.g., S. Flynn, Interview with Bob Swehla, Mike Fierro, and Ken Farnsworth, Oct. 18, 1985, in which Flynn describes Hofmann's supposed dealings with Hinckley. When pressed for the source of his information, Flynn replied, "A great deal of what I say is what he [Hofmann] told me."

47. George, Interview, May 3, 1980; George, Handwritten Notes, Dec. 9, 1985.

48. See notes 35, 88–89, and accompanying text.

49. George, Handwritten Notes, Dec. 9, 1985; Farnsworth, Interview, Oct. 26, 1989; George, Interview, May 3, 1989.

50. George, Interview, May 3, 1989; George, Handwritten Notes, Dec. 9, 1985.

51. Hinckley, Memorandum, June 12, 1985.

52. Glenn N. Rowe, Memorandum, Jan. 2, 1988.

53. "Preliminary Hearing," 6:54.

54. George, Handwritten Notes, Dec. 9, 1985; Farnsworth, Interview, Oct. 26, 1989; George, Interview, May 3, 1989.

Reflecting investigators' theory, three books on the bombing case suggest that Steve Christensen had been called to replace Mark Hofmann as a church agent to acquire documents, implying therefore that church officials' denials of this theory constituted a cover-up. *The Mormon Murders*, 213, 307; *A Gathering of Saints*, 231, 267; *Salamander*, 127–28, 178. The theory rests on the premise that Hofmann was an acquisition agent for the church. A more complete view of the evidence, however, shows that although Hofmann once proposed becoming a document agent for the church, church officials refused to accept his proposal, opting instead to treat him as a dealer. See chapter 4, notes 56–60, and accompanying text. Because Hofmann had not been appointed as the church's acquisition agent, the conclusion that Christensen was to replace Hofmann in that capacity does not follow.

Christensen's associate Tom Moore recalled that when he last saw Christensen on October 11, 1985, they had a heart-to-heart talk about Christensen's future. Christensen had talked to him earlier about the McLellin deal, but when they spoke that day, Christensen was clearly bent on remaining in the finance and securities business and gave no hint of making a career out of acquiring documents. Tom Moore, Telephone Interview, Oct. 3, 1989.

Hugh Pinnock's brother-in-law, Franklin Johnson, was another associate of Christensen who discussed the McLellin collection with him repeatedly in the weeks before the bombings. "But he was not ever representing himself as an employee of the church, or as an agent of the church," Johnson said later. "I don't think he ever did that. And I knew him very well at this time. I think he would have told me if he had, . . . but he never did." Christensen called Johnson at about 10:00 P.M. on October 14, 1985, just hours before the Judge Building bomb killed him. He told Johnson he would have to postpone a meeting with him on the fifteenth because he was going to close the McLellin deal. "He was very happy," Johnson recalled. "He thought that everything was accomplished, and that he would be through with it, and that he would be able to move on business-wise and otherwise in his life."

"He was trying to make a new start in life . . . financially," Johnson recalled, "and this [the McLellin transaction] was a drag. It was really pulling him down because he had to spend so much time. . . . I don't think he was looking towards any future deals on documents or anything like that that I knew of. And . . . in fact, I think he was shying away from it." Instead, Johnson said, Christensen seemed intent on "putting together deals for financing, where he would do the paperwork." Johnson said Christensen "thought there was a big future in it, and he was very excited about doing it." Franklin Johnson, Interview, Oct. 5, 1989.

Assuming that Christensen was planning a career in acquiring documents has led to other misinterpretations of evidence in the case. For example, *Salamander*, 351, relates that Christensen told his attorney that "a bankruptcy might not be necessary" because he had "something cooking that could clear the decks." The book observes that the attorney "gathered that the mixed metaphor referred to some kind of document deal, probably the lost 116 pages. Christensen obviously was feeling better about his financial situation. His sense of urgency regarding the bankruptcy seemed to have evaporated."

The deal to which Christensen alluded, however, was almost certainly unrelated to historical documents. Christensen was working with Salt Lake businessman Doug Snarr to complete the financing of a satellite network company. In discussions with Snarr, Christensen had implied that his debts totalled several million dollars. Snarr later said that had he lived, Christensen could have made up to $9 million from the project, an amount which might well have served to clear his troubled financial decks. "If I could get this thing going with you, Doug," Christensen had said repeatedly to Snarr, "and it works like I'm convinced that it will work, . . . I'm going to make it in life." Snarr, Interview, Dec. 9, 1989.

55. Farnsworth, Interview, Oct. 26, 1989; George, Interview, May 3, 1989.

56. Rowe, Journal, Dec. 10, 1985; Wayne Allen, Memorandum, Dec. 11, 1985; Claron E. Swenson to J. Martell Bird, Dec. 12, 1985; Larry Klenk to

Ronald D. Francis, Dec. 13, 1985; Glenn N. Rowe to Dean L. Larsen, Dec. 13, 1985.

57. Dallin H. Oaks, Transcript of Remarks Delivered at Historical Department Christmas Dinner, Dec. 11, 1985.

58. Mike Carter, "Wife's Polygraph Test Boosts Alibi of 'Prime Suspect' in Bombings," *Salt Lake Tribune,* Dec. 12, 1985; "Wife's Polygraph Test Backs Statement That Hofmann Was Home during Bombing," *Deseret News,* Dec. 12, 1985.

59. See Historical Department Archives Call Slips for George Throckmorton signed by Rowe on Dec. 13, 1985, in Historical Department internal file labeled "Dec. 13, 1985: Call slips to prepare for George Throckmorton visit"; Rowe, Journal, Dec. 16, 1985; Historical Department, "Daily Register, Archives Search Room," Dec. 16, 1985; Throckmorton, Taped Reminiscences.

60. Glenn N. Rowe to Dallin H. Oaks, Dec. 9, 1985; "Preliminary Hearing," 11:8; Throckmorton, Taped Reminiscences.

61. See Historical Department Archives Call Slips for George Throckmorton signed by Rowe on Dec. 17, 1985, in Historical Department internal file labeled "Dec. 17, 1985: Call slips for materials requested by George Throckmorton"; Rowe, Journal, Dec. 17, 1985; Historical Department, "Daily Register, Archives Search Room," Dec. 17, 1985; Throckmorton, Taped Reminiscences.

62. Rowe, Journal, Dec. 17–18, 1985; Glenn N. Rowe, Receipt for Stowell letter, Dec. 17, 1985; F. Michael Watson, Receipt for Stowell letter, Dec. 18, 1985, written at the bottom of Rowe, Receipt, Dec. 17, 1985; "Preliminary Hearing," 10:114; Historical Department, "Daily Register, Archives Search Room," Dec. 18, 1985; Throckmorton, Taped Reminiscences.

63. Historical Department Office Journal, Dec. 20, 1985; Historical Department, "Daily Register, Archives Search Room," Dec. 19–20, 1985.

64. Linda Sillitoe and Jerry Spangler, "Bombings Probe Focuses on LDS, RLDS Documents," *Deseret News,* Dec. 22, 1985.

65. Robert L. Stott, Interview, July 26, 1989; Cannon to Kirton, Dec. 4, 1985.

66. Subpoena Duces Tecum directed to Glenn Rowe, In re Criminal Investigation of Hofmann, No. CS 85–121 (Utah 3d Dist. Ct. issued Dec. 27, 1985); Subpoena Duces Tecum directed to Gordon B. Hinckley, In re Criminal Investigation of Hofmann, No. CS 85–121 (Utah 3d Dist. Ct. issued Dec. 27, 1985).

67. Kathy Fahy, "Lawyer Expects Hofmann to Face Murder Charges," *Deseret News,* Dec. 27, 1985.

68. Mike Carter, "Hayward to Seek Grand Jury in Bombing Case," *Salt Lake Tribune,* Dec. 28, 1985.

69. T. L. "Ted" Cannon to Wilford W. Kirton, Jr., Dec. 30, 1985.

70. Mike Carter, "Let a Grand Jury Probe Bombings, Sheriff Asks," *Salt Lake Tribune,* Jan. 1, 1986; "Judges Consider S. L. Killings for Grand Jury Investigations," *Deseret News,* Jan. 1, 1986.

71. Maxine Martz, "Top Ten Utah Stories," *Deseret News,* Jan. 1, 1986.

72. Rowe, Journal, Jan. 2, 1986.

73. Rule 14(b) of the Utah Rules of Criminal Procedure provided, "A subpoena may command the person to whom it is directed to appear and testify or to produce in court or to allow inspection of records, papers or other objects. The court may quash or modify the subpoena if compliance would be unreasonable." Utah Code Ann. §77–35–14(b) (1982).

74. Rowe, Journal, Jan. 2–3, 1986; Church Historical Department internal file labeled "Jan. 2–3, 1986: Call slips for additional items for George Throckmorton"; "Preliminary Hearing," 11:34–35, 178; Throckmorton, Taped Reminiscences; Heaps, "Recollections," May 26, 1989.

75. Oaks, Journal, Jan. 3, 1986; Francis M. Gibbons to the First Presidency, Jan. 3, 1986. One of the two subpoenas ordered the church to produce fifty-four documents. The other sought just one document. By adding fifty-four and one, Oaks came up with a total of fifty-five documents. The Stowell letter was mentioned in both subpoenas, however, so that in reality, the total was fifty-four.

76. Gibbons to the First Presidency, Jan. 3, 1986.

77. Dawn Tracy, "McLellin a Mormon? News to Us, Descendants Say," *Salt Lake Tribune,* Jan. 3, 1986. The professor was Richard Lloyd Anderson.

78. Rowe, Journal, Jan. 6, 1986; Historical Department Office Journal, Jan. 6, 1986; Oaks, Journal, Jan. 7, 1986; Wilford W. Kirton, Jr., to T. L. "Ted" Cannon, Jan. 10, 1986; Stott, Interview, July 26, 1989; Throckmorton, Taped Reminiscences. The letter from Kirton to Cannon summarizes the meeting. Cannon signed and returned it to Kirton to confirm that it accurately reflected what went on.

79. These items are listed in Kirton to Cannon, Jan. 10, 1986. For photographs of and transcriptions from the letter book and diary, see Jessee, *Personal Writings of Joseph Smith,* 3–14, 58–195.

80. Kirton to Cannon, Jan. 10, 1986.

81. Historical Department Office Journal, Jan. 6, 1986.

82. Ronald D. Francis, Memorandum, Jan. 10, 1986 (summarizing telephone conversation with Dean L. Larsen).

83. Rowe, Journal, Jan. 6, 1986; Historical Department Administration Meeting Minutes, Jan. 7, 1986. The FBI agent who called was Steve Clark.

84. Rowe, Journal, Jan. 7, 1986; Historical Department Administration Meeting Minutes, Jan. 7, 1986.

85. Jerry Spangler, "Police End Bombing Probe, Say It's up to Attorney Now," *Deseret News,* Jan. 7, 1986.

86. Mike Carter, "Willoughby Tells Detectives to Go for Charges in Two Bombings," *Salt Lake Tribune,* Jan. 7, 1986.

87. Rowe, Journal, Jan. 8, 1986; Michael P. George, Handwritten Notes, Jan. 8, 1986; Subpoena Duces Tecum directed to Glenn Rowe, In re Criminal Investigation of Hofmann, No. CS 85–121 (Utah 3d Dist. Ct. issued Jan. 8, 1986).

88. Francis M. Gibbons to Dean L. Larsen, Jan. 7, 1986; Dean L. Larsen, Signed Receipt, Jan. 8, 1986, typed on the bottom of Gibbons to Larsen, Jan. 7, 1986; Rowe, Journal, Jan. 8, 1986; Gibbons, Interview, Oct. 25, 1989.

89. Gibbons to Larsen, Jan. 7, 1986.

90. Dallin H. Oaks to Glenn N. Rowe, Jan. 8, 1986; Glenn Rowe to Rick Turley, Oct. 26, 1989; Christy Best to Glenn Rowe, Nov. 8, 1989.

91. Oaks to Rowe, Jan. 8, 1986.

92. "In Apology, Bombing Answer, County Attorney Is Correct," *Salt Lake Tribune*, Jan. 11, 1986; Rowe, Journal, Jan. 8–9, 11–12, 1986; Jay Burrup, Journal, Jan. 8–10, 1986; Throckmorton, Taped Reminiscences.

93. "Hofmann Trial Set Feb. 3," *Deseret News*, Jan. 14, 1986; "Hofmann Investigation Could Conclude Soon," *Daily Universe*, Jan. 14, 1986.

94. Glenn N. Rowe, "Additional Materials Requested by Salt Lake County Attorney General," Jan. 14, 1986; Burrup, Journal, Jan. 14–15, 1986; Rowe, Journal, Jan. 14, 1986.

95. Jerry P. Cahill to Richard P. Lindsay, Jan. 15, [1986].

96. Rowe, Journal, Jan. 15, 1986.

97. Church Historical Department internal file titled "Jan. 15–17, 1986: Research on Cash Transactions with Mark Hofmann."

98. Burrup, Journal, Jan. 17, 1986 (describing previous day's events); Rowe, Journal, Jan. 16, 1986. The reporter who called was Duane Cardall of KSL Television.

99. Oaks, Journal, Jan. 16, 1986.

100. Mike Carter, "Charges Remain Elusive in Bombing Deaths," *Salt Lake Tribune*, Jan. 16, 1986; Bob Mims, "Flynn Says He'd Consider Deal to Testify at Hofmann's Trial," *Deseret News*, Jan. 16, 1986.

101. Receipt signed by Glenn N. Rowe and Steven F. Clark, Jan. 17, 1986; Receipt signed by Glenn N. Rowe, James F. Bell, and Ken C. Farnsworth, Jan. 17, 1986; Historical Department Office Journal, Jan. 17, 1986; Rowe, Journal, Jan. 17, 1986; Subpoena Duces Tecum directed to LDS Church, In re Criminal Investigation of Hofmann, No. CS 85–121 (Utah 3d Dist. Ct. issued Jan. 15, 1986); Glenn Rowe to Rick Turley, Oct. 25, 1989; Farnsworth, Interview, Oct. 26, 1989.

102. Patrick D. Murray to Ronald D. Francis, Jan. 21, 1986.

103. Burrup, Journal, Jan. 17, 1986; Rowe, Journal, Jan. 17, 1986.

104. Dallin H. Oaks, Handwritten Notes, Jan. 17, 1986.

105. Rowe, Journal, Jan. 20, 1986; Oaks, Journal, Jan. 20, 1986; Historical Department, "Items Retained by Salt Lake County Attorney's Office," Jan. 21, 1986; Historical Department internal file labeled "Jan. 20–22, 1986: List (Receipt) of 14 items retained by Co. Att. Office in Crime Lab."

106. Rowe, Journal, Jan. 21, 1986; Oaks, Journal, Jan. 22, 1986 (describing previous day's activities).

107. Rowe, Journal, Jan. 22, 1986; Michael P. George, Handwritten Notes, Jan. 22, 1986.

108. Historical Department Advisers Meeting Minutes, Jan. 22, 1986.

109. Boyd K. Packer and Dallin H. Oaks to the First Presidency, Jan. 27, 1986; Rowe, Journal, Jan. 23, 1986; Oaks, Journal, Jan. 24, 1986.

110. [Boyd K.] Packer to [Gordon B.] Hinckley, Jan. 28, 1986.

111. Oscar W. McConkie, Jr., Handwritten Notes, Jan. 31, 1986; Pinnock, Journal, Jan. 31, 1986; Church Administration Building Daily Visitor Log, Jan. 31, 1986.

McConkie took detailed notes of the interview. Farnsworth took none. "I don't have any notes on that because I wasn't doing the interview," he later said. "I was there with the lawyers who were preparing themselves for court." Farnsworth, Interview, Oct. 6, 1989. When asked for his notes of the interview, Stott said prosecutors took none. Stott, Interview, July 26, 1989.

112. O. McConkie, Handwritten Notes, Jan. 31, 1986; O. McConkie to Turley, Aug. 30, 1989.

113. O. McConkie, Handwritten Notes, Jan. 31, 1986. Milton V. Backman, Jr., *The Heavens Resound: A History of the Latter-day Saints in Ohio, 1830–1838* (Salt Lake City: Deseret Book, 1983), 418, notes, "Solomon Spaulding's name is spelled differently in contemporary records. Sometimes it is spelled Spaulding and other times Spalding. [Spaulding was] the spelling most commonly used in later histories and the one employed by his widow, Mrs. Matilda Davison." On the other hand, Charles H. Whittier and Stephen W. Stathis, "The Enigma of Solomon Spalding," *Dialogue* 10 (Autumn 1977): 70, observes that when he entered the Revolutionary Army in January 1778, his name was "listed as 'Spaulding,' though the variant 'Spalding' appears most often in his later life."

114. Pinnock, Journal, Jan. 31, 1986; O. McConkie, Handwritten Notes, Jan. 31, 1986.

115. O. McConkie, Handwritten Notes, Jan. 31, 1986; Rowe, Journal, Jan. 31, 1986.

116. O. McConkie, Handwritten Notes, Jan. 31, 1986; David Biggs, Telephone Interview, July 31, 1989.

117. Pinnock, Interview, May 30, 1989.

118. Stott, Interview, July 26, 1989; Biggs, Telephone Interview, July 31, 1989.

119. Pinnock, Journal, Jan. 31, 1986.

Chapter 11: The Malefactor Charged

1. Bird, Journal, Feb. 4, 1986; Ronald D. Francis, Memorandum, Feb. 4, 1986; Information, State v. Hofmann, No. 860003035 (Utah 5th Cir. Ct. filed Feb. 4, 1986); Information, State v. Hofmann, No. 860003041 (Utah 5th Cir. Ct. filed Feb. 4, 1986); Information, State v. Hofmann, No. 860003044 (Utah 5th Cir. Ct. filed Feb. 4, 1986); Information, State v. Hofmann, No. 860003045 (Utah 5th Cir. Ct. filed Feb. 4, 1986).

2. Transcript of News Broadcast, KUTV Channel 2 (Salt Lake City), Feb. 4, 1986, 12:00 noon.

3. Information, State v. Hofmann, No. 860003035 (Utah 5th Cir. Ct. filed Feb. 4, 1986); see chapter 5, note 76, chapter 6, note 43, and accompanying text.

4. See, e.g., Linda Sillitoe, "Documents Have Been Hofmann's Life since 1980—and They Provide Both Motive and Charges in Murder Case," *Deseret News*, Feb. 4, 1986; Mike Carter, "Prosecutors Charge Hofmann with Two Murders and Fraud," *Salt Lake Tribune*, Feb. 5, 1986; Dawn Tracy, "LDS Papers May Play Big Role in Charges," *Salt Lake Tribune*, Feb. 5, 1986; Jim Woolf, "Bomb Suspect Charged," *Washington Post*, Feb. 5, 1986; "Dealer in Rare Mormon Documents Charged in Two Utah Killings," *New York Times*, Feb. 5, 1986; Linda Sillitoe, "Dates, Names of Victims Shed Light on Identity of Documents," *Deseret News*, Feb. 5, 1986; Mike Carter, "Records Allege Hofmann Sold Forged Papers," *Salt Lake Tribune*, Feb. 6, 1986; Russell Chandler, "Letter Bought by Mormon Church Ruled a Forgery," *Los Angeles Times*, Feb. 7, 1986.

5. Jan Thompson and Jerry Spangler, "Hofmann Charged with Two Murders and Fraud," *Deseret News*, Feb. 4, 1986.

6. "Forgery and Fraud Alleged in Document Transactions," *Church News*, Feb. 9, 1986; Transcript of News Broadcast, KUTV Channel 2 (Salt Lake City), Feb. 5, 1986, 6:00 P.M.; Chandler, "Letter Bought"; Rowe, Journal, Feb. 5, 1986; Tracy, "LDS Papers"; "Dealer in Rare Mormon Documents."

7. Wilford W. Kirton, Jr., to T. L. "Ted" Cannon, Feb. 4, 1986.

8. Information at 5–6, State v. Hofmann, No. 860003035 (Utah 5th Cir. Ct. filed Feb. 4, 1986); Carter, "Records Allege"; Robert D. Mullins and Jerry Spangler, "S.L. Detective Describes Scene following Bombing," *Deseret News*, Feb. 6, 1986.

9. Carter, "Records Allege"; Jim Woolf, "Alleged Mormon Papers Called Fake," *Washington Post*, Feb. 6, 1986; Dawn Tracy, "Previously Unknown LDS Papers Come to Light," *Salt Lake Tribune*, Feb. 6, 1986; Jerry Spangler, "Released Papers Say Hofmann Was Involved in Fraud, Forgery since '80," *Deseret News*, Feb. 6, 1986.

10. Bird, Journal, Feb. 6, 1986.

11. Oaks, Journal, Feb. 6, 1986.

12. Transcript of News Broadcast, KUTV Channel 2 (Salt Lake City), Feb. 5, 1986, 10:00 P.M.; Spangler, "Released Papers."

13. FBI Laboratory Report, Jan. 27, 1986, FBI File No. 174–9847.

14. Rowe, Journal, Feb. 6, 1986.

15. Mike Carter, "Hofmann Sold Forgeries, Expert Says," *Salt Lake Tribune*, Feb. 7, 1986; Brett DelPorto, "Eastern Dealer Calls Documents 'Obvious Fakes,'" *Deseret News*, Feb. 7, 1986; Chandler, "Letter Bought."

16. Oaks, Journal, Feb. 6, 1986.

17. Bird, Journal, Feb. 7, 1986. The police captain was O. J. Peck.

18. Audiotape, Bail Hearing, State v. Hofmann, Nos. 86 FS 3035, 3041, 3044–45 (Utah 5th Cir. Ct. heard Feb. 5–7, 1986); Information at 6, State v. Hofmann, No. 860003045 (Utah 5th Cir. Ct. filed Feb. 4, 1986); Order Setting

Bond, State v. Hofmann, Nos. 86 FS 3035, 3041, 3044–45 (Utah 5th Cir. Ct. issued Feb. 10, 1986).

19. Bird, Journal, Feb. 10, 1986.

20. Wilford W. Kirton, Jr., to T. L. "Ted" Cannon, Feb. 10, 1986.

21. T. L. "Ted" Cannon to Willard W. Kirton, Feb. 13, 1986. Cannon's letter does not identify the detective by name.

22. T. L. "Ted" Cannon to Wilford W. Kirton, Jr., Feb. 18, 1986; Ted C[annon], Undated Handwritten Note, attached to Cannon to Kirton, Feb. 13, 18, 1986.

23. Cannon to Kirton, Feb. 18, 1986.

24. Subpoena Duces Tecum directed to Glen Rowe, In re Criminal Investigation of Hofmann, No. CS 85–121 (Utah 3d Dist. Ct. issued Feb. 19, 1986); Rowe, Journal, Feb. 18–19, 1986. Rowe's journal does not mention the name of the person who called from the county attorney's office.

25. Subpoena Duces Tecum directed to Robert Swenson, In re Criminal Investigation of Hofmann, No. CS 85–121 (Utah 3d Dist. Ct. issued Feb. 20, 1986); Robert P. Swensen to Wilford W. Kirton, Jr., Feb. 21, 1986. The investigator who delivered the subpoena was Richard W. Forbes.

26. See, e.g., Gary M. Peterson and Trudy Huskamp Peterson, *Archives and Manuscripts: Law* (Chicago: Society of American Archivists, 1985), 94–95; Richard Rubin, "The Threat to Library Circulation Records: *A Case Study,*" *Library Journal* 109 (1984): 1602–6; "NYPL Respects Confidential Reading Even of Fugitive," *American Libraries* 14 (1983): 5; Ernest P. Laseter, "Destroy the Records," *Library Journal* 107 (1982): 756; "Library Circulation Records Confidential in R.I.," *Library Journal* 107 (1982): 1366.

Using library records for criminal investigations remains a volatile issue in the 1990s. See, e.g., "Police Subpoena Library Records in Hunt for NYC's Zodiac Killer," *American Libraries* 21 (1990): 703–4, which includes statements made by Paul Fasana, Andrew W. Mellon Director of the Research Libraries, New York Public Library, about releasing information "only after a proper subpoena was served in accordance with state law." The article notes, "Fasana told *AL* library records are subpoenaed an average of twice a year, but the library does not necessarily comply. Subpoenas can be and often are contested."

27. Two letters from Wilford W. Kirton, Jr., to T. L. "Ted" Cannon, Feb. 27, 1986.

28. Three Historical Department internal files whose titles begin "Feb. 16–20, 1986: Compilation given to authorities . . ."; Rowe, Journal, Feb. 27, 1986. Rowe's journal does not specify who the caller was.

29. Dallin H. Oaks to Thomas S. Monson, Feb. 28, 1986; Dallin H. Oaks to Boyd K. Packer, Feb. 28, 1986.

30. Oaks, Journal, Feb. 28, 1986.

31. Glenn Rowe to Rick Turley, Mar. 30, 1990. Related entries were later found in the Central States Mission Historical Record, vol. 1, pp. 222, 224–29, HDC.

32. J. L. Traughber to the Librarian of the Church, Jan. 13, 1908, Ms 1325, box 10, fd. 19, HDC.

33. Joseph F. Smith, John R. Winder, and Anthon H. Lund to Samuel O. Bennion, Jan. 18, 1908, CR 1/20, vol. 43, pp. 520–21, HDC. The other church leader involved in the 1878 interview was Orson Pratt.

34. S. O. Bennion to Joseph F. Smith & Counselors, Feb. 12, 1908, Ms 1325, box 18, fd. 20, HDC.

35. Author's personal recollection; Hinckley, Interviews, Apr. 26, Dec. 15, 1989; Gibbons, Interview, Oct. 25, 1989.

36. William E. McLellin, Journals, HDC; Doctrine and Covenants (1981) 66:10.

37. William E. McLellin, Manuscript Books, HDC.

38. Rowe, Journal, Mar. 4, 1986.

39. Oaks, Journal, Mar. 4, 1986.

40. Utah Code Ann. §77-35-7(d)(1) (1982).

41. Subpoena Duces Tecum directed to Glenn Roe, In re Criminal Investigation of Hofmann, No. CS 85-121 (Utah 3d Dist. Ct. issued Mar. 4, 1986); Rowe, Journal, Mar. 4, 6, 1986; Wilford W. Kirton, Jr., to T. L. "Ted" Cannon, Mar. 6, 1986.

42. Mike Carter, "Flynn Admits He Had Unlisted Machine Gun," *Salt Lake Tribune,* Mar. 4, 1986.

43. Subpoena Duces Tecum directed to Russell Homer, In re Criminal Investigation of Hofmann, No. CS 85-121 (Utah 3d Dist. Ct. issued [Feb.] 28, 1986); Wilford W. Kirton, Jr., to T. L. "Ted" Cannon, Mar. 5, 1986.

44. Telephone Message for [Hugh W. Pinnock], Mar. 12, 1986; [Virginia Archer to Dallin H. Oaks, Mar. 12, 1986], Typed Note attached to telephone message for HWP, Mar. 12, 1986; [Dallin H. Oaks], Handwritten Note, Mar. 12, [1986], inscribed on [Archer to Oaks, Mar. 12, 1986]; Pinnock, Journal, Mar. 28, 1986; Hugh W. Pinnock, Telephone Interview, Oct. 26, 1989; Ronald J. Yengich, Interview, Sept. 20, 1989. The investigator was Ronald P. Harrington. Harrington had sought an audience with church leaders in November 1985 but had been turned down because the only charge that had been filed against Hofmann at that point was for possession of an unregistered machine gun, a matter about which church leaders knew nothing. Pinnock, Journal, Nov. 12–14, 1985.

45. Historical Department [Richard E. Turley, Jr.] to Boyd K. Packer, Dallin H. Oaks, and Dean L. Larsen, Mar. 6, 1986; Rowe, Journal, Mar. 12, 1986.

46. See, e.g., "Oberlin Conference on Theft Calls for Action," *Library Journal* 108 (1983): 2118; Slade Richard Gandert, *Protecting Your Collection* (New York: Haworth Press, 1982); Timothy Walch, *Archives and Manuscripts: Security* (Chicago: Society of American Archivists, 1977).

47. Richard E. Turley, Jr., to Boyd K. Packer, Mar. 7, 1986; Richard E. Turley, Jr., to Dallin H. Oaks, Mar. 7, 1986; Historical Department Office Journal, Mar. 12, 15, 1986; Historical Department Administration Meeting Minutes, Mar. 11, Apr. 22, 1986; Historical Department Advisers Meeting Minutes, Mar. 26, May 7, 28, June 6, 20, 1986; [Timothy Walch], "Security

Consultation—LDS Church Historical Department, Preliminary Findings," [Mar. 14, 1986]; Timothy Walch, "Security Consultation, Historical Department, the Church of Jesus Christ of Latter-day Saints," Mar. 1986; Timothy Walch to Dean Larson, Apr. 10, 1986; "Church Library and Archives Scheduled for Remodeling," Press Release, Church of Jesus Christ of Latter-day Saints, Aug. 8, 1986; "Remodeling of Historical Library Will Begin," *Deseret News,* Aug. 8, 1986; "Remodeling Scheduled for Historical Library, Archives," *Church News,* Aug. 10, 1986.

48. Rowe, Journal, Mar. 17, 1986.

49. [Virginia Archer to Dallin H. Oaks], Typed Note, Mar. 18, [1986]; Subpoena 86168643 directed to Hugh Pinnock, State v. Hofmann, No. 863045 (Utah [5th.] Cir. Ct. issued Mar. 13, 1986); Subpoena 86168644 directed to Gordon B. Hinckley, State v. Hofmann, No. 863035 (Utah [5th.] Cir. Ct. issued Mar. 13, 1986).

50. Stott, Interview, July 26, 1989. *The Mormon Murders,* 355–58, puts county investigator Michael George in the interview. George, however, says he was not present. Michael P. George, Telephone Interview with Glenn N. Rowe, Oct. 27, 1989.

51. Biggs, Telephone Interview, July 31, 1989.

52. Stott, Interview, July 26, 1989.

53. Biggs, Telephone Interview, July 31, 1989.

54. Stott, Interview, July 26, 1989; Biggs, Telephone Interview, July 31, 1989.

55. Biggs, Telephone Interview, July 31, 1989.

56. Hinckley to Oaks, Nov. 5, 1987.

57. Biggs, Telephone Interview, July 31, 1989. On the origins of journal keeping in the church, see Dean C. Jessee, "Joseph Smith and the Beginning of Mormon Record Keeping," in *The Prophet Joseph: Essays on the Life and Mission of Joseph Smith,* ed. Larry C. Porter and Susan Easton Black (Salt Lake City: Deseret Book, 1988), 150–51. Bitton and Arrington, *Mormons and Their Historians,* 162, notes that "Mormons have always been industrious record-keepers," and that "among these primary sources are many hundreds of diaries, a resource certainly found to no greater extent in any other comparable group."

58. Bruce R. McConkie, *Mormon Doctrine,* 2d ed. (Salt Lake City: Bookcraft, 1966), 397 (italics in original).

59. Joseph Fielding Smith, *Doctrines of Salvation,* vol. 2, comp. Bruce R. McConkie (Salt Lake City: Bookcraft, 1955), 204.

60. Author's personal recollection. Hinckley's habit of not recording details in his journal about office conversations was not unique. Perhaps no church leader in modern times advocated keeping journals more than Spencer W. Kimball. See, e.g., Edward L. Kimball, ed., *The Teachings of Spencer W. Kimball* (Salt Lake City: Bookcraft, 1982), 349–51. Yet his journal entry for March 17, 1981, the day on which the First Presidency met with Historical Department officials and advisers to discuss the disposition of the Joseph Smith III

blessing, reads simply, "Regular meetings, interviews and appointments at the office." Kimball, Journal, Mar. 17, 1981.

61. Stott, Interview, July 26, 1989; Biggs, Telephone Interview, July 31, 1989.

At the time of this interview, the Stowell letter charge still listed Hinckley as a private victim, despite prosecutors' assurances that they would amend the count to reflect that Hinckley had been acting for the church when he bought the letter. Church officials' repeated requests to amend the letter were later misinterpreted by two books on the bombings. *The Mormon Murders* claims that during the meeting with Stott and Biggs, Hinckley (in a "mellow voice") counseled, "I think it would be in the best interests of the Church if you simply dismissed the charge." "More fervently than the prosecutors could have imagined," the book asserts, "Gordon Hinckley must have wanted to say 'dismiss the charges' on *all* of Hofmann's crimes. Close the public record, lock him away or buy his silence, put the matter to rest." *The Mormon Murders*, 358 (italics in original).

Similarly, *A Gathering of Saints* maintains that when charges were first filed against Hofmann, church legal counsel "sought to have those listing Hinckley as one of his victims *dismissed*," and that during the meeting with Stott and Biggs, Hinckley "again and again . . . urged Stott to *withdraw* the charges against Hofmann naming him as a victim of fraud." *A Gathering of Saints*, 311 (italics added).

The evidence in the case, however, does not sustain either book's account. Both Stott and Biggs deny that Hinckley or Kirton asked them to dismiss the charges. "Nobody asked us to drop the case," Stott said. "Nobody asked us to drop the charge. Nothing like that." Biggs concurred. Stott, Interview, July 26, 1989; Biggs, Telephone Interview, July 31, 1989; "Like Hofmann, the Authors Made Up Stories, Ward Says," *Deseret News*, Oct. 16, 1988.

62. Stott, Interview, July 26, 1989; Biggs, Telephone Interview, July 31, 1989; Gibbons, Interview, Apr. 6, 1989.

63. Stott, Interview, July 26, 1989.

64. Biggs, Telephone Interview, July 31, 1989.

65. Stott, Interview, July 26, 1989. Apparently, Kirton was not the only one to suggest saving witnesses for the trial. See, e.g., *A Gathering of Saints*, 317, which explains that New York document dealer Charles Hamilton did not testify at the preliminary hearing "because he was being saved for Hofmann's trial." See also chapter 12, note 178.

66. Biggs, Telephone Interview, July 31, 1989.

67. Stott, Interview, July 26, 1989. Roberto Aron and Jonathan L. Rosner, *How to Prepare Witnesses for Trial* (New York: McGraw-Hill, 1985), 61, points out that "an unwillingness to take the time necessary to testify . . . is a particular problem with busy people" and recommends, "If the witness is too busy to testify, the lawyer should agree to try to find a replacement and indicate that the witness will be called only as a last resort."

68. Stott, Interview, July 26, 1989; Biggs, Telephone Interview, July 31, 1989.

69. "Press Release on History Matter," Draft, Mar. 26, 1986; Historical Department Advisers Meeting Minutes, Mar. 26, 1986.

70. Rowe, Journal, Mar. 27, 1986.

71. Rowe, Journal, Mar. 28, 1986.

72. Rowe, Journal, Mar. 31, 1986.

73. Rowe, Journal, Apr. 1, 1986; Glenn N. Rowe to Richard Turley, Earl Olson, et al., Apr. 1, 1986. See also note 78.

74. Rowe, Journal, Apr. 1–2, 1986; Subpoena Duces Tecum directed to Glen Rowe, In re Criminal Investigation of Hofmann, No. CS 85–121 (Utah 3d Dist. Ct. issued Apr. 2, 1986); Robert Stott, "Receipt of Documents," Apr. 8, 1986. Mike George also signed a receipt for a Historical Department document on April 8, agreeing to return it by May 1. Michael P. George, Receipt, Apr. 8, 1986.

75. Rowe, Journal, Apr. 2, 4–5, 7, 9–11, 14, 16, 1986; "Church Delivers Records to Illinois Court, Lists Documents Obtained from Mark W. Hofmann," Press Release, Church of Jesus Christ of Latter-day Saints, Apr. 11, 1986; "Preliminary Hearing," 6:26; Rowe to Turley, Mar. 30, 1990; Author's personal recollection. All the returned documents are listed in the Appendix.

76. Glenn N. Rowe to All Historical Department Employees, Apr. 2, 1986.

77. Information, State v. Hofmann, No. 860020193 (Utah 5th Cir. Ct. filed Apr. 4, 1986).

78. "Church Delivers Records to Illinois Court"; Dawn Tracy, "LDS Disclosing Papers Bought from Hofmann," *Salt Lake Tribune,* Apr. 12, 1986; "LDS Church Returns Records to Illinois," *Deseret News,* Apr. 12, 1986; Russell Chandler, "Mormons Tell of Dealings with Suspect," *Los Angeles Times,* Apr. 12, 1986.

Relying on Don Schmidt's recollections, Glenn Rowe had estimated the total value of items traded to Hofmann to be $82,045. Rowe to Turley, Olson, et al., Apr. 1, 1986. An unsigned, undated memorandum written by Glenn Rowe a few days later noted that Wade Lillywhite (then of Deseret Book) had appraised the same items on April 4 at $110,280. "The difference, therefore, between Donald T. Schmidt's estimate and Wade Lillywhite's estimate is about $30,000," Rowe concluded. "We may wish to add some to our figures to be safe." In his April 1 memorandum, Rowe had noted that the estimates did "not include printed (published) materials as records were not kept of those transactions."

79. Richard P. Lindsay to All General Authorities, Apr. 11, 1986; Jerry P. Cahill to Public Affairs Staff, Apr. 11, 1986.

Chapter 12: Probable Cause

1. "Preliminary Hearing," 1:3–8.

2. Ibid., 9–24.

3. Ibid., 25–34.

4. Ibid., 34.

5. Ibid., 36–38, 47–49.

6. Ibid., 42–43.

7. Ibid., 49–109.

8. Ibid., 113–44.

9. Ibid., 196–208. The woman was Margene Robbins.

10. Ibid., 227–44.

11. Pinnock, Journal, Apr. 14, 1986.

12. Jerry P. Cahill to Richard P. Lindsay, Apr. 15, 16, 17, 18, 21, 22, 23, May 6, 7, 8, 13, 14, 21, 22, 23, 1986; Richard P. Lindsay to Special Affairs Committee, Apr. 21, 22, 24, May 7, 8, 13, 14, 21, 22, 23, 1986; Richard P. Lindsay to Boyd K. Packer and Dallin H. Oaks, Apr. 16, 1986 ("As recommended by the Special Affairs Committee we will supply daily updates to you both on matters related to the current preliminary hearing for Mark Hofmann. We will plan to do the same during the trial that will likely follow in late summer").

13. "Preliminary Hearing," 2:3–45.

14. Ibid., 50–128. The thirteen-year-old neighbor was Aaron Teplick.

15. Ibid., 137–45. The neighbor was Nancy Earl.

16. Ibid., 145–88. The sheriff's detective was Jerry Thompson.

17. Ibid., 188–210.

18. Ibid., 210–38.

19. Ibid., 238–50. The Radio Shack employee was Kelly Maria Elliott.

20. Ibid. 3:3–8. The officer was James Bryant.

21. Ibid., 8–31.

22. Ibid., 31–53.

23. Ibid., 53–63.

24. Ibid., 63–64.

25. Ibid., 64–70.

26. Ibid., 70–73.

27. Ibid., 75–78.

28. Ibid., 78–79.

29. Ibid., 89–91.

30. Ibid., 92–129.

31. Ibid., 129–40.

32. Ibid., 140–41.

33. Rowe, Journal, Apr. 16, 1986.

34. "Preliminary Hearing," 4:22.

35. Ibid., 22–23.

36. Ibid., 28–96. The engraving company employees who testified were Jorgen Olsen of Utah Engraving; Jack Smith of DeBouzek Engraving; and Edwin Q. Cannon III, Sonda Gary, and Blanche Leake, all of Salt Lake Stamp.

37. Ibid., 99–114. The examiner was Scott L. Pratt.

38. Ibid., 115–54, 197–98.

39. Ibid. 4:155–86, 194–228, 5:3–57, 72–109.

40. Ibid. 4:186–93, 5:57–72.

41. Ibid. 5:109–26. The Denver witness was Barbara Zellner of Cocks-Clark Engraving.

42. Ibid. 5:127–34. The orthodontist was Ralph Bailey.

43. Ibid. 4:34–39, 83–87. The witnesses were Jack Smith and Sonda Gary.

44. Ibid., 99–103.

45. Ibid. 5:135–44, 164.

46. Ibid., 144–46.

47. Ibid., 146–50. Cardon's partner was Dixon Duke Cowley.

48. Ibid., 161–62.

49. Ibid., 150–58.

50. Ibid., 198–217.

51. Ibid., 215. The hymn, written by Eliza R. Snow, is known today by the title "O My Father." *Hymns of the Church of Jesus Christ of Latter-day Saints* (Salt Lake City: Church of Jesus Christ of Latter-day Saints, 1985), no. 292.

52. Glen Leonard to Rick Turley, Feb. 15, 1989; Richard Evans, "Exhibit Honors Hymn, Paintings," *Church News*, Mar. 31, 1985.

53. "Preliminary Hearing," 5:218–32 (italics added). The two letters are items 435 and 436 in the Appendix.

54. Pinnock, Journal, Apr. 17, 1986.

55. "Preliminary Hearing," 6:3–30.

56. Ibid., 30–52.

57. Ibid., 53–61.

58. Ibid., 61–62.

59. Ibid., 63–66.

60. Ibid., 67–70. On redirect examination, Stott suggested to Rust that the date might actually have been September 13. Ibid., 125.

61. Ibid., 70–74.

62. Ibid., 121–24.

63. Ibid., 126.

64. Ibid., 127–28.

65. Ibid., 131. See, however, note 30.

66. Ibid., 132–34.

67. Ibid., 135–39.

68. Ibid., 140–55.

69. Ibid., 154.

70. Ibid., 188–89.

71. Ibid., 197–200.

72. Ibid., 209.

73. Oaks, Journal, Apr. 21, 1986.

74. "Preliminary Hearing," 7:4–6.

75. Ibid., 7–12, 15–16.

76. Ibid., 29–30.

77. Ibid., 36–37.

78. Ibid., 38–42, 63–68. Al Lyter analyzed the ink and Bill Krueger the paper.

79. Ibid., 42.

80. Ibid., 42–59.

81. Ibid., 50–51.

82. Ibid., 61–62. Rendell's assistant was Leslie Kress.

83. Ibid., 171–74.

84. Ibid., 175–79.

85. Ibid., 179–84.

86. Ibid., 187–89.

87. Ibid., 189–92.

88. Ibid., 192–204.

89. Ibid., 216–17.

90. Ibid., 228–35.

91. Ibid., 235–37.

92. Ibid., 240–59.

93. Ibid., 259. Jacobs later said that he did not lie to Gordon Hinckley or Steve Christensen about who found the letter. He said he made up a story about finding the letter after Hofmann told Kenneth Rendell in April 1985 that he, Jacobs, had been the one to discover it. Jacobs, Interview, Jan. 25, 1991.

94. "Preliminary Hearing," 7:259–64.

95. Ibid., 267–74.

96. Ibid., 272.

97. Ibid., 277–79.

98. Ibid., 279–81.

99. "Hofmann Breaks His Kneecap; Hearing Delayed," *Salt Lake Tribune,* Apr. 25, 1986; "New Injury to Hofmann Prompts Delay in Hearing," *Deseret News,* Apr. 24, 1986; "Hofmann Recovering," *Deseret News,* Apr. 25, 1986.

100. "Preliminary Hearing," 8:3–36. The son's name was Gaylen Dean Rust.

101. Ibid., 36–61.

102. Ibid., 44.

103. Ibid., 82–83.

104. Ibid., 100–104, 111. The witness was Robert Dale Pitts.

105. Ibid., 128–36; Farnsworth, "Investigation of the 1985 Mark Hofmann Forgery of the 'Oath of a Freeman,' " 139–41, 169–70, 175–77. The witness was Jack Smith.

106. "Preliminary Hearing," 8:136–39; *The Judgment of Experts,* 139–40, 171.

107. "Preliminary Hearing," 8:143–44.

108. Ibid., 144–48; Charles Hamilton, *Great Forgers and Famous Fakes: The Manuscript Forgers of America and How They Duped the Experts* (New York: Crown, 1980).

109. Mike Carter, "Evidence Alludes to 'Oath' Forgery," *Salt Lake Tribune,* May 6, 1986.

110. Hinckley, Memorandum, May 6, 1986; Ronald J. Yengich, Interview, Sept. 20, 1989.

111. "Preliminary Hearing," 9:3–13.

112. Ibid., 13–21.

113. Ibid., 22–29.

114. Ibid., 9–15, 17–19, 23, 32.

115. Ibid., 30–33.

116. Ibid., 34–35, 137.

117. Ibid., 35.

118. Ibid., 36–39. Wilding's partner was Gary Smith.

119. Ibid., 39–44.

120. Ibid., 44–46.

121. Ibid., 46–50.

122. Ibid., 50–51.

123. Ibid., 51–64. Wilding's attorney was John Ashton.

124. Ibid., 64–68.

125. Ibid., 68; David C. West to Whom It May Concern, Oct. 10, 1985.

126. "Preliminary Hearing," 9:68–72.

127. Ibid., 72–77.

128. Ibid., 86–101. The woman's name was Frances Magee. The book dealer was a "Mr. Rounds" from Glendale, California, whose son was named William.

129. Ibid., 166–67.

130. Ibid., 171–72.

131. Preliminary Hearing Audiotape 86–936, State v. Hofmann, Nos. 860003035, 860003041, 860003044, 860003045, 860020193 (Utah 5th Cir. Ct. heard Apr. 14 to May 22, 1986) [hereafter "Preliminary Hearing Audiotape"]; "Preliminary Hearing," 9:172–73; Farnsworth, Interview, Oct. 6, 1989.

132. "Preliminary Hearing," 9:176–92.

133. Ibid., 192–94.

134. Ibid., 218–21.

135. Ibid., 186, 190, 206.

136. See text accompanying note 107.

137. B. Ashworth, Interview, Sept. 5, 1990.

138. B. Ashworth, Interview, Mar. 29, 1989.

139. "Preliminary Hearing," 9:231–32.

140. B. Ashworth, Interview, Sept. 5, 1990; C. Ashworth, Interview, Mar. 1, 1991.

141. Mike Carter, "Investors Met 'Arrogance' of Hofmann," *Salt Lake Tribune*, May 7, 1986; Dallin H. Oaks, Notation, on copy of Carter, "Investors Met 'Arrogance' of Hofmann."

142. "Preliminary Hearing," 10:3.

143. Ibid., 3–10.

144. Throckmorton, Taped Reminiscences.

145. "Preliminary Hearing," 10:10.

146. Ibid., 10–14.

147. Ibid., 14–15.

148. Ibid., 15.

149. Ibid., 19–21.

150. Ibid., 22–24.

151. Ibid., 27–28.

152. Ibid., 29.
153. Ibid., 36–71.
154. Ibid., 45–47.
155. Ibid., 55.
156. Ibid., 56–59.
157. Ibid., 60–61.
158. Ibid., 63.
159. Ibid., 67.
160. Ibid., 70–71.
161. Ibid., 71–73. The *Oath* that Flynn and Throckmorton evaluated was the second one Hofmann attempted to sell. Hofmann gave it to Thomas Wilding, and Wilding eventually turned it over to investigators. The first *Oath*, which was in the possession of Schiller and Wapner in New York, did not become available to investigators for forensic examination until June 25, 1986. *The Judgment of Experts*, 140, 143–44.
162. "Preliminary Hearing," 10:75, 78.
163. Ibid., 83, 94–95.
164. Ibid., 111–12.
165. Ibid., 132.
166. Ibid., 151–52.
167. Ibid., 153.
168. Ibid. 11:31–32.
169. Ibid., 51–65. The engraving company was Salt Lake Stamp.
170. Ibid., 65–89. The negatives came from Cocks-Clark Engraving of Denver, Colorado.
171. Ibid., 93–98. The negative came from DeBouzek Engraving of Salt Lake City.
172. Ibid., 98–115.
173. Ibid., 115–17.
174. Ibid., 117–97.
175. Ibid. 12:102–8.
176. Ibid., 109–10.
177. Ibid., 110–11.
178. These were not the only stipulations in the case. According to statistics furnished by Judge Grant, thirty-nine witnesses testified in the courtroom and eleven others via stipulations. Mike Carter, "State Sums Up, Says Hofmann Bought Time with a Bomb," *Salt Lake Tribune*, May 21, 1986. On stipulations to reduce the number of witnesses who had to testify in the courtroom, see "Preliminary Hearing," 2:129–36, 187–88, 3:84, 4:27–28, 197–98, 6:209, 8:131–32, 9:174–75, 232, 10:163–64, 12:117–20.
179. "Preliminary Hearing," 12:117–18.
180. Ibid., 118–20.
181. Ibid., 10:163, 12:118, 120; David Biggs, Telephone Interview with Glenn N. Rowe, Nov. 7, 1989; Robert L. Stott, Telephone Interview with Glenn N. Rowe, Nov. 7, 1989; Gerry D'Elia, Telephone Interview with Glenn N. Rowe, Nov. 7, 1989.

182. Mike Carter, "Hofmann Case: Officer Calls 'Threat' Motive," *Salt Lake Tribune*, May 14, 1986.

183. Gordon B. Hinckley, Handwritten Notes, on copy of Jerry P. Cahill to Richard P. Lindsay, May 14, 1986.

184. "Preliminary Hearing Audiotape," No. 86–1069; Carter, "State Sums Up"; Jan Thompson, "Prosecutor Says Hofmann Killed Christensen in a Bid to Buy Time," *Deseret News*, May 21, 1986.

The dismissed charges were counts three and four in Information, State v. Hofmann, No. 860003041 (Utah 5th Cir. Ct. filed Feb. 4, 1986). Count four was the one dismissed because of the date problem. Count three was dismissed because the misdeed alleged actually related to count two in the same information. The court had earlier sought clarification of the relationship between the two counts. "Preliminary Hearing," 9:33.

The amended charge was count five in Information, State v. Hofmann, No. 860003035 (Utah 5th Cir. Ct. filed Feb. 4, 1986). Stott also moved unsuccessfully to change count one in Information, State v. Hofmann, No. 860003044 (Utah 5th Cir. Ct. filed Feb. 4, 1986) from a third- to a second-degree felony.

185. "Preliminary Hearing Audiotape," No. 86–1084; Mike Carter, "Drop Charges, Hofmann's Lawyer Urges," *Salt Lake Tribune*, May 22, 1986; Jan Thompson, "Hofmann Attorney Says Prosecutors 'Glossed Over' Sheets Slaying," *Deseret News*, May 22, 1986. Yengich also urged the court to consolidate or drop various other charges.

186. Findings of the Court, State v. Hofmann, Nos. 860003035, 860003041, 860003044, 860003045, 860020193 (Utah 5th Cir. Ct. issued May 22, 1986); "Preliminary Hearing Audiotape," No. 86–1084.

Chapter 13: Plea, Sentencing, and Interviews

1. Rowe, Journal, May 22, July 1, 8, Aug. 11, Sept. 4, 11, 30, Oct. 24, Nov. 5–6, 1986; Subpoena Duces Tecum directed to Glen Rowe, In re Criminal Investigation of Hofmann, No. CS 85–121 (Utah 3d Dist. Ct. issued June 30, 1986).

2. "Preliminary Hearing," 7:188–92, 214–19, 227; Mike Carter, "Witness Says LDS Pressed Hofmann to Pay Back Loan," *Salt Lake Tribune*, Apr. 23, 1986; Jerry Spangler and Jan Thompson, "Bomb Victim Had Warned Hofmann of Possible Suit," *Deseret News*, Apr. 23, 1986; Carter, "Evidence Alludes to 'Oath' Forgery"; Carter, "Hofmann Case"; Jerry P. Cahill to Richard P. Lindsay, May 23, 1986; Dallin H. Oaks to Richard P. Lindsay, May 23, 1986.

3. "Preliminary Hearing," 7:188–89, 227.

4. Oaks, Memorandum, Oct. 22, 1985.

5. Pinnock, Interview, May 16, 1989.

6. Dallin H. Oaks, Handwritten Notes of Conversation with Hugh W. Pinnock, Dec. 10, 1986, written on draft of "Clarification of Facts Concerning Alleged Threats of Excommunication," Sept. 25, 1986, attached to Dallin H. Oaks to Hugh Pinnock, Dec. 5, 1986; Videotape, LDS Press Conference, Oct. 23, 1985.

7. Merrill F. Nelson to Dallin Oaks, May 21, 1986; Dallin H. Oaks to Gordon B. Hinckley, May 22, 1986.

8. Cahill to Lindsay, May 23, 1986; Oaks to Lindsay, May 23, 1986; Hugh W. Pinnock to Dallin H. Oaks, Handwritten Note, n.d., inscribed on Dallin H. Oaks to Hugh W. Pinnock, May 23, 1986; Dallin H. Oaks, Handwritten Note, inscribed on "Draft," n.d.; Dallin H. Oaks to [Wilford W. Kirton, Jr.], May 28, 1986; Dallin H. Oaks, Handwritten Note, June 5, 1986, inscribed on "Possible Statement on Alleged Threat of Excommunication," n.d.

9. Dallin H. Oaks, "Recent Events Involving Church History and Forged Documents," *Ensign* 17 (Oct. 1987): 67.

10. LDS Press Release, Oct. 16, 1986; "No Early History by Cowdery Found," *Deseret News,* Oct. 16, 1986; John Dart, "Mormons Deny Papers Exist That Contradict Origins," *Los Angeles Times,* Oct. 17, 1986; Jessee, *Papers of Joseph Smith* 1:230–64.

11. "Tried to Kill Self, Mormon Artifacts Dealer Says," *Los Angeles Times,* Aug. 1, 1987; Dawn Tracy, "Hofmann Told Others He Was Shown Secret LDS History," *Salt Lake Tribune,* Oct. 17, 1986. According to Dawn Tracy, "L. A. Times Says It Joins a Long List of Hofmann Victims," *Salt Lake Tribune,* Aug. 17, 1987, "[*Los Angeles*] *Times* religion writer John Dart said he asked Hofmann repeatedly through his lawyer to be released from his promise [of confidentiality], an assertion confirmed by Hofmann's attorney Bradley Rich. 'Dart was caught in the middle,' said Mr. Rich. 'He tried. He really tried.' "

12. Cahill to Lindsay, May 23, 1986; Lindsay to Special Affairs Committee, May 23, 1986; Mike Carter, "Hofmann to Stand Trial in Killings, Theft," *Salt Lake Tribune,* May 23, 1986; Jerry Spangler, "Strategy Time in Hofmann Case," *Deseret News,* Oct. 13, 1986.

13. See, e.g., note 1.

14. Mike Carter, "Just One Trial or Five for Hofmann?" *Salt Lake Tribune,* June 4, 1986; "Hofmann Attorneys Push for Five Trials," *Deseret News,* June 4, 1986; "Hofmann Will Be Arraigned on All Charges Monday," *Deseret News,* June 6, 1986; Russell Weeks, "Hofmann Says Not Guilty in Surprise Arraignment," *Salt Lake Tribune,* June 7, 1986; Jan Thompson, "Hofmann Slipped into Court for a 'Quiet' Arraignment," *Deseret News,* June 7, 1986.

15. "Hofmann's Trial March 2," *Deseret News,* June 13, 1986; "March 2 Trial Scheduled for Hofmann," *Salt Lake Tribune,* June 14, 1986; Jan Thompson, "Delay in Hofmann's Theft Trial Sought until after Murder Trial," *Deseret News,* July 10, 1986; "Judge May Delay Hofmann Trial on Theft Counts," *Salt Lake Tribune,* July 11, 1986; "Hofmann's Trial for Theft Delayed until August '87—after His Murder Trial," *Deseret News,* July 11, 1986; "Hofmann Is Facing Fourth Trial May 15," *Salt Lake Tribune,* Aug. 9, 1986; "Hofmann Faces May 18 Theft-by-Deception Trial," *Deseret News,* Aug. 9, 1986.

16. Mike Carter, "Motion Is Filed to Combine Hofmann Cases in One Trial," *Salt Lake Tribune,* Aug. 5, 1986; "Five-in–One Hofmann Trial Sought," *Deseret News,* Aug. 5, 1986; "Hofmann Lawyers: Separate Trials," *Salt Lake Tribune,* Aug. 22, 1986; "Hofmann Defense Files Objection to Combining Five Trials," *Deseret News,* Aug. 22, 1986; Mike Carter, "Judge Delays Hearing

for Hofmann Due to Stolen Computer Disc," *Salt Lake Tribune,* Aug. 23, 1986; Mike Carter, "Hofmann's Lawyers Say Combining Cases Interferes with His Right to Fair Trial," *Salt Lake Tribune,* Sept. 11, 1986; Peg McEntee, "Request to Join Five Hofmann Trials into One Is Denied," *Deseret News,* Sept. 12, 1986.

17. Mike Carter, "Complications Keep Hofmann's March to Trial at a Crawl," *Salt Lake Tribune,* Oct. 14, 1986.

18. Jan Thompson, "Get Hofmann Case Moving, Judge Orders," *Deseret News,* Nov. 18, 1986; "Judge Sets Dec. 5 Deadline for Hofmann's Motions," *Salt Lake Tribune,* Nov. 19, 1986; Mike Carter, "Hofmann Claims Alibi in List of Nineteen Defense Motions," *Salt Lake Tribune,* Dec. 6, 1986; Brett DelPorto, "Attorneys Want Polygraph Tests as Evidence Backing Hofmann," *Deseret News,* Dec. 6, 1986; "Prosecutors Ask for Hofmanns' Polygraph Tests," *Salt Lake Tribune,* Dec. 18, 1986; Jan Thompson, "Defense Gives State Permission to Evaluate Hofmann Polygraph Tests," *Deseret News,* Dec. 29, 1986.

19. Mike Carter, "Hofmann May Enter Plea Bargain," *Salt Lake Tribune,* Dec. 30, 1986.

20. Jan Thompson, "N.Y. Investigating Hofmann Document," *Deseret News,* Dec. 30, 1986; Mike Carter, "Prosecutor Quits as Feud with Yocom Comes to a Head," *Salt Lake Tribune,* Dec. 10, 1986.

21. Jan Thompson, "Many Callers Riled by Reports of Plea Deal with Hofmann," *Deseret News,* Jan. 1, 1987; Mike Carter, "Cannon Finds Plea Bargain for Hofmann 'Distasteful,' " *Salt Lake Tribune,* Jan. 9, 1987.

22. "Hofmann Bargains, Says KTVX," *Daily Universe,* Jan. 22, 1987; Mike Carter, "Hofmann Plea Bargain Expected Today," *Salt Lake Tribune,* Jan. 22, 1987; Jan Thompson, "Media Cited in Cancellation of Hofmann Hearing," *Deseret News,* Jan. 22, 1987; Mike Carter, "Judge Cancels Hofmann's Plea Hearing," *Salt Lake Tribune,* Jan. 23, 1987.

23. Plea Agreement, State v. Hofmann, Nos. CR 86–834, 86–838, 86–840, 86–842, 86–844 (Utah 3d Dist. Ct. entered Jan. 7, 1987).

Regarding the plea agreement, *Salamander,* 483, would later posit that "by choosing the salamander letter, which Christensen had purchased, and the McLellin fraud, which involved only Rust, Stott had precluded naming the Church as a victim." Stott found this assertion to be illogical. "I mean," he said, "to even think that somehow we would reason that by pleading to these two charges the church wouldn't be perceived to be involved or a victim [is] ridiculous." Stott felt that anyone who followed the case rationally would make a connection between the church and both the salamander letter and McLellin collection. Stott, Interview, July 26, 1989.

Of the involvement of New York law enforcement officials in the case, Salt Lake City police detective Ken Farnsworth would later write: "In the fall of 1987, the New York District Attorney's Office became involved in the case at our request. We thought that the additional pressure that would be brought to bear on the Hofmann defense team if multiple jurisdictions had charges filed against Hofmann would work to our advantage. Also, New York was probably the appropriate arena for the prosecution of the forgery of the first *Oath.* Most of the witnesses lived in that area, and a major part of the crime actually took place there. Our attorneys therefore contacted the district attorney's office in New York, and its staff began collecting the information needed to prosecute the case. Grand jury subpoenas were sent out to some of us as witnesses, but we never appeared in New York because of what transpired in Salt Lake City." Farnsworth, "Investigation of the 1985 Mark Hofmann Forgery of the 'Oath of a Freeman,'" 145–46.

24. Plea Agreement, State v. Hofmann, Nos. CR 86–834, 86–838, 86–840, 86–842, 86–844 (Utah 3d Dist. Ct. entered Jan. 7, 1987).

25. Transcript of the Remarks of Judge Kenneth Rigtrup, State v. Hofmann, Nos. CR 86–834, 86–838, 86–840, 86–842, 86–844 (Utah 3d Dist. Ct. delivered Jan. 23, 1987).

Rigtrup later explained why he felt the plea agreement was rational. He was generally aware of the evidence that the prosecutors had presented during the preliminary hearing and said "it was doubtful . . . that they had much more." Even though he thought prosecutors might get a first-degree murder conviction at trial, he "clearly felt it was unlikely that they would get the death penalty imposed" because he "knew that Hofmann hadn't had any prior convictions, that he was a family man, [and that] he was relatively young." Rigtrup further added, "It had also been communicated to me that the Sheets family and the Christensen family wanted to get it over." Kenneth Rigtrup, Interview, Apr. 21, 1989.

Detective Ken Farnsworth gave similar reasons why he thought the plea was justified. "The other thing I also knew," Farnsworth added about Hofmann, "is we had gathered enough information about him and his behavior and his activities that we were the best evidence that he was psychologically diminished at the time of the incident. We would be our own witnesses against ourselves, which would mitigate his getting the death penalty." Farnsworth, Interview, Sept. 5, 1989.

Terri Christensen likewise felt Hofmann would not get the death penalty, and she was glad to avoid the lengthy trial and repeated appeals that would have been required had prosecutors decided to seek capital punishment for the killer. She would also say, "Living in prison is probably more hell than dying for Hofmann." Jan Thompson, "Birth of Steve Jr. Gave Widow Courage to Begin a New Life," *Deseret News*, July 30, 1987.

Nearly five years after the bombings, Kathy Sheets's sister explained that executing Hofmann would not have brought Kathy back. "Let him live in prison and try to come to terms with himself and his acts," she wrote. "Justice has been served." Joan Gorton, "Hofmann Paying," *Salt Lake Tribune*, Aug. 24, 1990.

26. Jan Thompson and Jerry Spangler, "Judge Wants Life in Prison for Hofmann," *Deseret News*, Jan. 23, 1987; Mike Carter, "Hofmann Imprisoned for Murders," *Salt Lake Tribune*, Jan. 24, 1987.

27. "Church Statement on Hofmann Case," Press Release, Church of Jesus Christ of Latter-day Saints, Jan. 23, 1987.

Bob Stott later explained that he and his associates discussed the proposed plea bargain with several victims but "never once talked with anybody from the church . . . even though the plea bargain involved those charges directly dealing with the church and documents. . . . [We] never got any direction or any counsel or any input from the church whatsoever as to what we should or should not do. . . . In that respect we treated the church discriminatorily. We treated them more poorly than we treated the other people. But again, the reason was . . . so people couldn't say that we were favoring the church and getting influence from the church." Stott, Interview, July 26, 1989; see also Steven L. Kent, " 'Mormon Murders' Sparks Controversy," *Daily Universe*, Sept. 21, 1988.

County detective Mike George likewise said that although county officials discussed the plea with the families of the murder victims, "the church wasn't notified." George said the reason for deliberately not consulting church officials was to avoid any potential conflicts of interest. George, Interview, May 3, 1989. George's partner, Dick Forbes, agreed. Referring to church officials, he said, "There was never an attempt by any of them to use any influence on our decision-making process, and that goes clear through the end of the case up through the plea bargain." Richard W. Forbes, Interview, July 20, 1989.

28. "Church Statement on Hofmann Case."

29. Historical Department Advisers Meeting Minutes, Jan. 30, 1987.

30. Three weeks after Hofmann pleaded guilty, Hugh Pinnock was sleeping in a Mexican airport hotel en route to a church conference he had been assigned to attend. In the middle of the night, he suddenly awoke with a strong impression. Grabbing a piece of hotel note paper, he recorded his feelings. "If Mark Hofmann lies during the 30 day period he has been given to answer questions," Pinnock scrawled, "then I should take from my journal and notes, all of which the law enforcement people know and make public this information. It will be helpful to the church, [Gordon B. Hinckley], [Dallin H. Oaks] and [Hugh W. Pinnock]." Hugh W. Pinnock, Handwritten Note, Feb. 13, 1987.

31. "Interrogation of Hofmann Is under Way," *Salt Lake Tribune*, Feb. 12, 1987; "Hofmann Has Begun Talking to Prosecutors," *Deseret News*, Feb. 12, 1987; "Hofmann Transcripts Won't Be Made Public for a While," *Deseret News*, Mar. 3, 1987; Dawn Tracy, "Forensic Experts Suggested for Hofmann Talks," *Salt Lake Tribune*, Mar. 21, 1987; "No Documents Experts at Sessions with Hofmann," *Deseret News*, Mar. 24, 1987; "Hofmann's Disclosure May Be Released to Public by End of May," *Deseret News*, Apr. 11, 1987; Michael White, "Hofmann 'Holding Nothing Back' in Talks with Prosecutors," *Deseret News*, Apr. 14, 1987; Mark Peterson, "Lawyer Recounts Hofmann Saga," *Ogden Standard-Examiner*, May 7, 1987; "Sheets Murder Was out of Character for Hofmann, Attorney Says," *Salt Lake Tribune*, May 7, 1987; *Mark Hofmann Interviews*.

32. Richard P. Lindsay to Special Affairs Committee, May 4, 1987.

33. Historical Department Advisers Meeting Minutes, May 8, 15, 1987; Richard P. Lindsay to Special Affairs Committee, May 13, 1987. The day the transcripts were released to the public, the church issued a statement explain-

ing that "as one of the aggrieved parties in this tragic episode of murder and forgery, representatives of The Church of Jesus Christ of Latter-day Saints, as were others, were briefed" by prosecutors. Richard P. Lindsay, "Church Statement Concerning the Mark Hofmann Interviews," Press Release, Church of Jesus Christ of Latter-day Saints, July 31, 1987.

Four days after this release, County Attorney David Yocom was a guest on a Salt Lake radio program. A caller asked him "why . . . according to Dr. Richard Lindsay [were] members of the Church prepped on this matter prior to the Friday release of the transcript?" Yocom answered: "Caller, that is true. We did have a meeting with Mr. Lindsay. In fact, Mr. McConkie was present. The other individual from the L.D.S. Church[,] that name escapes me right now, and we not only briefed the L.D.S. Church media people, but we also briefed [T]err[i] Christensen, we briefed Mac Christsensen, we briefed all of the people that were involved with regard to the documents that wanted to be present. The Sheets family and those that wanted to be present[,] they also participated that same day on Thursday, in a briefing by my prosecutors. So we felt that they had to know in advance in order to respond to media questions after the transcripts were released and what was contained in the transcripts. There obviously wasn't time between the time we released them and the time we had our news conference that they'd be asked questions. So, in response to your question, everybody had an equal opportunity to be briefed." Transcript of "Vital Issues," KALL Radio (Salt Lake City), Aug. 4, 1987. Terri Christensen's pre-release briefing is noted in Anne Palmer, "My Life Has Gone on, Says Widow," *Salt Lake Tribune*, Aug. 1, 1987.

34. "Hofmann Interviews: From Fraud to Murder," *Universe*, June 11, 1987; Mike Carter, "Questioning Ends for Hofmann," *Salt Lake Tribune*, June 20, 1987; "Hofmann Transcripts Will Be out in a Few Weeks," *Deseret News*, June 20, 1987; Jan Thompson, "Hofmann Transcripts Focus Exclusively on His Multiple Forgeries," *Deseret News*, June 24, 1987.

35. Oscar W. McConkie, Jr., Handwritten Notes, July 30, 1987; Richard E. Turley, Jr., Handwritten Notes, July 30, 1987; Author's personal recollection.

36. *Mark Hofmann Interviews*, 3.

37. Ibid., 3–66.

38. Ibid., 36.

39. Ibid., 54.

40. Ibid., 68–103; see also ibid., 116–19, 122.

41. Ibid., 98–99.

42. Ibid., 105, 112–13. On Hofmann's feelings about the church, see also ibid., 99, 130.

43. Ibid., 115.

44. Plea Agreement, State v. Hofmann, Nos. CR 86–834, 86–838, 86–840, 86–842, 86–844 (Utah 3d Dist. Ct. entered Jan. 7, 1987).

45. *Mark Hofmann Interviews*, 132; see also ibid., 19, 43, 45–46, 62, 83–84. For similar comments Hofmann made about others of his forgeries, see, e.g., ibid., 159–61, 201, 393.

46. Ibid., 124; see also ibid., 35, 87, 394, 417.

47. Ibid., 133–34, 143, 166–73.

48. Ibid., 175.

49. Ibid., 175–222; see also Appendix, item 45, for the Smith letter.

50. *Mark Hofmann Interviews*, 223–29. Mormon rare-book dealer Peter Crawley, who had the hymnal in his possession and carefully examined it, has labeled Hofmann's account of how he altered the last page as "just nonsense from beginning to end." Peter Crawley, Interview, Nov. 14, 1989.

51. *Mark Hofmann Interviews*, 229–41.

52. Ibid., 243–44.

53. Ibid., 246–53, 262–63.

54. Ibid., 332.

55. Ibid., 264–72.

56. Ibid., 264–75. The testing occurred six months after the bombings. For a copy of the preliminary report of the test, as well as "Post-confession Commentaries" of the testers, see T. A. Cahill, B. H. Kusko, R. A. Eldred, and R. H. Schwab, "Compositional Comparison of the Mark Hofmann 'Oath of a Freeman' and the 'Whole Booke of Psalmes,' " in *The Judgment of Experts*, 75–96.

57. *Mark Hofmann Interviews*, 276–80. Marcus McCorison of the American Antiquarian Society later observed that because Schiller and Wapner found the society's offer for the document to be unacceptable, the society returned the document to the dealers. "I must reiterate that AAS returned the *Oath* to Schiller on September 11," he wrote, "and report that a vote on the purchase of the document was not on the agenda of the AAS Council when it met on the afternoon, E.D.T., of that fateful October 15." *The Judgment of Experts*, 69.

58. *Mark Hofmann Interviews*, 280–82.

59. Ibid., 282–83.

60. Ibid., 293–94.

61. Ibid., 301–2.

62. Ibid., 303–6.

63. Ibid., 309–11.

64. Ibid., 315.

65. Farnsworth, Interview, Feb. 21, 1990.

66. *Mark Hofmann Interviews*, 315–16.

67. Ibid., 354–55.

68. Ibid., 357–59.

69. Ibid., 307, 363–66.

70. Ibid., 380–81.

71. Ibid., 451.

72. Ibid., 452–53.

73. Ibid., 453–54.

74. Brent Metcalfe, Telephone Conversation with Ronald K. Esplin, Aug. 1, 1987.

75. *Mark Hofmann Interviews*, 455.

76. Ibid., 513.

77. Ibid., 514–15.

78. Ibid., 515–16.

79. Ibid., 527–28.

80. Rust, Interview, Apr. 6, 1989. Rust gave a similar statement to Dallin Oaks and Martell Bird when they interviewed him on October 18, 1985. In a memorandum that he made of the interview, Bird detailed Hofmann's visit to Hinckley on June 13. Rust then recorded: "At this point, Brother Rust stated, 'I think I understand what has happened,' and pointed out that he had received a telephone call from Mark Hofmann who claimed that he was in New York City the day after he had written a letter to President Hinckley. During their telephone conversation, Brother Rust was assured by Mark Hofmann that he would soon have the money to repay Brother Rust. Brother Rust then told Hofmann that he had prepared a letter to President Hinckley on the matter which seemed to upset Hofmann considerably. Brother Rust said that Hofmann told him that it was a sad mistake, that he should have kept the matter entirely confidential." Bird, Memorandum, Oct. 22, 1985.

81. Videotape, LDS Press Conference, Oct. 23, 1985.

82. Hinckley, Memorandum, June 12, 1985.

83. Steve Christensen's account corroborates Rust's and Hinckley's. About two weeks after Hofmann met with Hinckley, Christensen recorded what Hofmann told him about the McLellin deal. "From the beginning," Christensen wrote, "it had been Mark's intention to leave the Church out of the transaction totally. Mark had been keeping President Hinckley informed was all." Christensen, Journal, June 28, 1985.

84. See, e.g., "Preliminary Hearing," 9:6–13, 22–25, 165–66, 12:117.

85. *Mark Hofmann Interviews*, 408.

86. Ibid., 527; Hinckley, Memorandum, June 12, 1985.

87. Hinckley, Memorandum, June 12, 1985. Hinckley added, "I told him I thought he had better bring them here." A few days later, Hinckley would recommend to the Quorum of the Twelve that the gift be publicly announced when received. See text accompanying chapter 6, note 24.

88. *Mark Hofmann Interviews*, 528.

89. Hinckley, Memorandum, June 12, 1985.

90. See, e.g., chapter 9, note 12, and accompanying text.

91. *Mark Hofmann Interviews*, 528.

92. Ibid., 529. The transcript inadvertently punctuates "enemy's hands," as "enemy's, hands," which has been silently corrected.

93. Ibid.

94. Hinckley, Memorandum, June 12, 1985; see text accompanying chapter 10, note 39.

95. *Mark Hofmann Interviews*, 529–30.

96. Ibid., 530.

97. Hinckley, Memorandum, June 12, 1985; see text accompanying chapter 9, note 12.

98. *Mark Hofmann Interviews*, 530.

99. Hinckley, Memorandum, June 12, 1985; *Deseret News 1987 Church Almanac*, 119, 121, 292–93.

100. *Mark Hofmann Interviews*, 530–31.

101. Ibid., 532.

102. Hinckley, Memorandum, June 12, 1985.

103. *Mark Hofmann Interviews*, 533.

104. Hinckley, Memorandum, June 12, 1985.

105. *Mark Hofmann Interviews*, 537.

106. Ibid., 2, following page 537; Biggs, Telephone Interview, July 31, 1989.

107. *Mark Hofmann Interviews*, 2–4, following page 537.

108. Videotape, Salt Lake County Attorney's Office Press Conference, July 31, 1987, as broadcast by KSL-TV Channel 5 (Salt Lake City), July 31, 1987, HDC.

109. Farnsworth, Interview, Oct. 26, 1989.

110. *Mark Hofmann Interviews*, supplement, SS–1 to SS–14.

111. "Hofmann's Hidden Life as Killer and Forger Is a Secret No More," *Salt Lake Tribune*, Aug. 1, 1987.

112. "Plenty of Questions Remain after Hofmann Transcript," *Deseret News*, Aug. 1, 1987.

113. Charles Hamilton, Answers to Questions Posed by Ronald P. Esplin, attached to Memorandum from Esplin to Symposium Participants, Aug. 4, 1987.

114. Chuck Gates and Jeff Hunt, "Few Who Knew or Had Dealings with Hofmann Think Transcripts Tell the Truth and Nothing But," *Deseret News*, Aug. 1, 1987.

115. Jan Thompson, "Hofmann: Believe It or Not," *Deseret News*, Aug. 16, 1977. The author of the article, who had followed the case closely, expressed her feeling that "most of what Hofmann reveals in the two-volume transcript of his prison debriefing interviews must be taken with a megadose of skepticism and with the understanding that Hofmann is a self-trained lying machine."

116. Jan Thompson and Jeff Hunt, "Transcripts Unveil True Hofmann—Devoid of Human Conscience," *Deseret News*, Aug. 1, 1987.

117. Gates and Hunt, "Few Who Knew or Had Dealings." Thompson, in "Hofmann: Believe It or Not," points out that physical evidence from the bomb site belies Hofmann's suicide claim: "Hofmann contends he put the bomb on the driver's seat and placed two wires together to detonate it. Evidence from bomb experts, however, indicates the bomb was in a different location and possibly of different construction than Hofmann claims."

118. Mike Carter, "Let Hofmann Die in Prison, Prosecutors Tell Board," *Salt Lake Tribune*, Jan. 22, 1988; Jan Thompson, "Hofmann: Never Let Calculated Killer out of Prison to Trick or Murder Again, Prosecutors Say," *Deseret News*, Jan. 22, 1988.

119. Audiotape, Hearing for Mark Hofmann, USP #18186, Board of Pardons of the State of Utah, Jan. 29, 1988; Stephen Hunt, "Board Tells Hofmann He'll Spend Life in Prison," *Salt Lake Tribune*, Jan. 30, 1988.

The Mormon Murders, 445, described the board's decision on life imprisonment as being made "to the surprise of all." Similarly, *Salamander,* 526, declared it "a final twist" that the board "vindicated the prosecutors' strategy and expectations by throwing away the prison key." Mike George, one of the chief investigators in the case, found this notion offensive. "I mean I've been involved in the investigation of sixteen capital crimes," he said. "I don't know how many Bob Stott has been involved in. We knew what Hofmann was going to get. We're not stupid." George, Interview, May 3, 1989. Detective Ken Farnsworth, who considered himself "one of the prime movers of the plea," said, "I knew that if we got him in front of the Board of Pardons with the information we had that they would take care of him. They'd slam him." Farnsworth, Interview, Oct. 26, 1989.

Conclusion

1. JoAnn Jacobsen-Wells, "Foundations of LDS Church Unshaken by Hofmann Scandal, Spokesman Affirms," *Deseret News,* Aug. 1, 1987; Richard P. Lindsay, "Church Statement Concerning the Mark Hofmann Interviews," Press Release, Church of Jesus Christ of Latter-day Saints, July 31, 1987; "LDS Official Says Forgeries Were Used against Church," *Salt Lake Tribune,* Jan. 26, 1987.

2. Dawn Tracy, "Christensen Letter Reveals Devotion, Fearlessness toward LDS Church," *Salt Lake Tribune,* Jan. 25, 1987; John L. Hart, "Hofmann Imprisoned after Plea Bargaining," *Church News,* Jan. 31, 1987; Jan Thompson, "Betrayed by Hofmann," *Deseret News,* July 31, 1987.

3. Jan Thompson, "Hofmann's Letter to Families Expresses Regret for Crimes," *Deseret News,* Jan. 24, 1987.

4. Sonja Eddings Brown, "Terri Christensen On: Mark Hofmann, Church, Children, and Renewal," *Utah Holiday* 18, no. 10 (July 1989): 23; Videotape, "Eyewitness News," KSL-TV Channel 5 (Salt Lake City), July 31, 1987, 10:00 P.M., HDC.

5. Brown, "Terri Christensen," 23. Terri Christensen was not alone in viewing her husband as a martyr. In his book *Martyrs of the Kingdom* (Salt Lake City: Bookcraft, 1990), 152–55, Hoyt W. Brewster, Jr., characterized both Steve Christensen and Kathy Sheets as "victims of a deliberate effort by a modern anti-Christ to undermine the cause of Christ by discrediting His Church, His leaders, and His priesthood." Of Christensen, whom he also referred to as "my fallen friend," Brewster wrote, "It is ironic that Bishop Christensen, known for his magnanimous nature and Christlike character, should fall victim to one who was discovered to be a cold, calculating, criminal whose evil and cunning nature would bring pain, suffering, and sorrow to so many."

6. A. Dean Larsen, Telephone Interview, Oct. 1, 1990.

7. "The Hofmann Papers: Between the Lines," KSL-TV Channel 5 (Salt Lake City), July 31, 1987.

8. Rust, Interview, Apr. 6, 1989.

9. Agreement for Pre-Trial Diversion, United States v. Flynn, No. 85-CR–201S (D. Utah subscribed May 11, 29, 1987); Motion and Order for Dismissal of Indictment, United States v. Flynn, No. 85-CR–201S (D. Utah filed June 16, 1987); Order for Dismissal of Indictment, United States v. Flynn, No. 85-CR–201S (D. Utah issued June 23, 1987).

10. Videotape, "Nightcast," KTVX Channel 4 (Salt Lake City), July 31, 1987, 10:00 P.M., HDC. The television reporter was Fred Fife.

11. Mike Carter, "Is Hofmann behind Threats to State Pardons Board?" *Salt Lake Tribune*, Mar. 24, 1988; "Has Imprisoned Hofmann Made Threats against Three?" *Deseret News*, Aug. 5, 1988; Mike Carter, "Vengeance Plot in Coded Hofmann Letters?" *Salt Lake Tribune*, Aug. 5, 1988; Mike Carter, "Anxiety, Doubt Surround Claim That Hofmann Has Cash for Vengeance," *Salt Lake Tribune*, Aug. 6, 1988; Laurie Sullivan, "Yengich Denies Hofmann 'Hit List,' " *Deseret News*, Aug. 6, 1988; Michael P. George, Interview, Aug. 12, 1988.

12. Mark W. Hofmann, "Mormon and Mormon-Related Autographs That I Forged," and "Forged Non-Mormon Autographs," 1988; George, Interview, Aug. 12, 1988. A complete list of the names on the sheet appears in the Appendix.

13. Jan Thompson, "Hofmann's Wife Files for Divorce," *Deseret News*, Aug. 10, 1988; Jan Thompson, "Doralee Supportive—until Now," *Deseret News*, Aug. 10, 1988; Christopher Smart, "Hofmann's Wife Files for Divorce, Citing 'Irreconcilable Differences,' " *Salt Lake Tribune*, Aug. 11, 1988.

14. Jerry P. Cahill, "First Presidency Statement," Press Release, Church of Jesus Christ of Latter-day Saints, Sept. 15, 1988; Mike Carter, "Drug Overdose Leaves Hofmann in Coma," *Salt Lake Tribune*, Sept. 16, 1988; Jerry Spangler, "Hofmann Listed Serious after Suicide Attempt," *Deseret News*, Sept. 16, 1988; Jan Thompson and Marianne Funk, "Action Deepens the Mystery about Hofmann," *Deseret News*, Sept. 16, 1988; Stephen Hunt, "Hofmann Slowly Gains as Investigation Waits," *Salt Lake Tribune*, Sept. 17, 1988; "Hofmann off Respirator following Drug Overdose," *Deseret News*, Sept. 17, 1988; "Hofmann Improving, but Listed as Serious," *Salt Lake Tribune*, Sept. 18, 1988; "Hofmann Is Serious but Stable and Slowly Coming out of Coma," *Deseret News*, Sept. 18, 1988; "Hofmann Still Improving," *Deseret News*, Sept. 19, 1988; Stephen Hunt, "Hofmann Has Arm Surgery; Condition Fair," *Salt Lake Tribune*, Sept. 20, 1988; "Hofmann out of Danger but Will Stay in Hospital," *Deseret News*, Sept. 20, 1988; "Hofmann's Bill Exceeds $10,678 at U. Hospital," *Salt Lake Tribune*, Sept. 21, 1988; "Hofmann Is Fair as Bill Mounts," *Deseret News*, Sept. 21, 1988; "Hofmann Continues to Gain Strength," *Salt Lake Tribune*, Sept. 22, 1988; "Hofmann out of Bed; Skin Graft Fine," *Salt Lake Tribune*, Sept. 24, 1988; "Hofmann Returns to Prison after Twelve Days in Hospital," *Salt Lake Tribune*, Sept. 27, 1988; "Hofmann Is Returned to Prison," *Deseret News*, Sept. 27, 1988; "Hofmann Recuperating," *Deseret News*, Oct. 7, 1988; "Hofmann Recovering Well from Redone Skin Grafts," *Deseret News*, Oct. 9, 1988; "Hofmann Intended Suicide, Investigators Con-

clude," *Salt Lake Tribune*, Nov. 24, 1988; "Hofmann Refuses to Talk about Overdose," *Deseret News*, Nov. 24, 1988.

15. Farnsworth, Interview, Dec. 5, 1989. The Lafferty murders are detailed in the following series of five articles by Kris Radish and Michael Morris that appeared in the *Deseret News* in 1985: "Lafferty Family's Serene Facade Hid Panorama of Delusion, Destruction," July 21; "Boughs on the Family Tree Begin to Bend and Break," July 22; "One by One, the Brothers Were Pulled toward Dan," July 23; "Ron and Dan Carry Out Grisly 'Revelation,' " July 24; "Idyllic Young Love Evolved into a Nightmare for Brenda," July 25.

16. Farnsworth, Interview, Dec. 5, 1989.

17. Jess Gomez, "Hofmann Critical after Another Suicide Attempt," *Salt Lake Tribune*, Aug. 23, 1990; Joe Costanzo, "Hofmann Recovering from Drug Overdose," *Deseret News*, Aug. 23, 1990; Jess Gomez, "Hofmann Improves following Drug Overdose," *Salt Lake Tribune*, Aug. 24, 1990; Joe Costanzo, "Hofmann Goes back to Prison to Recover," *Deseret News*, Aug. 24, 1990; Jess Gomez, "Hofmann's back in Prison after Overdose," *Salt Lake Tribune*, Aug. 25, 1990.

18. Costanzo, "Hofmann Goes back to Prison to Recover"; Gomez, "Hofmann Improves following Drug Overdose." The official quoted was David R. Franchina, public affairs director for the Utah State Department of Corrections.

19. "Hofmann Gets Different Cell," *Deseret News*, Jan. 16, 1991.

20. A. J. Simmonds, Interview, Sept. 21, 1990.

21. Audiotape of Symposium, Church History and Recent Forgeries, Brigham Young University, Provo, Utah, Aug. 6, 1987, HDC.

22. Richard P. Howard, "Under the Cloud of Mark Hofmann," *Saints Herald* 134 (1987): 507, 510. Asked if the forgeries would have been discovered had Hofmann been able to meet his financial obligations, Bob Stott said, "No. In fact, if he would have had the money by October the fifteenth, there would be no need to kill Steve Christensen, and we would not have had the bombs. And without the bombs, the police would not have investigated the case, and his forgery would not have been detected." Max Evans, director of the Utah State Historical Society and acting state archivist, likewise concluded that "without the murders, it is unlikely that the forgeries would have been discovered at all." Audiotape of Symposium, Church History and Recent Forgeries, Brigham Young University, Provo, Utah, Aug. 6, 1987, HDC.

23. Oaks, "Recent Events Involving Church History," 69.

24. "Fraudulent Documents from Forger Mark Hofmann Noted," *Ensign* 17 (Oct. 1987): 79.

25. Historical Department Acquisition Sheet 90-0069; Simon, "Thomas Bullock as an Early Mormon Historian," 86 n. 11; A. Dean Larsen, Telephone Interviews, Oct. 12, 17, 1990. The Bullock journal donated to Brigham Young University was published in *Brigham Young University Studies* 31 (Winter 1991).

26. William Thompson, "Latterday Saints Song," n.d., Thomas Bullock Papers, HDC.

27. Lawrence W. Towner, "An End to Innocence," *American Libraries* 19 (Mar. 1988): 211.

28. W. Thomas Taylor, "Provenance and Lore of the Trade," in *Forged Documents: Proceedings of the 1989 Houston Conference,* ed. Pat Bozeman (New Castle, Del.: Oak Knoll Books, 1990), 6.

29. Oaks, "Recent Events Involving Church History," 65–66.

30. Jacobsen-Wells, "Foundations of LDS Church Unshaken."

31. Jerry Johnston, "Hofmann's Changed the Face of Document Dealing," *Deseret News,* Mar. 11, 1987; Mike Carter, "Worthless Forgeries? No, They're Hofmann Originals," *Salt Lake Tribune,* Aug. 1, 1987; "Hofmann's Reputation May Make Forgeries Valuable," *Odgen Standard-Examiner,* Aug. 2, 1987.

32. Carter, "Worthless Forgeries?"

33. Brent Harker, "The Black and the White," *BYU Today* 41 (Oct. 1987): 38; Carter, "Worthless Forgeries?"

34. Doctrine and Covenants (1981) 10:8, 10, 19.

35. For examples of Hofmann's claims about seeking the lost pages, see, e.g., "Hunting for LDS Documents: An Interview with Mark Hofmann," *Sunstone Review* 2, no. 9 (Sept. 1982): 18; Keller, "Making a Buck off Church History."

The person who catalogued the Book of Mormon words for Hofmann was his friend and college roommate Jeff Salt. Salt later said that Hofmann had claimed he was doing "a frequency study or something" and that Hofmann had "quoted several studies" done at Brigham Young University as an example. Jeffery P. Salt, Interview, May 9, 1989. On the BYU word analysis, see Wayne A. Larsen and Alvin C. Rencher, "Who Wrote the Book of Mormon? An Analysis of Wordprints," in *Book of Mormon Authorship: New Light on Ancient Origins,* ed. Noel B. Reynolds (Provo, Utah: Religious Studies Center, Brigham Young University, 1982), 157–88.

Those who acquired what Hofmann claimed to be pieces of the manuscript of the published portion of the Book of Mormon include the church Historical Department, Deseret Book, Utah State University, and Brent Ashworth. See Appendix, item 438; B. Ashworth, Interview, Mar. 29, 1989; *Book of Mormon Critical Text: A Tool for Scholarly Reference,* 2d ed., 3 vols. (Provo, Utah: Foundation for Ancient Research and Mormon Studies, 1986–87), 3:1310; "The Coming Forth of the Book of Mormon," *Ensign* 13 (Dec. 1983): 37–38; "Fraudulent Documents from Forger Mark Hofmann Noted," 79.

36. George, Interview, Aug. 12, 1988. For a long time, investigators had believed Hofmann intended to "set the church up" for the forgery. Jerry Spangler and Marianne Funk, "Police Sift Documents to Build Hofmann Case," *Deseret News,* Oct. 23, 1985; Mike Carter, "Prosecutors Charge Hofmann with Two Murders and Fraud," *Salt Lake Tribune,* Feb. 5, 1986.

On the purported examples of Martin Harris's handwriting, see Jessee, "New Documents and Mormon Beginnings," 405–7, 425–28.

37. Doctrine and Covenants (1981) 10:23, 26.

Appendix: Suspect Items Acquired by the LDS Church

1. "Church Delivers Records to Illinois Court, Lists Documents Obtained from Mark W. Hofmann," Press Release, Church of Jesus Christ of Latter-day Saints, April 11, 1986.

Items 16 and 28 were given to the circuit court clerk of Daviess County, Missouri, in April 1986. Glenn N. Rowe to Linda Adkins, Apr. 16, 1986; Linda Adkins, Receipt, Apr. 21, 1986.

Items 35–36, 47–48, 63–355, 382–87, and 393 were given to the circuit court clerk of Hancock County, Illinois, April 7, 1986. Rowe, Journal, Apr. 7, 1986.

Item 356 was given to the circuit court clerk of Peoria, Illinois, April 21, 1986. Glenn N. Rowe to Leo Sullivan, Apr. 16, 1986; Leo E. Sullivan (by Helen R. Schraeder, deputy), Receipt, Apr. 21, 1986.

Item 357 was given to the circuit court clerk of Warren County, Illinois, April 21, 1986. Glenn N. Rowe to Roger H. Johnson, Apr. 16, 1986; Roger H. Johnson, Receipt, Apr. 21, 1986.

Items 358 and 406 were given to the circuit court clerk of Ray County, Missouri, in April 1986. Glenn N. Rowe to Everet Lauck, Apr. 16, 1986; Everett Lauck, Receipt, Apr. 18, 1986.

Items 359–81 were given to the circuit court clerk of Walworth County, Wisconsin, in April 1986. Glenn N. Rowe to Peggy Mackelfresh, Apr. 16, 1986; Peggy L. Mackelfresh, Receipt, Apr. 18, 1986.

2. Glenn N. Rowe, Handwritten Notes of Telephone Conversations, Apr. 1986, attached to Glenn Rowe to Rick Turley, Sept. 10, 1990.

3. Mark W. Hofmann, "Mormon and Mormon-Related Autographs That I Forged," 1988; George, Interview, Aug. 12, 1988.

4. Mark W. Hofmann, "Forged Non-Mormon Autographs," 1988. On Hofmann's forged non-Mormon Americana, see, e.g., *Mark Hofmann Interviews*, 74, 308, 371, 414, 431–32, 491, 509–14.

Jennifer S. Larson of Yerba Buena Books, San Francisco, has devoted considerable attention to Hofmann's non-Mormon Americana forgeries. "Hofmann retained records of his preparatory research into various historical and literary figures, much of which was seized by investigators," Larson has noted. "He devoted a great deal of attention in particular to Mark Twain and Daniel Boone; however, others (excluding those relating to Mormon history) are: Nathaniel Hawthorne, Thomas Lynch, Button Gwinnett, Emily Dickinson, Herman Melville, Abigail and John Adams, Charles Dickens, Jack London, Betsy Ross, Ludwig van Beethoven, Edgar Allan Poe, and Abraham Lincoln." Committee on Questioned Imprints, *Questioned Imprints* (San Francisco: Southern California Chapter, Antiquarian Booksellers' Association of America, 1990), 2.

5. Historical Department Acquisition Sheets 80–157, 80–402.

6. Hofmann told prosecutors that he had "made just a single trade . . . involving Mormon money" with church librarian-archivist Donald T. Schmidt before the Anthon transcript. *Mark Hofmann Interviews*, 114. Schmidt, however, does not recall any such transaction. "Preliminary Hearing," 4:206; Schmidt, Interview, Feb. 8, 1989.

7. Photographs of the transcript were included in Jerry P. Cahill, "Newly Discovered Transcript May Be 1828 Example of Joseph Smith's Writing," Press Release, Church of Jesus Christ of Latter-day Saints, Apr. 28, 1980, and quickly appeared in newspapers, see, e.g., "LDS Scholars Study Joseph Smith Transcript," *Deseret News,* Apr. 28, 1980; George Raine, "Joseph Smith Handwriting and 'Ancient Characters'?" *Salt Lake Tribune,* Apr. 29, 1980. Excellent color photographs of the transcript were printed on the inside front and back covers of *Ensign* 10 (July 1980).

8. *Mark Hofmann Interviews,* 36–87.

9. Danel W. Bachman, "A Look at the Newly Discovered Joseph Smith Manuscript," *Ensign* 10 (July 1980): 69; Danel W. Bachman, "Sealed in a Book: Preliminary Observations on the Newly Found 'Anthon Transcript,' " *Brigham Young University Studies* 20 (Summer 1980): 328–29.

10. *Mark Hofmann Interviews,* 3–35, 87–103, 131, SS–14.

11. Bachman, Journal, Feb. 13, 1980; Godfrey, Journal, July 29, 1980.

12. Mark W. Hofmann, "The Prophet for President," *TAMS Journal* 20 (Aug. 1980, pt. 1): 150–52.

13. The earliest published photographs appear in Hofmann, "The Prophet for President," 151. Photographs also appear in Harry F. Campbell, *Campbells Tokens of Utah,* rev. ed. (Salt Lake City: Harry F. Campbell, 1983), 60; Rust, *Mormon and Utah Coin and Currency,* 32 and dust jacket.

14. Hofmann admitted both to detective Michael George and to Al Rust that the token was not authentic. George, Interview, Aug. 12, 1988; Mark Hofmann to Al Rust, Feb. 1, 1990.

15. Hofmann showed at least a photocopy of the document first to Danel Bachman, next to Dean Jessee, and then reportedly to Don Schmidt, all on March 24, 1980. Jessee saw the document itself on July 9, 1980. The church apparently acquired it sometime after that date but before February 1984, when Jessee published it, citing it as being in church possession. Bachman, Journal, Mar. 24, 1980; Jessee, Journal, Mar. 25, Apr. 17, May 22, July 9, 1980; Jessee, *Personal Writings of Joseph Smith,* 596–98, 697; "Preliminary Hearing," 5:80; Schmidt, Interview, Feb. 8, 1989; Jessee, Interview, Feb. 10, 1989.

16. For information on Maria and Sarah Lawrence, see Jessee, *Personal Writings of Joseph Smith,* 697.

17. Ibid., 598.

18. *Mark Hofmann Interviews,* 107–11.

19. George, Interview, Aug. 12, 1988.

20. Photographs of the blessing document were included in Jerry P. Cahill, "Historic Document Appears to Be Father's Blessing to Joseph Smith III," Press Release, Church of Jesus Christ of Latter-day Saints, Mar. 19, 1981, and soon appeared in "Joseph Smith's Blessing on Son Discovered, Given to RLDS," *Deseret News,* Mar. 19, 1981. A crisp, slightly enlarged reproduction of the document appears in Reorganized Church, *For He Shall Be My Successor,* [6–7].

21. *Mark Hofmann Interviews,* 133–73.

22. In interviews with prosecutors, Hofmann said he forged and sold the white notes to the church through Don Schmidt before the Joseph Smith III blessing transaction occurred. Schmidt feels the white note acquisition came in late March after the Joseph Smith III blessing. Hofmann claimed Schmidt showed the notes to Richard Howard on March 2, 1981. Howard said he did not become aware of the notes until much later. Hofmann also said he forged more notes later. *Mark Hofmann Interviews,* 134, 143, 168, 323–24; Schmidt, Interview, Feb. 8, 1989; Richard P. Howard, Telephone Interview with Glenn N. Rowe, July 17, 1989; "Preliminary Hearing," 4:167–72, 220, 5:7–16, 56.

23. Campbell, *Campbells Tokens of Utah,* 308–9. The notes pictured in figures 57, 58, and 61 in Rust, *Mormon and Utah Coin and Currency,* 48–50, were acquired by the church from Hofmann. The note pictured in figure 60 does not belong to the church, the photo credit for figure 61 having been inadvertently attached to figure 60.

24. *Mark Hofmann Interviews,* 134, 143, 175–82, 323–33.

25. "Preliminary Hearing," 5:16–17, 25, 56–57.

26. "Preliminary Hearing," 5:16–26, 56–57; *Mark Hofmann Interviews,* 143, 327–32.

27. Rust, *Mormon and Utah Coin and Currency,* 53–54, figs. 64, 66. The item pictured in figure 65 is not a Hofmann forgery and has been in church possession for many years. See, e.g., Fox, "Hard Money and Currency in Utah"; McGarry, *Mormon Money,* 17.

28. *Mark Hofmann Interviews,* 143, 327–28.

29. Historical Department Acquisition Sheet 81–236.

30. Rust, *Mormon and Utah Coin and Currency,* 85.

31. George J. Throckmorton to Glenn N. Rowe, Feb. 25, 1988.

32. Hofmann to Rust, Feb. 1, 1990.

33. Historical Department Acquisition Sheet 81–242.

34. Steven G. Barnett, Telephone Interview with Glenn N. Rowe, July 12, 1990.

35. Mark W. Hofmann, *Mormon Manuscripts List #1* (Salt Lake City: Mark W. Hofmann, [1981]), 6.

36. Historical Department, HMMS Masterfile Record ID No. ARCH–88–3557.

37. Hofmann, *Mormon Manuscripts List #1,* 4.

38. Ibid., 2.

39. Ibid., 3.

40. Historical Department Acquisition Sheet 81–330.

41. George J. Throckmorton to Glenn N. Rowe, Dec. 12, 1987.

42. Hinckley, Memorandum, Sept. 4, 1981.

43. "Church Delivers Records to Illinois Court," item 48.

44. *Mark Hofmann Interviews,* 309–11, 315–16.

45. Historical Department Acquisition Sheet 81–366.

46. George J. Throckmorton to Glenn N. Rowe, Nov. 17, 1987.

47. Throckmorton to Rowe, Feb. 25, 1988.

48. Historical Department Acquisition Sheet 81–406.

49. Lyndon W. Cook, "Isaac Galland—Mormon Benefactor," *Brigham Young University Studies* 19 (Spring 1979): 280–81, suggests Galland was not in Nauvoo on December 14.

50. Throckmorton, Taped Reminiscences; George J. Throckmorton, Telephone Interview, July 12, 1990.

51. Ronald E. Romig to Glenn N. Rowe, Mar. 31, 1989; L. Madelon Brunson to Donald T. Schmidt, Sept. 22, 1981.

52. During the preliminary hearing, Don Schmidt recalled acquiring this item from Hofmann. "Preliminary Hearing," 5:76. However, no acquisition sheet for it has been found. The date is based on a catalogue record, which shows the item was "Purchased, 1981," and a one-hundred-dollar check dated October 30, 1981, to Hofmann "for purchase of manuscript materials." Historical Department, HMMS Masterfile Record ID No. ARCH–88–6904; Corporation of the President of The Church of Jesus Christ of Latter-day Saints, check no. 5500C74059, drawn on Zions First National Bank, Salt Lake City, Utah, Oct. 30, 1981.

53. For a published account of the expedition, see O. B. Huntington, "A Trip to Carson Valley," in *Eventful Narratives* (Salt Lake City: Juvenile Instructor Office, 1887), 77–98.

54. Hofmann, "Mormon and Mormon-Related Autographs That I Forged," n.d; Cataloguing worksheet for photographic reproduction of "Guide to Carson," Ms 351, HDC.

55. Historical Department Acquisition Sheet 81–438.

56. *Document Containing the Correspondence, Orders, &c. in Relation to the Disturbances with the Mormons* (Fayette, Mo.: Boon's Lick Democrat, 1841), 159–63.

57. On January 15, 1982, Hofmann ordered stamps used in manufacturing the notes. *Mark Hofmann Interviews*, 191. Richard Marks testified that Hofmann sold him a set of Spanish Fork Co-op notes in February 1983. "I was of the impression in talking to Mark at the time that there was only one other complete set known, those that belonged in the Church archives." "Preliminary Hearing," 5:204–6.

58. Campbell, *Campbells Tokens of Utah*, 564–65.

59. "Preliminary Hearing," 11:51–65.

60. *Mark Hofmann Interviews*, 182–95, 200–202.

61. Historical Department Acquisition Sheet 82–290.

62. Historical Department Acquisition Sheet 80–9; Ralph Bailey, Telephone Interview with Glenn N. Rowe, Jan. 20, 1989; Brent F. Ashworth, Telephone Interview with Glenn N. Rowe, Jan. 23, 1989; Dan Olsen, Telephone Interview with Glenn N. Rowe, Jan. 24, 1989.

63. Throckmorton to Rowe, Dec. 12, 1987.

64. Historical Department Acquisition Sheet 82–313.

65. Hofmann, *Mormon Manuscripts List #1*, 5.

66. Schmidt, Memorandum, Oct. 20, 1982.

67. "The Coming Forth of the Book of Mormon," *Ensign* 13 (Dec. 1983): 39.

68. *Mark Hofmann Interviews,* 317–23, 411–17, 422–23.

69. Historical Department, HMMS Masterfile Record ID No. ARCH–88–10002.

70. Ibid.

71. "Preliminary Hearing," 5:92.

72. Glenn N. Rowe to Richard E. Turley, Jr., May 23, 1989.

73. George J. Throckmorton to Glenn N. Rowe, May 20, 1989.

74. Hofmann, Bill of Sale, Jan. 14, 1983.

75. A photocopy and transcript of the letter were included in Jerry P. Cahill, "Church Releases Text of Presumed Letter of Joseph Smith to Josiah Stowell," Press Release, Church of Jesus Christ of Latter-day Saints, May 9, 1985. Most news sources did not receive the press release until May 10, 1985. See Jerry P. Cahill to William S. Evans, May 9, 1985. Transcripts of the letter appeared in Dawn Tracy, "Letter Linking Joseph Smith, Magic to Be Released," *Salt Lake Tribune,* May 10, 1985; "1825 Joseph Smith Letter Is Made Public," *Deseret News,* May 10, 1985; "Joseph Smith Letter of 1825 Is Released by First Presidency," *Church News,* May 12, 1985. A photocopy appeared in John Dart, "Letter Revealing Mormon Founder's Belief in Spirits, Occult Released," *Los Angeles Times,* May 11, 1985.

76. *Mark Hofmann Interviews,* 75, 243, 260, 345–61, 368–72, SS–13 to SS–14.

77. Historical Department Acquisition Sheet 83–26.

78. Throckmorton to Rowe, Dec. 12, 1987.

79. Hofmann, Receipt, Mar. 4, 1983.

80. "The Coming Forth of the Book of Mormon," 41.

81. *Mark Hofmann Interviews,* 372–87.

82. Corporation of the President of The Church of Jesus Christ of Latter-day Saints, check no. 5500CE3825, drawn on First Interstate Bank of Utah, Salt Lake City, Utah, June 17, 1983.

83. Ibid.

84. Glenn N. Rowe to Gordon B. Hinckley, Jan. 21, 1986.

85. Corporation of the President of The Church of Jesus Christ of Latter-day Saints, check no. 5500CE3835, drawn on First Interstate Bank of Utah, Salt Lake City, Utah, June 27, 1983.

86. Ibid.

87. Rowe to Hinckley, Jan. 21, 1986. Some idea of the general nature of the unidentified document can be gained by studying Hofmann's *Mormon Manuscripts List #1,* which asks two thousand dollars for a brief 1839 letter signed by Joseph Smith that requested its recipient to credit a man sixty dollars for a horse.

88. Corporation of the President of The Church of Jesus Christ of Latter-day Saints, check no. 5500C56811, drawn on Zions First National Bank, Salt Lake City, Utah, Sept. 29, 1983.

89. Jessee, *Personal Writings of Joseph Smith,* 358–59.

90. *Mark Hofmann Interviews,* 214.

91. Historical Department Acquisition Sheet 83–342.

92. Though Schmidt could not recall acquiring this letter, his initials are listed on the acquisition sheet as the person who arranged the acquisition. Ibid.; "Preliminary Hearing," 5:74, 78.

93. Historical Department, HMMS Masterfile Record ID No. ARCH–88–138.

94. Throckmorton to Rowe, Dec. 12, 1987.

95. Historical Department Acquisition Sheet 83–350.

96. Glenn N. Rowe to David Painter, Apr. 16, 1986; David W. Painter to Glenn N. Rowe, Apr. 18, 1986.

97. Leonard J. Arrington, *Brigham Young: American Moses* (New York: Alfred A. Knopf, 1985), 429.

98. Historical Department Acquisition Sheet 83–381.

99. Throckmorton to Rowe, Nov. 17, 1987.

100. Marilyn McMeen Miller and John Clifton Moffitt, *Provo: A Story of People in Motion* (Provo: Brigham Young University Press, 1974), 103.

101. This case is mentioned in Stanley R. Gunn, *Oliver Cowdery: Second Elder and Scribe* (Salt Lake City: Bookcraft, 1962), 190.

102. The Cowdery law firm apparently took several cases in which this man was plaintiff. See Gunn, *Oliver Cowdery,* 189–90 (where the surname is spelled "Geotschin").

103. Historical Department Acquisition Sheet 83–398.

104. The judge recorded the event in his journal, observing that in the evening he "examined the subscribing witnesses to the last will and testament of Peter Horrocks deceased and confirmed the appointment of E. D. Woolley and George Goddard as the executors thereof." Elias Smith, Journal, Aug. 6, 1866, HDC.

105. Throckmorton to Rowe, Nov. 17, 1987.

106. H.R. 18984 was a bill "for the protection and perpetuation of the national resources of migratory birds which pass between the United States and Canada twice each year." *Congressional Record* (Washington, D.C.: Government Printing Office, 1917), 54:417.

107. Historical Department Acquisition Sheet 84–004.

108. Patriarchal Blessing Collection, bk. 9, no. 286, HDC.

109. Throckmorton to Rowe, Feb. 25, 1988.

110. Historical Department Acquisition Sheet 84–096. In addition to the original items listed, Hofmann also gave the church a photocopy of a purported Lorenzo Snow poem dated August 6, 1886, during Snow's confinement in the Utah Penitentiary for practicing plural marriage. It reads, "The body is confined. / The spirit is *free.* / The flesh is made to bow. / The mind can *never be!*" The original of this item is currently owned by George Throckmorton.

111. (New York: John B. Alden, 1890).

112. This revelation appears in Doctrine and Covenants (1981) as section 124.

113. [Rick Grunder], *The Mormons,* Rick Grunder—Books, Catalogue 5 (Bloomington, Ind., [1983]), item 48; Rick Grunder to Glen Rowe, Sept. 24, 1987.

114. Simpson Montgomery Molen, Journal, Jan. 1, 1877, HDC.

115. Throckmorton to Rowe, Dec. 12, 1987.

116. Don Schmidt acquired the notes for the church in one or more transactions but kept no records of them. Schmidt, Interview, Feb. 8, 1989. Acquisition must have occurred, however, after May 18, 1984, when Hofmann ordered the first printing plate for the notes, and before September 28, 1984, when Schmidt retired. *Mark Hofmann Interviews*, 202, 209; Historical Department Office Journal, Sept. 28, 1984.

117. Rust, *Mormon and Utah Coin and Currency*, 74–86; Arrington, *Great Basin Kingdom*, 188–92; McGarry, *Mormon Money*, 21–22; Bancroft, *History of Utah*, 291.

118. "Preliminary Hearing," 6:38–42, 88–90.

119. Ibid., 5:109–16; *Mark Hofmann Interviews*, 202–22.

120. Rust, *Mormon and Utah Coin and Currency*, 78–79 figs. 90–93. Even though the credit line was inadvertently left off the note appearing in figure 90, the note belongs to the church.

121. Harry F. Campbell, *Hofmann: Mormon Money Forgeries—Historical Aspects* (Salt Lake City: Harry F. Campbell, 1988), 38.

122. This confusion is reflected in Campbell, *Hofmann: Mormon Money Forgeries*, 37–38, where the one- and two-dollar notes are listed as forgeries. Note that the one-dollar note described as a forgery on page 37 of that publication is the same note featured as genuine on page 36.

123. George J. Throckmorton to Glenn N. Rowe, Feb. 23, 1988.

124. *Mark Hofmann Interviews*, 222–23, 230, 245–46; David J. Whittaker, "The Hofmann Maze," *Brigham Young University Studies* 29 (Winter 1989): 88.

125. Church Administration Building Daily Visitor Log, Apr. 12, 1985; First Presidency, Minutes, Apr. 12, 1985; Christensen, Journal, June 28, 1985.

126. Hart, "Letter Sheds Light on Religious Era." Excellent photographs of both sides of the document appear in Jessee, "New Documents and Mormon Beginnings," 418–19.

127. Plea Agreement, State v. Hofmann, Nos. CR 86–834, 86–838, 86–840, 86–842, 86–844 (Utah 3d Dist. Ct. entered Jan. 7, 1987); *Mark Hofmann Interviews*, 243, 432–500, SS–12 to SS–14.

128. Rowe, Journal, Apr. 12, 16, 1985; Historical Department Acquisition Sheets 85–150, 85–151; "Preliminary Hearing," 5:219–25, 6:4–9, 13.

129. "Preliminary Hearing," 5:220–21, 223–24.

130. B. Ashworth, Interview, Mar. 29, 1989.

131. *Mark Hofmann Interviews*, 319–23, 410–11.

132. "Preliminary Hearing," 9:195; B. Ashworth, Interview, Mar. 29, 1989.

133. Throckmorton to Rowe, Nov. 17, 1987.

134. Glenn N. Rowe, Untitled Note, Oct.-Nov. 1985, filed with *The Book of Common Prayer*; "Preliminary Hearing," 5:226–31, 6:9–11.

135. Tuckett and Wilson, *The Martin Harris Story*, 119.

136. Jessee, "New Documents and Mormon Beginnings," 428.

137. *Mark Hofmann Interviews,* 500–501, SS–14.

138. Schmidt, Interview, Feb. 8, 1989.

139. "Preliminary Hearing," 5:79–80.

140. Mark W. Hofmann to Jennifer S. Larson, June 25, 1990.

141. Rust, *Mormon and Utah Coin and Currency,* 17 fig. 23.

142. Hofmann to Rust, Feb. 1, 1990.

143. Campbell, *Campbells Tokens of Utah,* 53; Rust, *Mormon and Utah Coin and Currency,* 13 fig. 17.

144. Hofmann to Rust, Feb. 1, 1990.

145. Schmidt, Interview, Feb. 8, 1989.

146. George J. Throckmorton to Glenn N. Rowe, Jan. 26, 1988.

147. Hofmann to Rust, Feb. 1, 1990; Rust, *Mormon and Utah Coin and Currency,* 31 fig. 40.

148. Hofmann to Rust, Feb. 1, 1990; "Preliminary Hearing," 5:207–10, 215–17.

149. Schmidt, Interview, Feb. 8, 1989.

150. Rust, *Mormon and Utah Coin and Currency,* 33–35 and dust jacket. Examples of the first token have been known to exist since at least 1911. See McGarry, *Mormon Money,* 7–8.

151. Bachman, Journal, Feb. 13, 1980.

152. Hofmann to Rust, Feb. 1, 1990.

Index

Mormon Studies from the University of Illinois Press

Thomas G. Alexander. *Mormonism in Transition: A History of the Latter-day Saints, 1890–1930.* 1986.

Leonard J. Arrington. *Brigham Young: American Moses.* Illini Books edition, 1984.

Leonard J. Arrington and Davis Bitton. *The Mormon Experience: A History of the Latter-day Saints,* 2d ed. Illini Books edition, 1992.

Leonard J. Arrington, Feramorz Y. Fox, and Dean L. May. *Building the City of God: Community and Cooperation among the Mormons,* 2d ed. Illini Books edition, 1992.

Maureen Ursenbach Beecher and Lavina Fielding Anderson, eds. *Sisters in Spirit: Mormon Women in Historical and Cultural Perspective.* With a foreword by Jan Shipps. 1987.

Richard L. Bushman. *Joseph Smith and the Beginnings of Mormonism.* 1984; Illini Books edition, 1988.

Maria S. Ellsworth, ed. *Mormon Odyssey: The Story of Ida Hunt Udall, Plural Wife.* 1992.

Edwin Brown Firmage and R. Collin Mangrum. *Zion in the Courts: A Legal History of the Church of Jesus Christ of Latter-day Saints, 1830–1900.* 1988.

Robert Bruce Flanders. *Nauvoo: Kingdom on the Mississippi.* 1965; Illini Books edition, 1975.

Lawrence Foster. *Religion and Sexuality: The Shakers, the Mormons, and the Oneida Community.* Illini Books edition, 1984.

Jennifer Moulton Hansen, ed. *Letters of Catharine Cottam Romney, Plural Wife.* 1992.

B. Carmon Hardy. *Solemn Covenant: The Mormon Polygamous Passage.* 1991.

Michael Hicks. *Mormonism and Music: A History.* 1989.

Stanley B. Kimball. *Heber C. Kimball: Mormon Patriarch and Pioneer.* 1981; Illini Books edition, 1986.

Stanley B. Kimball. *Historic Sites and Markers along the Mormon and Other Great Western Trails.* 1988; Illini Books edition, 1988.

Roger D. Launius. *Joseph Smith III: Pragmatic Prophet.* 1988.

Larry M. Logue. *A Sermon in the Desert: Belief and Behavior in Early St. George, Utah.* 1988.

E. B. Long. *The Saints and the Union: Utah Territory during the Civil War.* 1981.

Edward Leo Lyman. *Political Deliverance: The Mormon Quest for Utah Statehood.* With a foreword by Leonard J. Arrington. 1986.

Dallin H. Oaks and Marvin S. Hill. *Carthage Conspiracy: The Trial of the Accused Assassins of Joseph Smith.* 1975; Illini Books edition, 1979.

Erich Robert Paul. *Science, Religion, and Mormon Cosmology.* 1992.

B. H. Roberts. *Studies of the Book of Mormon.* Edited and with an introduction by Brigham D. Madsen and a biographical essay by Sterling M. McMurrin. 1985.

Gene A. Sessions. *Mormon Thunder: A Documentary History of Jedediah Morgan Grant.* 1982.

Jan Shipps. *Mormonism: The Story of a New Religious Tradition.* 1985; Illini Books edition, 1987.

Roger Van Noord. *King of Beaver Island: The Life and Assassination of James Jesse Strang.* 1988.